Beyond Conventional Economics

Selected Works of E Ray Canterbery

Beyond Conventional Economics

Selected Works of E Ray Canterbery

E Ray Canterbery
Florida State University, USA

World Scientific

NEW JERSEY • LONDON • SINGAPORE • BEIJING • SHANGHAI • HONG KONG • TAIPEI • CHENNAI • TOKYO

Published by

World Scientific Publishing Co. Pte. Ltd.

5 Toh Tuck Link, Singapore 596224

USA office: 27 Warren Street, Suite 401-402, Hackensack, NJ 07601

UK office: 57 Shelton Street, Covent Garden, London WC2H 9HE

Library of Congress Cataloging-in-Publication Data
Names: Canterbery, E. Ray, author.
Title: Beyond conventional economics : selected works of E. Ray Canterbery /
E. Ray Canterbery, Florida State University, USA.
Description: New Jersey : World Scientific, [2016] | Includes bibliographical references.
Identifiers: LCCN 2015044966 | ISBN 9789814704373
Subjects: LCSH: Economics. | Economics--History.
Classification: LCC HB171 .C2758 2016 | DDC 330--dc23
LC record available at http://lccn.loc.gov/2015044966

British Library Cataloguing-in-Publication Data
A catalogue record for this book is available from the British Library.

In-house Editor: Shreya Gopi

CONTENTS

* *These works are not reprinted in this collection*

* *These works are not reprinted in this collection*

* *These works are not reprinted in this collection*

* *These works are not reprinted in this collection*

** These works are not reprinted in this collection*

** These works are not reprinted in this collection*

* *These works are not reprinted in this collection*

* *These works are not reprinted in this collection*

** These works are not reprinted in this collection*

NOTES

1. Other Editorships besides Canterbery-Johnson include Symposium on Galbraith and American Economics (*Journal of Post Keynesian Economics*, Fall 1984), papers by *Arthur Schlesinger, Jr., *Warren Samuels, *John Adams, *James Galbraith, *William Breit, *David Colander, and E. Ray Canterbery and; special *Proceedings issue of the *Eastern Economic Journal* (July–September 1985), which contains selected papers from the April 1984 Conference.
2. Most of the other books are either economics in a broad sense, such as **Wall Street Capitalism: The Theory of the Bondholding Class* (World Scientific, 2000), **Economics on a New Frontier* (Belmont, CA: Wadsworth, 1968), and **The President's Council of Economic Advisers* (New York: Exposition Press, An Exposition-University Book, 1961), or biographical, including **Alan Greenspan: The Oracle Behind the Curtain* (World Scientific, 2006) and **F. Scott Fitzgerald: Under the Influence* (St. Paul, MN: Paragon House, 2006), with Thomas D. Birch, or fictional, **Black Box, Inc.* (San Jose/New York/Lincoln/Shanghai: Writer's Showcase Press, 2000)

* *These works are not reprinted in this collection*

ACKNOWLEDGEMENTS

The editor would like to acknowledge and thank the co-authors for the papers contained in this volume, as well as the following publishers for permissions to the articles.

The following article is reprinted from the *American Economic Review* with permission from the American Economic Association.

Exchange Rates, Capital Flows and Monetary Policy, *American Economic Review,* Vol 59, No. 3 (June 1969), pp. 426–432

The following articles are reprinted from the *Journal of Economic Issues* by special permission of the copyright holder, the Association for Evolutionary Economics.

The Coase Theorem as a Negative Externality, *Journal of Economic Issues,* Volume 26, No. 4 (December 1992), pp. 1179–1185, with Akbar Marvasti

Two Coases or two Theorems? *Journal of Economic Issues*, Vol. 28, No. 1 (March 1994), with Akbar Marvasti

Boulding's T, Kaleckian Power, and Minsky's Fragility Hypothesis, *Journal of Economic Issues,* Vol. 28, No. 4 (December 1994), pp. 1227–1247

Thorstein Veblen and *The Great Gatsby, Journal of Economic Issues.* Vol. 33, No. 2 (June 1999), pp. 297–304

The Theory of the Bondholding Class, *Journal of Economic Issues* (June 2002), pp. 365–372

The following article is reprinted from the *Journal of Economic History* with permission from the Cambridge University Press.

Review of Philip Mirowski (ed.) *The Reconstruction of Economic Theory* (Kluwer Martin Nijhoff: Dordrecht, 1986) in *The Journal of Economic History* (Cambridge University Press: Cambridge, UK), Vol. 49, No. 1 (March 1989), pp. 257–260

The following article is reprinted from the *Cato Journal* with permission from the Cato Institute.

The Flat Tax, Negative Tax, and VAT: Gaining Progressivity and Revenue, *The Cato Journal* (Fall 1985), pp. 521–535, with Eric W. Cook and Bernard A. Schmitt

The following article is reprinted from the *Global Economy Quarterly* with permission from the International Trade and Finance Association.

Rational Bubbles and Uncovered Interest-rate Parity: Retrospective and Prospective, *Global Economy Quarterly* (Summer 2000)

The following article is reprinted with permission from Edward Elgar.

Input-Output Analysis, in Malcolm Sawyer and Philip Arestis (eds.), *The Elgar Companion to Radical Political Economy* (Cheltenham, UK: Edward Elgar, 1994), pp. 212–216

The following article is reprinted from the *Canadian Journal of Economics* with permission from John Wiley & Sons, Inc.

The Crawling Peg and Exchange Stability, *Canadian Journal of Economics,* Vol. 3, No. 2 (May 1970), pp. 291–299, with John N. Boorman

The following articles are reprinted from *Challenge* with permission from Taylor & Francis Group.

The International Monetary Crisis and the Delayed Peg, *Challenge,* Vol. 21, No. 5 (November-December 1978), pp. 4–12

Review: *A Tenured Professor* by John Kenneth Galbraith, Boston: Houghton Mifflin Company, 1990 in *Challenge*, Vol. 33, No. 4 (July/August 1990), pp. 60–63

Review Essay of George Brockway, *The End of Economic Man* (London and New York: W.W. Norton, 1995) in *Challenge: The Magazine of Economic Affairs* (November–December 1995), pp. 59–62

The Fine Line Between Politics and Economics, *Challenge, The Magazine of Economic Affairs*, Vol. 11, No. 10 (July 1953), New York: New York University, July 1963, pp. 28–31

The Awkward Independence of the Federal Reserve, *Challenge, The Magazine of Economic Affairs.* Vol. 18, No. 4 (*September-October 1975*), Armonk NY: M.E. Sharpe, pp. 44–48, reprinted in *Readings in Economics* (Guilford Connecticut: Dushkin Publishing Group, Inc.,1977), and in M.E. Sharpe (ed.), *The Challenge of Economics* (New York and London: Random House, 1977)

The Independence of Arthur Burns, *Challenge, The Magazine of Economic Affairs,* Vol. 19, No. 5 (November–December 1976). Armonk NY: M.E. Sharpe, pp. 63–64

The following article is reprinted from the *International Trade Journal* with permission from Taylor & Francis Group.

Irrational Exuberance and Rational Speculative Bubbles, *The International Trade Journal, Volume VIII, No. 1* (Spring 1999), pp. 1–35

The following articles are reprinted from the *Journal of Post Keynesian Economics* with permission from Taylor & Francis Group.

The Doctrine of Inherent Productivity: Keynes, Sraffa, and Kalecki, *Journal of Post Keynesian Economics*, Vol. 11, No. 4 (Summer 1989), pp. 630–640, with William McLeod

Galbraith, Sraffa, Kalecki and Supra-Surplus Capitalism, *Journal of Post Keynesian Economics*, Vol. 7, No. 1 (Autumn 1984), pp. 77–90

Tax Reform and Incomes Policy: A VATIP Proposal, *Journal of Post Keynesian Economics*, Vol. 5, No. 3 (Spring 1983), pp. 430–439

The following article is reprinted from *Economic Inquiry* with permission from John Wiley & Sons, Inc.

A. Marvasti and E. Ray Canterbery, Cultural and Other Barriers to Motion Pictures Trade, *Economic Inquiry*, Vol. 43, No. 1, January 2005, 39–54

The following articles are reprinted from the *Southern Economic Journal* with permission from John Wiley & Sons, Inc.

The Modern Theory of Foreign Exchange and the Net Speculative Residual (*Southern Economic Journal*, Vol. 41, No. 2 (October 1974), pp. 182–187.

On the Relevance of Hedging for the Modern Theory of Forward Exchange: A Reply (*Southern Economic Journal*, Vol. 42, No. 3 (January 1976, pp. 533–535.

Review of *Welfare Economics: A Liberal Restatement* by Charles K. Rowley and Alan T. Peacock (New York: John Wiley and Sons, A Halstead Press Book, 1975), *Southern Economic Journal,* Vol. 45, No. 4 (April, 1979), pp. 1304–1307

A Vita Theory of the Personal Income Distribution, *Southern Economic Journal*, Vol. 46, No. 1 (July 1979), pp. 12–48

The Forbes Four Hundred: The Determinants of Super-Wealth, *Southern Economic Journal*, Vol. 51, No. 4 (April 1985), pp. 1073–1083, with Edward J. Nosari

Cost Savings from Nuclear Regulatory Reform: An Econometric Model, *Southern Economic Journal,* Vol. 62, No. 3 (January 1996), with Ben Johnson and Don Reading, pp. 554–564

Cost Savings from Nuclear Regulatory Reform: Reply, *Southern Economic Journal*, Vol. 63, No. 4 (April 1997), pp. 1113–1116, with Ben Johnson and Don Reading

The International Mobility of Land and the Law of the Sea, *Southern Economic Journal,* Vol. 43, No. 3 (January 1977), pp. 1338–1345, with Thomas H. Cate.

The following article is reprinted from the *Western Economic Journal* with permission from John Wiley & Sons, Inc.

A Note on Recent Money Supply Behavior, *Western Economics Journal* (Fall 1965), pp. 91–98. Now *Economic Inquiry*, reprinted in John H. Lindauer (ed.), *Macroeconomic Readings* (New York and London: Macmillan, 1968)

The following articles are reprinted from the *Eastern Economic Journal* with permission from Palgrave Macmillan.

Co-Editor with Harry G. Johnson, Symposium on Justice, Nozick and Rawls, *Eastern Economic Journal* (January 1978). Papers by E. Ray Canterbery, Abba P. Lerner Jan Tumlir, and Vincent J. Tarascio.

Introduction to Justice, Nozick and Rawls, *Eastern Economic Journal,* Vol. IV, No. 1 (January 1978), pp. 1–7, with Harry G. Johnson

Further Reflections on Economic Justice, *Eastern Economic Journal,* Vol. IV, No. 1 (January 1978), pp. 67-82, with Harry G. Johnson

Welfare Economics and the Vita Theory *Eastern Economic Journal*, Vol. VI, No. 1 (January 1980), pp. 1–20

A Theory of Supra-Surplus Capitalism, *Eastern Economic Journal*, Vol. XIII, No. 4 (October–December 1987), pp. 315–332

The following article is reprinted from *Briefing Notes in Economics* with permission of Richmond, The American International University in London.

Necessities, the Marginal Utility of Money, and Saving, *Briefing Notes in Economics*, Issue No. 62 (September/October 2004), pp. 1–9

The following article is reprinted from the *Review of Industrial Organization* with permission of Springer Science+Business Media.

The U.S. Motion Pictures Industry: An Empirical Approach, *The Review of Industrial Organization,* Vol. 19 (July-September, 2001), pp. 81–98, with Akbar Marvasti.

The following article is reprinted from the *Quarterly Journal of Economics* by permission of the Oxford University Press.

Reflections Upon the Income Distribution as a Pure Public Good, *Quarterly Journal of Economics* (May 1971), with Howard P. Tuckman

The following articles are reprinted from the *American Journal of Agricultural Economics* by permission of the Oxford University Press.

The Green Revolution and the World Rice Market, 1967–75: An Econometric Study, *American Journal of Agricultural Economics*, Vol. 53, No. 2 (May 1971), pp. 285–294, with Hans Bickel

The Green Revolution: A Reply to Professors Ruttan and Mellor, *American Journal of Agricultural Economics*, Vol. 54, No. 2 (May 1972), pp. 355–368, with Hans Bickel

The following article is reprinted from the *Journal of Political Economy* by permission of the University of Chicago Press.

A Theory of Foreign Exchange Speculation under Alternative Systems, *Journal of Political Economy*, Vol. 79, No. 3 (May–June, 1971), pp. 407–436.

ABOUT THE EDITOR

A former Professor of Economics at Florida State University (Tallahassee), **E Ray Canterbery** is one of the most respected economists of his generation. In 2003, John Kenneth Galbraith, who knew both Michal Kalecki and John Maynard Keynes, called Canterbery, "the best". He conducted research as a Truman Scholar in 2004, which led to his recent book, *Harry S Truman: The Economics of a Populist President* (2014). Canterbery is the author of many acclaimed books (and articles), including *The Global Great Recession*, the tour de force *Wall Street Capitalism*, biographies of *Alan Greenspan and of F Scott Fitzgerald* (co-authored with Thomas Birch), the classic, *The Making of Economics*, and the best-selling *A Brief History of Economics*, many of which are available in several languages. After the Truman book was safely in press, he returned to his global concerns with the engaging *The Rise and Fall of Global Austerity* (2015), which is ahead of today's newspaper headlines.

Canterbery served as President of the Eastern Economics Association in 1986–1987 and of the International Trade and Finance Association in 1997–1998. In January 1996, Prentice-Hall, Inc. selected Canterbery for their Hall of Fame Economist Baseball Cards for "significant contributions to the economics discipline", including the development of one of the first complete mathematical theories of foreign exchange, a new theory of the labor market and of personal incomes (vita theory), which later was integrated into international trade theory.

The international Biography Centre in Cambridge, England includes Canterbery among 500 persons worldwide in its *Living Legends* (2004), among 2000 scholars worldwide in its *Outstanding Scholars in the 21st Century* (2002), among *One Thousand Great Intellectuals* (2002), among *2000 Outstanding People* (2003) worldwide, and among *One Thousand*

Great Americans (2002). The American Biographical Institute includes Canterbery in its *Great Minds of the 21st Century* (2002) and *American Biography* (2003). He is also listed in selected issues of Marquis *Who's Who in the World and Who's Who in America*, as well as many other biographical sources.

INTRODUCTION

When my editor and I decided to put together a collection of works, it seemed at the time to be a slam dunk. It did not require any new writing; everything was already in print. All I had to do was write an Introduction. That was then; this is now. It is astonishing how much thought is required in the selection process. Then, just when you think you have it altogether, getting permissions looms large. Some journal titles have changed; some have new publishers. The same goes for books. Some books are out of print and otherwise not available. JSTOR is a wonderful resource for downloading articles, but even this service does not have everything. All this is to say that I did not have control over the entire selection process. As I will explain, some important, well, at least to me, pieces are missing.

Because of the broad way that I approach economics, some arbitrary decisions had to be made. Much of my work does not fit neatly into the usual categories of, for examples, microeconomics, macroeconomics, economic thought, methodology, speculation, theory or econometric. It was my judgment as to what was put where. Early on, I did not see a clear distinction between microeconomics and macroeconomics. Eventually, the economics profession merged the two in the new classical "macroeconomics." I was not a fervent fan of that merger; I preferred my own approach, which does require some explanation. As one example, the orthodoxy always has prices determined by supply and demand. My inclination generally is to go with corporate reality in which markup pricing takes place. This is not to say that all the contributions are "radical," for I have had considerable orthodox support, and some of the articles are orthodox personified. I offer no apologies for sometimes being simply yoeman-like. The term "eclectic" often is used to describe my work, a term that I find unoffensive.

Having said this, the professional economist and students will find the usual categories in the detailed table of contents. The rules of thumb are simple. If the content is price-oriented, it is microeconomics, even if it be mark-up pricing. If the broader economy is involved, it is macroeconomics. If the writing is mostly about dead economists, it is history of thought and sometimes methodology. If foreigners are on the scene, it is foreign exchange, economic development or even global. Sometimes foreign exchange involves speculation. Sometimes the work is more theory than policy-oriented. While somewhat arbitrary, some pieces fall into the monetary and fiscal policy bin. Once the pieces were categorized as this or that, chronology took over.

In first place is Part I. The first article on the theory of foreign exchange covers exchange rates, short-term capital flows and monetary policy. The first item listed is a monograph or "study," *Foreign Exchange, Capital Flows and Monetary Policy,* published by Fritz Machlup at Princeton. It was a revision of my doctoral thesis. It is not reprinted here both because of its length and because the mathematics is rather crude. In my defense, the readers at Princeton, including Machlup liked it, as did my doctoral committee. The mathematics of foreign exchange was in its infancy at the time. Machlup, in his defense, was one of the leading theoreticians of international economics at the time. Later, we had a friendly chat about our misjudgments.

The *National Banking Review* (NBR) article, "A Dynamic Theory of Foreign Exchange," stands up a bit better. The mathematics was much improved and a remarkable solution emerged. Unfortunately, I do not have a copy of this article and could only re-read it online.[1] Until about this time, foreign exchange specialists had relied on John Maynard Keynes' interest-rate parity.[2] To Keynes, the percentage difference between the forward exchange rate and the spot rate equaled the raw interest-rate differential. As it turns out, the articles herein dispute this because of Keynes abstraction from any speculative variable. Only under the most rigid assumptions and perfect markets does interest-rate parity hold. Jerome Stein had the same result as the *National Banking Review* (*NBR*) article in a much more simple model. Others such as Stein, S. C. Tsiang, and Herbert C. Grubel, helped to modernize the theory of foreign exchange. While the NBR article might be criticized for its linear demand and supply functions, the reduced-form

[1]The U.S. Treasury did not allow me to download this article or my Comment on Leland Yeager's article in the same issue because I no long had a formal affiliation with Florida State University. However, you can read the two articles online by googling "National Bank Review" and going to the June 1967 issue.

[2]Later, Keynes' interest-rate parity was popularized by writer-journalist Paul Einzig (1898–1973), who wrote 57 books. See his *Dynamic Theory of Forward Exchange* (London: MacMillan, 1961), pp. 144–145.

solution could be used to highlight the problems of statistical estimation of forward premiums and thus spot exchange rates.

Even though the model is more complex than its predecessors, its solution *sans* lagged variables is similar to that of Jerome Stein, in a much simpler model.[3] I cast some doubt on using short-term interest rate increases to slow capital flows, as well as the efficacy of a narrow gold band. For the first time, in "A Skeptical View of the Band Proposal: A Comment," I argued in favor of a wide gold band and suggested that we had to go beyond that. At the same time, I attacked Leland B. Yeager (1924–) for endorsing freely-floating exchange rates. I now do not like the tone of the "Comment," and Yeager liked it even less. In his "Reply" in the same issue, he takes me to the woodshed. My mistake was to rely on debating tactics that I had learned on my college debate team at Southern Illinois University. In a later friendly conversation, we both agreed not to do that again.[4]

The forward premium solution was now known as the modern theory of foreign exchange (MT). The new definition of "interest rate parity" has a speculative variable that caused all kinds of specification problems for those pioneers estimating the equation. Herein lies a heated debate about whether the speculative variable in endogenous or exogenous. My MT solution suggested that all variance unexplained by the interest-rate differential is captured in a speculative residual. Later, I realized the implications of this result. While it left some statistically endowed economists less to do, simple arithmetic eliminated all the statistical biases. The importance of the speculative residual is explained in the October 1974 *Southern Economic Journal* (SEJ). The purposes of this article are to show that the inclusion of hedging in the MT does not alter the nature of the reduced-form solution and to show that the unwittingly slighting of hedging in the empirical studies leads to a misinterpretation but not a misspecification. The theoretical models do not ignore hedging but fail to realize that hedging is a function of the expected (future) spot rate.

[3] See Jerome Stein, "International Short-term Capital Movements," *The American Economic Review*, LV, March 1965, pp. 40–66.

[4] Again, the "Comment" and Yeager's "Reply" can be read online. Yeager can best be described as a market monetarist, not entirely under the influence of Milton Friedman.

The usefulness of this MT result is illustrated by the data (May 18, 1973–July 5, 1973) on the "Watergate net speculative variable." Revelations of the magnitude of Watergate related deeds during the Nixon Administration led to speculative selling of dollars, a sharp increase in the foreign exchange rate, and a large and rising negative net speculative residual. Simple arithmetic (the raw interest-rate differential plus the forward premium) yields an unbiased estimate of the net speculative residual. The assumptions made are highlighted in the article. Economists, who very much like Okum's Razor, generally liked this result. Some might question the assumed linearity of the underlying demand and supply relations. Reliance was placed on the *NBR* model.

The *National Banking Review* (June 1967) and part of the Princeton study provide the background for "Exchange Rates, Capital Flows and Monetary Policy" in the *American Economic Review*. The likeness of the titles of the monograph and the AER article is not entirely coincidental. Moreover, the *AER* article also highlights the early problems of estimation of foreign exchange demand and supply functions. It is essentially a survey of the then-current state of the art of foreign exchange theory. The characters included Sven Arndt, Stanley Black, H. Peter Gray, Peter Kenen, Arthur Laffer, Jerome Stein, Edward Tower, Hans Stoll, and Leland B. Yeager, among others. It was a virtual who's who in international finance. It is a polite critique of the statistical state of the econometric art at the time; Sven Arndt and I had a friendly conversation about the exchange of ideas at a recent International Trade and Finance Association Meeting.

"The Theory of Foreign Exchange Speculation under Alternative Systems," *Journal of Political Economy* (1971), came before the *SEJ* pieces. I mention it now because, while it replayed the MT theme, the main chords chimed about speculation in foreign exchange. As far as I know, it contains the only mathematical models of speculation under narrow and wide gold bands (later becoming SDR bands), as well as flexible exchange rates. It is not the first paper to treat speculation under freely-floating exchange rates, but it was the first complete mathematical model to do so. Nonlinear equations were introduced, which was an improvement over the "The Dynamic Theory of Foreign Exchange."[5]

[5]The title mimicked that of Paul Einzig's widely-read book, *A Dynamic Theory of Forward Exchange*.

The MT solution did not escape scrutiny, as evidenced by Van Belle and Sakbani's reaffirmation of (1) that the omission of the hedging constitutes a misspecification of the modern theory of foreign exchange (MT), (2) attempt to prove that even if the emphasis be placed upon indication in "accurate indication," covered margins should not be considered a good indicator of speculation, and (3) demonstrate that it is future, not past values of imports and exports that reflect hedging. My "Reply" was that the authors were incorrect on (1) and (2). As to (3), their reference is to a nonobservable variable since future imports and exports are unknown. Hedging is related to both interest-rate differentials and to the expected future spot rate. To understand all the punches and counter-punches, you really must read all the articles. The main thing was to show that it was possible to statistically isolate trade, hedging and speculative variables. Sometime in 1969, Dudley Dillard (1914–1995), renowned as a chronicler of John Maynard Keynes, cautioned me, "Ray, you are writing on the most difficult subject in economics." Perhaps he was right.

Part II covers income distribution and welfare economics. The two topics are combined because I have always — well, almost always — seen a connection among income-wealth distributions and welfare, if not welfare economics. The first article, "Reflections upon the Income Distribution as a Pure Public Good," co-authored with Howard Tuckman, was motivated by a *Quarterly Journal of Economics* article by Lester Thurow (1938–). He argued that the income distribution is a public good in the sense that it enters everyone's utility function and its consumption is nonrival. He concludes that some income redistribution, therefore, is necessary to achieve a Pareto optimum. The amount to be redistributed and the optimum size of individual tax payments are determined with a voluntary exchange model of the Lindahl-Musgrave-Samuelson type. Thurow argues that "to some extent the voluntary exchange approach may also explain the process that the political majority must go through before it can impose its welfare function on the rest of society."

Thurow's attempt to broaden the concept of Pareto optimality to include the utility derived from the income distribution is laudatory, and his article is forward-looking. Pareto himself defined, first, the ophelimity optimum, which avoids cardinal measurement and interpersonal comparisons of satisfaction. This is the first and primary Pareto optimum commonly invoked by economists. However, second, Pareto in his sociological discussion, changes the ophelimity to a utility criterion, where utility "is a social concept, deriving from ethical, moral, religious, political, etc., as well as economic causes." As it turns out, Thurow's optimum is closer to a utility than to an ophelimity optimum. Thurow has usefully broadened the scope of economic science because his optimum is similar to Pareto's socio-economic one rather than one of pure economic efficiency.

Can the income distribution be a public good? The short answer is "no," but the arguments pro and con along the way are rather intricate, all of which are supplied in our article. The public goods and voluntary transfer approaches involve income redistribution as a prerequisite for achieving a social optimum. But to the extent that income distribution is based upon collective rather than individual action, the attainment of a social optimum also requires some method for reflecting individual preferences. The individual cannot redistribute the income of the entire society, no matter how strong the will to do so. The superiority of Thurow's tactic as compared with the social welfare function (SWF) approaches must then depend upon the acceptability of his utility function and the usefulness of the public goods definition as a guide to public policy.

We argue that the search for the "perfect" income distribution variable that would qualify as a *pure* public good is destined to fail. Later, Lester Thurow and I got to know each other personally and by reputation. The income-wealth distribution as a public good issue never came up again. We both had moved on to a somewhat broader view. I had invited him to give a talk at the Eastern Economic Association meetings (when I was President) and I don't recall any reference to public goods. In his original paper he indeed considers a third optimum, which arises from the inclusion in individual utility functions of X, a vector that "uniquely" measures every possible income distribution. However, if some individuals consider Z to be the relevant vector, the maximization of X need not lead to a societal optimum unless X is a linear transformation of Z. Then, the "optimum" income distribution can be made available to all individuals. Still, measures of dispersion, such as Gini coefficients, quartile ranges, and standard deviations, are generally not familiar to the public.

The central point is that the search for the "perfect" income distribution variable that would qualify as a public good is destined to fail. As we note, Paul Samuelson in 1969 wrote, "…, it is striking how Wicksell and Lindahl and even Musgrave and Johansen...after getting a glimpse of pseudo-equilibrium descend to the swampland of mathematical politics...." Today I would say that Thurow's public goods model does not lead to the optimum defined by his calculus, but this is beside the main point. A social problem requires a political solution. The purist, Thurow not withstanding, wants a Paretian ophelimity solution, where no one is made "worse off." In the real political world, this may require that the minority cast more votes than the majority. This is an outcome considered repulsive in a democratic society, but it could still happen. "To the extent that the market system and effective voluntary exchanges do not give individuals the income distribution that they desire, further redistribution will be determined by political power. It is not individuals but individuals in economic, social, and other types of groups (including policy-action groups) who decide national policies."[6]

Economic power was not considered a legitimate topic for economists. With few exceptions, this continues to be the case. Way back in 1952, my late friend, John Kenneth Galbraith published a book on "countervailing power" in economics.[7] Galbraith suggested that voters, an informed public acting through their leaders, would determine, rather than so much neo-classical rules about marginal utility or competitive equilibrium, whether countervailing power succeeded as a means of delimiting the abuses of economic concentration. Much later, he wrote, "The large corporation is here to stay. Those who want to break it up or confine its operations within national boundaries are at war with history and circumstance."[8] More to the point of our *QJE* conclusions, "Liberalism will be identified with the buttressing of weak bargaining positions in the economy; conservatism — and this may well be its proper function — will be identified with positions of

---

[6]The book chapter cited at this point in the article appeared in a book earlier that year. It is E. Ray Canterbery, "Income Distribution, Human Property and Non-Property Rights," in E. H. Pollack, ed., *Human Rights* (Buffalo, N.Y.: Jay Stewart Publications, Inc., 1971), pp. 373–95. It was delivered as a paper at the International Association for Philosophy of Law and Social Philosophy, Rutgers University, February 1970. Neither a copy of the book nor paper could be found.

[7]John Kenneth Galbraith, *American Capitalism: The Concept of Countervailing Power* (New York:; Houghton Mifflin, 1952).

[8]John Kenneth Galbraith, *The Age of Uncertainty* (Boston: Houghton Mifflin 1977), p. 277.

original power."[9] In late 1974, my *QJE* co-author and I gave a paper to the American Economic Association Meetings regarding a theory of power. Ken Galbraith was among the few who liked the paper. Tried as we might, we could not get the paper published.[10]

Later in seventies, I spent some more time on philosophy and economics. The motivation was provided by two amazing and contentious philosophers. They dominated their fields in the seventies and eighties. Each had something significant to say about economic justice and economists would ignore them at their peril. On the "left" we have John Rawls, who wrote first (1971), and on the "right," Robert Nozick.[11] Both were easy to talk with, and they freely discussed their ideas with me. As we will come to note, Rawls was especially modest.

Harry G. Johnson (1923–1977), then President of the Eastern Economic Association, suggested that he and I co-edit a symposium on "Justice, Nozick, and Rawls." The symposium was conceived and developed by Harry and me. It had a sad and premature ending as Harry had a second and fatal stroke. When we started work on selecting papers, etc., he was walking with a cane; he had had a stroke at the age of 49, but was still lucid and writing furiously. At some point, he had difficulty holding the telephone and I knew that I might have to finish my own and his contribution. His second stroke came on May 9, 1977 (at 53). The other papers were by Israel M. Kirzner, Jan Tumlir, Vincent J. Tarascio, and my good friend, Abba P. Lerner (1903–1982). Harry was the most prolific economist of all time. Abba was a famous follower and interpreter of J. M. Keynes, among many other things. His paper was "Utilitarian Marginalism (Nozick, Rawls, Justice, and Welfare). My effort was "Further Reflections on Economic Justice": Harry's edited piece is not reprinted here. All the articles are summarized in the "Introduction." The concluding "Reflections" addresses issues in detail that are either ignored by the symposium authors or else touched upon lightly, though frequently referenced.

Canterbery sees the advantages in multiple criteria for the ideal or "good society" compared to a unidimensional criterion derived from the

[9] Galbraith, *American Capitalism: The Concept of Countervailing Power*, op. cit. p. 151.

[10] E. Ray Canterbery and Howard P. Tuckman, "Toward a Theory of Power," American Economic Association Meetings, December 1974. Again, a copy of this paper could not be found.

[11] The references are to John Rawls, *A Theory of Justice* (Cambridge, Mass.: Harvard, 1971) and Robert Nozick, *Anarchy, State and Utopia* (New York: Basic Books, 1974).

simplicity of natural law principles. This is not simple for there are multiple criteria for the multiple criteria. The origins of Nozick's natural law view are examined and the moral claims for natural law are challenged. Alternative hypotheses are advanced for the nature of Nature, including those of Hegel and Marx. Not willing to leave philosophy for the philosophers, Canterbery tip-toes into what Paul Samuelson doubtless would have called a "quagmire" for economics. The public goods issue is raised within the context of Nozick's and Rawls' system. Questions concerning economic justice are not simple, and we cannot expect the answers to be any more so. Still, Nozick and Rawls are in search of a prior principle, which raises the question of what the appropriate prior principle is. Nozick's is derived from a moral premise; we must assume that Nature is just. Then for people to be moral they must obey the laws of Nature. Abba Lerner and I were not convinced that Nature knows what it is doing.[12]

[12] More should be said about the Abba Lerner connection. Joan Robinson introduced the then unknown field of macroeconomics to young Lerner who at first was unconvinced. Then, he sat in on lectures by John Maynard Keynes at Cambridge (England) in 1935. As "notes," Keynes read from the galley proofs of his *General Theory* (1936). Abba was asked to write a review essay on the published work; the article remains one of the most lucid expositions on the *General theory*, much clearer than Keynes himself. Compared with Lerner, Keynes was timid on policy and they did not, for that and other reasons, get along with each other. An early bloomer, Abba wrote a number of path-breaking articles, including one published in 1934, Lerner's first year as a graduate student, which introduced the first clear, definitive statement of Pareto optimality. Lerner showed that P = MC is a necessary and sufficient condition of an optimum allocation of resources — that is, a necessary condition for maximizing welfare in an economic efficiency sense. Later in his first major book, *The Economics of Control — Principles of Welfare Economics* (1944), he went well beyond Pareto's ophelimity. Therein, he defined diminishing marginal utility (that satisfaction decreases with growing consumption of any good or service) and society's overall satisfaction will be highest if income is equal for all. The debate over that has yet to end, and Lerner presents a qualified version in his symposium article. The 1944 exposition was the first time that the idea of distributional optimality was introduced. After his year at Cambridge and Manchester, Lerner came to the United States. Like Thorstein Veblen, Lerner bounced from one university to another. After he retired from the University of California at Berkeley, he was a distinguished professor economics at Queens College of the City University of New York until 1978 and then at age 75 took a chair at Florida State University (FSU) until his death in 1982. As colleagues, he and I discussed every aspect of Rawls and Nozick. His article bears my imprint, especially on Rawls and Nozick, much more than the Johnson essay. The balance on distributional optimality is pure Lerner.

Nozick's system of liberty can be viewed as a 20th century back-to-Nature movement and a bolster for the moral claims of neoclassical economics. This moral claim still seems to emanate from a particular view of God, as one who constructed the rules we call natural laws.

In the "original position," Rawls subscribes to the economist's definition of rational man, where the range for choice is narrow and decisions are made independent of people's own contemporary perception of criteria for the "good society," since the judgments are made behind a "veil of ignorance." In the original position the difference principle leads to the idea that society is organized in such a way that the "worst off" is not so badly off. Lerner concludes that anyone put in such a position would indeed follow Rawls' "maximin" principle. He would maximize the minimum income by choosing to be born into that kind of world in which the worst off group is better off than the worst off group in any other of the possible worlds. Rawls is consistent. He views the initial or "natural" distribution of material assets, as well as of natural abilities, as "morally arbitrary," so that no person has a moral claim to any particular product share. Those who would be better off (if paid the value of the marginal product of their work and of the material factors they owned) should make transfers to the worse off. This is considered fair because it brings the distribution closer to what would be chosen if there were no bias, namely, what would be chosen in the original position.

Nozick ends where Rawls begins. Nozick has a principle of rectification that opens the door for redistribution without defining principles or procedures to be followed. Despite rectification, Nozick apparently wishes to avoid a unilateral transfer of income or wealth from one individual to another except in instances of voluntary private charity. From what we have learned in public finance this appears to be an unreasonable constraint on the satisfaction of individuals' preferences within a community. As Lerner and Johnson suggest, people may prefer more equality than that generated by a free exchange system. One can easily see why conservatives lined up behind Nozick and (20th century) liberals behind Rawls. To me, Rawls could be viewed as an inspiration for a fair "Rawlsian society." I told Rawls in a phone conversation that that is what I considered to be his

While at FSU, he was considered for the Nobel Prize in Economics. I, and others, wrote recommendations for him. That he was never awarded the Prize is shameful.

main contribution. The very modest Rawls said, "Perhaps you are right. I do not know for sure." He wrote three more books before his death at 81, but his *Theory of Justice* was his magnum opus.[13]

To invoke Rawlsian language, being both editor and contributor is not always "fair." The other papers were so well crafted that I was left with residual thoughts. It was not the last time that I waxed philosophically, but I never went so deeply into the Samuelsonian quagmire again.

The Review of *Welfare Economics*: *A Liberal Restatement* by Rowley and Peacock is included in this collection because I continued my critique of Rawls and Nozick. Rowley and Peacock's definition of liberalism corresponds to eighteenth-century liberalism and this liberalism-becoming-ideology in the nineteenth and twentieth century. They take on John Rawls, who also impaled himself on the horns of the power dilemma. Like Nozick, they use "Leviathan" as a synonym for government, which reflects their deep fear of anything but a minimal state. This Hobbesian government in which the control of citizens is forever given over to a sole sovereign is not the model of government that was eventually adopted by England or by the colonial renegade Thomas Jefferson. They nonetheless give a knowing nod to John Kenneth Galbraith's view of the planning system, but ignore, at their peril, Galbraith's discourse on the symbiotic nature of corporate and government interests and, therefore, power.[14] Yet a principle could be wrung from Rowley and Peacock: government and

---

[13] John Rawls (1921–2002) went on to become the leading political philosopher of the 20th century, based mostly on his *Theory of Justice*. The only disputes were about who was second.; Nozick certainly was a contender. Shortly before his death, Rawls published *Justice As Fairness*: *A Restatement*, which was a response to criticisms of *A Theory of Justice*. In it he backed off from some of his more controversial ideas. Nonetheless, it is a layman's guide to his great book. He revived political philosophy, which was in the doldrums at the time while giving economists and political scientists much to debate. Rawls received the National Humanities Medal in 1999 from President Bill Clinton, and was the subject of "A Theory of Justice: The Musical!" premiering at Oxford in 2013. The musical, along with posthumous books, extended his fame into the 21th century.

[14] See especially Galbraith's *Economics and the Public Purpose* (Boston: Houghton Mifflin, 1973). It was under the influence of Galbraith that I and Howard P. Tuckman gave a paper, "Toward a Theory of Power," to the American Economic Association Meetings in December of the next year. As I recall, it was Galbraith's countervailing power in matrix algebra , among other things.

other forms of coercion appear to be acceptable if they have the effect of dispersing power. However, they fail to develop this thesis. Economists since have left power to be explained by political scientists.

"A Vita Theory of the Personal Income Distribution" is a well-known, widely-cited article. At the time Vincent Tarascio, the editor, told me that it was the longest paper ever published in the *Southern Economic Journal.* It grew in pages as I digested the many comments that I received on the article draft. The readers included Kenneth Boulding (1910–1993), Martin Bronfenbrener (1914–1997), Harry G. Johnson, Joan Robinson (1903–1983), and Lester Thurow (1938–).[15] Besides Thurow and Johnson, I knew Boulding, Bronfenbrener and Joan Robinson very well. Joan and I carried on correspondence until just prior to her death. I could not ignore the comments of these notable economists. There was a heated rivalry between Joan and Abba Lerner that had been ignited when they first met in the 1930s. Joan had made extended comments on my chapter on John Maynard Keynes in an early edition of *The Making of Economics.* I made the mistake of showing the pages to Abba who immediately said she was wrong about this or that. Ultimately, I had to be the referee. I did not reveal Joan's comments on the Vita Theory paper to Abba. A layman's summary of the Vita Theory is found elsewhere, so I will be brief here.[16] First, a vita

---

[15] Ken Boulding was president of numerous scholarly societies, including the American Economic Association (AEA). He was a magisterial figure in the social sciences generally. He was a prolific writer, which included *Economics as a Science* (1970). Martin Bronfenbrener (1914–1997) was prolific, and was a Fellow of the American Academy of Arts and Sciences and a Distinguished Fellow of the AEA. Joan Robinson was a brilliant teacher who had at least two students who won Nobel Prizes in Economics (Amartyen Sen and Joseph Stiglitz). She was a left-wing Keynesian who turned down Ragnar Frisch's offer to be Vice President of the Econometric Society because she said she could not read the Society's journal. I recall that she received a standing ovation when she addressed the AEA in New Orleans. Frisch and I had an interesting exchange regarding a paper submission, but that is another story. Les Thurow is perhaps best known for his book, *The Zero-Sum Society: Distribution and the Possibilities for Change* (1980) He is an economic columnist for the *Boston Globe*, *USA Today*, and was once a columnist for the *New York Times* and contributing editor to *Newsweek.* A man of many talents, he helped to found the Economic Policy Institute and currently serves on the board of directors of three high-tech companies.

[16] See E. Ray Canterbery, *The Rise and Fall of Global Austerity* (Singapore and New Jersey: World Scientific, (2015), pp. 255–265. H. Peter Gray extended the vita theory into international trade adjustments [Employment Arguments for Protection and the Vita

is a brief summary of the main attributes and events of one's life, a kind of autobiographic sketch. The vita theory is a way of saying that an individual's life history is important in deciding his or her income, and that income is important in deciding the person's life. Now, imagine that one labor market exists for each general class of labor, such as plumbers, medical doctors, electricians, or elementary school teachers. The individuals' quality as a productive member of the economic system determines which labor market that person enters. A person "qualifies" for a particular labor market by the state of his or her vita at the time. The vita begins with birth, when race, sex, religion, national origin, inherent or initial mental and physical capacities, inheritances, and family background (endowments) are duly noted. As persons age they move into a career and finally, a mature vita. As you will see, there is much more to the theory.[17]

In "Welfare Economics and the Vita Theory," once again Paretian ophelimity takes a beating. The faults in traditional welfare optima go beyond the tendency to use ophelimity in a futile effort to avoid the ethics of distribution. First, there must be a theory of the personal income distribution. To avoid the treatment of labor as just another commodity, I use a human developmental model that describes the process of cumulative acquisition of competences or credentials over time. Traditional human capital theory, an approach that relies too strongly on static exchange optima and that continues to treat labor as an abstraction, is modified by integrating individuals into the labor supply in stages over time. These stages are benchmarks in the labor market vitae of persons and hence the term, vita theory. A vita theory of the labor market is used to highlight the true nature of welfare optima as well as to show the requirements of any new welfare economics approach.

I use representative poor and non-poor maximizing utility, which, I argue, is necessary to achieve Rawls's optima. Among the poor are

---

Theory, *Eastern Economic Journal*, Vol. 10, No. 1 (January–March, 1984), pp. 1–13], which was followed by E. Ray Canterbery, "A General Theory of International Trade and Domestic Employment Adjustments," in M. Landeck, ed., *The Empirical Content of International Economics: Regional and Global Issues* (London: Macmillan Press; New York: St. Martin's Press, 1994).

[17] To complete the lay summary, see Canterbery, *The Rise and Fall of Global Austerity*, op. cit. I go on the relate the vita theory to the "Great Gatsby Curve" of President Obama's Council of Economic Advisers.

Rawls's "worst off." Any income distribution beyond that which is determined by private institutions requires a deliberate economic policy presumably motivated by societal concerns and unrequited externalities. Although society can be viewed as a cooperative venture for mutual advantage, it is ordinarily marked by conflict as well as by identity of interests. Because of conflict, further redistribution will be decided by the balances of power among groups in the political system, an arrangement greatly controlled by ideological and ethical considerations so that only an approximation of a (mathematical) global maximum is possible.[18]

The realization of a social minimum awaits the perceived identity of interest with the poor of the nonpoor, or else their altruism. We should not, however, ignore Rawls' difference principle. As I told him, Rawls has presented a vision — not a program — which inspires thoughtful reconsideration of existing social arrangements. Most important, from the view of an ethic acceptable to economists, Rawls' system of justice approaches utilitarianism with constraints when we apply his principles to the income distribution of the ongoing society.

Rawls once again is the focus of "Income Redistribution and Rawlsian Justice" in the *Journal of Economics and Business* (May 1981). I have lost this paper. In it are interdependent utility functions, which are required in the ongoing society if utility is to be maximized. The article was widely cited in the evolutionary economics literature. With some difficulty, Rawls' difference principle is pushed into the real world.

---

[18]This research was supported by the National Science Foundation (NSF). Once again, readers of the draft included Boulding, Bronfenbrenner, Johnson, Lerner, Joan Robinson and Les Thurow. Added to the list were philosophers John Rawls, David Braybrooke, Jeffrey Burkhardt, and Alan Mabe. Ingrid Rima and Kathryn Freeman provided editing assistance. David Braybrooke (1924–2013) was, like Rawls, a political philosopher. He was both a philosopher and political scientist. He had an irreverent sense of humor and was a valuable consultant on the NSF project. We had fun and interesting conversations about Rawls, Nozick and economics. Braybrooke maintained that the purpose of public policy should be to meet human needs. His first journal article was "Farewell to the New Welfare Economics" in the *Review of Economic Studies* (June 1955), which turns out to be a very long goodbye. As an internationally known scholar, he was President of the Canadian Philosophical Association (1971–72), elected to the Royal Society of Canada (1980), and Vice President of the American Political Science Association (1981–82).

"The Forbes Four Hundred: The Determinants of Super-Wealth" is a well-known and widely-cited article, so I can be brief. Our initial goal was to collect enough data to arrange in the Vita Theory format. Since the Four Hundred are at the very tip of the top of the income and wealth distribution, the survey does not provide a data base sufficiently broad to test the Vita Theory. It is a test only if one considers wealth to be lifetime income, including inheritances. In Alfred Marshall's view, the net marginal productivity of labor depends upon the availability of complementary factors of production, such as land, which in turn depends in part upon alternative demands for these cooperating factors. Since the distribution of income (and wealth) influences the demands for outputs and inputs, marginal products cannot be independent of the prior distributions (which the theory is intended to explain). Prior distributions turn out to be important, especially material inheritance, to the Vita Theory, whose framework provided some strong inferences. In the regression results, the independent variables of age, active employment, and particular industries were highly significant. When the Four Hundred are divided by sex into two samples, inheritance is more important to females than to males and active employment is more significant for males.[19]

Part III is all about speculation, foreign and domestic. "The Crawling Peg and Exchange Stability (co-authored with John T. Boorman[20]) evaluates various plans for monetary reform that anticipated the breakdown of what remained of a gold standard, fixed exchange rate system. It is a well-known article: those who can read French have an abstract as their guide. John H. Williamson is credited with the idea of the **crawling peg** (1965). He was quickly followed by J. Black and J Carter Murphy. Black and Murphy suggested that pars be automatically set equal to the moving-average of exchange rates over a predetermined prior period, probably a year. In August 1971, Carter Murphy became a senior staff economist of the Council of Economic Advisers under President Nixon. Less than a week after his

[19] This study preceded a number of similar studies with broader data bases, including using multi-year Forbes Four Hundred data.

[20] John T. Boorman, not to be confused with famous film-maker of the same name, was the co-author's co-author. Fritz Machlup and Thomas D. Willett again were on the scene. I was visiting at Simon Fraser University on the way to Florida State University so it was a long-distance collaboration.

arrival at the White House, the U.S. left the "gold standard." Suddenly, floating exchange rates replaced essentially fixed rates. Carter said that it was the greatest surprise of his career. Variations of the discretionary plan included the sliding parity of James Meade and the gliding parity of William Fellner. Murphy objected to the discretionary crawling peg.[21]

These crawling peg (C-P) plans share the same dilemma. If the exchange rate moves at a sufficient speed (at least 2 percent yearly, we guessed) to equalize the money value of trade flows, the necessity of changing short-term interest rates by about the same percentage points to conserve official monetary reserves completely ties monetary policy to the balance of payments. At a lessor speed, very little change in monetary policy is needed to conserve reserves but the trade account remains in disequilibrium. Williamson admitted that his C-P would require the central bank to keep interest rates sufficiently high to prevent capital flows.

While similar in conception, the automatic moving-average peg devised by Murphy would tie par values to the price of gold and the one by Black favors a calculation of the geometric mean of past exchange prices in which rates are varied in terms of dollars. We thought that exchange rates would be tied to the dollar rather than to gold, so we critiqued the Black version. ((As it turned out later, the U.S. dollar became the unit for expressing exchange rates. The dollar also became the key currency (for trade and capital flows) and the world's reserve currency.)) We show mathematically that the exchange rate will probably move its maximum in one year. If the par rate moved much less than its maximum, such a movement probably would be insufficient for stabilizing the trade account. We encounter the same dilemma as with the aforementioned C-P. If the band were any wider than 3 or 4 percent, it would no longer be a narrow-band crawling peg and speculation, commerce, and arbitrage would be modified by increased uncertainty. We could not formulate a mathematical formula that automatically produced an exchange rate appreciation sufficient to adjust trade but too meagre to attract capital.

---

[21] J. Carter Murphy, who passed away at the age of 91 in 2012, was one of the most pleasant persons that I knew. While he was at Washington University (St. Louis) briefly, I met him there as graduate student. Like most University of Chicago graduates, he was quite prolific, confining his work mostly to international finance.

By 1968 I had formulated something called the **delayed peg.**[22] In its first incarnation, it tied par values to gold (like Carter Murphy's C-P). As noted above, by 1970 (above) I knew that the dollar would probably remain the key and reserve currency. After the events of August 1971, the dollar emerged again as the key, trade and reserve currency. With exchange rates untied from gold, it made sense to tie the hypothetical **delayed peg** to the U.S. dollar. Then, as the years too floated by, some developing nations which did not have independent monetary and fiscal policies anyway adopted versions of the crawling peg. The narrow-band C-P did not fare well whereas the wide-band did. In 2014 only 2 countries (Nicaragua and Botswana) had crawling pegs. Several countries have adopted a **wide band** where if the value of their currency shifts outside the band, they revalue the currency (up or down). This is essentially a **delayed peg**, though the name never caught on. They generally set the par value in U.S. dollars. In 1972 the U.S. Treasury proposed a similar plan, but was defeated by special interest pleas that were only drowned by the inescapable float in rates. In June 1974, the IMF Committee of Twenty proposed the establishment in principle of many of the features of the delayed peg, including a wider band and more par flexibility. Later, I tied the peg to SDR's, which brings us to the next article.

"The International Monetary Crisis and the Delayed Peg" appeared in *Challenge*, but not until 1978. By then the U.S. dollar was not floating, but was sinking, which endangered the dollar in its role as a reserve currency. The Triffin dilemma raised its two heads. If the value of the reserve currency depreciates, there is the danger of capital flight from dollars into a different currency. All this is explained in the first part of the article. The first major test of the floating regime came with the tripling of the price of oil during 1973. The following account of the analysis of the 1970s crisis can be read as cautionary history, for the theoretical attractiveness of floating exchange rates is tempered by the historical circumstances of huge dollar reserves, uncontrollable forces, exchange rate manipulation, and the temptation of raise interest rates. Stagflation was the problem

[22] See E. Ray Canterbery, "The Delayed Peg and the Adjustment Mechanism," A Paper before the Southern Economic Association Meeting (November 1968) and *Economics on a New Frontier* (Belmont, California, 1968) pp. 212–216. I could not find a copy of the paper; copies of the book can be found on the Internet.

then: stagnation and slow growth in the U.S., Europe and Japan is the problem now. So, it is history but it is still instructive.

When we get to a wide SDR band and the delayed peg, we are looking at a possible future.[23] A little background information about the present IMF will aid the reader. The SDR is an international reserve asset, created by the IMF in 1969 to supplement its member countries' official reserves. Some 95% of the world's countries are now member-nations. Initially defined in terms of gold, the SDR was redefined as a basket of currencies in 1973 after the collapse of the Bretton Woods system. Today the SDR consists only of the euro, Japanese yen, pound sterling, and the U.S. dollar.[24] The establishment of the euro-zone, anticipated in the *Challenge* article, collapsed 19 currencies out of 28 member states of the European Union into one currency — the euro. The SDR is neither a currency, nor a claim on the IMF. It is a potential claim on the freely usable currencies of the IMF members. Holders of SDRs can obtain these currencies by exchanging *their* currencies for SDRs. The SDR also serves as the unit of account of the IMF and some other international organizations. The IMF has expressed the value of all currencies, including the euro, in terms of the SDR.[25] The next step toward a delayed peg would be a small one with major implications.

The percentage quotas of SDRs and the percentage of votes held by member nations are very similar. The United States in 2015 had 16.74% of votes, Japan, 6.23%, Germany, 5.81%, the U.K., 4.29%, France, 4.29%, Italy, 3.16%. If Japan, Germany, the U.K, and Italy could agree, which is unlikely, they could outvote the U.S. The U.S., Japan, Germany, and the U.K. combined have a third of the votes. Thus, the financial power which reflects the trading power of these countries is considerable. This is

[23]The delayed peg is replayed in E. Ray Canterbery, *The Global Great Recession* (Singapore, New Jersey, London: World Scientific, 2011), pp. 298–306, and receives shorter play in E. Ray Canterbery, *The Rise and Fall of Global Austerity* (Singapore, New Jersey, London: World Scientific, 2015), pp. 195–199, where the expanded role of the SDR would "shift the current focus of the IMF away from austerity programs in such nations as Greece, Spain, and Portugal."

[24]The weights of the currencies (based on the value of exports, and the amount of reserves denominated in the respective currencies that were held by other members of the IMF) can be revised and the next IMF review is scheduled by the end of 2015.

[25]These current "exchange rates" can be found on the IMF's website.

dramatized by the fact that the emerging nations of Mexico, Korea, and India have a combined 5.17% of the vote. Worse, the developing nations each generally have a fraction less than 0.05% of the votes. The IMF may allocate SDRs to member countries in proportion to their IMF quotas. The general allocations of SDRs have to be based on long-term global need. For example, an allocation of SDR 161.2 billion was made on August 28, 2009 in response to the international financial crisis. Yet, more than one fifth of the current IMF membership never received a SDR allocation until 2009. They are the smallest, poorest member-nations. The delayed peg would even the playing field for the emerging nations and the poorest nations, with the loan window open (as it has been) at the IMF. It would be a workable compromise between (dirty) floating and absolutely fixed exchange rates.[26]

The next piece is a review article of a novel by John Kenneth Galbraith. Its inclusion requires some explanation. In the 1970s and 1980s rational expectations was the rage among conventional economists, though some considered the rational expectationists to be unconventional on the right. The novel, readable and humorous, contains a send-up of rational expectations. Galbraith also pokes fun at his own institution, Harvard, as well as limousine liberalism-becoming-ideology. Few are sparred Galbraith's insightful wit. To understand the novel and some of my articles to follow, we need a brief introduction to rational expectations.

Under rational expectations, all market participants have the same information and use it with equal efficiency. The market is efficient in the sense that all profits have been exploited. No one can make any money because it has already been made. One might wonder why speculators or investors would ever enter a market in which all profits already have been taken. But, unless persons do enter the market, it doesn't exist. The theory assumes a super-rational man, one-upping the usual assumption of merely a rational man. Most importantly, markets work perfectly with a futuristic view of prices.

[26]This would preempt the movement toward a tripolor regime with the dollar, the euro and the Chinese Renminbi as its key likely pillars. The main obstacle to this is not relative economic power, but political. Chinese trade is rapidly growing while U.K. and Japanese trade is slowing as shares of world trade. For an exposition of this view, see Agnes Benassy-Quere and Jean Pisani-Ferry, "What International Monetary System for a Fast-Changing World Economy?", Bruegel Working Paper, June 2011.

John F. Muth (1930–2005), a modest, shy but remarkable business school professor at Carnegie-Mellon fathered rational expectations for commodities markets in 1961, only to be ignored for a decade. Then, Robert Lucas (1937–), once a colleague of Muth's and admittedly under his influence, took the rational expectations strain from commodities markets and infected macroeconomics with it. Macroeconomics has been feverish ever since. Lucas, a graduate of the University of Chicago also was strongly influenced by Milton Friedman and the modern monetarists. Lucas, rather than Muth, was awarded the Nobel Prize in Economics in 1995. Mostly, the Prize came from Lucas' dramatic implications of rational expectations for macroeconomics in his most influential paper, "Expectations and the Neutrality of Money," one of the subjects of his Nobel lecture.[27] Further, in a series of technical articles Lucas claims irreparable flaws in Keynesian *and* monetarist macroeconomics. He and others showed that rational expectations is a necessary condition to obtain internal consistency in macroeconomic models. The prediction of the future values of economic variables which decision makers on average base their decisions cannot be systematically wrong. Errors must be random.

In Muth's original account, which was only about commodities, equilibrium prices are determined by supply and demand. The actual price will only deviate from the expected price if there is information unforeseeable at the time expectations were formed. In other words, price is anticipated to equal its rational expectation:

$$P = P^* + e \text{ and } E(P) = P^*,$$

where P* is the rationally expected price and e is the random error term, which has an expected value of zero, and is independent of P*. The macroeconomic models were a response to theories based on adaptive expectations (expectations based on the values of *past* variables), namely Keynesian and monetarist theories. The result is anti-government policies more radical than the monetarists.

Though individuals' expectations may turn out to be incorrect, they will not deviate systematically from the realized values. Not only does the rational driver keep their eyes on the road ahead, but their ability to correct

[27]The lecture is published in Tore Frangsmyr, ed., Robert Lucus, "Monetary Neutrality," *The Nobel Prizes 1995* (Stockholm, Sweden: Nobel Foundation, 1996.

the steering after a wrong turn leaves such errors or bad turns of the steering wheel on average uncorrelated with the important, relevant variables in future decisions (such as keeping on the road). The hypothetical human gyroscope is correct within a margin of error which itself is random.

In a later paper that was ignored to the same extent that his original account was laser-focused on, Muth maintained that his rational expectations applied only to microeconomic phenomena and was being misapplied by the new classicals in the macro arena. This shocking conclusion was in a paper that I accepted for a proceedings issue of the Eastern Economic Association.[28] Muth did not regret not receiving the Nobel Prize and said that Lucas deserved it for his work in macroeconomics. This kind of generosity, if rare, should happen more often.[29] Suffice to say, the new classicals have never had a strong interest in the real world.

All of which brings us back to Ken Galbraith and speculation in the 1980s U.S. stock market. In Galbraith's novel the young Harvard economics professor Montgomery Marvin has created a measure oi excessive investor optimism and pessimism, the amazingly accurate Index of Irrational Expectations (IRAT). His use of IRAT in the stock market makes him rich. Excessive gains is contrary to rational expectations in which all market participants have the same information and use it with equal efficiency. In other words, Marvin should not be able to make all these profits.

Marvin invents IRAT from his understanding of the delusions of the crowd — South Sea Bubbles, the manic speculation of the late 1920s, and the financial genius of those men who communicated the errors of euphoria to others. From this history emerges a principle of finance: "Find out who in any euphoric episode is the greatest hero, who is the most celebrated, and invest in his eventual fall."[30] Luckily, by the mid-1980s, "euphoria was becoming endemic and universal."[31] The Securities and Exchange Commission (SEC) determined that IRAT was an illegal manip-

---

[28] Muth's critical paper was presented at the Eastern Economic Association Meetings in Pittsburgh. See *Proceedings of the Eastern Economic Association*, July–September 1985.

[29] For the complete story of rational expectations and the new classicals, see E. Ray Canterbery, *The Making of Economics, 4th edition, Vol. II The Modern Superstructure* (Singapore, New Jersey, London: World Scientific, 2009), pp. 109–126.

[30] John Kenneth Galbraith, *A Tenured Professor* (Boston: Houghton Mifflin Company, 1990), p. 57.

[31] Galbraith, *op. cit.*, p. 83.

ulation of the markets. Marvin had an unfair advantage. Moreover, those following his trades had inside information on his purchases and sales, a clear case of insider trading based on inside information on Marvin's trading — insider trading based on non-insider trading, and market failure is the product of the rational use of irrationality.[32]

"Irrational Exuberance and Rational Speculative Bubbles," was given as the presidential address at the International Trade and Finance Association Meetings in Atlantic City. "irrational exuberance" is a phrase made famous by Alan Greenspan in late 1997. Greenspan apparently believed that an irrational bubble was driving the stock market. Trying to avoid raising interest rates and causing the greatest stock market crash in history, Greenspan, then the great defender of "free markets," tried in vain to talk the market down. In late spring 2015, Janet Yellen, the current chairperson of the Federal Reserve Board, was trying the same thing, after years of zero or near-zero Fed funds rates. Again, there is a fear of a bubble in stock prices.

Greenspan's and (now Yellen's) tactics fly in the face of theories of efficient capital markets based on rational expectations. There is some irony in the Greenspan case: throughout his chairmanship of the Fed he denied that asset bubbles could exist or worse, collapse. Most historians and a few economists side with Greenspan. Ultimately, they say, we must come to grips with the reality of financial excess, a form of mass hysteria. The great financial bull market of the 1990s seemed to be coming to such a gruesome finale by August 1998. Those who deny bubbles mus go to the barricades against the four great bubbles of modern history — tulipmania, the Mississippi Bubble, the South Sea Bubble, and the Great Crash of 1929. Yet, in the late 1990s and continuing thereafter, *rewriting* the history of bubbles became a cottage industry. These revisions have been written by rational expectationists.

In addition to the rational bubble models, their predecessors are put into play to "explain" the great bubbles. In what were then called perfect foresight models, Hahn, Samuelson, Shell-Stiglitz, and others nonetheless argued that in the absence of futures markets extending into infinity, no market forces could prevent bubbles. In many such models, every bubble

[32] This review was written while my time was split between FSU and Ben Johnson Associates, where I learned over about a three-year period a great deal about private business.

eventually burst, requiring only that a speculator be sufficiently long-lived to take profits. The rational expectations' models, though bearing a family resemblance to the Samuelson-Hahn type models, made contrary claims.

Perhaps the best known bubble ended in the Great Crash of 1929. Ken Galbraith and the eminent economic historian Charles P. Kindleberger described the bull market of the late 1920s as a bubble that burst. Though most historians agree with Galbraith and Kindleberger, the rational bubble economists claim that those who bought shares were behaving rationally and no bubble existed. Yet, in the late 1920s stock prices raced way ahead of dividends. Fundamentals cannot explain the divergence between dividends and prices. The downward slide continued through June 1933. The use of credit fueled the bubble. Nothing, including higher interest rates at the Fed, could deflate the bubble. But it had to collapse. We find that the mathematical models of the rational bubble theorists cannot undo the conclusions of the economic historians or the predecessors to the rational expectationists.

Those who have read the above papers on foreign exchange theory and speculation will have little difficulty with "Rational Bubbles and Uncovered Interest-Rate Parity: Retrospective and Prospective." The focus shifts from domestic bubbles to foreign exchange bubbles. In the rational bubble models of foreign exchange, even the "bubbles" are "rational" because investors can believe that the foreign asset's price is above its fundamentals value and they will continue to hold the asset anyway. If the foreign exchange rate keeps moving in one direction, it is because it is expected to continue to move in one direction. The rational bubble never collapses; its bursting would betray irrationality on the part of speculators, a reversal of the requisites of rational expectations. The antecedents of this bubbling literature include the use of rational expectations in the theory of covered and uncovered interest-rate arbitrage.

The core difference between the earlier discussions of interest-rate parity and those of the rational expectationists is the introduction of an expectations operator. They find that the future spot rate equals the current forward rate at the date of maturity of the interest-earning asset. This is because the forward premium or discount on foreign exchange is directly linked to the current raw (uncovered) interest-rate differential. Most of the empirical research did not find market expectations to be rational. There was an attempt to amend the uncovered interest-parity (UIP) equation by adding a risk premium. Such a change in specification contradicts rational expectations and the original UIP because, if the information set includes all relevant information it would include risk considerations. It doesn't because the information set is equal to the forward premium on forward exchange.

The modern theory (MT) solution of the earlier papers include a risk variable, which can be expressed as a expected value. Then, the difference between the expected future spot rate and the current rate depends upon both the uncovered interest-rate differential and the expected value of the risk proxy. As noted above, the modern interest-rate parity equation always has a residual. The residual can be defined statistically as an error term with zero mean. We have seen how this residual can be estimated arithmetically.[33]

The rational expectationists fair no better when we go to more sophisticated model.[34] In the model, the exchange rate can move exponentially away from its equilibrium or fundamental value. Thus, as economic historians would have it, a speculative bubble in foreign exchange expands. It is a rational bubble only if no events can reverse the trend in the exchange rate. Within my *JPE* model, risk can rise and burst the bubble. However, rational expectations requires that the bubble last forever. Moreover, the rational expectationists generally deny the existence of bubbles, so something that does not exist cannot burst.

Part IV covers microeconomics, some of which is rather conventional and some not so much. "Income Distribution, Human Property and Non-Property Rights," was a paper presented to the International Association for Philosophy of Law and Social Philosophy at Rutgers University in February 1970 and reprinted in the Pollack volume. As noted, this paper has been lost and I could not find a copy of it on the Internet. As I recall, it had a lot to do with collective action groups and the redistribution of income-wealth. It made a plea to distinguish between human rights and property rights, the two not being synonyms. It was a philosophical prelude to another lost paper, "Toward a Theory of Power," which marked a return to economics in 1974.

---

[33]The above E. Ray Canterbery, "The Modern Theory of Foreign Exchange and the Net Speculative Residual, *Southern Economic Journal* 41, 1974, pp. 182–87.

[34]The above E. Ray Canterbery, "A Theory of Foreign Exchange Speculation under Alternative Systems," *Journal of Political Economy* 79, 1971, pp. 407–436.

The mathematical modeling in "An Evolutionary Model of Technical Change with Markup Pricing" imitates to a considerable degree the pioneering simulation work of R. Nelson and S. Winter. They in turn owe some intellectual debt to Joseph Schumpeter and Herbert Simon, among others. There are, however, major departures from or modifications of the Nelson-Winter model. (1) Policy variables such as alternative depreciation allowances and R&D tax credits are introduced. (2) A strategy markup on prime costs is based upon the growth objectives of the firm. (3) Rather than a putty-putty assumption about the relationship between capital and techniques, I use a putty-clay version. In this way the expected prices of inputs matter prior to switches in technique but not after. (4) Latent or potential productivity in the industry does not necessarily grow at a constant rate. (5) The futuristic nature of the firm's decisions is modeled further by incorporating future expected capital, labor, and other costs rather than current input prices alone. (6) Wherever relevant, values such as gross investment are expressed in money terms rather than only in physical units.

One of the main departures from Nelson-Winter is the use of markup pricing. Markup pricing eases the financing constraint. My late friend Alfred Eichner (1937–1988) had a particular formulation of the markup, which I modify. I have planned innovation (prior to planned production) yielding a price that can generate internal funds.[35] The markup pricing rule is to have a percentage markup on variable costs. In turn, the markup is decided by the current number of firms in the industry and the expected or perceived price elasticity of demand to the firm. The greeter the number of firms in the industry and the greater the expected price elasticity of demand, the lower the percentage markup. A greater price elasticity means a market share gain for an innovative firm producing and selling at a lower price. Innovation eventually can reduce the number of firms in the industry. Then, the markup can be increased at the same price elasticity level. In the model, price turns out to be a double-edged sword. However, there is a price that will roughly equate the rate of growth in sales with the

[35]This essay was one of those written in memory of Alfred Eichner, who died prematurely and suddenly at the age of 50 while playing racquetball. I and others urged him to slow down, especially to see a Doctor when he had chest pains. But he insisted on soldiering on. In a shortened career, he had a great impact on the economics profession. He opened many Post Keynesian doors for me.

rate of growth in financial funding ability. To repeat, there is a unique price and markup that nearly equate the sales growth rate with the financial funding ability growth rate.

The next two papers, "The Coase Theorem as a Negative Externality" and "Two Coases or Two Theorems?" read somewhat like lawyer's briefs. They in this way pay tribute to Ronald Coase (1910–2013), who taught law and economics for many years at the University of Chicago. We summarize the Coase Theorem as follows: Under perfect competition, and in the absence of income effects and transactions costs, voluntarily negotiated agreements among private parties generating or being affected by externalities will lead to the same resource allocation (and output mix) regardless of how property rights are assigned among the parties. Coase did not originate the phrase, the "Coase Theorem," nor its precise formulation, both of which were done by his colleague, George Stigler.[36] Two of Coase's articles, "The Nature of the Firm" (1937) and "The Problem of Social Cost" (1960), are most frequently cited when economist's refer to the "Coase Theorem." In his Nobel Lecture Coase refers to the "infamous Coase Theorem," almost as a disclaimer. The Prize was "for his discovery and clarification of the significance of transactions costs and property rights for the institutional structure and functioning of the economy.[37]

A few definitions will help the reader understand the points and counter-punches. When a cost is imposed on a third party, it called a negative externality. When their parties benefit from activities in which they are not directly involved, the benefit is called a positive externality. Air and water pollution caused by industry imposes health and clean-up costs on the whole society, whereas the neighbor of an individual who chooses to fireproof his home may benefit from reduced risk to fire to their own home. Thus, unregulated markets in goods and services with significant

[36] Stigler, noted for his works on regulation, won the Nobel Prize "for his seminal studies of industrial structure, functioning of markets and causes and effects of regulation." (The Sveriges Riksbank Prize in Economic Science in Memory of Alfred Nobel 1982).

[37] Thorsten Persson, *Nobel Lectures, Economics 1991–1995* (Singapore, New Jersey, London: World Scientific, 1997). The Prize was awarded in 1991, but I did not know about it while drafting the first article. As I recall, I did not know about the Prize until after the "Reply" went to press, because we do not mention the wonderful news (for a very nice man) in the second piece.

externalities generate prices that do not reflect the full social cost or benefit of their transactions; such markets are dubbed inefficient.

The definitions used by Coase too were by example. He acknowledges that high transactions costs might preclude a voluntary contractual agreement in his first article on the subject. The government, given legal rights and enforcement powers, could eliminate externalities. Coase remained skeptical about such outcomes because he thought the administrative costs of correcting externalities could be high. His examples are very clever but mostly hypothetical. One has to do with the property rights to the use of a cave, another is the property rights to a lighthouse (his best example), and still another pits farmers against ranchers. We conclude that the Theorem is really a circular argument and with the "ultimate irony," which is that the search and information costs embodied in the literature on the Coase Theorem must have been high, even if we exclude our own efforts. It is best that you read the article and judge for yourself.

The second article is the better one, because we had the advantage of having a thoughtful commentary by Steven Medema.[38] He agreed that our critique of the Coase Theorem was "largely on the mark." He chose instead to deal with our treatment of Ronald Coase and his relation to Zero Transaction costs and the Coase Theorem. The Coase Theorem is not at the heart of Coase's message. Rather, Coase embraces the real world of positive externalities. This makes two Coase's: the one invented by George Stigler and the one who won the Nobel Prize. Coase is really attacking the Pigouvians who always prefer government action in the face of externalities. As it turns out, he favors a weighing of marginal benefits and marginal costs solely in terms of maximal production. The "precision" of Coase's cost-benefit analysis really does depend upon perfectly competitive prices. Since prices reflect private not social costs, the evaluation of social costs with private cost data is contradictory for Coase and Pigou alike.

To get the full picture, you really need to read not only the articles, but the comment by Steven Medema and Coase's Nobel Prize lecture.

The short contribution on "Input-output analysis" requires little comment. It was written sans mathematics because a complete understanding of the mathematics of such modeling would require the knowledge of

[38] Medema went on the become President of the History of Economics Society in 2009–2010.

matrix algebra. I aim only to convey a feeling for the topic and its most important implications. For this, I simply defined matrix and vector. Since Nobel prize-winner Wassily Leontief (1973) first developed such a model in 1941, it has been expanded in many ways.[39] Herein I draw a connection to radical economics of the left. The core question they tried to answer was whether the intermediate output supplied by all industries constituting the production system be reduced to only one type of fundamental input. This central issue has divided economists from the beginning. Karl Marx, as noted, based his answer on a labour theory of value. This and other "answers" can be expressed in input-output analysis, as it is done here. The neoclassical theory is more a capital theory of value.

Piero Sraffa, a lovable Italian who spent much of his life editing David Ricardo, gave one answer in his famous "Production of Commodities by Means of Commodities" (1960). Another approach is to consider the total value added required of the economy in terms of both labour value and profits. This problem was solved by Luigi Pasinetti (1981) in his vertically integrated model of production. Independently, Canterbery (1979, 1994) developed a similar model without sensing the vertically integrated nature of the production system. Once the wage rate (unit labour cost) is known in the Pasinetti or Canterbery models, we only need to find "profits" in order to derive the price solution. In this way the full cost of production necessary for replication or continuous expansion of the economy can be found.[40] In this regard Sraffa provided some wonderful insights. Later, Eichner (1987) proved that we need make no distinction between the markup and the profit margin, even in a growing economy.[41]

---

[39] Leontief's Nobel Prize was for the development of input-output theory. He was a short, modest and kind man who often came to the defense of older and younger radicals on the Harvard faculty. He and Kenneth Arrow were among those who left Harvard in protest when the Harvard economics department purged itself of the brilliant young radicals on its faculty, such as Samuel Bowles and Herbert Gintis, who went on not only to win many awards but to make contributions to orthodox and radical economics.

[40] The Canterbery model (1994 version) can be found in Part IX of this collection. However, the reader is not spared the mathematics.

[41] There apparently are two publication dates for Eichner's *The Macrodynamics of Advanced Market Economies*, 1987 and 1991. The 1987 version is the one that I first read. I recall a meeting at some AEA meeting with several Post Keynesians and the then-editor

"Cost Savings from Nuclear Regulatory Reform: An Econometric Model," co-authored with my consulting colleagues, Ben Johnson and Don Reading, is pretty straight-forward. "Cost Savings from Nuclear Regulatory Reform: Reply" is not reprinted here. Both are widely cited. What we concluded in 1996 generally still holds today. Some 20 percent of U.S. electricity is nuclear-generated, no new plants are planned or on order, and some of the earliest units are up for decommissioning. There is a little bit of George Stigler in the paper. He would have liked the idea of an empirical approach with real-world data. Moreover, our premise is that the relevant costs are those of providing safe and environmentally clean electric energy. To the extent that the increased costs resulted from increasingly stringent regulations, they reflect the internalization of external costs. Thus, in this regulated industry, social and "private" costs are essentially the same. This is unique to the regulated industry; as Stigler contended, such a market is inefficient if unregulated. In this case, positive externalities were internalized.

There is much more to the article. We used ordinary least-squares to estimate the cost per kilowatt hour in the construction of nuclear projects. We also identified the sources of these costs. The cost per kw is less if the utility has moved down the learning curve by building other nuclear plants during the era studied. Our results confirm the existence of economies of scale (see Figure 1). As one might suspect, the level of regulation has contributed to the cost of nuclear projects. Some costs were associated with inefficient project management and with more complex, more costly designs. A second model, a policy simulation matrix adds to the case for regulatory reform and a need for pre-approved, standardized designs.[42]

"Cost Savings from Nuclear Regulatory Reform: Reply" (1997) gave us a chance to bolster our case. David Dismukes employs a data base that is similar — or, at least, overlapping with — ours. Moreover, he clearly states what he has accomplished. The dramatic contrast in sample design and empirical testing enhances the comparison. Having said this, we reassert the utility of our approach and the reliability of our findings. He states

for M.E. Sharpe in which we discussed possible changes in the book. In any case, a revised edition was published posthumously in 1991.

[42]The research and writing of the nuclear regulatory reform papers were conducted while I was a consultant to Ben Johnson Associates, Inc.

that we failed to recognize that the construction cost data has an unequal number of nuclear plants being constructed in an unequal number of years, and that we incorrectly used construction costs on a "per-project" rather than "per-plant" basis. This, he claims, led to irrelevance of the cumulative NRC regulations variable, and doubts about significant economies of scale.

Dismukes used a "first plant" variable which tends to "front-load" a significant amount of common costs onto the first unit, as he admits. This is one reason why we prefer to study the cost of entire projects. Each utility project involves a collection of common attributes that cannot be arbitrarily severed at the first unit level. Management, site location, design, transmission lines, and substations tend to be common to the entire project. However, management has the incentive to "front-load" costs onto the first unit to achieve faster cost recovery. We continue to favor the per-project approach to estimating costs and economies of scale.

Our dramatic comparison with the building of the Canterbury Cathedral in 1174 bears repeating. Similarities, including massiveness and wall thickness, exist between modern nuclear power plant construction and the building of the great cathedrals of the Middle Ages. In 1179 William of Sens laid the foundation for the enlargement of the church to build a chapel (a second unit) for St. Thomas a' Becket. The new foundation extended into the monks' cemetery, requiring careful exhumations and reburials (environmental reparations). In 1180 William directed the construction of the wall that encloses the choir and presbystery (third unit). He was forced to narrow the far end of the choir because of the placement of the existing towers (design error), whose massiveness precluded moving them (retrofitting). The reconstruction at Canterbury required about seven years (the average project duration in our nuclear sample was about ten years). In an accounting of the costs of construction, it would make little economic sense to use a dummy variable for the central nave costs (first unit) and then exclude the choir and the chapel in evaluating the overall scale of the project, since all areas were and are used for the production of religious services. Further, we would not doubt that duration contributed to the costs of construction (clerics meddled with the plans while William, the architect, continued to collect his handsome stipend).

The Theory of the Leisure Class and the Theory of Demand highlights Thorstein Veblen's contribution to demand curve theory. Mainstream economists are of several minds regarding Veblen, but few would hesitate in mentioning Veblen's contribution of such evocative terms as "conspicuous consumption," "conspicuous emulation," "pecuniary culture,": vicarious consumption," and "the leisure class" to the language of economics. The mainstream has even ratified Veblen with "Veblen effects."

Veblen entered the mainstream in a classic article by Harvey Leibenstein on "bandwagon, snob, and Veblen effects." The bandwagon, snob, and Veblen effects are due to *external* effects on utility. The *bandwagon effect* derives from the demand for a commodity increasing because others, too, are consuming the same commodity. Social taboos that effect consumption are bandwagon effects in reverse. The *snob effect* derives from the demand for a commodity decreasing because others are also consuming or increasing their consumption of the same commodity. The snob effect has an opposite but otherwise symmetrical relationship to the bandwagon effect. The snob jumps off the wagon because they do not want to associated with those jumping on. The "Veblen effect" refers to conspicuous consumption in which the demand for a consumer's good is increased because it bears a higher rather than a lower price. Taking all these influences into proper account, the most plausible demand curve is shaped like a backward S in which the schedule is upward sloping against price in some range, a range exhibiting the "Veblen effect."

Leibenstein's treatment of Veblen is not perfect. Some effects cannot be captured in the demand curve, even if S-shaped. To Veblen the standard of living shared by a particular class determines the "accepted standard of expenditure." That is, contrary to Leibenstein, price is not necessarily a yardstick in demand. As Veblen put it: "To accept and practise the standard of living which is in vogue is both agreeable and expedient, commonly to the point of being indispensable to personal comfort and to success in life." Veblen takes the bandwagon beyond a trip around the block. When it comes to emulation, the rich are more likely to take note of the higher prices of luxury goods than the middle-class emulator seeking status at any cost. The upper middle class or even middle class who want to emulate the rich leisure class but must do so by buying cheap imitations or by borrowing, even at the risk of bankruptcy or worse, which might be called the "Gatsby effect." *The Gatsby effect*, of course, intimates disasters beyond bankruptcy from which recovery is possible. As noted at some length,

F. Scott Fitzgerald's The Great Gatsby is the supreme Veblenian parable of conspicuous consumption, of conspicuous emulation, of pecuniary culture, and of vicarious consumption — even of waste and the leisure class itself. Like the orthodox neoclassical, Jay Gatsby fails to realize that Daisy is priceless, putting her out of reach of his standard of living.

The mainstream has recognized some of the deficiencies in Leibenstein's theory. In particular, Bagwell and Bernheim have attempted to deal with the Veblenian cases that Leibenstein excludes. First, they show that some individuals might prefer to purchase a larger *quantity* of conspicuous goods at a lower price, or a higher *quality* of conspicuous goods at a higher price. For instance, social climbers do not have be rich to buy Ralph Lauren's Polo brand clothes; yet the label signals exclusivity. Second, Bagwell and Bernheim rebut the "single-crossing property" of models with asymmetric information. The indifference curves depicting substitutability between inconspicuous and conspicuous goods are, contrary to neoclassical theory, concave rather than convex to the origin. The "single crossing" occurs where the higher-income individual's indifference curve crosses the lower-income individual's indifference curve from below, reflecting the possibilities for cheap emulation. Contrary to the single-crossing property, Bagwell and Bernheim show that the upper-class households can increase their utilities, without causing imitation, by purchasing more of the conspicuous good at a lower price.

Most economists acknowledge the influence of Veblen on John Kenneth Galbraith's view of demand, which is most visible in *The Affluent Society*. Concealed behind Galbraith's "much reduced urgency" of consumption is the idea of economic surplus, the means whereby the remaining economic insecurity could be banished. Enhanced production comes at the cost of a paradox, or, in Galbraith's words, "as production has increased in modern times concern for production seems also to have increased." He invokes the image of a hierarchy of goods whereby those required for daily living were more important to the average consumer than luxuries. Such a view is contrary to neoclassicial economics in which no rank ordering of goods according to biological need or psychological satisfaction is possible (because cardinal utility is implied). As production surpluses mount (from rising productivity), consumers increasingly must be persuaded regarding adequate consumption. The producer must take on an ancillary role of synthesizing wants "by advertising, catalyzed by salesmanship." That wants are "shaped by the discreet manipulations of the persuaders show that they are not very urgent. A man who is hungry need never be told of his need for food."

Still, the idea that discretion is the better part of value is an incomplete account of capitalism. In a theoretical system of perpetual scarcity the capitalist can barely be a prime mover. Any self-respecting capitalist is rightly embarrassed when they fail to produced a net surplus. Since the upper 1 percent now control roughly 40 percent of total household wealth, a surplus must exist on the income side either in a reflection of production surplus or as rentier income. American capitalism is indisputably an economy of surpluses. In what I have called a "supra-surplus economy," a hierarchy of absolute physical necessities and "wants" coexist. "Higher standards of living" usually are associated with the satisfaction of a greater number of wants, not the satisfaction at the margin from one more unit of the same good.

The implications for this new view of demand found their way into macroeconomics via James Duesenberry and his relative income hypothesis. His hypothesis is based on two assumptions: (1) the household's consumption depends in part upon the consumption patterns of other households (i.e.; utility functions are interdependent); (2) consumption is in great part dependent upon habitual patterns of behavior and therefore depends in part upon past consumption behavior. These assumptions are purely Veblenian, the first being based on pecuniary emulation and the second on inertia or the unwillingness or reluctance to break with former behavioral patterns. Econometrically, Duesenberry estimates a series of short-run consumption functions that exhibit a ratchet effect. The nonlinear short-run function ratchets upward in response to a new peak level of real disposable income, but consumption backslides reluctantly along the new (nonlinear) short-run curve in response to income declines. Duesenberry's relative income hypothesis is consistent with the cross-section data results. A low-income family experiences more pressure from the demonstration effect to attempt to match the consumption patterns of a high-income household. The average propensity to consume falls as one moves up and through higher-income households. Besides Duesenberry, direct utility functions and extended linear expenditure systems empirically confirm the importance of standards of living in consumption behavior.

"The U.S. Motion Pictures Industry: An Empirical Approach" was a rare econometric look at the industry. Studies of the success of individual films explain the films, but not necessarily the industry. A review of the then sparse literature on films revealed important facts about the industry's structure. The main finding in these studies was that the major studios must incur rising costs (from stars and their promotion) not only to have rising revenues, but to maintain market shares. Through advertising the studio can capitalize on the star as an input. The major studio/distributors distinguish themselves through their efforts to produce "hits" or blockbusters. It is not unusual for the top four movies to generate a fifth of total box office revenue. The "star system," born with Adolph Zukor's full-length films featuring such then luminaries as Mary Pickford, Douglas Fairbanks and Gloria Swanson, led to domination of the industry by a few majors. In the 1960s Elizabeth Taylor and Richard Burton broke the million-dollar level and literally set the stage for the action stars such as Burt Reynolds and Clint Eastwood to begin the multimillion-dollar star spiral in the 1970s, extended by such stars as Bruce Willis in the 1980s (and 1990s).

Typically the top four studios have about 60 percent of the market. Although membership among the top four has rotated among those having blockbusters, only six studios dominated the market during our sample era. The oligopoly of the 1920–50 era, based upon the old star system, has evolved into its presently more complex form, but it remains an oligopoly.

Most of the econometric equations are easy to follow. The most difficult variable to obtain was the identity of the stars. We did a survey of the stars, pretested the questionnaire, and distributed the final questionnaire, containing 429 "stars." From the "votes" for the stars, we created a rather complex index. Its conversion to an integer or index number scaled the vote count down to the range of 0 to 15. For example, Kim Basinger is a 10, whereas, ironically, Bo Derek, the star of *10,* is only a borderline 7. In turn, the index for each star was multiplied by the appearances of the star during a particular year. Finally, the products of the index and appearances of all stars in each year's movies were summed. These sums became the observations for the variable, "star." The simple correlation between our measure of stars and blockbusters was 0.80, so that 80 percent of the movies with stars turn out to be blockbusters. This was encouraging.

We used vector autoregression (VAR) log-log estimates for three demand for movies functions. The significantly estimated price elasticity of demand ranges from –0.23 to –0.52, suggesting highly inelastic demand. This inelasticity may be a measure of the success of the majors in differentiating their products though non-price competition. Total revenue estimates were consistent with the estimated price-inelastic demand. Consistent with all this was some evidence of economies of scale. By filling more seats and extending movie runs, the theaters create economies of scale for the major studios. Despite many seemingly unique characteristics in the movies industry, the movie star model may be applicable to the recording, television, and sports industries where stars receive large rents.[43]

We caution that these econometric results only apply to the 1965–1991 years. Though, some rough estimates carried the conclusions through 1999. Foreign films rather than foreign-born stars may be making inroads on the majors. Old blockbusters are being remade.

Part V is on Economic Thought and Methodology

"What Do We Mean by Asking Whether Economics is a Science?" with Robert J. Burkhardt is an easy read, especially for those with a taste for methodology and philosophy. Bob and I had been working on a philosophical critique of economics, and, after Alfred Eichner had seen a draft, asked us to prepare a condensed version for his newly edited book.[44] The question of whether economics is a science is complex. The answer has a lot to do with what we mean by the word "science." The tendency in the academy is to compare economics with physics or astronomy. Yet to describe economics as a science merely implies a standard which economists continuously seek to realize in practice but which, at the present time, is realized in neither the whole of economics nor any part of it.

[43] Some studies by economists since have found very little difference between the star performer and the also-ran. As a casual observer of recent films and the PGA golf tour, the public seems to lean toward stardom as a standard. Tiger Woods was *the* golf star when this article was published, and he still gets headlines even when he fails. He and Greg Norman, and even Jack Nicklaus and Arnold Palmer, still sit in the TV booth and earn income from advertisements. There are emerging "stars," such as Jordan Spieth and Rory McIlroy, who are being called "the next Tiger."

[44] It is an unpublished report, E. Ray Canterbery and Robert J. Burkhardt, Economics: The Embarrassed Science, National Science Foundation, Washington, D.C., 1980. It indeed *was* revised as a book manuscript, which was lost in a flooded warehouse in Tallahassee. Burkhardt was a superb editor and greatly improved the article and the book manuscript. Others who worked as consultants on the NSF project included (the aforementioned) David Braybrooke, Piero Mini, Leonard Rychtanek, Walter Zenner, and Robert Veatch.

Still, economics has certain basic features of a science. Thus, in this essay it is useful to consider what philosophers of science mean when they say "science" and what criteria they submit for its application.

A self-conscious conception of science emerged only with the rise of the logical positivist school of philosophy in the early 1900s. This school offered criteria for evaluating theories, and ones for evaluating whole areas of investigations as well. The ten criteria are listed in the article. According to the logical positivists, science must necessarily *progress* if it follows the positivists' ten commandments. That no scientist actually does follow all of those rules, led philosopher of science Karl Popper to introduce the notion of "falsifiability" in order to save the sinking positivist ship. Science is a moving picture of conjectures, refutations, new conjectures and so forth. Rather than try to prove theories true, scientists should — and do — really try to prove them false.

The positivists argued that, even with a principle of falsification supplanting that of verification, real science retains the logical structure outline in the positivist canons. Others, especially Thomas Kuhn and Imre Lakatos maintained that the whole of science was process, research programs, and paradigms. Science is definable not by either its content or its empirical methodology but rather by what scientists who are accepted as scientists by other scientists hold it to be. Science is whatever scientists do. In Kuhn's view a sociological analysis is more instructive than a logical construction for understanding the nature of science. At the heart of Kuhn's view is the concept of the paradigm. The paradigm defines who are indeed "really scientists."

One of the tests of whether the economist-writer is within the paradigm is publication in certain refereed journals. The ranking of departments is strongly dependent upon the number of articles published in the "leading" journals. The holders of doctorates from these schools also are among the majority of authors in the leading journals and among convention participants.[45] The departments are distinguished because the "best" departments are those who publish in their own journals, which are "best" since they publish the "best" departments. We called this "academic incest." Indeed,

[45] This trend continued, at least for a considerable time after publication of the data in this article.

the "truth," resides in seven academic departments whose membership comprises a small share of the registry of all economists.

In these leading journals the tendency is to continue to support theories that support the paradigm, without even attempting, or at least rarely attempting, to falsify the results of a hypothesis testing theory. In 542 full-length "empirical" articles in the major economics journals from 1973 to 1979, we found that only three articles actually attempted to falsify the hypothesis proposed.[46] Nearly all of the hypotheses accepted support the fundamental presuppositions of the orthodox paradigm. Paradigms can only define truth within them, as they define the limits of acceptable discourse, acceptable practice. The rank-ordering of paradigms requires an Olympian vista. In the final analysis, all we can say is that, at present, orthodox economics is the dominant paradigm. If a scientific revolution is afoot, it is not because theirs is not a scientific paradigm. Rather, it is because it is not *our* paradigm. The shift in paradigms only once in each generation is not due to mere chance.

The Review of *The Reconstruction of Economic Theory* (1989), edited by Philip Morowski, is reprinted because it covers some of the same ground as the first edition of my *The Making of Economics* (1976). Mirowski defines normal-science economics as the bigemony of neoclassicism and Marxism, the center of gravity for any reconstruction. He identifies a possible "third stream" flowing from such journals as the *Journal of Post Keynesian Economics, Journal of Economic Issues, Cambridge Journal of Economics, and Economic Development and Cultural Change*, with the contributors drawn from these pages. They are all opposed to the theoretical imperatives of neoclassical theory and include David Levine, Randall Bausor, David Ellerman, Donald Katzner, and Morowski.

None of the contributions are bound by tradition. Levine describes a classical price theory in which persons acting in their self-interest cannot be relied upon for general systemic coherence. Levine suggests that that production price (based on the cost of production) often fails to do so.[47] Bausor and Mirowski attack the "law of one price." Price, Bausor says,

[46] The hypotheses tested appear in Appendix 10A of Canterbery and Burkhardt, Economics: the Embarrassed Science, *op. cit.*

[47] This was the case in our study of the nuclear power plants (above).

cannot embody enough information to be a dependable means of economic coordination. He develops an alternative mathematical model using an idea from G.L.S. Shackle. Mirowski attacks the perspective that price is merely the simple ratio of physical quantities. Commodities are nonhomogeneous and cannot be properly quantified in physical units. Pride of place for neoinstitutionalism[48] goes to Ellerman, who sees the absence of a theory of property appropriation in neoclassical economics as a problem. Ellerman uses double-entry property accounting and activity analysis to identify appropriations or transactions with nature. Levine treats the firm as a semi-autonomous institution and Katzner models the firm as a case application of formalism to economic analysis. Mirowski's essay on "Mathematical Formalism and Economic Explanation" is a brilliant discourse on physics, mathematics, and economics.

The essays are extremely well written, with at least their first halves fully accessible to all economists and their second halves accessible to those trained in advanced algebra and integral calculus. I recommend the book.

"The Doctrine of Inherent Productivity: Keynes, Sraffa, and Kalecki" traces the history of the idea that capital has inherent value. Marshall's idea of value flowed from the independent schedules of supply and demand. That turned out to be a misapplication of David Ricardo. Ricardo defined land as having a natural and indestructible capacity for production, the return to which was the inherent property of the soil. However, in the industrial sector, changes in relative machine-labor costs create changes in all final prices. There is no measure of capital-labor intensity that is price independent. Marshall's notion of dual scarcity out of production with diminishing returns and out of consumption with diminishing utility has dominated the neoclassical short run. The value of capital is derived from the short-run spot prices of capital and final product, This turns out to be circular argument because we cannot assign values to capital until the final product is priced.

Even Keynes' struggle to escape marginalism and the influence of Marshall is incomplete. The enigma of dynamic capital accumulation

---

[48] Neoinstitutionalism is a theory that focuses on developing a sociological view of institutions, the way they interact and the way they affect society. It is often contrasted with the "old" institutionalism of John Dewey, Thorstein Veblen, John Commons, and has been advanced by such scholars as Richard Rorty, Amartya Sen, Donald (Deirdre) McCloskey, Warren Samuels, Dan Bromley, E. J. Mishan, and others. Among these alone, Amartya Sen won the Nobel Prize (1998).

through dynamic income and market shares cannot be resolved with short-term tools fashioned to solve the critical problem of short-term unemployment. At one point Keynes suggests that the market for physical capital is governed by the principle of scarcity under conditions of diminishing marginal productivity, and through consumption under the law of diminishing marginal utility. Marshall could not have put it better. Keynes theory of capital scarcity (derived primarily from supply and demand in the capital goods industry) is evident in his marginal efficiency of capital (MEC). His MEC reflects both the laws of diminishing returns in the capital-producing sector and the derived demand for capital based on the principle of diminishing marginal utility.

Sraffa repudiates the doctrine of inherent productivity. Given a particular level of effective demand, commodities are produced by means of commodities. Capital equipment is viewed as a "commodity," so its price varies with the price of the final product, which cannot be known in advance of production. Besides, the value of capital varies with wage and profit rates. There is a possible escape hatch for Sraffa (within an earlier Sraffa); it is only sketched here and we will return to the issue in more detail later in this volume.[49]

Kalecki replaces the doctrine. Capital goods are not priced according to short period scarcity principles, but instead once acquired receive their value from conditions prevailing in the final market for the commodity produced. As the market for finished goods always exists at a date ahead of that when capital is purchased, installed, and used, capital valuation becomes applied *ex post*. From a cyclical perspective Kalecki explained the self-propelling movement of dynamic capital value replacing the static doctrine of inherent productivity. As noted, there is much more to Kalecki than this. In a face-saving gesture, we find elsewhere in Keynes the idea that capital accumulation must conform to those market conditions prevailing when its product is ready for sale. In this instance, Keynes anticipates Sraffa and Kalecki.

"Burke, the French Revolution and Public Choice Theory" was written in response to an invitation from a friend, Warren Samuels

[49] For a brief but understandable summary of Sraffa, see *The Making of Economics, 4th edition, Vol. III The Radical Assault* (Singapore, New Jersey, London: World Scientific, 2010), pp. 142–143.

(1933–2011). He must rank among the top editors in economic history; he always had an interesting topic, this on the French Revolution.[50] Modern conservatism, which had its roots as a counterrevolution against the French Revolution, continues today.

The government of Louis XVI, beginning in 1774, was always on the brink of bankruptcy because the propertied failed to bear their share of the fiscal burden and because the French economy was growing slowly. He brought together an Assembly of Notables, leaders of the French aristocracy, to remedy the situation. Instead, the king got in return a tax revolt. The aristocrats who benefited most from the ancient regime took advantage of the king's fiscal deficit to reverse the trend of modern French history toward a strong monarchy. The aristocrats hoped to use the Estates General, last convened in 1614, to draft a government of the people, by and for the aristocracy. The Constituent Assembly swore (the Tennis Court oath) that they would disband only when France had a written constitution. Louis XVI, whose kindness was said to greatly exceed his intelligence, legalized the extralegal actions of the commoners. Voting by head count ended the aristocratic revolt and started the anti-aristocratic revolution. Reforms to meet the needs of the peasants and urban middle class while depriving the nobles of their special privileges, including the manorial obligations of the feudal system, followed. Much intrigue and one war later, the experiment with a limited monarchy failed. The democratic phase of the Revolution began.

The events of the French Revolution bequeathed the historical Edmund Burke. His *Reflections on the Revolution in France* (1790) was a literary success that created controversy. Burke made an impassioned attack on a political development which embodied the aspirations of vast segments of the population of Europe and seriously threatened the established order. At first, especially with the English Revolution in 1688, Burke was labeled an alarmist, a negative perception that changed in 1793 when France's Committee of Public Safety initiated "The Terror." The guillotine sharply vindicated Burke. Burke's ideas became the foundation for modern conservatism, a doctrine in defense of privilege which could serve as an antidote for future revolutions. The themes of this counterrevolution were echoed by

[50] Samuels described himself as an institutionalist.

public choice theorists during the 1980s and 1990s, a coalition of academic conservatives led by the formidable James Buchanan (1919–2013).[51]

Burke expressed the further fear of public debt. The economies of the 18th century states were economies of public debt. Still, all was in its rightful place as long as intellectual energy was controlled by the clergy or similarly by the patronage of "great men," that is, landed aristocrats who Burke considered the foundation of the social order. While public debt and the state were important, to Burke the institution of private property was in many ways, more important than the state. Since property is a natural right, the state cannot be a proprietor, only a guardian and regulator. Excluded from the roles of the state was the right to redistribute wealth, for the virtuous essence of property was inequality. His brief for public property, influenced by Adam Smith and dedicated to the virtues of inequality, was admired by public choice theorists who perpetuate Burke's synthesis of the Whig principle of freedom and the Tory principle of order. We find that Thomas Hobbes' state of nature — or more exactly, the Hobbesian state of mind — validates Burke's view and is the point of departure for the public choice theorists. The Reign of Terror became Burke's metaphor for Hobbes' state of nature. Out of brutish nature comes the social contract. John Locke and Jean-Jacques Rousseau developed other social contract theories, revived by John Rawls and Robert Nozick (see above).

Buchanan's constitutional attitude requires him to merge the Hobbesian state of nature with the unanimity test of Knut Wicksell. There is a Rawlsian "veil of uncertainty" about what the future holds. From these conditions Buchanan asks which social contract would conceptually elicit unanimous consent. This social contract is a strict constitution to be strictly interpreted. Its purpose is to provide constraints on political action. However, in Buchanan's "original position," unanimity is achieved through the coercion of fear for life and property. When we fear for our lives, most of us are willing "to bargain with the devil" without equivocation. A constitution then fills the void left by people fleeing for their lives.

[51] Buchanan won the Nobel Prize in 1986 "for his development of the contractual and constitutional basis for the theory of economic and political decision-making." His founding of the public choice school of economics was also mentioned. Gordon Tulloch (1922–2014) is often given credit for co-founding public choice. As one might suspect, I found both to be contentious and formidable debaters.

As the history of the French Revolution demonstrates and Burke admonishes, constitutional conventions sometimes fall into the hands of those who not have in mind the same conceptual constitution as the elite. So much the worse for public choice theory.

I could not find a copy of my introduction to Ben B. Selligman, *Main Currents in Modern Economics* (1990). Selligman (1912–1970), a well-known author of books on unemployment and poverty, had long since passed. The publisher, who I knew, asked me to write the introduction. The only thing I remember was "It deserves to to be the classic that it is."

The Review Essay–Countervailing Persuasion, on John Kenneth Galbraith's *Economics in Perspective* was another Warren Samuels project. It is an easy read and requires little comment. The first part is a mini-biography because I found it difficult to separate the man from his writings. Galbraith, at 83, was very much alive at the time, so the essay reflects this. At Berkeley, JKG was introduced to the writings of Veblen and Veblen's ironic skepticism made a lasting impression upon young Galbraith. His early life was an excellent background for his later career as a social critic, among other things.

The general theme of the book is that public policy and private decision making cannot be understood apart from its history. Moreover, that history cannot be understood apart from the circumstances that shaped the belief of the time. *Perspective* is typically Galbraithian because it replays his favorite themes. They are: (1) the neoclassical orthodoxy is irrelevant; (2) Economics in practice is theology; (3) power, especially as it relates to industrial concentration, is important in explaining economic outcomes; (4) great inequalities characterize advanced capitalism; and (5) an incomes policy is critical to the survival of the advanced capitalistic system. Galbraith sees the perfect competition retention of present-day economists in an age in which it is rejected by businesspeople (except as prescription for others), related both to theology and to the rise of mathematical economics.

Hopefully, this Review has aged gracefully.[52]

[52] Ken Galbraith continued to write almost to the end at age 97. In our last telephone conversation, just a couple weeks before his death, he said that he had published a book that "you will like very much." It is *The Economics of Innocent Fraud.*

Speaking of aging gracefully, you have to include my late friend, George P. Brockway (1916–2001, among them.[53] He published the third edition of *The End of Economic Man* at 79, and went on to publish *Economists Can be Bad for Your Health* in 1996. He was blessed with common sense graced with erudition, wit unspoiled by rancor, wisdom undiminished by pretense, and humanity unsullied by gratuitous moralizing.[54] I am not the only one to speak highly of George and his writings. Jeff Faux of the Economic Policy Institute called him "a national Treasure." Robert Heilbroner, a mutual friend and an amazing author himself, wrote: "In Brockway's hands economics becomes entirely understandable." Of Brockway's last book, Post Keynesian Paul Davidson wrote, "... Each piece is a gem in a string of pearls."

Brockway was an amateur economist-writer who deserves to be read by professionals. Adam Smith, one of the first amateur economists, was a moral philosopher who dabbled in economics only when he wrote *The Wealth of Nations*. David Ricardo was a stockbroker first, a parliamentarian second, a landowner third, and an amateur economist last. Jeremy Bentham, who laid the utilitarian foundations for modern microeconomics, would today be consigned to the belfry; he not only wrote books but bestsellers. Irving Fisher, highly regarded by professional economists, was an inventor, mathematician, statistician, businessman, reformer, and lastly a teacher. The regrettable loss of status for the amateur as as public intellectual brought me to George Brockway and his Third Edition of *The End of Economic Man.*

Once Chairman of the Board of W.W. Norton, which burnished the reputations of many economists by publishing their more readable works. Brockway also wrote wise, clear, and amusing essays for *The New Leader* and also contributed to *Challenge*, the *Journal of Post Keynesian Economics*, and the *New York Times*. As an amateur historian, he wrote *Political Deals that Saved Andrew Johnson* and was an honorary fellow of the Society of American Historians. In *The End of Economic Man, Third Edition,* he again opens with a rapier attack on "the economic man."

[53] Again, this is a *Challenge* piece, and it bears the earmarks of the editing skills there.

[54] We became friends during the final decade of his life: I regret that I did not know him sooner. George was remarkable, and anyone who knew him came away a better person. In his final days, when he was in considerable pain, he spoke with me about his future writing plans.

His ambition was to bury the hypothetical, self-interested and yet "rational," economic man. Brockway succeeds admirably, dancing on the grave of this hypothetical for fifteen chapters with what he calls the "Three Antinomies of Greed."

He goes on to lay to rest the saving-investment conundrum, define the dichotomy between speculation and enterprise, dismiss the notion of a natural rate of unemployment, and mounts an attack on then-current monetary policy. In the short run he has rising interest rates actually contributing to inflation, which he bases on his business experience at Norton. The new classical theory justified business cycles caused by "technological shocks," but it was a theory that once again justified the natural rate of unemployment. When the economic man is alive, the economy makes inadequate use of its labor and inappropriate use of its money. For more, you really must read the Review.

This spot was originally reserved for my 'The Theory of the Leisure Class and the Theory of Demand." Instead, you will find it in Part IV, chapter 8. Microeconomics was a close call for it for in it I showed how demand theory changes by including Thorstein Veblen's ideas on conspicuous consumption or the ostentatious display of wealth, pecuniary emulation ("keeping up with the Joneses"), and the presumption of surpluses superseding scarcities.[55]

In "Thorstein Veblen and The Great Gatsby," early on parallels between Thorstein Veblen's *The Theory of the Leisure Class* and F. Scott Fitzgerald's *The Great Gatsby* are drawn. My contention is that much of the socioeconomic satire informing *Gatsby* is not original with Fitzgerald, but reflects the influence, both directly and indirectly, of Thorstein Veblen. Admittedly, the indirect evidence which immediately follows, is circumstantial. Here is my brief.[56]

---

[55] For much more on Veblen, see E. Ray Canterbery, *The Making of Economics, 4th Edition, Vol. III: The Radical Assault* (Signapore, New Jersey, London: World Scientific, 2010), pp. 44–54.

[56] An earlier version of this paper was presented to the AEA Meetings in New York (January 4, 1999). This happily led to an encounter with the very talented Thomas D. Birch of the University of New Hampshire. We talked about co-authoring a biography of Fitzgerald with my paper as perhaps one chapter. This led to E. Ray Canterbery and Thomas D. Birch, *F. Scott Fitzgerald: Under the Influence* (St. Paul, MN: Paragon House, 2006).

F. Scott Fitzgerald's *The Great Gatsby* is set in the 1920s and, like its author and Zelda, it is strongly identified with the Jazz Age. However, Fitzgerald's original setting for *Gatsby* was the middle of the Gilded Age (1885), and the theme of the novel is widely recognized as an indictment not so much of the Roaring Twenties as of the "American Dream," which had attained an honored place in American mythology well before the opening of the twentieth century. Fitzgerald's masterpiece is the supreme Veblenian parable of conspicuous consumption, of conspicuous emulation, of pecuniary culture, and of vicarious consumption — even of waste and the leisure class itself. Surpluses, so essential to Veblenian economics, allow ostentatious display; they also promote advertising. While during the Gilded Age, the rich engaged in *self*-advertisement, by the 1920s, advertising had become an important industry. Daisy, in her turn, is attracted to Gatsby because he reminds her of "an advertisement." The cultural illusions are more important than wealth. As to snobbery, Gatsby again provides instruction. Tom and Daisy Buchanan live in a Georgian colonial mansion representing *established* wealth. In contrast, Jay Gatsby bought a vulgar imitation of a European mansion in East Egg. Even Gatsby's ivy is nouveau.

Now we turn to the *direct* evidence. Fitzgerald first described an East Egg type of Society in a March 30, 1924 syndicated article. Though he does not refer to Veblen in the article itself, his notes relating to the article make clear that he was consciously documenting the theme of conspicuous consumption and waste. The theme of "Our Irresponsible Rich" must have been very much on Fitzgerald's mind when, with three chapters of *Gatsby* in manuscript, he abandoned Long Island's lavish parties and escaped with Zelda to the more sedate Riviera, where he completed the draft, published in 1925. An earlier direct reference to Veblen appeared in a paragraph intended for a published review of a 1921 book by H.L. Mencken. The paragraph, deleted by a party unknown, was apparently a Fitzgerald joke, given that Mencken had earlier published an assault on Veblen.

We can only speculate about the motives for Fitzgerald's failure to acknowledge fully his debt to Veblen. Though he was generous in attributions, Fitzgerald prided himself in his originality. The parallels in the depiction of class may have been too close for comfort, and he distanced himself from Veblen. Other evidence may be lost to history because

Fitzgerald had no secretary until 1932. Out of 6,000 known letters, an estimated 3,000 were written prior to 1932. These have been lost.

The Report on The Turkish Financial System: Problems and Prospects (1967) is probably somewhere in the archives of U.S. State Department.[57] I could not locate a copy. I recommended some structural changes in the Turkish financial system. At the time the very conservative Turkish bankers were very reluctant to make loans to any firm or industry. The system was divided between private and public banks with the public banks closely allied with a nascent central bank. A major problem then was the lack of data from the banks and from the central bank. The Turkish money supply data were based on an extrapolation of two data points. The stock market consisted of a little, elderly woman keeping track of the few exchanges of the few stocks in a yellowing notebook. Her office was slightly larger than a broom closet. I further suggested that a viable bond market would depend upon development of a viable stock market.

Much has since changed. Recently the International Monetary Fund (IMF) issued a Report about how well the Turkish financial system weathered the 2008–2009 global financial crisis.[58] The pattern of contraction in credit was similar to that of the United States. Today, the IMF has complete consolidated balance sheet data on the private and public banks, and Turkey has a much more sophisticated central bank.

"The Green Revolution and the World Rice Market, 1967–1975" was another USAID project.[59] It was completed in 1971. The main purpose of

---

[57] A then energetic Barbara R. Bergman (1927–2015) at the University of Maryland and a Senior Economic Adviser with the U.S. Agency for Economic Development (USAID) recommended me as a consultant. She went on to become a prominent feminist economist. In Ankara I was lucky enough to meet briefly with another USAID consultant, the very impressive Edward S Mason of Harvard (1899–1992), who retired a couple years later. Among the things I recall most vividly is a Turkish cleaner losing most of Mason's monogrammed shirts. I was of no help since I was much shorter than him.

[58] IMF, Turkey. Financial System Stability Assessment, IMF Country Report No. 12/261 (September 2012).

[59] Michael Roemer, then at USAID, employed my services as a consultant in 1969 on the prospects of the Green Revolution. Based on this preliminary work, the Rockefeller Foundation and its social science director Michael P. Todaro (1942–), funded a project on the economic aspects of the Green Revolution. Roemer went on to the Harvard Institute for International Development (HIID) at Harvard, which was birthed in 1974 and died an

the study was to take into account the dramatic green revolution in rice production in making forecasts. We take into account the yield changes from technological advance and the impact of both production and consumption changes on the world price of rice. Rice consumption and production estimates were developed both from statistical equations and, in the case of production in the miracle-grain-adopting nations, from nonstatistical techniques. We were able to estimate statistically rice demand functions for the major consuming nations and for the world because of the stability of most of the consumption functions. The estimation for production and related elasticities was much more difficult. The many assumptions made are discussed in detail. The limitations of the purely statistical estimates make up a long list and should be read.

The period used for the least-squares regressions was 1955–1966. Rice consumption and production elasticities were estimated from the structural equations. Then, forecasts of the independent variables from 1967 through 1975 were made in order to estimate price changes. Thereafter, world and national production, consumption and trade estimates were made for the same period. We end by warning that the main problem from the Green Revolution probably relates to income distribution and levels.

In his "Discussion" of our paper, Vernon W. Ruttan (1924–2008), a well-known development economist at the University of Minnesota, concluded that "The authors do not know enough about the world rice economy to be playing the world rice market outlook game." Anyway, our "Reply" suggests otherwise. John W. Mellor of Cornell University's "Discussion" had more specifics.

"The Green Revolution: A Reply to Professors Ruttan and Mellor" is a easier read than the original article. Mellor criticizes our assumptions, but does not say which ones or how different assumptions would change the results. In retrospect our assumptions appear quite reasonable. Our methodology is unique, and the simultaneous estimates of rice price elasticities are made for the first time as far as we knew. Just why this methodology

---

unhappy death in 2000 because of controversy over HIID supervision of Russian aid. Roemer then went to New York University. Todaro, author of 8 books and more than fifty professional articles, recently published the 12th edition of his text, *Economic Development* (Philadelphia PA.: Trans-Atlantic Publications, 2014). He is the co-author of the famous Harris-Todaro model of rural-urban migration in developing countries (1970).

was considered to be so "ad hockery" as to offend Ruttan's "esthetic sensibilities" is not clear. In the "Reply" we list the several advantages of our methodology. Then, we compare our forecasts with those made by USDA, and find our world production estimate is 3.3 percent above USDA's, a difference probably explained by our development of the higher-yielding-variety production tables by hand. In the country estimates, only Japan's appear to differ significantly with both our production and consumption estimates under the assumption of "free markets" being about 13 percent higher. One would expect consumption of this basic necessity in the Asian diet to rise with production, and price elasticities to be zero or near-zero. Mellor says that we underestimated the demand elasticities. However, Mellor's cited elasticities are based on the Slutsky-Schultz condition which we find defective. The price behavior *assumed* by the USDA is relatively consistent with the price behavior that our model generates.

"The Employment Impact of the Green Revolution in Five LDC's" was, as I recall, a paper delivered at the Econometric Society Meetings in 1972. I do not have a copy of the paper. It statistically estimated employment changes directly related to the effects of the miracle-grain-adoption in five developing countries. It was based on research again funded by the Rockefeller Foundation.[60]

Aquaculture and the Developing Countries: *A Feasibility Study* had as the senior author Frederick W. Bell (1935–2006). It addressed the world food problem and the possibility of technology transfer in the fisheries industry. It included a study of the role of aquaculture potential for species transfer. It explored the nature of aquaculture enterprises and included a simulation model of technological transfers. We traveled up and down the east and west coasts gathering data from state offices and other sources. The data included biological information on various species. From those and productivity data by country, we were able to estimate parameters for the simulation model. The results included ocean and other suitability, production estimates by species, employment estimates and even foreign exchange earnings. It was a pioneering study.

The Foreword to Bernard A. Schmitt's book, *Protein, Calories, and Development*, is included for a several reasons. Bernie was one of my

[60]I do recall making a presentation for Todaro on some high floor of the Rockefeller building, which swayed with the wind.

graduate students at Florida State who later co-authored a paper on tax reform (see Part VIII below).[61] As noted, he was involved in the USAID and Rockefeller Foundation studies of the Green Revolution as well as a pioneering study of aquaculture in developing countries (see above). He learned from these and went on to produce this remarkable book. Finally, there is a message here about the income and nutrition distribution, an inequality that cuts across nations also slices through them.

Even the largest share of the fruits of the Green Revolution have gone to those who already had the most, a tendency called the "Matthew Principle" by Kenneth Boulding (1910–1993). The affluent nations that have met the production challenge can confront the distributional one. The impetus of the Green Revolution needs to be regained with more of the focus on distribution. New technologies and new products beyond miracle grains such as rice are need in the developing countries. Schmitt's treatise provides the information for a policy program.

My copy of the Global Report: Industry and Development (1985) has gone missing. It was published by the United Nations Industrial Development Organization (UNIDO), headquartered in lovely Vienna, Austria.[62] It shows the relationship between various industries and economic development. The goal given the consultants was the creation of an annual report.[63] The report currently published is the Industrial Development Annual Report with the 2013 report available on the Internet. Unfortunately, I do not recall enough of the Global Report to provide an overview. It endorsed the primary objective of UNIDO which is the promotion and acceleration of industrial development in developing countries and countries with economies in transition. Some 172 nation-states were members in 2015.

[61] Bernie is currently Deputy Chief of Staff of the U.S. Congress Joint Committee on Taxation, U.S. Congress.

[62] I fondly remember Vienna, which still is enamored with its past. My family and I spent much time with the Karl Zidek's, then I made short visits during the winter, staying in a comfortable Pension. We visited Kaffhous's (coffee houses) where the clock seemed to have stopped in 1910. Likewise, there was the Schonbrunn Palace, The Hofburg, the headquarters of the Hapsburg dynasty for 700 years, the Gothic Stephensdom (dark and gloomy), the Riesenrad (of *The Third Man* fame) in Stadpark, and so on.

[63] The consultants consisted of three Americans, two Koreans and a Russian. It was truly an international experience in which drinking the local red wine (or beer) was virtually a condition of employment.

The "North-South Conflict: Necessary Industrial Evolutions" (1990) paper has been lost. The title was quite descriptive of the content. The "North" and "South" referred broadly to the developed world and the developing countries. The industrial revolution does not have to be exactly copied, because advanced technology and techniques can be imported by developing nation-states. However the end of conflict which is related to production and income-wealth inequalities requires some level of industrialization in the "South."[64]

Part VII is about macroeconomics. The first paper, "A Note on Recent Money Supply Behavior" (1965) marks an early criticism of U.S. monetary policy, a habit broken recently by the ascension of Janet Yellen to the head of the Fed. My focus was on the behavior of interest rates and the consequent effect of open-market operations on the money supply.[65] The National Bureau of Economic Research (NBER), which keeps track of such things, dated three recessions relevant to this article — April 1960–February 1961; December 1969–November 1970; and August 1957–April 1958. Because of balance-of-payments considerations, the Federal Reserve placed a floor under the short-term Treasury bill rate from mid-1950 through most of 1961.[66] Setting an interest rate goal first results in the money supply doing essentially what the interest rate requires rather than vice versa. Lower interest rates and a more rapidly

[64] Mexico City, where the paper was presented, is as fascinating as the Mexican people are interesting. In many respects, it resembles a "Northern" city. A stroll down Paseo de la Reforma that connects the National Palace with the Castle of Chapultepec makes a trip there worthwhile.

[65] Shortly before that — in 1961–1962 — I was an Assistant Office Manager and Statistician for the Research Department of the Federal Reserve Bank of St. Louis. Homer Jones (1906–1986) was Director of the Department and was a firm believer in the money supply determining just about everything. Milton Friedman (1912–2006) said that he decided to become an economist because of his teacher at Rutgers (Jones) Judging from this article, I did not fall under the influence of Friedman, but my work at the Bank had an influence. Homer had the habit of rewriting the Bank's *Review* after it had been published. His wife, Alice Hanson Jones was a prominent economic historian. Monetarism did not become popular in the profession until the 1970s and 1980s, ending around 1990. Friedman won the Nobel Prize in 1976. Alice Vandermeulen was editor of the *Western Economic Journal* at the time and was a cheerful supporter of my efforts.

[66] This was prior to the era when the federal funds rate became the main policy target.

expanding money supply are thought to be expansionary in terms of GNP and employment compared to slower growth in credit (and money) and higher interest rates. From 1960 through 1963 the average annual rate of growth in the seasonally adjusted money supply was only 0.5 percent during the first half-year, while the rate rose to 4.7 in the last half.[67]

It seemed reasonable to conclude that the the change in the intra-yearly movement in the money stock was a consequence of "pegging" and pushing of the short-term Treasury bill rate.[68] In the early months of the year the monetary authorities supported higher yields by selling securities in the open market. During the fall and winter, when seasonal credit demands were strong, the System allowed the money supply to expand without endangering the support level for Treasury bill yields. This policy changed the behavior of one of the seasonally adjusted indicators used in evaluating monetary policy, that is, the money supply itself. It caused the money supply, between April and November of each year, to appear to have expanded faster than it actually did. Some analysts would say that the monetary contraction contributed to the plateau in employment and industrial production from May though the end of 1962.

"Inflation, Necessities and Distributive Efficiency" (1979) was not to be found. In it, I attempted to explain why the marginal utility of income does, in reality, diminish. Every individual's utility cannot be determined, but that is not an issue since we are concerned with probabilities. For that it is sufficient to measure marginal utility between one income interval and another. Individuals have a hierarchy of needs and wants; that is, basic needs trump other needs and some wants are more compelling than others. Properly defined, a hierarchy of bundles of goods and services can be lexicographically ordered. That is, individuals would rather have some goods and services (hereafter simply goods) from bundle-type one than to have any at all from the bundle-type ranked two and this holds for all subsequent rankings.

In this layered view personal income levels decide not only "marginal" but total utilities. If income rises adequately, all the basic

[67] Seasonally adjusted money supply was an innovation of the Federal Reserve Bank of St. Louis, which had the reputation of being the "maverick" Bank in the System.

[68] The later idea of the delayed peg would preclude the necessity or temptation to "peg" interest rates to slow short-term capital flows (see Part III above).

necessities will be consumed and the consumer moves on to satisfy wants. The threshold level of income for, say, bundle-type two, equals the satiation level of income for bundle-type one so that the satiation level of income in each case specifies a kink in the Engel curve (quantities consumed at different incomes). The personal income at the top provides the *least extra* utility but together with those beneath, the greatest *total* utility. The extended linear expenditure system (ELES) not only is a way of measuring consumer responsiveness to changes in income, but also can identify "necessities" versus "desired goods" for a society of a particular per capita income. That income devoted to non-necessities is supernumerary or purely discretionary income, giving rise to a supernumerary function (the ratio of expenditures on non-necessities to total expenditures). This ratio is higher in higher income countries and is higher for high-income families and lower for low-income families in the *same* country.

How does this relate to macroeconomics? The negative of the inverse of the supernumerary function is the expenditure elasticity of the marginal utility of expenditure or the Frisch parameter. Since the marginal propensities to consume of each discretionary commodity or bundle out of income can be estimated from the ELES equation their sum is the aggregate marginal propensity to consume (MPC). In turn, the MPC and the MPS can linearly transform the Frisch parameter into the income elasticity of the marginal utility of income. The integral, mathematically, of the income elasticity is the *marginal utility of income*.

There is a connection to savings in the economy. A general rise the price of necessities such as food, public utilities and medical care (at a given money income) requires a diversion of income away from discretionary items. As the subsistence share of total expenditures rises, savings will fall. The sensitivity of savings to the prices of the "most necessary" goods declines as per capita income rises. Put differently, as absolute necessities become smaller shares of incomes, savings become less responsive to price changes in the highest ranked (least desired) good. Therefore, we can expect the MPS and savings to rise at higher levels of per capita income, Keynes' long forgotten admonition.[69]

---

[69]This summary is based on "Necessities, the Marginal Utility of Money, and Saving" (see below).

The two short pieces, "Control of Inflation" and "Prospects for Social Security in a Half-Century" (1983) were written at the request of George Gallop. They are light works intended for the general public. I no longer have copies. In "Control of Inflation" incomes policies are recommended as substitutes for monetary policy. As I recall, I was optimistic regarding the future of Social Security.

"Galbraith, Sraffa, Kalecki and Supra-Surplus Capitalism" (1984) was an attempt to build a bridge from Piero Sraffa to Michal Kalecki to John Kenneth Galbraith.[70] This connection occurs because of Galbraithian notions of producer sovereignty and power. Sraffa nullifies demand theory and leaves open the theory of personal income distribution. Galbraith, introducing something more akin to producer sovereignty fills the demand vacuum left by Sraffa. In this way, Galbraith is the source of a demand theory that derives from the extension of the objective forces of production institutions. Sraffa moves from the classical subsistence economy to a production surplus economy; Galbraith moves on to the affluent society, a *supra*-surplus economy.

Kalecki's simplification of the income distribution, dividing income only between workers and capitalists, compels us to go beyond Kaleckian subsistence into the more complex distribution of supra-surplus capitalism, where we recognize the role of power in economic relations — a role epitomized by Kalecki's (and Weintraub's) price mark-up. Kalecki's "degree of monopoly" dovetails with Galbraithian "power." The configuration of a potential paradigm is drawn with some further intimations of the most realistic theoretical constructs of demand and income distribution.

In Sraffa's model of the surplus economy, basic commodities or goods that appear as inputs *and* as outputs are necessities only in a technological sense. Demand, even the demand for necessities, plays no role in deciding prices. However, non-basic commodities or goods and services enter only final demand and include both necessities and luxuries. Prices are production production prices or physical costs, not market prices. Only in Sraffa's subsistence model are basic commodities necessities in consumption as well as in production. He makes no attempt to separate the allocation of the extra-subsistence wage between necessary and "luxury" consumer goods. Still, his

[70]This article was part of a symposium celebrating Ken Galbraith's 75th year.

idea of a standard commodity group comprised of those basic commodities that enter into production in the same proportion that they exit production drives a wedge in the neoclassical system sufficiently wide to allow room for a new theory of demand *and* of income distribution.

A Kaleckian view of production can be made to conform with Sraffa's subsistence model, if we divide Sraffa's output sector into two distinct industries, one producing necessary consumption goods, the other producing necessary investment goods. We can introduce subsistence wages into Sraffa's subsistence model and transform it into a Kaleckian world of income distribution.[71] Since investment goods are combined with labor at a given technology, the demand for consumer necessities and investment goods determines the employment level. Such a model reveals that labor is best treated as a basic service, because labor is still necessary to produce subsistence commodities.[72]

We go on to show that mark-up pricing plays a strategic role in supra-surplus capitalism. Where corporate and union powers exist in supra-surplus capitalism and are symbiotic, *physiological* subsistence for the labor class must expand into *cultural* subsistence. The distribution of income re-enters the picture, but in a more complex way than in Kalecki. To fill the gap left for the personal income distribution, the vita theory of personal income is invoked. [73] As to demand, when hierarchical demand is considered, the true nature and importance of necessities, compared with luxuries in an advanced economy producing surpluses beyond physiological subsistence, is revealed.[74]

The first few sections of "Reaganomics, Saving, and the Casino Effect" (1993) comprise a lively account of Reaganomics and Supply-side economics, including the players who participated in the Reagan Revolution. As to saving, *personal* saving would be expanded through the incentives of tax cuts for the highest income earners. Supply-side economics became the Holy Grail of savers. Robin-Hood-in-reverse implied that

[71] The Italian Post Keynesians contended that Sraffa and Kalecki could not be combined this way. On the other hand, Ken Galbraith was pleased with the article.

[72] This is a stance I had taken in an early edition (1980) of *The Making of Economics*.

[73] Canterbery's vita theory is expressed in different ways in two aforementioned articles (see Part II and the articles in 1979 and 1980.)

[74] See the 1979 article above in the Gapinski-Rockwood volume.

the poor had *too much* after-tax income and the rich *too little*. Although the supply-side part stressed those elements crucial to the supply of labor and productive capacity, the full Reaganomics program went beyond tax cuts to slashes in government welfare spending and decreases in regulation. Its unique proclamation was its dual promise of stimulating economic growth and retarding inflation. Federal deficits far beyond the lively imagination of John Maynard Keynes were the consequence.

Rising inequalities were not just side-effects, the intent in word and deed was to redistribute income and wealth from the working class to the upper 10 percent, increasing both income and wealth concentration. The 1981 tax bill married federal deficits to higher interest rates. The rise in federal debt interest from $96 billion in 1981 to $216 billion in 1988 virtually guaranteed that nonearned income from holding paper would rise faster than the wages of workers. The top quintile of households were receiving 80 percent of the federal interest payments made to individuals, even as the top tax rate on such receipts fell steadily (to 28 percent in 1988). By 1983 the share of wealth held by the super-rich had risen sharply (to 26.9 percent) after falling for 40 years. Average CEO compensation increased from $900,000 in 1983 to $2,025,000 in 1988 (93 times the earnings of the average factory worker). As noted, this was a trend that was to continue.

As to saving(s), there is more than one measure. The Federal Reserve System measures individual savings — indirectly, using a flow-of-funds approach. It is a much closer approximation of changes in net worth, which, it is argued, comprises personal savings. The Federal Reserve measure adds increases in financial assets to net investment in consumer durables (such as a house purchase), and then subtracts the net increase in debts to arrive at savings. If one considers personal saving to be the increase in household net worth, the Commerce Department measure clearly undercounts personal savings, a discrepancy that greatly widened after 1981.

The other possible source of saving(s) is the business firm. The heart of the chapter uses a business and household net worth approach. It contains 10 accounting equations which are easy to follow (though the second commenter on the article seemed to reject them).[75] This section follows

[75] "Commentary by R. Jeffery Green," in James Gapinski (ed.), *The Economics of Saving* (Boston/Dordrecht/London: Kluwer Academic Publishers, 1993), pp. 187–192. Green was

the Fed's approach and considers the economy as a series of balance sheets. I was following the lead of Kenneth Boulding — in spirit if not in detail. Using a net worth approach, Boulding was able to integrate the income distribution into macroeconomic theory (1950). As he later became aware, he made several errors. In this account I attempted to correct those mistakes as well as introduce additional variables. Moreover, I express values in money rather than in real terms, whereas Boulding used the traditional definitions of real saving and investment. He corrected his 1950 version in *Challenge* in 1985.

Reaganomics culminated in the Casino Economy. The Wall Street raiders of the 1980s were encouraged — even cheered — as they used greenmail in the merger frenzy of the era. Between fiscal year 1980 and fiscal year 1988 merger filings soared more than 20 percent while the work-years allocated to antitrust enforcement plunged 40 percent. Raiders like Carl Icahn, Boone Pickens, and Ivan Boesky, as well as leveraged buyout masters such as Henry Kravis, built a large, profitable infrastructure that assured huge fees from questionable ventures and an unrealistic upward spin to stock market prices. Some of these actions result in changes in the balance sheets where there resides a transfer item (T) which consists of liquid assets and liabilities, while a comparable XT is found in the business sector. The various components of T and XT swirl about in the financial system without necessarily intersecting with *real* investment and saving.

From T and XT emanates the Casino Effect. Robert S. Chirinko of the University of Chicago wrote that "The Casino Effect and the instability of the credit process are the most novel and important parts of the analysis, bringing together strands from the public finance, macro/monetary, and Marxian literatures."[76] Furthermore, he adds that "some of these fluctuations [in asset values] reflect fundamental changes in the value of assets, while another, perhaps sizable, part is driven by the Casino Effect."[77]

"Boulding's T, Kaleckian Power, and Minsky's Fragility Hypothesis" (1994) will be easily accessible to those who have read the immediately preceding book chapter. Well, at least the balance-sheet mathematics will

---

a fan of Reaganomics or at least some verson of it. He is correct to say that I assumed a closed economy, but does not prove that this would much change my conclusions.

[76] "Commentary by Robert S. Chiorinko," *op. cit.*, p. 180.

[77] *Ibid.*, p. 182.

look familiar, while the geometry may be another matter. A draft of this article was presented as a paper for a conference in honor of Boulding, a few years prior to this passing.[78] I was inspired by his T (and XT) and by Minsky's hypothesis to attempt a more exact modeling. Boulding shows how his balance-sheet identities provide the foundation for a large number of macroeconomic models of comparative state equilibria and even of dynamics. Model I is driven by the functions in which the common Keynesian symbols of C, I, and Y are used. However, household consumption (or C) is the sum of household consumption and the accumulation of durables goods (as net worth). Further, C is a function of the wage share of output (W/Y), and business investment (I) is a function of the profits share (V/Y). If T is variable, the model is overdetermined. Then, we can write consumption, investment, and transfer functions as:

$$C = C(W/Y)$$
$$I = I(V/Y)$$
$$T = T(V/Y)$$

The identities of composition are:

$$Y = C + I$$
$$Y = W + V$$
$$W = C - T$$
$$V = I + T$$

Boulding provides only a geometrical "solution" for this model. My version of his geometry appears as Figure 1 and reveals a remarkable intuition. Consumption falls with the wages share and investment rises with the profits share. Total output initially rises as the profits share grows but peaks at a distributional equilibrium (which may or may not be at full employment).

[78] E. Ray Canterbery, "The Reconstruction of Boulding's Reconstruction of Economics," paper at Session Honoring Kenneth E. Boulding, Mississippi Valley Economics Association, Memphis, Tennessee, 1990. More should be said of Boulding (1910–1993). Knowing him was a privilege; in his presence, one felt like a better person. He was not only an economist and educator, he was a peace activist, poet, religious mystic, devote Quaker, interdisplinary philosopher, and co-founder of General Systems Theory. He was instrumental in organizing the first teachers protesting the Vietnam War at the University of Michigan (1965). He also was a leader in the evolutionary approach to economics.

Then we introduce a financial transfer function as T(V/Y), which is the sum of changes in money holdings by business, credit to households, bondholdings of households, and distributed interest and dividends. These components vary with V/Y. At one extreme where all investment is financed by the sale of securities to households, the change in bondholdings by households equals business investment. At another extreme, where all investment (I) is debt-financed, not only does V = D (dividends), but changes in bondholdings by households equal business investment (I), while the changes in money holdings by business plus the change in household credit is zero. A slight change in the underlying functions will cause a large shift in equilibrium or will even destroy the possibilities of equilibrium altogether. This could explain financial crises such as happened in 1929.

Boulding's distributional II has the same variables expressed in absolute terms. Since this model has less intuitive appeal than model I, I leave it and Figure 2 to the reader to understand.

Boulding appears correct in arguing that transfers and thus the financial system can alter the income distribution and the level of national income. Increases in consumer credit, decreases in corporate bond sales to households, and an increase in dividends because of a more liquid business sector will reduce the absolute level of wages. The use of profits as the growth in net worth and the introduction of financial variables at the fiirm level are a fruitful means to model this interrelationship between household and business expenditures and the distribution of income between profits and wages.

All of which brings us to Kaleckian power, the Lerner Index, and Hyman Minsky's idea of financial fragility. Profits as a share of national product or income is a macroeconomic version of the Kalecki-Lerner measure of the degree of monopoly power. Going from the microeconomics to the macroeconomics gives us

$$V = Q'U,$$

and,

$$Q'U/Y = V/Y,$$

where given the row vector of output levels (Q′), the larger the elements in U (the markup elasticities), the greater the power of firms generally to increase the aggregate profits share of V/Y. It is easy to show how Q′ can be determined in an input-output model in which average cost and demand also are determined.[79]

Minsky (1982) begins with Kalecki's accounting and accepts the Kaleckian markup. In Minsky's elaboration, however, the internal funds so generated by the firm are levered by debt to finance the acquisition of additional capital assets. In the aggregate, investment requires external financing. Thus, investment requires the issuance of bonds, which do appear in Boulding's T. Investment is financed by both internal (Kalecki) and external (Minsky-Boulding) funds. The income-distribution still plays a dominant role because Minsky sees household consumption depending upon household incomes, which includes, for the higher-income households, interest and dividend income from lending to business. A liquidity crisis ensues if the central bank attempts to reduce outstanding debt. Financial panics, such as market crashes, may occur as finance becomes more and more fragile.

"The Neo-Keynesian School of Economics," (1997) could not be found in my files. I have covered this school of thought elsewhere.[80]

"The Theory of the Bondholding Class" (2002) discusses the origins of the Class, its unique powers, the great inflation anomaly principle, and the NASDAQ crash of 2000–2001.[81] It closes with some policy prescriptions.

The bondholding class evolved and continues to thrive in an environment shaped for its own convenience. Its few families own not only virtually all bonds held by households but most of the value of stocks and other marketable assets. Its small population is strengthened by some investment bankers and security dealers on Wall Street. The class has yearly incomes that begin at around $200,000 and quickly go up into the tens of millions and billions of dollars (in 1992 dollars). These families number only about 1.1 million, but their average wealth is around $10.0 million. Its support group comprises a small number of professionals on Wall Street, the U.S.

[79] See Canterbery, "A General Theory of International Trade and Domestic Employment Adjustments" (1994) in Part IV.

[80] See E. Ray Canterbery, *A Brief History of Economics*, 2nd Edition (Singapore, New Jersey, London: World Scientific, 2011), pp. 235–250.

[81] This paper was originally given as an address in a joint session of the AEA and the Association for Evolutionary Economics, Atlanta, January 4, 2002. A more extended view of the bondholding class is found in E. Ray Canterbery, *Wall Street Capitalism* (Singapore, New Jersey, London: World Scientific, 2000), pp. 102–122, 192–221.

Treasury, and often the Federal Reserve System. The bondholding class even has its own editorial page — that of the *Wall Street Journal*.

Its ideology emanates from Wall Street. First, inflation or even rapid economic growth is bad for bondholders. Second the sole cause of inflation is a an excessively fast growth rate in the money supply. Third, federal budget deficits are inflationary if fed by rapid growth in the money supply and otherwise evil because they are the by-product of the redistribution of income and wealth from the rich to the poor. Fourth, household savings, seen as the main source of real investment and essential capital accumulation, will "trickle down" from the rich to the working class and the poor, assuring full employment. Moreover, when inflation turns from illusion to reality, the failure of enough people to volunteer for the Reserve's army of the unemployed is unacceptable.[82]

The bondholding class thrived particularly during the era of Alan Greenspan's terms as head of the Federal Reserve (August 1987–January 2006). He started his first term just in time for the stock market crash of 1987, and he resided over the 2000–2001 high-tech crash.[83] The sections on the great inflation anomaly principle, and the NASDAQ crash of 2000–2001 should be read as contemporary history. Much changed during Ben Bernanke's tenure (February 2006–February 1, 2014), as his terms included the Great Recession of 2007–2010 and the shift toward concern with deflation. Bernanke was succeeded by Janet Yellen who shifted the goal of the Federal Reserve toward full employment.[84] As indicated, we still need a transactions tax on financial instruments designed for

---

[82] This was written when inflation at least was a possibility. This era ended with the Great Recession of 2007–2010, from which slow economic growth emanated. For what happened, see E. Ray Canterbery, *The Global Great Recession* (Singapore, New Jersey, London: World Scientific, 2011). and Canterbery, *The Rise and Fall of Global Austerity* (Singapore, New Jersey, London: World Scientific, 2015). While the bondholding class no longer enjoyed substantial interest income from Treasuries, it had capital gains from bond price appreciation and interest from corporate junk bonds. Besides those gains, it had at least two periods of stock market gains, which continued, at least through June 2015. While it fluctuates with a volatile stock market, bond wealth remains more concentrated at the top than stock wealth.

[83] For much more on Greenspan, see E. Ray Canterbery, *Alan Greenspan: The Oracle Behind the Curtain* (Singapore, New Jersey, London: World Scientific, 2006).

[84] See *The Rise and Fall of Global Austerity*, *op. cit.*, pp. 199–201.

long-term holding but actually sold over a fortnight.[85] My long-term call for reform of the Federal Reserve System has not gone unheeded. With Janet Yellen in charge, any further reform may not be needed.

"Necessities, the Marginal Utility of Money, and Saving" (2004) is a paper written to honor the memory of Jim Gapinski, including his perseverance that led me to contribute chapters to books he edited. The content of this essay should be familiar to those who have read the earlier contributions.[86] The essay brings together in one place the themes of the two book chapters, publications separated by more than a decade but still relevant. The first ties inflation in necessities to distributive efficiency; the second ties "Reaganomics" to the Casino Effect, which generates a new kind of savings through asset inflation. The distributive effects of these two kinds of inflation — goods and asset — are linked by the marginal utility of money (or income) and the marginal propensity to save. The surprising macroeconomic implications of these relationships are explored within the context of the "new" welfare economics.

Part VIII contains mostly very readable articles on monetary and fiscal policy.

"The Fine Line Between Politics and Economics" (July 1963) is mostly about the President's Council of Economic Advisers. It was written while John F. Kennedy was still alive and President, and Walter W. Heller was Chairman of the President's Council of Economic Advisers (CEA).[87] There are several possible roles for the CEA, each with its risks

[85] For more details on a transaction tax, see *The Global Great Recession*, op. cit., pp. 306–313. Therein is a call for interest-free bond financing of local and state infrastructure during economic downturns (pp. 313–314).

[86] E. Ray Canterbery, "Inflation, Necessities and Distributive Efficiency," in James H. Gapinski and Charles Rockwood, Editors, *Essays in Post-Keynesian Inflation: In Honor of Abba P. Lerner* (Cambridge, MA: Ballinger, 1979) pp. 181–201 and E. Ray Canterbery, "Reaganomics, Saving, and the Casino Effect," in James H. Gapinski, Editor, *The Economics of Saving* (Boston/Dordrecht/London: Kluwer Academic Publishers, 1993), pp. 153–175. (See above.)

[87] There is still more on the CEA in E. Ray Canterbery, *The President's Council of Economic Advisers* (New York: Exposition-University, 1961. Later, after JFK's assassination, came E. Ray Canterbery. *Economics on a New Frontier* (Belmont CA.: Wadsworth, 1968), which in one part covers this ground and the economic advisers from Truman to Lyndon B. Johnson. The author had plenty of advice when writing the 1968 volume. Walter W. Heller

and shades of political meaning. As merely an *analytical* agency, it would gather, process and analyze data, distribute results to the President, the Congress and others, but make no recommendations. As strictly an *advisory* agency, it would go a step further to give suggestions to the President, possibly also to Congress, but make no attempt to seek public support for such suggestions. As a *policy-formulating* agency, it would go several steps further in the course of allowing itself to be heard in the early stages of drafting new legislation. And as a *policy-making* agency, it would move on to perform some of the tasks now performed by the President and Congress. The Council has played all of these roles to some extent.

When Walter Heller testified before Congress in support of the President's bill to grant corporations a tax credit for investment in new plant and equipment, he was acting as a policy formulator. Insofar as Congress enacted the bill and the President signed it, *they* were the policy makers. When the very persuasive Chairman Heller appeared on TV as a spokesman for the President, he certainly attempted to determine the fate of the legislation. The Heller Council was definitely active in the policy-making process.

In retrospect, the Heller role appears a natural evolution for the CEA through a variety of problems, five chairmen and the administrations of three Presidents. President Truman made the first appointment of a chairman after he signed the Employment Act of 1946, choosing Edwin G. Nourse, a highly respected Brookings Institution economist. This first Council, which also included Messrs. John Clark and Leon Keyserling,

---

(1915–1987), who was Chairman of the CEA from 1961 though 1964, and I carried on considerable correspondence related to the manuscript. Later, at an occasion celebrating the anniversary of the Employment Act of 1946, I had the pleasure of meeting Walter. He was very warm and personable, much as he appeared on TV. James Tobin (1918–2002), a Nobel Prize winner, (1981) said something about, "Ray is our (CEA) historian." Walter looked at him quizzically and said, "Soon I will write the history of *my* Council." Later, he published *New Dimensions of Political Economy* (1966). John Kenneth Galbraith, who was JFK's Ambassador to India, commented on several early chapter drafts and was a source of friendly encouragement. Tobin and Richard N. Cooper (1934–), both then at Yale, provided valuable critiques on the international chapters. Carl Kaysen (1920–2010), deputy special assistant to JFK (1961–1963), Arthur Okun (1928–1980) of Okun's Law fame, and Ted Sorensen (1928–2010), special counsel and speech writer for JFK, supplied useful information. When a very impressive Sorensen spoke at the University of Maryland, he was asked to sign a "loyalty oath." I apologized to him on behalf of the faculty.

was somewhat analogous to the research department of a large industrial firm such as General Motors. With no responsibility for drafting or promoting legislation, the advice which Truman accepted, at least up to 1948, became policy primarily through his efforts. He initiated the practice of occasionally having the Council appear at Cabinet meetings, although Nourse did not interpret this as ranking CEA members on the Cabinet level. Because Truman had ample political advice, Nourse believed the Council would be superfluous in plotting strategy. This all changed during the 1948 Presidential election campaign. Two of Truman's favorite targets were high prices and high profits. Nourse kept out of this debate, but Keyserling and Clark envisaged a less passive role for the government in the economy and backed the Administration.

The 1948 midyear Economic Report reflected the Truman-Keyserling-Clark policy of selective credit and price controls, the political role of the CEA was confirmed by Truman's election and disagreement was finally settled by the resignation of Nourse. His successor was Leon Keyserling. Under Keyserling the Council was primarily an advisory and policy-formulating group. And Keyserling often campaigned for the Fair Deal program. The danger of economic advisers following the advice of the President rather than vice-versa is illustrated by the subsequent chaos. Keyserling followed Truman's lead and advocated a $4 billion tax increase in 1949 to curb the inflation of "high profit levels." As the issue reached a heated peak, the CEA apparently failed to notice that the economy was in the throes of its first postwar recession. Truman and the CEA had to reverse themselves as Congress rightly rejected their program.[88]

Arthur F. Burns, appointed by President Dwight Eisenhower in 1953 pictured a less political role for the CEA than had Keyserling. It was the chairman's job, Burns said, to "speak out boldly within the halls of the executive, but prudently elsewhere." To some degree, Burns retreated to the style of Truman's first chairman. Both Burns and Nourse refused to appear before the Joint Economic Committee in public hearings. While Nourse *never* appeared, Burns did agree to appear at an off-the-record

[88] For much more on economic policy and consent during the Truman years, see E. Ray Canterbery, *Harry S. Truman: The Economics of a Populist President* (Singapore, New Jersey, London: World Scientific, 2014).

executive session. Burns, who was "an economist who happened to be a Republican," seldom had reason to disagree with Eisenhower. With no official record, his position before the Congress remains secret.

Raymond J. Saulnier was Eisenhower's second Chairman (1956–61), who carried on Arthur Burns' practice of attending most Cabinet meetings and reporting frequently on economic developments and their policy implications, attended all National Security Council meetings when economic questions were discussed and participated in several international conferences. All of which brings us full circle to the prominence of the Heller CEA.

At President Kennedy's urging, the Council's scope of action was broadened even more as it has taken "its place as a key element in the Presidential office," and Heller actively fought for JFK's pet projects. Heller stayed on another year to push for Lyndon B. Johnson's "War on Poverty." No CEA since has achieved the policy, advice and implementation luster of the Heller CEA. Part of this result was the consequence of the economic knowledge of JFK.

"A New Look at Federal Open Market Voting" (1967) could not be found on-line nor in my files. In it were described several different roles for the Federal Open-market Committee (FOMC) of the Federal Reserve System. Then, Chairmen were assigned different roles depending on the pattern of votes of the Committee. This is a widely cited article which was followed by other economists, particularly Thomas Havrilesky (1938–1995).[89]

"The Awkward Independence of the Federal Reserve" (1975) is another readable *Challenge* article. It calls for reform of the Fed based on its performance under Arthur F. Burns during the 1973–1975 economic recession. Since it is called "the Great Recession," some background will help. The 1970s recession was a period of economic stagnation in much of the Western world, putting an end to the general post-World War II economic boom. At the time, the 16-month contraction was the longest since the Great Depression. The period also has been described as one of "malaise," where

[89] For example, see Thomas Havrilesky and John Gildea, "The Biases of Federal Reserve Bank Presidents", *Economic Inquiry*, Volume 33, Issue 2 (April 1995), pp. 274–284. The article examines the voting patterns of Fed bank presidents when serving on the FOMC. I knew Tom as a hard-driving, hard-working professor at the University of Maryland. Thereafter, he taught for a long spell at Duke University. He passed prematurely of a heart attack at 56.

high unemployment coincided with high inflation. The unemployment rate did not peak until May 1975 at 9 percent. Though the recession "officially" ended in March 1975, its effects on the U.S. were felt through the Jimmy Carter presidency until the mid-term of Ronald Reagan's first term as president. This is the environment in which to judge Fed policy.

As late as June 1975, the Federal Reserve's chief policy-making body, the Open Market Committee (FOMC) saw its main priority as resisting inflationary pressures and achieving an equilibrium in the country's balance of payments. Burns insisted that an appropriate target for the increase in the money supply was 5 to 7 percent. Most economists, including many on the Fed's staff, believed 8 to 10 percent growth necessary to insure adequate recovery.[90]

A tax cut was aimed at stimulating the economy and lowering the unemployment rate. A main concern is how the Fed will respond to this fiscal easing. The tax cut, which added to the decline in revenues due to the fall-off in economic activity, will mean a deficit of perhaps $60 billion. What if the Federal Reserve absorbs none of the deficit? Bank reserves and the money supply will at best remain constant, interest rates will soar ever higher, and savings that otherwise would be loaned to the business community will have to be used by the government to pay debts. In effect, the monetary authorities will have confiscated much of the additional spending that Congress tried to induce through the tax cut. What actually happened (now that we know)? The Federal Reserve established a six percent target as full employment and the pre-recession level of 4.6 percent unemployment was not reached again until November 1997, when the Fed finally deviated from its anti-inflation stance.[91] At the time, Arthur Burns gave a vague promise to Congress to maintain a rate of expansion of the money supply of between 5 and 7.5 percent over the balance of the year. Generally the Fed did not even give a hint of what is *had* done until it publishes the edited record of FOMC policy actions ninety days after the event.

---

[90]This too was part of the era of monetarism wherein only the money supply mattered, and prior to the targeting of the federal funds rate as a policy tool.

[91]President Bill Clinton and Chairman Alan Greenspan's alliance was a trade-off between minimal budget deficits and lower long-term interest rates. For the full story, see Canterbery, *Alan Greenspan: The Oracle Behind the Curtain*, *op. cit.*, pp. 45–51.

Prudent judgment moderated by political reality recommends that the Federal Reserve System somehow be made more responsible to the body politic without taking away the Fed's power to avoid direct dependence on the Treasury. This could be accomplished by reforms that would generally enhance congressional authority. The Joint Economic Committee should be given authority to set up a watchdog committee, the Congressional Monetary Committee (CMC), comprised of academic and technical experts who would evaluate monetary policy on a continuous basis within the framework of the Employment Act of 1946. The responsibilities of the CMC would be comparable to the federal budget analysis now provided by the Congressional Budget Committees. The findings of this subcommittee, which could include dissident former Federal Reserve economists, should be published monthly, with a more lengthy year-end report issued. Another reform would be to change the internal workings of the FOMC, to end the practice of placing five regional Reserve Bank presidents on the FOMC, four of whom are on a rotating basis.[92] This would also weaken the close ties of the Fed to its financial constituency, especially the New York banking community.

"The Independence of Arthur F. Burns" (1976) is a letter to *Challenge* that restates polemically the positions taken in the above article and contends that Arthur F. Burns, then head of the Fed, has misread the Constitution. Burns is quoted extensively. It is an easy read, and the reader can decide who won the debate.[93] Since, the FOMC has become much more forthcoming, now releasing a statement immediately after its meetings, and releasing the minutes of the meetings three weeks later. Under Ben Bernanke and Janet Yellen's terms the Federal Reserve has become much more transparent.

With "Tax Reform and Incomes Policy: a VATIP Proposal" (Spring 1983) we switch from monetary policy to fiscal and incomes policies.[94] Some background on the value-added tax (VAT) and incomes policy may help. Worldwide VAT is a popular tax, the most commonly used tax. Some 140 countries (70.4% of all nation-states), including all the developed

[92]This also was a recommendation made later by Havrilesky and Gildea, *op. cit.*

[93]Edward J. Kane, "New Congressional Restraints and Federal Reserve Independence," *Challenge*, November/December, 1975, 37–44 took a similar stance. He is a well-known finance professor who has advised the Boston Federal Reserve Bank.

[94]An earlier version of this paper, VATIP: a New Incomes Policy," was presented at the Eastern Economic Association Meetings, April 1982.

countries except the United States, have a VAT. It has been proposed many times in the U.S. Congress; the most recent proposal was the Domenici-Rivlin Debt Reduction Tax Force call for a VAT in the U.S. in 2010. A VAT is applied to the sales price charged for goods at every point in the supply chain. All countries with a VAT either exempt exports and imports from the VAT or rebate the entire VAT paid on exports.

Incomes policies have been tried in numerous countries, including the United States. They have been most popular in developed nations during periods of high inflation, though UNCTAD in 2012 called for an incomes policy to complement exhausted monetary and fiscal policies. The term "incomes policy" includes specific measures aimed at moderating the rate of increase in wages and prices by curbing the power of business, labor and professional groups. The VATIP proposal combines VAT with an incomes policy feature.

In 1971 my late friend Sidney Weintraub (1914–June, 1983) and Henry Wallich (1914–1988) first proposed a Tax-Based Incomes Policy (TIP).[95] When TIP emerged politically in October 1979, President Jimmy Carter proposed a clumsy real wage insurance version because of the *perception* that it otherwise was unfair to labor. Congress wisely rejected the proposal. President Ronald Reagan, however, treated incomes policy as the third rail of economics. That proved unwise because the federal budget deficit from Reaganomics and the attendant recession exploded the federal budget deficit. An alternative inflation-fighting tax such as VAT would have been helpful.

I proposed: (a) an equitable VAT as a new revenue source and as the ideal tax base for the implementation of TIP; and (b) a simplified personal income tax program that would satisfy those critics of VAT who view it as inequitable. The closing of all tax loopholes, so that all income (including unearned income) would be taxed alike, would be the first step in raising revenue. The next step would require a second tax (VAT) based upon the understanding that every family, rich or poor, buys necessities. At the end

---

[95] Weintraub, a liberal, and Wallich, a conservative, shared a distaste for rising prices, hence the teamwork. Weintraub was one of the most prominent American members of the Post Keynesians, co-founder and co-editor (with Paul Davidson) of the *Journal of Post Keynesian Economics*. The American mathematician-economist E. Roy Weintraub (1943–) is Sidney's son. Henry Wallich was a long-time member of the Board of Directors of the Federal Reserve System and was instrumental in building the research capabilities of the Fed. Sidney Weintraub and I had some interesting conversations.

of the VAT chain the consumer pays the full amount of the tax in the sales price of the good or service and with *no other reform measure* would bear the full burden. This means that VAT should *not* be implemented without a reduction in the income taxes paid on the personal income allocated to necessities. As a *required* counterpart of VAT, the family income tax exemption should be raised for all taxpayers to a value equal to the cost of a market basket of necessities. A flat tax rate would apply to all income in excess of the minimal consumption budget (gross discretionary income) in each income interval, a rate progressively higher at higher income intervals. The minimal consumption budget value would be the sole exemption from taxation. Milton Friedman has recommended a negative income tax for poor households, which would guarantee a minimal income by providing income supplements. The supplement should be sufficient to maintain the social minimum for necessities and would be reduced by some fraction (less than 1) as the family earned additional income.

VAT is the ideal instrument for implementing a tax-based incomes policy (TIP). We know that if value added (or net sales) grows at the same pace as real output, inflation would be minimized. The Fed would be free to follow an easy money policy. A firm with a 1 percentage point increase in value added in excess of an *adjusted* real output growth norm could be penalized by adding 1 percentage point to its VAT. With the adjusted output growth norm of 6 percent, a giant firm allowing its value added from wages and salaries, net interest, rents, or profits to rise 7 percent would have to pay 1 percentage point extra in value-added taxes. The mathematical formulas for the implementation of VATIP are given in the article with a realistic example. Two objections were raised by Sidney Weintraub (who was defending the original Weintraub-Wallich unadorned TIP) and responded to in the article. A new social contract aimed at industrial peace could in a more perfect world eliminate the need for VATIP.

"The Flat Tax, Negative Tax, and VAT: Gaining Progressivity and Revenue" (Fall 1985), with Eric W. Cook and Bernard A Schmitt, was not in my files but was downloaded from the web.[96] This was a simulation model

[96] The first version of this paper was E. Ray Canterbery, "The Flat Tax, the Negative Tax, and VAT — Should the Three be Combined?" Conference on the Flat Tax, Florida State University, March 14–15, 1985. Representative Richard Gephardt also gave a speech on this occasion.

that estimated tax liabilities and revenue under a reform measure that included a simplified tax code (and fewer rates), a negative income tax and a value-added tax (VAT). In it we showed that progressivity and revenue gains would result. Representative Richard Gephardt and Senator Bill Bradley proposed a similar plan sans VAT which became the Bradley-Gephardt Fair Tax Act in 1982, and the Republican-controlled Senate Finance Committee proposed a similar plan. Bradley-Gephardt was rehashed again in 1986, but when Gephardt ran for President in 1988, he dropped the idea as too complex to explain. Both simplified personal taxes and VAT were discussed in reports by the Joint Committee on Taxation, U.S. Congress.[97]

A negative income tax, which would provide stipends to poor or low-income households, nearly passed Congress during the Nixon Administration. Since, only one nation-state, Israel, has adopted a negative income tax. Instead, in the U.S. the standardized deduction combined with an Earned Income Tax Credit (EITC), provides relief for poor or low-income households. For example, in 2015 the standard deduction ranges from $6,300 for singles, to $12,600 for married couples filing jointly, to $9,250 for the head of household. The EITC for poor or low-income households ranges from $503 for no children, to $5,545 for two children, to $18,110 for single taxpayers with one or more children. The combination of standardized deductions and EITC recognizes that income for necessities should not be taxed, though the threshold is generally below the poverty line. While the number of income brackets has been reduced to seven from fifteen, the U.S. tax code remains a tax attorney's dream machine.

Part IX 21st Century Development includes articles and books that have particular relevance for the 21st century. The selection is somewhat arbitrary because, for example, the delayed peg, price markups, tax reform and incomes policy will have relevance, especially if inflation resumes. The Part IV articles, however, also relate to economic development.

---

[97] See "Tax Reform Proposals: Rate Structure and Other Individual Income Tax Issues," For the Use of the Committee on Ways and Means and the Committee on Finance, Joint Committee on Taxation, August 12, 1986. Both Cook and Schmitt were staff economists at the time. Later, as noted earlier, Schmitt was named Deputy Chief of Staff. The Joint Committee is highly respected by both Democrats and Republicans for its objective analysis and revenue projections.

"The International Mobility of Land and the Law of the Sea," with Thomas H. Cate got a lot of attention *outside* the economics community.[98] It was a time-honored principle of economics that land was the one factor of production that did not "move," which may be the reason that in the twentieth century land was the least analyzed factor of production. In Hechscher-Ohlin models, land (and thus natural resources) were assumed internationally immobile (and, in fact, nationally immobile). We show that this assumption is confronted with numerous historical exceptions, the most visible being contemporary ocean resources conflicts such as the evolving international law on the use of ocean fisheries, seabed resources, and deep-sea minerals. We saw the exploitation of the oceans and seas as the last major earthly "land grab" in history and thus may have a massive impact upon world trade patterns.

Following John Stuart Mill's definition of land as all those natural agents which are not products of labor, land includes agricultural types, minerals, natural forests, wild-stock fisheries, natural water, solar energy, natural air, and air space. We further classify land into two general types: (1) Ricardian space; and (2) natural resources. *Ricardian space* is the three-dimensional solid geometry that for a given set of coordinates includes the globe's surface, its subsoil, and superjacent air space. Within broad limits, such space (land) is indestructable and *geologically* immobile. *Natural resources* include natural soil, natural water (including water power), natural air, solar energy, minerals, natural forests, and natural (wild-stock) fisheries.

We deploy N. Georgescu-Roegen's idea of production as a process. Some inputs are consumed in the process of production while others survive the process, usually with a few scars. The *fund* elements provide services and can be either inputs or outputs. Funds are not depletable if properly maintained. The use of a fund requires duration, where the size of the duration is decided within narrow limits set by the physical structure of the fund. The *flow* elements are used or acted upon by the fund elements, and are either only consumed *or* only produced by the process and are only an input *or* only an output. Whether a factor is classified as a fund or a flow nonetheless depends upon the duration of the production process. Time duration of production and clock (mechanical) time require

[98] Tom Cate was one of my graduate students at Florida State; he is currently Professor of Economics at Northern Kentucky University.

separate variables. Unlike the short-run (or neoclassical production function), the G-R production function is a functional, that is, a relation from a *set* of functions to *one* function. The agents of production are symbolically defined and a G-R production functional is given in Equation (1). We go on to show mathematically the domestic motivation for land mobility. Admittedly, this is rather complex.

We give three general types of international land mobility. (1) The transfer of the claims to ownership of Ricardian space and/or its associated resources from one nation to another. (2) The transfer of the claims to ownership from all nations (common property rights) to one. (3) The non-territorial transfer of natural resources through manmade or natural causes to another nation. The international transfer of claims to Ricardian space is a common historical occurrence. Under the jurisdiction of international law, Ricardian space is referred to as "territory," political boundaries that can be changed by political or economic (long-term production functional) forces.[99] Examples include the U.S. purchases of Louisiana and Alaska, the historically contested area of Alsace-Lorraine, and the dispute between the United Kingdom and France about the boundary between Niger and Chad.

The law of the sea and territorial limits of coastal states is presently of special importance. The territorial sea and its base line are sufficiently vague in terms of their geology to invite politically-determined definition. The continental shelf and the continental slope which appear in definitions of "economic zone" are not geologically precise. The eighteenth century "Cannonshot Rule" (about three miles) has been superseded by many forces, including modern rocketry. The Truman Proclamation of 1945 still provides the present legal doctrine regarding U.S. exploitation of the continental shelf, which for the U.S. was known to be large.[100] In 1976 the U.S. Congress, invoking the Truman Proclamation, extended the economic zone to 200 miles–that is, beyond the continental shelf. The U.S. at

---

[99] Nicholas Georgescu-Roegen (1906–1994) was one of the most innovative economists of the Twentieth Century. Nobelist Paul Samuelson called him an "economist's economist." He based his production analysis on the principle of entropy from thermodynamics rather than from Newtonian mechanics [see especially his *The Entropy Law and the Economic Process* (1971)]. He read several drafts of our article and we did not publish it until he was satisfied with it. We had some interesting correspondence.

[100] For much more on Truman and his economics, see Canterbery, *Harry S. Truman: The Economics of a Populist President*, *op. cit.*

the U.N. Law of the Sea Conferences in Caracas (1974) and Geneva (1975 argued for a 12-mile territorial sea and a 200-mile "economic zone" for the exclusive exploitation of minerals and fisheries (except for highly migratory species). Despite these attempts at unilateral extension of territorial or economic zone rights, the limits of coastal states still is not a settled issue.

Going beyond this 1977 article and coming up to date, the main change has happened through the U.N. The United States position has barely changed and the U.S. is merely an observer at the Conventions. At the 25th meeting of the U.N. Convention on the Law of the Sea (June 8 to 12, 2015), there were references to an "oceans constitution," based on the December 10, 1982 Conference, which would define the rights and responsibilities of all nations on matters ranging from the breadth of a nation's territorial waters to the conduct of ships on the high seas (UNCLOS). Membership in the UNCLOS would alter U.S. law and current practice. As of June 2015, 166 countries plus the European Union were members of UNCLOS. In May 2014 President Barack Obama asked the U.S. Senate to ratify UNCLOS, but it refused. As of June 2015, the U.S. Senate has yet to ratify UNCLOS.

"A Theory of Supra-Surplus Capitalism" (October–December 1987) was my Presidential Address to the Eastern Economic Association in Washington, D.C. (March 6, 1987). Sections I and II were covered in "Galbraith, Sraffa, Kalecki and Supra-Surplus Capitalism" (Part VII) and there is no need to repeat a summary here, except to say that under *supra-surplus capitalism*, production surpluses are so great that producers and governments must spend great resources to massage the interests and demands of the middle class (and beyond) to absorb supra-net-output. Further, in a supra-surplus economy, we have a hierarchy of absolute physical necessities and "wants." The satisfaction of a greater number of wants is usually associated with higher standards of living.

Uncertainty increases as we shift focus away from specific needs, such as the need to be housed, toward the particular way these needs and wants are met, such as through grandiosity and elegance. Households tend to eat more (and sometimes better) as incomes rise, but there is limit to the amount of extra money that people spend on food. The relation between reported personal income and expenditures by category for American families in 1985 is illustrated in Figure 1 in the article. The highest-quintile household spent about 9.6 percent of income on food, whereas the lowest-quintile household's share was 62 percent. The more "necessary" the product or service the sooner expenditure for that product or service begins to slow. And, there is a pattern suggesting a hierarchy of rankings. This means that the income distribution has a lot to do with the overall level of demand in the economy, as well as with the composition of production.

Engel's law places the role of discretionary income under supra-surplus capitalism into proper prospective. Discretionary income is to consumption what physical surplus (over-capacity) is to production; budget shares are to consumption what market shares are to production. The greater the surpluses, the greater the difficulty in convincing households to purchase goods they otherwise feel no need for. As John Kenneth Galbraith has noted, "mass communication was not necessary when the wants of the masses were anchored primarily in physical need. The masses could not then be persuaded as their spending — this went for basic foods and shelter." An excess of income above physiological subsistence leaves a demand wedge that provides breathing space for producers. Imperfect competition abhors wedges and sets into motion forces to fill the space. The price markup too accomplishes the task. The money wage — the actual wage negotiated — separates itself from the real wage or productivity. The mark-up could only be a return on capital in a fit of circular definition. A strategic role is played by the markup on unit costs (mostly wages) in the manufacturing sector.

Given the expected "price" elasticities, the corporation sticks with the market-bearing markup that will provide the target level of retained profits, a target that depends upon its dividend payout ratio to stockholders, its amount of debt relative to its equity, and, most importantly, its perceived investment needs. The firm will cling to the price derived from corporate strategy, the margin of prices over current average costs already reflects the degree of market power of the giant corporation. The markup and investment plans are inexorably linked. Because of the degree-of-monopoly element prices charged by the industrial firms do not reflect current demand conditions; they more closely mirror the funds requirements for the planned investment expenditures that the corporation deems sufficient to increase capacity (plant size or number of machines) to meet expected future demand. Only upon industrial maturity — near Engel curve peaks — will the producer select new labor-replacing techniques that create still greater excess capacity.

For the most part the industrial system has been successful in convincing consumers that they should expand the number of goods they consider necessary. Labor then demands higher wages so that workers can pay for the newly defined standard of living. Often enough, the corporation capitulates, if it can pass the costs along in higher prices. Still, in the history of capitalism, the idea that workers have to be employed in order to purchase the producer's goods has eluded producers. Though it is in the interest of any single manufacturer to minimize his total wage bill, if all producers succeed in that calculus they will find there is no outlet for their products. Keynes' concept of this fallacy of composition has yet to be denied effectively. The determination of wages and employment brings us to the broader issue of the personal income distribution. Section IV of the article deploys the Vita Theory of the personal income distribution, which has been covered in detail in Part II.

In Section VI of the article, we should say a word or two about Joseph A. Schumpeter's entrepreneur and the product cycle. Specialists in marketing research have known for a long time that products have a sales life cycle over the long run. Initially, a product innovation coming from one of Schumpeter's entrepreneurs will be sold (perhaps market-tested) to a handful of consumer pioneers, who are often the richest households in the society. (Sometimes it is sold to the government.) Since a new product usually is very expensive to develop, its introductory price will be very high. However, if a middle class exists, Veblen's class emulation emerges, and the product is gradually diffused among a larger and larger number of families. When the product hits Main Street, the sales growth is exponential; the product "takes off." Any market thus ignited is limited only by its human population and the distribution of income. When products are standardized in gigantic factories and produced with large-scale technology, they yield lower prices. When virtually every family has at least one of the "new products," the market is satiated. This product cycle looks like a flattened S and is often called, appropriately, the product S-curve and is illustrated in Figure 2.

Raymond Vernon's international product life cycles can be used to extend the idea of the product cycle into the developing and the newly industrialized countries. In the standardized stage, the markets in developing countries become a vent for surpluses because the supra-surplus economy encounters competition from other surplus economies as the monopoly position is eroded. The newly industrializing countries (NICS) become effective competitors because their adoption of the now-standardized technology is coupled with cheap labor. Come to think of it, Section X, the Summary, ties the complexity of this article into a neat package.

H. Peter Gray has attempted to develop a "pragmatic theory" of international trade by including specific human capital or "skill mix," the Vita Theory, the Linder thesis, and the product cycle. Originally, the Vita Theory was developed to explain the personal income distribution. Peter Gray saw the Vita Theory as the "Rosetta Stone which enabled [him] to formulate all [his] misgivings about the interaction of rapid changes in trade patterns and the rate of employment in industrialized nations."[101] Peter relied not only upon the 1979 and 1980 papers (see Part II) but also upon extensive discussions. The book chapter, "A General Theory of International Trade and Domestic Employment Adjustments," especially Section 16.3, has deliberate parallels with the Canterbery-Gray dialogue in Gray. The purposes of my new chapter are (1) to show how most trade theories can be summarized with a simplified production system that includes markup pricing, (2) to integrate my version of Raymond Vernon's (1966) product cycle theory with the Vita Theory, and (3) to suggest some broader policy implications.

We begin with a production system in which the technical methods of production are given by a matrix of interindustry coefficients in physical units. Equations (1) and (2) will be familiar to input-output theorists, and to those who have read the above article on "Galbraith, Sraffa, Kalecki and Supra-Surplus Capitalism" (1984) in Part VII. Equation 1 is only a production possibilities matrix since we have no assurance that Keynesian effective demand will be sufficient to purchase the implied outputs. All inputs except labour are treated as intermediate goods so that investment can only be identified as capital-type durable goods, including Gray's traditional or reproducible capital. These commodities (as inputs) are used up in each production period so that they have to be replaced entirely.

[101] See H. Peter Gray, *Free Trade or Protectionism: A Pragmatic Analysis* (London: Macmillan Press 1985 and New York St. Martins Press, 1985), p. x.

The residual replaced is the value added in the economic system. This is similar to Sraffa's production of commodities with commodities.

Value added is distributed as wages, net interest and profits. While generally wages are distributed in proportion to the physical quantity of labour of a particular type and quality, a specific money wage rate is determined in the labour market for the labour type and quality required. From here, the Vita Theory is followed. The markup over prime costs in each industry is the profit rate. The firm (industry) sets the markup and thus the profit rate according to the elasticity of demand for its product and, where applicable by rents on those inputs fixed in supply by quantity or quality. The markup includes than the returns paid to rent-earning inputs, a "residual" in Gray.

A row vector of prices depend on two general terms in Equation 3, the cost of using commodities to produce commodities and the variable costs of labour in production. Markups appear as variables in both terms. However, wage and profit rates are determined outside the production system and are thus "given" in equation 3. The system is solved for prices in Equation 4. From these equations we can find total production of each good and therefore form a matrix for production in the entire system, in which exports and imports are introduced. The output vector can be multiplied by a price vector to give gross income or gross output for the economy. Value-added or total income payments can also be derived (equation 10).

The Vita Theory is used to identify labor by its many types. From the unit labour requirements for all industries, we can construct a matrix of total labour required by the economy (at the particular output levels), which is expressed compactly in Equation 14. We go on to define labour markets as human capital types to be matched with n-1 labour markets in n-1 geographic areas. All labour markets can be represented by a partitioned row vector of D general human capital types matched with n-1 labour markets in n-1 geographic areas (Equation 15). Next, we consider the vitae of the workforce population. A vitae vector can be expressed for all human capital types (Equation 16). From here there is a national supermatrix of vitae that includes all labour markets and associated vitae (in rank order from most to least preferred employee characteristics). A still larger supermatrix of vitae would include all occupations (including professionals) and associated vitae (Equation 17).

The technical labor coefficients can vary in the long run. Moreover demand matrix evolution is related to exogenous and to induced changes.

Exogenous technological change or changes in the pattern of demand for goods alters the nature of the labour demand matrix. Also, patterns of labour and capital costs can induce changes in the labour intensity and the skill intensity of the selected capital-type goods. There is even a feedback mechanism in which changes in the personal income distribution will alter the level and mix of goods demanded, a feedback that can be related to the product cycle. Long-run evolutions in the supply matrix are mostly endogenous, as persons have time to adjust to changing patterns of excess labour demand and to anticipated future changes. However, the quality of training and education can alter the supply matrix. Over a long enough period, demographic movements and changes in the skill level of the population affect the supply matrices, and the demand matrices are transmuted by alterations in the vintages of physical capital-type goods in response to new technologies, changes in relative input costs, and changes in the mix of goods demanded.

We discussed the role of innovators and the product cycle across countries at different stages of economic development in the preceding article on supra-surplus capitalism. With this background and with the above discussion of vectors and matrices, Section 16.4 should be an easy read. However, the relation of standard of living to the production and price system may not obvious. Let E represent the complete vector of all household goods so that in the entire system the wage rate can be expressed as the vector [PE]. We can substitute PE for W′ in Equation 3, giving Equation 22. We now have the standard of living of the workers (and managers and professionals who receive a "shadow" standard of living). At a minimum society will expect the system to maintain a demand for consumption goods equal to E and a demand for raw materials and investment-type goods sufficient to maintain E. From this, by substituting a subsistence wage for PE, we can express individual prices in terms of an essentials' price index. This preliminary discussion is sufficient preparation to understand the final two sections on economic growth, employment adjustments, and the transfer of technology.

All in all, this chapter provides not only a general theory of international trade but a general theory of an open economy.

"Cultural and Other Barriers to Motion Pictures Trade" (2005) with Akbar Marvasti not only extends our analysis of the industry to international trade but employs cultural variables to explain U.S. success. The global success of the American film industry facing rising costs of production, foreign protectionism, and liberal trade policies at home is an enigma. The basis for American dominance is found in market size and structure. In turn market characteristics and microdata explain protectionist strategies — leading to a complex gravity-iceberg model of U.S. exports. Besides purchasing power and spatial distance, cultural variables as well as protectionist strategies are important influences on U.S. motion pictures trade. Competitors nonetheless are no match for the magical American combination of movie stars, economies of scale and popularity of English speech. The U.S. motion picture industry has been winning the global ball game despite three strikes against it — protectionism, rising real domestic costs of production and relatively stable real domestic ticket prices. We address the quandary of why protectionism fails in a culturally sensitive industry where protectionism is expected to succeed.

Why export? From the perspective of the studios, aggregate market size depends on gross domestic box office and the U.S. dollar value of exports (rentals, video tapes). Figure 1 presents gross domestic box office revenues in current dollars, and export earnings in the industry. Despite some volatility, the trend in both variables is upward. During 1980–2000 nominal domestic box office revenues increased by a multiple of nearly 2.8. Earlier we estimated the price elasticity for movie attendance between –0.23 and –0.51, suggesting highly inelastic demand so that a doubling in nominal ticket prices has contributed significantly to revenues. Export data show a steep rise in revenues from foreign markets rapidly converging on domestic box office revenues. Along with rising export revenue are rising production costs (which includes the cost of stars and cast). For exports, mostly marketing costs, potentially adding much more to revenues than to costs, are incurred. Thus economies of scale in distribution are enhanced with rising exports. Exports enlarge the total market (R + X) relative to optimal circulating capital costs [s in equation (2)], and therefore maintain the number of major studios that survive in a climate of soaring costs. In 1990 the share of market for the top eight U.S. studios (the majors) was 89.2 % of domestic box office and in 1997, 90.6%.

Virtually no U.S. tariff barriers have existed in recent years. In turn, the nature, magnitude and strategic choices countries make to limit U.S films vary. In Saudi Arabia, public exhibition of movies is strictly banned for religious reasons; in China, several hidden quantitative restrictions limit the importation of Western movies; in India severe quantitative restrictions limit film imports; in Thailand, imposed duties are mostly based on number of meters of imported films; and in many European countries a complex system of subsidies and taxes exists. Table 1 provides a general guide. The tariff, the most common barrier to most trade, is not used in Western Europe, Canada or the Middle East. It is deployed in Brazil, Indonesia, the Republic of Korea and Thailand. Where tariffs are used, they may be simply a source of tax revenue. Otherwise, quantitative restrictions are widely used as a substitute for tariffs.

The most popular trade barrier is the denial of property rights. Not only does film lend itself to piracy, black markets offer a way around quantitative barriers in the presence of strong demand for movies. Piracy is virtually universal; it is the protectionist strategy of choice everywhere except for Norway, Bermuda, Singapore, and New Zealand.

We next turn to mathematical models of cultural distance. Important characteristics of movies are aligned with the assumptions of gravity models, such as imperfect competition and economies of scale in production and distribution. Another common assumption of such models is significant transport costs sometimes used as a measure of spatial distance. Movies have negligible transport costs, but they do involve cultural distance. We begin with Samuelson's iceberg model wherein the value of a country's film shipments that arrive at their destination having "melted down" a fraction because of transportation costs and cultural distance between the countries. The total meltdown will be a weighted average from the effect all cultural differences for the importing country. Further, trade barriers can be included in the list of meltdown variables, barriers such as levies and subsidies in motion pictures often based on cultural considerations. All this is captured in Equation (3).

In Bergstrand's generalized gravity equation (1989) and Krugman's location model (1995) exports are positively related to the purchasing power of any country set but are inversely related by distance. Combining the Bergstrand-Krugman models with Samuelson's iceberg effect gives us a complex gravity-iceberg export model in Equation (4) Not only is the market larger, the greater is per capita income, but the market wealth effect is multiplicative, suggesting the potential for economies of scale in distribution. The econometrics which follow are based on this model. Equation (4) is rewritten in log transform, giving Equation (5). The data set yields 165 observations for 33 countries for 1991–95.

We generate two instrumental variables, one being a *count* of the number of trade restrictions imposed on imports of motion pictures (TBN), the second being an index of the complex trade barriers (TBI). From the theory of econometrics, we chose the Poisson model for TBN and the logit model as appropriate for TBI. The maximum likelihood estimates of the trade barriers equation (6) are in Table 4. The random effects regression estimates for U.S. exports or equation (5) appear in Table 5. Four different models are estimated. The gravity-iceberg export models that include specific cultural variables perform best. Taken together, the estimates corroborate the strategies revealed in the microdata, namely, that particular countries desire to develop local industry and that the cultural threat of proximity of the United States to Mexico and Canada is mostly expressed through protectionism. Explicit cultural variables (such as language, education, and religion) also are important indirect (via protectionism) influence on U.S. motion picture exports.

The United States continues to dominate the world as a popular cultural center through its export of films. Despite substantial barriers to film imports, other large economies apparently have been unable to internationally extend their domestic markets. Even India, where subsidies support the producer of the largest number of films in the world, has not successfully exported films to the U.S. market.

The Foreword to H. Peter Gray's *The Exhaustion of the Dollar* (2004) came just before a turning point in the American economy. The Great Recession was just around the corner. The U.S. dollar has been the dominant world currency for most of the past century. The perception of international money changers, including central banks, of U.S. financial markets as a safe haven made it so. Perception has been backed up by U.S. capital inflows, which have surged in the past two decades. Many believe that dollar dominance has allowed the U.S. to live beyond its means, running current account deficits financed by borrowing from the rest of the world on the cheap. At the same time prosperity in the rest of the world depends heavily on continued growth in U.S. aggregate demand while expanding its trade balance. Therein sets the Catch 22: American trade deficit financing depends on the generosity of strangers willing to lend to Americans (or buy their corporate equities) so as to maintain the U.S. standard of living. This led to what Ben Benanke famously called "a global savings glut." Indeed, current account surpluses of Japan, the eurozone, Denmark, Norway and Sweden rose some 67 percent between 1996 and 2004.

The dollar as a global reserve currency did decline from 70% of global holdings to about 62% in 2008–2013. The IMF and others were nervous about the possible collapse the the U.S. dollar as a world currency during the Great Recession. The global financial crisis altered conventional opinion regarding the reserves an economy needs to protect itself from crises. Still, the dollar prevailed (and to a considerable degree, continues to prevail). While many other currencies (and the euro) are tied to the dollar, the dollar has remained a key currency and the leading reserve currency by default. Peter Gray was premature, but not because of any fault in his analysis, but out of the dollar being the reserve currency by default. When will this end? It's already losing its reserve status in Europe and China. It would be unfortunate if its ultimate decline depends upon the continuing slowing growth in U.S. GNP. "The Multinational and Global Factor Mobility (unpublished, 2007) will hold few surprises for the readers of the earlier papers, especially the attempt to provide a general theory of international trade (1994) based on the vita theory, innovations, and the product cycle as well as technological change. Herein, I find that a gap exists between Gray's (and Dunning's) institutional analysis and my formal model. The purpose of the present paper is to provide some missing links and suggest how they could be used to build a bridge to this century's model. In this regard, one should recall that the MNC is involved in the production of every kind of good, including the S-good (the technology-reliant good). Although we are accustomed to think of trade as being between regions, we can say that the MNC's trade within their firms and industries. To the extent that their powers supercede or are an integral part of the powers of nation-states, the MNC's have established their own trading region, a zone virtually unconstrained by geography or politics.

The trading world can be divided into the following categories: The MNC zone (MNC), emerging nations (EN), less-developed non-oil producing nations (LDC-NO), and less-developed oil-producing nations (LDC-O). Defining the MNCs as comprising a new trading zone does not obliterate the usefulness of the old trading region pairings. Since MNCs generate the greatest value-added in the world trading system, the value of their trade is mostly North-North. That part which is North-South or South-North is mostly in the emerging economies of East Asia, Eastern Europe, and Latin America. In the LDC trade zones, prices and proceeds mostly are determined in competitive world commodity markets, the possible exception being the OPEC nations whose cartel power waxes and wanes.

We next superimpose this MNC world onto a formal trade model (Canterbery 1994). The production functions within the MNC zone are the most complex and therefore the most complete. Equations (3) through (14) complete the entire system, culminating in total labor requirements. The system for each country (and for the world) must be self-consistent in money prices. This consistency is reflected in the solution of the price system for an MNC-zone nation (Equation 4). A comparable price solution but including labor by human capital type is Equation 4A. Furthermore wage rates for different human capital types and the size of the mark-up are critical to understanding the economies of the MNC zone. To close the model, personal incomes must be generated and consumption take place, where incomes are based on wages and the workers' share of profits. In Section III. C, we show by comparison, the production relations for the LDC zones. Here, as noted, the prices of commodities are mostly determined in world commodity markets.

Section IV explains the effects of global integration and the resultant regional trade balances. For example, the MNC and the EN zones are tightly connected to the LDC-O zone by the necessity of importing oil. In turn, the LDC-O countries receive rents in the form of hard currencies. In this environment it is difficult to identify fundamental values of exchange rates. However, we know that the fundamental value of the U.S. dollar is decided by the trade balance and net financial capital flows. The actual exchange rate varies from its fundamental value with the buying and selling of official exchange reserves. Finally, Section V shows the implications of this world system for global economic growth. We find many reasons why full employment in the world system does not happen, not the least of which is inadequate incomes of the masses of unskilled labor and thus insufficient aggregate demand, though full employment may be achieved in one or more of the MNC nations. We conclude that the products and services produced and distributed by the multinational in the MNC zone cannot be explained by classical or Heckscher-Olin theories that require factor/technology immobility among nations and perfect competition in traded finished goods.

PART I

THE THEORY OF FOREIGN EXCHANGE

Chapter 1

EXCHANGE RATES, CAPITAL FLOWS AND MONETARY POLICY

By E. Ray Canterbery*

Debates on foreign exchange models, statistical tests of short-term capital flows, and implications for monetary policy have recently abounded in this *Review*.[1] Now a new statistical test by Hans Stoll [15, 16] focuses upon some important concepts overlooked by Jerome Stein's detractors [6]. Stoll's discussion also illustrates some of the problems in analyzing foreign exchange under partial equilibrium conditions, particularly when monetary policy conclusions are derived therefrom. There continues to be confusion in the literature between what is valid in theory and what is directly testable statistically, and between the forces that are endogenous and those that are exogenous.

To my knowledge there are two full equilibrium models of simultaneous spot and forward foreign exchange market transactions in print: those of Stein [12] and Canterbery [5]. Both authors later modified their models by explicitly specifying the speculative variable as endogenous rather than exogenous [14], [4]. As I owe a great debt to Stein's pioneering work [13], it is not surprising that my article [4, p. 32] derives a forward premium solution (though via more elaborate equation specifications) similar to Stein's [12, p. 56].[2]

I. *Interest Parity and Speculation*

Recent empirical studies can be interpreted in terms of both the behavioral equations and the interest parity solutions of the above theoretical models. Using the foreign exchange supply and demand equations specified by Canterbery [4], a simultaneous solution will yield equilibrium spot and forward rates. Given these rates, a new interest rate parity requirement is derived [4, p. 409, equation (24)]. Using Stoll's symbols, S = spot foreign exchange rate; F = forward foreign exchange rate; S^e = spot rate expected by speculators; r^d = U.S. interest rate; r^f = foreign interest rate; F^* = forward rate satisfying traditional interest parity

* The author is visiting associate professor of economics at Simon Fraser University and associate professor at the Florida State University. He expresses appreciation to J. Lawrence Hexter, Jerry Shipley and Paul Meyer for some very useful discussions on econometric estimation problems in foreign exchange. They share no blame for possible errors.

[1] Five "Comments" [6] were incited by an article by Jerome L. Stein [12].

[2] There are two main differences in the solutions: Stein includes a Central Bank intervention variable and also calls the net speculative variable "exogenous" in [12] even though it is endogenous. The reader is referred to [4, pp. 398–99] for a listing of other differences.

(IRPT), so $F = S - (\hat{r}^f - \hat{r}^d) + f(\Delta S^e)$.[3] Assuming identical forward rate and Treasury bill maturities, the percentage forward premium in the modern theory (*MT*) solution is

$$(1) \quad (F - S)/S = -(r^f - r^d) + f(\Delta S^e)/S.$$

There is no unique value for $(F-S)/S$ as the exchange rates are, in part, determined by a speculative variable. This *MT* solution implies that all variance unexplained by the interest differential can be explained by a speculative variable. This is a hypothesis crucial to the acceptance of recent empirical parity tests, and adds theoretical credibility to a number of statistical findings suggesting that interest differentials under narrow gold bands do not entirely explain forward premiums [e.g., 7, 1, 2]. Traditional interest rate parity would be

$$(2) \qquad (F - S)/S = -(r^f - r^d).$$

Stein does call attention to the interest rate parity implications of his solution in [11], and Peter B. Kenen [8] has emphasized the interest rate parity aspects of foreign exchange in a single-firm model. Kenen demonstrates definitionally what the present author has proven with behavioral relations: namely, traditional interest rate parity prevails only when speculation is nonexistent or stabilizing, that is, when the speculative coefficient in the above parity form solution (1) is zero or near-zero [8, p. 150]. Stoll's and Stein's statistical analyses could be viewed as either tests of the Stein-Canterbery solution or of Kenen's hypothesis.

Stein's final solution for the forward premium (though he confuses readers at various points by calling the forward premium the forward rate) is the beginning of his statistical test. Stein isolates, in theory, the speculative variable with his *MT* solution. Because of the way he specifies his model, however, the speculative variable netted between the spot and forward exchange markets must be endogenous rather than exogenous as Stein claims. (In the model speculative capital flows and both the forward and spot rates interact.) The statistical problem is to identify correctly the precise nature of the speculative variable and design an appropriate test.

Using a linear form of equation (2) Stein regresses the absolute forward premium $(F-S)$ on the uncovered interest rate differential $(r^d - r^f)$ and calculates the residual, the actual minus the predicted rate [12, p. 58]. Assuming speculation to be independent of interest rates, Stein presumes that this residual is an unbiased estimate of the speculative parameter. As Laffer [9, pp. 557–58] suggests, however, it is not possible to derive a statistically unbiased estimate of the parameter for an endogenous variable with this particular technique. A test of the new parity solution carries all the statistical problems associated with simultaneity.[4] In theory, nonetheless, the variable in this general solution is the net speculative function under flexible exchange rates or under a narrow gold band (away from the limits).

An overlooked significance of this new *MT–IRPT* solution is its isolation of two variables (the interest differential and the speculative) from real trade flows. Stein, in his *Reply*, unnecessarily accepts the argument by Heckerman [6, pp. 555–56] and Laffer [9, p. 557] that export–import variations can alter significantly the difference between the forward and spot rates (forward premium). In the Canterbery model, trade can affect the premium only insofar as exchange rate expectations affect hedging and this impact may be very marginal. Even when traders hedge to avert all risk, they are reacting to the same variable as are speculators, namely the expected future exchange rate (which can at times be constant). Assuming hedging then to be a function also of S^e, it is subsumed in the speculative coefficient of the forward market anyway. The relation between spot and forward

[3] The caret (^) signifies that values originally defined as percentages are now in absolute terms. In this modern theory (*MT*) solution the interest differential is the unitary exchange value of extra return from investing abroad rather than at home for the period of the contracts. See [4, p. 409n] for the precise calculation.

[4] If the estimated equation were $(F-S)/S = \alpha_4 + \beta_4 R + u$, the residual (u), in fact, is $[\beta_5 S^e + v]$, where v is an error term and S^e is not independent of $(F-S)/S$. Herein R equals $(r^f - r^d)$.

exchange rates is otherwise unaltered by the trade balance (exogenously given). The only other possible source of variation in the net S^e is a change in the interest rate, a second source of statistical bias in the coefficients.[5] The variation in the forward premium unexplained by interest rates must be then explained by some speculative variable. If the net speculative coefficient can be estimated as an endogenous variable and the speculative interest rate interaction is not present (or else the statistical bias from interaction minimized), there should be little objection to using speculative observations calculated from this indirect parameter estimate as a proxy independent variable along with interest differential observations explaining short-term capital flows.[6]

As Heckerman and Laffer advocate, a trade variable is missing from Stein's capital flows equation. But the suggested unlagged trade surplus variable is dependent under flexible exchange rates. It is, moreover, an accounting near identity with short-term capital flows (as Stein correctly replies) under either flexible or fixed rates. Given these considerations and having identified all the major independent variables, specifying trade as a distributed lag variable may yield an improved estimating equation for capital flows.

II. *Empirical Tests and Policy Implications*

A speculative variable that is correctly specified for all eventualities is needed; whether speculation interacts with exchange rates, is correlated with interest rates, interacts with interest rates, or is unrelated to interest rates. This would merge theory and empirical verification. In an inquiry "... only into the relationship of the forward rate to the spot rate" [15, p. 61], Stoll performs an improved test. The speculative variable is specified as a function of lagged spot rates, making it endogenous and of a form similar to that suggested (in theory) by Canterbery [4, p. 404n] and also tested elsewhere by Stein and Tower [14] and Sven Arndt [1].[7] Stoll's dependent variable is F/S rather than $(F-S)$ and his speculative variable is S^e rather than ΔS^e.

Arndt's distributed lag specification for the expected exchange-rate may lead ultimately to improved speculative parameter estimates.[8] But Arndt's estimates of the covered (and uncovered) interest rate and speculative parameters against capital flows also are biased, a bias (as Arndt correctly explains) resulting from the application of non-simultaneous techniques to what is (in theory) a simultaneous system. Stoll focuses upon a part of the Stein-Arndt type of statistical problem. Stoll specifies his endogenous speculative variable in such a way as to reduce interest rate coefficient bias. As Stoll wisely recognizes that past expectations can influence current expectations (unless random), the most general expression of his behavioral equations would have a as the coefficient of $(S-S^e_{-1})$ and b as the coefficient of S^e (of current expectations). His theoretical equation is reducible to

$$(3)\quad F/S = c + (1-b)R + b(1-a)S^e_{-1}/S,$$

where R is the interest rate differential. As S^e and S^e_{-1} are unknowns, however, they are defined functionally in terms of knowns $(S, F, F_{-1}, R, R_{-1})$ and hence eliminated from the final estimating equation. The statistical equation is then fitted in the con-

[5] A hypothesis of independence is a true one only if the monetary authorities do not change interest rates in reaction to exchange speculation. Even if speculator's responses to such interest rate changes are random the statistical collinearity is already present though of a sign opposite to what it would be with the reactions hoped for by the authorities.

[6] The statistical independence that would cause the two variables to be orthogonal simply means that the addition to the multiple regression (against capital flows) of the speculative variable would not alter the interest rate coefficient and one has the long sought statistical ideal coinciding with a theoretical solution. The coefficient of multiple determination also would be higher. It is emphasized, however, that as a reduced form estimate the speculative parameter in the *MT* solution is only a proxy for speculation in the capital-flows equation.

[7] Stoll's speculative variable is specified as $S^e = aS + (1-a)S^e_{-1}$, implying that S^e is a geometrically declining weighted average of past spot rates [15, p. 65]. A second order lag generated better results for the U.K.

[8] Data used in the test were for Canadian capital flows, 1952–60.

strained form:

$$(4)\quad F/S - (1-a)F_{-1}/S = 1 - b(1-a) + (1-b)\cdot[R-(1-a)R_{-1}] + z.$$

The coefficient $(1-a)$ is the weight given to prior expectations and $(1-b)$ is the interest rate coefficient.

Beyond pointing out the overlooked significance of Stein's preliminary solution and citing theoretically derived justification for Stoll's ingenious econometric test, some of the substantive discussion of Stoll in [16], wherein he apparently relies upon his model of [15], is challenged. Working through examples of capital-flow changes prompted by exogenous disturbances under both fixed and free exchange rate systems, Stoll attempts to illustrate that under certain conditions Keynes' "two interest rate" policy will fail and that even under flexible rates monetary policy is not independent of "international considerations." In two fixed rate cases his partial equilibrium analyses are based on changes in R that are exogenous. Throughout, all exchange rates are from U.S. point of view, i.e., the dollar cost of one foreign currency unit.

In Stoll's second fixed rate case between the U.S. and the U.K., the exogenous influence is a rise in the U.S. interest rate. Stoll states on the one hand, " . . . the spot rate cannot change and no reason exists for expectations about future spot rates to change, . . . " [16, p. 895]. On the other hand, he says that spot funds " . . . will be covered forward at F so that [the U.S.] F is driven up until $S^e = S < F = F^*$" [16, p. 895]. Why would interest rate arbitragers cover if it is expected that the spot rate will remain unchanged $(S^e = \overline{S^e})$? Interest arbitrage becomes a function of $[(r^f - r^d) + \overline{S^e}]$ rather than of $[(r^f - r^d) + (F-S)/S]$.[9] Without the forthcoming cover, the forward rate would not appreciate and U.K. capital outflows would simply continue on a mostly uncovered basis. The U.K. "two interest rate" policy would fail, as Stoll suggests, but not because the U.K. forward rate was falling, implying a lower future spot rate. An often overlooked contributor to this failure is the presence of *uncovered* interest arbitrage under a system that guarantees minimal losses for those who base some of their exchange activity on S^e.

A third case is under Canadian floating rates where the exogenous change is a rise in U.S. interest rates. The expected spot rate apparently is again exogenous. Stoll argues that " . . . the burden of the initial adjustment will be on S, · · · , and not on F so that $F = F^* = S^e > S$" [16, p. 896]. To assert that the burden of change is on the spot rate is *now* to presume that all interest-rate arbitrage is uncovered and exports-imports *unhedged* despite the greater risk of exchange rate fluctuation in a freely fluctuating system. Because of the necessity for Canadians to cover under free rates, it is more probable that the U.S. forward rate on the Canadian dollar will be appreciating while the spot rate falters.[10] The movement to a new equilibrium is that described by Stein [13, p. 32–35]. Rather than the continuing spot depreciation described by Stoll, *equilibrium* is reached at some lower value of S. Interest rate parity (equation (2)) is also likely achieved in a short time period.

Whether the exchange rate moves far enough to cause " . . . Canadian exports [to] increase . . . and inflationary pressure . . . " [16, p. 896] depends upon the arbitrage and import elasticities. The conclusion that " . . . the Canadian authorities refuse[d] to allow r^f to fall" in 1959 demonstrates only that the Canadian monetary authorities did not act independently of international considerations and contributed to a domestic recession; it does not prove domestic monetary policy could not have been independent.[11]

[9] Stoll's model excludes this possibility by defining all hedgers as those who take a riskless position. Canterbery [3, 4, 5] defines uncovered interest arbitrage as, in part, a function of ΔS^e. Importers and arbitragers only attempt to eliminate risk if in fact they have formulated some expectation about future rate movements, including expected no change. These reactions nonetheless are captured statistically in Stoll's estimates because of the residual nature of the speculative variable in equation (1).

[10] Normal leading and lagging by importers and exporters would reinforce these rate movements.

[11] A careful observer of Canadian economic policies

In estimating the modern interest rate parity equation (1), there can be two sources of simultaneity bias. In Stein's test, $(F-S) = h(\Delta S^e)$ and $\Delta S^e = g(F-S)$. However, monetary policy makers sometime change interest rates in reaction to changes in S and/or F. Thus, R may be also a function of past values of S and F, and hence of S^e (and vice versa).

Stoll in [15] estimates equation (2) in order to derive an intentionally biased estimate of the interest rate parameter. By specifying S^e as a function of predetermined spot prices in testing equation (1), however, Stoll eliminates the speculative exchange-rate bias encountered by Stein. Because of the nature of correlation and Stoll's technique, however, one cannot positively determine the direction of cause and effect[12] between R and S^e. The Canadian interest rate coefficient increased from .80 to .96 (under flexible rates) after addition of the speculative variable to the regression; and the U.K. coefficient *fell* from .80 to .60. Stoll attributes these R coefficient changes to the elimination of *all* bias in the interest rate parameter estimates. The cause-effect Stoll presumes [15, pp. 76–77] between interest differentials and speculative behavior may be at times of a direction opposite that which he asserts and at times nonexistent (qua Stein's independence assumption).

The Canadian authorities raised interest rates and S^e rose. Did S^e rise because of the interest rate advance or because of natural market forces? Speculation may have been stabilizing under freely fluctuating exchange rates. Yeager [18], Rhomberg [10], and Stein [14], have concluded that speculation tended to raise the rate on the Canadian dollar during the flexible rate period when it was tending to fall.[13] The U.K. authorities increased interest rates and S^e fell. Did S^e fall in perverse reaction to the interest rate or does this simply suggest that under a narrow gold band higher interest rates do not necessarily attract capital? In terms of monetary policy Stoll's comparative regression results may simply demonstrate that policy makers' reaction to capital flows was to change interest rates. Furthermore, under free rates the interest changes may have been unnecessary and under fixed rates, fruitless.

The foregoing discussion is not intended to fault Stoll's statistical test per se. Indeed, if all statistical biases were reduced, Stoll's coefficients approximate the true parameters for the reduced form equation in the Stein and Canterbery models. Stoll may have accomplished the statistical test only attempted by Stein and never tried by the present author. And Stoll's evidence does lend considerable support to the new, more general form of interest rate parity.

What general policy conclusions emerge from this debate? First, the new formulation of the *IRPT*, both theoretical and empirical, raises doubts concerning the advisability of using interest rates directly to influence capital flows. If traditional interest rate parity prevails with free exchange rates

has concluded that "... the primary cause in the ensuing difficulties should be sought in Mr. Coyne's [head of the Central Bank] attitudes towards monetary policy, and not to the flexible exchange rate mechanism as such ...". See [17, p. 235].

[12] Let the form of the *MT* estimating equation (1) be $F/S = \alpha_0 + \beta_1 R + \beta_2 S^e + v$, where v is the error term. If S^e is regressed against R, we have $S^e = \alpha_1 + \beta_3 R$. In turn, if the speculative variable is dropped for a test of the *IRPT* equation (2), the expected value of the estimated regression coefficient $(\hat{\beta}_1)$ is $E\hat{\beta}_1 = \beta_1 + \beta_2\beta_3$. In words, the estimated interest rate coefficient is biased by the slope coefficient of S^e regressed on R. Stoll is able, then to calculate an implied regression slope for S^e against R by comparing his estimated *MT* coefficients for R and S^e with his biased *IRPT* coefficient estimate for R. In Canada, $\beta_3 = -4.0$ and in the U.K., $\beta_3 = .5$. Even if the final *MT* estimates for β_1 and β_2 are unbiased, the direction of cause-effect between R and S^e can no more be inferred in this case than it can in any simple correlation between two variables, one arbitrarily defined as "dependent" and the other "independent." The failure to take this into account explains most of Stoll's subsequent interpretive errors. The reader, for the sake of accuracy, should bear in mind that Stoll's *MT* estimates for β_1 are derived from a constrained equation (4) rather than directly from (1). In the *IRPT* tests, $E\hat{\beta}_1 = .80$ in both Canada and the U.K. In the *MT* test, the coefficient moves close to parity in flexible rate Canada.

[13] This possibility escapes Stoll as he claims that in the U.K. "... a fall in the interest differential produces pessimism about the course of the pound relative to the U.S. dollar, thus causing S^e to fall relative to S." [15, p. 76] But one could obtain similar statistical results if a speculative variable outweighed the effect on capital flows of interest-differential changes.

(speculation being stabilizing), no interest rate alterations may be required. When independent speculative variable changes outweigh the effects of interest rate alterations under fixed exchange rates, interest rate policy is less relevant for exchange stabilization purposes. With flexible rates, *smaller* (self-limiting) amounts of capital may move more *rapidly* in response to interest rate changes. Because of the low-risk profitability of *uncovered* interest arbitrage with a narrow gold band, however, large capital amounts may flow as interest rates change and it is virtually impossible to separate speculative from interest-rate forces.[14]

It is not possible then for the monetary authorities to predict with any certainty the impact of interest rate changes on short-term capital flows under a narrow gold band. The Canadian monetary authorities may have used interest rate changes to support the Canadian dollar under a system that does not require artificial bolstering (flexible rates) and the U.K. may have used a similar device for pound support under a system and conditions in which such a policy cannot succeed. The failure of floating exchange rates may rest in the lack of desire of the monetary authorities to follow independent monetary policies under *any* system rather than resting on the precept that speculation necessarily will be destabilizing.

[14] For a model describing speculator response to interest rate changes under alternative systems, see Canterbery [3]. Uncovered interest rate arbitrage demand has been expressed elsewhere [4, p. 407]; [5, p. 36] as, in part, a function of the expected future price of exchange. The absence of traditional parity under a narrow gold band does not mean that capital will never flow in reaction to interest rate changes; such capital flows at times will be multiplied by associated rising, falling or stable expected spot prices.

References

1. S. W. Arndt, "International Short-term Capital Movements: A Distributed Lag Model of Speculation in Foreign Exchange," *Econometrica*, Jan. 1968, *36*, 59–69.
2. S. W. Black, "Theory and Policy Analysis of Short-term Movements in the Balance of Payments," *Yale Economic Essays*, Spring 1968, *8*, 5–78.
3. E. R. Canterbery, "The Delayed Peg and the Adjustment Mechanism," A Paper before the Southern Economic Association Meetings, Nov. 1968.
4. ———, "A Dynamic Theory of Foreign Exchange," *Nat. Bank. Rev.*, June 1967, *5*, 397–413.
5. ———, *Foreign Exchange, Capital Flows and Monetary Policy*, Studies in Internat. Fin., Princeton 1965.
6. H. P. Gray, D. G. Heckerman, A. B. Laffer, P. H. Hendershott, and T. D. Willett, "International Short-term Capital Movements: Comments," *Am. Econ. Rev.*, June 1967, *57*, 548–70.
7. H. Grubel, "A Neglected Aspect of Forward Exchange Theory and Policy," *Jour. Fin.*, Sept. 1963, *18*, 537–48.
8. P. Kenen, "Trade, Speculation, and the Forward Exchange Rate," in R. E. Baldwin (ed.), *Trade, Growth and the Balance of Payments*, Chicago 1965, 143–69.
9. A. B. Laffer, "International Short-term Capital Movements: Comment III," *Am. Econ. Rev.*, June 1967, *58*, 556–60.
10. R. R. Rhomberg, "A Model of the Canadian Economy under Fixed and Fluctuating Rates," *Jour. Pol. Econ.*, Feb. 1964, *72*, 1–31.
11. J. L. Stein, "The Forward Rate and the Interest Parity," *Rev. Econ. Stud.*, Apr. 1965, *32*, 113–126.
12. ———, "International Short-term Capital Movements," *Am. Econ. Rev.*, Mar. 1965, *55*, 40–66.
13. ———, *The Nature and Efficiency of the Foreign Exchange Market*, Essays in Internat. Fin., Princeton 1962.
14. ———, and E. Tower, "The Short-Run Stability of the Foreign Exchange Market," *Rev. Econ. Stat.*, May 1967, *49*, 173–85.
15. H. Stoll, "An Empirical Study of the Forward Exchange Market under Fixed and Flexible Exchange Rate Systems," *Can. Jour. Econ.* Feb. 1968, *1*, 55–78.
16. ———, "A Note on Exchange Rate

Changes and Capital Flows," *Am. Econ. Rev.*, Sept. 1967, *57*, 894–97.
17. P. WONNACOTT, *The Canadian Dollar* 1948–1962, Toronto 1965.
18. L. B. YEAGER, International Monetary Relations, New York 1966, 423–40.

Chapter 2

A Theory of Foreign Exchange Speculation under Alternative Systems

E. Ray Canterbery

Florida State University

Is speculation destabilizing? This paper explores the question of whether free exchange rates result in more stability than optional systems. The study includes development of a linear, stable equilibrium model of a free rate system; examination of speculative-induced movements in market exchange rates; and simplification of mathematics to allow for speculative shifts under a narrow gold band and for full interaction between spot and foreign exchange rates. Conclusion: Speculators are stabilizers under absolutely free rates, relative stabilizers under a wide gold band, and destabilizers under a narrow gold band, a theory qualified by political problems and uncontrollable exogenous forces.

I. Introduction

Since a major argument against completely free exchange rates is that speculation will be destabilizing, this paper addresses itself to the question of whether free rates are likely to result in more stability than optional systems.

We develop first a linear, stable equilibrium model of a freely fluctuating exchange system, determining equilibrium exchange rates independently from expected exchange rates. Next, speculative-induced movements in market exchange rates toward and away from equilibrium rates are examined in a sixth degree second-order differential equation. Knowledge from the equilibrium model that interest rate parity tends to prevail under free rates leads us to a solution which suggests a strong tendency for the market rate to approach stable equilibrium under free rates. Then, the mathematics is simplified to allow for speculative shifts under a narrow gold band and to allow full interaction between the spot and foreign exchange rates.

The author has benefited from discussions with J. Lawrence Hexter, John Boorman, A. Zafarulleh, John Chang, Christopher Clague, Leland B. Yeager, and Peter Morris and from comments by an unknown referee at this *Journal*.

We conclude that speculators most probably will tend to be stabilizers under absolutely free rates, relative stabilizers under a wide gold band, and destabilizers under a narrow gold band. This theoretical attractiveness of free rates is tempered, however, by both practical political problems (implementation) and uncontrollable exogenous forces (wars, riots, famines, etc.)

A major argument against completely free exchange rates is that speculation will be destabilizing under such a system. Evidence thus far is inconclusive. An often hidden presumption of the free-rate opposition is that fixed rates are by their very nature stable; this results in part from a confusion between the natural market rate and the arbitrarily fixed rate. Under fixed rates, instability can be transferred to official monetary reserves. In a world in which absolute stability may be an impossible or even undesirable criterion, attempts to demonstrate that free rates are absolutely stable would answer the wrong question. The relevant issue is whether free rates are likely to result in more stability than optional systems. This paper addresses itself to this more relevant question.

This discussion can best be oriented by comparisons with the well-known article by S. C. Tsiang (1958). The Tsiang theory is, of course, of a floating exchange rate system. Because of the assumptions and the specifications of his model, it cannot be used to describe comparative speculation under different systems. Moreover, by changing the assumptions, we can better explain the behavior of speculators under a floating system. We shall, however, abstract from the price level–exchange rate interactions under free rates so well described by Tsiang.

The following assumptions distinguish the models from Tsiang's and allow the outcomes to be useful for intersystem comparisons:

1. National governments successfully pursue a goal of full employment with price stability under free exchange rates. Thus, trade flows are not allowed to exert substantial pressures on average commodity prices. Even without this goal, an analogous result would follow when a nation's trade is so small a share of its GNP that the overall price level is insensitive to trade variations. Under fixed exchange rates, of course, there is no direct interaction between price levels and exchange rates.

2. While Tsiang assumes that the opportunity cost for speculators under free rates is the domestic interest rate, we assume that it is the opportunity cost under fixed rates while the covered differential between foreign and domestic interest rates is the relevant opportunity cost under free rates.

3. Rather than assuming that speculators always must borrow to speculate, we examine cases when they use available currency holdings and also when they use some currency holdings and borrow some at the going domestic rate.

4. The Tsiang risk factor is additive, whereas ours is multiplicative. This is important in comparing systems. If additive, there would be only a once-and-for-all shift in the speculative function in reaction to any new risk evaluation under a newly imposed system. If multiplicative, the risk factor will in great part determine whether or not the exchange rate is stable.

These new provisions turn out to be significant departures from the current theory of speculation. The second assumption is especially useful. While interest rate arbitrage tends to be covered against exchange risk under free rates, it often is uncovered under fixed rates or a narrow gold band. Thus the opportunity cost term can actually be altered as we move from one system to another. This specification also enables us to identify precisely an important source of speculation—uncovered interest rate arbitrage—under less flexible exchange rate systems.

II. A "Pure" Equilibrium Model

First, we shall develop a stable equilibrium model of a freely fluctuating exchange rate system. In it, equilibrium exchange rates are determined. The model is "purified" by abstracting from considerations of expected exchange rate movements. Interest rate arbitragers in such a system can be risk averters only if they completely cover all transactions in the forward market. Because of the high risk of exchange rate movements, we assume that all interest arbitrage is completely covered under free rates. Importers-exporters, it is assumed, do not react to expected exchange rate changes, but some will engage in forward transactions at times when the forward rate is different from the spot. Such traders unwittingly are the risk takers for covered arbitragers in the equilibrium model.

Although imports can be specified as, in part, a function of national income, we shall assume national incomes constant. Individual commodity prices are determined by perfect competition and do not change independently of exchange rates. For the longer run these assumptions are relaxed easily: an upward shift in incomes and demand for an income-elastic import could, *ceteris paribus*, raise its price, the demand for foreign exchange, and the price of foreign exchange. Domestic interest rates are exogenous variables and are independent of exchange-rate and balance-of-payments influences. The foreign currency values of imports (M) and exports (X) are dependent variables under freely fluctuating rates.

In this simplified model, the demands for spot (D, S) and forward exchange (FD, FS) depend only upon trade volumes and interest rate differentials (with short term government debt rates being proxy variables for all interest rates). Only two industrialized nations (or else two currency blocs) are involved. We shall let x be the daily spot rate, y the daily forward foreign exchange rate, z the absolute forward premium (+) or discount (−), where $z = y - x$, and m the interest-rate spread (foreign [v] − domestic [u] rate) in unitary exchange units.[1] The forward contracts and government obligations are assumed to be all of the same maturity, and transactions cost is negligible or cancelling.

With linear relations, the demand-supply functions in the spot market at constant levels of national income can be specified as:

$$D = a_1 - b_1 x + c_1(z + m) \; ; \tag{1}$$

$$S = a_2 + b_2 x - c_2(z + m) \; , \tag{2}$$

where the signs of the coefficients are taken from the partial derivatives. The linearity assumption is much more plausible if speculation is excluded, because responses to given price changes are more probably by the same magnitudes when price expectations are nonexistent. To avoid unnecessary (for our purposes here) and cumbersome mathematics, maturing forward contracts that augment spot supply and introduce a lag function are ignored.[2] Recognizing that the interest arbitrager sells a quantity of foreign exchange forward equal to his spot purchase,[3] the forward market becomes

$$FD = e_1 - h_1 z - c_2(z + m) \; , \tag{3}$$

$$FS = e_1 + h_2 z + c_1(z + m) \; . \tag{4}$$

It is hypothesized that $|h_1| < |b_1|$ and $|h_2| < |b_2|$. Forward demand and supply against the forward premium (z) have the same intercept (e_1) only if $m = 0$. Covered interest arbitrage is the only initial force that can cause the forward spot rates to diverge.[4] Note that total foreign exchange value demanded by importers in all maturities at any pairing

[1] The algebraic definition of unitary exchange units and the proof for this conversion appears in Canterbery (1967, p. 409, n. 28). To define m precisely, it is the extra return per unit of foreign exchange invested in foreign treasury bills. This definition of m greatly reduces the complexity of the algebra without significantly diminishing precision. The linear model solution also can be interpreted more easily. From the interest rate differential as a percentage, say $\hat{m}$, $m = \hat{m} \cdot x$, so that the amount of interest changes proportionately with the exchange rate. One could re-solve the linear model by substituting $[\bar{y} + x(\hat{m} - 1)]$ for $(z + m)$. Those who prefer the percentage expression also may use $[\bar{y}_0 + \bar{x}_0(\hat{m} - 1)$ for interest rate parity, $\hat{y}_0 - \bar{x}_0 + m)$, in the differential equations developed in Section III.

[2] For a model specification including such lags, see Canterbery 1967.

[3] For simplicity that does not affect outcomes, we are assuming that the amount of expected interest payment is not covered.

[4] The reasoning behind the specification of the arbitrage functions and the explicit signs of their coefficients appears in Canterbery (1965, chap. 4; 1967, pp. 397–414). The effect of maturing forward contracts on spot supply and price is incorporated into these models.

of (x, y) is $M = (a_1 + e_1) + (h_1 - b_1)\ x - h_1 y$; any supplied by exporters is $X = (a_2 + e_1) + (b_2 - h_2)\ x + h_2 y$. Set demand equal to supply in each market and simplify by letting $b_3 = (b_1 + c_1 + b_2 + c_2)$, $c_3 = (c_1 + c_2)$, $h_3 = (h_1 + c_1 + h_2 + c_2)$, $e_2 = c_3 m$, and $a_3 = [(a_1 - a_2) + c_3 m]$; then

$$b_3 x - c_3 y = a_3\ , \tag{5}$$

and

$$-h_3 x + h_3 y = -e_2\ . \tag{6}$$

Use Cramer's rule in solving for the equilibrium exchange rates, and

$$\tilde{x}_{0m} = \frac{(a_1 - a_2)}{(b_1 + b_2)} + \frac{c_3(h_3 + c_3)}{h_3(b_1 + b_2)}\ m\ , \tag{7}$$

$$\tilde{y}_{0m} = \frac{(a_1 - a_2)}{(b_1 + b_2)} + \frac{c_3[h_3 - (b_1 + b_2)]}{h_3(b_1 + b_2)}\ m\ . \tag{8}$$

Unless foreign buyers and sellers react to the independent variables in the same amounts as home buyers and sellers, the determinant of the coefficient matrix is nonzero and the equations are consistent.[5] The forward premium is

$$\tilde{z}_{0m} = -\beta m\ , \tag{9}$$

where $\beta \cong 1$. Because some importers-exporters switch to the forward market when forward exchange is cheaper (from their respective points of view), the coefficient of m will not be precisely one.

Leaving speculation out of the equilibrium model causes the premium solution to approximate traditional interest rate parity, which is

$$\tilde{y}_{0m} - \tilde{x}_{0m} + m = 0\ . \tag{10}$$

According to J. M. Keynes's original exposition of parity, short-term capital movements were stabilized by the movement of the forward premium to a discount matching the interest spread. For later purposes we can define a second set of equilibrium rates. When there is no interest rate differential (that is, $m = 0$), the equilibrium rates are:

$$\tilde{x}_0 = \tilde{y}_0 = (a_1 - a_2)/(b_1 + b_2)\ . \tag{11}$$

The tilde (~) is used to distinguish the nonspeculative equilibriums from other rates that occur at $t_0 = 0$, such as $x(t_0) = x(0)$ after an exogenous disturbance. Now we shall discuss speculative-induced movements in market exchange rates toward and away from equilibrium.

III. Speculation under Free Rates

Speculation may or may not contribute to stability of the exchange rate (or stability of official reserves when x is pegged). Destabilizing specula-

[5] Steps to solution appear in Appendix A. If equation (7) is subtracted from equation (8), the coefficient of m is $[-c_3\ (b_3 + c_3)]/(h_3 b_3)$, which would approximate -1.

tion can be defined as any behavior by speculators that tends to move the exchange rate away from its nonspeculative equilibrium level. In the Friedman (1953, pp. 157–203) and Telser (1959, p. 295) discussions, the nonspeculator is not influenced by the exchange rate he expects to prevail at some future date or, therefore, by recent exchange rate alterations. Thus the speculative function includes those transactions from leading and lagging by exporters-importers, uncovered interest rate arbitragers (to some degree), as well as transactions by pure speculators—those whose sole purpose is to make profits from exchange rate variations. Speculation is defined functionally, not in terms of who is doing what. Hence, where those who are reacting to exchange-rate changes begin to react exclusively to changes in the covered interest-rate differential, they are no longer "speculating." If speculation is stabilizing, the exchange rate will follow approximately the path it would have followed in the absence of speculation.[6]

Accepted economic theory plus currently available econometric tests suggest that adjustments under freely fluctuating exchange rates, equilibrating both the foreign exchange market and the balance of trade, will occur in the absence of destabilizing speculation.[7] Though there are unresolved political problems, the theoretical efficacy of more flexible exchange rates turns mostly upon the nature of speculation.

Under entirely free exchange rates, any temporary, nonspeculative excess market demand in either the spot (SED_{ns}) or forward (FED_{ns}) markets is a function of the prevailing spot market exchange rate; so

$$SED_{ns} = F(x) \; ; \qquad FED_{ns} = H(x) \, , \tag{12}$$

where $F(x)$ and $H(x)$ are assumed to be linear. The rate of change of the market exchange rates can be related to this excess demand. Looking initially at the effect of nonspeculators on this rate of change, we can argue that nonspeculators always respond in the same magnitudes over time to given exchange rate changes. We can assume an exogenously caused movement in the market exchange rate away from its equilibrium value (as determined in Section II). Using a constant proportionality factor, k in the spot market and q forward,

$$dx/dt = k \cdot F(x) \; ; \qquad dy/dt = q \cdot H(x) \, . \tag{13}$$

[6] This circumvents the type of debate engaged in by Telser and Baumol, in which Baumol argues that nonspeculators can be destabilizers. We can demonstrate that the general form of the linear equilibrium solution is the same for "legitimate" traders of goods and services as it is for banks that speculate (see Canterbery 1967, p. 410). This simply means that the leads and lags of commercial traders are in response to past or expected changes in the exchange rate. The same principle applies to uncovered interest-rate arbitragers.

[7] For a careful review and interpretation of this literature, see Yeager (1966, pp. 136–60). An algebraic derivation of the exchange stability condition appears in pages 158–60 (see also Haberler 1949; Mundell 1960; and Machlup 1939).

The positive constants' magnitudes (indicating direct proportionality) express the speeds of time adjustment to the equilibrium rate. For the purpose of solving our first model version, we further assume that $dy/dt = c \cdot dx/dt$, where c is a positive constant. In the absence of speculation, the equilibrium spot value will be approached when $F'(\bar{x}_0)$ is negative and the supply curve intersects the demand curve from below. The market then would be stable.[8]

Different magnitudes of response by speculators to the same exchange rate changes over time are probable. This is the consequence of speculative excess demand being in part a function of time. Even without the possibility that risk may rise with the volume of foreign exchange holdings, there is a psychology of free markets that says that the price of anything cannot continually move in one direction at a constant rate. To avoid unnecessary complication of the relations, we will not vary the risk coefficient itself with holdings, but we can plausibly hypothesize that under free rates the risk of exchange rate variation is great and, on the average, risk high.[9]

If we assume initially that forward exchange rates move in some constant proportion to spot, we can develop a realistic nonlinear specification of speculative behavior. We postulate that speculative magnitudes are determined by the difference between the expected spot rate change and the current rate of change in the spot rate $(dx^*/dt - dx/dt)$ adjusted for risk and opportunity cost. With the opportunity cost part of the speculative function linear, a moderate degree of foresightedness by speculators (reacting to the expected consequences of their own behavior) yields a sixth-degree polynomial function.[10] The precise degree of such relations may be more an empirical than theoretical question, and dis-

[8] The nonspeculative solution for the spot market rate determination alone has been presented by Vanek (1962, p. 147). His solution is: $x(t) = x_0 + A \cdot e^{k \cdot F'(x_0) \cdot t}$, where A is the initial difference between an exogenously determined market rate and the equilibrium rate (x_0). The market rate, therefore, converges to x_0 for small displacements from equilibrium.

[9] In effect, the stock-adjustments aspect of the model are subsumed in an exogenous risk factor and in the nonlinearity of speculative responses to expected exchange rate changes rather than in changes of an endogenous risk coefficient. Again, there may be advantages going either route. There is considerable empirical controversy concerning the importance of stocks versus flows (see Hendershott 1967; Laffer 1967; Stein 1967).

[10] The polynomial is derived by redefining what would otherwise be constants as functions of the original functions. Abstracting from opportunity cost and the risk factor, we have that part of speculative reaction to the expected exchange rate (x^*), the spot market rate (x), and time (t) as $f_0(x^*, x, t) = j_0 \cdot (dx^*/dt - dx/dt)$, where dx^*/dt is positively related to d^2x/dt^2, so $dx^*/dt = g_0 \cdot (d^2x/dt^2)$ while $g_0 = g_1 \cdot (d^2x/dt^2)$. Also, $j_0 = i_0 \cdot (dx^*/dt - dx/dt)$ and $i_0 = i_1 \cdot (dx^*dt - dx/dt)$. Therefore, $dx^*/dt = [g_1 \cdot (d^2x/dt^2)] \cdot (d^2x/dt^2)$. By substitution, $f_0(x^*, x, t) = i_1 \cdot \{[g_1(d^2x/dt^2) \cdot (d^2x/dt^2)] - dx/dt\} \cdot \{[g_1(d^2x/dt^2) \cdot (d^2x/dt^2)] - dx/dt\}\{[g_1(d^2x/dt^2) \cdot (d^2x/dt^2)] - dx/dt\}$ or $f_0(x^*, x, t) = i_1 \cdot [g_1 \cdot (d^2x/dt^2)^2 - dx/dt]^3$. With $i_1 = I$ and $g_1 = G$, the right-hand side of this relation is used in equation (14).

tributed-lag techniques have been applied to estimate the degree of the exchange rate variable against capital flows (Arndt 1968). The expected future change in the exchange rate is hypothesized as a function of the rate of change in the rate of change of the spot rate (d^2x/dt^2).

Speculative demand—it is hypothesized—therefore depends upon the expected rate of change in the exchange rate discounted by a subjective risk factor ($0 < \theta < 1$) minus the actual rate of change in the exchange rate. As this risk factor is multiplicative, risk would be zero when $\theta = 1$. But with freely fluctuating rates the risk of exchange variation is initially very high (θ is small). The speculator estimates future exchange rate changes from the rate of change in the rate of change in the exchange rate (d^2x/dt^2) and then—because of uncertainty—discounts this change by a fixed value. The decision to speculate is a portfolio one, as the holder of foreign exchange assets can invest alternatively in a (virtually) riskless asset—foreign treasury bills covered against exchange risk in the forward market. This cost of cover ($y - x$) plus the absolute interest rate spread (m) is assumed to be the relevant opportunity cost for the speculator.

The opportunity cost selected is not independent of risk. Also, because the possibility for daily exchange rate variation is great under free rates, the forward market is much more important to the commodity exporter-importer than under the current narrow gold band. The use of the forward market by risk averters becomes imperative. The same logic applies to interest rate arbitragers. Hence, opportunity cost tends to converge to zero, that is, to classical interest parity (equation [10]). In the solution to this model version, we presume that speculators have reasons for holding foreign currency inventories—they are bankers financing trade or commodity traders financing trade—and they do not need to borrow domestic funds for the purpose of speculation. We can relax this assumption later. (In this model where borrowing does occur, the solution varies only by the size of the domestic interest rate part of the opportunity cost parameter.)

The initial absolute cost of cover is the equilibrium cost ($\tilde{y}_{0m} - \tilde{x}_{0m}$) which is constant. But under conditions of excess demand the market rates (y and x) will be changing and the potential speculator will adjust his "normal" opportunity cost for the rates of change in both spot and forward exchange rates. Hence, in our equations, the equilibrium rates are adjusted by the rate of change in the two market rates (dx/dt) and (dy/dt).

With our derived polynomial, the spot market speculative excess demand function is

$$SED_s = I \cdot [G\theta \cdot (d^2x/dt^2)^2 - dx/dt]^3 - p_0 \cdot [\tilde{y}_{0m} + dy/dt - (\tilde{x}_{0m} + dx/dt) + m] \,. \tag{14}$$

Substituting for dy/dt, we have

$$SED_s = I \cdot [G\theta \cdot (d^2x/dt^2)^2 - dx/dt]^3 - p_0[(c-1)dx/dt] - p_0(\tilde{y}_{0m} - \tilde{x}_{0m} + m)\,. \tag{15}$$

Summing the nonspeculative and speculative spot excess demands, we have

$$SED_{ns} + SED_s = F(x) + I \cdot [G\theta \cdot (d^2x/dt^2)^2 - dx/dt]^3 - p_0 \cdot (c-1)dx/dt - p_0 \cdot (\tilde{y}_{0m} - \tilde{x}_{0m} + m)\,. \tag{16}$$

The last term of this expression will be recognized as the classical interest rate parity argument. In order to solve this second-order and sixth-degree differential equation, we need to assume that this term is zero. We learned from the equilibrium model that interest rate parity does tend to prevail under free rates.[11] If $(\tilde{y}_{0m} - \tilde{x}_{0m} + m) = 0$ and the equilibrium rate is unitary ($\tilde{x}_{0m} = 1$), then the general form of the solution in terms of the market exchange rate (for small values of t) can be derived by a Maclaurin's series. Letting $C = b^{2/5}[k(G\theta)]^{-3/5} \cdot [F'(x)]^{-6/5}$ and $\bar{D} = \bar{G}k^{-2/5}[\sqrt[5]{kP_0(c-1)} - 1]$,

$$x(t) = 1 + (C + \bar{D}) \cdot t + (C/5)(C + \bar{D}) \cdot t^2 + [(C + \bar{D})(C + 3\bar{D}) - (C^3/75)] \cdot t^3 + R_3\,, \tag{17}$$

where C and $\bar{D}$ represent the more complex versions of the constants and R_3 is a remainder.[12] Because of the probable smallness of k, C will tend to be very small. The remainder at $n = 3$ appears to be small for potential values of x ranging from 0.5 to 1.5. Thus, these terms may be sufficient to approximate a solution.

The difference between the equilibrium exchange rate and the prevailing market rate will depend mostly upon the size of the speculative coefficient (G), the risk factor (θ), the importance of opportunity cost (P_0), the slope of the excess demand function, $F'(x)$, and the smallness of the nonspeculative parameter (k). When $c > 1$, the large values of P_0 and (relatively) k under free rates would be forces reducing excess demand and raising the market rate toward equilibrium. If, then, $|\bar{G}k^{-2/5}[\sqrt[5]{kP_0(c-1)}]| < ||\bar{G}k^{-2/5}|$ by more than $|b^{2/5}[k(G\theta)]^{-3/5} \cdot F'(x)^{-6/5}|$, the market rate will fall short of the equilibrium (1.0). In this model speculators might push the exchange rate above equilibrium, "overshooting" it from the excess demand position. In general, this solution suggests a strong tendency for the market rate to approach stable equilibrium under free rates.

[11] All steps to solution appear in Appendix B. We assume a continuous function and that all derivatives are known.

[12] $R_3 = t^4 \cdot [(C^2/750) \cdot (2C^2x^{-7/5} + 14C\bar{D}x^{-9/5} + 12\bar{D}^2x^{-11/5}) + (2C/125)\bar{D}^3x^{-13/5}]$.

This polynomial version of the model, however, does not tell all the story well. In assuming interest rate parity we cannot discern shifts in speculation as a result of interest rate changes. This is particularly important if we wish to explain capital flows under fixed exchange rates. Also, full interaction between the spot and forward exchange rates is not allowed in this model type. And as indicated above, complete identification of the stability conditions may not be possible. To gain knowledge in both these respects, we need to simplify the mathematics. In doing so, we lose the precise form of the polynomial speculative path in theory but presume it can be recaptured in empirical tests.

We can specify a spot market equation analogous to (14), wherein speculation still is related to differences in expected and actual rates of change in the exchange rate and where still $dx^*/dt = f_1(d^2x/dt^2)$. But the mathematics is simplified by writing the equation as a second-order linear differential equation. We are losing one kind of information in order to gain other types of knowledge. In defense of this step, I invoke the dictum that mathematics is precise only in explaining itself.

The combined nonspeculative and speculative excess demands become

$$\begin{aligned} SED_{ns} + SED_s = {} & F(x) + j_1[j_2\theta\cdot(d^2x/dt^2) - dx/dt] \\ & - P_1[\tilde{y}_0 + (dy/dt) - (\bar{x}_0 + dx/dt) + m] . \end{aligned} \tag{18}$$

Considering the forward market, the speculator can now buy exchange to hold either for current or future delivery. The purchase (sale) is forward when the spot rate is rising (falling) faster than the forward. Hence, it is with respect to expected spot rates that speculators take forward positions. As the forward speculative transaction is usually on credit (say, on margin account), the risk factor (θ_1) is more significant relative to risk spot and $\theta_1 < \theta$. The opportunity cost is assumed identical in both markets. Therefore,

$$\begin{aligned} FED_{ns} + FED_s = {} & H(x) + s_1[j_2\theta_1\cdot(d^2x/dt^2) - dy/dt] \\ & - P_2[\tilde{y}_0 + (dy/dt) - (\bar{x}_0 + dx/dt) + m] . \end{aligned} \tag{19}$$

Solving simultaneously the spot and forward equation in order to eliminate one of the unknowns, $H(x)$, gives

$$\begin{aligned} & [\![q(s_1 + P_2)\cdot\{1 + P_1k + j_1[\theta j_2k^2\cdot F'(x) - k]\} \\ & \quad + \{P_1qs_1j_2\theta_1k^2\cdot F'(x) + P_2\}]\!]\cdot F(x) = -P_3q\cdot[(s_1 + P_2) + P_1] . \end{aligned} \tag{20}$$

As $k\cdot F(x) = dx/dt$,

$$\begin{aligned} dx/dt = {} & -\left(\frac{k^2\cdot[s_1j_2P_1\theta_1\cdot F'(x)] + P_2}{\{j_1[\theta j_2k\cdot F'(x) - k] + P_1k + 1\}(s_1 + P_2)}\right)\cdot F(x) \\ & + \left(\frac{P_3(s_1 + P_2 + P_1)}{\{j_1[\theta j_2k\cdot F'(x) - k] + P_1k + 1\}}\right)\cdot(\tilde{y}_0 - \bar{x}_0 + m) , \end{aligned} \tag{21}$$

which is the same expression (20) but in terms of the rate of change in the spot rate. When excess demand is positive, exchange rate changes also will be positive if $|P_1k + 1| > |j_1[\theta j_2k \cdot F'(x) - k]|$ as $F'(x) < 0$. The last term of equation (21) is the classical interest rate parity argument.

This evaluation facilitates the description of the movement of the market exchange rate, $x(t)$, from a nonequilibrium position with respect to the previously specified equilibrium rate (an equilibrium sans the speculative function).[13] We first solve at $m = 0$ and $(\tilde{z}_0 + m) = 0$. The market rate can now be determined if the function is continuous ($k \neq 0$, $q \neq 0$). Using Taylor's expansion, rearranging terms into a differential equation, then integrating, gives the nonequilibrium market rate as

$$x(t) = \bar{x}_0 + \left\{ \frac{P_3(s_1 + P_2 + P_1)}{-k^2[s_1 j_2 P_1 \theta_1 \cdot F'(x)] \cdot F'(\bar{x}_0)} \right\} \cdot (\tilde{z}_0 + m)$$
$$+ B \cdot \exp\left[-\left(\frac{k^2[s_1 j_2 P_1 \theta_1 \cdot F'(x)]}{\{j_1[\theta j_2 k \cdot F'(x) - k] + P_1 + 1\}(s_1 + P_2)} \right) \cdot F'(\bar{x}_0) \cdot t \right], \tag{22}$$

where B is the initial difference between the equilibrium and nonequilibrium rates.

For easy reference, the parameters are explicitly identified: k = nonspeculative spot coefficient; q = nonspeculative forward coefficient; j_1 = speculative spot coefficient; s_1 = speculative forward coefficient; P_1, P_2 = opportunity cost (covered interest rate coefficients), spot, and forward markets, respectively; θ, θ_1 = risk factor, spot, and forward markets, respectively.

The traditional stability condition that $F'(\bar{x}_0)$ be negative may no longer be sufficient. In the particular and general solutions of Appendix C,

$$\left\{ \frac{P_3(s_1 + P_2 + P_1)}{-k^2[s_1 j_2 P_1 \theta_1 \cdot F'(x)] \cdot F'(\bar{x}_0)} \right\} = a_0 \quad \text{and}$$

$$\left(\frac{k^2[s_1 j_2 P_1 \theta_1 \cdot F'(x)] \cdot F'(\bar{x}_0)}{\{j_1[\theta j_2 k \cdot F'(x) - k] + P_1 k + 1\}(s_1 + P_2)} \right) = a_1$$

At interest rate parity, $(\tilde{z}_0 + m) = 0$, the market exchange rate is

$$x(t) = \bar{x}_0 + B \cdot e^{-a_1 \cdot t} \quad (t \text{ large}) . \tag{23}$$

If there is excess demand or supply (B is negative or positive, respectively) and $|P_1k + 1| > |j_1[\theta j_2 k \cdot F'(x) - k]|$, a_1 is a positive integer, the exponent has a negative sign, and the market exchange rate will converge to equilibrium ($\bar{x}_0$). At constant interest rates, these are the necessary and sufficient conditions for stabilizing speculation. If, how-

[13] For the method used for this and subsequent solutions, see Appendix C.

ever, $|P_1k + 1| < |j_1[\theta j_2k \cdot F'(x) - k]|$, the exponent has a positive sign and the exchange rate will move away from the equilibrium exchange rate whether the conditions be excess demand or supply. These possibilities are described by figure 1.

The requirement for stabilizing speculation at $m = 0$, then, is a relatively large value for the spot interest rate arbitrage coefficient (P_1) and a relatively small value for the discounted (for risk) speculative coefficient ($j_1\theta$). Given the unfavorable state of an exponent of positive sign, however, larger values of $s_1j_2P_1\theta_1$ from the forward market will move the market rate even farther from equilibrium. To summarize, the more the weight attached to opportunity cost and the greater the risk evaluation

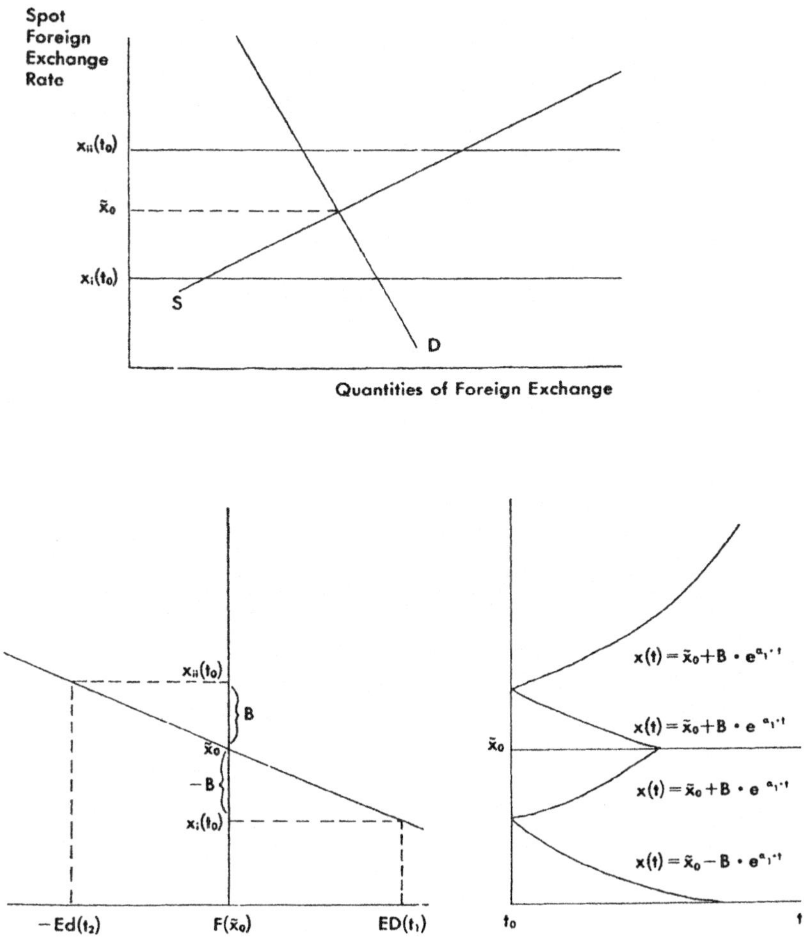

FIG. 1.—Equilibrium, excess demand, and speculation under free exchange rates

(the smaller is θ), the less the probability that speculation will be stabilizing under free rates. The interest rate differential can, of course, differ from zero. When it does, the equilibrium exchange rates become $\tilde{x}_{0m}$ and $\tilde{y}_{0m}$ (see equations [7] and [8]) and the time path of the market exchange rate may shift with these equilibrium movements, that is, with the shift parameter from equation (22) (now a_0). With a positive change in the interest rate differential (foreign interest rates rise relative to domestic),

$$dx/dm = d\tilde{x}_0/dm - a_0(d\tilde{y}_0/dm - d\tilde{x}_0/dm + 1) \,, \tag{24}$$

where the first term on the right side of this equation is the change to the interest rate equilibrium rate, $\tilde{x}_{0m}$, and the second term is the shift in the time path of the market rate from speculators, reactions to the new opportunity cost.

Returning to the original equilibrium equations, (7) and (8), we can set $[c_3(h_3 + c_3)]/[h_3(b_1 + b_2)] = \beta_0$ and $\{c_3[h_3 - (b_1 + b_2)]\}/[h_3(b_1 + b_2)] = \beta_1$. Substituting, we have

$$dx/dm = \beta_0 - a_0(\beta_1 - \beta_0 + 1) \,. \tag{25}$$

As the forward rate and spot rate changes will approximately offset the foreign exchange value of the interest differential change under free rates (that is, $[\beta_1 - \beta_0] = \beta \cong -1$), however, the interest differential parameter can be assumed to be β_0, and the market rate at nonzero values of m is

$$x(t) = \tilde{x}_0 + \beta_0 m + B \cdot e^{-a_1 \cdot t} \,, \tag{26}$$

or

$$x(t) = \tilde{x}_{0m} + B \cdot e^{-a_1 \cdot t} \,. \tag{27}$$

Suppose speculators borrow in the domestic money market a share of the funds used for speculation. This can be specified by subtracting $P_4 u$ and $P_5 u$ from the right-hand sides of equations (18) and (19), respectively. We have a different particular solution (interest rate parameters), in which m is separated into the domestic (u) and foreign (v) bill rates and the coefficient of u is no longer a_0. Let the new domestic bill coefficient[14] be a_2. Now, for any change in u under the stabilizing conditions,

$$dx/dm = \beta_0 - a_0(\beta_1 - \beta_0 + 1) - a_2 \,, \tag{28}$$

[14] The new particular solution is easily obtained by retracing the solution in Appendix C. The coefficient of u is

$$-\left\{\frac{(P_3 + P_6)(s_1 + P_2 + P_1)}{k^2[s_1 j_2 P_1 \theta' \cdot F'(x) \cdot F'(\tilde{x}_0)]}\right\} = a_2$$

and differs from a_0 only by a multiple of P_6, where $P_6 = (P_4 + P_5)$.

and

$$x(t) = \tilde{x}_{0m} - \alpha_2 u + B' \cdot e^{-\alpha_1 \cdot t} . \quad (29)$$

This suggests that any exogenously inspired upward movement in the market exchange rate will be lessened by the domestic bill rate and also implies, of course, that domestic interest rate increases are more effective in slowing outward speculation when the share of domestically borrowed funds for that purpose is high. (Note that B' is no longer only exogenously determined, as interest rate changes now can cause $\tilde{x}_{0m}$ and $x(t)$ to diverge.) Only domestic interest rate declines, encouraging borrowing for speculative purposes, could cause an endogenous depreciation of the domestic currency away from equilibrium. As long as α_2 is small, such excess foreign exchange supply shifts would be insignificant. To some magnitude, interest rate arbitrage (covered) would be substituted for pure speculation when foreign interest rates rise. These market rate solutions suggest that interest rate changes under free rates are not likely to cause sharp exchange rate movements; rather capital flows tend to be self-limiting.[15] As we shall see, these functions will not always remain in this form under a narrow gold band.

This model (or other models based on somewhat different assumptions) does not in itself answer all the questions posed in the choice of a new exchange system. The functions are discontinuous if q and k equal zero. Suppose a nation decides to move from a fixed exchange rate system to a completely freely fluctuating one. If importers just believe that speculation will be destabilizing, they may consider foreign trade so much more risky than domestic trade that they will purchase no foreign exchange and indeed will leave the foreign trade business. With k and q equaling zero or near zero, the speculators will dominate the market until it collapses. In short, even though speculation may be stabilizing under freely fluctuating rates, it may not be possible to adopt such a system without a transitional one or to maintain the system once adopted.

If history is a reasonable guide, the policy makers (in the U. S. Treasury and Bank of England, for instances) will be even greater risk averters than importers will be. If the policy makers believe that importers and exporters believe that speculation will be destabilizing, they will not adopt freely fluctuating rates.

In the policy area, especially, the economist-as-advocate faces some perplexing problems. Professor Yeager has argued that economists who advocate a compromise short of free rates "create a spurious impression

[15] This is simply one way of specifying relative insensitiveness of total capital flows to foreign interest rate changes under flexible rates. This magnitude of capital flow should not be confused with the speed with which the exchange rate adjusts to capital movements motivated by interest arbitrage. Indeed, where interest-rate parity dominates (under more and more flexible rates), the faster will exchange rates move (toward equilibrium) from capital flows.

of disagreement among themselves and undermine the authority of their technical knowledge." A compromise system, "far from gradually educating people in favor of free rates, is likely to make free rates even more politically impossible than they are now" (Yeager 1967, p. 297). If the importers, the public, and the policy makers could be educated about freely fluctuating rates and were agreed that speculation would be stabilizing, Yeager is correct. But can these doubts be erased with pure theory? If not, where will the empirical evidence come from if not from actual experience with the system? The parameters of equation (29) remain to be estimated, and perhaps only empirical studies under the new system in today's economies could eradicate these doubts. As yet, experimentation in the social sciences has not included trial runs with new systems.

Like it or not, the economist advocate also is faced with some messy political issues. As long as governments hold monetary reserves there will be a temptation to use them to fix exchange rates. Even if rates are allowed to float, the government may follow economic policies aimed at making the exchange rate seek a certain level. In short, governments must agree to follow purely domestic economic policies aimed at national goals independent of the foreign exchange markets and the balances of payments. Governments may not be sufficiently sophisticated to implement such lofty goals. Even if adopted successfully, severe exogenous disturbances such as strikes, abrupt fiscal changes, riots, famines, wars, and revolutions may compel a political resolution to curb widely moving rates by fixing them.

IV. Adjustment Consequences of Fixed Exchange Rates and the Narrow Gold Band

From the standpoint of the trade account, the present key currency system approximates an absolutely fixed, exchange rate system. While exchange rates are permitted to fluctuate within a narrow gold band (about 2 percent), such movements are sufficient only to cause capital flows but not trade-account adjustments. Balances in payments are achieved by substantial private capital flows and/or changes in official monetary reserves. The "normal" comparative-static condition in the foreign exchange market is one of disequilibrium.

The consequences of such a mechanism is illustrated with a foreign exchange model in which exports and imports are determined exogenously—that is, in which exchange rate variations affect the timing of foreign exchange sales and purchases (leading and lagging) but not the absolute foreign exchange volume of exports and imports. There are no linear schedules of demand and supply of traded commodities with respect to the exchange rate (as in the static equilibrium of Section II), simply because the exchange rate does not change sufficiently. The recognition of the roles of uncovered interest rate arbitrage, pure speculation, and leading-lagging by exporters-importers has led to the formulation of a more currently realistic theory of foreign exchange.[16] Reference to these models is useful in describing the more fixed exchange rate systems. But we shall ignore the lags involving interest arbitrage and hedging that complicate some such models (see Canterbery 1967).

Simultaneous balance of payments and foreign exchange market equilibriums are achieved when $M - X = 0$. This is not likely to prevail, as the determinants of M and X, such as national incomes, are outside the model while—most important—exchange rate variations do not influence the level of trade. When $M > X$, differential interest rates $(u > v)$ may achieve an equilibrium exchange rate consonant with the parity exchange rate. It is, however, improbable that a nation will be willing to peg interest rates to their exchange par for long time periods. Even so, a reserve currency nation such as the United States is able to achieve a balance-of-payments equilibrium at some value of x^* sufficiently high to generate capital outflows but not so high as to cause conversions of private home currency liabilities into central bank liabilities. This is symbolized in the modern theory as

$$(M - X) + f_2(z + m) + f_3(x^*) = 0 \,. \tag{30}$$

Where the foreign exchange value of commodity and service imports exceed exports, private short-term capital outflows will both balance payments and equilibrate the foreign exchange market as long as private foreign banks are willing to accumulate liabilities in the reserve nation's home currency.

A persistently positive dx^*/dt, however, is not consistent with a stable exchange rate equilibrium. Foreign official monetary institutions will have to take an increasing excess supply of the "depreciating" currency off the private market, and this can lead to reserve losses by the reserve currency nation. An analogous result follows for nonreserve currency nations, except the disequilibrium occurs sooner because foreign private banks are less willing to accumulate the liabilities of nonreserve countries. In short, what would otherwise be stabilizing or destabilizing movements in the exchange rate are transferred to foreign exchange reserves. The capital flow expression is altered by a central bank function. In absolute terms, supply and demand at the upper limit $(\bar{x}_u)$ can

[16] See the rudiments of such a theory in Canterbery 1965. The modern theory is further refined in the first third (theoretical section) of Stein 1965 and in Canterbery 1967 (see also Kenen 1965). A good attempt at econometric testing of the parity solution from the modern theory appears in Stoll 1968. A survey of the state of the theory vis-à-vis econometric testing attempts appears in Canterbery 1969.

be equalized by an official reserve (R) loss, so that

$$(M - X) + [f_2(y - \bar{x}_u + m) + f_3(x^*)] - \Delta R = 0 \,. \qquad (31)$$

It is not easy, of course, to discuss equilibriums in disequilibrium systems. Where exports (X) and imports valued in home currency units ($\bar{M}$) are exogenous and there are no other transactions, the "equilibrium" exchange rate can be empirically identified as ($\bar{M}/X$). This equilibrium is, of course, made more complicated by including interest rate and speculative variables (Canterbery 1967, p. 410, eq. 27). These data are available. But as Peter Kenen has suggested to me, the export-import observations have been determined at exchange rates in disequilibriums. Thus, we can have only an "approximate" equilibrium solution. This inability to match theoretical solutions precisely with empirical ones is a dilemma that is more likely to be resolved by changing the international financial system than by switching economists. Nonetheless, we can show in the modern theory (see Canterbery 1967, p. 410, eq. 32) that interest rate parity is not a guaranteed feature of nearly fixed or fixed exchange rates, rather,

$$z = -m + f_4(x^*) \,. \qquad (32)$$

Only if the net speculative function is zero will classical interest parity prevail. The odds are against it.

When the exchange rate (x) is rising and is no more than $\hat{m}$ (m in percent per contract period) above the lower limit ($\bar{x}_l$), most interest arbitrage becomes uncovered and is speculative.[17] If x is at the upper limit and devaluation is expected, interest arbitrage is uncovered, and hence, also speculative. At all times, the risks in speculation are minimal. Therefore, under a narrow gold band as well as under absolutely fixed exchange rates, speculative capital outflows can generate a long-term disequilibrium, inasmuch as M and X are insensitive to exchange rate changes. In short, the setting of interest rate parity to zero at the equilibrium spot and forward exchange rates is not valid for the nearly fixed exchange rate system. There is too little exchange uncertainty for that under a narrow gold band.

We shall bow to theoretical nicety in the analysis of the narrow gold band system. We can assume that commodity traders would react to exchange rate changes in the usual sloped demand and supply curves if in fact the exchange rate could change over a wide range. As this foreign exchange demand is a derived demand, perhaps the slope parameters could be estimated from commodity price elasticities. The equilibrium shifts from interest differential changes are only in part described by those postulated in Section II (although one could use the shift parame-

[17] There is little motivation for covering spot treasury bill purchases if the maximum exchange rate decline will leave the purchaser no worse off.

ters postulated in earlier models as full equilibrium shifts, such as in Canterbery 1967, p. 410, eq. 27).

In terms of the theory in this paper, a narrow gold band yields an objective value for θ in the key currency nations most of the time and often in other nations. The discounted risk will approach 1 when x is $\hat{m}$ percent or less above the lower limit in a key currency nation where devaluation is an unacceptable policy option or otherwise unexpected. The value of θ is constrained by the width of the narrow gold band. (There might even be negative risk with $\theta > 1$ after the upper limit has been sustained for long periods.) Also, at such times the relevant opportunity cost often becomes m rather than $(\bar{y}_0 + dy/dt) - (\bar{x}_0 + dx/dt) + m$. Whether foreign exchange is purchased in the spot or forward market—it is postulated—is dependent upon the differential rates of change $(dx/dt - dy/dt)$ in the two markets. We shall add a borrowing function (f_5u) to the excess demand equations, so

$$SED = F(x) + j_3[j_4(d^2x/dt^2) - dx/dt] + P_7[(v + dx/dt) - (u + dy/dt)] - P_{10}u\,, \tag{33}$$

$$FED = H(x) + s_3[j_4(d^2x/dt^2) - dy/dt] + P_8[(v + dy/dt) - (u + dx/dt)] - P_{11}u\,. \tag{34}$$

If the technique of Section III is used in solving for dx/dt and $x(t)$, the time path solution is

$$\begin{aligned} x(t) = \bar{x}_0 &+ \left(\frac{P_8[P_7 + (1 + P_8 - s_3)]}{\{k^2[s_3j_4P_7\cdot F'(x)] - P_7P_8k\}\cdot F'(\bar{x}_0)}\right)\cdot v \\ &- \left(\frac{P_{11}[1 + (1 + P_8 - s_3)]}{\{k^2[s_3j_4P_7\cdot F'(x)] - P_7P_8k\}\cdot F'(\bar{x}_0)}\right)\cdot u \\ &+ B''\cdot\exp\left[-\left(\frac{k^2[s_3j_4P_7q\cdot F'(x)] - P_7qP_8k}{\{j_3[j_4k\cdot F'(x) - k] + P_7k + 1\}(1 + P_8q - s_3q)}\right)\cdot F'(\bar{x}_0)\cdot t\right]. \end{aligned} \tag{35}$$

Again, the sign of B'' depends upon whether the excess is demand or supply. As suggested above, the opportunities for excesses at fixed rates or narrow bands will be frequent.

With the exponent coefficient a_3, the coefficient of the foreign interest rate (v) a_4 and the coefficient of the home rate a_5,

$$dx/dm = d\bar{x}_0/dm + a_4 - a_5\,, \tag{36}$$

and

$$x(t) = \bar{x}_0 + \beta_0 m + a_4 v - a_5 u + B''\cdot e^{-a_3\cdot t}\,, \tag{37}$$

or

$$x(t) = \bar{x}_{0m} + a_4 v - a_5 u + B''\cdot e^{-a_3\cdot t}\,. \tag{38}$$

Even if $|P_7k + 1| > |j_3[j_4k\cdot F'(x) - k]|$, the natural exponent will not be a positive integer if $|s_3q| > |1 + P_8q|$. Thus, the exponential stability conditions for the exchange rate are more strict than in the freely fluctuating exchange rate case. Moreover, the first condition is more difficult to achieve because the sizes of the spot speculative parameters are no longer reduced by the risk fraction (θ). Also, the use of the sign of the natural exponent as the test of the stability of the exchange rate is only applicable now at constant interest rates.

Speculation itself now appears to be responsive to interest rate changes. At constant home interest rates, an increase in v will cause a sharp upward movement in the exchange rate away from equilibrium equaling ($a_4 \cdot \Delta v + B''$). Interest rate changes now have effects on the exchange rate as abrupt (in theory) as strikes, riots, and wars. Because of the expectations regarding the exchange rate, the interest rate differential (uncovered) is viewed herein as a part of the windfall gain from speculation. The interest rate becomes an integral part of the speculative function, but the speculators are responding to actual and/or expected exchange rate changes (or lack of changes). Treasury bills are substituted for cash foreign exchange; and since the spot purchase for the bills is not covered by a forward sales, a speculative position has been taken.[18]

Now the increase in the equilibrium foreign exchange rate from covered interest arbitrage (when the foreign treasury bill rate is raised) is augmented by the speculator's response to the prospects for an extra windfall gain.[19] Hence the market exchange rate movements from interest rate changes under a narrow gold band will be (on the average) much wider than under more flexible rates. And the new equilibrium rate is likely to be unstable. The market rate movements (equation [35]) are no longer moderated by opportunity cost (P) and risk (θ) considerations. Unlike the function described by Tsiang (1958), under the narrow gold band risk does not necessarily rise as foreign exchange assets holdings are increased.

One-way-option speculation is characteristic at the limits. When x becomes a constant, dx^* will depend upon an exogenous estimate of the probability of devaluation. Even if this probability be evaluated as low,

[18] Interest arbitrage in the "nonspeculative" solution (7) is after an indeterminant (but very short) time lag. Ordinarily conservative covered interest arbitragers also may join the speculators.

[19] This aids in explaining recent econometric studies (Stoll 1968) suggesting that short-term capital is statistically more responsive to interest rate differentials under flexible than under fixed exchange rates. Such studies are simply able to accurately identify statistically the quantities of capital responding to interest rate changes. Under the narrow gold band it is virtually impossible to separate speculative from interest rate forces, and at times the speculative coefficient will completely overshadow interest rate considerations. With flexible rates, smaller amounts of capital move more rapidly in response to pure interest rate changes while relatively small amounts are being transferred for purely speculative reasons. Mundell (1960) has argued that instability will result from interest "sensitiveness" under fixed rates. In the narrow gold band case where the interest differential at times becomes a proxy for part of the speculative function, instability is inherent in the system.

speculation continues to be encouraged by low risk (large θ). Presumably, this would be reflected in official reserves changes and $F(R)$ and dR/dt would be substituted for $F(x)$ and dx/dt in our equations. The equations could then be solved for reserve stability conditions.[20] The time path might be substantially different from our exchange rate solution.

Interest rate changes as an inherent source of instability can be demonstrated graphically (fig. 2). Starting with the equilibrium exchange rate $\bar{x}_{0m}$, assuming that initially $(\alpha_4 v - \alpha_5 u) = 0$, you find that the initial market exchange rate also is $\bar{x}_{0m}$. Now, introduce a unitary increase in the foreign bill rate. The equilibrium exchange rate will shift up by β_0 to $\bar{x}'_{0m}$, and the market rate will move up by $\alpha_4 + B''$ more to

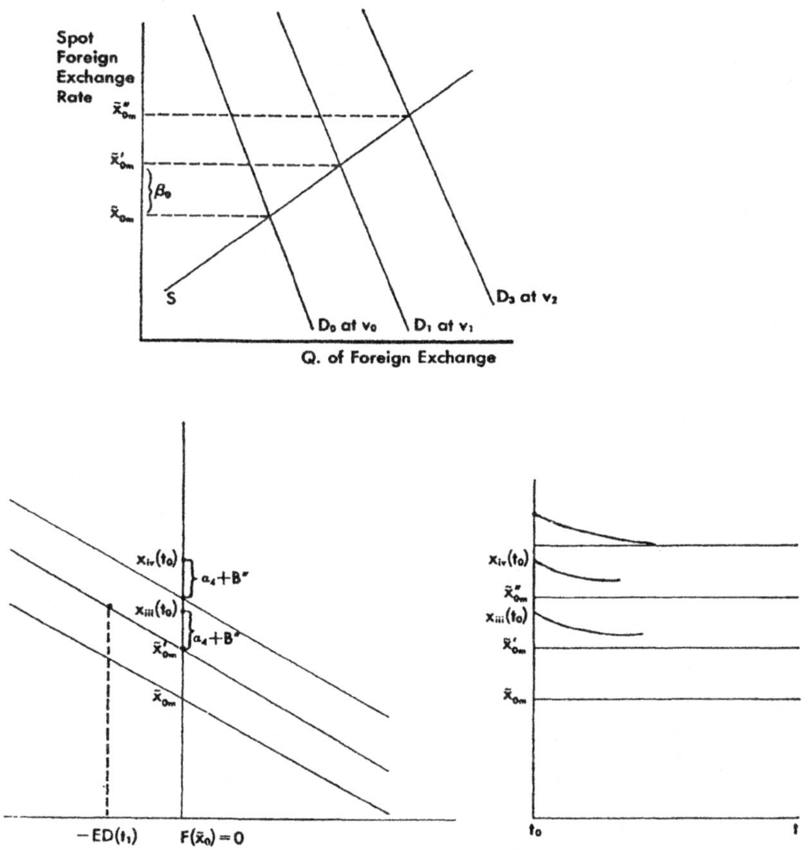

FIG. 2.—Equilibrium, excess demand, and speculation under narrow gold band

[20] There is a level of foreign currency reserves (the level when the market rate first becomes equal to the upper or lower limit) at which excess demand equals zero, that is, $F(R_0) = F(x^*) = F(\bar{x}) = 0$ at R_0.

$x_{iii}(t_0)$. If the sign of the exponent is negative, the market rate will tend to converge to $\bar{x}'_{0m}$. But assume a second round of foreign interest rate advances prior to convergence, a third round, etc., the market rate moves to $x_{iv}(t_0)$, etc. Continuous foreign interest rate changes can lead to erratic exchange rate behavior even when "convergence" occurs.

Two possible alternative time paths for the exchange rate under a narrow gold band is described by figure 3 (speculation stabilizing, as usually defined) and figure 4 (speculation destabilizing, as normally defined). Both unitary and nonunitary interest rate changes are illustrated. Contrasting exchange rate behavior under free rates with unitary interest differential changes appears in figure 5. (For simplicity, the exchange rate path in fig. 3 is assumed to be within the band while the path in fig. 4 is assumed unaltered by the substitution of dR/dt for dx/dt as x becomes hypothetical at the limits.) These figures suggest that exchange rate behavior can be erratic even when the rate tends to converge on "equilibrium."

V. Implications for Proposed Reforms

Among plans being considered for increasing exchange rate flexibility is the widening of the gold band to ± 3 percent or more either side of par (see Halm 1965). Under a wide gold band the interest differential will be less often a source of windfall speculative gains. As speculators usually

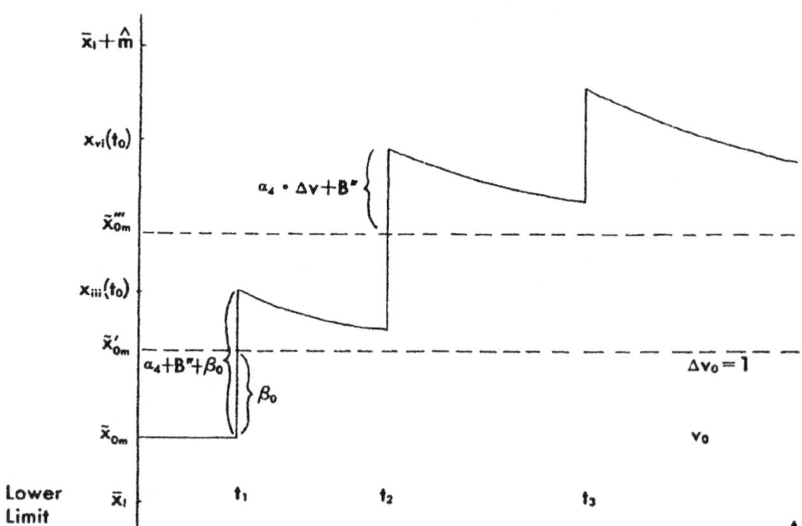

FIG. 3.—Exchange rate, narrow gold band, and "convergence"

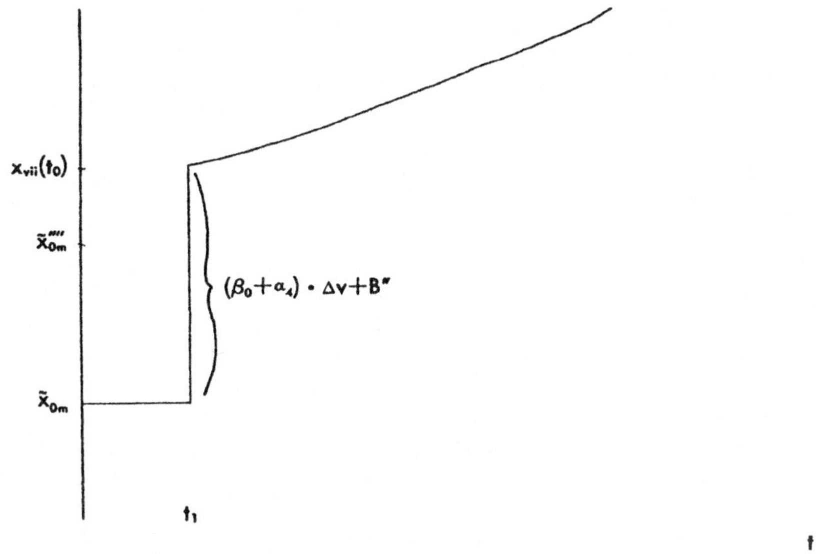

FIG. 4.—Exchange rate path, narrow gold band, nonconvergence

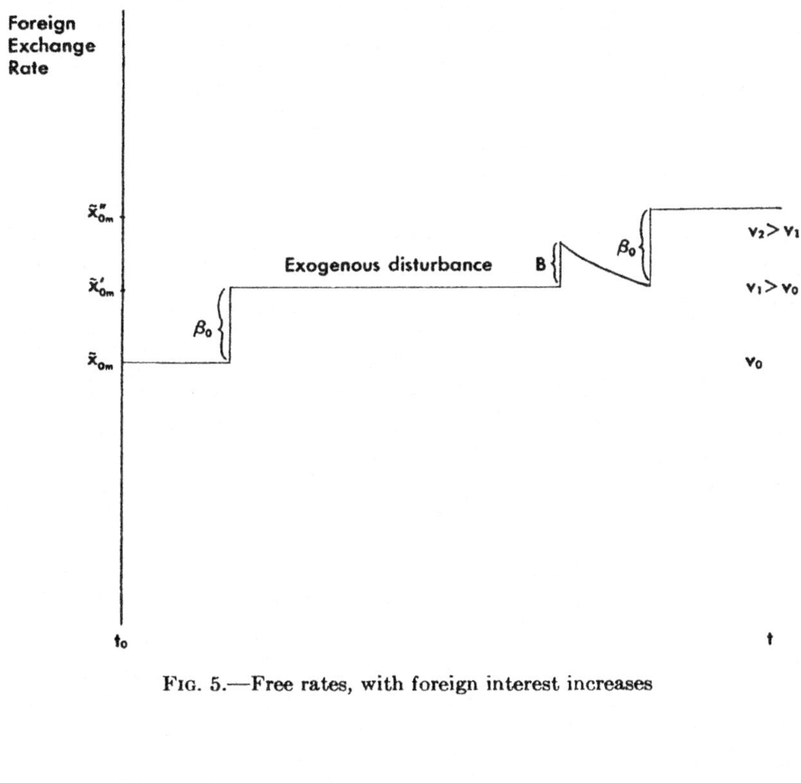

FIG. 5.—Free rates, with foreign interest increases

will have to consider the cost of cover, speculators will not tend to move the exchange rate to a level that would be much different from the new nonspeculative equilibrium. Also, under an ever-widening band θ will become increasingly smaller as exchange assets become larger (as in Tsiang). The reaction to interest rate changes mostly will be by conservative covered interest arbitragers who will quickly move the exchange rate to a new, stable equilibrium.

The $\hat{m}$ percent rule (wherein normal opportunity cost is irrelevant) would still apply to interest arbitrage, but the period of time in which this range would be relevant should be shorter. Also, outside the $\hat{m}$ percent range (a now wider space) the only riskless transaction would be a completely covered one. One-way option speculations are then possible, but such "crises" would be less frequent. Speculation is likely to be less in volume and more stabilizing than under the narrow band.

Using this theory, widening the gold band and allowing rates to move freely within it seemingly would have several advantages: (1) Doing so would create more uncertainty (lower the value of θ) for potential currency speculators and thus tend to lessen speculation based on too narrow a band. (2) Purchasers of foreign securities who do not always "cover" exchange risks under the narrow band would now be virtually compelled to enter forward exchange markets and "cover" their exchange position. This constraint would tend to broaden the forward exchange market in several maturities, providing a wider market for exporter-importer covering against the risk of exchange rate fluctuations and causing both speculators to be less sensitive to interest rate movements and interest arbitragers to be self-equilibrating as they increase their own covering costs. (3) The wider gold band would provide observations of some of the likely consequences of moving to even greater exchange rate flexibility. For example, the degree to which speculation is stabilizing or destabilizing to the market could be studied.[21] (4) With smaller flows from anticipated devaluation, short-term capital flows would probably be more stable. (5) Moderated short-term capital flows would eliminate one excuse for a monetary policy geared to "international considerations." (6) World liquidity needs would be lessened because some balance-of-trade adjustments within a wider band would reduce the magnitude and frequency of intervention and hence the level of required international monetary reserves.

Beyond the Wide Gold Band

A second step—made desirable by the $\hat{m}$-percent *caveat*—would be to move to even more exchange rate flexibility under the International

[21] Professor Yeager (1967) has raised some forceful objections to this. He has argued that speculators may not behave much differently than they would under a narrow band. Near the limits his arguments are valid for the wide gold band per se.

Monetary Fund. A "crawling peg" (C-P) has been recommended by several economists. The present model cannot describe well the implications of the C-P (for an alternative analysis and bibliography see Canterbery and Boorman, 1970). The main disadvantage of the narrow-band C-P is that domestic interest rates in the devaluing nation would have to be raised to prevent substantial short-term capital outflows. The present author has suggested a wide gold band plus a "delayed peg" (Canterbery 1968, pp. 212–16). Because the exchange prices would still have upper and lower limits, there would be an "early warning system" for identifying a par value level that differed greatly from the natural market exchange rate. If the U.S. exchange rate, for example, had to be supported near the lower end of its wider range (losing gold and foreign exchange reserves) for $t + h$ period, that necessity would be a signal for reducing—not devaluing—the par value of the dollar.

Market intervention by governmental authorities would, of course, characteristically occur where an exchange rate limit is reached. Several possible semiautomatic market rules could be used to determine a basic disequilibrium. A monetary reserve-base coefficient could be calculated by the IMF. With some base reserve value (R_b), the weekly value of reserves lost as a share of this base could be determined ($\Delta R_b/R_b$) and a record maintained. Hence both the speed and the volume of reserve attrition would be considered. (A 10 percent weekly reserve loss for three weeks would be viewed with as much concern as a 5 percent coefficient during a six-week span.) The critical range of coefficients for each nation as well as the reserve-base period selected would differ, would be altered from time to time on an unannounced basis, and would be secret until the IMF advised the national government that a basic disequilibrium existed according to the semiautomatic market rule, calling for a new band.

The gold band would be lowered (raised) with the old lower (upper) limit as the new par value. The announcement of the new gold band would come several weeks after its adoption in order to deter one-way-option speculators. (This feature of the delayed peg is being currently [May 1970] urged by West German monetary authorities.) The exchange rate is pegged while some trade adjustments continue. This par (or new midband) rate would be precisely supported to give those traders of goods and services not covered against exchange risks an opportunity for covering in the forward exchange market. Moreover, the maintenance of the new midband level for an indefinite period plus an initially controlled rate of depreciation (*if* the rate does indeed fall) would further deter heavy speculation in the appreciating currency. Because of this support preliminary to the actual rate change, the trade balance would continue to adjust in a way favorable to a higher rate. Speculators could be neither sure of the time required to hold currency purchases for profits nor certain that trade adjustments would fail to cause the rate to appreciate. The delayed peg could be analyzed by solving our theoretical system at the limits as suggested earlier, that is, substituting $F(R)$ and dR/dt for $F(x)$ and dx/dt. Near the limits, interest rate parity should cause speculation to be less attractive than under the wide gold band alone. In order to prevent the lower limit from becoming a "fixed for all times" rate, the IMF should be empowered to alter (when necessary) currency par values under the semiautomatic market rule.

VI. Conclusions

The theory of speculation expressed here focuses upon the impact of risk evaluation, opportunity costs, and interest rate variations under alternative exchange rate systems. The wider the range of permissible fluctuation in exchange rates, the higher the risk and in a seeming paradox, the less probable are wide speculative swings. The relevant opportunity cost under a narrow gold band and fixed exchange rates is the uncovered interest rate spread, causing the interest rate differential to become a proxy variable for a part of speculation. With greater permissible exchange rate variability, however, opportunity cost becomes the interest spread adjusted for exchange risks (covered interest differential) which tends to converge to zero, leaving speculators less sensitive to interest rate spreads and pure interest rate arbitragers more sensitive to hedging costs. If destabilizing speculation is defined as speculation that causes the exchange rate to diverge substantially from its nonspeculative path, speculators most probably will tend to be stabilizers under absolutely free rates, relative stabilizers under a wide gold band, and destabilizers under a narrow gold band.

The objections voiced by opponents to more flexible exchange rates are clearly modified under the proposed delayed peg. But would great uncertainty about rates still disrupt trade and capital flows? Quite the opposite would be true. The forward markets in which cover against exchange risks is possible would be even more viable than they are today. The necessity of trade covering would generate heavier markets in very long maturities, so that every reasonable exchange risk could be offset. The values of k and q would be different from zero.

The largest political obstacle to more flexibility in exchange rates has been the seemingly great risk taken in the transition from fixed rates. (As noted, economic and other forces creating a discontinuous function make this fear very tangible.) However, it is possible to move toward such a system in stages. Once the wider gold band *cum* delayed peg (or similar plan) proves workable, the worst that could happen would be for the free world to be forced back onto a fixed exchange rate system if nations feared instability in exchange rates. But such a development would only follow nations' efforts to fix their exchange rates at inappropriate levels. It is precisely the pegging of key currency par values at sometimes inappropriate levels that causes the current exchange rate system to be one of mankind's burdens. Hence, the main objection to a more flexible exchange rate system is the danger that it might become fixed. And where does that leave the defenders of absolutely rigid exchange rates? Although the theoretical attractiveness of free rates is tempered by both practical political problems (implementation) and uncontrollable exogenous forces (wars, riots, revolutions, famines, etc.), relevant economic theory is encouraging for free rate advocates, and the main problem in a freely fluctuating, exchange rate system may be a transitional one. Hopefully, this paper outlines a path relatively free in itself of risk.

Appendix A

The intermediate steps in the solution to the "pure," freely fluctuating, foreign model appear below:

If supplies and demands are set equal in each market from equations (1) through (4),

$$(b_1 + c_1 + b_2 + c_2)x - (c_1 + c_2)y = [(a_1 - a_2) + (c_1 + c_2)m] \,, \tag{4a}$$

$$-(h_1 + c_1 + h_2 + c_2)x + (h_1 + c_1 + h_2 + c_2)y = -(c_1 + c_2)m \,. \tag{4b}$$

The terms of equations (4a) and (4b) are simplified in equations (5) and (6) of the text. The determinants of those equations are:

$$x = \frac{\begin{vmatrix} a_3 & -c_3 \\ -e_2 & h_3 \end{vmatrix}}{\begin{vmatrix} b_3 & -c_3 \\ -h_3 & h_3 \end{vmatrix}} \;; \quad y = \frac{\begin{vmatrix} b_3 & a_3 \\ -h_3 & -e_2 \end{vmatrix}}{\begin{vmatrix} b_3 & -c_3 \\ -h_3 & h_3 \end{vmatrix}} \,. \tag{6a}$$

There is a unique solution, as the order of the coefficient matrix is equal to the number of unknowns. This is the case whether we solve the four structural equations, (1) through (4), or equations (5) and (6). It can be assumed that the determinants of the coefficient matrixes are nonzero, and hence the equations consistent.

Appendix B

Begin with equation (16) in the text,

$$\begin{aligned} SED_{ns,s} = {} & F(x) + I\cdot[G\theta\cdot(d^2x/dt^2)^2 - dx/dt]^3 \\ & - P_0\cdot(c - 1)dx/dt - P_0\cdot(\tilde{y}_{0m} - \tilde{x}_{0m} + m) \,. \end{aligned} \tag{16a}$$

As $d^2x/dt^2 = k \cdot F'(x) \cdot (dx/dt)$, and $(\tilde{y}_{0m} - \tilde{x}_{0m} + m) = 0$,

$$SED_{ns,s} = F(x) + I(G\theta)^3 \cdot [k \cdot F'(x) \cdot (dx/dt)]^6 - I(dx/dt)^3 - P_0 \cdot (c-1)dx/dt \,. \tag{16b}$$

Multiply through by k^2, and

$$-k^2F(x) = k^2I(G\theta)^3[k \cdot F'(x) \cdot dx/dt]^6 - k^2I(dx/dt)^3 - k^2P_0 \cdot (c-1)dx/dt \,. \tag{16c}$$

As $k \cdot F(x) = dx/dt$ and we can divide through by dx/dt, $-k^2I(G\theta)^3[k \cdot F'(x)]^6 \cdot (dx/dt)^5 = -k^2I(dx/dt)^2 - k^2P_0 \cdot (c-1) + k$, or

$$(dx/dt)^5 = [\![1/\{k^3(G\theta)^3 \cdot [F'(x)]^6\}]\!] \cdot [F(x)]^2 + P_0(c-1)/\{kI(G\theta)^3[F'(x)]^6\} - 1/\{k^2I(G\theta)^3[F'(x)]^6\} \,. \tag{16d}$$

Solve for dx/dt;

$$dx/dt = \sqrt[5]{1/\{k^3(G\theta)^3 \cdot [F'(x)]^6\}} \cdot [F(x)]^{2/5} + \sqrt[5]{[P_0(c-1)]/\{kI(G\theta)^3[F'(x)]^6\}} - \sqrt[5]{1/\{k^2I(G\theta)^3[F'(x)]^6\}} \,. \tag{16e}$$

Combine terms:

$$dx/dt = \{[k(G\theta)]^{-3/5} \cdot [F'(x)]^{-6/5}\} \cdot [F(x)]^{2/5} + \{(G\theta)^{-3/5} \cdot [F'(x)]^{-6/5} + I^{-1/5}\} \cdot k^{-2/5}[\sqrt[5]{kP_0(c-1)} - 1] \,. \tag{16f}$$

Because the final term includes a complicated multiplicative expression that is extremely small, $\{(G\theta)^{-3/5} \cdot [F'(x)]^{-6/5} + I^{-1/5}\}$, simplify by letting that term equal $\bar{G}$; so

$$dx/dt = \{[k(G\theta)]^{-3/5} \cdot [F'(x)]^{-6/5}\} \cdot [F(x)]^{2/5} + \bar{G}k^{-2/5}[\sqrt[5]{kP_0(c-1)} - 1] \,. \tag{16g}$$

Let $\{[k(G\theta)]^{-3/5} \cdot [F'(x)]^{-6/5}\} = \bar{C}$ and $\bar{G}k^{-2/5}[\sqrt[5]{kP_0 \cdot (c-1)} - 1] = \bar{D}$, and you have

$$dx/dt = \bar{C} \cdot [F(x)]^{2/5} + \bar{D} \,. \tag{16h}$$

As $F(x)$ is linear, it can be written $bx + c_0$, so that

$$dx/dt = b^{2/5}\bar{C}x^{2/5} + \bar{D} + \bar{C}c_0^{2/5} \,. \tag{16i}$$

As $\bar{C}$ and c_0 are very small (see above), $\bar{C}c_0^{2/5} \cong 0$. Let $b^{2/5} \cdot C = \bar{C}$, and simplify, so

$$dx/dt = C \cdot x^{2/5} + \bar{D} \,. \tag{16j}$$

If the variable x, can be expanded by its Taylor's series,

$$x(t) = x(t_0) + (t-t_0)dx/dt|_{t_0} + (t-t_0)^2/2!\, d^2x/dt^2|_{t_0} + [(t-t_0)^3/3!]d^3x/dt^3|_{t_0} + \ldots \tag{16k}$$

At equilibrium $F(\bar{x}_{0m}) = 0$ and $t_0 = 0$, giving a Maclaurin's series. For simplicity, assume that $x(t_0) = \bar{x}_{0m} = 1$; then

$$x(t) = 1 + t(dx/dt)\,|_{t_0} + t^2/2!\,(d^2x/dt^2)\,|_{t_0} + t^3/3!\,(d^3x/dt^3)\,|_{t_0} + \dots. \quad (16l)$$

As $dx/dt\,|_{t_0} = C \cdot x^{2/5} + \bar{D}$, and if all other derivatives of x can be derived from the first, the solution for $x(t)$ can be determined by substitution,

$$\begin{aligned} x(t) = 1 &+ (C + \bar{D})\cdot t + (C/5)(C + \bar{D})\cdot t^2 \\ &+ [(C + \bar{D})(C + 3\bar{D}) - (C^3/75)]\cdot t^3 + R_3 , \end{aligned} \quad (17)$$

where the remainder (R_3) is

$$R_3 = t^4/4!\cdot(d^4x/dt^4)(\xi)\,, \quad \text{where } \xi \text{ is between 0 and } t. \quad (17a)$$

Simulations of equation (17) at "possible" estimated parameters, for x between 0.5 and 1.5 yield "infinitesimally small" values for R_3. Equation (17) should approximate a solution at small values of t.

Appendix C

Begin with equation (21) in the text,

$$\begin{aligned} dx/dt = &-\left(\frac{k^2\cdot[s_1 j_2 P_1 \theta_1 \cdot F'(x)] + P_2}{\{j_1[\theta j_2 k\cdot F'(x) - k] + P_1 k + 1\}(s_1 + P_2)}\right)\cdot F(x) \\ &+ \left(\frac{P_3(s_1 + P_2 + P_1)}{\{j_1[\theta j_2 k\cdot F'(x) - k] + P_1 k + 1\}}\right)\cdot(\bar{y}_0 - \bar{x}_0 + m)\,. \end{aligned} \quad (21)$$

By Taylor's expansion near equilibrium (x_0),

$$F(x) = F(\bar{x}_0) + (x - \bar{x}_0)F'(\bar{x}_0) + 1/2!\,(x - \bar{x}_0)^2 F''(\bar{x}_0) + \dots. \quad (21a)$$

At equilibrium under free rates, $(\bar{y}_0 - \bar{x}_0 + m) = 0$, and $F(\bar{x}_0) = 0 =$ excess demand. Thus, all terms but the first-order term in the expansion are zero, and the right-hand side of expression (21a) can be substituted for $F(x)$ in equation (21). Let the coefficient of $F(x)$ be α, and

$$dx/dt = (x - \bar{x}_0)\cdot\alpha\cdot F'(\bar{x}_0)\,. \quad (21b)$$

Note that as long as $F(x)$ is linear, an identical result is possible without a Taylor's expansion and thus the "neighborhood" restrictions implied by Taylor's series do not apply. Since $d(x - \bar{x}_0)/dt = (dx/dt - d\bar{x}_0/dt) = (dx/dt) - 0$, we obtain

$$d(x - \bar{x}_0)/dt = (x - \bar{x}_0)\cdot\alpha\cdot F'(\bar{x}_0)\,. \quad (21c)$$

Rearranging the terms in (21c) by dividing by $(x - \bar{x}_0)$ and multiplying by dt gives the differential equation

$$d(x - \bar{x}_0)/(x - \bar{x}_0) = \alpha\cdot F'(\bar{x}_0)dt\,. \quad (21d)$$

Integrating (21d) gives

$$\log\,(x - \bar{x}_0) = \alpha\cdot F'(\bar{x}_0)t + \text{CONSTANT}\,. \quad (21e)$$

This is the general integral of the differential equation. Converting the log to an exponential form and letting $\alpha \cdot F'(x_0) = -\alpha_1$ gives

$$x(t) = \bar{x}_0 + B \cdot e^{-\alpha_1 \cdot t} \qquad (t \text{ large}), \qquad (23)$$

where B is a constant of integration.

For noninterest rate parity values of m, that is, when $(\bar{y}_0 - \bar{x}_0 + m) \neq 0$, the particular solution of equation (21) will give the coefficient relating any change in $(\bar{z}_0 + m)$ to x. Letting the coefficient of $(\bar{y}_0 - \bar{x}_0 + m) = \alpha_6$, rearrange terms of (21), using (21b), to obtain the differential equation

$$dx/dt + x\alpha_1 = \alpha_6(\bar{y}_0 - \bar{x}_0 + m) + \bar{x}_0\alpha_1 \, . \qquad (21f)$$

Solve for $x = x_p$:

$$x_p = \bar{x}_0 + (\alpha_6/\alpha_1)(\bar{z}_0 + m) - (dx/dt)(1/\alpha_1) \, , \qquad (21g)$$

where $\alpha_6/\alpha_1 = [P_3(s_1 + P_2 + P_1)]/\{-k^2[s_1 j_2 P_1 \theta_1 \cdot F'(x)] \cdot F'(\bar{x}_0)\}$, which equals α_0 in the text.

Adding the interest parity shift parameter from the particular solution to the general integral (21e) gives the general solution to (21) as

$$x(t) = \bar{x}_0 + \alpha_0(\bar{z}_0 + m) + B' \cdot e^{-\alpha_1 \cdot t} \, , \qquad (23a)$$

where B' (an integration constant) is now influenced by changes in m.

The solutions to equations (33) and (34) for the narrow gold band in the text are completely analogous to the above solutions. The most distinctive difference is that the particular solutions are in terms of v and u separately rather than together as m.

References

Arndt, Sven W. "International Short-Term Capital Movements: A Distributed Lag Model of Speculation in Foreign Exchange." *Econometrica* 36 (January 1968): 59–69.

Canterbery, E. Ray. *Foreign Exchange, Capital Flows, and Monetary Policy*. Studies in International Finance, no. 15. Princeton, N.J.: Internat. Finance Sec., Princeton Univ., 1965.

———. "A Dynamic Theory of Foreign Exchange." *Nat. Banking Rev.* 4 (June 1967): 397–413.

———. *Economics on a New Frontier*. Belmont, Calif.: Wadsworth, 1968.

———. "Exchange Rates, Capital Flows, and Monetary Policy." *A.E.R.* 59 (June 1969): 426–32.

Canterbery, E. Ray, and Boorman, John T. "The Crawling Peg and Exchange Stability." *Canadian J. Econ.* 3 (May 1970): 291–99.

Friedman, Milton. "The Case for Flexible Exchange Rates." In *Essays in Positive Economics*. Chicago: Univ. Chicago Press, 1953.

Haberler, Gottfried. "The Market for Foreign Exchange and the Stability of the Balance of Payments: A Theoretical Analysis. *Kyklos* 3 (1949): 193–218.

Halm, George N. *The 'Band' Proposal: The Limits of Permissible Exchange Rate Variations*. Special Papers in International Economics, no. 6. Princeton, N.J.: Internat. Finance Sec., Princeton Univ., February 1965.

Hendershott, P. H. "International Short-Term Capital Movements. Comment IV." *A.E.R.* 57 (June 1967): 560–63.

Kenen, Peter, B. "Trade, Speculation, and the Forward Exchange Rate." In *Trade, Growth and the Balance of Payments*, edited by R. E. Baldwin. Chicago: Rand McNally, 1965.

Laffer, A. B. "International Short-Term Capital Movements. Comment III." *A.E.R.* 57 (June 1967): 556–60.

Machlup, Fritz. "The Theory of Foreign Exchanges: Part I." *Economica* 6 (November 1939): 104–58; "Part II," 7 (February 1940): 23–40.

———. *Plans for Reform of the International Monetary System*. Special Papers in International Economics, no. 3. Princeton, N.J.: Internat. Finance Sec., Princeton Univ., 1967.

Mundell, Robert A. "The Monetary Dynamics of International Adjustment under Fixed and Flexible Exchange Rates," *Q.J.E.* 74 (May 1960): 227–57.

Stein, J. L. "International Short-Term Capital Movements." *A.E.R.* 55 (March 1965): 40–66.

———. "International Short-Term Capital Movements: Reply." Ibid. 57 (June 1967): 565–69.

Stoll, Hans. "An Empirical Study of the Forward Exchange Market under Fixed and Flexible Exchange Rate Systems." *Canadian J. Econ.* 1 (February 1968): 55–78.

Telser, L. G. "A Theory of Speculation Relating Profitability and Stability." *Rev. Econ. Statis.* 41(August 1959): 295–301.

Tsiang, S. C. "A Theory of Foreign-Exchange Speculation under a Floating Exchange System." *J.P.E.* 66 (October 1958): 399–418.

Vanek, Jaroslav. *International Trade: Theory and Economic Policy*. Homewood, Ill.: Irwin, 1962.

Yeager, Leland B. *International Monetary Relations*. New York: Harper & Row, 1966.

———. "A Skeptical View of the 'Band' Proposal." *Nat. Banking Rev.* 4 (March 1967): 291–97.

Chapter 3

THE MODERN THEORY OF FOREIGN EXCHANGE AND THE NET SPECULATIVE RESIDUAL

E. RAY CANTERBERY

Florida State University

Some confusions regarding statistical tests related to the modern foreign exchange model continue to abound in the literature. In particular, the impact of hedging upon the reduced-form solution, that is, the modern theory of forward exchange (MT), appears to be misunderstood. In a recent issue of this Journal, Van Belle attempts to "illuminate the misspecification of the MT caused by the neglect of the commercial hedgers' forward dealings" [20, 117]. This "neglect," even if it were endemic to the empirical studies, certainly is not characteristic of the theory.[1] Whether or not such a neglect exists or is benign is very important. The purposes of this article are to prove that the explicit inclusion of hedging in the MT does not alter the nature of the reduced-form solution and to show that the unwittingly slighting of hedging in the empirical studies leads to a misinterpretation but not a misspecification.

I. THE IMPORTANCE OF THE NET SPECULATIVE RESIDUAL

Assume two currency areas with one being a U.S. dollar bloc and the other, "foreign." Also, assume identical forward rate and Treasury bill maturities. Under assumptions that allow the coefficient of the interest-rate spread to be unitary [see 6], the MT says

$$(y - x)/x = -(r_f - r_{us}) + g(\Delta x^*)/x, \quad (1)$$

where x = spot foreign exchange rate, y = forward foreign exchange rate, x^* = spot rate expected by speculators and hedgers, r_{us} = U.S. interest rate, r_f = foreign interest rate.[2] Alternatively, the speculative variable can be written simply as $f(x^*)/x$. Thus, if (1) is a close approximation, the terms can be rearranged so that

$$(y - x)/x + (r_f - r_{us}) = f(x^*)/x. \quad (2)$$

Because the left-hand terms in (2) are officially reported statistics, the value of the net speculative variable, i.e. $f(x^*)/x$, can be derived arithmetically. Then, the preoccupation with statistical biases can be set aside.

The usefulness of this MT result is illustrated by the data on the "Watergate net speculative variable" reported in Table I. Revelations of the magnitude of Watergate related deeds led to speculative selling of dollars, sharp increases in the foreign exchange rate (x), and a large and rising negative net speculative residual. To the extent that f is independent of the current values of x, y, r_f and r_{us}, this calculated residual can be included as an independent variable determining short-term capital flows.

II. A CRITIQUE OF THE NEGLECTED-HEDGING VIEW

Van Belle is correct on three points: 1) hedging activity can not be separately delineated in the foreign exchange market; 2) H, the "forward exchange rate that equates the commercial hedgers' demand and supply of forward exchange," is not observable—indeed, I contend—is nonexistent; and 3) Stoll and Kesselman ignore hedging activity by those who are covering or partly cover-

[1] See the rudiments of such a theory in Canterbery [7]. The modern theory is further refined in the first third (theoretical section) of Stein [16], and in Canterbery [6], and at the firm level by Kenen [12]. The theory is used to identify theoretically the stability conditions for speculation under alternate exchange-rate regimes by Canterbery in [9]. The empirical studies include those by Stoll [17] and Kesselman [11]. Black [3] further refines the theory by including interest rates as endogenous for the first time (to my knowledge) and conducts new empirical tests. Black's conclusions [3, 53–54] regarding alternative systems are similar to those of Canterbery [9].

[2] To be precise, the interest differential is $-(r_f - r_{us})/(1 + r_f)$, but for theoretical discussions the r_f in the denominator is usually dropped.

TABLE I

THE WATERGATE NET SPECULATIVE RESIDUAL, U.S. AND U.K., MAY 18, 1973–JULY 6, 1973

[In per cent per annum for 91-day bills and forward maturities]

		$(r_f - r_{us})$	+	$(y - x)/x$	=	$f(x^*)/x$
May	18	.93		-1.80		-.87
	25	.62		-1.52		-.90
June	1	.19		-1.43		-1.24
	8	.04		-1.41		-1.37
	15	-.14		-1.38		-1.52
	22	-.26		-1.40		-1.66
	29	-.43		-1.68		-2.11
July	6	-1.11		-2.36		-3.47

Source: [4, A93].

ing assets and liabilities against indefinite and indirect exchange risks. Van Belle usefully reminds some of our authors that hedging and leading-lagging are important foreign-exchange activities.

Because H or a proxy for H, imports-exports, does not appear in the empirical tests by Stoll [17] and Kesselman [11], argues Van Belle, a specification bias results from a missing variable. First, as purely a technical matter, a specification bias cannot be defined for a nonexistent variable, H. Second, Kesselman *does* in several of his tests include lagged exports and imports as variables anyway, and these trade variables are insignificant. Third, Van Belle, like Laffer [13, 557] and Heckerman [10, 555–556] before him, presumes incorrectly that such export-import variations and associated hedging can alter significantly the difference between the forward and spot rates *independently* of the x^*, r_f, and r_{us} parameters.

A misunderstanding is caused by Stoll's and Kesselman's repeated references to their estimated parameters as purely interest-rate "arbitrage" and "speculative". Although the authors of these empirical studies do ignore hedgers, the theoretical models that generate the MT solution do not. Moreover, contrary to Van Belle, even the intentional or unwary slighting of hedging is not, in itself, a misspecification in Stoll's and Kesselman's tests. Their error is *interpretative* rather than statistical. Also, contrary to Van Belle, Aliber's observation that, with flexible rates, covered margins provide an accurate indication of speculative behavior [2, 180–181] still stands. But, I would place the emphasis on *indication* rather than accurate.

Those contentions of II requiring additional support will be defended by the theoretical model of III.

III. THE MODERN THEORY AND HEDGING ACTIVITY

In an attempt to clarify the derivation and characteristics of the MT and therefore bring some order out of the imbroglio, let me state in the barest possible form, the simultaneous equilibrium model for the foreign exchange markets.

The theory's contour is essentially the same under fixed or floating exchange rates.[3] However, imports-exports normally are viewed as exogenous with respect to the

[3] To show this, compare the solution in [9] with that in [6].

exchange rate under a fixed exchange rate system. Under either system the demand and supply for foreign exchange comes from both banks and commercial exporters and importers. Their activities involve the purchase and sales of foreign exchange for commercial trading purposes, interest-rate arbitrage (covered and uncovered), hedging, leading and lagging with respect to exports-imports or assets-liabilities (actually forms of hedging), and outright speculation.

Even under a fixed-parity-value system importers have four general alternatives at time t: 1) pay for imports immediately by engaging in a spot trade transaction at $x(t)$; 2) postpone payment by engaging in a forward transaction (hedge) at $y(t)$, given $x^*(t)$; 3) postpone payment to speculate on the price of exchange either by pure speculation, given $x^*(t)$ and $r_{us}(t)$, or uncovered interest-rate arbitrage at $r_f(t) - r_{us}(t)$, given $x^*(t)$; or 4) postpone payment and engage in pure interest-rate arbitrage, given $r_f(t) - r_{us}(t)$. Hedging in the home country on exports is in reaction to the same variables as in (2) but increases forward supply rather than demand. For simplicity, assume all delayed payments are completed in the next period, a time span that matches Treasury bills and forward maturities.

It is, of course, possible to exercise some combination of these choices. For instance, the home-currency value of a particular export or import may not be entirely "hedged." Except for direct transactions with respect to import-export activity, private commercial banks engage in the same foreign exchange dealings. Although the volume of imports is related to such variables as national income, prices, and tastes, spot transactions for commercial trade can be viewed like any other derived demand or supply, namely as a function of the price of foreign exchange.[4]

If importers purchase forward exchange, the bankers and in turn, the foreign-exchange dealers, will enter the market to supply the exchange spot in the next period. Thus, the total current (t) demand for spot exchange will depend upon both current purchases of foreign exchange by importers and the commodity purchases by importers in the preceeding period ($t - 1$) which were not paid for at that time, plus current private bank demands. Similarly, the value of the last period's exports that are just being paid for now will appear in the current supply of foreign exchange. The delayed demands and supplies are reflected theoretically by the appearance of each independent variable twice, the second time lagged by one period.

Thus, the demand for current spot exchange can be written as

$$D(t) = D(x_t, z_t, m_t, x_t^*, x_{t-1}, z_{t-1}, m_{t-1}, x_{t-1}^*), \tag{3}$$

and supply,

$$S(t) = S(x_t, z_t, m_t, x_t^*, x_{t-1}, z_{t-1}, m_{t-1}, x_{t-1}^*), \tag{4}$$

where $z = (y - x)/x$, and m is the interest-rate spread, that is, $m = r_f - r_{us}$. Again, for notational unadornment, I assume that all maturities match.

The current demand for *forward* foreign exchange equals the exchange value of imports hedged and other liabilities being covered (from the point of view of the home nation) plus the foreign-exchange value of dollars sold by foreigners to cover interest-arbitrage operations. The decision to hedge is related to the expected spot exchange rate (x^*) and the present forward premium or discount. Thus, continuing to assume that there is only one maturity forward, write the demand for forward contracts as

$$D_F(t) = D_F(z_t, m_t, x_t^*). \tag{5}$$

The supply of forward foreign exchange is the foreign-exchange value of exports (from the view of the home economy) hedged for the future delivery date plus other assets

[4] See [6, 402–403] for a treatment of this problem. The demand for foreign exchange for current imports under floating rates can, for example, be written simply as $D(M) = a - bx$.

being covered plus the quantity of foreign exchange sold forward as cover for interest-arbitrage transactions. Hence, the supply of forward contracts is

$$S_F(t) = S_F(z_t, m_t, x_t^*). \quad (6)$$

Simultaneous equilibrium in spot and forward markets occurs when

$$D(t) = S(t) \quad \text{and} \quad D_F(t) = S_F(t). \quad (7)$$

It has been shown elsewhere [6, 409] that—assuming linear demand-supply equations and assuming hedging solely a function of x^*—the forward market can be solved for $y(t)$, and

$$y(t) = x_t - \hat{m}_t + f(x_t^*), \qquad \text{or} \quad \hat{z}(t) = -\hat{m}_t + f(x_t^*), \quad (8)$$

where the caret (ˆ) indicates that the values formerly expressed in percentages are now in absolute terms.[6]

Let us incorporate all the arguments leading to (7). This complicates slightly the role of hedgers in the model. Because the expected spot rate can be specified as a monotonic function of all lagged variables, x_{t-1}, z_{t-1}, m_{t-1}, and x_{t-1}^* otherwise can be dropped for the purpose of determining $\hat{z}(t)$. Also, assume that $\hat{m}$ is one of the variables determining but not determined by x and y. Time's arrow makes x^* mathematically exogeneous, so only x and y are endogenous. Continue to assume that all demands and supplies are linear functions. From the steps-to-solution in the Appendix, the simultaneous solution for the spot and forward rate now is:

$$\hat{z}(t) = -\beta\hat{m}_t + \gamma x_t^*, \quad (9)$$

where (see Appendix) $\beta = [(c_3 + c_5)/(c_2 + c_4 + c_3 + c_5)]$ and $\gamma = [(d_2 + d_3)/(c_2 + c_4 + c_3 + c_5)]$. The coefficients, c_2 and c_4, represent exclusively hedging parameters while c_3 and c_5 stand for purely interest-rate arbitrage parameters. Because x^* probably overpowers the influence of z in hedging decisions, the smallness of $(c_2 + c_4)$ infers that $\beta \cong 1$. Therefore, (1) remains a close approximation of MT.

What are the implications of this solution? As indicated earlier [8, 427], even when traders hedge to avert all risk, they are mostly reacting to the same variable as are speculators, namely the expected future spot rate. If (9) is statistically estimated, x^* can be defined in terms of a weighted average of past spot rates. This essentially is the technique of Branson [5], Arndt [1], Thomas [18, 180–181], and Kesselman, although they all use different specifications. In the estimation there is no misspecification of the MT caused by neglect of commercial-merchant-hedgers' forward exchange dealings. Quite the contrary, their activities are subsummed in the speculative and interest-rate parameters. For the speculative parameter this is as it should be. The direction of the influence of hedgers on the forward exchange rate will be identical (although no doubt of a different magnitude) as that of pure speculators. If $(c_2 + c_4) = 0$, the arithmetical calculation of Table 1 is precisely correct. If $|c_2 + c_4|$ is non-zero, of course, the estimated interest-rate parameter is not unitary. But, neither is it necessarily a biased estimate: $\hat{\beta}$ is a reduced-form parameter, and the structural parameters, of c_2 and c_4, can only be determined with additional information. There *is* potentially a *simultaneity* bias discussed in [8] that is taken into account by Stoll and ignored by Kesselman.

IV. OTHER EMPIRICAL CONSIDERATIONS AND CONCLUSIONS

If "Hedging is primarily a function of the balance of trade" [20, 119], Kesselman should have captured it with his lagged import-export variables. But trade was insignificant [11, 292–293] because the non-exchange-rate-associated *level* of trade is reflected in the sizes of the intercept terms

[6] For the algebraic definition of unitary exchange units and the proof for this conversion, see Canterbery [6, 409, n. 28]. To be precise, $\hat{m}$ is the extra return (in currency units) per unit of foreign exchange invested in foreign treasury bills. This definition greatly reduces mathematical complexity without significantly diminishing precision.

of the foreign exchange supply and demand equations. As to Van Belle's contention that misspecification bias explains, in part, the differences in the Stoll and Kesselman estimates, two studies over divergent time periods using different variables and specifications are—by definition—not comparable.

The positive serial correlation found by Kesselman may be from nonlinearity, measurement errors, or perhaps is evidence that the exchange markets are underresponding to information through x^* [see 14 and 15]. Data may not match: for example, exchange rates usually are mid-day in New York or London and interest rates are at the time of peak volume.[6] Moreover, as Kenen [12] suggests, interest rates may be very responsive at times to arbitrage demand and the actual marginal interest rates paid may differ from those data points recorded in statistical series [also, see 3]. Underresponse may be a consequence of imperfect information among speculators, hedgers, and arbitragers dealing in foreign exchange.

Other explanations have been offered for the existence of f in (8). These include transactions cost, default risk, non-monetary returns, non-unitary correlation of returns, premature repatriation, and expected exchange controls.[7] To some extent, however, x^* captures the impacts of the last two items. The other "explanations" are not sufficient in themselves to cause the types of movements observed in the residual, including those exhibited in Table I. The effect of actual exchange controls as well as official reserve changes can be incorporated into the model theoretically [see 9, 423] and empirically, as by Kesselman [11, 292–293].

Because of the data-error problem that is inescapable anyway, the potential simultaneity bias, and the theoretical results discussed herein, the arithmetically calculated net speculative residual appears to be a useful and easily attainable approximation. Its usefulness is, of course, impaired when the monetary authorities engage in substantial counterspeculative purchases or sales. As Van Belle properly reminds us, however, the net speculative parameter at best includes a hedgers' component. Nonetheless, economists cannot create a distinction that even the market can not record. Not only is there no rate H that equates hedgers' supply and demand, but it is not necessary to imagine one.

[6] Moreover, non-Euclidian geometry dictates that noon in London be at a different earth-time than noon in New York.

[7] These are listed and discussed in the survey by Willett and Officer [19]. Also, I want to take this opportunity to correct a misunderstanding by Willett and Officer. The quotations they attribute to me are my restatements of Keynes' implicit assumptions that lead him to interest-rate parity. Their criticism of these statements as "incorrect" conditions for traditional parity [19; 250–251] should be directed at Keynes because I show later in the same source [7] why these assumptions do indeed fail to give traditional interest parity.

REFERENCES

1. Arndt, Sven W., "International Short-Term Capital Movements: A Distributed Lag Model of Speculation in Foreign Exchange." *Econometrica*, January 1968, 59–69.
2. Aliber, Robert Z., "Speculation in the Foreign Exchanges: The European Experience." *Yale Economic Essays*, Spring 1962, 171–245.
3. Black, S. W. *International Money Markets and Flexible Exchange Rates*, Studies in International Finance, no. 32. Princeton, N.J.: International Finance Section, Princeton University, 1973.
4. Board of Governors of the Federal Reserve System, *Federal Reserve Bulletin*, October 1973.
5. Branson, William H. *Financial Capital Flows in the U.S. Balance of Payments*. Amsterdam: North-Holland, 1968.
6. Canterbery, E. Ray, "A Dynamic Theory of Foreign Exchange." *National Banking Review*, June 1967, 397–413.
7. ———. *Foreign Exchange, Capital Flows, and Monetary Policy*, Studies in International Finance, no. 15. Princeton, N.J.: International Finance Section, Princeton University, 1965.
8. ———. "Exchange Rates, Capital Flows, and Monetary Policy." *American Economic Review*, June 1969, 426–432.
9. ———. "A Theory of Foreign Exchange Speculation Under Alternative Systems." *Journal of Political Economy*, May/June 1971, 407–436.
10. Heckerman, D. G., "International Short-term Capital Movements: Comment II." *American Economic Review*, June 1967, 548–570.
11. Kesselman, J., "The Role of Speculation in Forward-Rate Determination: The Canadian Flexi-

ble Dollar 1953–1960." *Canadian Journal of Economics*, August 1971, 279–298.
12. Kenen, Peter B., "Trade, Speculation, and the Forward Exchange Rate." in *Trade, Growth and the Balance of Payments*, edited by R. E. Baldwin. Chicago: Rand McNally, 1965.
13. Laffer, A. B., "International Short-Term Capital Movements: Comment III." *American Economic Review*, June 1967, 556–560.
14. Pippenger, J., "The Case for Freely Fluctuating Exchange Rates: Some Evidence." *Western Economic Journal*, September 1973, 314–326.
15. Poole, W., "Speculative Prices as Random Walks: An Analysis of Ten Time Series of Flexible Exchange Rates." *Southern Economic Journal*, April 1967, 468–478.
16. Stein, J. L., "International Short-Term Capital Movements." *American Economic Review*, March 1965, 40–66.
17. Stoll, Hans, "An Empirical Study of the Forward Exchange Market under Fixed and Flexible Exchange Rate Systems." *Canadian Journal of Journal of Economics*, February 1968, 55–78.
18. Thomas, Lloyd B., "Behavior of Flexible Exchange Rates: Additional Tests From the Post-World War I Episode." *Southern Economic Journal*, October 1973, 167–182.
19. Willett, T. D., and L. H. Officer., "The Covered Artibrage Schedule: A Critical Survey of Recent Developments." *Journal of Money, Credit and Banking*, May 1970, 247–257.
20. Van Belle, J. J., "A Neglected Aspect of the Modern Theory of Forward Exchange." *Southern Economic Journal*, July 1973, 117–119.

APPENDIX

Assume linearity and, for simplicity in solutions that does not affect significantly the outcomes, convert all percents to absolute values. All time is current and time subscripts can be dropped under our assumptions. As above, $\hat{z} = y - x$. All signs are taken from the partial derivatives. The demend for spot exchange for immediate payment for imports is viewed as downward sloping as $M(t) = -b_0x$. Thus, write (3), (4), (5) and (6) as

$$D(t) = a_0 - b_0x + c_0(\hat{z} + \hat{m}) + d_0x^*, \tag{3'}$$

$$S(t) = a_1 + b_1x - c_1(\hat{z} + \hat{m}) - d_1x^*, \tag{4'}$$

$$D_F(t) = a_2 - c_2\hat{z} - c_3(\hat{z} + \hat{m}) + d_2x^*, \tag{5'}$$

and

$$S_F(t) = a_2 + c_4\hat{z} + c_5(\hat{z} + \hat{m}) - d_3x^*. \tag{6'}$$

The forward demand and supply equations have the same intercept if the interest-rate spread and speculation are zero. In equilibrium, which may or may not be stable, $D(t) = S(t)$ and $D_F(t) = S_F(t)$. Let $(c_1 + c_0 + b_0 + b_1) = b_2$, $(c_0 + c_1) = c_6$, $[(a_0 - a_1) + (c_0 + c_1)\hat{m} + (d_0 + d_1)x^*] = h_0$, $(c_2 + c_3 + c_4 + c_5) = b_3$, and $[(d_2 + d_3)x^* - (c_3 + c_5)\hat{m}] = h_1$, then

$$-b_2x + c_6y = -h_0, \text{ and} \tag{A}$$

$$b_3x - b_3y = -h_1. \tag{B}$$

The determinants of (A) and (B) are:

$$x = \frac{\begin{matrix} -h_0 & c_6 \\ -h_1 & -b_3 \end{matrix}}{\begin{matrix} -b_2 & c_6 \\ b_3 & -b_3 \end{matrix}} \qquad y = \frac{\begin{matrix} -b_2 & -h_0 \\ b_3 & -h_1 \end{matrix}}{\begin{matrix} -b_2 & c_6 \\ b_3 & -b_3 \end{matrix}} \tag{C}$$

By Cramer's rule,

$$\hat{z} = h_1/b_3, \text{ or} \tag{D}$$

$$\hat{z} = -[(c_3 + c_5)/(c_2 + c_4 + c_3 + c_5)]\hat{m} + [(d_2 + d_3)/(c_2 + c_4 + c_3 + c_5)]x^*, \tag{9'}$$

which is re-written as (9) in the text. The equations are consistent and the solution is unique.

Chapter 4

ON THE RELEVANCE OF HEDGING FOR THE MODERN THEORY OF FORWARD EXCHANGE: REPLY

Van Belle and Sakbani [4] attempt to (1) reaffirm that the omission of hedging constitutes a misspecification of the modern theory of foreign exchange *(MT)*, (2) prove that even if the emphasis be placed upon indication in "accurate indication" [1, 183], covered margins should not be considered a good indicator of speculation, and (3) demonstrate that it is *future*, not past values of imports and exports that reflect hedging. On (1) and (2) the authors are incorrect. On (3), although "future" values is an unfortunate choice of terminology, the authors are correct in saying that trade flows are recorded upon delivery rather than at the transaction time. But their use of this fact is confused by conceptual, mathematical, and statistical errors. Moreover, the interdependence of hedging with other motives that the authors seek but cannot find is in the *MT*.

The authors take positions that are metaphysical. That is, whether they are correct or not, real world outcomes are unaffected. The authors go beyond metaphysics in the sense that they also are not logical. Why metaphysical? The authors reincarnate Van Belle's contention that a forward rate *(H)* exists at which the net hedgers demand for forward exchange is zero [3]. *There is no such rate.* And it is not only unnecessary to imagine one, it is awkward, inconvenient, and misleading. While the authors presume that it exists, it is (as the authors admit) nonobservable. There are, of course, many variables that do exist which scientists cannot observe. But with all the crucial rates that determine capital flows, trade, and exchange rates known and recorded, why insist on invoking a *proxy* for a nonobservable, nonexistent variable? Then, why compound the confusion by contending that the variable itself exists and that its absence in a statistical test is the cause of a specification bias? If the omission of proxies for nonexistent, nonobservable variables causes a bias, *all* statistical estimates are biased.

In reality, of course, the commercial export-import hedger will buy and sell at the current market rates for spot and forward exchange, given interest rates and expected future spot rates.

The logic and language whereby the authors conclude that hedging is not related to the expected spot rate (and hence the misspecification) is—to use a kindly verb—tortured. On the one hand, they state that "hedgers cover future foreign exchange commitments to eliminate the exchange risk generated by their foreign trade" and, on the other hand, they suggest that the expected spot rate is not an explanatory variable. If foreign exchange risk does not result from spot exchange rate fluctuations, then where is the risk?[1]

While admitting interdependence of exchange activity motives, the authors then suggest that we must ignore such interdependence because "there would be no basis for the standard version of the *MT* let alone its modification to include hedging." This is an error that apparently stems from a lack of understanding of a simultaneous equation system from which the reduced form solution [1, equation 9, p. 185] is derived. Perhaps we can clarify this by writing the reduced-form solution in its most general form. From equations (3) through (7) in [1] we have

$$z(t) = F(m_t, x_t^*, x_{t-l}, z_{t-l}, m_{t-l}, x_{t-l}^*), \quad (1)$$

where x = spot foreign exchange rate, x^* = spot rate expected by speculators and hedgers, z = forward discount or premium, and m = the interest-rate spread. All these variables are subsumed in the solution to the linear model. Because $z(t)$ is the *difference* between the forward and spot rates, the level of the trade balance which in part decides the

[1] Domestic price changes can, of course, alter the future values of commodity inventories, but the foreign exchange market can not be used to reduce or eliminate that risk.

spot rate (see the structural equations) does not influence the differential $z\ (t)$ except insofar as the traders engage in hedging, arbitrage and speculation. Thus the estimated coefficients for the reduced form reflect mixtures of hedging, speculation and interest-rate arbitrage motives.

Estimates of the reduced-form parameters are analogous to partial derivatives. Nonetheless, as with the calculus, a partial relation holds the other variables "temporarily" constant but is not independent of the level of these other variables. Thus the interdependence of the variety of exchange motives is captured. Contrary to Van Belle-Sakbani, the "pure" hedging impact also is defined in and derivable from the *MT* solution. Go to [1,185] and assume that β (the uncovered interest-rate differential parameter) and γ (the net speculative parameter) have been empirically determined. Consider the following ratios:

$$\beta/\gamma;\quad (1-\beta)/\gamma;\quad (1-\beta)/\beta. \qquad (2)$$

Transform the estimated parameters into their structural coefficient counterparts (defined in 1, 185). The ratios are, respectively, the relative importance of interest arbitrage to net speculation, "pure" hedging relative to net speculation, and "pure" hedging relative to interest arbitrage. "Pure" hedging is the reaction of commercial exporters-importers solely to the forward exchange costs of hedging. The *MT* thus meets both requirements of the two critics.

"Pure" hedging, however, is only relevant if hedgers cover from habit and not from uncertainty regarding exchange-rate movements. But such purity appears to be a contradiction in terms. Why would hedgers cover if they were certain that the exchange rate upon delivery of imports or exports would be the same as it was the day of the initial transaction?

For this reason, I argue that "x^* probably overpowers the influence of z in hedging decisions, the smallness of $(c_2 + c_4)$ infers that $\beta \cong 1$"[1, 185]. If β is *precisely* unitary, the two "pure" hedging ratios in (2) are indeterminant. Then, the direction of the effect of hedgers on exchange rates is identical to that of speculators but of a different magnitude. There would be no way of identifying the separate influences of the two types of exchange activity except by a carefully-designed questionnaire survey of a representative sample of foreign exchange participants. I see little purpose in gaining such information.

Also contrary to Van Belle-Sakbani, I did not say that hedging is "solely a function of the expected future spot rate," nor did I argue that only this particular specification of the model yields the *MT*-solution form. In [1] hedging is a function of x^* and z, and an alternative specification—such as the inclusion of interest rates as opportunity costs—does not alter the outcome [see 2].

As to my supportive illustration of the Watergate speculative residual, (when $\beta \cong 1$), the authors contend that "these large negative net speculative residuals . . . should reflect a speculative sell-off of pounds . . . and not a speculative sell-off of dollars . . ." As Figure 1 clearly reveals, the U. S. spot foreign exchange rate w.r.t. pound sterling was appreciating during the period questioned. For the price of pounds to *rise* from a "speculative sell-off" of pounds would require the demand curve for pounds to be downward-sloping and the supply-curve, upward-sloping! Even the British would find this rather unsettling.

The authors' test their *H*-proxy, future

FIGURE 1—Foreign Exchange Rates, U.S./U.K., January 1, 1972–July 6, 1973 (Watergate spot rate in shaded space).

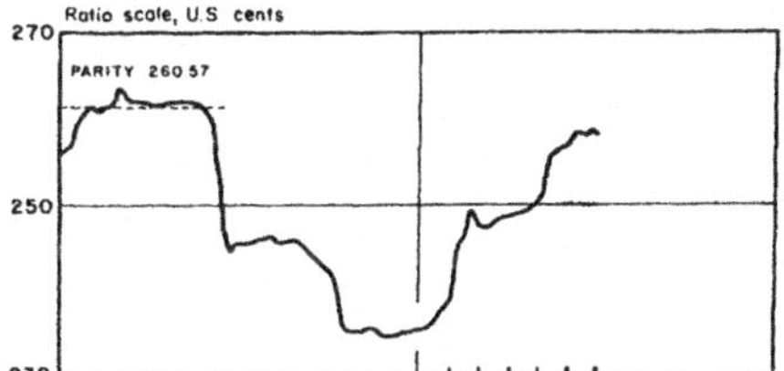

Source: Board of Governors of the Federal Reserve System, *Monthly Chart Book*, July 1973.
Latest figure plotted: July 6, 1973

trade balances, with the equation

$$(r_{us} - r_c) + (y_c - x_c)/x_c = f[(r_{us} - r_c), (M_c - X_c), (M_c - X_c)_{+3}, r_{us}, e], \quad (3)$$

where e= error term, and the subscripts denote the country viewing platform (c= Canada) and all values are in current time except for the future trade balance (+*3*). The same variables (r_{us}, r_c) appear on both sides of the equation (r_{us} appearing *three* times), *and* the *current* trade balance which is determined simultaneously with y_c and x_c is included as an "independent" variable. Also, the speculative variable has been omitted. Thus not only are the estimated coefficients unreliable, the estimators contain specification *and* simultaneity bias. Moreover, after contending that "lagged values of the trade imbalance can not effectively" be used "as the proxy for hedging" because "the trade balance is not a linear function of time," the covered margin is expressed as a linear function of the future trade imbalance. Because the future is destined to become the past, a special "time warp" assumption must have been made. But let us cut right through the metaphysics. Future recording of current transactions *do not cause* current actions. The hedgers are reacting to *current expectations* because they do not know what the *BT* statistics will be three months hence.[2]

There may well be a specification that improves the reduced-form estimation of the MT. Equation (3) is not it.

E. RAY CANTERBERY
Florida State University

REFERENCES

1. Canterbery, E. Ray, "The Modern Theory of Foreign Exchange and the Net Speculative Residual," *Southern Economic Journal,* October 1974, 182–187.
2. ———, "A theory of Foreign Exchange Speculation Under Alternative Systems," *Journal of Political Economy,* May/June 1971, 407–436.
3. Van Belle, J. J., "A Neglected Aspect of the Modern Theory of Forward Exchange." *Southern Economic Journal,* July 1973, 117–119.
4. Van Belle, John J., and Mahmoud Sakbani, "On the Relevance of Hedging for the Modern Theory of Forward Exchange: Comment," *Southern Economic Journal,* January 1976, 529–532.

[2] A better choice of terminology in any theory formulation would be "current trade contracts for future delivery" because the affirmative action is taken in current time. Nonetheless the authors are correct in referring to the balance-of-payments effect as "future."

PART II

INCOME DISTRIBUTION AND WELFARE ECONOMICS

Chapter 5

REFLECTIONS UPON THE INCOME DISTRIBUTION AS A PURE PUBLIC GOOD *

E. R. CANTERBERY AND H. P. TUCKMAN

Economists have analyzed the optimum distribution of income several ways. (1) In models with independent individual ophelimity functions, a Pareto optimum income distribution (P–O) automatically results from the determination of "efficient" ratios of factor and product prices. (2) In models where the incomes of other individuals appear as an argument in each person's utility function, the maximization of utility requires the redistribution of income in a voluntary transfer process.[1] (3) If a single measure of the societal distribution of income appears in individual utility functions, the income distribution becomes a pure public good. Optimization then is attempted through voluntary exchange.[2] (4) A social welfare function (SWF) is derived through a political process. The SWF represents society's collective decision as to which income distribution is best.[3]

The government plays no role prior to Optimum (3). This optimum is analyzed in a recent article by Lester Thurow.[4] He argues that the income distribution is a public good in the sense that it enters everyone's utility function and its consumption is nonrival. He contends that some income redistribution, therefore, is necessary to achieve a Pareto optimum. Although the amount to be redistributed and the optimum size of individual tax payments are determined with a voluntary exchange model of the Lindahl, Mus-

* We gratefully acknowledge the helpful comments of B. Tuckman, W. Mazek, and P. A. Meyer, who read an earlier draft of this material, and financial support from the Rockefeller Foundation. The authors are solely responsible for the results.

1. This approach usually emphasizes charitable transfers, as in H. Hochman and J. Rodgers, "Pareto Optimal Redistribution," *American Economic Review*, LIX (Sept. 1969), 542–57; R. Schwartz, "Personal Philanthropic Contributions," *Journal of Political Economy*, LXXVIII (Nov./Dec. 1970), 1264–92.

2. L. Thurow, "The Income Distribution As a Pure Public Good," this *Journal*, LXXXV (May 1971), 327–36.

3. See, for example, P. Samuelson, "A Diagrammatic Exposition of a Theory of Public Expenditures," *Review of Economics and Statistics*, XXXVIII (Nov. 1956), 350–56.

4. Thurow, *op. cit.*

grave, Samuelson type, Thurow argues that "to some extent the voluntary exchange approach may also explain the process that the political majority must go through before it can impose its welfare function on the rest of society."[5]

Thurow's attempt to broaden the concept of Pareto optimality to include the utility derived from the income distribution is laudatory, and his article is forward-looking. Nonetheless, we wish to clarify several issues that he raises and suggest some shortcomings of his model. (a) Thurow has, like other recent writers, unwittingly redefined Pareto optimality as commonly understood by economists. (b) The definition, income distribution = public good, has several weaknesses. (c) The model has several technical deficiencies. (d) Although the main purpose of bringing income distribution under the public goods umbrella is public policy analysis, this model leaves us with the problem of identifying preferences when it is extended to a multiperson world. Because of the latter three complaints, we believe that Thurow has failed to demonstrate that the public goods approach is superior to one using political variables or other methods of preference representation.

A "Socioeconomic" Definition of Pareto Optimality

In attempting to incorporate utility interdependence into the utility function, Thurow redefines the P–O concept. Pareto himself defined two optimums.[6] The first, the ophelimity optimum, avoids cardinal measurement and interpersonal comparisons of satisfaction. This is the Pareto optimum commonly invoked by economists. In Pareto's sociological discussion he changes the ophelimity to a utility criterion.[7]

Thurow's optimum is closer to a utility than to an ophelimity optimum. He wisely recognizes that the distribution of income may act as a proxy for a variety of utility-affecting forces such as "preventing crime and creating social or political stability . . . individuals may simply want to live in societies with particular distributions of income and economic power . . . [or] the individual is simply exercising an esthetic taste for equality or inequality."[8] Thurow's concerns go beyond pure economic efficiency. While this usefully

5. *Ibid.*, p. 336.
6. See Vincent J. Tarascio, "Paretian Welfare Theory: Some Neglected Aspects," *Journal of Political Economy*, LXXVII (Jan./Feb. 1969), 1–21.
7. Utility "is a social concept, deriving from ethical, moral, religious, political, etc., as well as economic causes" (*ibid.*, p. 7).
8. Thurow, *op. cit.*, p. 327.

broadens the scope of economic science, the optimum is a socio-economic one rather than one of economic efficiency.

Can the Income Distribution Be a Public Good?

The public goods and the voluntary transfer approaches involve income redistribution as a prerequisite for achieving a social optimum. But to the extent that income distribution is based upon collective rather than individual action, the attainment of a social optimum also requires some method for reflecting individual preferences. While personal gift giving can increase the utility of a person who wishes to favor a *particular* individual, the same individual cannot, through his own resources, redistribute the income of the entire society. Collective action is required. The superiority of Thurow's approach as compared with the SWF approach must then depend upon the acceptability of his utility function and the usefulness of the public goods approach as a guide for public policy.

Thurow considers Optimum (3), which arises from the inclusion in individual utility functions of X, a vector that "uniquely" measures every possible income distribution. But the income distribution can be treated as a pure public good in consumption only if all individuals' satisfactions (as Thurow implies) are related to similar objective measures of income equality and if therefore the "optimum" income distribution can be made available to all individuals. If some individuals consider Z to be the relevant vector, the maximization of X need not lead to a societal optimum unless X is a linear transformation of Z.

The search for the "perfect" income distribution variable that would qualify as a *pure* public good is destined to fail. Measures of dispersion, such as Gini coefficients, quartile ranges, and standard deviations, are generally not familiar to the public. Rather than reacting to a single abstract measure, individuals probably react to visible evidence of the plight of *certain groups* in the society and to events like unemployment or income increases received by family and acquaintances.

We end up with many subjective measures of the income distribution in which charity cannot complete the "desired" redistribution and public officials cannot perceive an optimum redistribution. Because different measures of the income distribution are utilized by different individuals, an improvement in the welfare of one individual need not be reflected in the utility functions of significant numbers of other individuals and the income distribution need not be a public good in consumption.

The Political Economy of the Model

Even if we accept Thurow's belief in a single measure, the voluntary exchange approach is questionable. The usefulness of the "public goods" model must be judged by what it adds to our knowledge rather than its provision of a set of "optimal" tax shares under unacceptable conditions. It is not sufficient, as Thurow implies, that "economic theory can tell us as much about the optimum distribution of income as it can about the optimum quantity of any other public good." In Samuelson's words,

> "whatever the relevance of the pseudo-equilibrium algorithm to a computer omniscient with respect to the F, u', and U functions, we must not forget that it has no relevance to motivated market behavior. Moreover, it is striking how Wicksell and Lindahl, and even Musgrave and Johansen . . . after getting a glimpse of pseudo-equilibrium descend to the swampland of mathematical politics. . . ."[9]

Does the model advance our knowledge of the process whereby income is redistributed? The model illustrates once again the great difficulty in separating means from ends in the making of public policy. Thurow revives the Kaldor-Hicks suggestion that the winners can compensate the losers and leave no one "worse off." Thurow's model presents a set of "benefit" curves, and it realistically allows one individual's curve (B_3) to decline as income is redistributed. This illustrates the fact that compensatory payments are required. The amount of income left over for redistribution must be *net* of compensation. Thurow's "market constraint curve" includes the money transfer payments required to achieve a particular income distribution *after* the necessary compensation payments have been made to those who must be bribed to accept a particular income distribution.

As formulated, Thurow's model does not lead to the optimum defined by his calculus. Moreover, under certain plausible conditions no positive income redistribution would be possible, and no optimum of any kind could be identified. Measured in Thurow's money terms, there are literally no significant costs to society resulting from income transfers, although minor costs may be incurred to

9. Paul Samuelson, "Pure Theory of Public Expenditure and Taxation," in J. Margolis and H. Guitton, eds., *Public Economics* (New York: St. Martins Press, 1969), p. 106.

distribute checks, etc. The positive slope of Thurow's market constraint (cost) curve results from the compensatory payments to reimburse the malevolent. But the sum of *all* transfers must be equal to zero, as shown in Thurow's own example (p. 332). It is the latter sum that appears in Thurow's mathematics inasmuch as *all* individual incomes are given in both equations (2) and (4). The "necessary transfer payments" (Y_{tp}) in equation (4) are a function of the incomes and utilities of both those individuals receiving compensatory payments and of those who do not; it is *not* the same optimum as that defined in Thurow's benefit-cost analysis.[1] As defined,

$$(1) \qquad \sum_{i=1}^{s} (\partial u^i/\partial Y^i) \;/\; (\partial u^i/\partial X) \neq \partial X/\partial Y_{tp},$$

the partial derivative on the right side cannot be found because $\partial X/\partial Y_{tp}$ is zero.[2] Instead the "optimum" would occur where the net benefit curve is its maximum distance above the (now) zero cost line, i.e., only at complete equality.

Thurow's benefit and cost curves are interdependent in the presence of malevolence and with a demand for equality that is income elastic. If the malevolent demand very large compensation payments, Thurow's net social benefit curve would lie *below* his cost curve, and no positive income redistribution would be possible. Moreover, a large share of the nonmalevolent population may demand compensation payments in return for their acceptance of a more "egalitarian" income distribution. If the demand for equality shifts downward with income reductions, Thurow's net benefit curve may shift downward and his cost curve upward; and again the net benefit curve could lie below the cost curve. These interdependencies can cause indeterminacy. Indeed, if the poor receive substantial benefits from income redistribution while the rich suffer a loss of utility, then Thurow's model implies that the rich should be paid compensation to be made poorer by the poor. Furthermore, since the poor benefit the most from income redistribution, they should pay the highest taxes!

Aware of this difficulty, Thurow refers to the "very peculiar type of dynamic instability" in his model.[3] He suggests that those who are relatively poor will be willing to pay for more equality since

1. Thurow apparently wants to retain his original Y_{tp} benefit-cost definition. But if he does, fewer persons are subsumed on the right than on the left side of the equation.

2. We have corrected the printing error in the equation originally published.

3. Thurow, *op. cit.*, pp. 332–33.

they will have more income after transfers. Thurow correctly suggests that "a limit is placed upon the movement toward equality by the preferences of those whose tax contributions for redistribution exceed the transfer payments that they receive." There is a much more severe restriction on the usefulness of the model than this statement implies. The poor will not be willing to vote for income redistribution if the compensation payments they make exceed the benefits they receive. This confirms the inequality of equation (1) — that the optimum defined by Thurow's graph is not a societal optimum after all. After the most greedy have been completely satisfied, the balance of the population is allowed to engage in voluntary exchange until they have achieved *whatever redistribution of income is possible with the (possibly meager) funds that remain.*

Thurow's solution is only an "optimum" through the eyes of those receiving compensation. And, of course, it is difficult to envision anyone *not* wanting to be compensated under this scheme so that the ultimate criterion for income transfers may rest upon who demands the most. The *order* in which compensation payments and transfers are made results in a system in which the greedy decide the income distribution. Income redistribution may be determined, for example, by thirty persons demanding $1 billion each as bribes for the otherwise "desired" income distribution. This initial step in income redistribution would not be acceptable to the electorate in an advanced industrial society if a reasonable, representative voting mechanism is used.[4] Because the majority would not view the redistribution of a residual amount as a social optimum, the economist ends up imposing a valuation that society finds undesirable. Even the strict P–O criterion is a *societal* optimum only if individuals value efficiency above all other criteria.

Thurow leaves unexamined the problem of identifying preferences. Yet realistic models of the income redistribution process must consider the methods by which preferences are represented. The empirical usefulness of the SWF approach has thus far been limited by our inability to find appropriate weights for the utility of each individual. Switching to the voluntary exchange approach does not make our task easier. As the number of individuals included in the Thurow model increases, so do the free riders. Each person's vested interest in disguising his true preferences is enhanced by

4. This does not preclude the possibility that this model might explain the process of income redistribution in certain LDC's where bribery is an acceptable part of the value system.

bribery. As Samuelson suggests, once the problem is thrown out of the "market place and into the legislature, it pays no one to behave according to the voluntary-exchange theory. So they will not."[5] The difficult problem of determining a set of societal preferences gives way to the difficult problem of revealed preferences. Both types of models thus far are nonoperational paradigms.

Alternative Approaches

A social problem requires a political solution. But Thurow attempts to have it both ways: he wants a purely Paretian solution, in the sense that no one is made "worse off," but this may require that the minority cast more votes than the majority in the realization of such an optimum. Thurow's model does not go far enough in providing a meaningful vehicle for preference representation. Models involving group behavior — including economic-interest groups, policy-action groups, and representative government interests — provide a more realistic approach to this research problem. It is not individuals but individuals in economic, social, and other types of groups (including policy-action groups) who decide national policies.[6] To the extent that the market system and effective voluntary exchanges do not give individuals the income distribution that they desire, further redistribution will be determined by political power.

Florida State University

5. Samuelson, "Pure Theory," p. 115. See also R. A. Musgrave, "Provision for Social Goods." in the same volume.

6. For a fuller discussion of this point, see E. Ray Canterbery, "Income Distribution, Human Property and Non-Property Rights," in E. H. Pollack, ed., *Human Rights* (Buffalo, N.Y.: Jay Stewart Publications, Inc., 1971), pp. 373–95.

Chapter 6

Editor‘s Note on:

Justice, Nozick, and Rawls: A Symposium

edited by *E. Ray Canterbery* and *Harry G. Johnson*

In May 1977 Harry Johnson, President of the Eastern Economic Association, passed on. The symposium contained in this issue was conceived and developed by Harry, and Ray Canterbery. Ray undertook most of the task of coordinating the contributions after Harry's untimely passing, and besides putting together the introduction and his own comments, edited Harry's contribution as well. Such a symposium, along a path of inquiry that Harry was just beginning to pursue, may be the best testament to the creativity and vigor of his thought and, it is hoped, a fitting tribute to his memory.

Chapter 7
Introduction

E. RAY CANTERBERY and HARRY G. JOHNSON*

The purposes of these introductory comments are to provide (1) a brief overview of Robert Nozick's principles of justice as they contrast with those postulated by philosopher John Rawls in *A Theory of Justice* and (2) a summary of the articles in this symposium. This introduction is the stage and the articles constitute the performance.

Nozick and Rawls ask the same question. What is a just society? Is it one that achieves the greatest possible degree of equality among its members, or one that pays the greatest possible respect to the rights of the individual? Or, for that matter, are the two types of society inseparable?

Rawls and the egalitarians appear to have had the advantage because of attempts to redress racial and economic inequalities during recent decades. Now, however, philosopher Robert Nozick argues that any state that pursues egalitarian goals as an *end state* condition is inherently unjust. This unjustness is not related in any way to the nobility of intent.

Nozick's book attacks government's redistributive efforts and, at its core, is perhaps the most tightly-argued defense of *laissez faire* since Adam Smith. At the same time it is providing a theoretical framework for the expanding libertarian movement.

I. Contending Philosophers: Nozick vs. Rawls

Nozick's book is the main philosophical counterpoint to the widely acclaimed 1971 volume by John Rawls. Both of these philosophers contend that classical utilitarianism does not provide a proper framework for basic rights. Nozick favors a social contract derived within the bounds of the laws of nature. Within such bounds, individuals should be free to order their actions and to dispose of their possessions as they see fit. He calls this "capitalism between consenting adults."

The laws of nature (following John Locke) state that no person ought to harm another in his life, health, liberty, or possessions. Certain "inconveniences" in the state of nature plus the advantages of division of labor and differentiation of services lead to the origination of private protective firms. Contending claims among clients give rise to a dominant protective association that has a territorial monopoly. This version of an *ultraminimal state* fails to provide protection and enforcement services to everyone in its territory. Therefore, Nozick recommends for the state an extension of its protective responsibilities to *everyone* within its boundaries. It nonetheless is a *minimal* or "nightwatchman state" limited in functions to protecting all its citizens against violence, theft, and fraud, and providing for the enforcement of contracts.

Friedmanesque protection vouchers are financed from tax revenues. All persons are given tax-funded vouchers which in turn can only be used for the purchase of protection from the state. In this concept of the state Nozick walks a fine line between the rejection of anarchy and a state which would have substantial redistributive functions. Moreover, he attempts to justify such a minimal state without recourse to the device of a unanimous contract.

Nozick's distrust of the state is stronger even than Adam Smith's. Nozick argues that

*Florida State University and University of Chicago.

"individuals have rights, and there are things no person or group may do to them (without violating their rights). So strong and far-reaching are these rights that they raise the question of what, if anything, the state and its officials may do" (p. ix).

At first glance it appears that some economic redistribution does occur in the minimal state. Because taxes are collected, *potential* protectees pay for the protection of others whose rights actually are violated. Such a form of redistribution might provide the pattern for other and more extensive redistributions in a more-than minimal state.

Nozick proceeds to argue, however, that "the minimal state is the most extensive state that can be justified. Any state more extensive violates people's rights" (p. 149).

Nozick's theory of economic distribution is an "entitlement theory." This theory states that a person is entitled to any holdings so long as their acquisition does not violate any individual's natural rights.

In a just world, the following definitions cover the subject of justice in holdings. (1) A person who acquires a holding in accordance with the principle of justice in acquisition is entitled to that holding. (2) A person who acquires a holding in accordance with the principle of justice in transfer from someone else entitled to that holding is entitled to the holding. (3) No one is entitled to a holding except by (repeated) application of (1) and (2). Nozick's "complete principle of distributive justice" states simply that a distribution is just if everyone is entitled to the holdings he possesses under the distribution. If any of the three of the original principles is violated, his principle of rectification comes into play as a fourth principle.

It is difficult, perhaps impossible, to avoid comparing Nozick's principles with those of John Rawls. Indeed it is clear that Nozick's main philosophical target is Rawls and 20th century democratic egalitarianism.

The Rawlsian principles of justice are chosen behind a "veil of ignorance" in "the original position" under a unanimity vote. No one can know his place in the ongoing society, and, therefore, people adopt a maximin rule for decisions in order to avoid risks. At this "constitutional convention", the people first adopt a basic liberty principle similar to Nozick's, except *individual* ownership of material resources for production is not required. The people choose a second principle requiring that sócial and economic inequalities meet two conditions: they must (a) be to the greatest expected benefit of the "worst off" members of society (the maximin equity criterion) and (b) be attached to offices and positions open to all under conditions of fair equality of opportunity.

Rawls claims a lexicographical ordering of principles with the basic liberty principle ranked first. Lexicographical (or lexical) ordering means that no quantity of a lower-ranked principle can be a substitute or a complement to a higher-ranked principle even though some quantity of all principles is desired. A Rawlsian social contract would therefore—given basic liberties—include the principle that those who have been favored by nature with talent, wealth, or other social advantages may gain in their good fortune only on terms that improve the situation of those who have otherwise lost out.

This appears to conflict directly with Nozick's entitlement theory of justice. Everyone, to Nozick, is entitled to his initial natural endowments and whatever returns they yield. Thereafter the justice of distribution depends solely upon acquisitions and transfers that do not violate the laws of nature.

Rawls views the distribution of natural assets as "morally arbitrary" and considers the distribution of natural ability as a "collective asset", much as European peasants once viewed the Commons. Everyone then has some entitlement or claim on the totality of natural assets. The "ideal Rawlsian society" is one that encourages co-operation within a setting in which the natural endowments of individuals and the natural endowments of resources are the society's common property. The "better off" in society make transfers to the "worst off" in order to gain and maintain their cooperation.

For arrangements in the on-going society, Nozick sides with Adam Smith in favoring free capitalistic exchange. He contends "I believe that the free operation of a market system will not actually run afoul of the Lockean proviso" (p. 182). He goes beyond most orthodox economists and argues that the prices of free exchange can be judged as "fair."

This contrasts with the on-going Rawlsian cooperative society in which the fairness of rewards based upon marginal products is brought into question. Economic inequalities in excess of those required for an efficient economy are assumed by Rawls to emerge under a system of free capitalistic exchange. Free exchange also cannot rectify inequalities that are derived from random endowments. Thus Rawls *openly advocates* the development of redistributive institutions within a democratic state.

In closing this introduction to Nozick and Rawls it is fitting that we return to Nozick's parallel with Adam Smith. Nozick expresses a methodological reason for preferring his system of liberty: it is an "invisible hand" theory of government. Here Nozick, literally and figuratively, joins hands with Smith.

Adam Smith's invisible hand explanation of the operations of the free private enterprise system is neatly summarized in his famous statement: "[Every individual] intends only his own gain, and he is in this, as in so many other cases, led by an invisible hand to promote an end which was not part of his intention." Smith saw unconstrained individual selfishness ending in a social harmony in which consumers reaped the benefits from the lowest possible prices. No one intended this outcome; it just "happened."

Nozick expresses the invisible hand notion somewhat more precisely. An invisible hand explanation shows how some overall pattern or design, which one would have *thought* had to be produced by an individual's or group's plan, instead was produced and maintained by a process that had no intrinsic pattern or design in mind.

The process is independent of the outcome. For this reason Nozick prefers such explanations. *Fundamental* explanations, says Nozick, do not use any notions of the process itself, and the less we use notions constituting what is to be explained, the more we understand. The invisible hand explanation suits this criterion because the outcomes are not the consequence of persons' desires or beliefs.

The opposite explanation would be one of "hidden hands". For example, in a conspiracy, what *looks like* an unintentional outcome is actually the product of a group's *intentional* design. Nozick offers a number of examples of invisible hand explanations in addition to his theory of government. Not surprisingly, among them is the neoclassical price theory that traces its roots to Adam Smith.

It would be misleading to suggest that Nozick is only concerned with the operation of the economy. He marshalls a reasoned plea for the protection of individual rights from several different perspectives. He no doubt will hit a responsive chord among both libertarians and democratic egalitarians when he contends that more laws and state regulations establish still more avenues for government coercion of citizens.

Nozick asks us to examine again the justification for state coercion and reassess the limits that apply to the state. Even for those who do not wish to put the limit of the state at the minimal threshold, the encounter with Nozick will cause them to think more clearly than ever about the proper limits of state coercion. Thus, even when the contributors to the present symposium disagree sharply with him, they have clearly been challenged by Robert Nozick's *Anarchy, State, and Utopia.*

II. The Articles: An Editors' Summary

The contributions presented herein have one conclusion in common: Nozick and Rawls have not provided theories of justice or else have given us incomplete principles of justice. Israel M. Kirzner sees Nozick's entitlement theory as incomplete. Jan Tumlir denies that immutable principles of justice ever exist. Vincent J. Tarascio views Nozick's and Rawls' theories as well-reasoned summaries of respectively, nineteenth century liberalism and contemporary American liberalism. Finally, Abba P. Lerner contends that principles of "justice" are derived from preferences, not from moral premises. But, we will see the authors go well beyond this theme.

It is the thesis of Israel M. Kirzner ("Entrepreneurship, Entitlement, and Economic Justice"), that Nozick's theory of entitlement does not—without significant reformulation—solve all the difficulties that may be alleged to exist in respect to the justice of the market. If the market depends upon the exploitation of profit opportunities made possible by the errors of others, and such profits are considered unjustly acquired, the justice of the market has been greatly compromised.

Kirzner argues that the only logical defense for the general morality of market transactions must be that the errors which characterize disequilibrium markets do not affect the voluntariness of the transactions completed. The profits won then would still fall under the rubric of Nozick's yardstick of discretionary justice in transfer. The particular insight into disequilibrium market transactions required to retain the market's morality is the "finders, keepers" ethic. The introduction of an ethic concerning entrepreneurial discovery and finders, keepers, according to Kirzner, justifies the free operation of the market system with fewer qualifications than those of Nozick.

Jan Tumlir ("The Unintended Society? Some Notes on Nozick") dramatizes the difference between invisible hand and patterned outcomes by asking a fundamental question: In what way is a society able or "free" to control and deliberately steer its own development, and to what extent, by what methods? How much is governed by the invisible hand, and how much is or can be governed by deliberate and effective use of various design devices?

Tumlir considers this the central question of the social sciences. It is also a political question. To Tumlir, Nozick's minimal state offers society a high degree of control over its future in the sense of allowing the individual citizen to plan his or her future. The much-more-than minimal state, through the very expansion of its specific commitments causes its policies to be increasingly unstable, and reduces *everybody's* control over the future, including that of the government and of the individuals composing the society.

State policy outcomes therefore are also invisible-hand outcomes. This is so because we do not know enough to use the patterning mechanism in a way that would guarantee planned outcomes.

The claim for justice in (greater) equality of results logically presupposes a belief in the possibility of social engineering. Thus, even if we accept Rawls' principles of justice, an inadequacy of knowledge causes social engineering failures. Planning efforts crash on the shoals of ignorance. Such failures have little to do with justice. Contrary to Nozick (and Rawls), Tumlir views the rules of law as all the justice that society presently agrees to and these laws are mutable.

Vincent J. Tarascio ("Theories of Social Justice, Social Action, and the State") develops a theoretical framework based upon his own extension of Paretian utility theory in order to assess Nozick and Rawls under the same umbrella. He considers both works to be, to some degree, an extension and modification of the principles of classical utilitarian philosophy, still the dominant theory in moral and political philosophy. The direct relevance of the theories to economics is displayed in Tarascio's article.

The moral foundations of classical political economy were essentially utilitarian in nature and modern economic science contains vestiges of utilitarian philosophy. Tarascio suggests that one of the basic differences between Rawls and Nozick is the extent to which "shared values" dominate over individual heterogeneity. Whereas Rawls sees individual and social (and economic) heterogeneity as a basis for possible injustice (resulting from inequality), Nozick sees in such heterogeneity the *only basis* for justice.

In the works of Nozick and Rawls the justification of the existence of the state remains tied to moral issues. From his general framework, however, Tarascio concludes that the *heterogeneity of individuals* is the basis for the state. He also concludes that the contention between both works concerning government's redistributional role is ex-ante and ex-post redistributional vs. ex-ante and ex-post compensatory. Each implies differences in degrees of government interference and individual and social action.

Abba P. Lerner ("Utilitarian Marginalism (Nozick, Rawls, Justice, and Welfare)") examines Nozick's entitlement theory of distribution and Rawls' difference principle of distribution within the economist's traditional utilitarian concept of distribution. Lerner suggests that Nozick and Rawls fail to understand the attributes of marginal products in deciding an efficient income distribution.

Lerner goes on to show how the free market exchange conditions can be met while a "social dividend" is redistributed among the population. In this way he builds the case for a maximax, a simultaneous allocative and distributional efficiencies optimum. Where the maximax is unattainable, Lerner restates his rule for income transfers from higher to lower income receivers.

This optimum, derived from the contemporary utilitarian principle, is based on the assumption that the marginal utility of income is diminishing. Lerner concludes that the three approaches—Nozick's, Rawls', and the modified utilitarian view—are three configurations of preferences with each claiming to exhibit higher levels of societal satisfaction. None of the three approaches can be considered a construction of social justice.

Lerner objects to Nozick's theory of entitlement because it states that *whatever* income distribution exists is the correct one. He objects to Rawls' conception because it is derived from a state (the "original position") which can never exist. Lerner favors his own axiom for the redistribution of income because it provides an explicit definition of what it is that satisfies.

Finally, the concluding comments of the co-editors ("Further Reflections on Economic Justice") address issues in detail that are either ignored by the symposium authors or else touched upon lightly.

Chapter 8
Further Reflections on Economic Justice

E. RAY CANTERBERY* and HARRY G. JOHNSON

The purpose of these comments primarily is to address issues in detail that are either ignored by the symposium authors or else touched upon lightly. Such comments are not, however, unrelated to these articles and indeed frequently reference them.

E. Ray Canterbery takes up Tumlir's implication that first principles of justice are suspect, as well as Lerner's contention that social justice is a function of preferences. Canterbery sees the advantages in multiple criteria for the ideal or "good society" compared to a unidimensional criterion derived from the simplicity of natural law principles. The origins of Nozick's natural law view are examined and the moral claims for natural law are challenged. Alternative hypotheses are advanced for the nature of Nature, including those of Hegel and Marx. The public goods issue is raised within the context of Nozick's and Rawls' systems.

Harry G. Johnson presents the economist's arguments for the determination of personal income distribution, as well as the basis for the inevitability of poverty and the demands upon public policy that inequality commands. He sees the basis for redistribution toward egalitarism in the cultural nature of poverty. The yields on natural endowments are decided by social institutions as well as individual choices about transactions under uncertainty. Therefore, Johnson rejects Nozick's view that the morality of the income distribution can be judged only in terms of the "initial conditions."

Professor Canterbery takes the role of a philosopher's devil's advocate as well as presenting the public finance perspective. Professor Johnson, as usual, is the economist's economist as he explains analytically the distribution of personal income and its relation to Nozick's system.

CANTERBERY

I. The Non-Simple Matter of Criteria for "Economic Justice"

Questions concerning economic justice are not simple. We cannot expect the answers to be any more so. A feature of mankind for per-

*I thank Robert Nozick and John Rawls for writing books so stimulating that they inspired this symposium and also for discussing with me some of their more recondite ideas. I express appreciation to Jeffrey Burkhardt, Edgar Fresen, William Laird, and Irvin Sobel for reading and commenting on an earlier draft. I am indebted to Abba P. Lerner and Alan Mabe for some profound discourse on the general topic. I am grateful also to Harry Johnson for giving me—what regrettably was my last—opportunity to collaborate with this intellectual giant. I nonetheless bear full responsibility for any errors.

Harry and I had not completed our comments for this symposium prior to his death. We had discussed in detail the choice of authors, the introductory statement, and the motivation for any concluding comments. In the absence of a draft of his concluding statements, I completed his contribution in the following way. First, I drew heavily from various sections of Chapters 17 and 18 of his *The Theory of Income Distribution*, London: Gray-Mills Publishing Ltd., 1973. Second, I considered his views on inequality as I understood them. Third, I organized these ideas around the symposium's theme. If I have made any errors of interpretation, I am quite certain that Harry will find a way to inform me in unmistakable terms, in a manner that even wounded egos learn to appreciate.

haps the last 100 thousand years, and no doubt the last 10 thousand years, is a preference for living together. Cooperation and community life must have advantages or it would not have had such a long history. Despite the instinct for community, conflict appears an inescapable element within the contemporary community. To the extent that we seek community, such conflict seems part of being human.

If conflict is human, so is the desire to end it —to have harmony. In human communities the resolution of conflict has always depended on certain criteria, only one of which is fairness in economic transfers. The unidimensional commutative criterion of Robert Nozick and equality criterion of John Rawls must be viewed with caution, because the settlement of differences and the move toward harmony depend upon multiple criteria.[1]

Personal and collective security probably was the first criterion of society, of a primitive society. Such a society is the starting point for Robert Nozick. In Nozick, conflict leads ultimately to the minimal state. The only, and therefore the highest task of the state, is to protect individuals from harm to their lives, health, liberty, or possessions. The initial purpose is security. In this system individuals do what they do out of their "rational self-interest," a behavioral assumption preserved by John Rawls in his "original position."

In a practical political sense the notion of a second criterion, basic individual liberties, originates in the 17th century with John Locke. Nozick and Locke appear to be primarily concerned with individual liberty *and* the security of property and person. One is tempted to say that exclusive concern with the criterion of security begins to diminish with a "civilized" state. For example, Nozick's hypothetical scenario of the development of the minimal state also serves as a plausible *real* history of the emergence of the nation-states.[2] Once the nation-state is secure within its own political boundaries, its citizens' demands for individual liberties become more persuasive. However, this is an oversimplification. Modern technology has given us the neutron bomb with which most of a people's possessions will survive while human populations are eradicated. This tool for fine-tuning security meets one of the Lockean provisos but violates all the rest. Surely this is not what Locke had in mind.

Of all criteria, widespread concern with economic equality probably has had the shortest history. Historical evolution has given us criteria roughly in the following order: security first; individual liberties next; and equality last.

However, we cannot construe this to mean that at every historical point the greatest utility is derived from security and therefore a community's concern should always be placed on that criterion above others. It is more plausible to argue that without *some degree* of security, there can be no individual liberties, and without some civil liberties, persons cannot be concerned with economic inequalities. The marginal utilities from each criterion diminish with levels of achievement. The realization of each criterion diminishes its importance because the citizen accepts these fulfillments as constants or the fulfillment of expectations in their lives.

So far we have suggested that there are three basic criteria by which individuals can be guided within a community setting. However, community life is not this simple. There are multiple criteria for the multiple criteria.

Historically we associate security with safe communities and protected nations, but an inadequate food supply to an individual or community provides direct endangerment to life.

[1] The references are, of course, to Robert Nozick, *Anarchy, State and Utopia* (New York: Basic Books, 1974) and John Rawls, *A Theory of Justice* (Cambridge, Mass.: Harvard, 1971).

[2] A description and analysis of this real history is included in E. Ray Canterbery, *The Making of Economics* (Belmont, Calif.: Wadsworth, 1976), pp. 6–22, 39–66.

It is a short step from the criterion of subsistence food supply (or subsistence income) to income security and still another short step to national security.

Today about two-thirds of mankind is living on less than thirty cents a day. If this condition continues or accelerates the other third of the world's population will not be secure. The provision of minimal incomes directly and indirectly affects human survival, and makes it a life security issue. Wherever income security is culturally determined, as it is in a technologically advanced society with a very small agricultural population, where do we draw the line for income security?[3]

If individuals have basic liberties, what are they free to do, with what, to whom? Nozick tells us that people should be free to do anything they want so long as the natural rights of others are not violated, but what constitutes "harm to others"?

An industrial plant emitting toxic fumes and effluents in the world's common property atmosphere and biosphere is engaged in free exchange. People voluntarily use aerosol spray products that are destroying the (world's) common property ozone layer. In an exercise of liberty an individual can purchase defective automobiles that are unsafe to others. (In the U.S. we know that this happens because automobiles are recalled by the manufacturer itself for modification.) The unconstrained use of fossil fuels as the energy base for a free exchange system may alter the world climate until New York, Miami, New Orleans, Los Angeles, and other cities around the world are beneath the oceans. Are people free to use up all essential national resources? The freedom to do certain things can be harmful, even death-inducing, but it appears to be a matter of opinion as to which liberties are fatal. Moreover, mortalities will be at different levels and rates during different historical epochs, depending in part upon the state of technology. Yet Nozick ignores compensation for pollution and other third-party damages except those affecting private property.[4]

It seems implausible to me that these three basic criteria—security, liberty, and equality—can be lexicographically ordered once and for all. Once the society is ordered for personal protection and judicial arbitration, Nozick appears to rank basic liberties as Number One. Yet his system does not provide for even a minimal—if he will excuse the term—national defense.

If a nation is conquered by an external oppressor, whence liberty? Although Rawls begins in the "original position" with a lexical ordering (basic liberties first), he quickly descends into the quagmire of trade-offs between liberty and equality as he discusses the ongoing Rawlsian cooperative society. As Nozick suggests, Rawls' demands also are not symmetrical; the rich are coerced by the necessity of gaining the cooperation of the poor, but the poor are not required to reciprocate.

This lack of symmetry results because Rawls sees the survival threat from the riot potential of the starving masses or from the withholding of their labor. The restraint of the poor (who are given alms) is the benefit received by the non-poor. If so, "charity" begins at personal and economic security. Under varient conditions social goals will be ranked and weighted differently, which suggests that the "true criteria" are not defined with sufficient precision when we say "security, liberty, and equality."

The complexities do not end with the interdependence of the basic criteria. Economic justice is a sub-category of social justice, the standard or standards used to evaluate the way in which social institutions distribute to individuals the benefits and burdens of their *shared*

[3] As Johnson suggests in his comments, the definition of the "socially decent" income line rises as average income per capita increases.

[4] Nozick, *op. cit.*, pp. 79–84.

social state. The criteria for "economic justice" include commutative, desert, merit, equality, need, and expectations.[5] Nozick wishes us to add entitlement.

Perhaps these criteria can be better understood with an example. Suppose you hire two men, Roy and Charles, in exchange for roofing your house in their spare time. You promise to pay $400 for their labor with $200 going to Roy and $200 to Charles. Roy is older and more experienced (presently skilled) than Charles but Charles is currently otherwise unemployed.

After the job has been completed, you note that Roy worked 25 percent more hours than Charles even though Charles is unemployed. Should you pay Roy more and Charles less than originally promised (contracted)? If so, how much more and less?

If you use the *commutative* contract criteria, you pay $200 to each. If you believe that Roy *deserves* more because he worked more hours, you would pay him $250 and Charles, $150. If you believe—in retrospect—that Roy *merits* more because of his longer preparation and superior skills, you might pay him $300 and Charles, $100. If you use the *equality* criterion, you would pay each $200. If you pay according to *need*, you might pay Charles $300 and Roy, $100. If Charles claims that he and his dependents are near starvation, you may widen this differential. If you pay according to *expectations*, each receives what he originally anticipated, $200.

The payment extremes run from a $300-$100 split in favor of Roy (merit) to a $300-$100 split in favor of Charles (need). If all criteria were given equal weight, Roy would receive $210 and Charles, $190.

However, additional issues might have a bearing upon your decision. Charles contends that, while Roy worked longer and is more skilled Roy would not have been able to contract for the job if Charles had not been willing to help (that is, the labor unit is defined as two-persons). Because of the jointness of production, the marginal product of each person's labor is undefined.

Entitlement as desert clearly is not a distinct criterion. It is not even clear whether commutative entitlement derives from the original contract or from job performance. As indicated above, if the contract is invoked as the basis for desert, $200 goes to each worker. On a pure exchange basis, however, if the two are assumed of equal skill (though they are not), Roy deserves $250 and Charles, $150, because Roy worked more hours. Even without considering capital and natural resource entitlements, the jointness of current production creates a confusion about whether Roy's marginal product *should* be valued as $250 because, without Charles, Roy produces a real exchange value of zero dollars. If neither has a marginal product in the absence of the other, in what sense are products marginal?

What is the Rawlsian solution to the two-person, one labor unit production function case? Rawls would argue that Charles should receive an equal payment (as long as this does not cause Roy to cease work effort) because, irrespective of initial endowments of abilities, production is joint in a cooperative society and Charles is disadvantaged.

What is the solution in the "good society"? It all depends. It depends upon: (1) the criterion selected; (2) the weights given to each criterion; and (3) the feasibility of making awards according to the weighted criteria. These will all vary over historical time and space.

Among these criteria, only the first is relatively easy to define. Commutative justice is "justice" which results from contract or free exchange. Its simplicity, however, is deceptive. Although *what* is commutative is clear, whether the results of free exchange are "just" is not so

[5] This list is taken from H. Scott Gordon, "Ideas of Economic Justice," *Daedalus* (Summer, 1963), pp. 433–446.

obvious. The presumption by Nozick is that the voluntary nature of such exchange meets his basic liberty criterion and therefore causes free exchange outcomes to be just.

Unfortunately these multiple criteria of "economic justice" also are not mutually exclusive. Moreover, at certain levels of satisfying, other criteria and orderings of criteria lurk behind these *apparent* criteria, suggesting that the latter are not fundamental criteria. Despite this complexity Nozick has reduced the number of criteria in our list from six to one by combining commutative, desert, and merit into commutative entitlement and by ignoring need, equality, and expectations.

Because prior criteria lurk behind the apparent "economic justice" criteria, we have a technical problem similar to that posed by the fundamental criteria. The measure that satisfies an "economic justice" criterion at one level will not necessarily satisfy it at another. That is, some levels of satisfying Criterion A may be lexical with respect to Criterion B (at A's present level of satisfying) while still other levels of satisfying Critérion A may be *substitutible* are *complementary* for B's level.

One measure of satisfying need is a subsistence income. Subsistence needs are ranked above other criteria because survival (security) is fundamental to further earthly satisfactions. This is because life is preferred to death. If any lexical ordering is permanent, it is this one.

The self-sufficient English manor in feudal society had two basic aims: producing enough to sustain the manor, and providing a surplus that could be used for defense (security). Above subsistence, material need may be traded off for the liberty to exchange. Agricultural surpluses appear to have been a precondition for the development of a free exchange system.[6]

All this is to say that there may be a hierarchy of criteria which are hierarchical only in a historical *ex post* sense. This is because the upper reaches may not even be visible until individuals have moved several steps up the need ladder. What, therefore, are the criteria for the need criterion?

There is a similar problem with *desert*. Nozick suggests that one is entitled to receive payment in proportion to one's *exchange* of productive services. Desert is commutative. Within the context of the social institution of free market exchange one therefore deserves the income that he receives as yields from one's natural endowments. Why is this a criterion for justice?

Nozick's assumption is either that Nature is just in its distribution of endowments or else that the justice of Nature is irrelevant. If the former, the institution of free exchange retains a just distribution because of the voluntariness of its participants. If the latter, natural endowments are "given" and the justice begins (and ends) with free market institutions because of the voluntary nature of transactions. If Nature is just only *by assumption* (certainly the justice of Nature is not a provable hypothesis), Nozick has a circular argument. Nature is "just" and voluntary exchange keeps a "just distribution" intact. (Most neoclassical economists today are not willing to *explicitly* embrace free exchange as a system of justice even though they might otherwise appear comfortable with the implied ethic.) If this is what Nozick means, commutative is not a criterion for justice after all and he has no theory of economic justice.

If Nozick assumes that the distribution of endowments is irrelevant to the issue of justice, then he is giving priority to the voluntary nature of free exchange and he has lexicographically ordered liberty *in the acquisition and transfer of possessions* above other criteria. The endorsement of voluntary exchange itself as a principle of justice is to say that *whatever* income and wealth distributions exist under such exchange are the just ones. However, this is not a theory of economic justice either. Payments

[6]For further elaboration, see Canterbery, *op. cit.*, pp. 8-16, 41-46, 61-69.

to those who produce a market value in exchange for income is still commutative, but it is liberty to contract and exchange, not entitlement as a first principle of justice, that is served.

This fails to answer the question of whether there are other socially just reasons (criteria) for which non-*quid-pro-quo* income payments should be made. Need may be one of those criteria for certain income ranges, but not for others. The commutative criterion therefore appears to be an instrumental variable (or system) and not a fundamental criterion of justice.

Need, equality, merit and expectations appear to be criteria in Rawls system. Rawls would like to see an efficient economy with no absolute poverty and a minimum of inequality. Rawls considers a society with great inequalities as an unjust society because he views the distribution of the sources of inequalities—natural endowments—as random and, therefore, having no moral basis. The merit criterion is met only in so far as it is required to obtain necessary services from able individuals and to maintain efficiency.

This argument illustrates the 20th century Western shift in measures and in criteria. Minimum life-sustaining need at low levels of production is probably a fundamental criterion behind egalitarianism. Then when moderate needs are generally met, egalitarianism ceases to be a criterion or else has to be based upon non-basic material need criteria.[7] If some levels of satisfaction of the criteria for economic equality cause them to be lexical, not only are such criteria multiple, the criteria themselves change with the conditions and values of society.

If Nature provided sufficient abundance relative to people's wants, and the society enjoyed moral solidarity, multiple criteria for the "good society" would not emerge and indeed harmony would exist. The classes and levels of wants are derived from the relative selfishness or generosity of people. With sufficient abundance, rapacious egoism would disappear (except as an occasional aberrant condition). With sufficient income, scarcity would be irrelevant.

In the presence of scarcity the issue of social justice emerges whenever each person does not, or cannot, treat other persons as the other persons wish to be treated. This conflict does not end with the establishment of a free exchange system and a minimal state: it requires resolution by social ideals, mores, and rules.

I prefer to think of the multiple criteria as defining the contemporary view of the utopian or "good society," a view (and criteria set) that changes—one would hope, progresses with an increased number of criteria—as production constraints are removed. The "good society" is not simple. A theory of economic justice, especially one that is not a theory of justice, does not help. Except for procedural justice, which is really the rule set for fairness, there is no justice in this world, only relative preferences for criteria of distribution of benefits and costs. To slightly modify Tumlir's view, the rules of law are all the *fairness* that society presently agrees to.

The scarcity-selfishness nexus and the exploitation it engenders is related to Professor Kirzner's extension of Nozick's system. Nozick agrees with Locke that the original acquisition, especially of limited, life-giving resources must leave enough in common for others. Nozick argues that the operation of a free market exchange system will not (in practice) run afoul of this Lockean proviso.

The concept of relative scarcity nonetheless tells us that we can deplete and pollute out of existence *natural* resources. We mentioned above examples where voluntary exchange depletes and pollutes common property. To avoid exhaustion may require us to decrease wants below expectations, or else to conserve collectively. (Technological change is an uncertain and mixed insurance against these requirements.) These natural resources are demanded

[7] Again, see Johnson's discussion of the cultural definition of poverty.

for meeting the essential needs for human nutrition, shelter, and transportation.

Indeed, some would question whether *any* goods and services are outside the category of limited, life-giving. In a cultural sense, and to different degrees, *all* goods and services involve life-giving or life-denying properties. The automobile may be life-enhancing at 55 miles an hour but life-denying at 85 miles an hour.

II. The Origins of Natural Law and Its Moral Claims

The unidimensional criterion for justice is suspect. This raises the question of why such simple formulas have been postulated as principles of justice, even by philosophers. This predilection appears to derive from the Western definition of rational man as one who makes consistent choices in his self-interest, where self-interest is legitimitized by an alleged first principle, the "invisible hand." This idea of rationality is derived from natural law. A first principle is difficult to find in the best of scientific circumstances but one that is invisible is especially elusive. For Nozick, nonetheless, rational self-interest generates an "invisible hand" theory of politics and economics.

Present-day fascination with natural law goes back at least to Isaac Newton (1642-1727). The Newtonian system put in concrete form the idea that all phenomena, all experience, consisted of the arrangement of atoms following mechanical, mathematically regular laws. In his theory of gravitation, Newton had found a cosmic law subject to precise mathematical proof and as applicable (he thought) to the smallest object as to the entire universe.

The idea that natural effects are caused by mechanical motions had occurred to scientists before Newton. As early as 1605 Kepler wrote to a friend:

> I am now engaged in investigating physical causes; my goal is to show that the celestial machine is not the likeness of the divine being, but a likeness of a clock (he who believes that the clock is animate ascribes the glory of the maker to a thing made). In this machine nearly all the variety of movements flows from one very simple magnetic force just as in a clock all the motions flow from a simple weight.[8]

This passage is closely related to the paradigm that Newton developed. It has two significant implications for philosophy: first, God is an artisan or craftsman who constructed an immensely complicated but reliable piece of machinery called "the universe"; second, after God created the universe and the rules by which it operated smoothly, He then more or less retired and left the machine to run "on its own."

This does not mean, however, that the universe was immoral or valueless, for with Newtonian science a God emerged who was derivable from natural law and in harmony with the order of the universe He made. God, like His universe, was rational and dependable. This optimistic conception of reliability—intensified by the conviction that the Creator was kind and charitable—produced a profound sense of relief. For example, the American clergyman Cotton Mather (1663–1728) could argue: "Gravity leads us to God and brings us very near to Him." To understand the forces of gravity was to better comprehend God's wondrous ways.

Newton's great scientific synthesis was a source of inspiration for much of the liberal philosophy and theology of later centuries. Although one now had difficulty believing that the world had been constructed with only humans in mind, one could at least believe that the mechanics of the universe were so perfect that nothing could go wrong. Because cause and effect were so certain and clear in physics and astronomy, many scholars assumed that history, human behavior, and economics would all be governed by natural laws. If laws are divinely predetermined, scholars reasoned, people should discover what these laws are so

[8]C. Frisch, ed., *Johannes Kepler Opera,* Vol. 2 (Frankfurt/Main: Heyder and Zimmer, 1859), pp. 83–84.

that they can cooperate with the "pre-established" natural order that controls them.

John Locke's (1632–1704) task was to "discover" natural laws in the political universe. This concept of order also was the basis of the political philosophy of the French physiocrats who preceded the English classical economists. We are reminded that the physiocrats were named for physiocracy, the law of natural order. The ideas of these philosophers—taken from the natural sciences—were representative of those spreading through the literate classes in France and England by the middle of the 18th century. The physiocrats' motto, *laissez faire, laissez passer*, neatly summarizes the shared view of the physiocrats and Adam Smith (1723-1790) that the natural advantages of free market competition should not be spoiled by government interference.

Smith believed that once the economy had been set in motion by the "invisible hand" of God, there was no need for any improvements. Repairmen would only upset the mechanism and disturb its ability to function in an orderly way. In his founding of classical economics, Smith was no doubt driven by a desire to emulate the most widely respected scientific system of his time, and thus the impact of Newton on social science and society continues to this day.

People exhibit "rationality" in this metaphorical transfer so long as they respect natural political laws, remain self-interested in economic exchanges, and make consistent choices in terms of these guides. The consequences for each scientific system are the same: harmony and order in the physical and in the social world. Let natural law do this, the people will assuredly be trusted to do what is left undone, which is virtually nothing. As to third-party damages, "rationality" is never having to say that you are sorry.

When the invisible hand is further invoked as theory, it is at the other end of the arm of natural law. Beginning with the distrust of tyranny in 1776 and continuing today, invisible hand explanations have enjoyed considerable popularity. It is a theory buoyed by the optimistic belief that Nature is automatic and structured to reward persons according to their merit. However, there are some obvious objections to the reliability of invisible hand explanations.

First, one can not distinguish invisible hands from hidden hands because they are equally unseen. Are oil prices decided by free market forces of competing interests or by a round-table of conspirators? Either way the outcome is to see and experience a "market price" for oil. Richard Nixon initially stated that the Watergate break-in was *unintended*, the unplanned actions of zealots fulfilling a higher cause. Now we know: the "invisible hands" wore gloves.

This brings us to a second criticism. Invisible hand explanations invariably serve the *status quo*. If outcomes are inexplicable, so much the better for those whose interests are currently served.

"Who me? . . . Raise the price of automobiles?" rhetorically asks the head of General Motors. "The invisible hand of the market once again served the public's interest." If you don't like the price of Chevrolets, blame the invisible hand! But, then, no one wishes to cast the first stone at God.

There is a third weakness. The inability to explain an outcome by describing the process that led to it can also be attributed to something else—ignorance! If we do not *understand* the process, say, whereby prices and distributions are decided, how do we *know* whether it is spontaneous or planned, perhaps by conspiracy? To wave aside all competing explanations with our (visible) hands is a repudiation of modern science.

The Western definition of rationality therefore is striking for its simplicity and also for its view of the individual as a mammal with remarkably limited reasoning capacity. The range for choice is narrow and decisions are made independent of people's own contemporary perception of criteria for the "good society."

Nozick and, in the "original position," Rawls, subscribe to this view of rationality. To Nozick, Nature provides endowments which are either automatically fair or morally irrelevant. (Which, we cannot discern.) In Rawls, the rational man chooses a "fair" principle because of an ignorance that is nearly total. In neither case are higher reasoning faculties brought into play. It is natural law that leads Robert Nozick, to a unidimensional commutative concept of justice. Even though the trains of justice leave the same station, Rawls—given basic liberties—arrives at a unidimensional criterion of equality.

Nozick and Rawls are in search of a prior principle. This raises the question of what the appropriate prior principle is. For Nozick's principles to be derived from a moral premise, we must assume that Nature is just. Then for people to be moral they must obey the laws of Nature. Abba Lerner and I are not convinced that Nature knows what it is doing.

With the help of Newton and Locke, Nature in part displaced God. The Romantic philosophical movements of the 19th century displaced contractarian theory. Only in economic theory did contract theory remain in use and it remains there today. Nozick's system of liberty therefore can be viewed as a 20th century back-to-Nature movement and a bolster for the moral claims of neoclassical economics. This moral claim still seems to emanate from a particular view of God, as one who constructed the rules we call natural laws.

Most of today's neoclassical economists stress the positive scientific elements of general equilibrium and generally leave the moralizing to philosophers and "radical economists." If now the economists and Robert Nozick interlock invisible hands, the theory of general equilibrium conditions might enjoy apparent moral certification.

I do not believe that this will happen. As Kirzner suggests, there are many competing ethical principles. Kirzner does not demand that we adopt his. To be persuasive to economists as a moralist, Nozick must tell us more about the nature of Nature. Is God as formulator of natural rules a verifiable hypothesis? If so, why are there so many views of God—those of Calvin, Luther, Lao Tse, Mary Baker Eddy, Mohammed, Zaroaster, and so on?

The notion that Locke "discovered" natural laws is fantasy. Natural laws (as defined) were a product of Locke's mind. It seems a paradox that intelligent people endorse such rules because they mistakenly presume that they are not derived from intelligence. People only have the capacity to discern the order in Nature, whereas Nature exhibits the greater faculty of understanding what is best for people. However, a natural law cannot claim moral superiority to man-made law if natural law itself is man-made!

If philosophers accept Nozick's commutative principle of justice, ethics becomes economics. This spectre is not as frightening (to economists) as the reverse. If economists accept Nozick's "entitlement theory" as moral, positive economics will become ethics. This is not to say that the schools of economic thought have no ethical bases. As long as such ethical bases are diverse, however, economics will enjoy the liveliness of competing philosophies and systems of thought.

As Kuhn has persuasively argued, even in the natural sciences the choice of premises greatly influences the type of science that we practice.[9] Einstein dispensed altogether with Newton's "law" of gravity. The implication of quantum theories combined with relativity is that Nature itself is only probable and not "definite." The content of philosophy and economics is highly

[9]See Thomas S. Kuhn, *The Structure of Scientific Revolutions*, 2nd ed. enl. (Chicago: University of Chicago Press, 1970). The nature of revolutions in economic science is explored in Canterbery, *op. cit.*

sensitive to the choice of scientific metaphor.[10] However, not all social scientists have selected the same metaphor.

All this is not to say that it is easy to separate God and Man or whether it is possible or even desirable. Perhaps we can do no better than the following exchange from Joseph Heller's *Catch-22*:

"What the hell are you getting so upset about? I thought you didn't believe in God."

"I don't," she sobbed . . . "But the God I don't believe in is a good God, a just God, a merciful God. He's not the mean and stupid God you make Him out to be."

III. Hegel, Marx and Alternative Hypotheses

There are alternative views of Nature, views which allow natural laws to change or be overcome through history. G.W.F. Hegel (1770-1831) saw the course of history as the gradual realization by human beings of their own nature, which is identical with Mind, Spirit, or God, terms that Hegel used interchangeably. Spirit is a self-generated creative energy whose ultimate goal is to become fully conscious of itself in its role as Spirit. Matter and Mind are not ultimately separable and all things, all earthly events, are the result of the growth of the Spirit toward the ideal. We can follow the course of this growth to some extent by using Hegel's *dialectic*: feudalism (thesis) encountered a new force, the market economy (antithesis) and the result of this encounter was an entirely new system, capitalism (synthesis). Properly understood, history is a dialectical progression of the self-realization of the Spirit, the goal of which is perfect freedom.

[10]In the Newtonian metaphor individuals' actions are inferred from the behavior of inanimate objects. In the latest craze, sociobiology, the understanding of human behavior is assumed derivative of the social activities of living ants, an improvement of sorts. At the risk of seeming radical, I suggest that considerable insight into human behavior might be gleaned from studying humans.

However, humanity's progress toward self-realization is not smooth, as the defenders of the natural order presume. The Spirit can become alienated from itself. Alienation occurs when the Spirit confronts a world that appears real (i.e., aligned with the Spirit) but is in fact of human origin. A person is alienated when he or she becomes hostile toward a former attachment to an object, a behavior, or an idea for reasons that do not emanate from a higher spiritual source but from human imperfection. Alienation is resolved when the Spirit recognizes the object of the hostility for what it is—human error—and unites itself once again with itself. (An obvious difficulty with Hegel is that he tends to be abstract, but so is the notion of the "invisible hand.") The God view accepted by Newton is easily reconciled with the world of free exchange capitalism. But for Hegel, because humanity itself is Spirit or God *in the process of self-realization*, contentment with capitalism is illusory, and alienation is the eventual result. For Hegel, humanity is the manifestation in history of the self-alienated God.

In a sense, Karl Marx (1818-1883) turned Hegel inside out. (In this respect Marx was following Feuerbach's transformational criticism of Hegel.) Instead of seeing Man (used here to mean all people) as self-alienated God, Marx saw organized religion ("God") as a reflection of self-alienated Man. The human species creates God in its own image through organized religion. Thus, Man projects an idealized image of himself as "God" and worships this imaginary spirit. As soon as Man discovers the error of artificial image-worship, Marx believes that Man becomes estranged from himself and his own ungodly earthly creation becomes hateful to him.

Man overcomes alienation by taking God back into himself and recognizing that *human individuals* are the proper objects of love, care, and worship. Religion is a phenomenon of human self-estrangement. Whereas Hegel saw history as a series of detours on the road to the self-realization of God in Man, Marx, although he also had a progressive idea of history, saw God as yet another roadblock.

The basis of Marx's world view is broadly humanistic, affirming the worth and dignity of Man and Man's capacity for self-realization through reason. There is little evidence that Marx himself had any great affection for the masses of people that his system is supposed to free. He was dedicated to Man's thinking powers, and his own reasoning told him (as did Hegel's) that the forces of history and self-realization were inescapable.

Marx is an evolutionary determinist: the course of history is predetermined, not by "God" but by the evolutions of entire social systems from lower (slavish) to higher (democratic and socialistic) forms. Institutions such as organized religion slow the progress from lower to higher social orders, and the historical process could be speeded up by destroying them. Marx believed he was putting Man and his "true" rationality back at the center of the universe. Man did not have to subordinate himself to immutable natural laws.

Marx saw in the relationship of human beings to their government a process of alienation similar to the one he perceived in religion. Just as humans extend the idealized attributes of the species to a supreme deity, so they project social power into a separate sphere—the state. And the state dominates them. Political alienation, however, is an institutional reality and its resolution requires an actual social revolution—that is, a collective act in which the citizens repossess the social power that they gave to the state.[11]

The state is intertwined with and at times indistinguishable from the economic life of society, which is yet another sphere of human self-alienation. Here we can clearly see the influence of Hegel: the Spirit, or God, did not create a materialistic world; the production of material goods was an entirely human undertaking and hence alienating. Marx believed that the workers and the owners of the means of production would be prevented from developing their full human potential because of their slavish devotion to producing more and more goods for the marketplace. Eventually the "animal spirits" that drove men to the accumulation of profit would be exposed as simply a lower stage in human intellectual development.

Because of the intensity of alienation, of obscured self-realization, that the capitalist stage of economic development caused, Marx preferred feudalism to capitalism as a form of economic organization; its social relations were paternalistic and personal and work was not solely a means for making and accumulating money. Under pure feudalism labor was used only to produce consumer goods that were more or less consumed at the site of production rather than sold in exchange for money. To Marx, when the middle-income group or bourgeoisie "got the upper hand," it left no other access between persons than naked self-interest, and egotistical calculation resolved personal worth into exchange value.

Free exchange capitalism was an extension of Man's self-interest that he would grow to dislike, a stage of history's progress that was alien to Man and not the culmination of civilization. When Man's final "scientific" state is achieved, it will be what it *should* be, and, moreover, objectively determined. That is, Man's self-realization that *what is* (capitalism) is unendurable *should* and *will* alter the historical process. At the same time, the technology of capitalism makes it materially possible for alienated labor to escape. Abundance leaves Man free, free of the drive to accumulate property. The process of the self-development of the human species will, according to Marx, culminate in communism.

Thus, because they are concerned both with

[11]Marx has a theory of revolution because conflict remains in the ongoing society. In Nozick revolution is unnecessary because order and harmony are presumed present after the formation of the minimal state.

"what is" and "what should be," Marx's arguments provide a valuable description of the interconnection between positive and normative economics. When Man arrives at a true perception of reality, he will at the same time experience the economic system that is best for him. This view, of course, is contrary to Nozick's conclusions, in which the commutative criterion is first, last, and always.

Still another description of the nature of Nature can be formulated, one that has implications also divergent from those that view natural laws as immutable. This formulation will use Hegel's method but avoid the functional role of alienation. This view also is conceivable. Suppose that Nature is a Universal Mind which is not ultimately distinguishable from the individual "minds" of persons. The Universal Mind (Nature) can be viewed as an indescribably complex computer with each person's mind being a computer terminal. Different people have varying abilities to gain access to the knowledge of the Universal Mind.

A mentalist, for example, has greater accessability than the average person. People's progress can be defined as incremental gains in accessability to all knowledge, that is, to the Universal Mind. All things are known when every person's mind knows itself as the Universal Mind or becomes one with Nature.

Locke's "discovery" of natural laws (beneficial as it was in the defense for constitutional government against monarchy) and its widespread understanding and acceptance is viewed as only one step toward ultimate self-knowledge. Rawl's "discovery" of the principle of minimizing inequalities, the collective judgment of democratic egalitarianism, can be viewed as a recent incremental step.

The implications for social rules are quite different from the Lockean view of natural law. The greater the number of people in a society that gain Universal Knowledge, the greater the agreement (or the greater is Tarascio's homogeneity of persons) to higher order social rules. The rules become increasingly collective (in agreement) as they approach the total knowledge of the Universal Mind. (This does not preclude influential persons from advancing competing ideas about what is true.)

When everything is known, the knower is the Universal Mind and the need for individual differences and the cause of conflict disappears. This view is consistent with multiple and variable criteria for the "good society." Ultimate knowledge would include many criteria related to each other in intricate ways. The liberty for intellectual thought experimentation would be the most important freedom in gaining Universal Knowledge and awareness. Freedom of thought cannot in itself harm anyone.

The foregoing view of Nature is also speculative and metaphysical (not verifiable), characteristics equally shared with Locke's, Smith's and Nozick's view of natural laws as first principles. This departure is consistent with the idea of progress evolving from historical experience and learning from having done. Most importantly, these alternative views of Nature have practical consequences for social theory and practice. In the Lockean-Smithian system, order and harmony are the natural conditions. "Rational" people conclude that the less they do to control outcomes, the better. In Hegel, Marx, and my speculations, conflict and disorder are the natural conditions prior to the "ideal" state. Conflict does not end at the edge of the minimal state. In Nozick, whatever *is*, is right. In Hegel and Marx, whatever is, is *wrong*.

Moreover, the existence of alternative views of Nature raises still more doubts about the one interpretation of Nozick's parable of initial endowments as a morality play. The competing pictures of Nature have equal moral claims even where—as in Feuerbach—the distinction between Man and God is hopelessly blurred. The proposition that God is created in Man's image is far more demonstrable (and has had far more social impact) than the reverse. Nature also has no meaning except that placed upon it by individuals and social institutions.

IV. Public Goods and Friedmanesque Vouchers

One of the advantages that Nozick claims for the free exchange system is that outcomes are unintended (invisible hand). However, he is quite selective in describing what these unintended outcomes are. For the voluntary nature of his system to remain intact goods, services, and factors must be exclusive; that is, everyone but the buyer of the good must be excluded from the satisfactions or dissatisfactions it provides. No one must receive pleasure or harm from interdependence of utility and production functions. This feature of exclusiveness no doubt explains why the only public good in Nozick's system is police protection and the judicial system. It also explains why his theory does not cover national defense.

In cases of negative externalities (as mentioned above) as well as positive externalities, exclusivity is violated even in private consumption and production. It nonetheless is more common to find nonexcludability with public goods. Indeed, public goods often are defined thusly.[12] If one of the nation's citizens receives protection from foreign invasion, all do. A more mundane example is city street lighting. Once the lights are in place and turned on, it is very difficult to imagine how it would be either possible or worthwhile to exclude certain nonpaying individuals from the lighting benefits. If a good is a public good, it probably will not be produced privately and sold in the free exchange system. Still, according to economic theory (and common sense), it would be in society's interest to have it provided.

The financing of public goods normally requires a redistribution of income and benefits. Obviously, Nozick goes to great lengths to avoid the establishment of a state which would have such redistributive functions. However, it is difficult to conceptualize a system of redressing economic grievances through a principle of rectification that does not require redistribution. In fact, as with protection, compensatory payments require a revenue source.

To further complicate matters the violation of a natural law of acquisition or transfer may have occurred in a different historical period from the recognition of the violation. The classic example is the violation of the human economic rights of the American black population. "Affirmative action" is the contemporary principle of rectification in this case. The first violations extend back in time to the capture of the African Black on the African continent. The tracing of the "roots" of this violation and its history (as Nozick defines history, the record of individual transactions and transfers) is incredibly complex.

Imagine the difficulties of writing the history of acquisition and transfers of all income and properties for every living person back to Adam and Eve. If justice is decided by these principles, no person is being treated justly until all incremental violations have been rectified in some sense. This raises the still more complex question about the division of inheritances of incremental retribution payments otherwise owed to dead ancestors.

In these problem areas, there are at least five reasons why the public finance specialists will prefer Rawls to Nozick. (1) Rawls *begins* with

[12] Nonexcludability cannot be the *only* reason for public goods because some private goods exhibit this feature and some presentday "public goods" do not. This is often the consequence of the difficulty in identifying subdemands in joint consumption and subcost curves in joint production. For a discussion of these problems and of some of the other ambiguities in the standard definitions of the public good as well as other justifications for public expenditures, see Alan Abouchar, *Transportation Economics and Public Policy: With Urban Extensions* (New York: John Wiley and Sons, 1977), pp. 3-18.

a principle of redistribution. (2) Nozick *ends* with a principle of rectification that opens the door for redistribution without defining principles or procedures to be followed. (3) Nozick's system of liberty depends upon exclusiveness that rules out most public goods except the one Nozick himself selects. (4) Rawls' discussion of public finance in the ongoing society presupposes that people have learned from the experience of the 18th, 19th and 20th centuries. (5) Rawls' system allows the economist to postulate a type of social welfare function for income and wealth redistribution. In Nozick's utopian system, in which people are otherwise free to imagine whatever they want, they presumably cannot imagine an effective and fair nonminimal government.

Despite the principle of rectification, Nozick apparently wishes to avoid a unilateral transfer of income or wealth from one individual to another except in instances of voluntary private charity. From what we have learned in public finance this appears to be an unreasonable constraint on the satisfaction of individuals' preferences within a community.

As Lerner and Johnson suggest, people may prefer more equality than that generated by a free exchange system. A society may be comprised of a large number of people who are charitable or who for other reasons (including gaining cooperation) wish to eliminate absolute poverty in the society. (The Rawlsian society allows for this.) They have sympathy for others or else their version of the "good society" has no impoverished members.

There are at least two cases in which individual charity is not effective. (1) Sympathy may extend only to relatives or to persons whom the potential giver knows. There may be a large population which has no relations or friends or at least none with sufficient resources or charitability to end their poverty. This condition is most likely to be found in a highly mobile society such as the United States or under the type of free immigration advocated by Nozick in his utopian framework. (2) Some poverty problems and other social problems requiring transfers may be so extensive that individual charity is not sufficient. This raises the question of whether tax coercion is justifiable.

Where preferences in a democratic society can only be fulfilled by public income transfers, public finance specialists recommend that all be taxed. If everyone is not taxed, there are free riders who would potentially or actually derive benefits without making payments. This—even by Locke's provisos—would be unfair.

Individuals have preferences to do certain things so long as they know that others of their type share more or less equally in the effort. There would be a greater probability that the individual's expenditures will be effective and a lesser probability that others will not receive the free ride. This is the message of the free rider argument. Voluntariness still is present, but it is at the constitutional level when persons agree to be taxed.[13]

There is a way around Nozick's objection to income transfers within his own system. As with the financing of protection and the judiciary, a Friedmanesque voucher system could be used to reduce poverty. Taxpayers would receive a second voucher, this one to be used only to reduce poverty. If one has as much faith in the free market system as Nozick, one could believe that private poverty reduction agencies would materialize. Such agencies would see the profit in reducing poverty, just as the private protection association gains profit from the provision of protection. Private enterprise could use its imagination in designing funding projects to ease the burdens of the poor. If poverty became sufficiently profitable, poverty reduction might become a growth industry.

Some might argue that poverty is the golden

[13]An excellent discussion of the free rider argument *vis-a-vis* Rawls appears in Martin Bronfenbrenner, "Equality and Equity," *The Annals of the American Academy of Political and Social Science* (September, 1973), pp. 9–23.

egg of the agency and the goose is killed by its own success. Such negativists are not true believers. Clever advertising and sound packaging can convince consumers that the poor are always with us. Without the technology of modern media organized religion maintained this self-fulfilling prophecy for centuries.

I would suggest a marketing campaign centered on the theme that poverty is cultural and therefore relative (see Johnson below). Just as automobile producers are careful not to produce a car that lasts forever, the poverty reduction agencies must avoid being so effective that personal incomes become equal.

Would Nozick object to such agencies? The purpose of tax coercion in the minimal state is not redistributive. Therefore Nozick contends that the minimal state is not redistributive. With equal logic the *purpose* of the poverty reduction system would be minimal income security and since no redistributive purpose is expressed, the antipoverty program is not redistributive.

V. Beyond Critique

Thus far I have provided a critique of the natural law view and its relation to neoclassical economics and to public finance. If this appears to be an assault, Nozick's book provides a remarkable defense. Therefore I have not dwelled on the virtues of his work. This is so even though I believe that he has developed the definitive theory which justifies the existence of a state.

Anarchy cannot survive the brilliance of his arguments. At the same time Nozick has not fulfilled his purpose of providing a theory of the *limits* to the state. He claims to show that no state more extensive than the minimal state can be justified, but his principle of rectification opens the door to justifying *any* size state with ad hoc and subjective arguments.

Even if Nozick's book had been published in 1932, at the leading edge of massive government intervention, the New Deal nonetheless would have expanded the tentacles of government. If the Great Depression had failed to mobilize government activity, World War II most assuredly would have. The absence of a theory of national defense would not have reversed the reactions to Pearl Harbor.

I agree when Nozick argues that economic inequalities often lead to inequalities in power. The economically well-off use political power to give themselves differential economic benefits. That certainly appears to fit the U.S. model in many respects. He goes on to contend that the minimal state precludes the multiplicative use of such power, but this gun can be turned either way.

The reduction of economic inequalities can reduce unequal political power and so can a breakage of the institutional linkage between economic and political power. Moreover free market capitalism itself in the presence of decreasing cost industries favors wealth concentration.

Why is the presence of economic inequality an argument in favor of the minimal state? It is more plausible to argue that increased economic equality would reduce demands upon the state and therefore allow the establishment and workability of a minimal state. The minimal state is no guarantee that the power of the wealthy in society will be neutralized. The minimal state may end up with the best judiciary and police system that money can buy, particularly in a system whose highest rewards are through exchange. American history already has traveled this road. Can we trust the system that failed, to extricate us from our present dilemmas?

Still, the questions which Nozick raises are fundamental: "How much room do individual rights leave the state?" His answers are inspirational. "Individuals have rights, and there are things no person or groups can do to them without violating their rights. So strong and far-reaching are these rights that they raise the question of what, if anything, the state and its officials may do."[14]

In this respect I find Nozick's chapter on utopia persuasive and mind-stretching. His utopia consists of utopias—of many different and divergent communities in which people lead different kinds of lives under different institutions. Utopia is a framework for utopias, a place where people are at liberty to join together voluntarily to pursue and attempt to realize their own vision of the "good life" in the ideal community.

He contends that utopia is the equivalent of the minimal state. This, he argues, is because the minimal state treats individuals as inviolate. People cannot be used as means or tools or instruments or resources. People are treated with respect by respecting persons' rights. People choose their lives and realize their ends and their conception of themselves, in so far as they can, aided by the voluntary cooperation of others possessing the same dignity.

Nozick concludes "How *dare* any state or group of individuals do more. Or less."[15] Yes, this is inspirational, but it is also utopian. The minimal state is utopian, however, only if people behave as Nozick wishes them too, independently of existing social institutions. As its literal meaning states, Utopia is Nowhere, and it will remain in a never never land until humans achieve their full potential.

The 17th century concept of the minimal state originated in an environment of political absolutism and economic agrarianism. Progress was seen as deriving from a stationary base, a set of first principles, but the efforts to find first principles of justice are destined to fail. This is not an adverse reflection upon the abilities of philosophers. Little onus should be placed upon the failure to find something that does not exist in the first place. Since the search is futile, it should end.

In this respect philosophy is like neoclassical economics. If general equilibrium can be proven to exist, the world no longer needs economists. If first principles of justice are found, society can also dispense with philosophers. If Nozick is accepted, economics becomes an ethic derived from first principles and members of both specialties will be technologically unemployed and will have to rely upon private charity distributed by presumably, self-seekers, who are unaware of other people's interests.

This is precisely the fundamental objection. The liberty of material objects does not guarantee an ideal society: this is the unsolved philosophical transformation problem of Nozick. He devotes far too much analytics to the defense of private property so that one is led to believe that individuals' dignity depends solely upon the freedom to exchange possessions and accumulate.

I believe that Nozick's system of liberty is better applied to civil liberties than to commutative "justice." Yet neither "civil liberties" nor "freedom of expression through media" appears in his book's index. This is unfortunate, for he is the ideal author of such a work. His system is more persuasive when applied, for example, to "homosexual acts between consenting adults" than to "capitalism between consenting adults."

Commutative justice may give freedom of migration to possessions while impugning the liberties of persons. People have a greater capacity for appreciation than do objects. Indeed, to become an influential force in modern society, the libertarian movement must do more than make the world safe for orange juice.

[14] Nozick, *op. cit.* p. ix.
[15] *Ibid.* p. 334.

Chapter 9

Review:

Welfare Economics: A Liberal Restatement.
By Charles K. Rowley and Alan T. Peacock. New York: John Wiley and Sons,
A Halstead Press Book, 1975. *Pp. viii, 198.*

Economists see Paretian welfare economics as a product of nineteenth-century liberalism. Rowley and Peacock challenge this view and contend that policies derived from Paretian welfare economics may not be liberal solutions. They offer an alternative, a perspective that leads to such "liberal" economic policy suggestions as a negative income tax, antitrust action, and a monetary rule for the growth of the money supply. Rowley and Peacock claim John Stuart Mill and the neo-Austrians (especially Hayek) as their worldly liberal philosophers. The authors' purpose is to persuade fellow economists to end their love affair with Paretian welfare economics and embrace reconstructed liberalism.

The strength of Rowley and Peacock is their transfusion of a rich range of topics, frequently connected to real life, into the usual bloodless abstractions in welfare economics. However, in their attempt to rescue nineteenth-century liberalism they encounter conflicts of the most confusing kind. This is hardly surprising for a liberal view that embraces both of Mill's tracts, *On Liberty* and *The Principles of Political Economy*. Mill advanced moral principles derived from utilitarianism in *Liberty* and then tried to adjust these principles to social facts in *Principles*. Now Rowley and Peacock are confronted with new facts, but their version of reality will not be satisfactory to everyone.

The first three chapters of this book provide a detailed but critical account of present-day Paretian welfare economics. In addition to highlighting the ethical premises of welfare economics, the authors attack this orthodoxy on its own ground, hammering the Paretian armament of mathematics and formal logic into weaponry against itself.

Chapter four summarizes the philosophical challenge to the Paretian hegemony thundering out of the New Left. Rowley and Peacock do not agree with the New Left's value assumptions, its inner logic, nor its factual interpretations. They are otherwise "sympathetic" to the New Left.

The remaining chapters restate the liberal philosophy and offer detailed applications for economic policy.

Paretian welfare economics is a formidable target; it has survived murder at least three times. It was (1) shot down by Arrow's General Possibility Theorem, (2) mortally wounded by Lipsey and Lancaster's general theory of second best, and (3) strangled by the intricate cobweb of compensation criteria. Still, it lives.

Rowley and Peacock correctly conclude that the Arrow-type of social theory cannot account for real-world outcomes because it does not take into account the intensity of preferences. (Moreover, common sense tells us that all nations do not have to be equally undemocratic.) The second-best theorem dramatizes how completely the requirement for the Paretian optimum depends upon general equilibrium, in which there is no such thing as "being a little bit monopolistic." The initial suggestion of the compensation principles that individuals who would benefit from a policy change would get together and pool either money or commodities to "bribe" the harmed individual into "voting" for the policy was recognized as a moral judgment conducive to blackmail, only the most embarrassing of many implications. The "new" welfare economists retreated, their desks drawn in a cricle, and restated their arguments: the compensation principle asks only that the losers *could* be compensated; it does not require that they *should* or *would* be compensated. The final statements became vacuous or else counterfactual. Rowley and Peacock restate all of these principles, providing excellent critiques. It is a persuasive indictment of welfare economics.

Next, liberalism is confronted with the "facts." As defined by Rowley and Peacock, liberalism is concerned with the maintenance and extension of individual freedom in which coercion of some individuals by others is reduced to the minimum possible degree.

Central to the liberal thesis is "rule of law," "equality before the law," and majority rule. Several advantages are claimed for rule by laws, by majority consent. It restricts the effective power of "Leviathan." It reduces administrative discretion in policy implementation. It places overriding authority for the control of market regulation in the hands of the judiciary, "the least corruptible of all the possible control organizations" (p. 161).

Freedom is divisible and encompasses the moral and intellectual and political sphere—the freedoms of *On Liberty*—and the economic sphere, including freedom of work, enterprise and trade, travel and migration, contract, markets, competition and entry, choice in consumption, and choice in occupation.

There can be little disagreement about the desirability of minimal coercion. Such a principle is in league with Motherhood, the Queen, apple pie, crumpets, and Chevrolets. The problem is the authors' failure to identify clearly what constitutes coercion within their own framework of fighting power with power.

Rowley and Peacock's definition of liberalism corresponds to *eighteenth*-century liberalism and this liberalism-becoming-ideology in the nineteenth and early twentieth centuries. The earlier Lockean-Smithian view of liberty tied freedom of the person to the individual's property. Property, in turn, was an inalienable right. No social obligations accompanied rights to ownership. This conception fit well an economy of large numbers of small entrepreneurs. Freedom implied self-contained, autonomous persons.

The industrialized economies have since become far more complex, with a smaller number of corporations, competition largely replaced by administered prices and wages, the government part of big business, advance planning in industrial manufacturing, and corporate ownership increasingly divorced from management. The owner of capital can no longer be described as a swashbuckling innovator. The corporation itself, however, inherited the autonomy without obligation that was once the sole privilege of the individual. This made labor weak so that it had to organize. Consumer complaints led to government regulations—government became responsible for corporations which otherwise had no specified civic duties.

For these esentially economic reasons, liberalism was redefined in the twentieth century. The opportunity for individual growth depended upon equal opportunities. In this way government became involved with individuals' economic chances. Business became less private, more public, so that the economic activities of individuals and corporations were also no longer completely private. It was not so much freedom that was redefined as the conditions under which liberty was otherwise handicapped.

Rowley and Peacock seem torn between proposed twentieth-century policies (negative income tax, effective inheritance tax) to gain the degree of equal opportunity required for freedom and a desire to restore competition (antitrust policies and open shop, i.e., no effective unions) to its rightful eighteenth-century condition. If the latter is achieved, the monetary rule and its implicit Say's Law assumption make some (but not much) sense. One might view this as an attempt to embrace simultaneously eighteenth-, nineteenth- and twentieth-century liberalism. This can be done with impunity with respect to freedom from arbitrary physical abuse. However, freedom in its broader twentieth-century liberal definition is a separate issue.

It is to the immense credit of Rowley and Peacock that they recognize the conflict of liberal principles with industrial and wealth concentration. However, they are to be mildly admonished for recommending policies that cannot be implemented prior to political reform, failing to see the historical connection between law, the corporation, capital accumulation, and political power, and being too timid in addressing the interrelated problems of economic and political inequalities.

Although the Hayek liberal apparently prefers unplanned market to planned economic outcomes,[1] Rowley and Peacock suspect that the prices and quantities of oil, steel, automobiles, tires, computers, soft drinks, and so on are no longer freely determined in the market. They give a knowing nod to John Kenneth Galbraith's view of the planning system, but ignore, at their peril, Galbraith's discourse on the symbiotic nature of corporate and government interests and, therefore, power.[2] Galbraith's description of the modern industrial corporation highlights both the necessity for professed liberals to retain "unplanned outcomes" by selected interventions and the improbability of such a feat in the modern corporate state.

Obviously, numerous conflicts exist among positive freedoms, because the *objectives* of those exercising positive freedom are diverse. The majority in society may rank some of these goals above others. Some level of coercion is often required to prevent a still more coercive outcome. Rowley and Peacock argue that one of the advantages of liberalism is its flexibility in the selection of these coercive trade-offs, and they ask us to believe that they know which is which. However, these advantages end at the water's edge of negative freedoms; that is, their liberalism disintegrates into subjectivism as soon as trade-offs are required. They want unions to counter corporate coercion, but only powerless unions. They want the corporate person to accumulate capital without accumulating power. They want to protect the majority from the "tiny minority," the poor, who might coerce others (how, with what?) with abusive taxation. They like the intuitive appeal of "workers' democracy" but conclude that it must be inefficient "since labour-controlled firms are rarely found in Western economies" (p. 166). We might as well conclude that democracy around the world must be inefficient because of its rarity. Even if we accept Rowley and Peacock's choices, existing power imbalances can preclude counter-coercion.

Stated in more general terms, where are the precise or even rough guides in the making of trade-offs among competing social ends? Moreover, why are coalitions suspect in this choice process? Why are the freedoms of market, competition and entry, and choice (to the extent possible) in consumption and occupation more important means of resolving conflict than the freedoms of contract and coalition? Is it

1. See also Robert Nozick, *Anarchy, the State and Utopia* (New York: Basic Books, 1974). This "invisible hand" theme is replayed by the neolibertarians.

2. See especially his *Economics and the Public Purpose* (Boston: Houghton Mifflin, 1973).

because the magnitude of evil stalemated by market freedoms is greater than that prevented by coalition and contract? What degree and type of coercion is permissible in countering what degree and type of coercion?

This trade-off problem between negative and positive freedoms crystallizes in the chapter on justice, in which the authors take on John Rawls.[3] Although the chapter is interesting, insightful, and provocative, it exposes the authors to all the embarrassing inconsistencies confronted by Rawls.

Rawls—a representative of twentieth-century liberalism—also impales himself on the horns of the power dilemma.[4] Freedom as equal liberty is the same for all, but the worth of liberty is not the same for everyone. Those who have greater authority and wealth have greater means to achieve their aims (positive freedom). Rawls, like Peacock and Rowley, leaves us in doubt about the ability of a modern industrial state to disperse its wealth and therefore its power more evenly. In this respect the main hope for a Rawlsian solution rests in his "vision" which might motivate a society to gain order *and* power balance through mutual interests.

If liberalism is to be extended, it should be from its strength, that is, from its focus on "negative freedoms." The list of negative freedoms can be lengthened by conversion of some of the "positive freedoms" into negatives. This can only be achieved, however, through coalitions. Negative freedom is not just the absence of coercion by other individuals. Other negative freedoms to be valued include the absence of coercion by circumstance, such as genealogy, place of birth, time of birth, events, negative economic externalities, institutional coercion (even when passive) by giant corporations, and deplorable conditions such as absolute poverty in an affluent society.

The benefits from coalitions depend on their objectives and the means used to achieve them. The *means* need not violate moral, intellectual and political freedoms. There is no *a priori* reason why one particular form of coalition is necessarily coercive. This raises the question of why the reconstituted liberals single out the government as *the* evil coalition.

The authors' misuse of "Leviathan" as a synonym for government reflects the deepness of their fear. Yet, the Hobbesian government in which the control of citizens is forever given over to a sole sovereign is *not* the model of government that was adopted by England or the colonial renegade Thomas Jefferson. Government ≡ Leviathan is a literary device that obscures. Indeed, if it is true that man's natural state is brutish, nasty, and hopelessly quarrelsome, what hope does liberalism offer with its emphasis upon laws decided by the majority?

Rowley and Peacock's preoccupation with Leviathan obscures their rallying point and appears to be a highly improbable route to the balanced society. Yet a principle could be wrung from their book: government and other forms of coercion appear to be acceptable if they have the effect of dispersing power. However, the authors do not develop this thesis and fail to discuss power in sufficient detail. The logical end of power balance is most probably achieved by substantial redistribution of income and wealth.

E. Ray Canterbery
Florida State University

3. *A Theory of Justice* (Cambridge, Mass.: Harvard University Press, 1971). For further explication of Rawlsian principles, see the articles in E. Ray Canterbery and Harry G. Johnson (eds.), "Symposium on Justice, Nozick and Rawls," *Eastern Economic Journal*, January 1978.

4. Hayek also develops at least one principle of justice: administrative laws, those specific rules formulated to direct the actions of government agencies with respect to citizens, should be minimal. Yet, he offers no principle whereby conflicts between liberty and other ethical values

Chapter 10

A Vita Theory of the Personal Income Distribution*

E. RAY CANTERBERY
Florida State University

I. Introduction

The purpose of this paper is to develop a testable theory of the personal income distribution in which the distribution of endowments is endogenous. Human capital theory is modified by integration with labor market theory (hence, the term vita theory) and with the results of the discrimination and migration literature. This approach provides a general framework for otherwise diffuse empirical findings in which personal income differentials are attributed to education, experience, training, dual labor markets, as well as to differences in race, sex, class, and region.[1] Variables over which individuals have personal control and those in which they as members of society have collective control are delineated; thus the relation of endowments to public policy choices also is made clear.

The main thrust of a vita theory can be simply stated. Assume that one labor market exists for each general human capital classification. The individual's quantity of human capital determines *which* labor market the person enters. A person "qualifies" for a particular labor market by the state of his or her vita at that point in time. Determination of vita begins at birth when one's race, sex, religion, national origin, inherent mental and physical capacity, inheritances, and family background are duly noted.

The vita is "added to" over one's lifespan by education, other training,

*The author has greatly benefitted from comments on various drafts of the ideas in this paper by Kenneth Boulding, Martin Bronfenbrenner, Thomas Espenshade, Chris Hunter, the late Harry G. Johnson, William Laird, A. L. Rhodes, Joan Robinson, Lester Thurow, the members of a seminar at Ohio State University, and an especially astute referee. The author also thanks Camille Nichols for editing advice. These parties are not otherwise implicated in the results.

1. Such studies include [4; 6; 7; 16; 18; 20; 22; 24; 26; 27; 28; 30; 33; 34; 35; 36; 38; 44; 46]. The comprehensive survey by Sahota [32] calls for an eclectic theory that includes all such variables. This article is my response to this need.

and experience. The individual has some control over the "length" and "depth" of his or her vita. Since labor demand is related to product prices and a changing technology, however, only the rare individual can predict with any accuracy the derived demand for workers with vitae of his or her type. Moreover, specific labor supply conditions are a collective consequence outside personal control. Then, *given* one's vita and the characteristics of the applicable labor market, as a first approximation, the individual's basic wage rate depends upon the wage of central tendency for such labor services. Upon further approximation, however, the individual's personal income exhibits differentials from potential labor market earnings. The differentials—occupational, geographic, inter-industry, union-nonunion, discriminatory, and so on—often can be traced back to the first vita stage, which we will call the *birth vita*.

Empirical studies that find geographical, industrial, occupational, racial, and sexual wage and earnings differentials abound. Such studies, by their very design, do not explain all such differentials simultaneously. The eclectic nature of the vita theory offers a more complete explanation, and its complexity does not preclude empirical verification. Path analysis, a statistical model uncommon to most economists, is suggested. Parameter estimates from a prior study lend empirical support to the vita theory. Path analysis is recommended because of the importance of identifying both direct and indirect impacts of the numerous variables deciding personal incomes.

II. Vitae, Human Capital, and the Labor Market

The Vitae

The vitae of full life-cycle endowments and acquired capabilities of individuals can be viewed in terms of three stages: (1) the birth vita; (2) the pre-career vita; and (3) the career or mature vita. The purpose of delineating the three stages in human capital development is to highlight those variables and times in which the individual often loses control over important choices.

The Birth Vita. Assume that G and E are indices that take on larger values when they are more favorable for augmenting human capital (earnings capability) at birth. The *birth vita* is:

$$k = B(G, E); \qquad \kappa \equiv I_0, \tag{1}$$

where the initial nonhuman endowment (I_0) is equal to the total nonhuman capital available (κ). Nonhuman capital includes the stock of owned or controlled financial assets and physical capital from which returns are received. The birthright human capital endowment is decided by genetics (G) and family environment conducive to earnings potential (E). The genetic code decides innate IQ, sex, race, and initial state of health. (For simplicity, assume health to be independent of lifetime earnings.) Individuals have no control over their birth vitae.

The Pre-career Vita and Education. Human capital in the pre-career stage can be incrementally increased by hours of education within the sole control of the individual (s_1), hours of mandatory formal schooling provided by the State (s_2), hours of initial on-the-job training within sole control of private industry (s_3).[2]

Parental contributions through living allowances, tuition payments, books, training devices, and so on are taken into account by including parental schooling subsidies as a part of the nonhuman capital endowment from the birth vita. Thus, the initial nonhuman capital endowment (I_0) includes these education subsidies plus all other material inheritances. This initial endowment of material capital can be augmented by savings derived from further human capital development. Now we can write the *pre-career vita* as:

$$k = P(G, s_1, s_2, s_3, E) \tag{2}$$

and

$$\kappa = C\left[I_0, P(G, s_1, s_2, E\right], \tag{3}$$

where all partials of k and κ have positive signs.

Only education and training under the control of the individual (s_1) compose an individual choice variable. For this reason, s_1 dominates the traditional human capital theory. In reality, however, individuals have only moderate control over their pre-career vitae because the level of voluntary schooling and training is related both to the hours allocated to human capital development and to inherited material endowments. Since increases in h_1 may subtract from working hours, a positive I_0 can be a replacement source for foregone income. With this in mind, substitute h_1 for s_1 as an independent variable determining k and κ in equations (2) and (3). Therefore, I_0 can be a direct source of "unearned" income and for financing increases in h_1.

The empirical evidence supplied by Becker and others suggests that the rate of return on education is roughly comparable to the rate of return on nonhuman capital. The initial material endowment, therefore, can be viewed as a perfect substitute in adding to income directly or indirectly (through increases in human capital).

The Mature Vita and Human Capital Building. We can now rewrite (2), and, by substitution, (3) for the *mature vita*.

2. These same variables receive a detailed treatment in Johnson [25, 205–06]. Also see Thurow [40, 47–67].

The expression "education within the sole control of the individual" needs qualification. Empirical human capital studies suggest that the dominant share of formal schooling beyond secondary is financed by parents (see especially Schultz [33, 57]). While considerable choice is involved, the pre-career person of high- or middle-income parents will most likely be subsidized by his or her parents through living allowances, tuition payments, books, training devices, and other fees.

$$k = F(G, h_1, s_2, s_3, E, \tau), \tag{4}$$

and

$$\kappa = H\left[I_0, F(G, h_1, s_2, s_3, E, \tau)\right], \tag{5}$$

so that net additions to total capital can be derived from increases in the hours devoted to human capital accumulation. A new variable, years of experience (τ), enters the mature vita. We will return to these functional relations in Section IV.

The Vitae, Noncompeting Labor Markets and the Labor Supply

General Human Capital and Spatial Distinctions. The labor force, the supply side of the labor market, consists of those persons who are of working age, wish to work, and have either *pre-career* or *mature vitae*. These vitae (V's) identify the persons' human capital types, classifications that are decided simultaneously at any time (t_0) by individual characteristics and training (as defined above) and by the labor markets and occupations currently available in the economy.

Initially assume a one-to-one correspondence between general human capital classifications and labor market types. There are many homogeneous and, thus, noncompeting national labor types where, for example, HC_1 denotes Human Capital Type 1 (the greatest quantity of human capital). For n human capital types, however, each is potentially available in any particular geographically defined area. One distinguishing characteristic, therefore, of each market for a particular labor type is its spatial location, a characteristic shared potentially by members of n types. For example, there may be unskilled labor markets in two selected metropolitan areas that may otherwise be differentiated only by their spatial separation.

Thus, a homogeneous noncompeting labor market is defined as one bounded geographically and one in which the elasticity of substitution in production between the labor of its type and the other types within the area approaches zero.[3] The geographic limits are set by "reasonable" commuting distances (at current state of transportation technology) from the selected labor population center.

The short run is defined as a period of labor immobility among homogeneous labor markets. Substitution even of "like" labor types across spatial boundaries is precluded. Thus, *under*employment cannot be shifted *among* noncompeting markets in the short run.

The long run is a period sufficient for persons to accept employment in a lower-yielding homogeneous market within or outside of the geographical area, move spatially to a labor market with "like" but higher-paid HC types, or increase their human capital and in this way "qualify" for a higher-return

3. The concept of noncompeting groups is not new. It is discussed by Taussig [37, 134–38]. Martin Bronfenbrenner has indicated to me that one of his teachers, Frank Knight, was always reminding his class members of the "manyfold typology" of labor. Also, the idea of "technical limitationality" discussed by Finkel and Tarascio [15, 111–13] leads to noncompeting groups.

labor market. As we will see, these potential movements are listed in their relative order of economic ease. However, the personal and social stigma to "downgrading" oneself to a lower-paying labor market often delays labor adjustments.

All labor markets can be represented by a partitioned row vector,

$$HC' = [HCI_1 HCI_2 \ldots HCI_n | HCII_1 HCII_2 \ldots HCII_n | \ldots HCD_1 HCD_2 \ldots HCD_n], \quad (6)$$

in which n general human capital types are matched with n labor markets in D geographic areas for a total of $n \cdot D$ labor markets. For example, a person in good physical condition and with an undistinguished scholastic record in geographic area D may be in the HCD_n market.

There is, of course, more than one person who has a *pre-career* or *mature* vita suitable for each labor market. In general, the number of vitae directly applicable to a labor market decreases with increases in the skills, special aptitudes, and credentials requirements of the market. For example, the number of persons who can qualify as unskilled labor greatly exceeds the number who can qualify as medical doctors.

For each labor market we can write a column vector of vitae whose elements equal that vitae population. Assume that the largest number is s in the Dth area, representing the workforce population for the lowest-skilled market, the nth, in the most populated geographical area. The nth vitae vector for *all* geographic areas is:

$$V_n = \{VI_{1n} VI_{2n} \ldots VI_{\gamma n} | VII_{1n} VII_{2n} \ldots VII_{rn} | \ldots VD_{1n} VD_{2n} \ldots VD_{sn}\}. \quad (7)$$

The nth HC-type labor supply is γ in quantity in area I, r in II, and s in D, with an s by n matrix of labor force population in area D. There are numerous zero elements available to be filled by new entrants. Expressing the complicated notation for the implied national supermatrix of vitae is unnecessary for this paper's purposes. The labor supply in each noncompeting labor market is equal to the number of available vitae that match requirements for that market.

The vitae are in rank order (e.g., 1, 2, . . . γ) from most to least preferred employee characteristics. These orderings can be thought of as Thurow's labor queue [36], but at either a local or national level.

There is no assurance that all vitae will be employed at any particular time. The employment levels depend upon the demand factors discussed below. It is presumed that wherever involuntary unemployment exists it will involve the persons of lowest-ranked vitae. This would include young persons with pre-career vitae who lack job training or are being newly considered for on-the-job training.

Population growth is the main source of the total labor supply. Changes in labor force participation rates also will affect many if not all labor markets. In the interest of simplicity, we will abstract from those factors that alter the overall labor force size and its participation rate. Suffice it to say that most new entrants will appear at the end of the vitae rankings.

Specific Human Capital. Even in the short run there may be varying elasticities of substitution of labor *within* given labor markets. Human capital can be defined more precisely, say in years of experience performing a particular task, so that *occupations* can be associated with a *specific HC* identification. In general, the elasticity of substitution will be greater among occupations that are within unskilled labor markets, with the lowest elasticity of substitution within the most specialized. At the higher-skilled extremity, in fact, the professional occupation *is* also the labor market for the defined geographical area.[4]

Two extreme occupational descriptions—that for handling and that for surgery—can be used as comparative examples of specific human capital (see Appendix A). The "handler's" task can vary from frog farm laborer to morgue man. Both the handler and the surgeon need physical stamina and perform tasks with their hands. However, the earnings of the highest-paid handler are only a fraction of the earnings of the highest-paid surgeon in the United States. The handler's lower earnings are in part related to the high elasticity of substitution among handlers' tasks as well as among handlers and other unskilled workers. The *Dictionary of Occupational Titles* [41] lists several pages of occupations under "handling," but only three occupations under "surgery," with each of the three being a unique specialty and each having its own labor market.[5]

Return to the labor market row vector (HC') and for each homogeneous labor market we can write alternatively a *column* vector of occupations, also in rank order. The lowest-skilled labor market will have the largest number of occupational elements and specialized professions, one. If the lowest-skilled market contains m occupations, this column vector is:

$$HCO_n = \{HCOI_{1n} HCOI_{2n} \ldots HCOI_{mn} | HCOII_{1n} HCOII_{2n} \ldots HCOII_{mn} | \ldots HCOD_{1n} HCOD_{2n} \ldots HCOD_{mn}\}. \tag{8}$$

For each of I through D geographic areas there is an m by n matrix (HCO) of specific human capital with a large number of zero elements. These elements are available to be filled by new occupations generated by technological

4. Although my definition of homogeneous labor markets includes human capital quantities of a "general" type, in the occupations of greater specialization the quality (exact nature of training and skills) of human capital causes a qualitative distinction to be attached to what otherwise would be only a quantity. We might say that mechanical engineers and lawyers have about the same quantity of human capital, but the nature of demand for such specialized labor services plus the distinctly unique skills and training of each labor type generate qualitative differences. The labor market for engineers is therefore distinct from that for lawyers defined in general *or* specific human capital terms. Irrespective of qualitative considerations, there is a "threshold" quantity of human capital required for each labor market.

5. We will refer back to these comparative examples from time to time.

and social change. The occupational matrix (*HCO*) could be defined as a submatrix of its labor force population. A larger matrix would have as its elements the vitae populations associated with each occupation.[6]

Wherever the *HCO* matrix is not identical with the broader labor market (*HC*) there is some latitude for shifts in employment *within* the *HCO* matrix in the short run. During periods of reductions in output and employment, the persons of low-ranked vitae may move down the occupational ladder unless prohibited by occupational entry barriers, creating underemployment. Likewise, during a time of production and employment expansion *upward* occupational mobility in the *HCO* matrix can happen. By our definition of noncompetitive labor markets, however, mobility among the *general* labor markets (*HC*'s) can occur only in the long run. The real-world nature and implications of mobility are explored below.

Labor Institutions and Market Duality

Labor market entry conditions include union shops and licenses. *Occupational* entry conditions include licenses, apprenticeship regulations, and seniority practices. There also may be other types of entry barriers.

Craft Unions and Licensing. A particular *HC* type in any given geographical area can be further identified as unionized, licensed, or non-controlled. Craft unions and professional licensing requirements have the same effect: they limit the supplies of labor of their types. In turn, craft unions and professional licensing affect wage rates by controlling the supply of labor. Some union members (such as bartenders) may also be licensed.

The elements representing the craft-union workers and those representing licensed professionals of the labor market vector (*HC'*) would reappear as the same elements in the occupational matrix (*HCO*) because their skills are sufficiently specialized so that the occupational pool is identical with the labor market. This division between "general" labor and specialized labor provides an exact definition of the dual labor market.

The craft-union and licensing requirements reduce the population of the affected vitae vector. For example, the vector for the surgeons' vitae would have more elements in the absence of licensing. Finkel and Tarascio [15, 72–77, 122–126], following Georgescu-Roegen, call these "limitational factors."

Industrial Unions. The balance of the occupational matrix (*HCO*) consists of labor that is nonorganized or organized into industrial unions. The industrial union organizes an entire industry. Therefore, a (rather complex) partitioning of the *HC* and occupational matrices would be required to capture the

6. Again, supermatrix notation is a complication avoided in this paper.

industrial-union population, for it comprises different human capital types and occupations, including both unskilled and semiskilled workers.

The main economic effect of the industrial union is negotiation of a wage-rate floor for its members. However, the industrial union attempts to gain some of the advantages of the craft union through apprenticeship regulations, seniority practices, and (in some cases) discrimination. The main impact of these regulations and practices is to alter the mobility conditions for the union member as he or she attempts to change occupations within the unionized plant. These are the supply conditions in the labor markets.

The Demand for Labor

The vita theory points toward a structural view of labor demand. Employment and wages are not always determined by the same forces, although the deciding elements are more highly correlated in the long run. In describing such a process we lose the determinism of the neoclassical labor market but gain some realism.

Just as there is a dichotomy between the professional's and the industrial union's labor supplies, the analysis of the professional's labor demand cannot proceed along the same lines. The demand schedule for the professional's services *is also* the demand for labor time. With this caveat we can proceed to generalize.

In the short run the state of technology, industrial competition and product prices (ρ's) are given. Let σ_i be the labor hours required of the ith human capital type (HC_i) per unit of physical output in a selected geographical area. Assume that employment is a fixed proportion of production. The quantity of labor demanded is

$$Z_i = \sigma_i q_j , \tag{9}$$

where q_j is the total output of product j, which is assumed to be homogeneous across the labor market.

If labor is paid its value in production, the wage rate is

$$w_i = \sigma_i^{-1} \rho , \tag{10}$$

where ρ is the price of the product or service produced by this labor type. (In Knightian terms ρ would be the expected price.) Generally, no person alone can influence this price. Again, the exception is the professional whose remuneration is linked to services demanded rather than to productivity and who may operate under near-monopoly conditions.

Technology and Demand. Technological progress can alter directly the demand for a particular labor type by changing labor-quantity requirements. That is, while capital and labor tend to be complements (fixed factor coefficients) in the short run, they potentially are substitutes in the long run. The magnitude of the *direct* effect of technological progress upon the demand for labor depends upon whether the new technology is labor-using.

In modern capitalism the main purpose of new tools and equipment is to reduce unit labor requirements. Machines are more responsive to managerial commands. Moreover, the long-term trend of wages is known to be upward, especially in the already capital-intensive industrial sector that is unionized.

Technological change can also exert an *indirect* effect. A new, more complex technology can result in a producer's *shifting* to labor that embodies a much greater quantity of human capital, a different *HC* type. These shifts are institutionalized via job description changes (often required by union agreements). Those workers with the "older" skills are, in the short run, unemployed, as they cannot move (along with demand) to the alternative labor market. Either direct or indirect shifts in labor demands from technological change can be represented as changes in the values of the σ's.

III. Labor Market Returns

The Wage of Central Tendency

Supply and the Short Run. We can now state the complete short-run conditions. Technology and the state of industrial competition (σ and ρ) are constants on the demand side, while labor mobility among markets is absent on the supply side. Demand and supply conditions vary with the *HC* type as well as with labor union and licensing practices. We will consider, in turn, the wages for professional, skilled craft union, industrial union, and unskilled-nonorganized workers. The wage rates of central tendency are those of the market for each general *HC* type in a specific area.

Figure 1, which illustrates four of the many noncompeting labor markets in the *D*th geographical area, has one short-term market. The height of the supply curve is determined by the subsistence wage or the social minimum (w^s). From *A* to *B* (as in Panel *a*) is the labor market segment between the minimum work hours decided institutionally for the given labor force size and the upper limit dictated by the biological nature of labor in the short run. It is a short schedule in which the hours supplied can be increased through "overtime." The labor supply schedule becomes perfectly inelastic at the biological limit and may be backward-bending at some "high" wage.[7]

In the professional labor market, services usually are unique and the demand curve will be highly inelastic as in panel *a*, Figure 1. Thus the perfectly inelastic short-run supply of professional labor, restricted by licensing, decides the wage rate as given by a highly inelastic fee. The price of the

7. As Barzel and McDonald [1, 625] have shown, simply the presence of wealth in the utility function can give a backward-bending labor supply curve.

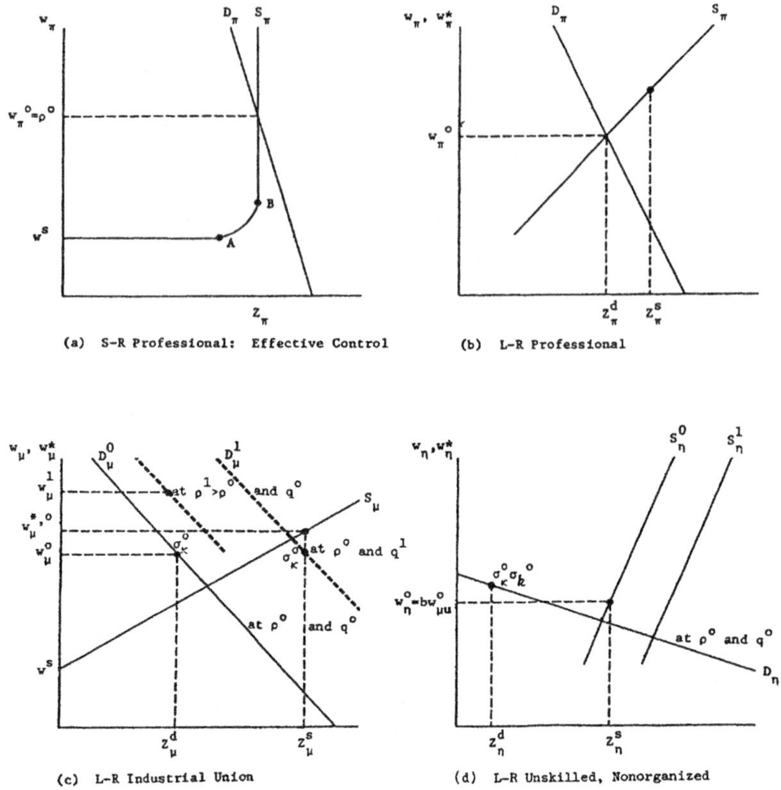

Figure 1. Labor-Market Prototypes, *D*th Geographical Area

service *is* the wage rate ($w_\pi^o = \rho^o$), although it may include a capital rental cost. In a similar way, managers (a separate labor market) may be paid a share of profits as quasi-rent on physical capital. In neither case are wages closely connected to productivity. If the professional has effective control, operating as a services *and* labor supply monopolist, the wage rate will—by definition—clear the market because labor supply will be restricted to the quantity of services demanded at the service market fee.

In any given geographical area the craft union influences the wage rate by strictly controlling entry; in the short run the supply of labor tends to be perfectly inelastic. Bargaining theory suggests that the labor market wage rate will be somewhere between the "competitive" wage and a premium wage in which all economic profits are paid to labor. Assume imperfect product market conditions and the bargained craft union money wage rate is $w_v = \sigma^{-1}\bar{\rho} + P$, where P = the economic profits allocated to workers per hour of effort.[8] Employment levels, independent of the wage rate, vary with output levels. However, in a period of rising demand for craft-produced products, full employment may ensue and wages will be bid up by firms attempting to lure labor away from competing firms. Craft labor then may receive a larger share of economic profits.

Although bargaining theory also applies to the industrial union, the union's instrumental variable is the wage rate rather than the labor supply. The average product price influences management's ability to pay, an ability usually enhanced under imperfectly competitive product market conditions. However, cause-to-effect does not reliably point in one direction: management may yield to union demands with the assurance that higher wage costs can be passed on through a constant or rising mark-up. The likelihood of full-cost pricing increases with greater product market imperfection. On the other hand, price rises may stimulate union demands. The literature refers to such prices and wages as "administered." In this case the elasticity of substitution of the various specific labor types—probably high—is largely irrelevant.

In the short run employment is not related to the wage rate and the wage rate is geared to employment only when full employment extends across the partitioned occupation matrix. A high wage can be associated with a high unemployment rate because employment is decided by the level of production.

Let us now consider unskilled, nonorganized labor. The general consensus is that nonunion wages are proportionately related to union wages, but lower. Thus the short-run wage rate for unskilled, nonorganized labor in an area can be expressed as $w^o_\eta = bw^o_{\mu u}$, where $0 < b < 1$ and $w^o_{\mu u}$ is the union rate for unskilled labor. In the absence of unionized labor in an area, unskilled labor is paid a wage near subsistence. As suggested above, unskilled labor tends to be homogeneous and is highly substitutable across all firms employing it in the area. It is reasonable to postulate a perfectly elastic supply curve that equals in length the number of vitae of that *HC* type. Unskilled labor employment can be *any* point (but only *one* point) in the wage plane, depending upon the output of employing firms. The related production is very labor-intensive, but any quantity of labor demanded that is less than the vitae number leaves a reserve of unemployed.

This completes the discussion of the short-term wages of central tendency.

Central Tendency and the Long Run. In any particular labor market the wage rate of central tendency is responsive in the long run to changes in the type and nature of unionism of licensing, new entrants, changes in average product

8. Bars (–'s) above variables denote their constancy for the purpose of the analysis.

prices, and improvements in technology of the employing industry and firms.

It is important to distinguish between the usual graph depicting a cause-effect relation between the wage rate and the quantity of labor demanded and a graph of the *loci* of wage rates and labor quantities. It is the latter that is represented in panels *c* and *d* of Figure 1. (Linearity is assumed in panels *b*, *c* and *d* for simplicity.)

If the growth of technology reduces the labor-output ratio, the loci of $w = \sigma^{-1}\bar{p}$ and $Z = \sigma\bar{q}$, where Z is employment and q and p are at given levels, trace out what appears to be a downward-sloping labor demand curve. Retain the Sraffa-type assumption of fixed production coefficients at each new level of technology and the labor-output ratio equals the marginal labor-output ratio. As more capital-intensive production reduces labor per extra unit of output, *by definition* the marginal physical product of labor rises as Z declines. At higher levels of output, the wage-employment loci shift rightward: at higher product price levels, the loci shift upward. However, just as a higher average product price and wage rate do not necessarily imply a higher employment level, neither does a lower amount of output *necessarily* result in a lower wage rate.

The illustrations in Figure 1 are unique for still another reason. The long-run supply of labor is not a function of the *actual* wage rate. The long-run labor supply is a function of the *expected* wage rate (w^*) because the supply over time represents the maturing of vitae that have been directed along a path designed years earlier. Increases in the expected market wage rate are likely to attract new entrants and the relevant human capital vector is lengthened. (This labor expansion, however, may be controlled by craft unions or licensing.) Also, technological change may generate new occupations to fill some of the present zero elements in the occupational matrix (*HCO*).

Even in the long run, labor supply in craft union markets will be fairly inelastic because of the union's ability to control entry. The w-Z loci also will trace a rather "inelastic" curve because of limited possibilities for capital substitution. We would expect to see relatively stable wage behavior and therefore it is probable that in the long run $w_v \simeq w_v^*$ and the labor market is cleared. Thus it is not mere historical accident that skilled workers were the first to organize into craft unions and successfully raise wage rates (see [15] for more details). An increase in the average price of products produced with such labor will raise both the actual and expected wage. This, of course, does not preclude unemployment in the short run.

The long run professional labor supply has similarities to craft labor but tends to be less inelastic because expected wages are so high. Market clearing, however, is more problematical. The labor supply depends upon a multitude of life plans along complex paths over a long gestation period. Although the labor quantity (services) demanded is rather assured, the vitae number may be a level such as Z_{π}^{s} in panel *b* while the wage rate or service fee is an "equilibrium" one, w_{π}^{o}. Unemployment or underemployment would result (Z_{π}^{d} − Z_{π}^{s}).

The employers of industrial labor have an incentive and ability to substitute capital for labor in the long run. Thus, the *w*-*Z* loci trace an "elastic" curve. At any time labor demand, however, is represented by only one point, such as σ_{K}^{o}, which is given by the current state of technology. The labor supply curve, being based upon wage expectations, tends to be relatively price elastic. Although the actual *and* expected wage rates may be nearly equal (as in panel *c*) capital substitution may have advanced to the point where labor demand is Z_{μ}^{d} (σ has declined to σ_{K}^{o}) so that only an output increase sufficient to shift the demand to D_{μ}^{1} (at σ_{K}^{o}) would bring full employment to this labor market. At a constant or rising price mark-up a wage increase to w_{μ}^{1} will bring along a price rise to ρ^{1}. Alternatively, a price rise to ρ^{1} may result in an increase in the wage rate to w_{μ}^{1}. The direction of cause-to-effect depends upon timing in the bargaining process and may be unrelated to output changes (as illustrated).

In the unskilled, nonorganized labor market there is little incentive or ability to substitute capital for labor. Expected wage rates are low and unskilled workers cannot operate complex machines. However, the labor is highly substitutable for itself, perhaps swamping the capital source of "inelasticity." This is shown in panel *d*, Figure 1 by multiplying σ_{K} by σ_{k}, a labor substitution parameter. On net, the *w*-*Z* loci would probably trace a highly "elastic" curve. Long-run supply of unskilled labor is decided mostly by nonwage elements. The unskilled might be viewed as failed life plans so that the long-term supply is inelastic. This, however, does not preclude sharp rightward shifts in supply from economic recession or technological change that reduces employment in other markets. Employment is decided independently of the wage rate (w_{η}^{o}), and may be at any point in the *w*-*Z* loci, say Z_{η}^{d}. If the actual wage rate approximates the expected ($w_{\eta} = w_{\eta}^{*}$), the vitae available are given by that respective point on the long-run supply curve. In panel *d*, such a combination results in unemployment. An unused supply of unskilled labor is not necessarily a permanent condition. Modest increases in demand (ceteris paribus)—though presently improbable—would quickly eliminate the unskilled reserve.

The Wage Rate Vector. The wage rate at t_0 is the short-run wage rate which may or may not be near the long-term rate. As suggested above, the process that decides wage rates differs by general type of human capital and by labor market type.

Assume that national industrial unions cover workers of μ general *HC* types. At any time then, there are $n \cdot D + \mu$ labor market wage rates of central tendency associated with *n* human capital types, including some wages at minimums. This gives a partitioned vector of wage rates of central tendency with (say) π professional labor market wages, m managerial wages, v craft-union wages, μ industrial union (administered) wages, and η residual wages of the unskilled, nonorganized, so

$$w = \Big[w_1 w_2 \ldots w_\pi \,\Big|\, w_{\pi+1} w_{\pi+2} \ldots w_{\pi+m} \,\Big|\, w_{\pi+m+1} w_{\pi+m+2} \ldots w_{\pi+m+v} \,\Big| \\ w_{\pi+m+v+1} w_{\pi+m+v+2} \ldots w_{\pi+m+v+\mu} \,\Big|\, w_{\pi+m+v+\mu+1} w_{\pi+m+v+\pi+2} \ldots w_{n \cdot D+\mu}\Big], \tag{11}$$

where $\eta = n \cdot D + \mu - (\pi + m + v + \mu)$.

Differential Wages and Labor Mobility

The foregoing provides an explanation for several kinds of wage differentials. The levels and types of unionism or licensing requirements create wage differentials. Occupational differentials are based upon skill requirements, but also upon job specifications and union rules, including credentials. Differences in average product prices also can create wage differentials. Once these differentials are identified, only those remaining differences can be described as truly geographical. The growth rate characterizing the dominant industry in a locale may set a "traditional" wage rate with the wage rates of those of other professions or industries forming contours around it. Thus "country doctors" in a farming community receive lower fees than their equally trained cohorts near the industrial plants of Detroit.

If we make the usual assumption of "rationality" with respect to income, these differentials represent an opportunity to "arbitrage," but any adjustments certainly cannot be expected to approach the efficiency of foreign exchange markets. The mobility of labor is a complex, difficult, and cumbersome process. Studies attribute 53 to 69 percent of migration to a purely economic motive, leaving considerable room for the motivations of regional preference, health, education, available housing, marriage, life style, family ties, and so on.[9] A share of the geographical residual differential may be attributable to such preferences.

According to the vita theory, the *individual* achieves a higher wage rate via his or her labor mobility, either through time (temporal) or across space (spatial). The high-wage seeker would look to a labor market of licensed professionals with monopolistic supply control over high-priced services of inelastic demand with little prospect for capital-intensive technological advances located in a traditionally high-wage geographical area.

Most job shifts are in the same occupation because persons are most likely to "qualify" for an occupation they already know. Such job changes require switching employers within the same locale in the short run or moving geographically in the long run. The new labor market may have a

9. See [29] for sources and some possible explanations.

higher wage rate because of union, licensing, product price, geographical, or other differentials.

The professionals or semiprofessionals who are said to be in "national" labor markets can be thus described because they have relatively high levels of capital and, hence, mobility. However, this mobility must be facilitated by national information networks. In our long run, these professionals hopscotch from one "local" market to another (wherever no entry barriers exist).

An upward or downward occupational movement in terms of status or wage may occur with no change in human capital, although such transfers are unlikely to be by more than one rung on the job ladder. Such movements might be in the same producing unit (in the absence of entry barriers) or outside the unit but within the same labor market. As indicated above, in the short run such changes are in response to the ups and downs of production at given levels of technology. Downward transfers are usually involuntary. The greater share of internal (same occupation) job and wage shifts are among those in highly skilled occupations (professionals, managers, craftspeople).

In entry and reentry situations there is no presumption of perfect knowledge on the pat of either employer or employee. The unemployed may, by downplaying credentials, successfully apply for a lower-level job. The underqualified may gain a position in the hope of learning the requisite skills before being "found out."

Entry jobs are those filled by persons from the bottom of the vitae queues. Technological progress tends to raise the skill requirements for entry positions so that the employer moves to higher-ranked human capital types. Such technological improvements tend to reduce mobility between occupations because of the lags between training response and vita requirements. It takes about 16 years to produce an unskilled worker and 19 or 20 years to produce a skilled one.

Significant upward temporal mobility requires the acquisition of a greater quantity of human capital (moving from HC_n and toward HC_1). Whether this be a response to changing skills requirements from technological change or a result of the person's desire to increase status and income, the training and education augmentation requires substantial blocks of time and, unless the employer offers a training program, a substantial personal investment commitment.

Unfortunately, low levels of capital which inhibit upward temporal mobility also slow spatial mobility. Such transfers are related to desire, *ability*, and prospects for success. Although social barriers to labor migration no doubt vary with the quantity of human capital, the main economic inhibitor to successful migration is the cost of physical transport, financed from one's capital stock ($k + \kappa$), and the level of capital itself.[10]

10. For a study finding that poverty reduces family mobility, see L. Kaluzny [26]. For a study that evaluates the risk of migration, see [43].

The search for higher earnings may end with still another obstacle to mobility. The individual may not receive the wage rate of the labor market and occupation of choice because of characteristics decided by his or her *birth vita*. Discrimination, be it racial, sexual, age, ethnic, or whatever, can preclude a particular individual from receiving the wage rate of central tendency. We expect, therefore, to find earnings differentials are wider than wage differentials.

The Wage Earner as an Individual. Although about two-thirds of all earnings in the U.S. are from labor markets, the *individual* may also receive a return independent of or related to the labor market wage from his or her nonhuman capital endowment.

Therefore, we will define the *individual's* "wage rate" as the "personal capital rate." An individual who is employed as "top management" in an industry receives a return from nonhuman capital either from ownership of physical or financial capital or from control of such capital. Such a person receives a shadow wage rate from the "labor market" for top managers plus a return from nonhuman capital. The self-employed also may receive returns from both k and κ.

Select (again) the ith human capital type and the labor market that pays the *highest wage* of central tendency for this labor type. The individual with this quantity of human capital is potentially a "price taker" of this wage rate. More probably the individual will not receive this wage rate but rather a personal capital rate that is lower. A lower return would be from *wage rate differentials* related to location, union-industry conditions, and the personal characteristics described above.

Let W_{ji} = the jth individual's personal capital rate (whose human capital quantity and type is HC_i) at t_0, w_i = highest wage rate of central tendency for HC_i, D_{gi} = a residual geographical-location wage differential, D_{ui} = union condition wage differential, D_{oji} = occupational wage differential, D_{pi} = industry wage differential based upon product price, $D_{\sigma i}$ = industry wage differential based upon the state of technology, and D_{Rj} = wage differential based upon discrimination against a person of j's personal characteristics. Then, individual j's personal capital rate at t_0 is

$$W_{ji} = (w_i + D_{gi} + D_{ui} + D_{oji} + D_{pi} + D_{\sigma i}) \cdot D_{Rj}. \tag{12}$$

All the D's except the discrimination differential are $\leqslant$ zero. If less than zero, the differential reduces the personal capital rate. The discrimination differential is multiplicative because discrimination can prevent entry altogether into a labor market or occupation. Therefore, if $D_{Rj} = 0$, no return is possible. If $0 < D_{Rj} < 1$, discrimination reduces the return. If $D_{Rj} = 1$, discrimination does not exist. Therefore, $0 \leqslant D_{Rj} \leqslant 1$.

Personal Income and the Income Distribution. The before-tax personal income (y) is y = (hours worked) · ("wage rate"), so

$$y_j = h \cdot \left[(w_i + D_{gi} + D_{ui} + D_{oji} + D_{\rho i} + D_{\sigma i}) \cdot D_{Rj}\right] + y_{\kappa j}, \quad (13)$$

where $y_{\kappa j}$ = rents from the quantity of nonhuman capital owned or controlled by the jth person at t_0.

The income distribution is a rank-order vector of all persons' (of vitae in the V matrix) before-tax personal incomes, that is,

$$y = [y_1 y_2 \ldots y_\nu] \quad (14)$$

Such a distribution can be arrayed in the usual ways. (We are reminded that $y_{\nu-\lambda}$ through y_ν may be zero because some population members may be unemployed.) Our rank ordering of human capital quantities *does not* match our rank ordering of personal incomes.

From the view of economic policies that might alter the personal income distribution the degree of control by the individual in the design of his or her own life plan is very important. For this reason a formal model from the individual's view that incorporates the elements of the vita theory is developed below. This formulation is placed within the traditional context because economists have stressed the liberal idea of maximizing individual choice. The key choices are in the area of occupational and labor market mobility.

IV. Control over Personal Incomes: A Formal Model

Individual Incomes in Noncompeting Labor Markets

Explanation of the Variables. A general personal income function for the jth individual is[11]

$$y = y(h, k, \kappa, \rho, m, \theta, M, R), \quad (15)$$

where the subscript, j, is deleted, y = before-tax personal income, h = hours worked, k = the jth individual's human capital, κ = the jth individual's nonhuman capital endowment (as defined above), ρ = the average price of the product or service produced by this individual's labor (or *expected* price), m = an index of mobility, θ = a variable that measures risk and uncertainty regarding income opportunities at alternative geographical locations, M = an

11. I consider the individual rather than the household because my purpose is general conceptualization. Similar but more complex functions can be generalized with respect to the household. If the adults' human capital were homogeneous, the household function could be similar to equation (15) except that some income would have to be allocated to child care. If two adults were of two distinct human capital types, the nuclear household version of (15) would contain two income functions, one for the male and another for the female adult. Such an approach that includes the effect of children and their ages upon family productivity is used by Gramm [17]. Also see Gronau [19].

index of monopolistic power that would equal zero for individuals with "ordinary" or average human and nonhuman capital endowments under free entry conditions in groups of large numbers, and R = a discrimination (racial, sexual, ethnic, and other) index that is negatively related to income for those who suffer economic effects from discrimination.[12]

The amount of time available for work effort is limited by the biological constraint of the total number of waking hours ($\bar{h}$). Let us divide the hours of "leisure time" between hours allocated to augmentation of human capital (h_1) and those devoted to "pure" leisure (h_2).[13]

We hypothesize that monopolistic power (M) depends upon both the level of total capital endowment ($k + \kappa$) and the labor market entry conditions or occupation entry conditions of the relevant labor market. Let EN be an index of entry in which larger values of EN represent greater ease of entry. The value of EN for most blue-collar occupations is described by the type and level of unionization.

In the long run the relation between race, sex, or ethnic identification and income can be eliminated by societal attitudinal changes and laws that require equal treatment in hiring practices. Thus, although the coefficient of R may change, suffice it to say that $(\partial y / \partial R) < 0$ where discrimination exists.[14]

The Income Function. We can now be more specific about functional relations. Whereas *temporal* mobility is a direct function of the quantity of human capital (k), worker *spatial* mobility is a direct function of k, κ, and θ, so $m = m(k, \kappa, \theta)$, where $\partial m / \partial k > 0$, $\partial m / \partial \kappa > 0$, and $\partial m / \partial \theta < 0$. The monopolistic power function is $M = M(EN, k, \kappa)$, where $\partial M / \partial EN < 0$, $\partial M / \partial k > 0$, and $\partial M / \partial \kappa > 0$.

Finally, there is a labor demand shifter (professional) or wage rate shifter (union or unskilled)—associated with product price changes—$\partial y / \partial p > 0$. As suggested above, the main impact of technological improvements is upon employment; that is, upon h, which may become zero unless the individual becomes underemployed. As this is a discrete phenomenon, we will assume that the individual responds by *attempting* to increase his or her human capital.

Let the function W be the personal capital rate and (15) can be written as

$$y = h \cdot W\left[k, \kappa, p, m(k, \kappa, \theta), M(EN, k, \kappa), R\right]. \tag{16}$$

The "wage rate" is the entire function W.

12. If equation (15) were to contain the variables for the representative worker in the ith labor market, then (15) is properly viewed as a reduced-form equation for the HC_i labor market.

13. The terms h, h_1, h_2, are interdependent, because they are constrained by $\bar{h}$. The trade-offs—h for h_1, h_1 for h_2, or whatever—can be defined by assumption.

14. For a sampling of the literature on discrimination, see [4; 20; 21; 22]. Also see [5; 6; 16; 18; 27; 28; 30; 34] for a sample of the migration literature. For a study that blends discrimination and migration, see [44].

Initially calendar time is undefined so as to express the model in the most general terms.[15] The partials with respect to income are given below.[16]

The Utility Function. Traditional microtheory has the worker optimizing in work-leisure trade-offs. In human capital theory, the optimum is sought in education-training and leisure trade-offs. An assessment of the meaning of such trade-offs for optimal personal incomes requires a utility function.

As recent analyses recognize, the satisfaction from one's own income is relative, because the person's utility from income is related to other known or "perceived" incomes (and implied consumption) in the society. To keep our arguments simple and focused upon earnings, we will assume that the utility from own-income (y) is derived within a given sociological environment in which the jth individual views his or her income in relation to any other relevant incomes.[17] In general, then

$$u = u(y, h), \qquad (17)$$

where y = before-tax personal income of individual j, $h = \bar{h} - h_1 - h_2$, $\partial u/\partial y > 0$, and $\partial u/\partial h < 0$. The partials are noncontroversial.

Optimal Vitae

Total differentials of the earnings function and the utility function identify optima.[18] In the neoclassical short run only dh in the earnings function will be

15. The variables can be expressed in any time units desired. As an example, the income variables can be defined as expected lifetime or average lifetime earnings (see Ben-Porath [3], Weiss [43], and Fair [14]). Because we abstract from calendar time, age is not included explicitly as a variable determining income. However, years of experience (a proxy for age or vice versa) is included as a human capital variable.

16. The personal income partials are:

$h \cdot (\partial y/\partial k) > 0;$
$h \cdot (\partial y/\partial \kappa) > 0;$
$h \cdot (\partial y/\partial \rho) > 0;$
$h \cdot [(\partial y/\partial m) \cdot (\partial m/\partial k)] > 0;$
$h \cdot [(\partial y/\partial m) \cdot (\partial m/\partial \kappa)] > 0;$
$h \cdot [(\partial y/\partial m) \cdot (\partial m/\partial \theta)] < 0;$
$h \cdot [(\partial y/\partial M) \cdot (\partial M/\partial EN)] < 0;$
$h \cdot [(\partial y/\partial M) \cdot (\partial M/\partial k)] > 0;$
$h \cdot [(y/\partial M) \cdot (\partial M/\partial \kappa)] > 0;$
and $h \cdot (\partial y/\partial R) < 0.$

17. Hochman-Rodgers [23], for example, include the income of one other person in the utility functions of their two-person Mutt-Jeff model. In [39; 42; 47] the societal distribution of income itself appears in individual's utility functions. A critique of these voluntary exchange models appears in [9]. A different version of utility interdependence is developed by Canterbery [8].

Empirical research finds the first-order partial derivative w.r.t. income positive in all income ranges. Marginal disutility from hours worked is derived from loss of leisure and increased marginal labor effort. The individual's labor supply curve would become backward-bending at $|\partial u/\partial h| > |\partial u/\partial y|$. See Clark's [11] survey of the empirical literature and his own statistical test.

18. Without defining precise units of time, and with the assumption of additivity of the W-

nonzero. In the long run, the differentials can be viewed as discrete changes (Δ's) that are larger for larger units of calendar time (assuming linear approximations are possible). Alternatively, the integral of dy/dt can be taken over the life-cycle vita in order to derive lifetime income.[19] Then, $y(t_0)$ from equation (16) gives an individual's income at a point in time in that individual's vita.

The traditional "optima" have limited meanings.[20] The neoclassical "optimum" w.r.t. hours worked occurs at a socially static time in which public policies as well as capital levels are unchanging. Our version of the standard "optimum" with respect to hours worked is[21]

$$\begin{aligned} dy/dh &= Y'_h(k,\kappa,\rho,\theta,EN,R) = W\left[k,\kappa,\theta,m(k,\kappa,\theta),M(EN,k,\kappa),R\right] \\ &= -U'_h(y)/U'_y(h). \end{aligned} \tag{18}$$

This marginal utility condition differs at alternative values for human capital, nonhuman capital, own-income itself, product prices, and the state of fulfill-

---

function arguments, the total differential of equation (16) is:

$$\begin{aligned} dy = &\left\{h\cdot\left[\partial y/\partial k + (\partial y/\partial m)\cdot(\partial m/\partial k) + (\partial y/\partial M)\cdot(\partial M/\partial k)\right]\right\}\cdot dk \\ &+ \left\{h\cdot\left[\partial y/\partial\kappa + (\partial y/\partial m)\cdot(\partial m/\partial\kappa) + (\partial y/\partial M)\cdot(\partial M/\partial\kappa)\right]\right\}d\kappa \\ &+ \left[h\cdot(\partial y/\partial\rho)\right]\cdot d\rho + W\left[k,\kappa,m(k,\kappa,\theta),M(EN,k,\kappa),R\right]\cdot dh \\ &+ \left[h(\partial y/\partial m)\cdot(\partial m/\partial\theta)\right]\cdot d\theta + \left[h\cdot(\partial y/\partial M)\cdot(\partial M/\partial EN)\right]\cdot dEN \\ &+ \left[h\cdot(\partial y/\partial R)\right]\cdot dR. \end{aligned}$$

Time is the implicit common denominator of the differential.

The total differential of u (equation (17)) is, very simply, with the same assumption of additivity,

$$du = (\partial u/\partial y)\cdot dy + (\partial y/\partial h)\cdot dh.$$

The relation of the comparative-static with the life-cycle utility is analogous to the above treatment of income.

19. The income distribution implications of the life-cycle approach are well described by Johnson [25, 207–]10].

20. At this point we need to be very clear on the meaning of our notation. Posit a function $z = f(x,y)$, and the value of $\partial z/\partial x$ at a point (x,y) depends, not only upon the value of x from which we start the limiting variation that defines the partial derivative, but also upon the value of y that is kept constant during the limiting process. Thus the precise meaning of partial derivatives in multi-variable functions is made obvious with more appropriate notation. Write $\partial z/\partial x$ as $f_x'(y)$, and it is clear that the partial derivative w.r.t. x at a point (x,y) is a function of both x and y where the term(s) in parentheses is (are) constant. Further simplifying notation, partial derivatives are written as the "dependent" variable capitalized with subscripts denoting the independent variable with respect to which the derivative is taken. For example, now the partial of the person's income with respect to human capital is:

$$h\cdot\left[\partial y/\partial k + (\partial y/\partial m)\cdot(\partial m/\partial k) + (\partial y/\partial M)\cdot(\partial M/\partial k)\right] = Y_k'(h,\rho,R).$$

21. Begin with the differential of the utility function, and substitute the income differential for dy. Then set the resultant differential equal to zero and divide through by dh.

The first-order condition for a constrained optimum is $du = 0$. Because certain variables are independent of h at this juncture, $dk/dh = d\kappa/dh = d\rho/dh = d\theta/dh = dEN/dh = dR/dh = 0$, and none of these variables are now *mathematical* constraints. Use our abbreviated notation and we have the simplified "optimum" w.r.t. hours worked, equation (18). The more complex form of the derivatives can be seen by inspection of their counterpart in the differential equations of the text. Note, however, that the ratio of the differentials can be written as a partial derivative when all other derivatives are zero.

The higher-order optimality conditions for (18) require that the second-order determinant be negative definite.

ment of public policies regarding barriers to mobility (through I_0, EN, θ, s_2, and R).

This "optimum" is derived from *non-changing opportunities* for maximizing personal income, *except* for changing hours worked that themselves are constrained by institutional arrangements, biological work effort limits, employment offers, and technological change (see Figure 1). Moreover, a poor person's "optimum"—without some substantial change in endowments—leaves him or her still poor. Can we not presume that, given more advantageous endowments, one might prefer to "optimize" at a higher personal income level? Any optimal *societal* income distribution thus is related to a complicated interrelation of economic variables, institutions, and national policies.

With these constraints, how do individuals improve their economic status? The vita theory suggests that any significant improvements are derived from switching to a higher wage rate.[22] As such a change can only be made via temporal or spatial mobility, we must consider the human capital optimum.

The earnings function is not at "first causes" in terms of *birth*, *pre-career*, and *mature vitae*. Therefore, substitute the capital functions of (4) and (5) from Section II into the earnings equation (16). Assume that $dh_1/dh_2 = 0$ and therefore $dh_1/dh = -1$. At any time the individual is optimizing w.r.t. the rate of voluntary education-training if[23]

$$\begin{aligned} dy/dh_1 &= Y'_k(\rho,\theta,EN,\partial y/\partial R)\cdot K'_{h_1}(G,s_2,s_3,E,\tau) + Y'_K(\rho,\theta,EN,\partial y/\partial R) \\ &\quad \cdot K'_k(I_0,G,s_2,s_3,E,\tau)\cdot K'_{h_1}(G,s_2,s_3,E,\tau) - W \\ &= -U'_h(y)/U'_y(h)\,. \end{aligned} \tag{19}$$

Voluntary education and training over the life plan is optimized by a life-cycle of optima that begin with the *pre-career vita*. Note also that, by the assumption that hours allocated to human capital production detract from work hours ($dh_1/dh = -1$), the income derived from work effort is reduced by the value of W.

Endowments and Assets. As suggested in Section II, if $I_0 \simeq 0$, or the individual is at the institutional or biological working-hour limits, one cannot seek a

22. Returning to an earlier consideration, the hours-worked restriction will not be as severe on the nuclear household. The two adults might enter two different labor markets so that their combined hours of work is much greater than is implied by either one's supply curve.

23. After substitution of equations (4) and (5) into (16) in the text, take their differentials. Substitute the differentials of the earnings function (dy) into the differential of the utility function. Then set the differential of the utility function equal to zero and divide by dh_1. (Again, the first-order condition for a constrained "optimum" is $du = 0$.) By assumption, $dh_1/dh_2 = 0$, and h_2 is no longer a mathematical constraint. Use our abbreviated notation (see footnote 20) and we have the "optimum" w.r.t. hours devoted to human capital development.

The higher-order optimality conditions for (19) require that the second-order determinant be negative definite.

higher income. On the other hand, the case where I_0 is sufficiently large that reduced work effort is not a constraint on human capital development is approximated by assuming $dh_1/dh = 0$.[24] Large initial endowments free the individual to increase the hours devoted to human capital without having to be concerned about the reduction in current income via the diversion of hours away from work effort. Therefore, material inheritance can be important in defining the initial conditions that greatly impact the lifetime income path.[25]

Costs of Increasing Human Capital. Even where $I_0 \simeq 0$ the individual can consider borrowing in order to finance human capital increases. In the private market, however, the terms for borrowing are directly related to present asset holdings, current income, and the individual's vita. Interest costs may be prohibitively high or even infinite where collateral is required for the loan.

The optimum human capital level depends *upon the same constraints* as those that determine current incomes. Given G, E, s_2, and s_3, the rational parent or (later) individual maximizer of income will select the Human Capital Type with a net positive capital value and that yields the highest expected income. In short, if one could ignore costs and claims a favorable genetic code and family background (G and E), the "rational" individual would decide to become Human Capital Type 1.

However, expected cost cannot be ignored. In reality the parents and (later) the individual rank the expected costs of acquisition (C^*'s) of human capital types. Assume that costs are ranked in the same order as the general human capital quantity requirements (*HC*'s), then $C_1^* > C_2^* > C_3^* > \ldots C_n^*$. The accessibility to a human capital type that yields a higher return depends strongly upon the individual's initial capital endowments as well as the current income that such endowments yield.[26] Not every individual can acquire the surgeon's vita even if each desires it: this observed failure often can be traced back to the *birth vita*.

The individual's investment potential may be restricted to a Human Capital Type and hence a labor market that will yield a small stream of lifetime income. We are merely suggesting that capital tends to beget human capital

24. If I_0 is assumed large and therefore

$$\begin{aligned} dh_1/dh &= 0, \\ dy/dh_1 &= Y_k'(\rho, \theta, \partial y/\partial R) \cdot K_{h_1}' (G, s_2, s_3, E, \tau) + Y_K'(\rho, \theta, EN, \partial y/\partial R) \cdot K_k(I_0, G, s_2, s_3, E, \tau) \\ &\quad \cdot K_{h_1}' (G, s_2, s_3, E, \tau) \\ &= -U_h'(y)/U_y'(h). \end{aligned}$$

25. The initial material endowment plays no functional role in the traditional human capital literature (see Becker [2] and Chiswick and Mincer [10]).

26. If inheritance (I_0) is limited, any current costs to the individual must be financed by borrowing if h_1 hours must be substituted for work hours (h). The implied interdependence between I and k is exhibited in our model by the freedom given to persons with large endowments to increase human capital hours while ignoring the impact of such changes upon current income from work effort.

tends to beget income tends to beget capital, and so on. Kenneth Boulding has called this the Matthew principle—"to him that hath shall be given."

Our labor market analysis in Section III suggests that human capital will not even do this if every person is equally "rational" or demand conditions are not favorable. The greater the number of persons who have vitae that fit a particular labor market, the greater the probability (ceteris paribus) for unemployment ($h = 0$) or underemployment. College professors should find this argument persuasive.

Public Policy and Welfare Implications

The standard microtheory approach has been to seek an income-optimal w.r.t. hours worked. However, the wage rate of central tendency in the labor market and the differential effects upon personal capital returns may be more important in deciding income. Moreover, the social-political milieu can alter human-nonhuman capital endowments, the present state of competition and technology (labor demand), and taxes or grants.

The vita theory is rather a description of the process whereby persons attempt to move toward a higher income. With a noncompeting labor market for each human capital type, placed in rank order beginning with the highest expected capital return, the individual potentially can move to a significantly higher income interval by changing his or her vita and then shifting from one occupation or labor market to another. Such shifts nonetheless often involve discrete (and perhaps large and lumpy) changes in capital as well as barriers to entry and discrimination.

Certain conditions are always destined. *Birth vitae* represent "initial states" that in part determine the configuration of "final states" in the *mature* vitae.[27] In the initial state the individual has no control. Individual control is abrogated once again after the individual has selected among the choices available, given the initial state, the "best possible" number of hours devoted voluntarily to work and human capital augmentation. The individual alone cannot decide the market wage rates or—in some instances—whether he or she will even receive the market return.

Any income distribution other than that determined by labor market conditions (given persons' vitae) requires a deliberate economic policy in which individual action recedes into social policies at that point where no further unilateral human capital changes are possible. Social goals need to be defined and further redistribution will be decided by the political process because many desires will be in conflict.

Some public policies relate to human capital variables.[28] It is only pos-

27. Future exceptions can be imagined here. Total genetic engineering could equalize IQ's in a Brave New World society.

28. These policies are not necessarily motivated by a concern with the income distribution. For example, mandatory education may be urged by those who see minimum education for the

sible, however, to "optimize" the individual's utility through some collective decision-making process. At a practical level, these variables translate into public policies to increase mobility such as inheritance tax changes, altered licensing requirements, increased flow to the public of reliable information on future skill shortages, moving subsidies, federal and private training programs, changes in educational financing, antidiscrimination legislation, subsidies for geographical transfers, and perhaps policies to reduce the risks of spatial movement.

The mandatory state-supported schooling level (s_2) illustrates an "optimum" to be decided by collective choice. For a representative individual the optimum with respect to state-supported schooling is at a known value of dy/ds_2.[29] The incremental income from k is now allowed to change because s_2 is no longer a given parameter. However, if schooling does not detract from hours worked, the optimum must be defined in social terms; otherwise, no constraint exists.[30]

All such policies do have common constraints, namely the implementation of public preferences and the size of governments' budgets. There is no assurance that the equilibrium conditions for the *individual* will be met, because there is no guarantee that governmental budgets will include positive

---

population as necessary for the effective functioning of a democracy. Indeed, the lack of specific redistribution intent may be a force leading to direct redistribution policies.

29. In deriving dy/ds_2 the same steps are used as in deriving dy/dh_1 except we divide through the fully specified utility differential by ds_2. The following simplified definitional reminder will aid the reader in understanding the steps to solution and its meaning: $dy/ds_2 = dy/dk + dy/d\kappa - dy/dh$. Thus,

$$\begin{aligned} dy/ds_2 &= Y_k'(\rho, \theta, EN, \partial y/\partial R) \cdot K_{s_2}'(G, h_1, s_3, E, \tau) + Y_\kappa'(\rho, \theta, EN, \partial y/\partial R) \\ &\quad \cdot K_k'(I_0, G, s_3, E, \tau) \cdot K_{s_2}'(G, h_1, s_3, E, \tau) - W[k, \kappa, \rho, m(k, \kappa, \theta), M(EN, k, \kappa), R] \\ &= -U_h'(y)/U_y'(h). \end{aligned}$$

The higher-order conditions require that the second-order determinant be negative definite. Simplify by assuming $\kappa = 0$ for the nonpropertied. Then,

$$\begin{aligned} dy/ds_2 &= Y_k'(\rho, \theta, EN, \partial y/\partial R) \cdot K' \ (G, h_1, s_3, E, \tau) - \\ &\quad W[k, \kappa, \rho, m(k, \kappa, \theta), M(EN, k, \kappa), R] \\ &= U_h'(y)/U_y'(h). \end{aligned}$$

30. Alternatively, assume that the policy variable is the inheritance tax so that net inheritance of the representative person is altered. The optimum is then at some value ot dy/dI, and it cannot be identified in terms of individual marginal utilities, and therefore a social optimum condition would have to be specified.

The same steps are followed in deriving dy/dI as with dy/ds_2 except that the utility differential is divided through by dI. In the solution it is assumed that $dh_1/dI = 0$ since the returns to k to κ are presumably similar. So:

$$dy/dI = Y_\kappa'(h, \rho, \theta, EN, \partial y/\partial R) \cdot K_I'(G, s_1, s_2, s_3, E, \tau);$$

and no relative utility optimum exists because, strictly from the view of the individual, there is no constraint.

Each change in the ordering of policies, however, alters the nature of the next "optima." As (19) illustrates, "optima" conditions depend upon the levels of the nonchanging parameters selected and these selections are varied by the order of policies. Thus, these "optima" are not independent.

values for ds_2, dEN, and so on up to the equilibrium points for all persons. For that matter, there is considerable doubt that such policies can be effective.[31] The climb of the individual toward the utility mountain peak can be stopped on a contour of the mountain by the government's budget constraint as well as by the shortness of the umbilical rope that ties the person to his or her *birth vita*.

V. Path Analysis: An Empirical Application

Let us now consider the possibilities for empirical applications. The reality of wage differentials is not in question. Absent are a general theory, hypotheses, and tests for the determination of incomes that exhibit and to some degree reflect these wage differentials.

A Regression Model for Path Estimates

Variables of Approximation. Suppose that we could identify ten measures or proxy measures (x_1–x_{10}) which would accurately capture the variables of the vita theory. The ultimate variable to be explained is, of course, current personal income $[y(t_0) = x_{10}]$. The proxy measures for genetic endowment (G) are IQ at age 12 (x_1), race (x_2), and sex (x_3). The proxies for family environment (E) are family head's formal education in years completed (x_5) and family head's occupation (x_6). Years of completed formal education of the individual (s_1, s_2) are known (x_8) and age for (x_4) can be used to measure years of experience (τ).

An index for occupations (x_9) can be used as a proxy variable for the average product price and other industry characteristics as well as specific entry conditions. (Admittedly, the latter is an overly aggregated measure.) Finally, let the individual's number of children (x_7) be a proxy measure of the capital available (which decreases with increases in the number of children) for the extension of adult formal education and training.[32]

Vita Hypothesis and Path Theorem. The hypothesis can be expressed in a general, yet testable form. Current personal incomes (x_{10}) are determined by labor market (and occupational) choice (x_9) in which temporal income improvements are facilitated mostly by years of formal education (x_8), spatial improvements mostly by capital endowments and accumulations ($k + \kappa$), all of which are constrained by the initial state conditions of genetic (x_1, x_2, x_3) and family endowments (x_5, x_6). Thus, the effects of the independent variables upon personal incomes are both direct and indirect. The linkages of the

31. See, for example, the arguments of Thurow [38].
32. We know that—for whatever reason—formal education completed is negatively related to number of children.

"dependent" variables of schooling (x_8), occupation (x_9), and personal income (x_{10}) can be expressed as a recursive multiple regression model in which

$$x_8 = b_8 + b_{81}x_1 + b_{82}x_2 + b_{83}x_3 + b_{84}x_4 + b_{85}x_5 + b_{86}x_6 + b_{87}x_7 + b_{8u}x_u \quad (20)$$

$$x_9 = b_9 + b_{98}x_8 + b_{91}x_1 + b_{92}x_2 + b_{93}x_3 + b_{94}x_4 + b_{95}x_5 + b_{96}x_6 + b_{97}x_7 + b_{9v}x_v \quad (21)$$

$$x_{10} = b_{10} + b_{10,9}x_9 + b_{10,8}x_8 + b_{10,1}x_1 + b_{10,2}x_2 + b_{10,3}x_3 + b_{10,4}x_4 + b_{10,5}x_5 + b_{10,6}x_6 + b_{10,7}x_7 + b_{10,w}x_w, \quad (22)$$

where x_u, x_v, and x_w are residual terms and linearity is by assumption.

Path analysis can be best understood by stating its central theorem and using a path diagram. The basic theorem may be written as:

$$r_{ij} = \sum_q P_{iq} r_{jq}, \quad (23)$$

where i and j denote two variables in the model and the index q runs over all variables from which paths lead directly from variable x_i to variable x_j, r_{ij} is the total correlation between i and j through path q, and P is the *path coefficient* that is comparable to the beta coefficient.[33] The beta coefficients can be derived from ordinary partial regression coefficients, the estimated "b's" (equations (20)–(22)). In path analysis, however, some betas can be "solved for" in the absence of a coefficient estimate.

The measures of our variables were preselected because their path coefficients have been estimated by Duncan [12]. His model is expressed as a path diagram in Figure 2. The path coefficients are for white U.S. males aged 25–34 years in 1964. Thus, the effects of race (x_2), sex (x_3), and age or experience (x_4) are determined by subpopulation structuring.

One-way arrows lead from each determining variable to each variable dependent on it. The quantities attached to such arrows on the diagram are the values of the path coefficients derived from the multiple regression equations (20)–(22). The two-headed arrows are unanalyzed correlations (simple correlation coefficients) and are exogenous. The one-headed arrows coming from "outside" the diagram are the residuals of the three regressions.[34]

Why Path Analysis. Several features distinguish path from ordinary regression analysis. (1) The path diagram provides a pattern of interpretation that expresses the logic for a set of regression calculations. (2) The assumptions about the ordering of variables, about unmeasured variables, and about uncorrelated residuals are made explicit. (3) It provides an algebraic computa-

33. $P_{ij} = b_{ij}(\sigma_j/\sigma_i)$, which is the change in the standard deviation of the dependent variable from a unitary change in the standard deviation of the independent variable, other variables constant. The reader will recognize that equation (23) would be the coefficient of correlation if the sum were over all independent variables of a multiple regression equation. Here, however, the path q may trace variables across several regression equations.

34. The .003 is the correlation between two of these residuals.

Figure 2. Path Model of Genetic-Family Endowments and Personal Earnings

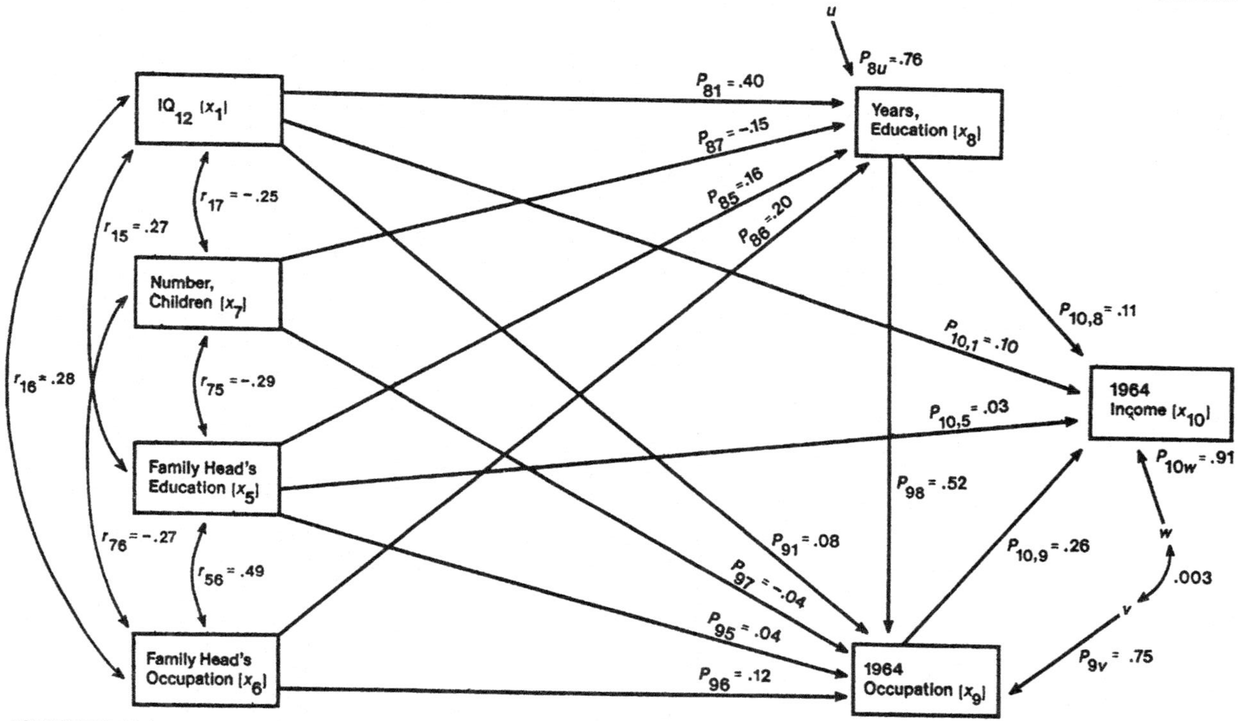

Source: Adapted from Duncan [12].

Notes: The path coefficient estimates pertain to the U.S. population of white males 25–34 years old in 1964. Among the estimates, the values for $P_{10,6}$ and $P_{10,7}$ were not significant. The x_2, x_3, and x_4 parameters are held constant by sample structuring.

tional scheme for indirect effects, which equal the sum of the products of all intervening path coefficients between a dependent and independent variable. (4) The total explained correlation along a particular path can be calculated via expanding the basic equation (23) along it. (5) Path analysis provides for an interpretation of the effect of unmeasured variables (via its estimate of the residual path coefficient).

The rule for expansion is to read *back* (counterclockwise) from variable i, *then forward* (clockwise) to variable j, forming the products of all paths ($P_{iq}r_{jq}$) along the traverse and then summing these products for all possible traverses.[35] The same variable cannot be intersected more than once in a single traverse, and in no instance can one trace back having once started forward. The bidirectional correlations are used in tracing either forward or back, but only one can be used in a single traverse. A coefficient pertaining to an entire path connecting two variables is a *compound path coefficient*.[36]

Contribution of Duncan's Index. Duncan's main data sources are the questionnaire supplement to the October 1964 Current Population Survey (CPS) and an earlier CPS supplement carried out by the Bureau of Census in March 1962. Agreement between the two sources is found to be very close. Income is expressed in thousands of current dollars.

Duncan's occupational index has a special meaning within the context of the vita theory. His index—a two-digit score ranging from 00 to 96—is highly correlated with the "performance demands" of an occupation. Our "handlers" would have scores ranging between 00 and 20, while our surgeon would score somewhere between 92 and 96.[37]

Computing Indirect Effects. The rules for computing indirect effects and *compound path coefficients* are useful in evaluating the path model in Figure 2. The bulk of the influence of intelligence (IQ measure) on occupation is indirect, via education. The direct path from IQ to occupation is only .08, whereas the indirect path via education is (.4)(.52) = .21, or more than twice as large. The sum (.29) is the entire effect of intelligence upon occupational choice apart from joint effects with the other three social background variables.

The effect of intelligence (IQ) on earnings, net of the effects of education and occupation, likewise is appreciable. The direct effect of IQ on earnings is .10 while the sum of indirect effects via education and occupation is .12. The combined effect (net of the three social background factors) is .22. Therefore, white males aged 25–34 with the same schooling and in the same line of work received differential rewards for IQ because of social contingencies.

The direct effect of the family head's education upon the respondent's

35. The endogenous correlation coefficients are continually expanded into path coefficients and exogenous correlation coefficients.

36. The "entire path" may consist of subpaths. This procedure also can be used to calculate the residual path.

37. More information on data use and sources appears in [12] and [13, 69–105].

income is .03 while the indirect effect through education and occupational choice is .04, for a total impact of .07. This excludes correlation due to common (joint) causes such as respondent's number of children and the family head's occupation.[38]

The effects upon income from our proxy for capital costs (number of children) are all indirect. The effect through education is −.04 and through occupation is −.01 for a total impact of −.05, excluding joint causes.

Total Variance. The basic theorem can be used to calculate the total correlation (including compound path coefficients) between any two variables. These values squared are comparable to coefficients of determination or the percents of explained variances.[39] Explained variance includes that from the direct effect, indirect effects, and joint causes.[40]

In a recursive model variables intervene between the "initial state" exogenous variables and the final dependent variable. In the path diagram genetic influence, capital costs, and family environment have greater total measured impacts upon education than upon (in turn) occupational choice and income. Each of these "dependent" variables can be viewed as a stage in one's life plan in which new possibilities or life paths are diminshed after each vita stage—genetic and family endowments, education, occupation—in turn is reached.

IQ alone accounts for 21 percent of the variance in education, number of children, 4 percent, the family head's education, 6 percent, and the family head's occupation, 13 percent. The shares of explained variances in occupational choice are 12 percent, 2 percent, 5 percent, and 15 percent, respectively. The family head's occupation is somewhat more important in determining the respondent's occupation than in deciding years of education.

In looking at the "filtered" impacts of the initial state variables upon income, IQ alone explains 5 percent of the variance in income, the capital-cost variable, 1 percent, the family head's education, 3 percent, and family head's occupation, 5 percent. The total variance in education explained by the four variables is 44 percent, occupation, 33 percent, and income, 13 percent. In terms of the vita theory educational achievement (years) does not translate proportionately into income even though the other genetic factors (sex and race) as well as (roughly) years of experience are held constant. Moreover, between occupation and income the effects of initial state conditions are greatly muted by occupational types and labor market conditions that include

38. Actual data references the respondent's father. For the white males there was no significant difference between the two designations. We use the term "family head" because it is significant for the black male population.

39. Again, however, the path selects the independent variables rather than any one regression equation. I refer here to "explained variance" because of the very large sample size.

40. The direct and indirect effects are obvious (see above) while the joint causes are based upon the expansion of the basic theorem equation. The zero order correlations required in these estimates appear in [13, 267].

differential geographic effects. However, this does not alter the reality of favorable initial endowments enhancing occupational (including locational) choice, nor does it alter our conclusions about many labor market conditions being nonindividual choice variables.[41]

The Structure of Racial Discrimination. Race also is one of the elements outside the purview of personal choice. The impact of race can be estimated by subpopulation structuring.[42] One procedure is to calculate incomes by substituting subpopulation means into structural regression equations from base subpopulations. Duncan [12] provides the necessary data to estimate the effects of racial discrimination for black males in the 25–34-years-old category.

Convert the path coefficients for white males in Figure 2 into partial regression coefficients for equations (20)–(22) and insert means for black males on the explanatory variables. For each "dependent" variable black and white males are equated for family background, number of children; then for the combination of these determinants plus education; then for all these plus occupation. This procedure provides components of the difference based upon race with respect to each dependent variable.

The interpretation of IQ scores requires some explanation. Intelligence tests are culturally specific: they tend to measure the performance goals of a white male society and are not otherwise entirely genetically determined. Thus the IQ scores for white males may be a fairly reliable measure of rewardable, innate mental ability, but the same scores for blacks are more apt to capture intraenvironmental influences (poverty) and extraenvironmental effects (culture). Therefore, we call the differential black-white IQ, "culturally specific mental development" differences.

Table I shows the white-black differences in culturally specific (white) mental development attributable to the socioeconomic level of family of origin, number of siblings; the differences in education attributable to the above plus specific mental development; the differences in occupation (score) attributable to the above plus education; and income differences resulting

41. The possible importance of "initial states" also is dramatized by recent studies of the variance of the earnings of cohorts. Unfortunately, these studies tend to abstract from labor market and industry conditions. Taubman's [36] study from a sample of male twins born in the years 1917–27 suggests that 40 percent of the variance in earnings can be explained by genetic endowments (*G*), 16 percent by family environment (*E*), and 35 percent by formal education. Jencks's [24] survey of earnings differentials estimates that 15 percent of the variance in earnings can be explained by *G*, 15 percent by *E*, and 58 percent by formal education. These studies suggest that most earnings inequalities are determined *before* the individual even enters the labor market.

However, Taubman makes a more cautious interpretation of his results than what we have inferred. He states: "It is possible that the proportion of the variance [in earnings] due to events transpiring before entry into the labor force accounts for half the total variance" [35, 868]. He also agrees that "the variance of schooling is more determined by common or family environment than that of earnings" [36, 867].

42. A similar procedure could be used for sexual and other forms of discrimination, but comparable data on females were not available.

Table I. Differences in White and Black Means with Respect to Vita Theory Components

Culturally Specific Mental Development	Education	Occupation Score	1964 Income	Net Differences Due to [a]:
1.9	1.0	6.5	$ 560	Family Background
0.5	0.2	1.3	100	Capital Costs
7.6	0.9	5.5	650	Culturally Specific Mental Development
	0.2	0.9	70	Education
		8.7	350	Occupation
			1,200-1,400	Income
10.0	2.3	22.9	2,930-3,130	Total Gap (White - Black)

Source: Based upon data from [12].

[a] White means for each variable were: culturally specific mental development = 51.0; education = 12.1 years completed; and occupation score = 40.6.

from the above plus occupation. The residuals (unexplained differences) may be assignable to direct racial discrimination.

Of the entire gap of 10 in the mental development means, 1.9 is explained by family environment. The "unexplained" gap of 7.6 can be attributed to cultural differences.

Of the total education gap of 2.3 years, 1.2 are accounted for by family background and number of children combined; an additional 0.9 year by culturally specific mental development, and only 0.2 year by unexplained causes. There is not much discrimination effect there. Net of family environment and number of children, culturally specific mental development accounts for 5.5 of the 22.9 points gap between black and white occupational status. However, 8.7 points of the remaining gap might be a result of racial discrimination.

Probable employment discrimination carries over into an income differential of $350. Even given this, the combination of family environment, number of children, mental development, education, *and* occupation leaves $1,200 to $1,400 of a total $3,600–3,800 income gap that might be a consequence of wage discrimination in 1964.[43]

Experience. The impact of years of experience (x_4) also can be estimated because Duncan et al. [13] have structured the white nonfarm males by age group.[44] Use the same procedure as above and assume that the mean age difference between any two age groups is 10 years. The 35–44 age group member earned a total differential of $2,440 (in 1961) over the 25–34 age group or an average $244 extra per year of experience. The return to experience is not linear because the 45–54 group member received an average of only $95 per year of experience more than the 35–44 group member.

All these findings provide considerable support for affirming the vita theory hypothesis. Certainly, they lend credence to an eclectic theory of the personal income distribution.

Migration. The subhypothesis that spatial migration is a function of capital endowments and accumulations (traceable in great part to the birth vita) emerges from the vita theory. With a subpopulation structuring but somewhat less sophisticated regression equations Duncan et al. [13, 224–32] compare white male migrants with nonmigrants, 25 to 64 years old. Duncan finds that migrants (those reporting a different location from that at age 16) have higher mean occupational indices than nonmigrants, and migration is positively related to advantageous family backgrounds and education. While these results

43. The exact mean income differences could not be established because incomes reported by black males are not strictly comparable to those by whites.

44. In these estimates the *direct* effect of IQ on earnings is not calibrated so that a small share of the differentials attributed here to experience may be a result of mean IQ differences between age groups.

are consistent with the mobility subhypothesis, more conclusive findings await improved modeling of this phenomenon.

More elaborate path models, with more complete measures (such as specific industry and labor market variables) and including perhaps feedback effects (such as own-earnings upon own-schooling and training), may provide a more reliable estimate of vita theory parameters. However, such models await the completion of comprehensive long-term longitudinal studies.[45]

In Reference to Our Example. Let us reflect upon these empirical findings with our common sense comparison of the handler and the surgeon. The handler is in an unskilled labor market which is noncompetitive with the professional labor market of the surgeon. "Physical stamina" is the only requirement that is probably related strongly to the *birth vita* of the handler, whereas the surgeon must have the "intellectual capacity" to understand a wide variety of subjects, "verbal ability," and "spatial perception," in addition to the physical requirements shared with the handler. Furthermore, the surgeon requires 11 to 15 years of premedical and medical training in the *pre-career vita*.

The handler's wage will be influenced by union conditions as well as the industry of employment. The surgeon is licensed and must meet the further requirement of certification and "professional recognition." These elements in great part explain wage differentials among handlers and surgeons. Yet, the person's occupational choice has been dominated by education-credentials requirements wherein the highest attainments have the greatest probability of completion given favorable genetic and family background conditions.

VI. Concluding Statements

The weakness of individual control over certain human capital variables leads to policies often urged collectively by society to satisfy social goals. The definition of a social optimum is altered as a society devises more and more policies that alter the base parameters from which individuals can move toward the next elusive optima. In this view social policies reduce constraints.

Yet a number of studies—including the one interpreted here—find that inherent capabilities and family environment have important impacts upon life plans that culminate in occupational selection and personal incomes. The advantageous *birth vita* starts the individual on the optimum vita path, aiding the selection of the "optimum" years of schooling and other training. Genetic and family endowments directly and indirectly affect occupational choice and

45. Very promising in this respect are the National Longitudinal Surveys [31] because of their subsample of young cohorts. On the demand side we need a standard occupational classification system, manpower requirements by occupational class, and occupational data further organized on an industry basis. With 4–7 million persons completing educational and training courses each year, on the supply side we need a reliable breakdown on an occupational basis. Furthermore, representative subsamples should be available at local and regional levels.

thus earnings. In the mature vita, the genetic code can impinge again in the way of job and wage discrimination.

The acceptance of the vita theory raises profound social and economic questions. The crucial and cumulative impacts of the initial state conditions suggest that a program of equal schooling for "equal opportunity" may leave the income distribution virtually unaltered even while contributing to economic growth. Are economic and social policies aimed indirectly at reducing income and wealth inequalities effective? Can job training programs and migration subsidies succeed where education might fail?

The distributional issue, of course, is of concern only to those in the society who find the existing income distribution unacceptable. However, if unequal *birth vita* in a society of ideally equal opportunities leave the society with unacceptable income and wealth inequalities, more equal distribution could only be achieved by such *direct* redistributional policies as John Stuart Mill's inheritance tax proposal and Friedman and Tobin's negative income tax.

Appendix A. Two Occupational Classifications: Handling and Surgery

I. Handling

Work Performed

Work activities in this group primarily involve performing routine, nonmachine tasks involving little or no latitude for judgment. Adherence to rigid standards or specifications is not involved.

Worker Requirements

An occupationally significant combination of: Physical stamina; an inclination toward routine, repetitive activities; some dexterity with the fingers and hands; eye-hand coordination; form perception; and the ability and willingness to follow instructions.

Clues for Relating Applicants and Requirements

Good physical condition
Undistinguished scholastic record
Expressed preference for "outside" or factory work

Training and Methods of Entry

The work is usually so elemental in nature that no previous training is required, and entry workers generally receive only a short demonstration or explanation of the tasks involved. The most important hiring factor is the ability of the applicant to meet the strength requirements, ranging from light to very heavy according to the job. Personal characteristics very often play a significant part. An employer usually will have much latitude in engaging people because of the nature of the work and the fact that many applicants can qualify for it. He or she frequently will be influenced by an applicant's record of reliability, honesty, and industry. These factors are also taken into consideration when it is decided who will receive training in more complex work and who will be promoted.

II. Surgery

Work Performed

Work activities in this group primarily involve diagnosis and treatment of human disease, injury, and deformity by manual or instrumental operations.

Worker Requirements

An occupationally significant combination of: Intellectual capacity to comprehend a wide variety of subjects in basic medical sciences and college-level courses in humanities and social sciences; ability to learn and apply principles and substance of medical disciplines; analytical ability to derive nature, origin, and probable course of illness or injury from diagnostic and historical information; verbal ability to learn and use medical terminology; spatial perception to visualize position and arrangement of unseen organs, bony structures, and body tissue from X-ray photographs and knowledge of anatomy; form perception to see details in body tissues and structures; combination of finger and manual dexterity and motor coordination as required to use surgical instruments and apparatus with precision and speed; ability to make quick decisions and perform difficult tasks under stress; and stamina to maintain high level of concentration, alertness, and performance during prolonged periods.

Clues for Relating Applicants and Requirements

Demonstrated intellectual ability at college or university level. Interest in science as it relates to health and welfare of people.

Training and Methods of Entry

Preparation to practice requires 8 to 9 years of pre-medical and medical training leading to the doctor of medicine degree, followed by 3 to 6 years of advanced training and experience directed toward development of specialized skills required in the operating room. Successful completion of a licensure examination is required in all states and the District of Columbia. In addition, doctors of medicine seeking to specialize in surgery must satisfy the requirements specified by an examining board in order to gain certification and professional recognition.

Source: [41, 360, 471]

References

1. Barzel, Y. and R. J. McDonald, "Assets, Subsistence, and the Supply Curve of Labor." *American Economic Review*, September 1973, 621–33.

2. Becker, G. S., "Investment in Human Capital: A Theoretic Analysis." *Journal of Political Economy*, October 1962, 9–49.

3. Ben-Porath, Y., "The Production of Human Capital and the Life Cycle of Earnings." *Journal of Political Economy*, August 1967, 352–65.

4. Bergmann, B. R., "The Effect on White Incomes of Discrimination in Employment." *Journal of Political Economy*, March/April 1971, 294–313.

5. Borts, G. H., "The Equalization of Returns and Regional Economic Growth." *American Economic Review*, June 1960, 319–47.

6. Bowles, S., "Migration or Investment: Empirical Tests of the Human Investment Approach to Geographical Mobility." *Review of Economics and Statistics*, November 1970, 356–62.

7. Bowles, S. and V. I. Nelson, "The 'Inheritance of IQ' and the Intergenerational Reproduction of Economic Inequality." *Review of Economics and Statistics*, February 1974, 39–51.

8. Canterbery, E. R., "Income Distribution, Human Property and Non-Property Rights," in *Human Rights*, edited by E. H. Pollack. Buffalo, N.Y.: Jay Stewart Publications, Inc., 1971, 373–95.

9. Canterbery, E. R. and H. Tuckman, "Reflections upon the Income Distribution as a Pure Public Good." *Quarterly Journal of Economics*, May 1973, 304–10.

10. Chiswick, B. R. and J. Mincer, "Time Series Changes in Personal Income Inequality in the United States from 1939, with Projections to 1985." *Journal of Political Economy*, Supplement, May/June 1972, s34–s71.

11. Clark, C., "The Marginal Utility of Income." *Oxford Economic Papers*, July 1973 (new series), 145–59.

12. Duncan, O. D., "Ability and Achievement." *Eugenics Quarterly*, March 1968, 1–11.

13. Duncan, O. D. et al. *Socioeconomic Background and Achievement*. New York and London: Seminar Press, 1972.

14. Fair, R. C., "The Optimal Distribution of Income." *Quarterly Journal of Economics*, November 1971, 551–79.

15. Finkel, S. R. and V. J. Tarascio. *Wage and Employment Theory*. New York: The Ronald Press Company, 1971.

16. Gallaway, L. E., "The Effect of Geographic Labor Mobility on Income: A Brief Comment." *Journal of Human Resources*, Winter 1969, 103–09.

17. Gramm, W. L., "Household Utility Maximization and the Working Wife." *American Economic Review*, March 1975, 90–100.

18. Greenwood, M. J., "The Geographic Mobility of College Graduates." *Journal of Human Resources*, Fall 1973, 506–15.

19. Gronau, R., "The Intrafamily Allocation of Time: The Value of the Housewives' Time." *American Economic Review*, September 1973, 634–51.

20. Gwartney, J., "Changes in the Nonwhite/white Income Ratio—1939–1967." *American Economic Review*, December 1970, 872–83.

21. Harrison, B., "Education and Underemployment in the Urban Ghetto." *American Economic Review*, December 1972, 796–812.

22. Haworth, J. G. et al., "Earnings, Productivity, and Changes in Employment Discrimination during the 1960's." *American Economic Review*, March 1975, 158–68.

23. Hochman, H. M. and J. D. Rodgers, "Pareto Optimal Redistribution." *American Economic Review*, September 1969, 542–57.

24. Jencks, C. *Inequality: A Reassessment of the Effect of Family and Schooling in America*. New York: Basic Books, Inc., 1972.

25. Johnson, H. G. *The Theory of Income Distribution*. Lectures in Economics, 3. London: Gray-Mills, 1973.

26. Kaluzny, R. L., "Determinants of Household Migration: A Comparative Study by Race and Poverty Level." *Review of Economics and Statistics*, August 1975, 262–74.

27. Laber, G., "Human Capital in Southern Migration." *Journal of Human Resources*, Spring 1973, 223–41.

28. Long, L. H., "Migration Differentials by Education and Occupation: Trends and Variations." *Demography*, May 1973, 243–58.

29. Mazek, W. F. and W. E. Laird, "Size Preferences and Population Distribution: The Analytical Context." *The Quarterly Review of Economics and Business*, Spring 1974, 113–21.

30. Miller, E., "A Note on the Role of Distance in Migration: Costs of Mobility Versus Intervening Opportunities." *Journal of Regional Science*, December 1972, 475–78.

31. Parnes, H. S., "The National Longitudinal Surveys: New Vistas for Labor Market Research." Proceedings of the American Economic Association, *The American Economic Review*, May 1975, 244–49.

32. Sahota, G. S., "Theories of Personal Income Distribution: A Survey." *Journal of Economic Literature*, March 1978, 1–55.

33. Schultz, T. W., "Investment in College Instruction: Equity and Efficiency." *Journal of Political Economy*, Supplement, May/June 1972, s2–s30.

34. Sjaastad, A., "The Costs and Returns of Human Migration." *Journal of Political Economy*, Supplement, October 1962, 80–93.

35. Tannen, M. B., "The Distribution of Family Income: A Reexamination." *Southern Economic Journal*, April 1976, 666–74.
36. Taubman, P., "The Determinants of Earnings: Genetics, Family, and Other Environments; A Study of White Male Twins." *American Economic Review*, December 1976, 858–70.
37. Taussig, F. W. *Principles of Economics*. Vol. II. New York: The MacMillan Co., 1915.
38. Thurow, L. C. *Generating Inequality*. New York: Basic Books, Inc., 1975.
39. Thurow, L. C., "The Income Distribution as a Public Good." *Quarterly Journal of Economics*, May 1971, 327–36.
40. Thurow, L. C. *Investment in Human Capital*. Belmont: Wadsworth Publishing Co., 1970.
41. U.S. Employment Services. *Dictionary of Occupational Titles*, 3rd ed. Vol. II. Washington, D.C.: U.S. Government, 1965.
42. von Furstenberg, G. M. and D. C. Mueller, "The Pareto Optimal Approach to Income Redistribution: A Fiscal Application." *American Economic Review*, September 1971, 628–37.
43. Weiss, Y., "The Risk Element in Occupational and Educational Choices." *Journal of Political Economy*, November/December 1972, 1203–13.
44. Weiss, L. and J. G. Williamson, "Black Education, Earnings, and Interregional Migration: Some New Evidence." *American Economic Review*, June 1972, 372–83.
45. Wright, S., "The Relative Importance of Heredity and Environment in Determining the Piebald Pattern of Guinea Pigs." *Proceedings of the National Academy of Science*, 6, 320–32.
46. Yezer, A. M. and L. Thurston, "Migration Patterns and Income Change: Implications for the Human Capital Approach to Migration," *Southern Economic Journal*, April 1976, 693–702.
47. Zeckhauser, R. J., "Optimal Mechanisms for Income Transfers," *American Economic Review*, June 1971, 324–34.

Chapter 11

Welfare Economics and the Vita Theory

E. RAY CANTERBERY*

I. Introduction

A useful welfare economics died giving birth to Paretian ophelimity.[1] However, the elegance associated with the most refined version of general equilibrium theory seems to assure ophelimity's life after death. Nonetheless, a theory that treats the functional distribution of income as given and the personal distribution as nonexistent cannot draw robust conclusions regarding a fundamental welfare issue, namely the equity of the personal income distribution.

In this article I argue that the faults in traditional welfare optima go beyond the tendency to use ophelimity in a futile effort to avoid the ethics of distribution. First there must be a theory of the personal income distribution. In order to avoid the treatment of labor as just another commodity, I use a human developmental or anthropogenic model that describes the process of cumulative acquisition of competences or credentials over time. Traditional human capital theory, an approach that relies too strongly on static exchange optima and that continues to treat labor as an abstraction, is modified by integrating individuals into the labor supply in stages over time. These stages are benchmarks in the labor market vitae of persons and hence the term, vita theory. The vita theory of the personal income distribution itself has been developed in greater detail elsewhere [7]. In the present article a vita theory of the labor market is used to highlight the true nature of welfare optima as well as to show the requirements of any new welfare economics approach.

The focus of the vita theory is on the ways in which persons are able to increase their options in seeking higher incomes over a life-plan. Once those variables over which individuals have personal control are identified, it is clear that some individuals have far more options than others. Then, the goal of a welfare economics is to identify the constraints and to judge whether and show how they can be eliminated. In other words, the distant peak of a utility mountain is of little

*The Florida State University.

*The author has greatly benefited from comments on various ideas developed in this paper by Kenneth Boulding, David Braybrooke, Martin Bronfenbrenner, Jeffrey Burkhardt, Kathryn Freeman, the late Harry G. Johnson, Abba P. Lerner, Alan Mabe, John Rawls, Ingrid Rima, Joan Robinson and Lester Thurow. They are not otherwise implicated in the results. This research was supported by the National Science Foundation (Grant No. OSS77-16566). Any opinions, findings, and conclusions or recommendations expressed in this publication do not necessarily reflect the views of the National Science Foundation.

[1] Pareto's ophelimity optimum is the Pareto optimum as commonly understood by economists. Ophelimity assumes: (a) want-satisfaction is a function only of private goods and services; (b) individuals' want-satisfactions are independent; (c) preferences are revealed only in a market; (d) individual preferences are given; and (e) property and human capital distribution is given rather than determined (see Tarascio, [23, 20]). On the other hand, Pareto's sociological definition of utility from his *The Mind and Society* has been discussed by Tarascio as "a social concept, deriving from ethical, moral, religious, political, etc., as well as economic causes" [23, 7]. This sociological definition would extend to the broader interpretation of utility used in this article. Samuelson [21, 213–214] as well as others mistakenly equate Pareto's *ophelimite* with Pareto's *utilite*.

relevance to those confined to the initial base camp by circumstances beyond their personal control. In this view human welfare can be enhanced by policies that enable persons to start the climb along a path that leads to the preferred destination.

The equity with which options or the endowments that provide the options are distributed becomes a legitimate enquiry for welfare economics. Problems of equity—especially distributions at birth—take economists into a terrain of collective choice and ethics that most would rather leave to others. As I show, however, because utility functions are interdependent in reality, only a homogenizing force such as an ethic can leave persons otherwise satisfied with unequal marginal utility conditions. Among those to whom economists have relinquished equity principles is philosopher John Rawls. It thus seems appropriate to appraise the Rawlsian difference principle within the construct of the vita theory modified through its merger with interdependent utility functions. Whether one agrees with Rawls, he has forced the equity issue into the open. When economists come out of the ethics closet they find themselves again confronted with utilitarianism, an ethical system from which they have been retreating during the past century.

II. The Vita Theory of the Personal Income Distribution Redux

The purpose of this section is to provide a summary of the vita theory.[2] Its main thrust can be simply stated. Assume that one labor market exists for each general human capital classification. The individual's quantity of human capital determines which labor market the person enters. A person "qualifies" for a particular labor market by the state of his or her vita at that point in time. Determination of vita begins at birth when one's race, sex, religion, national origin, inherent mental and physical capacity, inheritances, and family background are duly noted.

The vita is "added to" over one's lifespan by education, other training, and experience. The individual has some control over the "length" and "depth" of his or her vita. Since labor demand is related to product prices and a changing technology, however, only the rare individual can predict with any accuracy the derived demand for workers with vitae of his or her type. Moreover, specific labor supply conditions are a collective consequence outside personal control. Then, given one's vita and the characteristics of the applicable labor market, as a first approximation, the individual's basic wage rate depends upon the wage of central tendency for such labor services. Upon further approximation, however, the individual's personal income exhibits differentials from potential labor market earnings. The differentials—occupational, geographic, inter-industry, union-nonunion, discriminatory, and so on—often can be traced back to the first vita stage, which I call the *birth vita*.

The *pre-career vita* retains the initial characteristics at birth and includes education and "first-time" on-the-job training. The *mature vita* that also carries work experience is the labor-market vita. The individual confronts a large number of homogeneous and, thus, noncompeting labor markets in which each exhibit a wage of central tendency.[3] In the short run technology and the state of industrial competition are constants on the demand side, while labor mobility among markets is absent on the supply side. Demand and supply

[2]See Canterbery [7].

[3]A homogeneous noncompeting labor market is defined as one bounded geographically and one in which the elasticity of substitution in production between the labor of its type and the other types within the area approaches zero. The geographic limits are set by "reasonable" commuting distances (at current state of transportation technology) from the selected labor population center.

conditions vary with the human capital (HC) type as well as with labor union and licensing practices.

In any particular labor market the wage rate of central tendency is responsive in the long run to changes in the type and nature of unionism and licensing, new entrants, changes in average product prices, and improvements in technology of the employing industry and firms. It is nonetheless true that the actual wage rate facing the worker is always the short-term wage rate, which may or may not be near the long-term rate.

General Labor Market Conditions

As the concentrated manufacturing sector and industrial unions are the pacesetters in the modern industrialized economy, I will focus exclusively on what John Kenneth Galbraith has called the "planning system" to illustrate wage determination in a labor market.[4]

Initially assume a one-to-one correspondence between general human capital classifications (HC's) and labor market types. We can think of the members of the labor supply of a human capital type as being in rank order (for example, *1, 2, . . . , γ*) from most to least preferred employee characteristics, a labor force queue at either a local or national level. It is presumed that whatever involuntary unemployment exists it will involve the persons ranked lowest within the *HC* classification.

In the short run the wage rate and the employment level are decided by different forces. Essentially, this separation of forces stems from the static nature of production processes combined with union regulations in the short run. Union rules usually specify the number of workers assigned to a machine and floor area as well as their work speed. The production process—otherwise designed by technology—cannot be altered in the short run. Let σ_i be the labor hours required of the *i*th human capital type (HC_i) per unit of physical output in a selected geographical area. As employment is a fixed proportion of production, the quantity of labor demand is

$$z_i = \sigma_i q_j, \qquad (1)$$

where q_j is the total output of product *j*, which is assumed to be homogeneous across the labor market.

If labor were paid its value in production, the wage rate would be

$$w_i = \sigma_i^{-1} \rho, \qquad (2)$$

where ρ is the price of the product or service produced by this labor type. (In Knightian terms ρ would be the expected price.) No union worker alone can influence this price. Technological progress, a change in the production process, can alter the demand for a particular labor type directly by changing labor-quantity requirements. That is, while capital and labor tend to be complements (fixed factor coefficients) in the short run, they potentially are substitutes in the long run. The magnitude of the direct effect of technological progress upon the demand for labor depends upon whether the new technology is labor-using.

Technological change can also exert an indirect effect. A new, more complex technology can result in a producer's shifting to labor that embodies a much greater quantity of human capital, a different human capital type. These shifts are institutionalized via job description changes (often required by union agreements). Either direct or indirect shifts in labor demands which emanate from technological change can be represented as changes in the values of the σ's. The industrial union's instrumental variable is the wage rate rather than the labor supply. The union is aware of the pricing power of the concentrated indus-

[4]For a more general theory of how this sector is interrelated with demand conditions and therefore contributes to inflation, see [5, 79–103].

try in which higher wage costs can be passed on through a constant or rising mark-up over variable or average costs. The likelihood of full-cost pricing increases with greater product market imperfection.

Whereas the level of employment is decided by the production technique and the level of product demand (output) in the short run, in the long run the connection between productivity and the wage rate is closer but of a different character than often described. The demand for labor is responsive to changes in average product prices and improvements in technology of the employing industry and firms. As the labor supply of a particular *HC* type usually requires a gestation period of several years, the long-run labor supply is a function of the expected wage rate (w^*) rather than the actual.

The motives for capital accumulation are not always clearly defined. However, even if producers do not desire growth to maintain market shares or for other reasons, a remaining salutary effect of adopting a new mode of production is the potential it gives for replacing labor. Beyond the reduction of the wage bill, replacement of workers with machines has further advantages: machines do not demand fringe benefits and are more responsive to managerial commands. Moreover, the long-term trend of wages is known to be upward, especially in the already capital-intensive industrial sector that is unionized. It is not surprising, therefore, that the price markup is used to generate investment funds for the purpose of acquiring a production process that utilizes less labor.

It is important to distinguish between the usual graph depicting a cause-effect relation between the wage rate and the quantity of labor demanded and a graph of the *loci* of wage rates and labor quantities. It is the latter that is represented in Figure 1, which shows the labor market for one unionized human capital type in a particular geographic area. (Linearity is assumed for simplicity.)

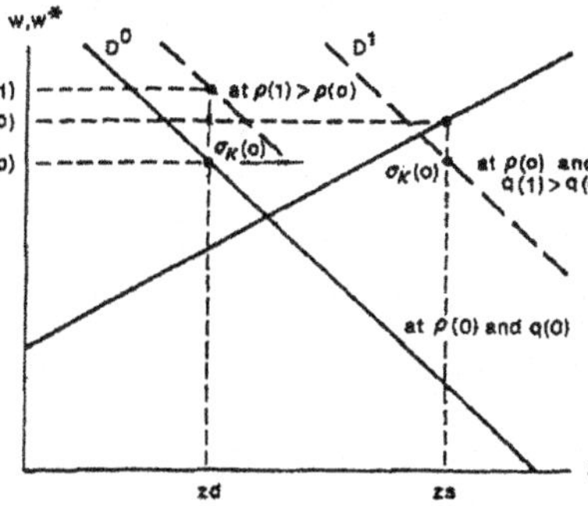

Figure 1. Wage-Employment LOCI, An Industrial-Union Labor Market

If the growth of technology reduces the labor-output ratio, the loci of $w = \sigma^{-1}\bar{\rho}$ and $z = \sigma\bar{q}$, where z is employment and q and ρ are at given levels, trace out what appears to be a downward-sloping labor demand curve. As fixed production coefficients pertain at each new level of technology, the labor-output ratio equals the marginal labor-output ratio. As more capital-intensive production reduces labor per extra unit of output, by definition the marginal physical product of labor rises as z declines. At higher levels of output, the wage-employment loci shift rightward: at higher product price levels, the loci shift upward. However, just as a higher product price and wage rate do not necessarily imply a higher employment level, neither does a lower amount of output necessarily result in a lower wage rate.

The employers of industrial labor have an incentive and ability to substitute capital for labor in the long run. Thus, the w-z loci trace an "elastic" curve. At any time labor demand, however, is represented by only one point, such as $\sigma_\kappa(o)$, which is given by the current state of technology. The labor supply curve, being based upon wage expectations, tends to be relatively price-elastic. Although the actual and expected wage rates may be nearly equal (as illustrated), capital substitution may have advanced to the point where labor demand is zd (σ has declined to $\sigma_\kappa(o)$ so that only an output increase sufficient to shift the demand to D^1 (at $\sigma_\kappa(o)$) would bring full employment to this labor market). At a constant or rising price markup, a wage increase (motivated by attempts to maintain or increase discretionary income) to w(1) will bring along a price rise to $\rho(1)$. Alternatively, a price rise to $\rho(1)$ may result in an increase in the wage rate to $w(1)$. The direction of cause-to-effect depends upon timing in the bargaining process and may be unrelated to output changes (as illustrated). The wage rate at $t(0)$, the short-run wage rate, may or may not be near the long-term rate. Within such an environment it is unrealistic to presume that any particular worker has control over his or her contract wage rate.

In the long run, the manufacturer reduces his dependence on labor by adopting new capital-intensive processes purchased with the investment funds generated by the price mark-up. The long-run physical marginal product of labor is merely an artifact derived from new technologies.[5] The actual relation between labor and capital is that decided by the new human capital required to match the skill requirements for operating the new machines and equipment. As the labor force does not know what these future skill requirements entail, the mismatch of human capital and machines often results in unemployment even when wage rates are rising. As labor is not paid its marginal revenue product, any welfare inferences based upon the Paretian marginal conditions are spurious.

Differential Wages and Labor Mobility

The vita theory of the labor market provides an explanation for several kinds of wage differentials. If we make the usual assumption of "rationality" with respect to income, these differentials represent an opportunity to "arbitrage," but any adjustments certainly cannot be expected to approach the efficiency of foreign exchange markets. The mobility of labor is a complex, difficult, and cumbersome process.

According to the vita theory, the individual achieves a higher wage rate via his or her labor mobility, either through time (temporal) or across space (spatial). The high-wage seeker would look to a labor market of licensed professionals with monopolistic supply control over high-priced services of inelastic demand with little prospect for capital-intensive technological advances located in a traditionally high-wage geographical area.

Significant upward temporal mobility requires the acquisition of a greater quantity of human capital (moving from HC_n and toward HC_1). Whether this be a response to changing skills requirements from technological change or a result of the person's desire to increase status and income, the training and education augmentation requires substantial blocks of time and, unless the employer offers a training program, a substantial personal investment commitment.

Unfortunately, low levels of capital which inhibit upward temporal mobility also slow spatial mobility. Such transfers are related to desire, ability, and prospects for success. Although social barriers to labor migration no doubt vary with the quantity of human capital, the main economic inhibitor to successful migration is the cost of physical transport, financed from one's capital stock ($k + \kappa$), and the level of capital itself.

The search for higher earnings may end with still another obstacle to mobility. The individual may not receive the wage rate of the labor market and occupation of choice because of characteristics decided by his or her birth vita. Discrimination, be it racial, sexual, age, ethnic, or whatever, can preclude

[5] I do not intend to imply that the marginal product case is any better supported outside of manufacturing. Quite the contrary, a glance at the salaries of professional service workers will be no more reassuring.

a particular individual from receiving the wage rate of central tendency. We expect, therefore, to find earnings differentials are wider than wage differentials.

III. The Issue Regarding Control over Personal Incomes

In vita theory language, a general personal income function for the *j*th individual is[6]

$$y = y(h, k, \kappa, \rho, m, \theta, M, R), \qquad (3)$$

where the subscript, j, is deleted, y = before-tax personal income, h = hours worked, k = the jth individual's human capital, κ = the jth individual's nonhuman capital endowment, ρ = the average price of the product or service produced by this individual's labor (or expected price), m = an index of mobility, θ = a variable that measures risk and uncertainty regarding income opportunities at alternative geographical locations, M = an index of monopolistic power that would equal zero for individuals with "ordinary" or average human and nonhuman capital endowments under free entry conditions in groups of large numbers, and R = a discrimination (racial, sexual, ethnic, and other) index that is negatively related to income for those who suffer economic effects from discrimination.[7]

The amount of time available for work effort is limited by the biological constraint of the total number of waking hours ($\bar{h}$). Divide the hours of "leisure time" between hours allocated to augmentation of human capital (h_1) and those devoted to "pure" leisure (h_2) and the terms h, h_1, h_2, or whatever can be defined by assumption.

In the vita theory monopolistic power (M) depends upon both the level of total capital endowment ($k + \kappa$) and the labor market entry conditions or occupation entry conditions of the relevant labor market. Let EN be an index of entry in which larger values of EN represent greater ease of entry. The value of EN for most blue-collar occupations is described by the type and level of unionization.

In the long run the relation between race, sex, or ethnic identification and income can be eliminated by societal attitudinal changes and laws that require equal treatment in hiring practices. Thus, although the coefficient or R may change, suffice it to say that $(\partial y/\partial R) < 0$ where discrimination exists.

I can now be more specific about functional relations. Whereas temporal mobility is a direct function of the quantity of human capital (k), worker spatial mobility is a direct function of k, κ, and θ, so $m = m(k, \kappa, \theta)$, where $\partial m/\partial k > 0$, and $\partial m/\partial \kappa > 0$, and $\partial m/\partial \theta < 0$. The monopolistic power function is $M = M(EN, k, \kappa)$, where $\partial M/\partial EN < 0$, $\partial M/\partial k > 0$, and $\partial M/\partial \kappa > 0$.

Finally, there is a labor demand shifter (professional) or wage rate shifter (union or unskilled)—associated with product price changes—$\partial y/\partial \rho > 0$. As suggested above, the main impact of technological improvements is upon employment; that is, upon h, which may become zero unless the individual becomes underemployed. As this is a discrete phenomenon, I assume that that the individual responds by attempting to increase his or her human capital. Let the function W be the personal capital rate and (3) can be written as

$$y = h \cdot W[k, \kappa, \rho, m(k, \kappa, \theta), M(EN, k, \kappa), R]. \qquad (4)$$

The "wage rate" is the entire function W.

Initially calendar time is undefined so as to

[6]Similar but more complex functions can be generalized with respect to the household.

[7]If equation (3) were to contain the variables for the representative worker in the ith labor market, then (3) is properly viewed as a reduced-form equation for the HC_i labor market.

express the model in the most general terms.[8] The partials with respect to income are given below.[9]

The Utility Functions

Satisfaction from one's own income is relative, because the person's utility from income is related to other known or "perceived" incomes in the society. Utilities are interdependent.[10] Granted, the perception of utility from other persons' incomes, irrespective of whose or how many, will normally be fuzzy.

With the fuzziness caveat initially hypothesize that relative income satisfaction is derived from own-income, the income of a "representative" person in a higher income interval that can be aspired to by the individual, and the income of a "representative" member from a lower income interval. In theory the "representative" persons might be individuals that one personally knows but more likely one has a vague image of an amorphous group with incomes above and below one's own.

In general, then

$$u = u(y, y^a, y^P, h), \qquad (5)$$

where y^a = before-tax personal income of a representative of the aspiration interval, y^P = income of a representative of the interval immediately below the income of the individual whose income is y, and $h = \bar{h} - h_1 - h_2$, where h_2 is pure leisure.[11]

Marginal disutility from hours worked has two components: (1) loss of leisure; (2) labor effort. Traditionally the disutility from work is assumed the same at all income and capital levels. However, an income unit from nonhuman capital normally can be generated with less labor effort than from human capital. Moreover, the productivity increases commonly associated with larger amounts of either human or non-human capital imply that work effort can decline with increases in either kind of capital. In common sense terms, time and effort used in calling a stock broker is small relative to the expected return. As Scitovsky has suggested, "such lightening of the work burden might well turn out to be no less or even more important for people's welfare than the reduction in working hours" [22, 16]. Further, some empirical work suggests that leisure is valued more at higher income levels.[12] Moreover, in "desirable"

[8]The variables can be expressed in any time units desired. For example, the income variables can be defined as expected lifetime or average lifetime earnings. Age is not included explicitly as a variable determining income. However, years of experience (a proxy for age or vice versa) *is* included as a human capital variable.

[9]The personal income partials are:

$h \cdot (\partial y/\partial k) > 0;$
$h \cdot (\partial y/\partial \kappa) > 0;$
$h \cdot (\partial y/\partial \rho) > 0;$
$h \cdot [(\partial y/\partial m) \cdot (\partial m/\partial k)] > 0;$
$h \cdot [(\partial y/\partial m) \cdot (\partial m/\partial \kappa)] > 0;$
$h \cdot [(\partial y/\partial m) \cdot (\partial m/\partial \theta)] < 0;$
$h \cdot [(\partial y/\partial M) \cdot (\partial M/\partial EN)] < 0;$
$h \cdot [(\partial y/\partial M) \cdot (\partial M/\partial k)] > 0;$
$h \cdot [(\partial y/\partial M) \cdot (\partial M/\partial \kappa)] > 0;$
and $h \cdot (\partial y/\partial R) < 0.$

[10]Also see the critique of the voluntary exchange models in [9]. An alternative version of utility interdependence is developed by Canterbery [3].

[11]This section introduces a broader definition of the utility function than applies in the vita theory.

[12]Empirical research finds the first-order partial derivative w.r.t. income positive in all income ranges. Marginal disutility from hours worked is derived from loss of leisure and increased marginal labor effort. The individual's labor supply curve would become backward-bending at $|\partial u/\partial h| > |\partial u/\partial y|$. See Clark's [11] survey of the empirical literature and his own statistical test.

An unresolved research problem is the separation statistically of diminishing marginal utility of income through an increased taste for leisure from disutility from other sources such as concern for others' incomes, work effort required per income unit, failure of worker opportunities to meet societal goals, and others that are discussed in this paper.

The risk of human capital losses also may have some affect upon utility. However, these risks do not appear to be correlated with the persons' human capital levels.

Some persons may believe that risk of property loss is positively correlated with property holdings. The accumulation of tangible property, therefore, might lead to perceived rising risks, a risk factor that would appear occupations or professions, work may even yield positive utility, rather than disutility. Thus the disutility from hours worked is modified by some function of K, κ, and y. Take these elements into account by writing utility from hours worked as a function of $h \cdot f(k, \kappa, y)$, where $\partial f/\partial k < 0$, $\partial f/\partial \kappa < 0$, $|\partial f/\partial \kappa| > |\partial f/\partial k|$ and, more tentatively, $(\partial f/\partial y) \gtrless 0$. The function f qualitatively alters hours worked: the value of the function decreases with effort-reducing increments of capital, increases as income increments augment the value placed upon leisure or, for that matter, decreases as work itself might become more valued at higher income levels.

Utility from income interdependencies depends in great part upon the individual's attitude toward the equality of the income distribution. More precisely, the existence and the sign of certain incremental utilities depends upon whether the individual is relatively egoistic, malevolent, or altruistic toward the receivers of the incomes in other intervals.

Also there are explicit "goals of society" that affect individual utilities more indirectly, as ethical judgments. "Equality of opportunity to maximize personal income" is an example of such an ethic. Freedom of market entry, worker mobility and nondiscrimination are among those variables that reflect the reality of such opportunities. Although equal opportunity is widely contended as an American ethic, an identical type of analysis could hypothesize a different ethic.

Let S be an index of proxy variables that measures the contribution toward fulfillment of the social objective. The social, economic, or political policies influencing EN, $\partial y/\partial R$ and θ are instrumental in maximizing the social goal of (for illustrative purposes) "equal opportunity." The impact of personal tastes or value judgments is in part moderated, therefore, by the broader social goal that could augment the satisfaction otherwise derived from one's own income. Let g be a monitonically increasing function and write $y \cdot g(S)$.

By substitution of the qualitative hours function and the social goal index in (5) the individual's utility function becomes

$$u = u[y \cdot g(S), y^a, y^p, h \cdot f(k, \kappa, y)] \quad (6)$$

where, by hypotheses, $y \cdot (\partial u/\partial g) \cdot g'(S) \gtreqless 0$, $(\partial u/\partial y) \cdot g(S) \gtreqless 0$, $h \cdot (\partial u/\partial f) \cdot f'(k, \kappa, y) \gtrless 0$, $(\partial u/\partial h) \cdot f(k, \kappa, y) < 0$.

Obviously, economists know little about which signs to select. However, from one's own income in isolation, always $\partial u/\partial y > 0$. The existence and sign of the other marginal utilities will depend upon individuals' relative altruism and consequent responses.[13] Obviously, any one or a few altruistic individuals cannot significantly alter the average income within an income interval. A measurable impact upon the national income from altruism or egalitarianism is most likely to emerge from the "mandatory" application of a collective decision.[14]

Let us see what *mathematical* optimization of this formulation implies. Divide the income distribution into only two intervals, the "poor" and "nonpoor." The precise poverty threshold is not crucial. The poor (p) will

even in locations where such risks are imaginary. However, we do not know to what extent private measures are taken in an effort to protect human life versus property.

Because I cannot be precise about the meaning of the evidence or the ability of persons to otherwise avoid these various risks, only risks related to worker relocation appear in this model.

[13]Such altruism may or may not include a voluntary willingness to give up part of one's own income to augment the income of another. Altruism is defined as regard for the economic well-being of others.

[14]What is "mandatory" at one level of implementation is not necessarily mandatory at another. In a representative democracy society's members voluntarily agree to a social pact with the government in which powers are delegated voluntarily so that certain policies are enforced in such a subsequently mandatory way that the numbers of "free riders" are minimized.

have little, if any, non-human capital. Assume initially that it is zero. Because the poor are, by definition, in the lowest interval, $y = y^p$, and $y^a = y^n$ where n denotes the "nonpoor." But, for notational simplicity, drop the "p" superscript for all variables that relate to the poor, so

$$y = h \cdot W[k, \rho, m(k, \theta), M(EN, k), R], \quad (7)$$

for a representative poor person. The nonpoors' (n) income sources are less restricted because of non-human capital endowments: the n-income equation is the same as the general equation (4). The total differential of (7) is given below.[15] However, in the short run only dh will be non-zero.

In the long-run, the differentials can be viewed as descrete Δ's that are larger for larger units of calendar time (assuming linear approximations are possible). Alternatively, the integral of dy/dt can be taken over the lifecycle in order to derive lifetime income. Then, $y(t_0)$ in equation (7) gives the individual's income at a point in time in the individual's life cycle.[16]

Write the utility function for the representative poor as:

$$u = u[y \cdot g(S), y^n, h \cdot f(k, y)]. \quad (8)$$

Again, the total differential appears below.[17] The income constraint, utility function, and differentials for the representative nonpoor are comparable to those of the poor except they follow (4) and (6), respectively and, in the two-interval model, $y = y^a = y^n$.

IV. Implications for Microtheory, Human Capital Optima, and Income Maxima

The unconstrained maxima for the poor and nonpoor respectively can be defined as

$$\max u, \max u^n, \quad (9)$$

where the sufficient conditions require that all first-order increments be zero and all second-order increments be negative. The maximization of life-cycle utility implies that at any point in time maximum utility is a point on the optimum life-cycle utility path. Let us denote these unconstrained maxima as "ultra-maxima." Ultra-maxima are ideals achievable only in utopias. Not only are current incomes and hours worked constraints that preclude ultra-maxima but so are the other independent long-run variables—human capital, non-human capital, risk, entry conditions, and discrimination. The peaks of the utility mountains represented by (9) are inaccessible.

The conventional "optimum" with respect to hours worked occurs at a socially static time, a period in which social attitudes and public policies as well as capital levels are non-changing.[18] Because these conditions pre-

[15] Without defining precise units of time, and with the assumption of additivity of the W-function arguments, the total differential of equation (7) is:

$$\begin{aligned} dy = \{&h \cdot [\partial y/\partial k + (\partial y/\partial m) \cdot (\partial m/\partial k) + (\partial y/\partial M) \cdot (\partial M/\partial k)]\} \cdot dk \\ &+ [h \cdot (\partial y/\partial \rho)] \cdot d\rho \\ &+ W[k, m(k, \theta), M(EN, k), R] \cdot dh \\ &+ [h(\partial y/\partial m)] \cdot (\partial m/\partial \theta)] \cdot d\theta + [h \cdot (\partial y/\partial M) \cdot (\partial M/\partial EN)] \cdot dEN \\ &+ [h \cdot (\partial y/\partial R)] \cdot dR. \end{aligned}$$

Time is the implicit common denominator of the differential.

[16] The income distribution implications of the life-cycle approach are well described by Johnson (13, 207–210].

[17] The total differential of u (8) is

$$\begin{aligned} du = &[(\partial u/\partial y) \cdot g(S) + h \cdot (\partial u/\partial f) \cdot (\partial f/\partial y)] \cdot dy \\ &+ (\partial u/\partial y^n) \cdot dy^n + [(\partial u/\partial f) \cdot (\partial f/\partial k) \cdot h] \cdot dk \\ &+ [(\partial u/\partial h) \cdot f(k, y)] \cdot dh \\ &+ [(\partial u/\partial g) \cdot (\partial g/\partial S) \cdot y] \cdot dS. \end{aligned}$$

The relation of the comparative static with the life-cycle utility is analogous to the above treatment of income.

[18] At this point we need to be very clear on the meaning of our notation. Posit a function $z = f(x, y)$, and the value

exist, however, the optimum is at a higher or lower *level* of utility than it otherwise would be. The more broadly defined vita "optimum" for a representative poor person would be:[19]

$$dy/dh = Y'_h(k, \rho, \theta, EN, R) = -\frac{U'_k(S, y^n, k, y)}{U'_y(S, y^n, k, h)}. \quad (10)$$

The similar "optimum" for the nonpoor interval would include a constant value for κ. These "optima" are derived with *non-changing opportunities* for maximizing personal income, *except* for changing hours worked. Even the hours worked can only be varied within the boundary conditions decided by institutional arrangements and biological work effort limits. Moreover, the poor's own "optima" without some substantial change in endowments leaves them still poor. The nonpoor "optimum" also is very limited because the constraints preclude any means for capturing any externalities from the redistribution of income.

Utility interdependence brings into question the meaningfulness of using the standard marginal conditions for optima. First, the variables determining the respective *income constraints* are independent because the capital endowment for p is unrelated to the n endowment, but the utilities from the two incomes are interdependent. There is no assurance that p's utility can be maximized with respect to y^n when p has no control over n's income and vice-versa. Positive and negative externalities are present, not rationalized by markets, not likely resolved by private transfers, and therefore preclude simultaneous true optima. Second, (10) and its n-interval counterpart themselves are only *obtainable* with current human-non-human capital endowments, the present state of competition (including the prices of products produced), and no taxes or grants altering current income from all sources.

The above specification alters the traditional relation between hours worked and leisure. The wage rate is only part of the personal capital return for the *nonpoor*. If we include the impact upon income of non-human capital and assume that utility is constant (i.e. form indifference curves), the individual will choose more leisure time. That is, in part personal income determines the amount of leisure time rather than the one-

of $\partial z/\partial x$ at a point (x, y) depends, not only upon the value of x from which we start the limiting variation that defines the partial derivative, but also upon the value of y that is kept constant during the limiting process. Thus the precise meaning of partial derivatives in multi-variable functions is made obvious with more appropriate notation. Write $\partial z/\partial x$ as $f'_x(y)$, and it is clear that the partial derivative w.r.t.x at a point (x,y) is a function of both x and y where the term(s) in parentheses is (are) constant. Further simplifying notation, partial derivatives are written as the "dependent" variable capitalized with subscripts denoting the independent variable with respect to which the derivative is taken. For example, now the partial of the poor's income with respect to human capital is:

$$h \cdot [\partial y/\partial k + (\partial y/\partial m) \cdot (\partial m/\partial k) + (\partial y/\partial M) \cdot (\partial M/\partial k)] = Y'_k(h, \rho, R).$$

[19]Begin with the differential of the utility function for the poor (8) from the text. Initially, there are two constraint equations, (4) and (7), where the dependent variable in (4) is designated as y^n. Their differentials can be substituted for dy and dy^n, respectively, in equation (8). Then set (8) equal to zero and divide through by dh.

The first-order condition for a constrained optimum is $du = 0$. Because certain variables are independent of h at this juncture, $dy^n/dh = dk/dh = d\rho/dh = d\theta/dh = dEN/dh = dR/dh = dS/dh = 0$, and none of these variables are now *mathematical* constraints. Use our abbreviated notation (see footnote 18) and we have the simplified "optimum" w.r.t. hours worked for the poor, equation (10). The more complex form of the derivatives can be seen by inspection of their counterparts in the differential equations of the text. For example, $U'_y(S, y^n, k, h) = [(\partial u/\partial y) \cdot g(s) + h \cdot (\partial u/\partial f) \cdot (\partial f/\partial y)]$. Also, note that $dy/dh = Y'_h(k, \rho, \theta, EN, R) = W[k, \rho, m(k, \theta), M(EN, k), R]$. That is, the ratio of the differentials can be written as a partial derivative when all other derivatives are zero.

The higher order optimality conditions are met by assumption.

way causality wherein the leisure-time decision determines income.[20]

With the limitation upon augmenting income by increasing the number of hours worked, how does the individual improve his economic status? The vita theory suggests that any significant improvements are derived from switching to a higher wage rate. Since such a change can only be made via temporal or spatial mobility, we must consider the human capital optimum and therefore changes that can occur (if at all) over the long run.

The earnings function is not at "first causes" in terms of birth, pre-career, and mature vitae. As these vitae are defined elsewhere [7], detail is omitted and the mature vita is represented as

$$k = F(G, h_1, s_2, s_3, E, \tau), \tag{11}$$

and

$$\kappa = H[I_0, F(G, h_1, s_2, s_3, E, \tau)], \tag{12}$$

where I_0 is the initial nonhuman capital endowment, G represents the genetic code, E represents family environment conducive to earnings potential, s_1 is the hours of education within the sole control of the individual, s_2 is the number of hours of State-required formal schooling, s_3 is the hours of initial on-the-job training within sole control of private industry, and τ is years of experience. Net additions to total capital can be derived from increases in the hours devoted to human capital accumulation. Assume that G and E are indices that take on larger values when they are favorable for augmenting human capital (earnings capability) at birth.

Assume now that the poor have some positive value of non-human capital so that the *forms* of the p and n optimums are identical. Also assume that $dh_1/dh_2 = 0$ and therefore $dh_1/dh = -1$. Substitute the capital functions of (11) and (12) into the earnings equation (4). At any time the individual is optimizing w.r.t. the rate of voluntary education-training if[21]

$$\begin{aligned} dy/dh_1 = {} & Y'_k(\rho, \theta, EN, \partial y/\partial R) \\ & \cdot K'_{h_1}(G, s_2, s_3, E, \tau) \\ & + Y'_\kappa(\rho, \theta, EN, \partial y/\partial R) \\ & \cdot K'_k(I_0, G, s_2, s_3, E, \tau) \\ & \cdot K'_{h_1}(G, S_2, s_3, E, \tau) - W \\ = {} & -U'_h(y)/U'_y(h). \end{aligned} \tag{13}$$

Voluntary education and training over the life plan is optimized by a life-cycle of optima that begin with the pre-career vita. Note also that, by the assumption that hours allocated to human capital production detract from work hours ($dh_1/dh = -1$), the income derived from work effort is reduced by the value of W.

If $I_0 \simeq 0$, or the individual is at the institutional or biological working-hour limits, one cannot seek a higher income. On the other hand, the case where I_0 is sufficiently large that reduced work effort is not a constraint on human capital development is approximated by assuming $dh_1/dh = 0$. Then,

[20]The reader can easily verify this with the standard wage rate-hours utility map by comparing equilibria at lower and higher "wage rates" with total hours awake (available hours) constant.

Returning to an earlier point, the hours-worked restriction will not be as severe on the nuclear household. The two adults might enter two different labor markets so that their combined hours of work is much greater than is implied by the supply curves in the individual labor markets.

[21]After substitution of equations (11) and (12) into (4) in the text, take their differentials. Substitute the differentials of the earnings function (dy) into the differential of the utility function. Then set the differential of the utility function equal to zero and divide by dh_1. (Again, the first-order condition for a constrained "optimum" is $du = 0$.) By assumption, $dh_1/dh_2 = 0$, and h_2 is no longer a mathematical constraint. Use our abbreviated notation (see footnote 18) and we have the "optimum" w.r.t. hours devoted to human capital development.

The higher-order optimality conditions are met by assumption.

$$dy/dh_1 = Y'_k(\rho, \theta, \partial y/\partial R) \cdot K'_{h_1}(G, s_2, s_3, E, \tau) + Y'_k(\rho, \theta, EN, \partial y/\partial R) \cdot K'_k(I_0, G, s_2, s_3, E, \tau) \cdot K'_{h_1}(G, s_2, s_3, E, \tau) = -U'_h(y)/U'_y(h). \quad (14)$$

Large initial endowments free the individual to increase the hours devoted to human capital without having to be concerned about the reduction in current income via reduced work effort. Therefore, material inheritance can be important in defining the initial conditions which affect the lifetime income path.[22]

Costs of Increasing Human Capital

In human capital theory the person invests in an educational or training program that has a positive net present capital value.[23] However, in reality the optimum human capital level depends upon the same constraints as those that determine current incomes. In short, if one could ignore costs and claim a favorable genetic code and family background (G and E), the "rational" individual would decide to become Human Capital Type 1.

However, expected costs cannot be ignored. Assume that parents and, subsequently, individuals rank costs in the same order as the general human capital quantity requirements (HC's), then $C_1^* > C_2^* > C_3^* > \ldots C_n^*$. The accessibility to a human capital type that yields a higher return depends strongly upon initial capital endowments and the current income that such endowments yield.[24] The observed inability of individuals to acquire any HC type they desire cannot be attributed to "imperfect capital markets": this failure often can be traced back to the birth vita.

The individual's investment potential may be restricted to a Human Capital Type and hence a labor market that will yield a small stream of lifetime income. We are merely suggesting that capital tends to beget human capital tends to beget income tends to beget capital, and so on. One moves to a higher income interval by altering one's vita and then shifting from one labor market to another. Any movement toward social optimization (either in comparative statics or in life-cycle terms) requires some sequential ordering of optima (in a climb up the poor and nonpoor utility mountains) as a part of the sociopolitical process. Mathematically, this process is replicated by a chain of differentials that implies diminishing individual control over the independent variables with each additional differential "link" that "lengthens" the chain. But this only holds in a linear approximation because the movement of a person from one labor market to another involves descrete (and perhaps large and lumpy) changes in capital.[25]

V. Collective Choice, Ethics and the Income Distribution

Just as we cannot deny the roles of human and non-human capital in determining

[22]The initial material endowment plays no functional role in the traditional human capital literature (see, for example, Chiswick and Mincer [10]).

[23]The net capital value of investment in Human Capital Type 1 (k_1^*) is

$$k_1^* = \sum_{t=0}^{n} \frac{y_t^*}{(1+i)^t} - \sum_{t=0}^{n} \frac{C_{1,t}^*}{(1+i)^t},$$

where y^* = expected income, C_1^* = expected cost of acquisition of k_1, and i = market interest rate.

[24]If inheritance (I_0) is limited, any current costs to the individual must be financed by borrowing if h_1 hours must be substituted for work hours (h). The implied interdependence between I and k is exhibited in our model by the freedom given to persons with large endowments to increase human capital hours while ignoring the impact of such changes upon current income from work effort.

[25]Beyond these problems, as Thurow [24, 22–23] has indicated, identical levels of acquired formal education do not by any means guarantee that such persons will be in the same income interval.

income, we also cannot ignore the role of collective decision-making.

Any income distribution beyond that which is determined by private institutions requires a deliberate economic policy presumably motivated by societal concerns and unrequited externalities. Although society can be viewed as a cooperative venture for mutual advantage, it is ordinarily marked by conflict as well as by identity of interests. Because of conflict, further redistribution will be decided by the balances of power among groups in the political system, an arrangement greatly controlled by ideological and ethical considerations so that only an approximation of a global maximum is possible.

This reality can be illustrated with a human capital variable. Assume that $\partial k/\partial G = \partial k/\partial E = 0$. Then, the individual's utility can be maximized with respect to any one of the variables amenable to policy influence—I, EN, θ, s_2 or $\partial y/\partial R$. Consider State-supported schooling (s_2). Because the hours devoted to schooling are mandatory, assume that such hours are taken away from work effort hours, and the "optimum" for someone in the poor interval is[26]

$$dy/ds_2 = dy/dk - dy/dh = -[U'_k(s, y, y^n) - U'_h(s, y, y^n)]/U'_y(s, y^n, h). \quad (15)$$

The same process w.r.t. s_2 applies to the nonpoor except that the level of I_0 and κ are non-zero and

$$dy^n/ds_2 = dy^n/dk + dy/d\kappa - dy^n/dh \quad (16)$$

where dy^n/dh may not be a constraint.

The more complex solution for the nonpoor illustrates the tenuous nature of such "optima." If in fact schooling does not detract from hours worked, the optimum must be defined in social terms; otherwise, *no constraint exists*. Let T be tax revenue for public schooling and we know that if $dy/ds_2 = dT/ds_2$, then $dy^n/ds_2 \neq dT/ds_2$; that is, the marginal benefits are not equal for every interval in the personal income distribution. Therefore, any "optima" have to be defined in social terms because marginal tax rates are constraints on public funding. A similar problem attaches to the inheritance tax as a policy variable: From the view of the nonpoor there is no constraint regarding their increase in income from an inheritance tax reduction—unless the nonpoor are concerned about their *relative* income increases compared with a static income level of the poor. However, such a concern is collectively expressed in the social goal index (S) and probably requires the presence of, at a minimum, biased altruism (see Section III). Moreover, as society changes the mere ordering of policies, the nature of the next "optima" is altered. That is, the various "optima" are not in fact independent and thus the overall social configuration is crucial.

In the history of economics in the English-speaking world the dominant ethic used to judge the worth of economic arrangements has been utilitarianism in one form or another. The assignment of utility to each individual mirrors utilitarianism. With sustained economic growth in a society, the belief that everyone can become equally better off is a convenient ethic to counter those who would suggest any willful redistribution of income. Nonetheless, the transformation of utilitarianism into Pareto ophelimity has taken from economists the capability to judge the personal income distribution on utilitarian grounds. Although it is argued that only the individual can judge his or her own satisfactions, the "given" nature of preferences precludes any evaluation of the meaning of ophelimity welfare optima. This analytical

[26]In deriving dy/ds_2 the same steps are used as in deriving dy/dh_1 except we divide through the fully-specified utility differential by ds_2. Only $dS/ds_2 = 0$, and only this (initial) mathematical constraint is dropped. The second order conditions for an optimum can only be assumed, not assured.

trick still has left the escape from value judgments incomplete, because all ophelimity optima are presumed to be ones of engineering efficiencies and therefore such efficiencies are prized above all other things. It is not surprising therefore that some scholars, especially philosophers, conclude that Paretian ophelimity is incapable of yielding the liberal solutions traditionally associated with utilitarianism.[27]

The paretian dilemma has led many economists to the principles of justice of Harvard philosopher John Rawls [19]. The vita theory also points to the issues raised by Rawls regarding the random and thus "arbitrary" nature of initial endowments in deciding the income and wealth distributions. As we shall see, to raise and clarify the issues—though helpful—does not resolve all the analytical difficulties.

The Rawlsian Principles of Justice

In Rawls' "original position" the principles of justice are chosen behind "a veil of ignorance" so that no one is advantaged or disadvantaged in the choice of principles by the outcome of natural choice or the contingency of social circumstances. The "veil of ignorance" is such that persons do not know particulars concerning their own capacities, personal likings or aversions (such as risk aversion), or the positions they would occupy in an ongoing society.

The persons in the original position are "rational:" having a coherent set of preferences among options, the individual ranks the options so as to advance his own interests. Rawls makes the special assumption that individuals do not suffer envy because envy tends to worsen everyone's lot. With no other side conditions, the prototypical person of the original position would be indistinguishable from the prototype of the Paretian economic man.

The Paretian economic man, however, is completely autonomous—to the point of not even considering himself to be a member of society. Although the rationality in Rawls is one of mutual disinterest, the parties are nonetheless capable of a sense of justice because of their knowledge about the general facts of society [19, 142–145]. This preference for social intercourse diverges from the autonomous economic man prototype.

In the original position persons prefer more to fewer primary goods because the individual has greater probability of advancing his or her own ends (which are not known in particulars) if he or she possesses more such goods. In the vita theory context the increased quantity and quality of human and nonhuman capital would best advance one's own ends.

Among the primary goods are opportunities and powers, and income and wealth. Rawls couples powers and wealth: "greater powers and wealth tending to go together . . ." [19, 94]. By "powers" Rawls apparently means the ability to achieve one's ends. However, it is difficult to separate these abilities from the exercise of power (over others) in a general, political sense.

The assumed "finality" of the social contract leads to a unanimous decision from the "original position" in which the "worst off" representative person will be in the best circumstances possible. This "maximin" solution yields two principles, the second of which concerns us most directly. The difference principle holds that social and economic inequalities are to be arranged so that they are (a) to the greatest expected benefit of the "worst off" members of society (the maximin equity criterion) and (b) attached to offices and positions open to all under conditions of equality of opportunity [19, 12]. The difference principle is applied by open competition

[27] See, e.g., Rowley and Peacock [20]. For further explication of the liberal dilemmas that emanate from various versions of utilitarianism, see Canterbery [6].

for offices and positions, and then, subject to this constraint, by the arrangement of social and economic inequalities so that everyone benefits [19, 61].

By assuming that powers and wealth go together, Rawls narrows the residual social and economic inequalities to those of wealth and income. Such inequalities are permitted only when they can be shown to be to the advantage of the economically "worst-off" societal group. Then, because everyone benefits from economic and social equalities, "there is an identity of interests since social cooperation makes possible a better life for all" [19, 126].

Rational Individualism and Social Cooperation

An ostensible paradox derives from what appears to be an unduly individualistic concept of rational persons in the abstract original position, in contrast to Rawls' early call for "social cooperation" [19, 4]. At first glance, Rawls too appears to be caught in the ophelimity trap. This seeming paradox can be resolved in two ways.

First, embedded in the original position is the notion of a "well-ordered society," a society in which persons share the same views about justice derived from their general knowledge about human society. The conception of justice is not egoistic (as, e.g., Paretian ophelimity is), but is based upon individuals' understanding that social cooperation makes possible a better life for all than any would experience, should each live solely by his own efforts. Furthering one's ends requires the cooperation of other members of society. As Rawls sees it, mutual disinterest (as to particulars appended to others) and the veil of ignorance "forces each person in the original position to take the good of others into account" [19, 148].

Second, the value of community is established by Rawls (in Part II), using the idea of "reflective equilibrium." The members of society reexamine the principles of justice (especially in comparison with what Rawls too considers the main competing principle of utilitarianism and its individualism) and find, upon reflection, that the correct principles have been chosen. As Rawls states, "not until later is justice seen as part of our good and connected with our natural sociability" [19, 584].

Rawlsian Utility Functions

We now come to a second apparent paradox. The interdependent utilities outcome in the original position is analogous to that for pure altruism. The conditions assumed achieve the same purpose as interdependent utility functions such as those formulated in this article. When one makes a decision in the original position, the choice is made simultaneously for oneself and for everyone else, because any individual has an equal expected probability of ending up in the same socioeconomic condition as *any one* of all others. The assumptions force one's own utility to be determined *as if* it were everyone's utility, making the inclusion of other persons' income in one's own utility function redundant. In the ongoing society the "as if" outcome is no longer sufficient, however, and interdependent utility functions are *required.* Only in social union can each person participate in the sum of the realized natural assets of others.[28]

The Problem of Social Conflict

Although society is a cooperative venture for mutual advantage, Rawls admits that on a micro level "it is typically marked by a conflict as well as by an identity of interests" [19, 14]. It is on the subject of conflict that

[28]Also, see the long footnote beginning on page 523. Rawls also believes that entitlements are "... very often derived from social institutions and the legitimate expectations to which they give rise" [19, 10].

TABLE 1. The Control-Level Matrix

Optimum w.r.t.		Time Order	Given Conditions	Individual Control	Corporate Control	Public Policies: Democentric	Public Policies: Public Interest
a	destiny	0	G				
a		0	E				
b	core micro-economic theory	1	ρ				
c		2		dh			
d	human capital	3		ds_1			
e	modified human capital	4			ds_3		
f		5				ds_2	
g	all other economic institutions	6				dI	
h		7				$\partial y/\partial R$	
i		8				dEN	
j		9				$d\theta$	
k	pure collective choice	10					dy^P, dy^n through taxes and grants on current income

the possibility of incompleteness in Rawls' difference principle appears.[29]

In the ongoing society there is little basis for societal conflict as long as everyone's income is advanced (economic growth) and as long as the poor see their fortunes tied to those of the nonpoor. However, a greater potential for social conflict begins when the national income is viewed as a constant in which the poor can only achieve further benefits through direct redistribution. Moreover, as the analysis of Section IV requires, the Rawlsian framework gives rise to the notion of the State's redistributive function even at the level of initial natural endowments.

The schema of Table 1 is useful for analyzing the relation between Rawls' priorities and institutional arrangements. The initial condition is nature's distribution of endowments (wealth), a distribution that is, according to Rawls, "arbitrary." These initial states affect every personal income determined thereafter, and the difference principle can be used to appraise the justness of the resultant inequalities. Once the construct of a society is introduced, such endowments affect occupational selection. Due to social mores, inherent characteristics—sex, race, and so on—determine which persons are rewarded. A free market economy rewards those who have skills in high demand, but only under *ceteris paribus* social conditions.

[29]For those seeking a critique of Rawls' principles of justice per se, see [1] and [17]. For a collection of papers by economists contrasting Rawls [19] with Nozick [17] who goes beyond Pareto ophelimity to defend the justness of all free exchange outcomes, see [8]. Also, see [4] for a more general appraisal of Rawls and more details on the issues of this section of my article.

There are at least two types of public policies that can alter vitae, which I will call Democentric and Public Interest policies. 1) *The Democentric Policies:* Policies that influence geographic-occupational mobility and the income effect of discrimination (through θ, EN, I_0, s_2, $\partial y/\partial R$) also *indirectly* alter the income distribution. The individual exerts indirect control over incomes (including own-income) through society's institutions. These parameters give us the income in equation (4). Because these policies may lack the expected impact, be incorrectly perceived, or not be pursued vigorously, society moves to a second classification of policies.[30] 2) *The Public Interest Policies:* Society may choose to alter *directly* the resultant incomes (enter Friedman's and Tobin's negative income tax proposals as well as Boulding's Grant Economics). Although the maximization problem is attacked more directly through pure collective choice, decisions on relative incomes nonetheless are delegated to the governing fiscal institution as one part of a social contract.

The individual yields some personal sovereignty. Taxation always involves a mandatory rule for collection which normally precludes an optimum tax rate from the view of every *person* taxed. Some lost sovereignty, however, is pre-existing in the State at the inception of a social contract. Long ago Buchanan characterized political voting "as an alternative power structure which may be deemed preferable to that of the market" [2, 341].[31]

[30] Although all these policies change the income distribution, they may not have been motivated entirely by such a goal. For example, mandatory education may be urged by those who see minimum education for the population as necessary for the effective functioning of a democracy. Indeed, the lack of specific redistribution intent may be a force leading to the Public Interest Stage policies. For example, empirical studies show that increases in education can contribute to economic growth without significantly changing the distribution of income.

[31] For an excellent discussion of "social coercion" in the voting process, see Buchanan [2, 339].

Democentric policies would work on the constraints related to a, b, and c, attempting to provide equality of opportunity and to keep offices and positions open to all. These policies would have Rawlsian priority over public interest policies, and might include free public education, a public library system, judicial actions against discrimination, free medical services to those born frail, anti-trust policies, and so forth. However, if democentric policies fail or are otherwise inadequate in meeting Rawls' difference principle, public interest policies would emerge to directly redistribute incomes by taxes and grants.

A socially optimum condition depends upon the nature of the utility function of each interval. Let p and n denote the most representative members from each social group. At a fixed level of national income simultaneous optimum for each representative requires

$$dy^p/dy^n = -(U^{p\prime}_{y^n}/U^{p\prime}_{y^p}) = -U^{n\prime}_{y^n}/U^{n\prime}_{y^p}) \quad (17)$$

which states that the ratios of the marginal utilities from nonpoor and poor incomes are equal for the representatives from either income interval! Recall, however, that social values and goals may be such that the nonpoor individual might receive smaller increments of satisfaction from the same unit of own-income than he or she otherwise would. If the utility ratios *are* equal governments can select the y's in such a way that the maximum implied by (17) is realized.

Suppose, however, that $(U^{p\prime}_{y^n}/U^{p\prime}_{y^p}) \neq (U^{n\prime}_{y^n}/U^{n\prime}_{y^p})$ so that what is optimal for each separately is not optimal for the society. A global maximum would require the aforementioned homogenizing agents, say β^p and β^n, so that

$$dy^p/dy^n = -\beta^p \cdot (U^{p\prime}_{y^n}/U^{p\prime}_{y^p}) = -\beta^n \cdot (U^{n\prime}_{y^n}/U^{n\prime}_{y^p}). \quad (18)$$

The homogenizing agents may come from

increased information flow, a change in the *g* function, or altered personal value judgments. The difference principle itself may ultimately provide the homogenizing ethic.

Any movement toward the difference principle optimum is contingent upon both groups benefiting (in some sense) from a transfer of income from the nonpoor to the poor. In economic terms the necessary conditions for such a move depend upon a diminishing marginal utility of income and the actual interdependence of utilities. The sufficiency conditions require that the nonpoor have reason to transfer diminishingly satisfying but nonetheless positive increments of expected income utility to the poor. Neither the representative poor nor nonpoor have "fairness" as an impartial observer of their utilities. They are their own utility beholders. And, as Musgrave contends, a social optimum requires "the mandatory application of the voting decision . . . to secure revelation of preferences" [16, 992].

Unless ideology dissuades them, the poor view existing income inequalities as undesirable, if not unjust. If the nonpoor resort to the rationality of Paretian ophelimity and the self-interest assumed in Rawls' original position, they will not respond by making income transfers. However, if human nature is as Rawls describes it in reflective equilibrium, and the nonpoor perceive the advantages of social cooperation (perceivable even in the original position), the nonpoor will realize that natural endowments are common assets and that the society will lose its stability if the poor are not compensated in a way that retains their cooperation. The poor presumably know, however, that they cannot push the nonpoor too far in redistributive efforts, because then everyone would lose income. That is, the poor desire to live in a well-ordered, stable society as well.[32]

[32]Following Rawls, we abstract from any influence that ideology might impose on the poor's degree of acceptance of their socio-economic rank.

Ironically, Rawls' assumptions about human behavior, in the absence of commitment to principles agreed to in the original position, lead to a utilitarian outcome. That is, an income redistribution from the nonpoor to the poor raises the sum of utilities and therefore societal utility (in a utilitarian sense).[33] However, the wealth-power duality in Rawls prevents his system from resolving social conflict in a society pervaded by substantial inequalities. In such a society, a very wealthy group, would, under Rawls' assumption, also be very powerful in achieving the ends of *its* representative member. Suppose this well-financed group retained the rational self-interest assumed in Rawls' original position and therefore used its power to maintain (at the least) the status quo. Suppose such a group can effectively influence policymakers by campaign financing and lobbying as described by Okun [18, 22–31]. Dollar vote outcomes in an income distribution determined at the margin by the government would leave the distribution with income differentials that closely approximate those of a market economy. Obviously, there is no distribution that would give a simultaneous optimum in terms of the poor and the newly-assumed wealthy group.

VI. Concluding Statements

Paretian ophelimity optima, at their best, require that factors of production be paid their marginal products. The vita theory raises serious doubts: the processes of production, for the most part, decide the productivity of all factors concurrently. Then, the level of employment in any particular labor market is decided apart from the wage rate, an outcome that precludes matching wage payments with labor's marginal product. The Paretian optima are not even "second best" under these conditions and welfare optima

[33]As with most expressions of utilitarianism, Rawls' is utilitarianism "with constraints," see [1].

based upon efficiency conditions become more remote from reality.

Unconstrained ultra-maxima are achievable only in a utopia which is literally, "nowhere." Interdependent utilities and the weakness of individual control over crucial variables lead to social policies. The definition of a *social* optimum can be altered as a society devises more and more policies that reduce existing constraints that limit optima selection.[34] While the traditional Pareto criteria on Samuelson's Utility Possibility Curve give infinite efficiency optima at one given income distribution, my model provides the basis for a large but finite number of social welfare optima out of nearly infinite income distributions. Whereas the expansion of the core to include collective choice facilitates the definition of a maximum feasible social welfare optimum that does not rely upon the Pareto ophelimity conditions, a renewal of welfare economics would require the use of an ethic regarding the social desirability of an income distribution selected from all possible distributions. When economists are pressed to select an ethic, they historically have retreated into utilitarianism. John Rawls claims to offer a competing set of principles.

However, there is a curious puzzle in Rawls. He says that "the motivation of the person in the original position must not be confused with the motivation of persons in everyday life who accept the principles that would be chosen and who have the corresponding sense of justice" [19, 148]. Given our knowledge about human nature, in the original position persons are not trusted to be fair to anyone but themselves. Why should we suppose that persons in the ongoing society without the benefit of the original social contract suddenly would behave in a benevolent way, especially since the same knowledge of human behavior pertains? Why is Rawls not willing to advance the two competing systems (Rawls' principles and utilitarianism) on their own merits?

The answer appears to be roughly as follows. Rawls wants to justify his principles in the accepted "scientific" sense (i.e., using rational choice and social contract theory), with no direct appeal to moral values as such. However, he is in danger of being in the same dilemma as is the Paretian welfare economist. If the economist equates the self-interest of the original position to egoism in society and ignores persons' "natural sociability," optima still are of the Paretian ophelimity variety. As a result, the Rawlsian assumptions about behavior in a cooperative society provide an incomplete model of income redistribution. The optimal income distribution depends upon the interdependent utility functions from the view of persons in the ongoing society.

The realization of a social minimum awaits the perceived identity of interest with the poor of the nonpoor, or else their altruism. This does not mean that Rawls' difference principle should be ignored. With a fate formerly reserved for John Stuart Mill, Rawls has presented a vision—not a program—which inspires thoughtful reconsiderations of existing social arrangements. Most importantly—at least from the view of an ethic acceptable to economists—Rawls' system of justice approaches utilitarianism (with constraints) when we apply his principles to the income distribution of the ongoing society.

[34]For example, if there were no restrictions on the order in which the policies are introduced in Table 1 and we assume that all "optima" are independent of each other, the combination of time order and lettered "optimums" provide 3,628,800 optima permutations for each income interval. If at the other extreme, we assume that the time order can follow only the chronology illustrated, there are nine "optima" per income interval.

References

1. Braybrooke, D., "Utilitarianism with a Difference: Rawls' Position in Ethics." *Canadian Journal of Philosophy*, December 1973, 303–31.

2. Buchanan, J. M., "Individual Choice in Voting in the Market." *Journal of Political Economy*, August 1954, 334–43.
3. Canterbery, E. R., "Income Distribution, Human Property, and Non-property Rights." *Human Rights*. Edited by E. Pollack. Buffalo, New York: Jay Stewart Publications, Inc., 1971, 373–95.
4. Canterbery, E. R., "Income Redistribution Amidst Rawlsian Paradoxes." Paper before the Southern Economic Association Meetings, Washington, D.C., November, 1977.
5. Canterbery, E. R., "Inflation, Necessities and Distributive Equity." *Essays in Post-Keynesian Inflation*. Edited by James Gapinski and Charles Rockwood. Cambridge, Mass.: Ballinger, 1980, 79–103.
6. Canterbery, E. R., Review of *Welfare Economics: A Liberal Restatement* by C. K. Rowley and A. T. Peacock. *Southern Economic Journal*, April 1979, 1304–07.
7. Canterbery, E. R., "A Vita Theory of the Personal Income Distribution." *Southern Economic Journal*, July 1979, 12–48.
8. Canterbery, E. R. and H. G. Johnson, eds. Symposium on Justice, Nozick and Rawls. *Eastern Economic Journal*, January 1978.
9. Canterbery, E. R. and H. Tuckman, "Reflections upon the Income Distribution as a Pure Public Good." *Quarterly Journal of Economics*, May 1973, 304–10.
10. Chiswick, B. R. and J. Mincer, "Time Series Changes in Personal Income Inequality in the United States from 1939, with Projections to 1985." *Journal of Political Economy*, Supplement, May/June 1972, s34–s71.
11. Clark, C., "The Marginal Utility of Income." *Oxford Economic Papers*, July 1973 (new series), 145–59.
12. Henderson, J. M. and R. E. Quandt, *Microeconomic Theory: A Mathematical Approach*. New York: McGraw-Hill, 1971.
13. Johnson, H. G., *The Theory of Income Distribution*. Lectures in Economics, 3. London: Gray-Mills, 1973.
14. Lipsey, R. G. and K. Lancaster, "The General Theory of Second Best." *Review of Economic Studies*, 1956–57, *24* No. 63, 11–32.
15. Morganstern, O., "Thirteen Critical Points in Contemporary Economic Theory." *Journal of Economic Literature*, December 1972, 1163–89.
16. Musgrave, R. A., "Pareto Optimal Redistribution: Comment." *American Economic Review*, December 1970, 992.
17. Nozick, R., *Anarchy, State and Utopia*. New York: Basic Books, 1974.
18. Okun, Arthur M., *Equality and Efficiency: The Big Tradeoff*. Washington, D.C.: The Brookings Institution, 1975.
19. Rawls, J., *A Theory of Justice*. Cambridge: Harvard University Press, 1971.
20. Rowley, C. K. and A. T. Peacock, *Welfare Economics: A Liberal Restatement*. New York: John Wiley and Sons, A Halstead Book, 1975.
21. Samuelson, P., *Foundations of Economic Analysis*. Cambridge: Harvard University Press, 1947.
22. Scitovsky, T., "The Place of Economic Welfare in Human Welfare." *Quarterly Review of Economics and Business*, Autumn 1973, 7–20.
23. Tarascio, V. J., "Paretian Welfare Theory: Some Neglected Aspects." *Journal of Political Economy*, January–February 1969, 1–20.
24. Thurow, L. C., *Generating Inequality*. New York: Basic Books, Inc., 1975.

Chapter 12

The Forbes Four Hundred: The Determinants of Super-Wealth*

E. RAY CANTERBERY
E. JOE NOSARI
Florida State University
Tallahassee, Florida

I. Introduction

Research on richness is rare. Since the Age of the Moguls, roughly from the Civil War to the Great Depression, the super-rich in the United States have gone underground. This privacy has now been shattered by *Forbes* magazine which began publishing "The Richest People in America: The Forbes Four Hundred" in 1982. This compilation of the richest rich was not easily accomplished, inasmuch as the majority of the people in it, including Malcolm S. Forbes, Chairman and Editor-in-Chief, would have preferred not to have been listed. Therefore, this annual survey by *Forbes* provides a rare glimpse "into the nature of wealth and the wealthy, into how they got that way as well as who they are, and how they conduct their lives" [3, 100].

The purposes of this article are to compile a data base from the *Forbes* study, analyze insofar as possible the causes of super-wealth and suggest areas in which such a data base falls short of perfection. Before describing these new data, however, we will summarize some theories of richness.

II. Theories of Wealth

From the beginning of their speciality, economists have been ambiguous about wealth. The most widely cited classical on the subject of "richness" is probably John Stuart Mill; in the *Principles* he bemoans the accumulation of unearned wealth. His main targets are landlords and inheritors. The landlords, earners of economic rent, ". . . grow rich as if they were in their sleep, without working, risking or economizing . . ." [6, 818]. The inheritors receive wealth without any exertion. Even though Mill may be writing of both the income and the wealth distributions when he states: "The distribution of wealth, therefore, depends upon the laws and customs of society" [6, 200], his most controversial reform proposal favors changing the law by taxing inherited wealth.

If we move forward to the neoclassicals, we find that a *simpliste* marginal productivity

*We wish to thank an anonymous referee who provided insightful and usable suggestions that greatly improved the article and Susan Williams who provided able editing assistance.

theory sheds little light on the causes of wealth. The neoclassicals generally agree that marginal productivity theory serves, at best, as a theory of the demand for factor inputs. The postulates of marginal productivity theory are satisfied indirectly by Euler's theorem of product exhaustion only if production functions are homogeneous of the first degree or directly if the firm's maximum profit equals zero and the production functions are non-homogeneous.

In Alfred Marshall's view, the net marginal productivity of labor depends upon the availability of complementary factors of production, such as land, which in turn depends in part upon alternative demands for these cooperating factors. Since the distribution of income (and wealth) influences the demands for outputs and inputs, marginal products cannot be independent of the prior distributions (which the theory is intended to explain) [5, 517–18]. The neoclassicals could not ignore these interdependences once Walras's general equilibrium theory was understood. Therefore, the neoclassicals began to use a factor price frontier deduced from the zero-profit conditions of competitive general equilibrium and which indicates, at each level of interest rate, for each productive technique, the maximum wage rates that a competitive firm can pay without incurring a loss. Generally, then, only in long-run competitive equilibrium with no firms earning economic profits would the distributional postulates of marginal productivity theory be met.

The requirement of long-run competitive equilibrium not withstanding, neoclassical economics has long since accomodated its analyses of price-setting and excess returns to the real-world presence of variant degrees of monopoly power. Even though the knowledge that degrees of monopoly power have distributive consequences has resulted in few systematic studies of these effects, it is frequently noted that monopoly power extracts consumer payments in excess of marginal costs. Although current owners of the enterprise (or ownership shares) may be receiving excess returns, monopoly profits are often capitalized into the value of the firm at the time of its creation so that when current owners acquired their ownership rights, the price they paid included the present value of the expected future stream of monopoly returns. Such wealth, then, is generated through the capitalization of monopoly profits. Through wealth conservation the original owners of the monopoly can pass along most of their gains through inheritance. Inheritance itself could be viewed as a source of monopoly returns lagged. In this perspective present wealth is based upon current monopoly ownership or past capitalization of monopoly profits.

In modern neoclassical theory, excess returns also can flow from rent in a way well-described by Johnson [4, 87–89]. As with Ricardian rent associated exclusively with land, the supply of a key factor is fixed or nearly-fixed for an economically relevant period. For any factor completely fixed in supply, the price it commands is determined by the demand for its services. Neither its alternative opportunity cost nor its original cost of production plays any part in determining its price. All returns to the factor, above zero or a reservation price, will be rent.

Lester Thurow, one of the few contemporary economists who has theorized about the causes of wealth, begins with Mill's hypothesis: "If one examines the very rich, about 50 percent of the great fortunes are gotten through inheritance" [10, 172]. Except for the observation that the very rich can pass wealth unimpaired to their children, Thurow offers no source for his "50 percent" solution. Rather, Thurow suggests that the "more interesting half" is "the half that did not inherit their fortunes." According to Thurow, two elements explain the "newly-acquired fortunes" in the form of entrepreneurial "instant wealth"—the capitalization of above-average returns and the random walk hypothesis.

Wealth from capitalization depends upon real capital markets being in disequilibrium. Thurow points to the wide variance in after-tax rates of return on stockholder equity by industry (3.6 to 18.6 percent) as evidence of disequilibrium [9, 143–46]. In an example [9, 173], an entrepreneur invests $10 million in real investment in plant and equipment and earns $3 million per year. At a market rate of interest or discount rate of 10 percent, the capitalized value of the investment is $30 million ($3 million/.10). The initial investor has quickly increased his wealth from $10 million to $30 million. Thurow's capitalization case nonetheless falls under the neoclassical monopoly returns rubric where the failure of long-run firm equilibrium and the presence of non-zero economic profits result in "disequilibrium rates of return." Thurow's capitalization idea only describes the Fisherian discounting mechanism whereby the returns to physical capital are instantly realized as individual financial wealth holdings. The same mechanism can be applied in the case of a fixed factor so that rent also can be capitalized. (A contemporary example is provided by the football player who receives a $5 million annuity.)

The capitalization process does not explain *which* individuals capitalize, nor how the rich stay wealthy. Thurow uses the random walk to explain how these instant fortunes are allocated to individuals. Since no one can predict where these opportunities for capitalizing real disequilibria will be, the winners emerge from a lottery. These nouveau riche are simply lucky [10, 175; 9, 142–54]. These large fortunes are buttressed either because the real capital market disequilibrium remains or because the rich then diversify their investments until they earn the market rate of return. A compound interest formula can keep the rich wealthy, and then the inheritors can benefit from the "good fortune" of the new rich.

Nobelist George Stigler also stresses the importance of compound interest and portfolio diversification in the accumulation and conservation of wealth [8, 308]. However, Stigler sees dynasties limited to no more than a century because of (1) stupid or profligate heirs and (2) an unstable environment.[1] With employment based upon labor participation rates, Stigler estimates lifetime labor earnings of living Americans (1960 census) at the *average* yearly wage per worker. He further assumes that each worker saved 10 percent of their labor income plus interest on savings, and upon retirement, purchased an annuity with the accumulation. Inherited wealth is that share of total wealth unexplained by the lifetime accumulation of this average worker. The estimated share of total wealth inherited on this basis ranged from zero to 73.9 percent (in "current" dollars). Stigler concludes that "... inherited wealth may be a very modest share of present wealth or it may be a dominant share" [8, 310].

Canterbery's vita theory [1] cuts across many of these theories because it is a modified "human capital" theory. Although the vita theory is about the personal income distribution and imperfect labor market and product conditions, it nonetheless places inheritance (genetic and material) in a central role. Canterbery's theory can be viewed as a theory of wealth if personal income is expressed in terms of the life-span. Canterbery views the vitae of full life cycle endowments and acquired capabilities of individuals in terms of three stages: (1) the birth vita, (2) the pre-career vita, and (3) the career or mature vita [1, 13–15].

1. Stigler shows that $1 invested at Caesar's death (44 B.C.) at a 5 percent annual interest rate would have amassed an incomprehensible $\$33.65 \times 10^{40}$ by 1964 in the absence of bad luck.

The three stages in human capital development highlight those variables and times in which the individual often loses control over important choices. Somewhere among these three stages entrepreneurship qualities may emerge.

We realize that these theories do not exhaust all possibilities. For example, traditional human capital theorists "capitalize" the returns to human capital as a measure of lifetime wealth. We have selected these particular theories because the Forbes Four Hundred data have something at least to say about the variables underlying these rather incomplete explanations.

In consideration of the selected theories and the data limitations, we examine the following propositions:

- That material inheritance accounts for a large share of wealth;
- That, among the inheritors, wealth is conserved (in a linear relation) through a diversified portfolio yielding average rates of return;
- That entrepreneurship, which capitalizes disequilibrium or "monopoly returns" (in a random walk), provides an exponential growth rate in wealth; and
- That rentmanship, which capitalizes the returns on a fixed factor, provides an exponential growth rate in wealth.

III. The 1982 Forbes Four Hundred Data Base: The Rules of the Chase

The sample is only of the richest rich, not of ordinary millionaires. The individual has to be a centimillionaire or worth at least what they call in Texas "a unit," to make the list. Since the *Forbes* researchers do not have much cooperation from the four hundred in the data compilation, certain valuation rules are followed.

1. Owned, traded stocks are priced at their mid-August 1982 market prices. 2. The values of privately held companies are computed as a multiple of estimated earnings, where the multiplier is based upon the multiples then prevailing for publicly traded companies in similar businesses. 3. The rule-of-thumb convention used within the particular industry is applied when earnings estimates are not available. (A newspaper company for example, is valued at $500 and up per subscriber, or 10 to 15 times earnings, or 1.0 to 1.4 times revenues, with a subtraction for probable liabilities.) 4. The worth of a TV station is evaluated by reputable media brokers. 5. In some cases, the researchers settle for estimates of book value, especially among private oil producers, where *Forbes* often does not go beyond placing a "fair estimate" on the company's oil reserves.

Trusts are especially difficult to evaluate and are valued by *Forbes* virtually on a case-by-case basis. Trusts are usually established to assure a normal pattern of inheritance (to wives or husbands, or offspring) and exist mainly to minimize inheritance taxes. 6. The trusts are generally attributed to the person (if alive) who created the wealth or else to the principal controlling family member when the creator is deceased. The assets of "spendthrift trusts" (meant to keep control of fortune *out* of the hands of beneficiaries) are credited to the controlling family members whereas the estimated trust income is assigned to the beneficiaries. 7. Irrevocable charitable trusts are not counted as wealth, even though, as in the case of the Pews of Sun Oil, they serve to retain control over the family company. 8. Foundations are not counted as wealth sources. 9. Wealth in the name of a spouse or child is considered to be part of the still-active principal's wealth, especially when family ties are close and family members share interests in an ongoing business. There are exceptions to this rule: (a) where a fortune is so great that another family member's share qualifies them for the Four Hundred (as with Wang Laboratories' An Wang and his wife, Lorraine), (b) where family and business ties are broken or badly frayed.

The researchers and writers provide examples of the ninth rule. They consider Joseph Meyerhoff as patriarch-in-charge of Magna Properties, whereas Henry Ford II is not considered in charge of Ford Motor Company. In the case of Ford, he is retired, and his children are "scattered" (maintaining their own inheritances), born of wives Ford has since divorced. (Besides, the researchers could come up with "only" $80 million for Henry Ford II himself, and that consists of "depressed Ford stock and his 4 percent interest in California's Irvine Ranch." Meyerhoff, on the other hand, still goes to his office, and his son, a major shareholder, is "in the business." The founder of Mary Kay Cosmetics, Mary Kay Ash, is not listed, whereas the president-son and largest share holder, Richard Rogers, is, because of the strong claim by both that he is and has been firmly in charge of the company.

Forbes acknowledges assistance from 82 sources and indicates that the more than 80 other sources insisted upon anonymity—mainly brokers, lawyers, and financial advisors [3, 172].

IV. The Regression Model

Our initial goal was to collect enough data to arrange in the vita theory format. These data would include values of the initial material endowment (inheritance) and the birthright human capital endowment decided by genetics and family environment conducive to earnings potential. The genetic code decides innate IQ, sex, race, and initial state of health. These are the variables of the birth vitae over which individuals have no control. However, no data are available on IQ, and Caucasians so dominate the Forbes Four Hundred population that race cannot appear as a variable. (As far as we could ascertain, for example, the sample contained only one Black whose presence left the estimated parameters essentially unaltered.) Since 82 percent of the Four Hundred is male of average age 61.58 years, we can safely infer that they have generally been of good health. Very little family background data (such as education of parents) are available, but we do know that 40 percent of the Four Hundred inherited a portion of their wealth. Later, for the career or mature vita, Canterbery [1, 13–15] contends that the type of industry of employment and geographical location create differential incomes because of differential benefits from degrees of monopoly power (including rents). Industry of association and employment as well as its location, is available from the Forbes data.

Although the Forbes Four Hundred data provide for strong inferences, the survey does not provide a data base sufficiently broad to test the vita theory.[2] Nonetheless, the vita theory provides a framework for organizing the data. Moreover, since the role of material inheritance is a theme running throughout the vita theory, the *framework* appears to be the best currently available for examining the inheritance propositions.

The Forbes Four Hundred data reveal many interesting characteristics of the richest rich. Average wealth is $231 million. The greatest number of the population resides, in

2. Canterbery [1, 36] suggests path analysis as a statistical procedure for testing the theory, but path analysis requires data from all the life stages.

Table I. State of Residence

State	Number	Percent of Total
New York	85	21
Texas	66	17
California	53	13
Florida	22	6
Other	174	43
Totals	400	100

Source: [3].

Table II. Industry of Source of Wealth

Industry	Number	Percent of Total
Manufacturing	133	33
Oil	73	18
Real Estate	67	17
Publishing	47	12
Shipping	4	1
Other	76	19
Totals	400	100

Source: [3].

rank order, in New York, Texas, California, and Florida. In fact, 57 percent of the Four Hundred are residents of only these four states (see Table I). Almost three-quarters are still actively employed (despite the high average age). One-third of the individuals are associated with manufacturing, while 18 and 17 percent are connected with the oil and real estate industries, respectively. Individuals in manufacturing industries include such names as Forrest Mars Sr., "the Howard Hughes of candy," David Packard of Hewlett-Packard Co., the third-largest minicomputer company, and William R. Hewlett of the same company. Among the richest-rich in oil are the three sons of H. L. Hunt's "first family," Lamar, William Herbert, and Nelson Bunker Hunt. At or near the top in real estate are Harry Brakmann Helmsley, who controls the Empire State Building, William Walter Caruth Jr., who owns 30,000 acres in North Dallas, and Trammell Crow, also of Dallas. Some 81 percent of the Four Hundred are associated with the five major industries noted in Table II.

The variables considered to be important in explaining wealth consist of a subset of the individuals' characteristics discussed above. Ordinary least squares is used to estimate a model in which the dependent variable is wealth (in billions of dollars) and the independent variables are age (in years); sex (a dummy variable equals 1 if individual is male, 0 if female); material inheritance (a dummy variable equals 1 if individual has an inheritance, 0 if not); active employment (a dummy variable equals 1 if individual is "actively employed," 0 otherwise); and industry of major source of wealth (a set of five dummy variables denoting the oil, shipping, real estate, manufacturing, and publishing industries with the category "all other" the omitted class).

Table III. Regression Results: Total Sample

Independent Variable	Coefficient	t-Value
Age	.00286	3.43000[a]
Sex	.03921	1.21118
Inheritance	.10001	4.01267[a]
Actively Employed	.10164	3.69172[a]
Oil Industry	.13643	4.08055[a]
Shipping Industry	.46939	4.57305[a]
Real Estate Industry	.00351	.10470
Manufacturing Industry	.00318	.10784
Publishing Industry	.00567	.15268
Constant Term	−.12237	−1.70708
F-Statistic	8.80742	
R-Squared	.1500	

a. Significant at the .001 level.

Whether we use the Mill, Thurow, or vita theory viewpoints, we expect the sign of the coefficient for inheritance to be positive. For Stigler the sign is indeterminant. Age is a proxy variable for wealth conservation: we expect the linear age coefficient to be positive if we consult Thurow's or Stigler's diversified portfolio proposition. However, if entrepreneurship garners monopoly or disequilibrium rates of return, we expect the compound interest factor (the age proxy) to be exponential for the non-inheritors. The same expectation holds for capitalized rents. We expect all other coefficients to be positive, according to either the capitalized monopoly or rents propositions. The variables related to these propositions are the "active employment" and industry variables. However, since 40 percent of the Four Hundred have an inheritance of some amount, "active employment" may in many instances be viewed as purely honorific, because "unemployment" or retirement leaves these magnitudes of wealth intact. Alternatively, the estimated coefficient for "active employment" for the non-inheritors subset of the Four Hundred might be viewed as a return to entrepreneurship (Thurow's disequilibrium real capital returns) or to fixed factor ownership.

Table III gives the empirical results of the linear OLS regression model for the entire sample of the super-wealthy.[3] The adjusted coefficient of determination is 15 percent while the F-ratio is highly significant. Each coefficient possesses the expected (positive) sign.

The material inheritance variable, an important variable in the vita theory, is the most interesting. Ceterus paribus, a top Four Hundred heir, is $100 million richer than a person with no inheritance. Inheritance "explains" 43 percent of mean income for the sample, a value surprisingly close to Thurow's "guess." The result also confirms the importance that the vita theory places upon material inheritance. The statistically significant age coefficient indicates that each year of age adds about $2.9 million to wealth holdings so that age—as a proxy for linear returns from diversified portfolios—alone would "explain" about $176 million of wealth at the mean age. Thus, the wealth conservation proposition is supported. Finally, the "actively employed" person—as a proxy for entrepreneurship—can expect to

3. Several other functional forms of the model (log-linear, semi-log, and quadratic) were estimated but the overall fit was not significantly improved.

A similar model was also estimated with place of residence dummy variables included as explanatory variables. A partial-joint test indicated that place of residence did not add significant explanatory power to the equation.

have about $102 million more in wealth than the inactive rich person.[4] An individual with an inheritance at about the mean sample age and "actively employed" can expect to have at least $378 million in net assets. Among those who closely fit this description from the Forbes Four Hundred are Charles Cassims Gates ($420 million), Henry Lea Hillman ($500 million), and Edwin L. Cox ($450 million).

The industry of one's source of wealth, a second vita theory variable, is important in explaining wealth. The empirical results confirm an often-expressed suspicion that the oil and shipping industries are especially lucrative: the oil and shipping industries have significant positive differentials from the "all other" or base category. Other things being the same, a placement in the shipping industry adds a $469 million differential to one's net worth, while oil adds $136 million. This result helps explain why shipping tycoon Daniel Keith Ludwig heads the Forbes Four Hundred list at $2 *billion* in net worth. Ludwig combined the two most lucrative industries by using contracts with major oil companies as collateral to build his ships. A father and son team, Perry Richardson Bass and Sid Richardson Bass, built the second-largest oil empire (after the Hunts) and together have a fortune in excess of $2 billion. Likewise, Philip Anschutz made a fortune (now worth $1 billion) in the oil industry. These industry findings suggest that the capitalization of monopoly profits and rents contributes to the amassment of wealth.

When the sample is divided between inheritors and non-inheritors (Table IV), the coefficients for age and "actively employed" are significant in the non-inheritors group and insignificant in the inheritors subsample. Moreover, the significance of the oil industry is suggestive, for inheritors, of past capitalization of monopoly returns, and for non-inheritors, of current monopoly returns on rents. Although those results shown in Table IV might point toward disequilibrium returns, the growth rate of wealth with respect to age was not exponential.[5]

We next consider whether a third birth vita variable, sex, alters net worth. In Table V, the Four Hundred are divided by sex into two samples. As common knowledge might suggest, inheritance appears to be more important to females than to males and "active employment" more significant for males than for females. The significance of the oil industry for females lends further support to the past capitalization proposition. The females had the misfortune (no pun intended) of by-passing the shipping industry altogether. The male's age contributed more to wealth than the female's (for which age is insignificant); however, this result probably reflects the dominant role of inheritance for the female subsample.

We do not have a direct estimate of the degree of monopoly power (even for the oil and shipping industries) or the assignments of its capitalized wealth value, past or present. However, some inferences can be drawn from an earlier study by Comanor and Smiley [2] who estimate the impact of past and current enterprise monopoly profits on the distribution of household wealth in the United States. They find that "the effect of monopoly is to increase the relative share of household wealth held by the wealthiest families by something

4. "Actively employed" might be coded as "active entrepreneur." However, when we divide the respondents between "actively employed" and not employed, the estimated coefficients are not significantly different in the subsamples.

5. Since no one in the shipping industry received an inheritance, the inheritors "model" is not identical to the non-inheritors "model." Therefore, we cannot draw the usual statistical inferences in comparing coefficients between the two sets of results. Moreover, our tests for non-linearity may have failed because of missing variables. For these reasons, we do not have sufficient confidence to draw strong inferences in comparing the two sub-samples.

Table IV. Regression Results: Inheritors versus Non-Inheritors

Independent Variable	Inheritance(161)[a]	Non Inheritance(239)[a]
Age	.0025(1.83)	.0033(3.10)[c]
Sex	.0363(0.79)	.0675(1.01)
Actively Employed	.0857(1.80)	.1252(3.60)[b]
Oil Industry	.2106(3.33)[b]	.0811(2.03)[d]
Shipping Industry		.4521(4.82)[b]
Real Estate Industry	.0594(0.72)	−.0118(0.34)
Manufacturing Industry	.0312(0.54)	.0051(0.15)
Publishing Industry	.0514(0.67)	−.0036(0.09)
Constant Term	−.0331(0.32)	−.1836(1.62)
F-Statistic	4.099	6.256
R-Squared	.119	.150

a. *t*-ratios are in parentheses
b. Significant at the .001 level
c. Significant at the .01 level
d. Significant at the .05 level

Table V. Regression Results: Male versus Female

Independent Variable	Coefficient (326 Male Observations)[a]	Coefficient (74 Female Observations)[a]
Age	.00335(3.303)[b]	.00144(1.045)
Inheritance	.10047(3.642)[b]	.14732(2.162)[d]
Actively Employed	.11452(3.437)[b]	.07316(1.580)
Oil Industry	.13132(3.409)[b]	.18735(2.811)[c]
Shipping Industry	.46498(4.321)[b]	
Real Estate Industry	.00527(0.142)	.03133(0.355)
Manufacturing Industry	.00651(0.192)	.02501(0.419)
Publishing Industry	−.00706(0.166)	.11552(0.144)
Constant Term	−.12291(1.446)	−.10479(0.826)
F-Statistic	7.89378	2.62677
R-Squared	.14507	.13494

a. *t*-ratios are in parentheses
b. Significant at the .001 level
c. Significant at the .01 level
d. Significant at the .05 level

over 40 percent" [2, 193]. Their class of wealthy households, however, account for .27 percent of the total number of households which is substantially greater in number than the Four Hundred richest rich.

The role of pure chance or "luck" also is difficult to test directly. Again, we would mention inferences from an earlier study. Scherer [7, 146] conducts a computer-simulation experiment for an imaginary industry having none of the usual "reasons" for asset concentration such as economies of scale and legal entry barriers. Each firm was given a random probability of growing somewhat faster or slower than the industry average. The average industry growth rate and firms' growth variance were set equal to the actual averages from *Fortune*'s 500 during 1954–60. After a simulated century had elapsed, it was not uncommon to find a single leading firm holding 25–35 percent of the market. Some firms got a head start by pure chance and—once in front—the other firms could not catch up. Could such luck explain the capitalized net worth derived from Mary Kay Cosmetics, Hewlett-Packard Co., or other companies which made some individuals rich?

V. Conclusions

The results strongly confirm the material inheritance propositions: material inheritance accounts for a large share of the wealth of the Forbes Four Hundred. Support is found for the proposition that wealth is conserved (*apparently* through a diversified portfolio). The evidence regarding entrepreneurship and monopoly returns is indirect and mixed. "Active employment" and the industry source of wealth are significant explanatory variables, variables suggestive of disequilibrium rates of return. There was no evidence that wealth grew exponentially, at least over the lifetimes of the respondents: this result, however, may be the consequence of missing variables or our inability to identify "sudden wealth" in cross-section data. Finally, although we identify industries that have enjoyed disequilibrium rates of return, in the case of the super-rich it would be impossible to assign these returns to human capital (entrepreneurship) or physical capital (rents).

Our empirical results tend to confirm Stigler's "dominant" estimate of the importance of inheritance as well as Thurow's "guess." Once a large inheritance is invested in a diversified portfolio, Stigler's (and Thurow's) compound interest formula goes to work on a much larger base than that provided by the average worker's incremental savings. Moreover, our method—unlike Stigler's residual but similar to Thurow's—suggests the possibility of disequilibrium rates of returns for the nouveau riche. The large percentage of unexplained variance (even though data are cross-sectional) nonetheless does suggest missing variables. Canterbery's [1] recommendation of path analysis as a method for handling large numbers of variables in a recursive system such as the vita theory should be taken seriously. Therefore, we end with the usual plea of the econometrician; namely, we need data on more variables.[6] Unfortunately, in any analysis of present-day super-wealth, the Forbes Four Hundred data base probably is as good as we can expect.

6. We are compiling and coding data from the *Forbes* Four Hundred studies for 1983 and 1984. We do not expect our findings to be changed significantly. However, a comparison of these data bases may enable us to identify a few cases of instant wealth.

References

1. Canterbery, E. Ray, "A Vita Theory of the Personal Income Distribution." *Southern Economic Journal*, July 1979, 12–48.
2. Comanor, Williams S. and Robert H. Smiley, "Monopoly and The Distribution of Wealth." *Quarterly Journal of Economics*, May 1975, 177–94.
3. "The Forbes Four Hundred." *Forbes*, September 12, 1982, 99–170.
4. Johnson, Harry G. *The Theory of Income Distribution*. London: Gray-Mills Publishing LTD, 1973.
5. Marshall, Alfred. *Principles of Economics*, 8th ed. London: Macmillan and Company, 1920.
6. Mill, John Stuart. *Principles of Economics*, edited by Sir W. J. Ashley. London: Longmans, Green and Company, 1929.

7. Scherer, F. M. *Industrial Market Structure And Economic Performance*, 2nd ed. Boston: Houghton Mifflin Company, 1980.

8. Stigler, George J. *The Theory of Price*, 3rd ed. New York: The Macmillan Company, 1966.

9. Thurow, Lester. *Generating Inequality*. New York: Basic Books, Inc., 1975.

10. ______. *The Zero-Sum Society*. New York: Penguin Books, 1981. Reprint of the 1980 edition by Basic Books, New York.

PART III

SPECULATION : FOREIGN AND DOMESTIC

Chapter 13

THE CRAWLING PEG AND EXCHANGE STABILITY*

E. RAY CANTERBERY *Florida State University*

JOHN T. BOORMAN *University of Maryland*

Le taux de change à crémaillère et la stabilité des changes. Avec le système actuel, il n'est possible de procéder à un changement de taux de change que s'il y a évidence d'un « déséquilibre profond » et présence des attitudes politiques appropriées. De plus, la perspective de tels changements tend à susciter des mouvements de capitaux importants, à cause du degré de risque restreint associé à cette opération de conversion d'une monnaie en train de se déprécier vers une monnaie en train de s'apprécier. L'insatisfaction générale eu égard à ce système a donné lieu à grand nombre de suggestions visant la mise sur pied de mécanismes automatiques ou semi-automatiques d'ajustement des taux de change. Parmi ceux-ci, on trouve les nombreuses variantes du mécanisme de taux de change à crémaillère (« crawling peg »).

Les auteurs en font un relevé. Ils s'attachent aux effets probables sur les taux de change, la balance commerciale, et les fonds de réserve de changes officiels. De plus, ils démontrent que ces mécanismes sont susceptibles de créer des contraintes sérieuses pour la politique fiscale et monétaire.

Dans la version discrétionnaire de John Williamson, on se propose de corriger les « déséquilibres profonds » des taux de change au moyen d'une autorisation de procéder à des réajustements à un rythme maximum de un vingt-sixième de un pourcent par semaine. Dans la version de J. C. Murphy et J. Black, il serait possible de laisser varier les taux de change à l'intérieur d'un intervalle de part et d'autre d'un taux moyen, calculé comme une moyenne mobile des taux d'une période passée définie.

Les auteurs notent que dans la version de Williamson, l'initiative de la constatation d'un « déséquilibre profond » et de l'action appropriée est encore laissée entre les mains des autorités. De plus, toutes les versions conduisent à la nécessité du maintien d'une différence importante entre les taux d'intérêts du pays en difficulté et ceux des autres pays, par les autorités monétaires du pays qui fait face à une dévaluation. Ainsi, même avec un intervalle de variation de seulement un pour cent de part et d'autre du taux moyen, il y aurait nécessité d'un écart des taux d'intérêts d'au moins quatre pourcent. Certains ont soutenu qu'une partie du caractère de prévision facile des mouvements des taux de change dans le cadre de tels systèmes peut être annulée en incorporant des facteurs d'incertitude à ces mécanismes, au moyen de la politique fiscale. D'autres ont prétendu qu'il est toujours possible d'utiliser la politique fiscale dans la réalisation d'objectifs intérieurs, même si l'usage possible de la politique monétaire est limité. Ces deux types d'actions sont incompatibles. On ne peut sortir d'un dilemne qu'au moyen de contrôles directs des changes pour les pays dont les monnaies se déprécient. De plus, on doit se demander quels sont les fondements logiques d'un système de taux de changes flexibles qui nécessite un caractère d'incertitude au bénéfice des spéculateurs, caractère qui ne peut être obtenu que par des changements des politiques économiques internes, ou encore que par des contrôles directs des changes. Les auteurs sont d'avis que ces difficultés sont évitées dans le cadre d'un système « d'ajustements retardés des taux de change » (« delayed peg ») recommandé par l'un d'eux parce que l'incertitude est partie inhérente d'un tel mécanisme.

Introduction

Under serious consideration for foreign exchange-rate reform is some version of the crawling peg. This exchange mechanism has been proposed in both a dis-

*We wish to thank J. Carter Murphy, Christopher Clague, and Thomas D. Willett for their useful comments and George N. Halm and Fritz Machlup for their encouragement. The usual *caveat* applies.

This article was completed while Professor Canterbery was visiting at Simon Fraser University.

Canadian Journal of Economics/Revue canadienne d'Economique, III, no. 2
May/mai 1970. Printed in Canada/Imprimé au Canada.

cretionary and an automatic guise and has been endorsed in one form by Guido Carli and Otmar Emminger, two influential European central bankers. These academic proposals are welcome additions to the literature. They have stimulated discussions in which the appropriate questions are being asked. The purpose of this paper is to: (1) indicate the overlooked probable behaviour of resultant exchange rates, the trade account, and official monetary reserves; and (2) emphasize the consequent constraints on domestic monetary-fiscal policies from the narrow-band varieties of the crawling peg.

The narrow-band versions of the crawling peg assure that under most relevant conditions exchange speculators and interest arbitragers will know precisely each day's calculated par values. In these plans daily par rates are changed by an administratively predetermined per cent or set equal to a moving average of past market exchange rates. In *theory*, the market exchange rate is allowed to fluctuate within a narrow gold band. John Williamson has suggested the form whereby a currency would, upon devaluation, be reduced in price by 1/26 of one per cent per week. J. Carter Murphy and J. Black have suggested that pars be automatically set equal to the moving-average of exchange rates over a predetermined prior period, probably a year. Variations of the discretionary plan include the sliding parity of James Meade and the gliding parity of William Fellner.[1]

The discretionary crawling peg

The discretionary crawling peg leaves no doubts concerning the future value of exchange rates or the *necessary* course of monetary policy. Given a devaluation at a predetermined weekly rate, commercial traders, interest arbitragers and pure speculators know precisely what the minimum exchange rate will be at the end of a year. Home-nation importers will lead in purchases of exchange and foreign importers will lag in payments. Interest arbitragers could purchase foreign treasury bills on an *uncovered* basis (assuming constant interest rates).[2] Clearly, if domestic interest rates of the devaluing nation remain unchanged or fall, and foreign interest rates remain constant, international monetary reserve losses will be substantial as the monetary authorities will have to sell official foreign currency reserves to prevent exchange appreciation at more than a crawl. Unless home interest rates are increased, mounting official reserve losses

[1]See John H. Williamson, *The Crawling Peg*, Essays in International Finance, no. 50 (Princeton, 1965); J. Carter Murphy, "Moderated Exchange Rate Variability," *National Banking Review*, III (Dec. 1965), 151–61; and J. Black, "A Proposal for the Reform of Exchange Rates," *Economic Journal*, LXXVI (June 1966), 288–95. These and the Meade-Fellner proposals are detailed in George N. Halm, *Toward Limited Exchange-Rate Flexibility*, Essays in International Finance, no. 73 (Princeton, 1969).

J. Carter Murphy objects to the *discretionary* version in his "Reply," *National Banking Review*, IV (Sept. 1966).

[2]For a detailed explanation of these forces in the exchange market, see E. Ray Canterbery, *Foreign Exchange, Capital Flows, and Monetary Policy*, Studies in International Finance, no. 15 (Princeton, 1965), 7–47. Interest-rate arbitrage would become a function of $(R + S^*)$ rather than of $[R + (F - S)]$, where R is the interest differential, S the spot foreign exchange rate, S^* the expected spot rate, and F the forward rate. Leading-lagging and pure speculation are mostly functions of S^*, while interest arbitrage would now become, in part, a speculative function.

will convince speculators that the rate of appreciation of the foreign exchange rate will have to be increased and their own accelerated purchases will assure that it will.

All these C-P plans share the same dilemma. If the exchange rate moves at a sufficient speed (at least 2 per cent a year) to equalize the money value of trade flows, the necessity of changing short-term interest rates by about the same percentage points in order to conserve official monetary reserves completely ties monetary policy to the balance of payments; if the exchange rate crawls at a lesser speed or moves in a cycle, very little change in monetary policy is required in conserving monetary reserves but the trade account remains in disequilibrium. These versions of the crawling peg are not to be confused with a wide gold band and "delayed peg" advocated by one of the authors.[3]

Assuming a dollar devaluation (with gold as numéraire) under the discretionary C-P version and constant foreign interest rates, the foreigner purchasing US Treasury bills will have committed himself on the *first day* of the crawl (C-day) to a depreciation in the value of his bills of say, 1/26 of one per cent a week. Increases in US interest rates somewhat greater than the planned appreciation of foreign exchange might maintain *status quo* short-term capital flows. But this would require an increase in US interest rates on bills maturing in one year or less of more than two percentage points on C-day.[4] Premature upward movements in US interest rates would advertise the devaluation to currency speculators. This is in part recognized by Williamson, who states as the "essential corollary" of his proposal "... that countries should maintain interest rates at levels adequate to prevent such creeping changes in exchange rates from giving rise to capital flows."[5]

If such a crawling peg had been implemented in June 1969 by the United

[3]See E. Ray Canterbery, "The Delayed Peg and the Adjustment Mechanism, "A Paper before the Southern Economic Association Meeting (Nov. 1968), and *Economics on a New Frontier* (Belmont, California, 1968), 212–16.

Under the delayed peg, changes in pars would not be announced nor otherwise precisely predictable by speculators, and par changes would equal one-half the total gold band width while exchange rates *within* the band are market-determined. The D-P plan usually is subsumed under the C-P classification (e.g., see Halm, *Toward Limited Exchange-Rate Flexibility*, 18–20). But at the limits par changes are by *discrete* amounts while daily exchange-rates are still market-determined under the D-P. Under *any* par-change plan, there is more independence between the exchange-rate and par when the band is wide. While the D-P is a wide gold band that moves, it does not "crawl." This distinction may justify the distinctive name; if not, avoidance of confusion does. The D-P provision that par values (band movements) be determined by official reserves changes possibly could be used to define the rate of crawl under any of several plans.

[4]Would other nations voluntarily *lower* their interest rates by, say, half as much? The US authorities have immense difficulty deciding what monetary and fiscal policy *should* be, much less co-ordinating such policies. Free world co-ordination of monetary-fiscal policies and the necessary relinquishing of domestic political independence would be a major miracle *and* would eliminate the immediate necessity of changing exchange rates anyway.

[5]Williamson, *Crawling Peg*, 2. As Williamson correctly anticipates "... since income is generally taxed more highly than capital gains, it is probable that the interest-rate differential needed to prevent capital flows would be rather greater than the rate of depreciation of currency" (p. 3). Proponents of the several versions of the crawling, sliding, gliding parities presume that capital flows will be stabilized if an interest *differential* of 2 percentage points is maintained. This is not *necessarily* the case. As another exception, interest rates would have to be more than 2 percentage points higher in a politically unstable country devaluing its currency.

States for one year, the prime rate on short-term money would have been at least 10.5 per cent and long-term loan rates (including private mortgage money) would have been raised by something less than two percentage points for nearly the entire subsequent year. The necessary increase in long-term rates would depend upon the length of the period of expected appreciation relative to the maturity of the obligation. In Great Britain the Bank Rate under such a planned devaluation by the UK would have been 9 per cent.

Assuming that the shortest maturities are 30-day T bills *and* assuming (unrealistically) that one year's appreciation is sufficient, on May 1, 1970 interest rates on these securities could have been allowed to adjust back to their previous level. Similar reductions in the rates on other maturities could be affected over the course of the year in expectation of an end to the planned devaluation. Under conditions of perfect knowledge in the securities markets, the term-to-maturity structure of interest rates might adjust back to its original level (or its new equilibrium level) at an even pace over the course of the year. However, in the face of uncertainty about the size and duration of the devaluation, the burden on the Federal Open Market Trading Desk to keep markets "orderly" would be substantially increased. Furthermore, substantial (and frequent) administrative adjustments of the rates paid on commercial bank time deposits (Regulation Q) and other such instruments would be required for banks to maintain their competitive position in attracting funds.

Advocates of a discretionary crawl might argue that restrictive money policy would be precisely the policy needed for balance-of-payments equilibrium. But even in an inflationary economy, the necessary relative (or absolute) contraction in the money supply (plus the resulting two or more additional interest percentage points on C-day) may do severe damage to capital formation (especially construction). The policy's impact on housing and family-welfare would have serious social overtones. And, of course, such an interest-rate policy would make domestic monetary policy at times pro-seasonal.[6] Some might argue that fiscal policy could be used to offset necessary monetary-policy changes, but current institutional arrangements – at least, in the US – make fiscal policy inflexible yearly, quarterly and certainly seasonally. Hence, even under the most ideal domestic conditions for workability of the proposal, there would be severe domestic economic repercussions.

Even if the monetary authorities decided not to co-operate with the crawl in the peg, there would initially be a rising credit demand and substantial upward pressures on interest rates. After an announcement of the devaluation domestic borrowers would expect a more restrictive monetary policy or anticipate a contraction in the money supply from capital outflows. These self-

[6]For a discussion of the observed consequences on the money supply of setting short-term US interest rates to accommodate "international considerations" in the late 1950s and early 1960s, see E. Ray Canterbery, "A Note on Recent Money Supply Behavior," *Western Economic Journal*, IV (fall 1965), 91–8, reprinted in John Lindauer, ed., *Macroeconomic Readings* (New York, 1968), 99–104. For a discussion of the consequences of monetary policies dependent upon "international considerations" under alternative systems, see E. Ray Canterbery, "Exchange Rates, Capital Flows, and Monetary Policy," *American Economic Review*, LIX (June 1969), 426–32.

fulfilling expectations would lead to a rush to borrow and the authority initially may have difficulty preventing interest-rate increases from *exceeding* the year's exchange appreciation. After these early-stage credit demands are met, the monetary authority would probably become a net seller of securities. At best, post-C-day would be marked by very disruptive forces in the money and capital markets.

The two major trading areas, the United States and the United Kingdom, might provide the most embarrassing test for the discretionary crawling peg. Both have experienced balance-of-payments deficits during periods of both rising prices *and* economic recession. Suppose the crawling peg had been implemented in the US during the economic recession of 1960–1. (There were rumours of dollar devaluation at that time.) Instead of interest rates being pegged (as they unfortunately were), short-term interest rates would probably have been increased immediately by at least two percentage points. Using one estimate of the consequences, such an increase in interest rates (and required absolute or relative money-supply contraction), gross national income would have contracted by another $11 billion, *ceteris paribus*.[7] Using "Okun's Law," this additional contraction in 1960 would have been translated into about one-half million fewer employed workers and an unemployment rate of about 6.3 per cent instead of the prevailing 5.6 per cent. The main disadvantage of this exchange-rate system is that it completely destroys the flexibility of monetary policy, making it *dependent* on the international financial system.

The automatic moving-average peg

The automatic moving-average peg has similarities with the discretionary plan but also some important differences. The present authors agree with Professor Murphy that the current system "... virtually eliminates risk of capital loss for those who transfer funds from a weak to a strong currency."[8] It likewise is agreed that the IMF "... provides no *orderly* (original italics) means for adjustment of exchange rates."[9] The Murphy Plan calls for a daily par calculation equalling the moving-arithmetic-mean of exchange rates over a past period, say one year. Gold prices would be varied to gain exchange-rate changes, and a band of permissible gold price variability of ± 1 per cent to ± 1.5 per cent either side of par would be established. Professor Black favours a calculation of the geometric mean of past exchange prices in which rates are varied in terms of US dollars. Gold is only an accounting numéraire. The geometric-mean calculation provides for symmetrical rates for any two nations.

As most probably exchange rates would be set via changing the dollar prices rather than altering the price of gold, we shall examine the Black version. Where x_{t-i} is the spot market exchange rate for the *i*th day *prior* to C-day (t),

[7]Myron H. Ross, "'Operation Twist': A Mistaken Policy?," *Journal of Political Economy*, LXXIV (April 1966), 198.

[8]Murphy, "Moderated Exchange," 152. See also Canterbery, *Foreign Exchange, Capital Flows, and Monetary Policy*, 30–1.

[9]Murphy, "Moderated Exchange," 153.

and n is the number of days selected for the averaging period, the C-day parity rate, P_t, is

$$(1) \qquad \ln P_t = \frac{1}{n} \sum_{t=1}^{n} \ln x_{t-t}.$$

The change in the parity rate between C-day and the next day could be calculated as

$$(2) \qquad \ln P_{t+1} - \ln P_t = (1/n)\,(\ln x_t - \ln x_{t-n}).$$

For the par alterations between any two days, the change in terms of the arithmetic average is

$$(3) \qquad P_{t+j} - P_{t+j-1} = (1/n)\,[x_{t+j-1} - x_{t+j-(n+1)}].$$

The maximum annual rate of appreciation would depend upon the width of the band, the length of the period of the calculation and (overlooked by Black) the trend of exchange rates prior to establishing the crawling peg. Both Murphy and Black would calculate the maximum annual depreciation or appreciation for a currency as $(100)2b/a$, where $\pm(100)b$ equals the band percentage (say ± 1 per cent) and a is the number of years used in the calculation.

The first problem is getting the system started. Let us assume – as the authors of these plans apparently do – that par values are not realigned to equilibrium positions prior to the C-day.[10] Assume that the US foreign exchange rate on German marks (DMs) has been at its upper limit for n days, the dollar price of pounds at the lower limit and the pound price of marks near the upper limit. Let there be continuous upward pressure on the US-DM foreign exchange rate as the dollar is "devalued" against DMs. Under Black's assumptions all non-dollar currencies are tied to the dollar. The upward pressure will be caused by either the "natural" market forces or an exogenous shock (say, comparable to the French student-worker strikes of summer 1968). The value of the initial par is

$$(4) \qquad P_t = P_{IMF} + bP_{IMF},$$

where P_{IMF} is the old IMF par with (for simplicity) a $(100)b$ per cent band. With the continuous upward pressure the exchange rate rises the first day by its maximum within the "new" band (b), so that $x_t = P_t + bP_t$ while $x_{t-n} = P_t$. Using equation 3, the second day's $(t+1)$ arithmetic par calculation is

$$P_{t+1} = P_t + (1/n)\,[(P_t + bP_t) - P_t], \text{or}$$

$$(5) \qquad P_{t+1} = P_t + (1/n)\,(bP_t),$$

Substituting equation 4 into 5,

$$(6) \qquad P_{t+1} = P_{IMF} + bP_{IMF} + (1/n)\,(bP_{IMF} + b^2P_{IMF}).$$

The second-round change in pars would then be

$$(7) \qquad P_{t+1} - P_t = (1/n)\,(bP_{IMF} + b^2P_{IMF}).$$

[10] If exchange rates are realigned prior to C-day, most governments would argue that no further movements in exchange rates are required and the crawl would not be implemented.

Speculators and commercial traders would *assure* that the exchange rate would rise by the maximum during the devaluation. Suppose the trend of past exchange rates has been *steadily* upward. Commercial traders, pure speculators and interest arbitragers have calculated the new par-for-the-day and judge it to be too low ($P_t < x_t$). Increased demand for foreign exchange on day t assures that the calculated par for day $t + 1$ will be higher. The higher par calculation will assure another demand increase, etc., so that

$$P_{t+n} > \dots P_{t+2} > P_{t+1} > P_t.$$

The second calculated par ($P_{t+1} > P_t$) will virtually guarantee that the exchange rate will move its maximum during one year. On the other hand, if one could show that the par rate would move much less than its maximum, such a movement probably would be insufficient [if $(100)b = 1$ per cent)] for stabilizing the trade account.[11]

Continuing with the dollar-pound-mark example, if the dollar depreciates by the maximum during the year against the mark, and the pound (at the US lower limit) is devalued in terms of the dollar, the pound could depreciate in terms of the mark by about $(100)4b$ per cent. (This assumes no barriers to triangular exchange arbitrage, and the likely continuous downward pressure.) A band width equalling ± 1 per cent for one year would under these assumptions gain a depreciation in the dollar in terms of the mark of 2 per cent. This is not merely a hypothetical possibility; rather this relation approximates that among the mark, pound and dollar at various times in the 1965–8 years. Capital would flow rapidly from the relatively weaker to the relatively stronger currency nations. To avoid a rapid and complete monetary reserve attrition in the weaker currency nations, interest rates would have to be increased by at least 2 percentage points in the US relative to W. Germany, by at least 2 percentage points in Great Britain relative to the US, and at least *4* percentage points in Great Britain relative to W. Germany.

There are at least two other possibilities. Suppose the exchange rate had been at the floor the first half of the year used for calculation and at the upper limit during the last half of that year. The pars would be below x_t for less than one-half the subsequent year and the expected exchange rate would be rising. In the balance of the subsequent year, however, the daily exchange rate would be much closer to the beginning market rate values and speculators would expect a decreasing rate of increase in x. The appreciation the first year would be less than the maximum and very little appreciation would be forthcoming the second year of the crawl.

The behaviour of the rate during the period used for calculation may have been symmetrically cyclical. The behaviour of the calculated par would then be a guaranteed damped cyclical one. In all cases, the market-rate pattern would be determined by speculation, not by "normal" commercial trade. And whenever the resultant market-rate behaviour is cyclical, it is highly unlikely that rate behaviour would be stabilizing for the trade account. Monetary policy

[11]If the band were any wider than 3 or 4 per cent, it would no longer be a narrow-band crawling peg and the speculative, commercial and arbitrage parameters would be modified by increased uncertainty.

requirements still would be stringent; an agile Open Market trader would have to change interest rates at all inflection points, though the necessary movements would not be as wide.

There are other policy accommodations that could be attempted. Suppose the monetary and fiscal authorities attempt to build uncertainty into the crawling-peg system. Such a policy would require changes in money and taxing policies that would tend to move the exchange rate in a direction opposite that which the invoked crawl is taking it. Besides the many uncertain linkages among policy institutions, monetary-fiscal policy changes and their impact on exchange rates, this approach would add a *fiscal* policy constraint to the monetary policy constraint.[12] Even the fiscal-monetary policy mix advocated by R. Mundell for the current system could not be invoked. Also, if successful, such domestic policies may prevent the exchange rate from moving a sufficient distance to provide (by itself) trade adjustments. An option independent of fiscal-monetary policies would be direct exchange controls. If more flexibility in exchange rates fails to yield substantial domestic economic policy independence and balance of payments adjustments based on exchange-rate changes themselves, such a system of flexible exchange rates loses most of the advantages it claims. Beyond these fundamentals, one can question the logical foundations of a system of flexible exchange rates that requires an uncertainty for speculators that can only be gained via domestic economic policy changes or else requires direct exchange controls.

In practice, therefore, the narrow-band moving-average peg would sometimes behave differently from a discretionary peg. For most relevant devaluations, either home interest rates would have to be *immediately* increased by percentage points equalling the maximum expected depreciation in the foreign exchange value of each credit instrument over its maturity, or else fiscal-monetary policies would have to counter the exchange-rate movements, or else direct exchange controls would have to be administered. In the first case monetary policy independence is lost; in the second monetary-fiscal policies are substituted to some indefinable degree as the adjustment mechanism rather than exchange rates. Even those economists who advocate monetary rules rather than authorities – such as Milton Friedman – would be offended because the crawling peg in these instances would eliminate the possibility for a stable rate of money-supply expansion. If for any reasons the moving-average peg crawls by less than the maximum allowed by a 2 per cent band, trade balance improvement would depend, at least in part, upon other policies.

Conclusion

The crawling peg most likely to be workable would be one with a wide gold band. But even a conceivable version of this has defects. The few foreign

[12]The tying of domestic policies to the foreign exchange rate assumes that the monetary and fiscal authorities are autonomous, making accurate decisions sometimes independently of the people's will, of irrationality, and of severe disturbances (usually exogenous to the economic model such as riots, strikes, and wars). Even if governments prevent large changes in aggregate spending by their nationals, can they avoid steep and protracted changes in their own spending?

exchange dealers in New York City might fix each day's exchange rate at the day's par calculation if a *crawling par* is instituted. This would eliminate uncertainty for speculators and interest arbitragers, assuring a predictable exchange-rate behaviour and necessary interest-rate (and/or fiscal policy) changes. A delayed peg in conjunction with a wide-gold band (or floating exchange rates) would, however, greatly reduce certainty and free monetary and fiscal policies for domestic ends.[13] Also, after par changes all exchange-rate movements under the delayed peg are market-determined rather than being mechanically determined by a moving average or by an arbitrary discretionary percentage.[14]

This paper raises some serious questions regarding the advisability of a discretionary or moving-average crawling peg. Perhaps there is a mathematical formula that automatically would produce an exchange rate appreciation sufficient to adjust trade but too meagre to attract capital, but such a formula has thus far eluded us. The discretionary peg probably would not be credible to speculators and hence would, in practice, not be allowed to crawl. To be "workable," both ordinary types would require the tying of domestic monetary and fiscal policies to international balances of payments for most relevant devaluations. The main burden of the ordinary crawling peg is the certainty it provides. The necessary monetary-fiscal policy mix for the movement toward national socio-economic goals may then be unattainable.

[13]Completely free exchange rates have some disadvantages widely discussed in the literature. Excellent defences for floating rates have been advanced by Milton Friedman and Leland B. Yeager.

[14]An excellent discussion of the advantages of a wide gold band *cum* crawling peg appears in Halm, *Toward Limited Exchange-Rate Flexibility*, 20–4. Also, see Thomas D. Willett, S. I. Katz, and W. H. Branson, *Essays in International Finance*, no. 78 (Princeton, 1970). Although Branson and Willett do not make a choice between the narrow- and the wider-gold band, Willett (pp. 11–2) and Katz (p. 25) discuss cogently the advantages of the latter.

Chapter 14

E. RAY CANTERBERY

The International Monetary Crisis and the Delayed Peg

Traditional "floating" or "fixed" exchange rates can no longer solve the problem of international monetary instability. Fundamental reform is needed, in the shape of a workable compromise between those two extremes.

Floating foreign exchange rates, in which the price of the dollar to foreigners is more or less determined by supply and demand in the market, functioned well for a few years, but now the international monetary system is in disarray. The United States dollar has not been floating: it has been sinking. American tourists in Germany or Japan do not know from one hour to the next how much less their dollars will buy. Banks holding dollar-denominated accounts and U.S. Treasury securities cannot predict what foreign currency value these items will have when bank doors open. The main U.S. response has been higher interest rates and a tighter federal budget even when key domestic economic indicators have pointed downward. The troubled international monetary system is now endangering the health of the American economy.

The uncertainty shrouding the price of the dollar also is threatening the relatively liberal trading system of the "free world." Britain has been discussing quota schemes, Italy has imposed a tax on foreign exchange purchases, and France has moved toward stricter currency and import controls—trade restrictions aimed at the common goal of limiting the influx of goods from other nations, including such commodities as machine tools and Marlboro cigarettes from the United States. This economic warfare is ultimately counterproductive,

E. RAY CANTERBERY is Professor of Economics at Florida State University; Visiting Scholar, University of Texas at Austin.

for nations will sell less to each other, retarding world economic growth. Remedial measures notwithstanding, the fundamental forces still point downward—toward the bottom of a sea of international dollar balances.

The most recent causes of the sliding dollar have been a trade deficit (about $20 billion yearly) with the oil-producing countries and the slow growth in U.S. exports to Germany and Japan due, at least partly, to their weak economic growth. The total resultant U.S. trade deficit approaches $30 billion annually. The surge in demand by Americans for the foreign currency (exchange) to pay for these imports relative to the weaker demand by foreigners for our dollars has led to a decline in the dollar's value, a trend accentuated by the gnomes of Zürich and speculators elsewhere.

According to the theory of floating or flexible exchange rates, the plunge of the dollar in the face of a large U.S. trade deficit is precisely what is supposed to happen. The U.S. foreign exchange rate is the price an American importer pays for the currency used to purchase foreign goods: an increase in the foreign exchange rate is the equivalent of a rise in the price of Toyotas, Beefeater gin, or Italian silk. A lower price for dollars (the foreigner's foreign exchange rate) gives foreign buyers bargain rates for U.S. exports of Ford Mustangs, Jack Daniels bourbon, and Brooks Brothers suits, and makes foreign goods expensive to Americans. In due course the trade deficit should right itself as Americans buy fewer Toyotas and Japanese buy more Mustangs. Why, then, has the U.S. deficit persisted under floating exchange rates?

The adjustable parity exchange rate system of the post-World War II era did not function according to theory either. This earlier system was one in which exchange rates were fixed (pegged) by the buying and selling of foreign currencies (exchange) within narrow intervention limits (pegs) by foreign central banks. In a classic case of history repeating itself, the reasons are the same for the failures of two apparently opposite systems; the policies fostered under each as well as the institutions and special interests which decided how each should function are also alike. The United States dollar has played a central role in the difficulties, and the history of the dollar illustrates the story of either system equally well.

Bretton Woods and the dollar heritage

The Bretton Woods Agreement, ratified by the United States and most of its allies in 1944, provided for fixed exchange parities (or par values) which member nations of the International Monetary Fund (IMF), the "custodian" of the system, were obligated to defend. Exchange rates were allowed to fluctuate within a narrow band of about one percent on either side of the parity, or official rates of exchange. Member nations could alter these official rates only in the face of chronic deficits or surpluses in nations' balances of payments called "fundamental disequilibria." Less serious imbalances were to be dealt with by temporary financing based partly on newly created IMF lending facilities, as well as by appropriate national economic policies.

Although the prices of foreign currencies were expressed by the IMF in terms of ounces of gold, in practice currencies were fixed in terms of the price of a dollar. In turn, foreign currencies were only convertible into gold by their convertibility into dollars. For example, in 1968 the U.S. gold price was $1.00 = 13.7 grains of gold and the British gold price was £1 = 32.9 grains of gold. The par value of the dollar was 32.9/13.7, about $2.40 per £1. However, the Bank of England agreed to buy an unlimited number of pounds with dollars at $2.38 and to sell unlimited pounds *for* dollars at $2.42 to establish the lower and upper pegs. In practice, the Bretton Woods system became a rigid dollar standard.

Over the years the American economy came to lead and then to dominate trade expansion in the West. Through the fortunes of finance, the dollar, a *national* currency, began to serve a dual purpose as *the* international currency. In recent decades it has been the main unit of account for valuing trade, the key currency for trade payments and—most important in connection with its difficulties—a store of wealth in the form of reserve currency. The German mark was considered to be "worth" about 25 cents, the price of a Mercedes Benz was quoted in dollars, and the German central bank willingly accumulated dollars in order to maintain the mark at a level roughly equivalent to an American quarter-dollar. No economist, government or international agency consciously designed the dollar's multi-faceted role.

By the late 'fifties, the United States experienced large balance of payments deficits while continental European countries (and later Japan) registered huge surpluses. To maintain the par values of exchange rates the European central banks had to intervene and buy more and more of these "excess" dollars. These, as well as private dollar balances, became so large that the dollar emerged as the main vehicle for reserve storage and maintenance of par values.

The dollar utilized as international money *and* as a store of wealth is a contradiction: a national currency used to finance expanding trade cannot forever be a reliable reserve currency. With the dollar as the main reservoir of wealth, total trade financing potential (international liquidity) could be expanded only through still larger U.S. payments deficits. As such deficits led to larger dollar reserves, however, confidence that the dollar parity in terms of gold could be maintained was eroded. A small crack in confidence widened, threatening to engulf the system as central banks began to demand gold from Fort Knox in exchange for dollars.

With the bulk of the world's monetary gold locked up in the Kentucky citadel, the unabated accumulation of dollar reserves abroad presented a very awkward problem. If the United States devalued its currency (possible only in terms of a higher dollar price for gold), foreign central banks holding dollars as reserves would find their assets shrunken in value. Equally important was the fact that official and private foreign dollar balances in New York banks would be worth less, and foreigners might convert such balances into other currencies or assets, creating a "run" on the dollar and on gold simultaneously. The holdings of official and private dollar accounts were and still are sources of enormous profits to the largest New York banks. Under the pressure of foreign central bankers and private commercial and investment bankers, the Eisenhower, Kennedy, and Johnson administrations rejected devaluation or par value changes. Although traders and bankers often feared it, "devaluation" under "fundamental disequilibria" was almost as empty a threat as the cry that "the Russians are coming."

Par values really were fixed. The United States was left with the alternative of restrictive economic policies. Higher interest rates could be used to reduce the level of aggregate demand, thus reducing imports. It was also hoped the higher interest rates would attract foreign capital. Direct controls on trade and capital flows could be tried: taxes and quotas on imports, tourism, and the export of U.S. capital. All these policies were imposed at one time or another.

Despite such measures, the troublesome payments deficit persisted and dollars continued to finance trade growth. Traders and speculators finally came to believe that a realignment of exchange rates—so long rejected—was now inevitable, and speculative crises emerged. Massive private selling of British pound sterling forced its devaluation in 1967. There was a rush to buy gold from the United States: by 1971 it was widely agreed that the U.S. dollar had to be "devalued."

The American authorities again were in awkward straits. As other currency prices were now in dollars, the U.S. dollar could be devalued in terms of foreign currencies only at the option of other countries. Other nations finally allowed their exchange rates to float upward freely against the dollar in mid-1971. The arrangement whereby dollars could be exchanged for gold officially ended. Without the float toward lower dollar prices, foreign central banks would have been flooded with dollars and, had the gold window stayed open, Fort Knox would have become a vacant warehouse.

The major trading nations signed the Smithsonian Agreement at the end of 1971, resolving to return in the near future to a pattern of fixed exchange rates, with somewhat wider bands than had characterized the previous system of fixed rates. Unfortunately, the balance of payments continued to run red, accompanied in January 1973 by massive speculation and in February by a proposed further 10 percent "devaluation." By the end of March, several European Economic Community (EEC) member nations decided to stabilize their currencies against each other but to let them float against the dollar, an arrangement called the "snake." This action dealt a final blow to the Bretton Woods system.

The shape of the present crisis

The first major test of the floating regime came with the tripling of the price of oil during 1973.

Dollar reserves shifted *en masse* into nations in the Organization of Petroleum-Exporting Countries (OPEC), and the central banks intervened sharply—buying dollars again—to influence the market price of currencies. Bankers began to call for "corrective strategies" by the United States, such as tighter fiscal and monetary policies and a slowdown of energy imports. The responsibility for guaranteeing that the dollar would not depreciate was again thrust upon the United States.

Why has a condition developed under ostensibly "floating" exchange rates that is identical to that under the felled fixed-exchange-rate regime? The answer is found in the continued multiple role of the dollar as a unit of account, trading vehicle, and reserve currency, as well as in some overlooked defects in a flexible-exchange-rate system.

The way the dollar's price falls does not matter as much to foreign governments as does the fact that it falls at all. A dollar which is devalued under fixed exchange rates depreciates under floating rates. Ultimately the outcome for traders and bankers is the same.

A cheaper dollar means a more expensive German mark; the United States can now undersell Germany in world markets. Likewise, a higher British pound undercuts the competitiveness of Britain's exports and worsens its rate of unemployment. Japan, France, and Italy, with no oil reserves, have deliberately undervalued their currencies in order to encourage trade surpluses and to export—among other things—their unemployment. Moreover, foreign central banks still hold in reserve accumulating dollar assets that decline in value with each drop in the dollar's exchange price, and private New York banks and investment houses still worry about the decline in the value of their clients' dollar-denominated assets which might spur them to move their accounts elsewhere, into gold or other currencies. Furthermore, the Carter administration must contemplate the consequent dollar outflows which would worsen the payments deficit and accelerate the dollar's descent.

With about $500 billion held in banking balances outside the U.S., neither the U.S. authorities nor the foreign central banks have much chance of stopping the dollar slide. (The United States has only $.7 billion in liquid international reserves.) At best, the foreign central banks can only temporarily control swings of the exchange rate under this managed or "dirty" float—and then only at enormous costs in terms of official reserves expended. Within this system the Carter administration must turn to the same policies followed by prior administrations under fixed exchange rates.

Therefore, the theoretical attractiveness of floating exchange rates is tempered by the facts that: (1) the historical circumstance of huge dollar reserves introduces an uncommon element of instability; (2) uncontrollable forces (OPEC, coal strikes, riots, wars, famines, Watergates, and so on) cause sharp and unpredictable movements in exchange rates and; (3) flexible exchange rates at the option of national governments offer the delightful temptation to intervene and set exchange rates which would accommodate national economic and political demands.

The worst may be yet to come. OPEC is concerned about the dollar slump because the lower-valued dollars it receives impair its members' ability to buy non-American goods. OPEC has expressed an intent to raise the price of oil to compensate, should the decline continue.

Stagflation, old pleas, and tired policies

American stagflation—simultaneous inflation and unemployment—makes matters even worse. The rising price of oil worsens the balance of payments problem, which in turn causes the fall of the price of the dollar. OPEC retaliates. Another round of balance of payments deficits brings another round of dollar declines. The falling price for the dollar to foreigners allows American producers in concentrated industries to raise their prices. (Automobile and steel producers were quick to raise prices as the U.S. foreign exchange rate rose.)

A flexible exchange-rate system is not supposed to work in this way. The prices of American exports are supposed to remain low, but the contributors to stagflation—giant corporations and powerful unions—are also obstacles to cost and price movements favorable to the balance of payments.

Even though the present exchange rate regime is alleged to be the "flip side" of the Bretton Woods system, rhetoric from the 1960s echoes through the canyons of Wall Street today. Henry Kaufman, chief economist at the securities firm of Salomon

Brothers, is quoted by the *Wall Street Journal* (August 18, 1978): "With the dollar going down, you have an international monetary system without a rudder." Willard C. Butcher, president of Chase Manhattan, expresses (in the same *Journal*) the sentiments of David Rockefeller during the 'sixties, when he called for swift action to restore "confidence in the U.S. dollar." "We think the Fed ought to raise the discount rate," said Mr. Butcher.

Three days later the Federal Reserve raised its discount rate, an interest rate closely tied to the interest charged prime business borrowers by private banks, from 7.25 percent to 7.75 percent, citing the dollar as the Fed's main concern. Although this action came upon the heels of indications of an economic slowdown, Chase Manhattan was not entirely satisfied. Mr. Butcher urged "a significant cut ($25 to $40 billion) in government spending to reduce our massive budget deficit" (*Wall Street Journal*, August 21, 1978).

It is even more hopeless in the 'seventies than it was in the 'sixties to use tighter fiscal and monetary policies at home in an effort to maintain product prices which are more attractive to foreign buyers. Stagflation is a common affliction of the industrialized nations; to slow inflation, these monetary-fiscal policies must squeeze the domestic economies until a substantial fall in output and employment occurs. The problem is that wages and prices are not very flexible downward. Despite this fact, U.S. Treasury officials at times have seemed even rhapsodic about the current prospect for a slowdown in the U.S. rate of economic growth and hence in the dollar outflow.

Fundamental reform

The profit concerns of a small number of powerful New York bankers cannot be ignored, but dollar chauvinism has been costly to the general public in terms of production shortfalls, fewer jobs, and less housing construction. The United States controls the greatest number of votes in the IMF and has had many opportunities to lead the Western world into planned international monetary reform. Each time, apprehensions about a sovereignty that is ephemeral in an interdependent world and the elusive prestige of a self-tarnishing dollar have caused government officials to limit themselves to shouting slogans that are the envy of private bankers in their vain attempt to bolster the dollar. However, we have played out our string of dollars: they are going to start coming home whether we push or pull the string.

The reform initiative has now passed to other governments. Spurred by West German Chancellor

Culver Pictures

Helmut Schmidt and French President Valéry Giscard d'Estaing, the Common Market is moving toward a new plan to stabilize currencies of the nine member nations and enhance trade among them. At the core of the new system would be the European Currency Unit or ECU, whose value would be based upon a weighted average (market basket) of the prices of European currencies. Within this proposed currency union, payments between nations would be made in ECUs rather than in dollars and member nations would intervene in foreign exchange markets with their own currencies in order to isolate Europe as much as possible from the deleterious effect of the unstable dollar. The European currencies would fluctuate in a wide band around the ECU and the ECU would float more or less freely against the dollar. The effect of this new arrangement is likely to be even slower economic growth in Europe, in what they consider to be a fair trade-off for greater economic stability. This "slowth," however, will worsen the trade balance for the United States. Moreover, the existence of reserve substitutes for the dollar invites current dollar holders to dump them.

The embarrassing truth is that the "free world" has never really had a formal, comprehensive "monetary constitution." Although U.S. oil dependence is the most recent "excuse" for the international crisis, the roots of the problem lie in the special role of the dollar. International monetary reform must lead away from the dollar and toward a faceless world currency. A feature of my own reform plan is the worldwide extension of the concept of a "European" currency. The European initiative should provide extra incentive for such an extension. True reform, however, requires rejection of all proposals—and they come most frequently from private bankers—to return to a narrow-band exchange rate system and rather to adopt a new type of limited exchange rate flexibility that has the advantages of fixed *and* floating rates without the most injurious disadvantages.

Under a born-again narrow band, any disequilibria in the American balance of payments would still have to be corrected either by an up-valuing (against the dollar) on the part of trade surplus nations, or by a government-created economic recession in the United States. In the former case, surplus nations must consider the domestic political repercussions of up-valuation, which is viewed by producers as a penalty for their efficiency and by governments for their financial discipline. In the latter case, the U.S. President would have to consider the political risk of rising unemployment. An "adjustable" system simply cannot be expected to work unless some "politically safe" mechanism exists for causing and enabling nations to adjust whenever conditions warrant.

Successful limited exchange rate flexibility involves: (1) short-run exchange rate variation sufficient to create uncertainty among speculators and therefore slow speculative money (capital) flows; (2) long-run par value changes sufficient to alter effective international prices significantly and hence reduce trade deficits, but administered in a way that minimizes speculative capital flows; (3) assurance of an international reserve growth rate adequate for stabilizing par values; and (4) a strengthened role for the IMF in order to wrest the political responsibility (and repercussions) of par value adjustments from the exclusive hands of national governments. A wide SDR band would meet these requirements.

A wide SDR band

Because gold reserves were inadequate and further dollar amassments precarious, a new type of international monetary device, Special Drawing Rights (SDRs), was established in 1968 to add to world liquid reserves. Thus far, however, the role of SDRs has been minor. SDRs, often called "paper gold," are bookkeeping entries at the IMF in the names of member nations. SDRs can be exchanged (under certain conditions) by central banks for other foreign exchange reserve currencies. The SDR unit, originally expressed in terms of gold (at about \$1 = 1/35 ounce of gold), has been calculated since 1974 in terms of a complicated weighted average of the prices of sixteen major currencies. Although the current trend is toward expanded dependence on SDRs, the dollar remains the main reserve currency for use in moderating exchange-rate movements. (Any SDR rate can be calculated in terms of dollars.) One task of monetary reform would be to establish conditions that would enhance SDRs as a truly international money.

The first step toward limited exchange-rate flexibility would be to reinstate par values. However, all par values should be expressed in terms of SDRs rather than the dollar, in the same way in which the dollar was once linked to gold. If, for example, \$1 = 1 SDR and if £1 = .25 SDR, then \$1 = £4 would be the par value.

The universal use of the SDR-denominator would: (1) allow increased U.S. control of the dollar exchange rate as a means to influence trade and capital flows; (2) allow a wider permissible band of fluctuations in exchange rates; and (3) enhance the prestige of SDRs as an international unit of account. The use of other national currencies for pegging operations would be further encouraged because the central banks could draw dollars, marks, or whatever through their SDR balances at the IMF. With the dollar as the denominator currency, the pound sterling price of German marks, for example, could vary as much as twice the difference in the rates between the dollar and each country individually. Bankers and traders cannot fathom, much less predict, the present SDR market basket valuation. Businessmen understandably tend to fear what they do not understand, and they presently continue to use the dollar as a unit of account, as do most central banks. The simple SDR valuation would facilitate its widespread use for accounting purposes. Such familiarity should breed content and enhance the SDR's stature.

The second step of our proposed course of action would be to establish a wide band of variability of exchange rates, 3 percent either side of par. The old narrow gold band led to highly volatile capital movements and therefore to hikes in interest rates by the Federal Reserve that tended to dampen further an often sluggish domestic economy. Higher interest rates abroad usually are attractive only if investors consider the investment to be relatively free of risk. Movements in the exchange rates in which securities are valued could erase the expected gain from investment in the higher-yielding foreign securities. For example, a Japanese businessman holding a \$10,000 one-year U.S. Treasury bond yielding 8 percent at the beginning of 1978 would have experienced a net loss of about 14 percent by mid-year (upon conversion to the fewer yen that the dollar bought). Investors can protect themselves from this risk through arrangements (which offset risk) in the forward exchange market, a market in which currencies can be sold or bought for future delivery.

Investors tend to think alike. If all investors are engaged in the forward market, their actions will increase the cost of offsetting their risks and diminish the incentive to continue investing abroad even though interest rates are higher than at home. The details of this process need not concern us here. Suffice it to say that short-term investment or capital flows tend to be self-limiting when the forward market is engaged.

Under the Bretton Woods narrow-band system, capital flows were not self-limiting. The risk from losses through foreign exchange rate variations was limited by the narrowness of the band. Therefore, the protective actions in the forward market were not taken and the self-stopping mechanism failed.

The narrow distance between pegs (the upper and lower limits to the exchange rates) under the Bretton Woods system also reduced the necessity for importers and exporters to use the forward market. One-way speculation—attempts to gain profits solely from variations in the exchange rate—also was encouraged by this system. Speculators knew that their maximum losses were restricted by the narrow limits to exchange rates while their potential for gains was virtually unlimited if in fact any devaluations occurred. Speculation was rampant. Therefore, in the waning days of the system, when par value alterations became unavoidable, such changes were hastened in a climate of crisis by massive speculative currency flows.

A wide SDR band would diminish these disadvantages. Purchasers of foreign securities would be virtually compelled to enter forward exchange markets to protect their exchange position so that such capital flows would tend to be self-limiting. Within most of the band, speculators would be uncertain, for example, whether the yen would next move up or down, and such uncertainty would exert a sobering influence in the market. The moderate nature of short-term capital flows would eliminate one excuse for higher interest rates geared to "international considerations," a policy that might conflict with a domestic goal of economic expansion.

Beyond such benefits, there is a bonus to the widened band. The exchange rate movement should be sufficient to alter the effective price of competitive commodities such as wheat, so that some reductions in any trade deficits or surpluses would accompany exchange-rate variations within the band. This advantage of floating rates would be retained.

The delayed peg

The wide SDR band works well—up to the limits of allowed variation in the exchange rate. However, the upper or lower limit of currency will eventually be reached because of economic forces pushing the exchange rate in one direction. At and near the limits difficulties would arise because speculators would foresee an impending alteration in par values and behave accordingly. What could be done at the limits to avoid the speculative crises of the old adjustable-peg system?

We need a wide SDR band that moves. In 1968 (in *Economics on a New Frontier*) and again in 1971 (in the May/June *Journal of Political Economy*) I suggested the "delayed peg." According to this system, the wide SDR band would be lowered (raised) with the old lower (upper) limit as the new par value. The announcement of the new band would come several weeks after its adoption, deterring speculation. This par (or new mid-band) rate would be precisely supported to give those traders not protected against exhange risk an opportunity to protect their commitments (this action could be completed within hours or days). The maintenance of the new mid-band level for an indefinite period plus an initially controlled rate of depreciation (if the rate does indeed fall) would further discourage speculatior in the appreciating currency. As the effective price of such commodities as corn and cotton fell with the foreign exchange rate, exports would tend to grow, which would favor a higher exchange rate even before the par value change.

Speculators could be neither sure of the time required to hold purchased currencies for profits nor certain whether trade balance changes (which necessarily lag behind exchange-rate movements) would cause the exchange rate to reverse its direction. By the time the rate was set free within its band again, the exchange rate would have given domestic policy-makers the opportunity to make changes in domestic policies favorable to the balance of payments.

This time lapse is crucial, especially for domestic adjustments in a stagflation-prone economy. The floating rate system does not provide enough time for domestic policies to change productivity, alter wages, or dampen consumer demand. The wide band of the dollar could, if required, be pegged and repegged over a period of one or two years.

In order to prevent the lower limit from becoming a rate which is "fixed for all times," parity adjustments should be *mandatory*, once the international rules for such adjustments are formulated. The IMF should be empowered to alter currency par values (when necessary) under a semi-automatic market rule. Some formal or informal indicator would have to be recognized explicitly in the IMF articles of agreement as a trigger for par value changes in the various currencies. Otherwise, some nations might reject changes in currency values. Although the market exchange rate would be its own indicator under the delayed peg, IMF machinery to prevent competitive depreciation, such as the Japanese pushing the yen price downward despite a huge trade surplus, still would be needed.

Several possible semi-automatic market rules could be used to determine the "fundamental disequilibrium" that would require a change in par values. A monetary reserve base coefficient could be calculated by the IMF. With some base reserve value, the weekly value of reserves lost (or gained) as a share of this base could be determined. Hence, both the speed and the volume of reserve attrition (or accumulation) would be considered. (A 10 percent weekly reserve loss or gain for three weeks would be viewed with as much concern as a 5 percent coefficient during a six-week span.) The permissible losses (or gains) and the reserve rule would be decided in consultation between the national governments and the IMF. The critical range of coefficients for each nation as well as the reserve base period would differ, would be altered from time to time on an unannounced basis, and would be secret until the IMF advised the national government that a basic problem existed according to the semi-automatic market rule, calling for a movement of the band. The intervention responsibilities would rest equally with the deficit and surplus nations. The use of non-dollar intervention currencies would now be possible with the expansion of German mark, Swiss franc, French franc, and Japanese yen holdings.

Further reforms

Although the volume of required official international monetary reserves to finance trade growth under the delayed peg would be smaller than that under the old Bretton Woods system (and indeed smaller than under the current managed floating exchange rate system), we need a provision for adequate growth in official reserves. A truly international money is potentially the best reserve asset, and one whose growth is not dictated by pure national interest or by the vagaries of mining technology and the fixed natural endowment of world gold. Therefore, further measures should be taken to replace gold and a large share of dollar reserves with SDRs. This move would require some additional changes and technical arrangements, including the payment of a still higher interest rate to central bank holders of SDRs. The strongest national currencies would be used as the intervention currencies during the foreseeable future. As SDRs became more acceptable as reserve assets, their use would extend to private transactions; eventually the SDR unit would be *the* international unit of account and currency for trade.

Is the delayed peg reform idea politically palatable? In 1972 the U.S. Treasury proposed a similar plan, but was defeated by special interest pleas that were only drowned by the inescapable float in rates. In June 1974, the IMF Committee of Twenty completed an *Outline of Reform*, proposing the establishment in principle of many of the features of the delayed peg, such as the use of "objective indicators" to obligate a country to make politically risk-free parity changes, a band of ±2.25 percent for any new par value system, more par flexibility, and the use of an international unit of account. The Committee for Economic Development (CED), a private research organization that avoids special interest entanglements, had endorsed an almost identical plan the preceding year.

With the exception of the private banking choir singing the praises of the dollar, widespread agreement has emerged regarding the specific features for international monetary reform. Further delay in implementing such reform will surely prove hazardous to the common interest of Europe, Japan, and the United States.

GLOSSARY OF FOREIGN EXCHANGE TERMS

Par value or parity—An official exchange rate used as a reference point in pegging currencies. Under the Bretton Woods system currencies were pegged at points about 1 percent either side of parity.

Devaluation—A reduction in the par or "official" value of a currency under adjustable parities. The British pound, for example, was devalued in November, 1967 when the U.S. foreign exchange rate was reduced from \$2.80 = £1 to \$2.40 = £1.

Undervalued exchange rate—An exchange rate at which a country's balance of trade is chronically in surplus.

Overvalued exchange rate—An exchange rate at which a country's balance of trade is chronically in deficit.

"The Snake"—The system by which EEC nations have agreed to fix par values against each other within a ±2.25 percent band but to let them float against the dollar. The "snake" breaks apart from time to time. Its current membership includes Belgium, Denmark, the Federal Republic of Germany, Luxembourg, the Netherlands, and Norway.

Special Drawing Rights (SDRs)—A unit of account entered as a reserve asset in a member nation's IMF balance. The IMF issues SDRs to each member nation according to the country's quota size (based upon trade volume) with the IMF. The SDRs can be used to settle accounts between nations. The SDR unit was originally expressed in terms of gold and the dollar with 1 oz. of gold = \$35 and \$1 = 1 SDR.

U.S. foreign exchange rate—The number of dollars it takes to buy one unit of a foreign currency (e.g., 40 U.S. cents = 1 D-Mark).

Forward foreign exchange rate—The number of dollars it takes to buy one unit of a foreign currency for future delivery.

Peg—The term which denotes the intervention rate, that is, the exchange rate at which the monetary authorities of a country intervene in the foreign exchange market in order to keep a currency from falling or rising. There are two pegs: an official selling price, and a buying price for the currency.

Adjustable parities—Parities that are adjusted at once by more than one-half of the band width at a time. The original Bretton Woods intent was to adjust parities in this way when "fundamental disequilibrium" existed.

Wide Gold Band—A system in which the total distance between pegs is more than four percent. The band need not be centered on parity.

Narrow Gold Band—A system in which the exchange rate pegs are four percent or less in total width. The band need not be centered on parity.

Mandatory parity adjustment—A parity adjustment to which the country in question is firmly committed under international rules and which is enforceable by an international agency.

Flexible or floating exchange rates—Exchange rates which neither of two countries in question undertakes to keep invariant within narrow limits.

Managed float—An exchange rate system similar to the floating one, except that national monetary authorities intervene in the foreign exchange market either to moderate the speed of exchange rate movements or to push them intentionally one way or another.

Chapter 15

REVIEW

A Tenured Professor

By John Kenneth Galbraith, Boston: Houghton Mifflin Company, 1990.

E. Ray Canterbery

Two decades ago John Kenneth Galbraith took a sabbatical from economics with *The Triumph*, a satire on U.S. foreign policy. Now America's most literate—and wittiest—economist returns to fiction with a very amusing, multidimensional satire on the greed of the 1980s and the timeless arrogance of academia. The tides of greed ebb and flow but the manners of the Academy remain stilted and stoggy.

My impression is that *The Triumph* ill-served Galbraith's reputation as a writer of fiction. Even so, he is the sole economist to be a fellow in literature of the American Academy of Arts and Letters, and, I venture, *A Tenured Professor* will greatly elevate Galbraith's stature as a satirist. The quality of his satire, wit, and mastery of the boomerang phrase in this new novel leaves little doubt that his literary style is unique, perhaps nothing less than Galbraithian.

Galbraith's amiable maliciousness deftly uncovers society's hidden agendas in a morality parable that is both comic and timely. In broad outline the plot has Harvard's economics faculty looking for a professor with impeccable credentials, an impressive publication, and the right political attitudes. They find Montgomery Marvin, a scholar from all the right places (Harvard, Cambridge University, and Berkeley—a road similar to the one traveled by Galbraith), a published treatise on the theory and mathematics of refrigerator pricing (symbolic of Galbraith's past as a price freezer during World War II), and the right political attitudes (liberal but responsible). To their immense surprise and discomfort, Harvard gets more than it bargained for. Professor Marvin has created a measure of excessive investor optimism and pessimism, the amazingly accurate Index of Irrational Expectations (IRAT).

Goaded on by a very assertive wife, Marvin and IRAT make millions in the stock market. Soon this respectable professor becomes a financial power player and—God, man, and Harvard forbid—a successful corporate raider. If this quickly acquired wealth isn't galling enough for the Harvard bluebloods, the Marvins decide to put their money where their progressive causes are. The faculty knives are unsheathed and events spin out of control. As it turns out, spin control by the Marvins involves a Harvard "bail out." Sound like fun? Well, it is.

Rational expectations

The summer between Marvin's undergraduate days at Harvard and a year at Cambridge University is spent in Vienna, a setting that enables Galbraith to give us "twin peeks" at Vienna and Budapest. There is romance and sex as young Marvin falls in love near lovely Schoenbrunn, where many others have succumbed. With Galbraith as our guide, we glide down the Danube to Budapest and hear the tale of two great Hungarian economists—Nicholas Kaldor and Thomas Balogh, or Buddha and Pest, as they were called. The transition from romance to money is smoothed by Marvin's musings regarding the perfect environment of Cambridge.

In order to understand the incredible money-making machine soon to be invented by Marvin, the reader needs some introduction to the idea of *rational expectations*:

All market participants have the same information and use it with equal efficiency. The market ends up being efficient in the sense that all profits have been exploited. No one can make any money because it has already been made. (This is not satire. It is where *rational expectations* logically delivers us!) The naive economist must wonder why speculators or investors would ever enter a market in which all profits already have been taken. Yet, unless people do enter the market, it doesn't exist.

At Cambridge an old mentor advises Marvin to obtain tenure before revealing his liberalism or other broad interests. This caution does

E. RAY CANTERBERY is Professor of Economics at Florida State University and Consulting Economist at Ben Johnson Associates, Inc., Tallahassee, Florida.

not prevent Marvin's contrary mind from drifting frequently to the delusions of the crowd—to South Sea Bubbles, the manic speculation of the late 1920s, and the financial genius of those men who communicated the errors of euphoria to others.

Marvin reads of the glowing reputations of the men who helped produce the stock market boom of the late 1920s. For example, "there was Richard Whitney, the quintessential Harvard clubman, deeply committed to his own economic acuity, a symbol of the highest standards of financial morality as expressed by the New Stock Exchange, who passed quietly into Sing Sing."

From this history emerges a principle of finance: "Find out who in any euphoric episode is the greatest hero, who is the most celebrated, and invest in his eventual fall." Donald Trump springs to mind, though Galbraith resists this forecast. As F. Scott Fitzgerald once wrote: "Show me a hero and I will write you a tragedy."

Charting euphoria

At Berkeley, Marvin realizes that he needs a measure of the euphoria in a company and its stock. Marvin takes measure of a banking legend, the Bank of America. With reality as 100, Marvin set the measure of euphoria in the bank as twice that figure. With the lights of Berkeley below, those of San Francisco aglow in the distance, he and his cooperative Canadian wife, Marjie, invent the Index of Irrational Expectations. Galbraith, who predicted the 1987 stock market crash in an *Atlantic* article, is toying with the rational expectationists.

IRAT no doubt has some symbolic meeting. It reminds me of my first encounter with experimental economics, during an interview at an institution generating experimental data on the "token economy." Rats were rewarded with tasty pellets only if they behaved in a purely self-interested way. The behavior of the rats was exactly as predicted by orthodox economics. Through the methods of natural science the economists claimed proof that capitalism worked and capitalists responded correctly to the proper market incentives. I, very young and irreverent, suggested that the experiments only proved that "capitalists are rats." I did not land the job.

Marvin had his own experiment to conduct with IRAT. Armed with the knowledge that eventual losses of the many clearly come from the eventual gains of the few, a short position in the BankAmerica stock could lead to profits. Marjie understood: borrow stock, sell it at current prices, and then when the price goes down, replace it, keeping the difference.

Marvin is cautious; not so his aggressive wife. Marjie opens a Merrill Lynch account and makes all the right moves. The return was to give her "powerful leverage in influencing and, indeed, governing Marvin in the years to come." Marjie is the political flywheel that balances the faint-hearted Marvin. By now, the same Harvard that produced Marvin, the undergraduate, has recruited Marvin, the Berkeley Ph.D.

Galbraith takes us along on a commentary-filled travelogue of America as Marvin and Marjie construct indices in Oklahoma and Dallas at a time prior to the oil, real estate, and S&L debacle there. After a stop in Washington, D.C., they eventually settle in a comfortable apartment on Prescott Street behind the Faculty Club, only a block from Harvard Yard.

Of course, Galbraith knows this terrain intimately. Marvin and spouse set up an elaborate computer network at their home in order to calibrate IRAT and apply it to stock market gains. Then, Marvin, attending his first economics department meeting, is warmly congratulated on his cool work on refigerator pricing.

Unlike most young (or old) professors, Marvin is rich before he has tenure. Galbraith walks us through a very funny tenure meeting at Harvard, at which Marvin ultimately prevails. Of course, since no one knew, no one was influenced by the newness of Marvin's wealth or the means of its acquisition.

Galbraith, a life-long Democrat, manages to reach the Gipper and his economists with a few jabs. We are told of the "compelling doctrine that the rich were not working because they had too little money, the poor because they had too much. And . . . the Laffer curve."

The Laffer curve is appealing to the Marvins, as well as to Reagan. By greatly reducing taxes on the top incomes, it left the Marvins with a great deal more cash than would otherwise have been the case. "According to accepted legend, the original curve had been drawn on a paper napkin, possibly toilet paper, and some critics of deficient imagination held that the paper could have been better put to its intended use."

By the mid-1980s, "euphoria was becoming endemic and universal." Securities prices across the board are going up. The Marvins discover index and program trading and begin to use heretofore undreamed-of leveraging. At a time when Ivan Boesky is in descent for using inside information, the Marvins carefully avoid any improprieties. They are honest speculators. The Marvins, going short as usual, become very rich from the stock market crash of October 19, 1987.

The green light

The author of *The Great Crash* makes much of the parallels between the roaring 20s and the casino economy of the 1980s. The stock market crash of October 1929, had, until the 1980s, extinguished the bright lights and levity of the 1920s. The memories of the gin, sex, and dances of the 1920s took on an almost legendary aura in the grimness of the Great Depression. In *A Tenured Professor*, the Yuppies—unisex, perhaps even giving the woman the edge—replace the Flappers of the 1920s. Soon, I suspect, we too will remember only the legends of the 1980s.

F. Scott Fitzgerald's morality tale, *The Great Gatsby*, helped to define the earlier Jazz Age. The *nouveaux riches*, such as Gatsby and those like him, made huge fortunes but lacked the traditions associated with inherited wealth and were therefore vulger.

Others, such as the Buchanans, who had establishment wealth and thus possessed inherited traditions, lacked the vulgarity, but were corrupted by the purposelessness and ease their money provided. Both kinds of wealth resulted in similar human failings, though they were manifested differently.

Gatsby's spirituality enables him to construct and preserve a vision. At the end of the first chapter, Gatsby appears in the attitude of a worshipper, alone and stretching his arms toward the single, faraway green light—the one that might be at the end of a dock across the water—the visible symbol of his vision. Green is the color of promise, of hope and renewal, and ultimately, at the end of the final chapter, it fuses Gatsby's vision with that of the explorers who discovered the promise of a new continent.

In American culture as well as in Gatsby's personal dream, ideals are almost always wrapped up with wealth, and so the means corrupt the ends. Gatsby's description of Daisy's voice as being "full of money" defines the charm she embodies for him. Youth and beauty are inextricably part of the package, imprisoned, and preserved by money. Daisy has an ethereal, insubstantial quality that radiates insincerity. The irony: Daisy is unworthy of the vision, and Gatsby's only attraction is her "vulgar, meretricious beauty." The sacred green light becomes nothing more than a bulb burning at the end of Daisy Buchanan's dock.

As Galbraith suggested in *The Affluent Society*, the material aspect of the American dream is most prominently displayed in advertising. Gatsby resembles an advertisement, remarks Daisy. Eternal youth, beauty, and wealth are on permanent display there. Daisy does not want Gatsby for what he is, but for the superficial illusion of what he represents. Gatsby's corruption is related historically to the destruction of America's early idealism by its involvement with a materialistic ethic. In Gatsby, Nick Carraway is the Scottish moralist who realizes that an ideal based on materialism alone is a corruption rather than a fulfillment of the American dream.

John Kenneth Galbraith, another Scot, is the moral presence in *A Tenured Professor*. Marvin embodies his economics and Marjie his penchant for political action. Galbraith, the writer, is one person expressing himself as many. The Marvins had agreed that the wealth was just a means to an end—a greater end. Galbraith lampoons the limousine liberal taking the high road paved with good intentions. The "positive power of wealth" embues it with elevated purpose.

Limousine liberalism

Liberalism resolves the moral dilemma confronted by Fitzgerald. The limousine liberal takes the vulgar out of wealth by using money to "do good" and to speed progress. The idealism of the American Dream is transformed into the new American prospect. Money nonetheless remains the lubricant.

Marjie teams with New Englander Helen Winthrop Wentworth in an effort to place a tag or sticker on products conveying the share of women in the executive ranks of the producer. Meanwhile, under increasing heat from Harvard as information of their activities become known, the Marvins decide to "bail out" Harvard by offering to buy all of its securities subject to criticism because of corporate participation in the South African economy. Marvin's offer was at 10 percent over closing prices.

Harvard becomes anti-apartheid only after Marvin makes it profitable to be so. Old wealth again takes the easy street of Fitzgerald's Buchanans, but new wealth (like that of Gatsby), fails to fill the moral void. Galbraith's earlier story about the houses of Harvard takes on a new meaning. The original seven red-brick houses were to be named—like Dunster House—for Harvard presidents in their order of succession, a design that faltered with the presidency of Dr. Leonard Hoar.

The novel also shows just how unpopular waging peace, one of Galbraith's lifelong missions, can be. Marvin offers an endowment of $2.5 million to establish Professorships for Peace in each of the three service academies.

The academies are slow to respond. "What seemed to cause the greatest concern was whether this might make peace as a concept unduly prominent in the academies' routine." Critical congressional reaction was that "the professorships were a design for making the academies and their graduates soft on defense."

The American Legion went further: the teaching was no less than an insertion of "subversive Communist propaganda into . . . patriotic and otherwise sacred institutions." The terror of training officers to prefer peace to war ultimately is overwhelmed only the by size of the endowments.

In *A Tenured Professor* there is no Daisy. Marjie has a well-defined progressive vision and knows how to make the conversion to reality. She can do what a Gatsby cannot, though Galbraith seems a bit put off by her apparent aggressiveness. Yet she is the necessary foil to Marvin's hesitant nature. Her sexual fidelity places her as much in the 1990s as Daisy's infidelity helped to define the Jazz Age.

Marjie's special role enables Galbraith to continue his *ju jitsu*. Marjie's new idea is to fight political action committees (PACs) with a countervailing PAC. For every dollar that an incumbent receives from a PAC, the counter-PAC would provide a dollar to the opposing candidate. "A liberal would get the money and then beat the moneyed interests with their own weapon."

Marjie's suggestion for the name of the new PAC, Political Rectitude and Integrity Committees or PRICs did not survive the indelicacy of its acronym because it was considered sexist. Unwittingly, Marvin and Marjie "had crossed the great divide, that which separates benign and agreeable liberalism, of which all politicians are known to be tolerant, from action, which often means serious and highly unwelcome trouble."

Stepping on the toes of congressmen inevitably leads to hearings and sometimes even action, actions taken by such regulatory agencies as the SEC. Galbraith provides a description of the hearing room and the hearings of the House Banking Committee that becomes ever more hilarious as it approaches accuracy.

The hearings nonetheless do not prevent Marvin from a leveraged buyout of "Special Electric" and a rumored buyout of General Electric. A bill is introduced in the House and Senate forbidding any corporation with more than a one-half-billion-dollar commitment in the arms industry to own a TV station.

The president embraces the new law as "supporting the First Amendment. In its assurance of free, untrammeled speech it removes our defense industry, the men and women of our armed forces, all who so serve our country, from the effects of ill-motivated, ill-spirited, unpatriotic propaganda."

The red light

The turning point is provided by the SEC. IRAT, it had been determined, was an illegal manipulation of the markets. It was a case of unfair competition with a certain winner. IRAT not only gave Marvin an unfair advantage, but those following his trades had inside information on his purchases and sales. Hence, we have a clear case of insider trading based on inside information on Marvin's trading—insider trading based on noninsider trading! Market failure is the product of the rational use of irrationality.

When the SEC denies Marvin the use of IRAT, he buys stocks in a random walk, informs the SEC, and provides full information of his transaction to the press. Marvin's undiminished reputation is sufficient to bring others onto a bandwagon. Complete information leads to a one-way speculation that guarantees Marvin's profits. Even the efficient use of complete information shakes the markets. At the end Marvin still has tenure.

Galbraith once again is sending up the rational expectationists. But, there also is subtle symbolism. Galbraith at Harvard always was an "outsider" because he sought a larger audience. His verbal dexterity, acerbic put-downs, and mordant understatements gained not only a wider audience but a *Playboy* interview and political clout in Democratic party circles.

Galbraith became an insider in national politics by being an outsider at Harvard where the green might have represented envy rather than Gatsby-like hope. Galbraith nonetheless has brought hope to economists by reminding us of how much fun we could have if only we were more like him.

Chapter 16

IRRATIONAL EXUBERANCE AND RATIONAL SPECULATIVE BUBBLES

E. Ray Canterbery

* * * * *

I. INTRODUCTION

"Irrational exuberance" is a phrase famously coined by Alan Greenspan, head of the Federal Reserve, in December 1997. Sensing an overpricing of some 20 percent in the Dow, Greenspan hoped to talk the market down without a crash. Though the market immediately recoiled in reaction to Greenspan's remarks, it quickly recovered. The Dow had climbed *another* 20 percent by spring 1998. Still concerned with overvalued assets, Greenspan was reluctant to raise interest rates for fear of setting in motion the greatest stock market crash in American history. Greenspan apparently believed that an *irrational* bubble was driving the stock market. Some will see the irony; Greenspan, an outspoken opponent of any regulation of financial markets, repeatedly has praised such markets for their "efficiency."

A variety of formal definitions of a bubble exist. However, the intuition remains the same. If the price of an asset is high today only because buyers *believe* that the selling price will be high tomorrow, a bubble exists. Put differently, today's price is not fully explained by fundamentals (variables having a direct effect on future income streams

---

E. Ray Canterbery is Professor of Economics at Florida State University.

An earlier version of this article was given as the presidential address at the international meeting of the International Trade and Finance Association in Atlantic City, New Jersey, May 29, 1998.

The author thanks H. Peter Gray for his helpful comments. Any remaining errors remain unshared.

from, for example, equities). Often, it appears, a self-fulfilling prophecy is underway, because asset prices will cleave to the high side as long as buyers believe they will. In the short run, the high asset price is "justifiable," because it yields a return (dividends) equal to or greater than returns on alternative assets, including, say, bonds.

Still, Greenspan's view is contrary to the theories of efficient capital markets based on rational expectations. In the stronger version of rational expectations all asset prices are not only always correct, they reflect market fundamentals. In the rational bubble models, even the "bubbles" are "rational" because investors can believe that the asset's price is above its fundamental value but continue to hold the asset anyway. That is, they believe that someone else (a greater fool?) will buy the asset for a higher price in the future, preventing a pricking of the bubble. In a rational bubble, therefore, asset prices can deviate from their fundamental values for a long time because the bursting of the bubble cannot be predicted and so there are no unexploited profit opportunities. A single player in the market, such as George Soros or Warren Buffet (or even a pirate like Jimmy Buffet), can never beat the market, even one with a bubble. Not only will any differences from the "optimal forecast" of any asset's price (its fundamental value) sum to zero, so will differences from the optimal forecast of the bubble; such deviations, therefore, are unpredictable. Asset prices walk a random walk.

For now, we will not trifle with the efficient market theories. Suffice it to say that most historians and some economists side with Greenspan. Ultimately, they say, we must come to grips with the reality of financial excess, a form of mass hysteria. Patsy-Cline-like "crazy" behavior—manic, obsessed, haunted, mesmerized, and orgasmic—leads to abnormal outcomes. When the players overdo financial opportunities, a mania follows that must somehow end, usually an atrabilious end. In this view, the great financial bull market of the 1990s seemed to be coming to such a gruesome finale by August 1998, if not sooner.

Rather than differences in fundamental and bubble prices, it is sometimes useful to contrast tranquil markets with turbulent markets.[1] A tranquil market has no internal contradictions and no external shocks; expectations based upon past experience are confidently held and constantly justified. Current prices can be confidently expected without rational (or forward-looking) expectations. Still, internal contradictions can evolve in any market, especially in a financial market. Moreover, when a market turns from tranquil to turbulent, it is difficult to say whether the turbulence is "caused" by external shocks. If a market is so delicate that a particular shock causes it to collapse (become il-liquid), we might even question the basis for the players' confidence based on past experience or even forward-looking expectations. Besides, since markets are interdependent, does one market adversely affecting a second comprise an "external shock"? In particular, since the interest rate on a long-term bond may be used as the discount rate on valuing equities, an unexpectedly dramatic fall in bond prices may be an "internal" shock to stock markets. If an equity-market player behaves as if movements in bond prices do not matter, is the player being rational?

We cannot answer all such questions in one article, but we can shed some light on the issues involved. Certainly, irrational exuberance defies the rational individual behavior and general equilibrium models based on rational behavior, including Lucas' critique as well as *rational* bubbles in assets. Then, irrespective of theory, those who deny bubbles must go to the barricades against the four great bubbles of modern history—tulipmania, the Mississippi Bubble, the South Sea Bubble, and the Great Crash of 1929. This is precisely what has

---

[1]The conditions under which a tranquil market can remain robust (i.e., liquid) were well defined by Gray (1992). In reference to Hicks' famous "snake diagram," Gray reminded us, "once within the unstable range, the instability feeds on itself (a crisis) so that the range of instability can be substantial" in a financial asset market (1992, p. 250).

happened; recently, rewriting the history of bubbles has become a cottage industry. If these revisionists were to write the history of the Titanic, the *iceberg* would have sunk! Meantime, a dramatic end to the Great Bull Market of the 1990s may provide still another historical case.[2]

We will proceed to restate the history of the classic bubbles. Notably, these revisions have been written by rational expectationists. Then, we will critique the revisionist histories of these bubbles. Along the way we will consider the standard model for such bubbles. Finally, though considering the lessons learned from history, we will suggest an alternative theoretical approach.

First, we return to the first great historic bubble, tulipmania.

II. TULIPMANIA

The Traditional History

A tulip bulb craze pervaded Holland during the early 17th century. Though popular and expensive by 1593, many tulips became infected after that with a nonfatal virus and the petals developed contrasting colored stripes or "flames." Wealthy Dutch people, who called these infected bulbs "bizarres," greatly valued them. Inevitably, the more "bizarre" the bulb, the higher its price. Speculators, however, did not enter the market until late 1636, as prices of many varieties soared from November through December 1636.

Then, tulipmania set in; prices began to rise wildly. The higher the prices went, the more attractive the bulbs became to buyers. Even

[2]This address, of course, was delivered prior to the 19 percent "first phase" decline from a "peak" of 9368 in the Dow during August 1998. This was the greatest decline from a major peak in the 20th century.

common bulbs became part of the speculative bubble. Farmers, mechanics, seamen, footmen, and nobles shifted out of their usual industry and speculated in tulip bulbs. People apparently thought tastes would never turn against the bizarres and prices would rise toward infinity. The few who thought otherwise were left behind, feeling foolish, as the prices continued to climb and their friends made great profits.

A herd instinct took over, and few could resist temptation. Near the end people were exchanging their personal property—jewels, furniture, land—for the bulbs that they expected would make them rich. In the final stage of the mania during January 1637, prices of *ordinary* tulip bulbs increased twentyfold, only to drop to about 1/20 of their peak value in February.

Speculators began cautiously to take their profits as they tiptoed out of tulips. Prices began to wilt, like petals in a dry summer. Though the Dutch government reassured citizens that "there was no reason for the bulbs to fall in price," dealers continued to go bankrupt. Eventually, most tulip bulbs became no more valuable than onions. The end was poetically, well, bizarre. Not only the speculators but the conservative buyers and dealers went down with the bulb prices. We return to some of the details.

Applying the Standard Models

Paul Samuelson associated tulipmania with "the purely financial dream world of indefinite group self-fulfillment" (1967, p. 230). Samuelson's students, Shell and Stiglitz (1967, p. 593) stated that "the instability of the Hahn model is suggestive of the economic forces operating during 'speculative booms' like the Tulip Bulb mania." In his presidential address to the American Finance Association, Van Horne (1985, p. 627) invoked the possibility of tulipmania, in which a "single bulb sold for many years' salary." In what were then called perfect foresight models (today, called rational expectations models), Hahn (1966), Samuelson (1967), Shell–Stiglitz (1967), and others nonetheless argued that in the absence of futures markets extending into infinity, no market forces could prevent bubbles.

In many such models, every bubble eventually broke, requiring only that a speculator be sufficiently long-lived to take profits. Shiller (1984, 1986), too, advanced the hypothesis that asset prices are driven by crowd behavior or fads. Shiller (1986) wrote that the standard and accurate view, until the last few decades, has been that asset markets are driven by capricious investors acting on the basis of fads and bubbles. He cites tulipmania as an example.

In these models the terminal price of the asset becomes trivial if the asset price increases more slowly than the discount factor. Then, only if the value of the asset were just equal to the discounted value of the stream of returns it yielded, would no bubbles exist. Otherwise, as long as no one has an infinite planning horizon, nothing could ensure that the asset price equaling the discounted stream of returns condition (the transversality condition) would prevail. Put differently, if the rate of price increases of an asset equals (or exceeds) the rate of interest, then the share of the value of all assets accounted for by this asset would grow without bound, a condition *inconsistent* with long-run (fundamentals) equilibrium. A bubble would persist (not burst) only in the special case where the growth rate in the asset's price equaled the interest rate. Though these models assume a fixed interest rate, a rising interest rate (as suggested previously) *could* cause a financial bubble to collapse.

Today's rational expectations' models, though bearing a family resemblance to the Samuelson–Hahn style models, make contrary claims. The evaluation of errors in an "optimal" forecast model (the sum of which are *assumed* zero), "proves" the efficient market hypothesis. As defined previously, a bubble in an asset price requires a comparison with its "fundamental" price. The fundamental price is derived from an ***estimation*** of returns received over time (such as dividends on stocks), sometimes an estimate of the terminal value of the asset, and the proper selection of a discount rate or rates for transforming future returns into current values.[3] Once we have a formula for a price based on fundamentals, or course, we need a solution that includes a bubble. The initial bubble then can have an

[3] In the standard formula, people are risk-averse and they discount future returns at a constant rate. R. Then, for example, the price of one equity share, P_t, equals the expected discounted present value of the accrued dividends during the ownership period, D_{t+1}, plus the price at which the share can be sold at the end of the ownership period, P_{t+1}. Thus,

$$(1)\quad P_t = E_t(D_{t+1} + P_{t+1})/(1 + R),$$

where $E_t(D_{t+1} + P_{t+1})$ is the expected value of the future dividend and the future price based on information available at time t. An asset pricing formula can be derived from equation (1) by a recursive process. Update equation (1) by one time period to derive P_{t+2} and substitute the right-hand side of the expression for P_{t+2} into equation (1), giving

$$(2)\quad P_t = E_t[D_{t+1} + E_{t+1}(D_{t+2} + P_{t+2})/(1 + R)]/(1 + R).$$

Update equation (1) again, and substitute for P_{t+2} into equation (2). Use the law of iterated expectations, $E_t[E_{t+1}(D_{t+2})] = E_t(D_{t+2})$, which assumes that the expected value today of what we will expect about the future when we have more information in the next period is simply what we expect about the future today with much less information. After an infinite number of substitutions, the current price equals the expected present value of all future dividends or

$$(3)\quad P_{f,t} = \sum_{i=1}^{\infty} [1/(1 + R)]^i E_t(D_{t+i}).$$

In this equation the subscript f defines price as the market fundamentals price, as defined above. Since the share is held infinitely long, it has no terminal value.

innovation attached to it. We could conceive even of a model in which many innovations take place, perhaps into infinity.[4]

Besides the assumption that forecast errors sum to zero, the main departures under rational expectations are an "information set" behind the equations and the assumption that the representative agent

---

[4]One way of introducing bubbles into the earlier fundamentals equation is to consider equation (3) in footnote 3 as only one mathematical solution to equation (1). Other solutions can include a bubble, denoted with B_t, or

$$(4)\quad P_t = P_{f,t} + B_t.$$

The bubble represents a deviation of the current market price of the asset from the value based solely upon fundamentals. To satisfy equation (1) the current value of the bubble must be the expected discounted value of the future bubble in the next period, or

$$(5)\quad B_t = E_t(B_{t+1})/(1 + R).$$

However, a bubble is a possible outcome of this model only as long as it is expected that the bubble will continue. Sometimes the bubble definition has been written as

$$(6)\quad B_{t+1} = B_t(1 + R) + b_{t+1}$$

where

$$(7)\quad b_{t+1} = B_{t+1} - E_t(B_{t+1}).$$

Whereas B_t is a bubble in the equity price, b_{t+1} is the innovation in the bubble at time $t + 1$ which has mean zero. Then, if bubbles exist, they must grow at the real rate of interest. Burmeister, Flood, and Garber (1983) discussed several indeterminacies in the homogeneous part of the solution to the difference equation (1). Since the bubble process is the homogeneous part of the solution, $(1 + R) > 1$ generates an explosive indeterminancy. If the bubble were negative in equation (5), it would be expected to be larger and negative over time until it exceeded the fundamentals price, a price that could not grow as fast as the bubble would shrink. The equity would have a negative price in finite time, something we never observe in the stock markets, though some stocks can disappear from the market. This result has led some economists to conclude that bubbles cannot exist. Alternative conclusions, however, could be either (1) the asset price should be constrained by market institutions to a positive value or (2) the bubble equation is incorrect. After all, the Russian stock market can drop 90 percent in a few days without going all the way to 110 percent.

lives forever. In the Hahn–Samuelson model, a bubble would persist *only* if the representative agent lives forever. Samuelson and his followers, however, always *knew* that only an infinitely lived "representative" agent could prevent the bursting of a bubble, but considered such a condition irrelevant in the real world. We revisit rational expectations in Section IV.

Problems with the Revisionist Interpretation

Despite the problematic econometrics of "rational" bubbles, Peter M. Garber (1989), a longtime champion of rational expectations who disavowed irrational bubbles,[5] gave us not so much a revisionlist parable of tulipmania, as a revisionist interpretation. Despite his providing a wonderfully detailed history, he claimed that "most" of tulipmania was not obvious madness. In his view, high but rapidly depreciating prices for rare bulbs is a *typical pattern* in the flower bulb industry. "Only the last month of the speculation, during which common bulb prices increased rapidly and crashed, remains as a potential bubble" (1989, p. 535).

As Garber correctly related, "the market for bulbs was limited to professional growers until 1634, but participation encompassed a more general class of speculators by the end of 1634" (1989, p. 543). Formal futures' markets in bulbs developed in 1636, the primary focus of trading before the collapse in February 1637. By the summer of 1636 traders began meeting in taverns in groups called "colleges" where trades were regulated by a few rules. Since bulbs are not available until June and must be replanted by September, any purchase between September and June has to be a contract for future delivery. The impetus for higher prices initially came from a rising demand

---

[5]See Flood and Garber (1980) for empirical tests for the existence of bubbles.

from wealthy Frenchmen competing to adorn their favorite women with the most bizarre of the flowers.

As with today's futures markets, neither party intended delivery on the settlement date; only a payment equaling the difference between the contract and settlement price was expected. The timing of events was hypothesized by Posthumus (1929, p. 444):

> At the end of 1634, the new nonprofessional buyers came into action. Towards the middle of 1635 prices rose rapidly, while people could buy on credit, . . . About the middle of 1636 the colleges appeared; and soon thereafter the trade in non-available bulbs was started, while in November of the same year the trade was extended to the common varieties, . . .

Counter to Garber, however, the accounts of tulipmania, including his own, *do* include speculation in common bulbs. Besides, even if Garber is correct in claiming that the prices of bizarres traded among the serious and wealthy tulip fanciers reflected fundamentals, he *does not* and *cannot* dismiss the bubble in prices of the common bulbs. Besides, the pattern described by Posthumus (now deceased) is precisely what is usually seen in speculative bubbles. At first, professionals and wealthy people control trading, bidding only on bizarres or blue chips. Later, when something dramatic, such as the dazzling prices paid for the bizarres, happens, common people desire part of the action. They could not afford the high-priced bulbs. Often, because they have minimal resources, they and the traders bringing their business to them have to be innovative (using futures, margins, meeting conveniently in taverns) to participate in markets normally serving only the rich. Participation by the masses drove up the price of common bulbs, causing it to soar well above any fundamental price. If the NASDAQ increased twentyfold in one month and fell to 1/20 of its value the next, it would attract the attention of many people.

III. A FRENCH–ENGLISH INTERNATIONAL FINANCIAL CRISIS

Elsewhere, Garber (1990, p. 40–52) dismissed—with greater conviction than with tulipmania—the Mississippi and South Sea bubbles as rational events, based irretrievably on solid fundamentals. Garber nonetheless correctly connected the fates of the players in both episodes in what might be described as the first *international* financial crises. In its beginning, the Garber parable once again follows standard historical accounts.

The Traditional History of the Mississippi Bubble Phase

By 1715 the French government had been bankrupted by the wars of Louis XIV. Despite France's repudiating its debt and gaining a reduction in interest on the remainder, it was still in arrears. A combination of forces, including high taxes riddled by special exemptions, had led to a depression. In 1717 John Law organized a company to monopolize trade with Louisiana and in Canadian beaver skins. (Apparently, "Mississippi" comes from the river being located in the Louisiana territory.)

The French, in effect, privatized the treasury under Law's scheme, in the hope that a *general* commercial recovery would support market prices of the company's (Company d'Occident's) shares. Law issued shares to be paid partly in cash but mostly in government debt. Then he converted the debt into *rentes* and offered the government an interest-rate reduction. Law's idea was to generate a cash flow that could be leveraged into wonderfully expanding commercial activity. Indeed, the company managed to gain a tobacco monopoly in September 1718 and the Senegalese Company (trading with Africa) in November 1718.

Meantime, the French government allowed Law to open a conventional, note-issuing bank, the Banque Generale. In January 1719, the Banque Generale was renamed the Banque Royale, with a note issue guaranteed by the crown. Remaining in control of the bank, Law acquired the French East India and China companies. Then he created a conglomerate of all his companies (the Compagnie des Indes) which monopolized all French trade beyond Europe. Law issued shares against the conglomerate at 1,000 livres per share to acquire the right to mint new coinage valued at weights of gold or silver which varied greatly during Law's regime. Share prices rose to 1,800 livres within a few months. Between August and December 1719 Law took over the administration of the French tax system. Share prices soared to 3,000 livres.

Law proceeded to refund the national debt (with a face value of 1,400 million livres but a market value of much less) with new shares sold at 5,000 livres per share, payable in monthly installments. Conveniently, payment could be made in the notes issued by Law's Banque Royale. By August 1720 he had acquired the government debt, guaranteeing him a steady flow of income from the treasury. Then, share prices immediately rose to 10,000 livres. By now he was France's Controller General and Superintendant Generale of Finance while heading the Banque Royale. Law now was CEO of a private conglomerate that controlled France's overseas trade and the development of its colonies, collected France's taxes, minted its coins, and held three-quarters of France's national debt. By controlling all markets, Law was able to issue junk equity to buy junk bonds. Not surprisingly, King Louis XV was a principal shareholder.

Law's Banque Royale issued new bank notes to fund each new issue of shares. Sensing the debasing of the bank's notes, people began to sell shares, converting their capital gains into gold. By the end of January 1720, share prices fell below 10,000 livres. The king, seeing the downside to this venture and an inside trader if there ever was one, sold his shares back to the conglomerate at 9,000 livres per share. The Banque Royale ceased supporting the share prices with new bank notes. Despite Law's devaluation of bank notes relative to gold, share prices had fallen to 2,000 livres by September 1720 and to 1,000 livres by December. By September 1721 the share prices had fallen to 400 livres, or roughly to its value in May 1719. This would be the equivalent of the Dow going from 1,000 to 10,000 in $1\frac{1}{2}$ years, then crashing to 400, a decline of 96 percent, one year later!

A Revisionist's Account: Mississippi Was not a Bubble

Garber claimed that Mississippi was not a bubble. Again, the quarrel is not so much with his excellent historical account, but his interpretation. "After all," he wrote, "behind the price rise lies Law's program to revitalize the French economy through financial innovation and fiscal reform." As to the downward slide in share prices, "it is even easier to understand, given the radical shifts in monetary policy and the intimate connection of Compagnie shares to Banque Royale note emissions" (1990, p. 46). A *rational* macro-model underpinned John Law's program, for "elements of [Keynesian economics, supply-side economics, monetarism] were primary components of Law's scheme (1990, p. 47)." Rational expectations were at work because the French buyers of the shares had this convincing model apparently embossed on their silk cockades. "It is the centerpiece of most money and macroeconomics textbooks produced in the last two generations and the *lingua franca* of economic policymakers concerned with the problem of underemployed economies" (1990, p. 47).

The Traditional History of the South Sea Bubble Phase

The English seldom have wished for exclusively good fortune for the French without a tinge of envy. Thus, not only did English nobles participate in the Mississippi Bubble, but the British South Sea Company emulated Law's program by acquiring British government debt in January 1720. The British scheme nonetheless was much simpler. About 40 percent of the British debt was held by the South Sea Company, the Bank of England, and by the East India Company. Besides its holdings of government securities, the South Sea Company had a monopoly on British trade with the Spanish colonies of South America (the South Seas).

To finance the acquisition of the government's debt, the South Sea Company was allowed to expand its shares outstanding. Its shares had a par value of Ł100. For each Ł100 of the long- and short-term securities acquired, the company increased its shares outstanding by Ł2,000 and Ł1,400 pounds, respectively. Though the government interest rate was reduced, the company still could enjoy a steady cash flow from holding the debt.

The company paid Ł1.3 million in bribes to leading members of Parliament and favorites of the king to assure passage of the refunding act (Scott 1911, p. 315). Direct, unconstrained bribery in the pursuit of favorable policies was common. Moreover, members of Parliament and the government "bought" 17 percent of the new issues and received Ł1.1 million in cash loans against those shares.

The South Sea's share, beginning in January 1720 at about Ł120 per Ł100 par value, immediately rose to Ł200, leaping to Ł300 with the passage of the refunding act on March 21. The company issued sufficient new shares during April to pay its bribes. Late in April the company began to convert its shares into government securities. Once it was clear that the company would be able to acquire all of the government debt, share prices soared to Ł700. In June the company issued still more shares at Ł1,000 per share: buyers bought on margin with 10 percent down and the balance due within $4\frac{1}{2}$ years. Again, to compare the appreciation in shares to the Dow, it was like the Dow going from 1200 to 10,000 in six months for an annualized gain of 1467 percent!

Euphoria spread from the South Sea Company to other companies, some of which were sound and some of which were fraudulent. Fearing that such companies might reduce South Sea's profits, the South Sea Company convinced Parliament to pass the Bubble Act in June 1720, banning the formation of unauthorized corporations or the extension of corporate charters into new ventures. Upon enforcement of the act in mid-August, a selling wave overwhelmed South Sea's potential competitors. The contagion spread to the South Sea Company. Because the shares were mainly held on margin, liquidity quickly evaporated. Then, the collapse of John Law's conglomerate in September 1720 drained still more funds from British markets.

The price collapse began at the end of August. Share prices fell from about 775 on August 31 to about 290 on October 1, 1720, or 62.5 percent, an annual rate of 750 percent. If the Dow fell 62.5 percent in a single month, it would eclipse the Crash of 1929 by indescribable proportions. (It took almost three years for the market to drop 83.3 percent in the 1929–33 collapse.) Although the total market value of all shares stood at Ł164 million on August 31, some Ł103 million of those were lost within a month. The losses exceeded twice the value of the original government debt! Even Parliament, reacting to a shift in public opinion against the South Sea Company, abandoned it.

The Problems with the Revisionist History That South Seas Was not a Bubble

Again, Garber declared that South Seas was not a bubble. Only Garber's representation of the macroeconomic theory behind Law's program seems more implausible than the program itself. At a moment in time when kings and queens still ruled on the continent, patients were bled to cure them, the masses were impoverished, the nobles fed off the labors of masses of peasants, slaves worked the colonies, witches and heretics still were being burned, the nobility (despite already questionable intelligence diminished by inbreeding) not only understood macroeconomics ***before its invention***, but fully fathomed a hybrid of ***three*** 20th-century macro-models. Besides, the amalgam of Keynesian economics, supply-side economics, and monetarism (very much resembling Garber's theory) was tried during the early 1980s and was—according to macroeconomists at the time and today—an unmitigated disaster because of its internal contradictions.[6] Even rational expectations fail if the agents in the economy have ***the wrong model.***

Garber made other dubious claims. South Sea's revenue from the government, at a 4 percent discount rate, created an asset, he wrote, having "a value of about 40 million pounds." Still, "share prices [on August 31] exceeded tangible net assets by five times or more" (1990, p. 52) Garber cited Scott's (1911, pp. 313–314) justification for a share price of 300 to 400, based upon the predicted commercial expansion from the capital raised. The fundamentals, Garber claimed, were sound.

At some point reality must intrude. If commercial expansion was so promising, why did South Sea fear competition from other companies? Moreover, commercial expansion, the buying and selling of existing goods, creates little value-added, unlike a full-fledged factory system, a structure not yet on the horizon. Besides, even after those competing companies were eliminated by Parliament, the rapid deterioration in their share prices quickly spread to a "sound company," the South Sea Company. Even the buyer paying £300 per share, Scott (1911, pp. 313–314) suggested, "may have been unduly optimistic, but there was at least a possibility that his confidence would be rewarded in the future."

A possibility? The £300 price is beside the point; in the final subscription of shares, people were paying £1,000. Scott's problematic "fundamental price" is 70 percent below the subscription price, a gap in excess of that revealed in the single-month collapse. The buyers must have been not simply "unduly optimistic," but irrationally exuberant. Still, Garber concluded, "the episode is readily understandable as a case of speculators working on the basis of the best economic

---

[6]For accounts of the Reaganomics disasters, see Canterbery (1987, 1995) and Krugman (1994).

analysis available and pushing prices along by their changing view of market fundamentals" (1990, p. 52). That is, rational expectations fully explains the South Sea bubble. If all price behaviors, no matter how bizarre, are based on "rational expectations," of what value is rationality?

IV. THE GREAT CRASH OF 1929

The Histories

At last we come to the Great Crash of 1929. Its broad outlines and even its specifics are well-known among economists. Many have read John Kenneth Galbraith's enduring classic, *The Great Crash 1929*, recently reprinted. Galbraith (1988 [1954]) and economic historian Charles P. Kindleberger (1989 [1978]) described the bull market of the late 1920s as a bubble that burst. Though most historians agree with Galbraith and Kindleberger, some economists have claimed that those who bought shares were behaving rationally and no bubble existed.

Even early on, Charles Amos Dice (1929) of Ohio State University wrote that economic fundamentals were driving the market. Well after the crash, Irving Fisher (1930) restated his faith in share prices, contending that his own impression was that the market went up principally because of sound, justified expectations of earnings, and only partly because of unreasoning and unintelligent mania for buying.

More recently, Sirkin (1975) expressed support for Dice and Fisher's views. Assuming a normal price-to-earnings ratio of 15, Sirkin found that earnings would have had to grow 9 percent per year for another 10 years to justify the peak P/E ratio of 20.4. Since 9 percent was the average growth rate of 1925–29, Sirkin claimed that no "speculative orgy" existed. Fundamentals were simply undone by the policy errors of the Federal Reserve and the Congress that led to the Great Depression.

Still more recently, Eugene N. White presented a contrary account of the causes of the bubble and the Crash. He wrote, "the qualitative evidence assembled in this paper favors the view that a bubble was present in the 1929 market" (1990, p. 67). Yet, he claims, the market boom initially was based on some realistic expectations related to the rise of high technology industries.

White's account of the causes of the upswing is interesting because—with a few substitutions with today's corporate names, new technologies, and surging industries—he could have been writing about what President Clinton and *Business Week* have called the "New Economy." The 1920s' growth in GNP can be attributed partly to the "emergence of large-scale commercial and industrial enterprises that took advantage of new continuous process technologies" (1990, p. 69). The capital requirements for commercial banks restricted their ability to provide expanding finance needs. (Though he does not mention it, the real bills' doctrine limited bank lending to the provision of working capital.) Though the market for industrial securities had emerged in the 1880s, it necessarily came of age during the 1920s, as old and new corporations issued equities to finance new plants and equipment going unfinanced by commercial banks. Like today, many of the new buyers of shares were neophytes. Unlike then, the peak P/E ratio in the Great Bull Market of the 1990s was 27, making 1929's 20.6 appear anemic.

Rather than sitting on the sidelines during the 1920s, commercial banks circumvented capital restrictions by setting up wholly owned securities affiliates, permitting them to enter investment banking and the brokerage business. The banks not only enthusiastically underwrote securities and distributed existing issues to the public but entered the insurance business. In a similar fashion today, banks have been superseded by the growth in capital markets and are using holding companies to circumvent various legal restrictions, so that they can move back into investment banking, brokerage services, and insurance.

Many of the firms embodying new technologies, like many firms on today's NASDAQ (soon to be part of the American stock exchange), *had never paid a dividend.* (Using the standard pricing formula based on fundamentals, a stream of zero dividends would put the fundamental price of the stock at zero.) The non-dividend-paying stocks included RCA, Radio-Keith-Orpheum, ALCOA, and the United Aircraft and Transport Corporation. As the electric utilities comprised a frontier industry undergoing consolidation and expansion, many were paying no dividends, including Commonwealth and Southern Corporation, Electric Bond and Share, and the North American Company.

The true stock market boom got underway in 1927, by the end of which the *Times* industrials (forerunner of the *Dow-Jones* industrials) had gained 69 points to end at 245. Though indices of dividends and stock prices moved in tandem from 1922 to 1927, stock prices raced way ahead of dividends in 1928 and 1929.[7] Fundamentals cannot explain this divergence between dividends and prices. During 1928 the *Times* industrials gained 86 points, climbing from 245 to 331, a remarkable advance of 35 percent. Zero-dividend Radio had gone from 85 to 420, DuPont from 310 to 525, and Wright Aeronautic from 69 to 289. Trading on the margin—on borrowed money—soared like Wright Aero: The speculator could buy $1000 of stock with only $100 down—a 10-to-1 leverage, just as with the South Sea Company shares. Ultimately, the public utilities index experienced a bigger bubble than industrials. Still, the orgy of unrestrained speculation had to end.

The panic of 1929 began on Black Thursday, October 24. Shortly after a normal opening of the exchange, prices began to fall on rapidly rising volume. The stampede of selling by 11:00 a.m. was so wild, it would have scared even the Merrill-Lynch bull. Fear became genuine panic, as a crowd gathered outside the Exchange at the corner of Broad and Wall Streets.

---

[7]See White (1990, p. 73, Figure 3).

The first wave of panic subsided at noon, when word spread of a meeting at 23 Wall Street, the offices of the venerable J. P. Morgan and Company. The assembled bankers pledged to pool their resources and turn the market around. But they could only lean—despite their great bulk—into the wind. By Monday afternoon the *Times* industrials were down 49 points for the day, with General Electric alone down 48. Since the ticker tape could not keep abreast of trading, no one knew how bad it was by the day's end. By 4:30 p.m., the bankers now would try to save themselves, reducing their losses by selling short.

The next day, Tuesday, October 29, was the most devastating. On many issues no buyers at all were anywhere in sight; liquidity had dried up. The *Times* industrials closed down 43 points on enormous volume. Alarm again gripped Wall Street. Save for a mild rally during the first quarter of 1930, the stock market would continue its relentlessly downward slide week after week—through June 1933.

The reallocation of credit from the real economy to the stock market tends to confirm the bubble. The Federal Reserve had hoped (as Alan Greenspan apparently has during 1998) that high real interest rates would slow the stock market. The use of credit in the market continued even though the call rate on brokers' loans, perhaps the correct rate to discount earnings, soared to 20 percent. Nothing, it would appear (just as with the Great Bull Market of the 1990s, until July 1998), could slow the asset inflation.

What Really Caused the Great Crash?

Galbraith and Kindleberger's argument that the market was so overvalued that anything could have shattered the confidence of those in the market remains convincing. White nonetheless attributed the crash to "evidence of an oncoming recession" (1990, p. 81). Although it is true that the Federal Reserve's index of industrial production dropped in July 1929, the declines in the Federal Reserve's other indices beginning in August and September were not published until

October, after the crash. Retrospectively, though the peak of the business cycle has been dated from August 1929, the prestigious Harvard Economic Services (HES) and Irving Fisher, arguably the two preeminent forecasting services of that time, could not detect any signs of a downturn as late as March 1930. Moreover, Fisher's forecasts were published weekly in a nationwide syndicated newspaper column on economic affairs.

In the week prior to Black Friday, the HES assessment was that

> If recession should threaten serious consequences for business (as is not indicated at present) there is little doubt that the reserve system would take steps to ease the money market and so check the movement.[8]

HES confidence continued through August 1931. The day before Black Friday, Irving Fisher continued to be bullish despite some small movements that had rocked the stock market in recent weeks. He wrote:

> The [stock market] break certainly exhibited signs of a market rendered top-heavy by the activities of shoals of speculators, acting unintelligently, who at last became frightened and dumped millions of shares in a way temporarily to swamp the Exchanges.... The only event which can bring about a serious decline in stock value is a severe business slump, which does not seem likely from present indications.[9]

---

[8]Quoted from the HES weekly report by Dominguez, Fair, and Shapiro (1988, p. 606).

[9]*Ibid.* p. 607.

Fisher did not see any change in the fundamentals; if they did change, he had confidence that the Federal Reserve would take effective corrective actions. Even immediately after the Crash, Fisher remained optimistic. As late as December 30, 1929, Fisher's optimism bordered on cheerleading:

> ...While the stock exchange endured the severest panic in history, this did not suffice to shake the price level of stocks off a warrantable high new plateau, which had been built up since 1922. ... The function of the stock market is to reflect the discounted value of future increased business, as clearly foreshadowed in the increasing rate at which earnings are plowed back into industry.[10]

The expressions of optimism by HES and Fisher regarding prospects for economic recovery in the midst of the Great Depression are, retrospectively, embarassing.

If the best economic forecasters in the world did not see the Crash *after* it happened, much less forecast it, can we reasonably expect that the least experienced buyers of stock in history could have seen the recession coming and surmise the end of the bull market? If they had a full set of information, would it not include the reports from HES and Fisher? Even ordinary traders should have been hanging on every word of Irving Fisher's weekly newspaper column. If HES and Fisher were their information sources, the market players should never have sold, pricking the bubble.

Could orthodox economists today provide more accurate forecasts? Some have tried. They estimated a number of vector autoregres-

---

[10] *Ibid.*

sive (VAR) models using the Harvard and Fisher data plus five additional modern historical variables unavailable to Harvard or Fisher.[11] These modern-day economists—using techniques and some data unavailable to Harvard or Fisher—failed to predict the large declines in output at the beginning of the Great Depression either in the months before the Crash or afterward, taking account of the news of the Crash. Though we might argue that those who publish in the *American Economic Review* are using the wrong model, their failure to predict the past does not bode well for their predicting the future.

Doubtless some economists will be tempted to say that the failure of Harvard's and Yale's best forecasters proves that stock prices follow a random walk. Oddly, Flood and Hodrick (1986) used precisely this logic in a no-bubbles defense. But, rational expectations cannot have it both ways. According to Flood and Hodrick, apparent evidence of bubbles could be a result of misspecification by econometricians who select a time series not used by the market participants as a measure of fundamentals. That is, market participants know which data series decide fundamentals whereas economists are sufficiently ignorant to turn the Lucas–Barro critique on its head. (Lucas and Barro claimed that not only have economists selected the correct model, but blue-collar workers essentially have a copy of the model taped to the lid of their lunch buckets.) If it is true that neophytes know more about the fundamentals than economists, how can we trust economists' judgments or evidence that this is so?

What Thomas W. Lamont, J. P. Morgan's partner, told the governors of the Stock Exchange on October 24, 1929, Black Thursday, is much more instructive. "Gentlemen," he said, "there is no man nor group of men who can buy all the stocks that the American public can

[11] *Ibid.*, pp. 599–605.

sell." Thereafter, J. P. Morgan and the private bankers gave up trying to stop or reverse a market driven by irrational forces. Rational expectations to the contrary, it is difficult to fault the neat summary of what happened by John Kenneth Galbraith (1988, pp. 11–12):

> Early in 1928, the nature of the boom changed. The mass escape into make-believe, so much a part of the true speculative orgy, started in earnest... the time had come, as in all periods of speculation, when men sought not to be persuaded of the reality of things but to find excuses for escaping into the new world of fantasy.

V. RATIONAL EXPECTATIONS VERSUS THE HISTORY OF MANIAS

The Illogic of "Rationality"

The defenders of efficient markets and rational expectations cannot make up their minds whether all the financial players have the same information or not. Sometimes, it is argued, the appropriate move in the market requires only a substantial number of smart agents. Sometimes the agents have to be smarter than Ph.D. economists. If so, the representative agent model is not a complete model of such behavior unless the "representative" selected is especially astute (for example, Warren Buffet or George Soros). If the representative eliminates unexploited profits before they happen, he or she still must have made profits that had not been exploited.

The same contradictions apply to differing risk preferences of agents. If the agent is representative, what does he or she represent—heterogeneity or homogeneity? Can an agent be both representative and have infinite life; for instance, an "Oral Roberts" type? Using an overlapping generations (or even genetic transfer) model whereby the securities are inherited within the family until the end of time overlooks not only disinheritance but the tendency of the newly rich to liquidate in their attempt to gain elusive pecuniary decency.[12] In reality, if all players in any financial market have the same information and the same view of risk, the market would collapse because all would be either buyers or sellers. Indeed, when everyone perceives the need to be a seller, the market does crash. Demand and supply curves disappear and the market converges to a singularity. Price, and thus the seller, much like light, cannot escape the black hole. Since rational expectations have invaded theories of foreign exchange, these same difficulties apply to those theories.[13]

Logic has not prevented defenders of the rational faith from claiming that market crashes prove the reliability of their theories. After all, they argue (perhaps contrary to the facts), the historical crashes were not predicted. Therefore, the sum of the errors in the optimal forecast was zero. Beyond the observed changes in volatility, economists can legitimately question the value of a theory in which the "optimal forecast" has an unbounded standard error, much less a

---

[12] The term, of course, comes from Veblen (1899). Veblen is relevant to this discussion for two other reasons: (1) he considered emulation to be the strongest of human motives; and (2) financial assets are luxury goods. If a herd instinct is important or prevails in goods markets, it could be even more prevalent in financial markets. The idea of "Veblen effects" is pursued further in Canterbery (1999).

[13] The original address given included a section on foreign exchange theory. To economize on space this section has been deleted. However, a supplementary paper on foreign exchange will be published elsewhere next year.

theory in which all observations support it by circular definition.[14] Besides, if any and all outcomes are consistent with the theory, it can never be subject to falsification.

Rational expectations faces a formidable problem if people do not know (or do not behave as if they know) the true model describing a market. Survey research by Shiller (1990) and his coauthors suggested that the broad masses of financial actors do not use economists' models. When asked about the 1987 stock market crash, the respondents could not name a theory. Instead, about a third of both individual and institutional investors said the market was "overpriced." A third, in one way or another, spoke of investor irrationality–"that investors were crazy or that the fall was due to investor panic or capricious change in opinion" (1990, p. 56). In a 1987–88 survey related to the housing bubble in many California cities, Case-Shiller (1989) found respondents expecting housing prices to rise indefinitely. (They did not.) Price increases themselves serve to increase

---

[14] If the regressor associated with a bubble explodes, as predicted from the solution to the standard bubbles equation (1), the time series sample—irrespective of its largeness—is always from a small sample, and the standard central limit theorems are not applicable. In the somewhat tortured language of rational expectations, if the regressor explodes as t increases, the information content of its latest observation never goes to zero as a fraction of the information content of all prior observations.

This problem dates to the Black–Scholes model. Its assumption that asset prices follow geometric Brownian motion implies that the percent change in price over the next time interval is independent of both the percent change over the last time interval and the level of the asset's price. "Brownian" motion, whereby microscopic particles follow a random walk was explained much earlier (1906) by Albert Einstein. Like the particles in physics from which Brownian motion is derived, prices are "memoryless." Since volatility is constant for a particular asset, the assets' prices are homoskedastic, showing no tendency toward "volatility bunching." That is, a market crash on one day is as likely to be followed by a bull run on the next as by another crash. Despite this assumption, during the past two decades U.S. bond and stock prices have experienced the greatest volatility in their recorded histories. By treating prices as Brownian particles, of course, we eliminate the human psychology driving a bull or bear market.

For more on the implications of metaphors from physics for markets, see Canterbery (1987, chapters 2 and 9).

prices, creating a vicious circle common to the great speculative bubbles in history. Again, emulation and bandwagons come to mind. Still, Shiller et al. (in press) found unique elements ascribed to each bubble and crash, supporting the heterogeneity among players.

Lessons from History for Theory

If these events—tulipmania, the Mississippi–South Sea bubbles, and the Crash of '29—were the result of rational behavior, Holland, France, England, and the United States could have benefited from having some irrational people. These were ***manias***: players threw rationality to the winds. As to the truth, in 1929 few were willing to believe this to be the end of the good times, and so they ignored the signs and made the trauma worse. Prior to August 1998 few traders or brokers were willing to believe that the Great Bull Market would end. Manic prices come from the crazy collective behavior of people. Since history provides some important lessons, we should be wary of ahistorians reinterpreting history.

During these bubbles, entire markets were at risk. In these manias it was not a matter of whether one tulip bulb or another was rising or falling in price, nor was it a matter of Radio rising in price and Wright Aeronautic falling. The markets for every bulb and every stock disappeared. Liquidity dried up. If the market in question embodies the quintessence of risk, even risk-averters have no place to run. The systems fail, giving credence to the value of a lender of the last resort restoring liquidity.

Though each historical event is unique, they share some common characteristics. The first common characteristic is the ***involvement of wealthy or powerfully placed persons*** at the inception. During the early phase of tulipmania the high rollers were wealthy Dutch families and professional growers. Initially, John Law's investors were the nobility (including the king himself) and the well-placed, powerful members of Parliament. Some of the same English nobles participating in the Mississippi bubble put money into the British South Sea Company. Those who first bought stock during the 1920s were professionals and wealthy households. In recent years, one very rich man, George Soros, has pricked bubbles in national currencies.

A second common characteristic of these bubbles is a *change in the rules of the game.* Tulipmania (as applied to common bulbs) would not have happened without a mechanism for involving common wage earners. They were brought in by the evolution of nonprofessional trading in those taverns. In turn, trading could be extended beyond the wealthy buyers through the use of margins. John Law not only changed the rules of the game, but he invented a new game. His was a pyramid scheme in which only those first-in and first-out could win. Law also established the infrastructure for the new game whereby his *own* bank would print notes to buy shares in his *own* conglomerate under his *own* supervision in commanding government posts. The cash then was used to acquire income-earning government debt. In turn, this income would be used to expand his conglomerate's commercial activity to justify his selling shares at ever higher prices. Only the *un*worldly philosophers (to rephrase Heilbroner 1986 [1953]) could characterize this as anything other than fraud.

During the 1920s when commercial bank lending was constrained, rapidly expanding industrial firms and merging utilities used equities to raise funds on a vast scale for the first time. Commercial bankers skirted existing laws, and redefined themselves as investment bankers and brokers. Moreover, margin requirements for share purchases were minimal. The share buyer had no regulatory protection. Even so, the early stock buyers enjoying the rapid appreciation of shares could not lose.

A third common thread is *general irrational exuberance*. Rather than a representative agent, the mix between risk-averters and risk-takers changes over time. Under the new rules of the game in which the first buyers cannot lose, rising prices of bulbs, shares, or whatever create the illusion of easy riches. The masses become enchanted and, at the height of euphoria, are the biggest gamblers of all, using easy credit and risking their well-being in the reckless pursuit of wealth or what this author has called the "Gatsby effect" (Canterbery 1999, pp. 142–146). Pure speculation takes over whereby players buy for resale rather than income. Through emulation, most everyone jumps on the bandwagon.

In each case, the bulbs or shares were bought on small margins, usually 10 percent, or paid for in installments. In the Great Bull Market of the 1990s, ordinary households were using home equity loans and credit cards to purchase stock at a time when the average dividend rate reached an all-time low of about 1.5 percent. (The net worth of households earning $50,000 or less declined during the Great Bull Market.) It is the engagement of the masses that usually leads to manias and irrational bubbles. Market prices no longer are linked to reality, much less fundamentals.

A fourth common thread is spun. With rising speculation by more and more players, *credit eventually becomes scarce and real interest rates rise*. Not only does speculation become more costly, but a rising interest rate decreases present values. At an early stage, the "smart money" of the insiders begins to move out of the market. In the Mississippi bubble, King Louis XV took his profits and so did many members of Parliament. In the Crash of 1929, J. P. Morgan and the New York bankers began to reduce their long positions and sell short. Warren Buffet began selling stocks and buying silver or bonds long before the July 1998 peak in the Dow. At the top of the bubble, the bid prices of those getting in and the ask prices of those getting out must be about evenly matched. However, the leveling off in prices is a frightening prospect for those who have borrowed at rising interest rates to gamble. The smaller market players panic and take their losses.

Worse, the bubbles eventually burst, some more abruptly than others. No common external event applies. When assets are overvalued beyond any reasonable prospect for future returns, any untoward event can precipitate a panic. A king selling his shares, a J. P. Morgan with too little wealth to buy all the stock people are willing to sell, failing banks, or a central banker raising the specter of "irrational exuberance" could prick the bubble. The rush to cash leads to a liquidity crisis. Only a lender of last resort can end the crisis without massive losses.

These untoward events provide some important lessons for theoretical modeling.[15] The representative rational agent model is hopelessly defective: no single agent can represent mass behavior. Initially the players are rich; however, at the top of the bubble almost everyone is a participant. Initially, the players are risk-averse; however, at the top the new players are reckless. In the bursting of the bubble, those whose insanity led to the debacle recover their senses. However, their final act of sanity provides the final collective irrationality. The assets that on one day were highly priced are the next day, nearly worthless. Each agent, at last acting rationally, leads the masses, lemming-like, to an irrational termination. The otherwise simple logic of the fallacy of composition is missing from all models of rational expectations. His-

[15] In a modest version of such a theory, this author (Canterbery 1993, pp. 171–173) deploys most of the common characteristics revealed by the great historical bubbles. In the simple model developed, Canterbery was attempting to explain the U.S. real estate bubble of the 1980s that burst late in the decade, contributing to the S & L debacle. Wealth is created by the dynamics of a precursor model (Canterbery 1993, pp. 164–170). Then, real wealth or net worth of the upper quintile of the distribution (W), the value of real estate (RE), and the value of total mortgages held by the financial industry (K) are connected in a circular way even though the circle can expand and contract in space over time. In the simplest model, the circles do not intersect, so that $[RE(t) - W(t)]^2 + [K(t) - W(t)]^2 = [W(t)]^2$. As W gets larger, the center of the circle moves away from the origin along a line bisecting the angle between the axes (45° line), and the radius of the circle increases. Because the values of mortgages as financial assets are colinear with the value of real estate (probably with some lag), RE and K most likely will follow the 45° line as W becomes larger. When real wealth rises, so too will the value of real estate and mortgages. If much of the real wealth is tied to real estate and the price of real estate drops, however, this event can shrink the circle (real estate prices dropping faster than goods prices generally). During a crash the circle converges to a point (the black hole).

tory, of course, cannot inform models that are ahistorical, nor can revisionist historians who are ahistorical.

REFERENCES

Burmeister, E., Flood, R. P., and Garber, P. M. 1983. On the equivalence of solutions in rational expectations models. *Journal of Economic Dynamics and Control*. May 5: 224–34.

Canterbery, E. R. 1987. *The making of economics*, chapter 14. Belmont, CA: Wadsworth.

Canterbery, E. R. 1993. Reaganomics, saving, and the casino effect. In *The economics of saving*, ed. J. H. Gapinski. Boston/ Dordrecht/ London: Kluwer.

Canterbery, E. R. 1995. *The literate economist*, chapter 22. New York: HarperCollins.

Canterbery, E. R. 1999. The theory of the leisure class and the theory of demand. In *The founding of institutional economics*, ed. Warren J. Samuels, pp. 139–56. London: Routledge.

Dice, C. A. 1929. *New levels in the stock market*. New York: McGraw-Hill.

Dominguez, K., Fair, R. C., and Shapiro, M. D. 1988. Forecasting the depression: Harvard versus Yale. *American Economic Review* September 78: 595–608.

Fisher, I. 1930. *The stock market crash—and after*. New York: Macmillan.

Flood, R. P., and Garber, P. M. 1980. Market fundamentals versus price level bubbles: The first tests. *Journal of Political Economy* August 88: 745–70.

Flood, R. P., Garber, P. M., and Scott, L. 1984. Multi-country tests for price level bubbles. *Journal of Economic Dynamics and Control* December 8: 329–40.

Flood, R. P., and Hodrick, R. J. 1986. Asset price volatility, bubbles and process switching. *Journal of Finance* 41: 831–42.

Galbraith, J. K. 1988 [1954]. *The great crash 1929*. Boston: Houghton Mifflin.

Garber, P. M. 1989. Tullipmania. *Journal of Political Economy* June 97: 535–60.

Garber, P. M. 1990. Famous first bubbles. *Journal of Economic Perspectives* Spring 4: 35–54.

Gray, H. P. 1992. Hicksian instability in asset markets and financial fragility. *Eastern Economic Journal*. Summer 18 (3):249–58.

Hahn, F. 1966. Equilibrium dynamics with heterogeneous capital goods. *Quarterly Journal of Economics* November 80: 633–46.

Heilbroner, R. L. 1986 [1953]. *The worldly philosophers*. New York: Simon and Schuster.

Kindleberger, C. 1989 [1978]. *Manias, panics, and crashes*. New York: Basic Books.

Krugman, P. 1994. *Peddling prosperity*. New York, London: W. W. Norton.

Posthumus, N. W. 1929. The tulip mana in Holland in the years 1636–37. *Journal of Economic and Business History*. May 1: 434–55.

Samuelson, P. A. 1967. Indeterminancy of development in a heterogeneous capital model with constant saving propensity. In *Essays on the theory of optimal economic growth*, ed. K. Shell. Cambridge: M.I.T. Press.

Scott, W. 1911. *The constitution and finance of English, Scottish, and Irish joint stock companies to 1420*, vol. II. Cambridge: Cambridge University Press.

Shell, K., and Stiglitz, J. E. 1967. Allocation of investment in a dynamic economy. *Quarterly Journal of Economics* November 81: 592–609.

Shiller, R. 1984. Stock prices and social dynamics. *Brookings Papers* 2: 457–98.

Shiller, R. 1986. ***Fashions, fads and bubbles in financial markets***, paper prepared for Conference on Takeovers and Contests for Corporate Control, February.

Shiller, R. 1990. Speculative prices and popular models. ***Journal of Economic Perspectives***. Spring 4 (2): 55–65.

Shiller, R., Fumiko, K., and Tsutsui, Y. in press. Investor behavior in the October 1987 stock market crash: The case of Japan. ***The Journal of Japnese and International Economics***.

Sirkin, G. 1975. The stock market of 1929 revisited: A note. ***Business History Review*** Summer 44: 223–31.

Van Horne, J. 1985. Of financial innovations and excesses. ***Journal of Finance*** July 40 (3): 621–31.

Veblen, T. 1994 [1899]. ***The theory of the leisure class***. New York, London: Penguin Books.

White, E. N. 1990. The stock market boom and crash of 1929 revisited. ***The Journal of Economic Perspectives*** Spring 4 (2): 67–83.

Chapter 17

Rational Bubbles and Uncovered Interest-rate Parity: Retrospective and Prospective

Global Economy Quarterly

I. Introduction

The Asian currency crisis of 1997 led some economists to the conclusion that foreign exchange bubbles not only exist but can burst. The Asian crisis began when the peg of the Thai baht to the U.S. dollar was abandoned on July 2, 1997. The baht lost 15 percent of its external value within two weeks. By mid-July the Philippine peso and the Malaysian ringgit could no longer be successfully defended. The Indonesian rupiah lost about 10 percent of its value in the second half of July. By the end of October, these currencies had lost between 25 percent (Malaysia, Philippines) and 35 percent (Indonesia, Thailand) of their values. Unexpectedly, the Korean won crashed. The contagion spread to Brazil by early 1999 as the *real* went from a crawling peg to a float and a depreciation of 40 percent by March.

We have long understood that international short-term capital flows are related to interest rates and to currency crises. Nonetheless Brazil found that a real interest rate of 30 percent was insufficient to stem the outflow of capital and to prevent the collapse of its exchange rate. In Thailand, capital inflows created a bubble in real estate prices only to burst with capital flight. Although different conditions led to the bubbles and their bursting in each country, these global events nonetheless provide an introduction to some abstract ideas, including the concept of rational bubbles and uncovered interest-rate parity, that may or may not be related to foreign exchange crisis.

In recent years the expanding literature on rational bubbles has laid claim to all asset markets and has itself become a bubble. Even revisionist histories suggest that the Mississippi-South Sea bubble, the first international financial crisis, was not only a rational event but was based irretrievably on solid fundamentals.[1] In rational bubbles, foreign exchange rates embody all available information. In the strong version of rational expectations not only are all asset prices correct, they reflect market fundamentals. In the rational bubble models, even the "bubbles" are "rational" because investors can believe that the asset's price is above its fundamentals value and continue to hold the asset anyway. If the foreign exchange rate keeps moving in one direction, it is because it is expected to continue to move in one direction. The rational bubble never collapses; its bursting would betray irrationality on the part of speculators, a renting of the requisites of rational expectations. If the foreign exchange rate suddenly reverses itself, it is for good reason, such as a change in fundamentals. A bubble, therefore, did not exist in the first place.

The antecedents of this bubbling literature include the use of rational expectations in the theories of covered and uncovered interest-rate arbitrage. In the telling of the arbitrage story, rational expectations has defined the efficient market hypothesis. Thus, such arbitrage provides an initial basis for an evaluation of rational bubbles. Thereafter, we retreat to the haven of an earlier literature to consider whether erudition too has ballooned from the infusion of rational expectations into bubbles.

II. The Pillars of Contemporary Foreign Exchange Theory

At the core of today's theory of foreign exchange are various interest rate parity relationships, all based on particular conditions regarding arbitrage. Uncovered interest rate parity (UIP) states that the expected rate of depreciation on the domestic currency equals the difference between the domestic and foreign interest rates over the same time period; that is,

$$(1) \qquad E_t s_{t+1} - s_t = i^*_t - i_t ,$$

where E is an expectations operator and the spot exchange rate s is defined as the logarithm of the foreign currency value per unit of the domestic currency, while i and i^* represent the domestic and foreign interest rates, respectively. This equation often is written in its rational expectations form as

(2) $E[s_{t+1} - s_t \mid \Theta_t \mid] = i^*_t - i_t$,

where Θ is the information set, a set that is usually equal to the forward premium on foreign exchange. Then, UIP is transformed into covered interest rate parity (CIP), whereby the forward premium or discount (when negative) on foreign exchange is directly linked to the current raw interest rate differential, or

(3) $f_{t+1,t} - s_t = i^*_t - i_t$,

where $f_{t+1,t}$ is the current forward rate at the date of maturity (t + 1) of the interest-earning assets. All the variables, they write, are "forward looking," implying that they know where they are going. For example, since the current spot rate is a function of the expected future exchange spot rate (in addition to the current "fundamentals") and since today's forward rate is a perfect predictor of the future spot rate,

(4) $s_{t+1} = f_{t+1,t}$.

For reasons obscured in the mists of history, the recognition of the role of exchange rate expectations is traced back to the "overshooting" model of Dornbusch (1976), where the uncovered interest rate parity condition (UIP) is used to generate the dynamics of the exchange rate. However, once rational expectations was unleashed, so too was a giant and steady torrent of papers testing the rationality of exchange rate expectations and the efficiency of the foreign exchange market. Most tests found the forward rate to be a biased predictor of the future spot rate in violation of UIP. Beginning with Dominguez (1986) and Frankel and Froot (1987), market survey data was substituted for the interest rate differential. This research, however, did not consistently find market expectations to be rational. For example, most of the UIP-macro fundamentals models failed to predict the collapse of the European Exchange Rate Mechanism in September 1992 (Rose and Svensson, 1994). A vast number of studies have rejected UIP (Meese, 1992). One attempt to amend UIP has been to introduce a risk premium term, so that

(5) $$E_t s_{t+1} - s_t = i^*_t - i_t + r_t ,$$

where r_t is a risk premium. Such an amendment contradicts rational expectations *and* the original UIP because, if the information set includes all relevant information, it would include risk considerations.

In response to these failures, two new lines of inquiry were opened. One approach is based on the possibility of self-fulfilling expectations (Obstfeld, 1994, 1995; Jeanne and Mason, 1996). A second approach is based on the idea that financial markets fail to process information related to future exchange rate changes. In turn, this has led to attempts to construct non-financial market-based early warning systems for foreign exchange crises.

III. Theories in the "Dark Ages" that Preceded Rational Expectations

A myth dying slowly is the belief that during the Dark Ages prior to the Enlightenment Age of Rational Expectations, expectations were not considered in foreign exchange theory. Quite the contrary, expectations were at the heart of American developments in the literature near the end of the 1950s and continuing in the 1960s (see Tsiang 1958; Rhomberg 1964; and Canterbery, 1965, 1967). Later, Canterbery (1969, 1971) provided mathematical models of foreign exchange speculation under alternative systems. Empirical models closely related to these theories also flourished (Arndt 1968, Stoll 1968). The following discussion will focus on Canterbery, not only out of vanity, but from familiarity having not yet bred contempt.

Though the mathematics was rather crude early on, it was finely tuned by 1967 or 1969. The models initially were derived from the demand and supply of foreign exchange in both the spot and forward markets. The demands and supplies both spot and forward were derived from exports, imports, leading and lagging, interest-rate arbitrage, and speculation. The general form of the simultaneous solution turned out to be the same irrespective of the model *or* the levels of mathematical sophistication. Structural equations determine the interest parity conditions so that the solution to the equations is not simply an *ad hoc* reduced-form equation. This solution (Canterbery 1965, 1967, 1969, 1974; Stoll 1968), with exchange rates transformed below into logs to conform with the above, was called the modern theory (MT) solution, or

(6) $\quad f_{t+1,t} - s_t = (i^* - i) + E_t(ds_t)$,

where E(ds) or the expected value of current spot rate changes was formed from several mathematical permutations over the decade or so. Equation (6) can be re-written as

(7) $\quad E_t s_{t+1} - s_t = (i^*_t - i_t) + E_t(ds_t)$

Initially, equation (6) applied to the old Bretton Woods system in which the spot rate was fixed within narrow limits. Interestingly, even though spot rates were virtually fixed, traditional covered interest-rate parity did not prevail; that is, interest differentials did not entirely explain forward premiums. Always there remained a "speculative residual" or $E_t(ds_t)$. In today's language the forward rate was *not* a good predictor of the future spot rate, and Equation (4) becomes an inequality since the forward rate can be greater or less than the future spot rate. If the market were efficient in a rational expectations sense, a *reduced-form* estimating equation would look the same as equation (7) but the properties of "the residual" would be defined statistically. Then, the process generating the exchange rate would be stochastic and the "speculative residual" would become an error term with zero mean.[2]

One problem with this rational expectations specification is the failure to initially specify a speculative variable, and *then* to generate an error term that is independent not only of the interest-rate differential but of the trade balance and of speculation.[3] A zero mean can be disputed by the simple averaging of the differences between forward premiums and interest rate differentials (Canterbery 1974): statistical estimates only confound interdependencies that cannot be unbundled whereas simple arithmetic suffers not this defect.[4] Contrary to rational expectations, these solutions suggest that, in theory, the foreign exchange markets are not efficient and do not meet the conditions of rational expectations. Commodity exports and imports comprise parts of the demands and supplies of foreign exchange (including leading and lagging by importers and exporters), unlike the later reduced-form efficient market models.

IV The Anticipation of Rational Bubbles

In one of the more mature models (Canterbery 1971, 411-415), ordinary trade and interest rate differentials provide a "fundamentals" or "equilibrium" exchange rate in the absence of any expected spot values. Once expectations are introduced—whether related to speculation or not--movements away from the exchange rate determined by fundamentals happen. In turn, speculative demand depends on the expected rate of change in the exchange rate discounted by a subjective risk factor minus the actual rate of change in the exchange rate. With freely fluctuating rates the risk of exchange variation is initially very high. The speculator estimates future exchange rate changes from the rate of change in the rate of change in the spot exchange rate (d^2s/dt^2) and then–because of uncertainty–discounts this change by an initially fixed value. Since the holder of foreign exchange assets can invest alternatively in a (virtually) riskless asset--foreign treasury bills covered against exchange risk in the forward market, the cost of cover (F - S) in absolute values plus the absolute interest rate spread in unitary exchange rate units (I* - I) is the relevant opportunity cost for the speculator. (The capital letters represent values in absolute rather than log or percentage values.) Because of the greater risk under floating rates, the forward market is much more important to the commodity exporter-importer than under various kinds of bounded exchange rate systems.[5]

This model was expanded to one in which opportunity cost was not the interest parity condition (1971, 416-429) and where full interaction between spot and forward rates was allowed. If interest rates between the countries are equal, the general solution is

$$S(t) = S_{om} + Be^{-a_1 t} \qquad \text{(t large)}, \tag{8}$$

where *B* is the initial (exogenous) difference between the fundamentals equilibrium and non-equilibrium rates. If there is excess demand, *B* is negative; if there is excess supply, *B* is positive. In this equation, as in the original, the spot rates are natural numbers. The size and sign of a_l is based on some complicated conditions in the model's structural equations. If a_l is a positive integer, the exponent has a negative sign, and the market exchange rate will quickly converge to equilibrium (S_o). If, however, a_l becomes negative, the exponent has a positive sign, and the exchange rate will move exponentially away from its equilibrium value. As defined by economic historians, a speculative bubble in foreign exchange would exist. It is a *rational* bubble, however, only if no events can reverse the sign of a_l.

All of which brings us back to the Enlightenment literature; a bubble is rational only if it *never* bursts. An obviously odd characteristic of this definition is its difference from the historical definition of bubbles. We discovered bubbles because historically they *did* burst: bubbles were called that for their tendencies. If they never burst, such bubbles never existed. After redefining the meaning of a bubble as a rational bubble, any reversal of an exchange rate would have to be a consequence of a change in "fundamentals." This definitional slight of hand, however, is deficient.

Monetary authorities, in efforts to reverse exchange rate movements, often will change interest rates (fundamentals in arbitrage operations) when an exchange rate has moved too far too fast in one direction. Moreover, a government might impose trade barriers to slow a soaring foreign exchange rate. Trade flows eventually would be reversed, bursting the bubble. That is, an intentional change in particular fundamentals can burst the bubble. The rational bubbles devotees would argue that the bubble did not burst because the exchange rate reversed course as a result of *a change in fundamentals*! Rational expectations throws out the bubbles with the bath water.

Other reasons for bubbles bursting in mid-air also exist. In equation (8), as noted, the a_l part of the exponent embodies many things, including a risk coefficient. The risk that the exchange rate will move against the speculator's position can increase as the exchange rate continues to move in one direction. In fact, in equation (8) the requirement for stabilizing speculation is a relatively large value for the spot interest rate arbitrage coefficient and a high degree of risk (in the risk coefficient of the speculative parameter). Private market changes in trade and interest rates also can burst a bubble. Only a player who is a fool would expect the exchange rate to move in one direction indefinitely. Of course, if fools are in suitable supply, buffoons of higher and higher order can keep the exchange rate moving in one direction for a very long time (the greater buffoon theory). Rational bubbles, however, must rise *forever*, which is *very* long time. Besides, a "rational" bubble that depends upon a rising supply of irrationally-behaving speculators seems, too, to redefine rationality.

The solution of the model in the more realistic case in which interest rates in any two countries are *un*equal, illustrates the influence of exogenous interest-rate or import-export changes on a bubble. That is,

(9) $S(t) = S_o + \beta_0(I^* - I) + Be^{-a_2 t}$.

The interest rate differential (in capital letters) is now in unitary foreign exchange units.[vi] Suppose, again, that speculators are driving the market exchange rate away from the current fundamental equilibrium rate or S_o. Furthermore, suppose that the foreign exchange rate is falling, making foreign goods cheaper in domestic currency. The domestic monetary authorities could lower short-term interest rates (assuming no retaliation) to encourage the movement of capital to the foreign country and perhaps reversing the decline in the foreign exchange rate. Of course, the larger a positive value for the (mostly) arbitrage coefficient β_0, the greater the beneficial effect of the home country's interest rate policy.

A secondary effect of falling domestic interest rates would be an expansion in construction and durable goods sales at home. This stimulus is likely to spill over into the trade sector as imports began to rise. The rising imports would raise the fundamentals exchange rate (S_o). These second-order effects might further slow or even reverse the fall in the foreign exchange rate. If the bubble bursts, it then is because the fundamentals changed. Contrary to the rational bubbles literature, however, the movement in fundamentals that extinguishes the bubble does not redefine the bubble out of its prior existence. Put differently, the disappearance of a bubble does not mean that it never existed.

IV. Conclusions

The recent empirical literature on foreign exchange does not support the efficient market hypothesis in its rational expectations incarnation. This is so whether the tests are of the forward rate as an unbiased predictor of the spot or whether the tests are of rational bubbles. As some economists have suggested, it is difficult, perhaps impossible, to design a proper test for rationality. If whatever people do, no matter how bizarre, is considered rational, rational expectations is not simply as circular as a perfect donut, it is at its core, the donut's hole--an empty set. Nonetheless, the defenders of rational bubbles, living lives of harmonious desperation, have redefined all bubbles out of existence. If bubbles do not exist, they cannot burst. At the same time, a richness in the structural equations of earlier models has been lost. It is as if the rising and falling tides of foreign trade and imprudent speculation do not exist; only uncovered interest-rate arbitrage under the conditions of rational expectations. Much of the literature of short-term capital flows has lost touch with the fundamentals. Having lost that touch, ironically, it also has lost touch with evanescent bubbles. The rational expectations theories cannot explain events such as the East Asian currency crisis. If the currency collapses of recent history were the consequences of speculators operating at the peaks of their rationality, the global economy could use a good dose of irrationality.

References

Arndt, Sven W. 1968. International short-term capital movements: a distributed lag model of speculation in foreign exchange. *Econometrica* 36: 59-69.

Canterbery, E. Ray. 1965. *Foreign Exchange, Capital Flows, and Monetary Policy.* Princeton, N.J.: International Finance Section, Princeton University Press.

Canterbery, E. Ray. 1967. A dynamic theory of foreign exchange. *National Banking Review* 4:397-413.

Canterbery, E. Ray. 1969. Exchange rates, capital flows, and monetary policy. *American Economic Review* 59: 426-32.

Canterbery, E. Ray. 1971. A theory of foreign exchange speculation under alternative systems.

Journal of Political Economy 79: 407-436.

Canterbery, E. Ray. 1974. The modern theory of foreign exchange and the net speculative residual. *Southern Economic Journal* 41:182-87.

Canterbery, E. Ray. 1999. Irrational exuberance and rational speculative bubbles. ITFA presidential address. *International Trade Journal* 13:1-33.

Canterbery, E. Ray. 2000. *Wall Street Capitalism: The theory of the bondholding class.* Singapore/London/New Jersey/ Hong Kong: World Scientific.

Chen, Zhaohui and Charles A. E. Goodhart. 1998. Inferring market expectations using currency option price and volume data. In Zhaohui Chen, Editor, pp. 183-96. *Currency options and exchange rate economics*. Singapore/London/New Jersey/Hong Kong: World Scientific.

Dominguez, K. 1986. Are foreign exchange forecasts rational? New evidence from survey data. *Economics Letters* 21: 277-281.

Dornbusch. R. 1976. Expectations and exchange rate dynamics. *Journal of Political Economy* 84, 1161-1176.

Frankel, Jeffrey and Froot, Kenneth 1987. Using survey data to test standard propositions on exchange rate expectations. *American Economic Review* 77: 133-153.

Jeanne, O. and Masson, P. 1996 *Was the French Franc Crisis a Sunspot Equilibrium?* Washington D. C.: International Moneary Fund, unpublished manuscript.

Meese, R. 1990 or 1992 Currency fluctuations in the post-Bretton Woods era. *Journal of Economic Perspectives* 6: 117-134.

Obstfeld, M. 1994. The logic of currency crisis. In *Mouvements de Capitaux et Marchés des Changes, Cahiers Économiques et Monétaires,* pp. 189-214. Paris: Banque de France.

Obstfeld, M. 1995. Models of currency crisis with self-fulfilling features. *National Bureau of*

Economic Research Working Paper: 5285. Cambridge, MA.

Rhomberg, R. R. 1964. A model of the Canadian economy under fixed and fluctuating rates. *Journal of Political Economy*. 72: 1-31

Rose, Andrew K. and Svensson. Lars E. O. 1991. Expected and predicted realignments: the FF/DM exchange rate during the EMS. *National Bureau of Economic Research Working Paper*: 3685. Cambridge, MA.

Stoll, Hans. 1968. An empirical study of the forward exchange market under fixed and flexible exchange rate systems. *Canadian Journal of Economics* 1: 55-78.

Tsiang, S. C. 1958. A theory of foreign-exchange speculation under a floating exchange system. *Journal of Political Economy* 66: 399-418.

NOTES

1 Canterbery (1999) provides a critique of the rational bubbles literature that has evolved around stock market valuations in the Great Bull Market of the 1980s-1990s while disputing the revisionist histories of famous bubbles. Canterbery (2000), while explaining the origins of the Great Bull Market, develops a more general theory of of hyper-speculation in a "casino economy," a term applicable to Japan during the 1980s and to the United States during the 1980s and the 1990s.

2 For a best-case estimate of Equation (7) defined as an uncovered interest-rate parity equation, see Chen and Goodhart (1998, pp. 194-95). The sample is from the U.S. and the U.K. for beginning-of-the-month observations between January 1989 and December 1993. However, not only is their estimate of the interest-differential parameter large and negative (-1.991) rather than being positive and unitary, but their constant term is even larger and negative (-14.6337), implying that the interest-rate differential is a wildly inaccurate predictor of future exchange rate changes. However, their error term may not have met the classical standards for regression analysis for reasons noted in footnote 4 below.

3 These interdependencies causing econometric problems in the estimation of short-term capital flows were identified in the midst of the Dark Ages (Canterbery 1969).

4 During the Watergate crisis of the Nixon administration, speculation against the U.S. dollar became as popular as President Nixon was not. In Canterbery (1974) the speculative residual between the U.S. and the U.K. is calculated as the sum of the interest rate differential and the forward premium for weeks ending during May 18, 1973-July 6, 1973. This "covered" interest-rate differential is hugely and increasingly negative during those weeks. The mean of this exponentially increasing speculative residual is *not* zero. (It could be argued, though it was not, that this was a speculative bubble in pound sterling.) Although ordinary least squares estimates involve a mean-reverting process, the zero mean value of the error term is conditional and must be independent of the variables included in the regression. As noted, such a statistical requirement is virtually impossible to meet when the variables are the spot rate, forward rate, interest rates, imports, exports, *and* expectations based on these variables. Since the estimates are from a reduced-form equation, interdependency is not the only consideration since important variables (i.e., imports, exports, leading and lagging, protectionism, fiscal and monetary policy changes, etc.) are otherwise excluded but *assumed* to be represented in the error term. While it may seem dreadfully inelegant, arithmetic is superior to econometrics in this particular application.

5 Under *floating* exchange rates a bank's foreign exchange department typically quotes the forward margin as equaling the interest rate differential (plus a small transactions fee). Under such conditions, one would expect covered interest rate parity to hold. The same, however, does not apply to uncovered interest rate parity. When the quoted interest rate differential fails to reflect players' expectations, then

they can get out of the domestic currency by selling the currency in the spot or forward markets.

[vi]For the algebraic definition of unitary exchange units and the proof for this conversion, see Canterbery (1967, 409, n. 28).

PART IV

MICROECONOMICS

Chapter 18

E. Ray Canterbery

An Evolutionary Model of Technical Change with Markup Pricing

It is commonly held that tax policy influences innovation both through its contribution to the general macroeconomic climate and through direct effects on specific kinds of innovation, and that tax incentives can have a positive effect on the level of R&D expenditures (Mansfield, 1981, 1984; Eisner, Albert, and Sullivan, 1983; Nadiri, 1980, 1981). However, these otherwise valuable studies do not provide an all-encompassing model in which policy simulations can be utilized. In part, this defect stems from the dual nature of such studies: they either focus exclusively on the cost of capital (e.g., Hulten and Robertson, 1983; Auerbach, 1983) or upon the impact of tax policy changes on cash flow (Mansfield, 1984). The present model can account for the effects of various tax policies upon both the cost of capital *and* cash flow (the financial constraint). Moreover, unlike other models, the *indirect* effect upon R&D from general tax policies influencing total investment through changes in the cost of capital and cash flow can be considered.

An evolutionary approach is used so that individual firm decisions are altered as the industry evolves. The firms are presumed to establish long-term policies with respect to the funds allocated to efforts of obtaining new processes of production. The history of each firm and each industry is known. This history provides a pre-policy "baseline" for the study of innovation in each industry. That is, the historical patterns of actual policies are "givens" that have influenced firms' decisions in each industry. If the modeling is successful, the "hypothetical" decisions made by the firms will result in an approximation of the firms' historical allocations of funds to investment and R&D activity and the observed net sales and income growth from such outlays. Although data suggestions and empirical applications are recommended, this paper does not otherwise cross the boundary between theory and empirical testing.

The modeling will imitate to a considerable degree the pioneering simulation work of R. Nelson and S. Winter, who owe an intellectual debt to Joseph

Schumpeter and Herbert Simon as well as to R.M. Cyert, A.D. Chandler, and J.G. March. This literature shows that the goal of capital acquisition permeates the organizational structure of the firm (see, e.g., Chandler, 1962; and Eichner, 1976). Nelson and Winter (1976) have provided a breakthrough procedure that I expand conceptually and shape for policy simulation purposes. Professors Nelson and Winter hoped to stimulate new empirical research on technological advance, productivity growth, and market structure through their demonstration that formal evolutionary models could be constructed. The Nelson-Winter model and its extension in this paper focuses upon the place of innovation in the growth strategy of the firm.

In this evolutionary/behaviorialist view, the individual firm is governed by its current decision rules, criteria that link its actions to environmental stimuli. Nonetheless, I make significant departures from the published Nelson-Winter modeling. These departures derive from the policy-oriented goals of the research as well as from developments in post-Keynesian economic literature, especially with regard to the relation of the firm's capital accumulatiòn goal to its pricing strategy. The relevant post-Keynesian contributions include those of Eichner (1976), Levine (1975), Marris (1964), Penrose (1959), Ong (1981), Shapiro (1981), and Wood (1975). This literature and that of the behavioralists are complementary. Other important influences include the work of David (1975), Gold, Pierce, and Rosegger (1970), Sylos-Labini (1962), and Williamson (1975).

The following summary statements comprise the main departures from or modifications in the Nelson-Winter simulation model:

1. Policy variables such as alternative depreciation allowance rates and R&D tax credits are introduced.

2. A strategy markup on prime costs is based upon the growth objectives of the firm whose success is determined in part by the number of (evolving) firms in the industry and historical price elasticities. A markup pricing rule now has been widely used in econometric modeling (Eckstein, 1972; Okun, 1981; Nordhaus, 1974). In Nelson-Winter, market price elasticity is constrained to unitary and the number of firms play a different role. In Nelson-Winter *and* here, however, the number of firms is determined by the evolutionary process of Schumpeterian competition, which in turn has an impact on intermediate decisions.

3. Rather than a putty-putty assumption about the relationship between capital and techniques, I use a putty-clay version. In this way the expected prices of inputs matter *prior* to switches in technique but not after. This also means that—unlike the Nelson-Winter modeling—latent or potential productivity in the industry does not necessarily grow at a constant rate.

4. The futuristic nature of the firm's decisions is modeled further by incorporating future expected capital, labor, and other costs rather than current input prices alone.

5. Wherever relevant, values such as gross investment are expressed in money terms rather than only in physical units. This is especially important for the firm's financial constraint.

The measurement of the impact of direct and indirect R&D policies is presently in an undeveloped stage. The proper model must be sufficiently general to be applicable to the selected industries and adequately specific to be used as an evaluative tool for R&D policy. My intention is to present a model that meets these requirements.

The Model of Innovations and Imitations

Since the model's development uses the Nelson-Winter simulation as the starting point, the conceptual differences from that simulation are noted as these departures arise.

Initial State Conditions for the Firm and the Industry

At t_0 each firm in the selected industries has a particular production technique characterized by technical labor, capital, and other technical coefficients (a_L, a_K, a_S). Throughout it is understood that input requirements and productivities are expressed in terms of an "appropriate" time unit or production period. It also is understood that the amount of an output per machine is different for one year than it is for one week. The firm's scale relative to the industry is defined by its level of essential primary physical capital goods.

Nonetheless, there are "necessary" inputs and their related productivities. The inputs, of course, are viewed as necessary only with the current production technology. That is, I presume that an essential raw material (such as petroleum in airlines) has a productivity that might in a new process swamp the effect of a change in productivity attributable solely to labor (such as number of pilots). Although productivity always can be defined in terms of capital goods—or, at least, *a* capital good—a "set" of input requirements (a's) enables us to take into account changes in input requirements and their variable costs.

The initial distribution of techniques (the a's) can be decided for each industry by the historical state of production processes in firms at t_0 (which, say, might be twenty-five years ago). These values of the a's can be compared with estimated values of a's in selected firms over time. A probability distribution can be estimated for the values of a's. This range comprises the set of techniques from which the firms in the industry can "draw" during the (say, twenty-five years of) production history. The allocation of the productivity draws is decided by various decision rules that are applied over the history of each industry. The history of each firm would include its primary physical capital goods, labor force size, number of research personnel, R&D expenditures, total investment expenditures, debt-equity ratio, dividend payout ratio, sales revenue, and real output of dominant product or service. Historical industry data would include number of firms in the industry and estimates of the price or income elasticity of demand for the dominant product or service of the industry. During that history, of course, the bases of such decisions as prices, dividend payout ratios, wage rates, prices of inputs, etc., will be changing.

Following Nelson-Winter, the probability distribution for latent or potential productivity at $t_0 + 1$ depends only on the value of potential productivity at t_0 and is independent of other industry variables. However, the distribution of the next-period state for a given firm (say, Boeing) in the (aerospace) industry depends directly on the levels of variables of Boeing, and other firms in the industry that influence Boeing through several intervening variables, including the market price of the aircraft produced. In a departure from Nelson-Winter, price changes from period to period vary not only with output but also with the price markup strategy of the individual firm.

For any particular industry the state of firm j in time t can be characterized by:

- K_{jvt}, or its primary physical capital stock of vintage v at t. *K is measured in physical service units*. For example, in the airline industry the primary physical capital good characteristic or service might be defined as carrier capacity or available horsepower. Productivity of capital or a_K^{-1} might be defined as passenger miles and cargo weight per carrier capacity or horsepower. The *value* of capital goods can be expressed in nominal terms from their prices but—as Canterbery and McLeod (1989) show—the true economic value of such goods is ambiguous since it depends in part upon the future unknown demand for finished goods. Unlike Nelson-Winter, depreciation and tax credit allowances are variables and the capital need not be fully utilized.
- L_{jt}, or the firm's full-employment labor force. With fixed factor coefficients (at a point in time) it is possible to move back and forth between capital, labor, and other requirements. In a departure from Nelson-Winter, R&D expenditures in some cases could be usefully related to labor rather than to capital. Again, a firm and industry can operate at less than full employment of capital and (after a time lag) less than full employment of labor whose productivity is a_L^{-1}.

Innovation and Imitation Policies

The adoption of a new technique requires acquisition of new capital goods. The original putty-clay hypothesis is that factor proportions can be varied while capital is being designed but not after it has been built. Capital is putty ex ante, but ex post, it is hard-baked clay. Any new capital vintage, once installed, can be utilized only in fixed proportion with labor. My use of this idea runs as follows: Prior to the firm's selection of a new technique *already in use* somewhere in the industry (imitation), the wage rate, user cost of the new equipment, and cost of primary materials influence the choice of technique. Once the innovation or imitation is adopted and installed, factor coefficients (the a's) are fixed so that primary capital goods services to labor services to other requirements' ratios are immutable until still another change occurs and another technique is adopted.

This approach allows negative quasi-rents to appear for capital goods of older vintage. As an example, older vintages may be highly labor-intensive: even though the wage rate is rising rapidly, the firm cannot reduce the number of workers allocated to each "older" machine and losses may occur. To avoid losses the firm eventually scraps the capital earning nonpositive quasi-rents. This scrapping may involve an entire plant. Since the present value of capital depends upon future interest rates and since labor costs are to be incurred after the installation of the new technique, the user cost of capital and the wage rate used in choosing that technique are expected future values.

R_{jt} or j's Research Policy

A research policy is a commitment to a certain level of research expenditures that is decided by the growth objectives of the firm. This commitment can be expressed in terms of dollars of R&D expenditures and in terms of the number of research personnel. Thus, in a variation of the Nelson-Winter approach, policy dimensions can be expressed in some cases as dollars per period per research employee and (where applicable) in terms of research personnel costs. For computational convenience, R&D dollars can always be expressed in terms of shares of total investment dollars.

The first possible R&D result may be to facilitate the acquisition of an innovation, a process heretofore unavailable to the industry. The research policy increases productivity of capital services, labor, or other key inputs through innovation if it results in the "drawing" of a new technique or technical-coefficients combination that has productivities higher than the firm's current technique. The a's are based upon productivities that have yet to be adopted at time t by *any* firm in the particular industry being studied. The firm's research expenditure (R_{jt}) buys a probability of sampling the latent a's. $P(R_{jt})$, or the probability of a successful research draw from the distribution of a's, is positively related to the firm's investment expenditures devoted to R&D and to the size of the firm's research staff. That is,

$$P(R_{jt}) = f(RD_{jt}, RL_{jt}), \qquad [1]$$

where RD is the level of R&D expenditures and RL is the size of the research staff. (In Nelson-Winter the probability is proportional to the level of expenditures.) The first-ever draw is independent of the wage rate, user costs, and the costs of primary materials. I am presuming that the advantages of being the first innovator overwhelm the current and expected production costs. The firms with the largest R&D expenditures and research staff already have decided to use innovation to achieve their goals. When a successful research draw occurs and results in a higher productivity level, the firm moves to this new technique in a subsequent period, $t + \iota$, the value of which can only be determined empirically.

IM_{jt} *or j's Imitation Policy*

The second possible R&D result would be the acquisition of the best available technique already in use in the firm's industry. There are also, of course, favorable effects upon production processes from the acquisition of extant "more advanced" equipment and tools, newer vintages. This purchase of the latest vintage of capital is described as "imitation policy." Normal replacement investment would tend to follow a historical trend line for a particular firm. However, the aggressive acquisition of new equipment and tools would be reflected in a more rapid than "normal" growth in total investment (adjusted for the effects of the business cycle). The *indirect* effects upon process innovation from accelerated depreciation or non-R&D investment and from increased investment tax credits would most likely be reflected in an "above-norm" growth rate in total investment.

Let IM_{jt} represent the firm's imitation policy, a policy with similarities to R_{jt}. However, the distribution of a's from which the drawings are made is comprised only of actual a's of firms in the industry at t. In this case, R&D expenditures buy a probability of drawing the current "best available practice" technique, in which the highest productivity technique in use would be selected. $P(IM_{jt})$, or the probability of a successful *imitation draw* is positively related to the firm's total investment growth rate above the "norm" (defined above) and to the size of the firm's research staff, but is assumed to be a decreasing linear function of the quantitative difference between the existing and the adopted technique. (The time period over which the investment growth rate is computed is an empirical issue.)

The values of the linear coefficients (or weights) in this case depend upon the expected prices of the physical capital, labor, and primary inputs. The model thus takes into account the effect of expected changes in the relative prices of inputs in the selection of techniques. That is, let I be the above-norm investment growth rate, RL the size of research staff, z the capital vintage of the most productive or hth firm in the industry. Then—for the jth firm—we can write:

$$P(IM_{jt}) = F(\dot{I}_{jt}, RL_{jt}) - WTK^{*}(a_{K,jvt} - a_{K,hzt}) - WTL^{*}(a_{L,jt} - a_{L,ht}) \qquad [2]$$

where the weights WTK^{*} and WTL^{*} depend upon the expected prices of the primary physical inputs (only two in this example) and $WTK^{*} + WTL^{*} = 1$. Only when $WTL^{*} = WTK^{*}$ would the choice of techniques be unbiased. The weighted averages of the input coefficients mean that the probability of adopting the "best available practice" decreases as firms become more "dissimilar." The expected prices or other user costs of key pieces of capital equipment can be determined in the orthodox way. In a variation of the Hall-Jorgenson formula,

$$c_k^* = q_k\,(r* + \delta_k)\,\frac{1 - c_0 - T - PV\,(DEP_k)}{1 - T}, \qquad [3]$$

where c_k^* = expected cost of a unit of capital services of the kth type, q_k = the current price of capital equipment (or plant) of the kth type, r^* = required expected real rate of return after corporate taxes (further defined below); δ_k = exponential rate of economic decay of kth capital type; c_0 = percentage tax credit; T = statutory corporate tax rate; and $PV(DEP_k)$ = the present value of depreciation allowances of kth capital type discounted by $r^* + \Pi^*$, the expected *nominal* rate of return where Π^* is the expected inflation rate. In order to take into account debt financing, the expected and required real rate of return is defined as:

$$r^* = bi(1 - T) \;+\; (1 - b)e - \Pi^* \qquad [4]$$

where b = the fraction of the investments the firm finances with debt; i = nominal rate of interest of debt; and e = the nominal return to equity required by its owners. This definition of $r*$ closely follows Auerbach (1983).

The estimation of unit labor costs is straightforward. Such costs are published for the United States by the Bureau of Labor Statistics (BLS) for each major industry. The inclusion of labor costs means that capital goods prices need not be expressed as relatives.

We can write:

$$WTK^* = G(c_k^*) \qquad [5]$$

to show that the capital weight is a function of the expected cost of capital and, of course, $WTL^* = 1 - WTK^*$.

In each period there are three possibilities regarding productivities. Potentially, the firm may have the options of a new "exogenous" set of a's, an interindustry set, or its current set. The independent variables determining $P(R_{jt})$ and $P(IM_{jt})$ provide the estimated probabilities for an innovation or imitation of best available practice. At equal probabilities where $P(R_{jt}) = P(IM_{jt})$, the results from each set of a's are compared by the firm with its current set. Wherever a draw only from $P(R_{jt})$ or $P(IM_{jt})$ is made, that set of a's is the highest productivity set. If the industry studied were airlines, for example, heretofore unadopted productivities for the innovative firm in the airline industry would levitate potential *outputs* of the aerospace industry. The "best available practice" available for imitation would be the best available carriers in use by the lowest-cost airline. Once a new set of a's is acquired, input coefficients are fixed at the lower levels until the next successful innovation draw.

Markup Pricing and the Financing Constraint on Investment

Firm Costs, Profits, and Net Income

Costs include variable costs (from noncapital-type inputs), depreciation of capital goods, and costs of financial capital (interest). If R&D is fully expensed for tax purposes, such expenditures are included in variable costs. (Except for tax credits, that will be the assumption, but such expensing can be varied to simulate tax policy changes.) In a policy modification of Nelson-Winter, the depreciation rate and the nominal interest rate are variables. The firm's net income (y_{jt}) is current economic profits or:

$$y_{jt} = [(P_{jt} \cdot a_{K,jvt}{}^{-1}) \cdot K_{jt} - (i_j + D_{jvt} + VCP_{jt}) \cdot K_{jt} \cdot q_k] \cdot (1 - T) + c_0 I_{jt} \qquad [6]$$

where P is the product price; a_K^{-1} is productivity (measured via primary capital or capital good services); i is the nominal rate of interest; D is the rate of depreciation; VCP is variable costs (mostly current labor costs) as a percentage of the current value of primary capital services of type k; q_k is (as above) the current price of (primary) capital; T is the statutory corporate income tax rate; and c_0 is the effective percentage tax credit on total investment I. Let c_1 be an effective tax credit percentage on R&D expenses; then VCP can be adjusted (for policy simulation purposes) by $VCP - c_1 RD$. The effective percentage tax credits, c_0 and c_1, can vary with the level of R&D expenditures. (Mansfield, 1984, and Eisner et al., 1983, explain these relationships.) Dividends based upon e are paid out of net income or y; however, as a part of "financing costs," e enters the model as part of the user cost of capital (equations 3 and 4 above).

Whether at or below full employment, the primary capital stock changes if the quantity of primary capital (in physical service units) changes. For example, in the airline industry, net additions to the airplane fleet would add carrying and horsepower capacity. When this happens, a variable depreciation rate can be applied to the "old" capital vintage and the "new" capital vintage. Different vintages of capital emerge in any historical simulations and will have different depreciation rates.

The Role of the Markup

Markup pricing can ease the financing constraint. In a modification of Eichner, I envision planned innovation (prior to planned production) as yielding a price that can generate internal funds. The markup pricing rule followed is:

$$P_{jt} = VC_{jt}\,(1 + M_{jt}) \qquad [7]$$

where VC is variable costs and M is the percentage markup. These costs are expressed in terms of the same time units as the productivities. In turn, the markup is determined as:

$$M_{jt} = n_t^{-1}\,E(N_{jt})^{-1} \qquad [8]$$

where n_t is the current number of firms in the industry, and $E(N_{jt})$ is the perceived or expected price elasticity of demand to firm j at time t and has a negative sign. The greater the number of firms in the industry and the greater the expected price elasticity of demand, the lower the percentage markup (normally). At the same time, however, a greater price elasticity means a market share gain for an innovative firm producing and selling at a lower price. Innovation eventually can reduce the number of firms in the industry. Then, the markup can be increased at the same price elasticity level. The perceived deviation of the firm's price elasticity of demand from the industry elasticity (N_t), therefore, is assumed to be based upon expectations of a market share gain from j's ability to further differentiate its product and to lower relative production costs. That is, if N_{jt} is greater than N_t, it is because a market share gain is expected.

The perceived or expected firm price elasticity is:

$$E(N_{jt}) = N_t + INN_{jt}, \text{ where } INN_{jt} = C(VC_{mt} - VC_{jt}) + \varepsilon \qquad [9]$$

which says that firm j's expected price elasticity equals the industry market price elasticity plus an incremental elasticity (INN), which is a positive linear function of the difference between the variable costs of the highest cost firm (firm m) and firm j's current variable costs plus an error term (ε). That is, an expected market share gain is based, in part, upon the cost differential between firm j (say, Boeing in aerospace) and the other firms in the industry. In this way, the markup can potentially be varied in order to provide funds for investment purposes.

Price setting may vary with industry characteristics. For example, if price leadership characterizes the industry at a particular time, a markup formula (which may differ from the one above) might be used for the price leader, and the other $n-1$ firms might behave as perfectly competitive firms. The price leader could plan production to yield a price markup that generates internal funds to finance planned investment. This would constitute an Eichnerian markup in which investment strategy is considered when the markup is set.

The Financial Constraint of the Firm

Returning to Nelson-Winter, the amount of fundable gross investment ($I_{g\,jt}$) depends upon whether the firm is making economic profits. Such profits nonetheless are not independent of investment strategy or the markup. In Nelson-Winter the firm earning positive excess returns can obtain "matching funds" by borrowing. In the present model, rather than matching, such borrowings are decided by the firm's historical asset-debt ratio. Thus, for the positive economic profit-maker, I_g depends upon its depreciation allowances ($D \cdot K \cdot q_k = DEP$), its net income ($y$), and its debt-to-asset ratio, or:

$$I_{g\,jt} = DEP_{jvt} + (1 + B)y_{jt}, \quad [10]$$

where B is a function of the historical log difference of assets (A) and debt (d) over some past time (not yet known empirically), or:

$$B = \beta(\log A - \log d). \quad [11]$$

If y is zero or less, then:

$$I_{g\,jt} = DEP_{jvt} + y_{jt} \quad [12]$$

so that a firm with zero or negative economic profits contracts. Wherever shrinking firms are encountered in an economy ($y \leq 0$), the history of such firms can be examined to determine whether they are scrapping plant and equipment over time so that appropriate adjustments can be made in levels of K. Thus, negative quasi-rents have feedback effects on innovation as K and perhaps the value of a_K changes. In the 1980s such firms, among others, became takeover targets.

The Desired Investment of the Firm

Price is a double-edged sword. The rate of growth in fundable gross investment (I_g) depends on changes in depreciation allowances and net economic profits (y). In turn, the growth of y is positively related to price (P). However, for the firms with a downward-sloping demand curve (and $N_{jt} > N_t$), a product price rise leads to a falling growth rate in sales. If all the other variables deciding y are held constant, there is a price that will roughly equate the rate of growth in sales with the rate of growth in financial funding ability. (We should bear in mind that a set of a's with higher productivities will generate this particular price at a lower level.) At a particular perceived price elasticity (N_{jt}), the two growth rates are (approximately) equal where marginal revenue equals output in primary capital productivity units (from the net-income-equation 6) or:

$$P_{jt}(1 - 1/N_{jt}) = a_{K\,jvt}^{-1}K_{jvt} \cong dy_{jt}/dP_{jt}$$

or

$$dy_{jt} = P_{jt}(1 - 1/N_{jt})dP_{jt} \cong (a_{K\,jvt}^{-1}K_{jvt})dP_{jt} \quad [13]$$

so that the equalizing price (P^*) is:

$$P^*_{jt} \cong \frac{a_{K,jvt}{}^{-1} K_{jvt}}{(1 - 1/N_{jt})} \qquad [14]$$

where $N_{jt} > 1$. If $N_{jt} < 1$, price can be increased until the elastic range is reached. Hence, there is a unique price and markup that nearly equate the sales growth rate with the financial funding ability growth rate. If P_{jt} (as defined above in equation 7) is above the price equating the two growth rates (P^*_{jt}), the rate of gross investment spending can be increased (with R&D increased more or less proportionately, depending upon R_{jt}, IM_{jt}, and R&D tax policy) until an acquisition of more productive a's enables the two growth rates to be matched at the higher product price. This gap between P_{jt} and P^*_{jt} can lead to a surge in investment that raises the probability of a successful innovation or imitation draw. A higher productivity rate would be accompanied by a higher level of the new-vintage capital stock.

In the absence of any discrepancy between P_{jt} and P^*_{jt} desired gross investment, I^*_g is:

$$I^*_g = [D_{jvt} \cdot K_{jvt} \cdot q_k] + \{G \cdot [1 - (M^*_{jt} \cdot AC_{j(t+\iota)}) / P^*_{jt}] \cdot K_{jv(t+\iota)} \cdot q_k\} \qquad [15]$$

where M^* and P^* are the values of the markup and price that approximately equate the sales growth rate with the financial funding ability growth rate. The value G is an adjustment coefficient and $AC_{j(t+\iota)}$ is the firm's unit production cost at a higher future expected productivity level (following Nelson-Winter) in $t+\iota$ and by the cost rate values (nonconstant in this case), or:

$$AC_{j(t+\iota)} = [(i_t + D_{jt} + VCP_{jt}) \cdot K_{jv(t+\iota)} \cdot q_k] / a_{k,jv(t+\iota)} \qquad [16]$$

The lower expected average costs provide for the allocation of more of the product price to investment, raise current investment above depreciation, and therefore add to the capital stock.

Entry, Exit, and Evolution

Entry and exit from each industry is possible. The triggering "decision" will depend upon the firm's net income and expected future losses in the case of exit and between major firms' profit rates (or returns on primary capital services) relative to the long-term market rate of interest in the case of entry. As suggested above, negative net income implies negative quasi-rents on capital. Scrapping of plants (which reduces K) as well as outright firm failure is possible. Leveraged buyouts (LBOs) of such firms are possible. However, the increase in debt to equity ratios has a debilitating effect upon future investment, R&D, and innovation. Such LBOs provide a problematic route to innovation even as they scrap capital goods. The simultaneous selling of assets is likely to deflate their values as a source of future funding. The time lags for exit and entry can only be determined empirically as the industry evolves and as it becomes more or less concentrated over time. Successful innovation increases the firm's market share and can lead to business failures that reduce the number of firms in the industry.

Empirical Musings: A Data Base

Balance sheet data on investment spending for firms are available from Standard & Poor's Compustat Services, company annual reports, the Office of Tax Analysis, the Joint Committee on Taxation, the *Journal of Mergers and Acquisitions*, and Moody's Industrial Manual. These sources also provide much of the required information on physical characteristics of production such as employment and nature of capital equipment. Additional sources for physical data include academic studies such as those of Abernathy (autos), Brock (computers), Charles River Associates (semiconductors), Enos (petroleum), Hollander (rayon), and Phillips (aircraft) as well as the reports of the National Science Foundation (textiles, steel, etc.) and feature stories in *Business Week* and various trade journals. Another source for the airline industry are its regulatory bodies over the years, including the Central Aeronautics Board. After exhausting these sources the economist must be prepared to visit a sample of the major firms in each industry and to discuss production data by telephone with the remainder of the current industries' membership.

Perfect real-world data are not required for successful simulations. Indeed, a complete simulation model could be constructed from existing estimates of price elasticities of demand, unit costs of production, and so on. However, if the intent is to replicate the real world as closely as possible for establishing the basic parameters of the model, the policy simulations then are only limited by our imaginations. Unlike the valuable pioneering work of Nelson and Winter, such simulations would be based on historical data. The results could be tested for reliability by comparing each "actual" policy simulation with the actual history of the selected industries in terms of profits, real capital, sales revenues, productivities, and number of firms in the industries at various times.

Summary

I have presented an evolutionary model that includes the effect of tax incentives upon investment through the impact such policy has upon a firm's net economic profit. Given a firm's markup, these incentives have a positive effect upon the "financing constraint for investment" that a firm faces. The markup is determined by a firm's industry cost position, its ability to accomplish product differentiation, and the relative power that the firm enjoys within its industry. Although internal financing requirements are part of the markup strategy, the amount of fundable gross investment depends upon whether economic profits exist. Hence, with economic profits, the firm (or industry) maintains or expands, and without economic profits, it contracts.

Part of the investment strategy of the firm is to innovate. Hence, the markup is used, in part, to generate the internal funds that affect a firm's ability to reduce costs. In this way investment depends on changes in net economic profits as well as a planned level of internal funding. The growth in these net economic profits is positively related to price. A firm facing a downward sloping demand curve finds that a price rise leads to a falling growth rate in sales. If all other variables determining the growth in profits are held constant, there is a price that will equate the rate of sales growth with the rate of growth in financial funding ability. At a particular price elasticity, the two growth rates are equal where marginal revenue equals output in primary capital productivity units. Hence there is a unique price and markup that nearly equate the sales growth rate with the financial funding ability growth rate.

References

Abernathy, William J. (1978). *The Productivity Dilemma: Roadblock to Innovation in the Automobile Industry*. Baltimore: Johns Hopkins University Press.

Auerbach, Alan J. (1983). "Corporate Taxation in the United States." *Brookings Papers*, 2.: 451–505.

Canterbery, E. Ray, and Bell, Frederick W. (1976). *Aquaculture and the Developing Countries: A Feasibility Study*. Cambridge, MA: Ballinger, pp. 451–505.

Canterbery, E. Ray, and McLeod, William. (1989). "The Doctrine of Inherent Productivity: Keynes, Sraffa, and Kalecki." *Journal of Post Keynesian Economics* 11, 5 (Fall): 630–640.

Caves, R.E. (1980). "Corporate Strategy and Structure." *Journal of Economic Literature*, 18, 1 (March): 64–92.

Chandler, Alfred D. (1962). *Strategy and Structure: Chapters in the History of the Industrial Enterprise*. Cambridge, MA: MIT Press.

Charles River Associates. (1980). *Innovation, Competition, and Government Policy in the Semi-conductor Industry*. Lexington, MA: Lexington Books.

Cyert, Richard M., and Hedrick, Charles L. (1972). "Theory of the Firm: Past, Present, and Future: An Interpretation." *Journal of Economic Literature* 10, 2 (June): 398–412.

Cyert, Richard M., and March, James G. (1963). *A Behavioral Theory of the Firm*. Englewood Cliffs, NJ: Prentice-Hall.

David, Paul A. (1975). *Technical Choice, Innovation, and Economic Growth: Essays on American and British Experience in the Nineteenth Century*. London: Cambridge University Press.

Eckstein, Otto, ed. (1972). *The Econometrics of Price Determination*. Washington, DC: Board of Governors of the Federal Reserve.

Eichner, Alfred S. (1976). *The Megacorp and Oligopoly*. Cambridge: Cambridge University Press.

Eisner, Robert; Albert, S.H.; and Sullivan, M.A. (1983). "Tax Incentives and R&D Expenditures." Draft. 16th CIRET Conference, Washington, D.C., September 21–24.

Gold, B.; Pierce, W.S.; and Rosegger, G. (1970). "Diffusion of Major Technological Innovations." *Journal of Industrial Economics* 18, 3 (July): 218–41.

Hollander, Samuel. (1965). *The Sources of Increased Efficiency: A Study of Dupont's Rayon Plants*. Cambridge, MA: MIT Press.

Hulton, Charles R., and Robertson, J. W. (1983). "Differential Effects of the Accelerated Cost Recovery System on Investment: A Survey with Implications for Understanding Effects on High Technology Investment." Draft. Report to the Division of Policy Research and Analysis, National Science Foundation, October.

Levine, David P. (1975). "The Theory of the Growth of the Capitalist Economy." *Economic Development and Cultural Change* 24 (October): 64–76.

Mansfield, Edwin. (1981). "Tax Policy and Innovation: Provisions, Proposals, and Needed Research." *Preliminary Papers for a Colloquium on Tax Policy and Investment in Innovation*. Division of Policy Research and Analysis, National Science Foundation, April 24.

——— (1984). "Public Policy toward Industrial Innovation: An International Study of Direct Tax Incentives for R&D." Draft. University of Pennsylvania, March 1.

Marris, Robin. (1964). *The Economic Theory of Managerial Capitalism*. New York: Free Press.

Miller, Ronald, and Sawyers, David. (1968). *The Technical Development of Modern Aviation* London: Routledge & Kegan Paul.

Nadiri, M. Ishaq. (1980). "Productivity Slowdown." *American Economic Review* 70, 2 (May): 349–52.

———. (1981). "Tax Incentives and R&D Expenditures." *Preliminary Papers for a Colloquium on Tax Policy and Investment in Innovation*. Division of Policy Research and Analysis, National Science Foundation, April 24.

Nelson, R., and Winter, S.G. (1982). *An Evolutionary Theory of Economic Change*. Cambridge, MA: Harvard University Press.

Nelson, R.R., et al. (1976). "Technical Change in an Evolutionary Model." *Quarterly Journal of Economics* 90, 1 (February): 90–118.

Nordhaus, William D. (1974). "The Falling Share of Profits." *Brookings Papers on Economic Activity* 1: 169–217.

Okun, Arthur M. (1981). *Prices and Quantities: A Macroeconomic Analysis*. Washington, D.C.: Brookings Institution.

Ong, Nai-Pew. (1981). "Target Pricing, Competition, and Growth." *Journal of Post Keynesian Economics* 4, 5 (Fall): 101–6.

Penrose, Edith. (1959). *The Theory of the Growth of the Firm*. Oxford: Basil Blackwell.

Phillips, Almarin. (1971). *Technology and Market Structure: A Study of the Aircraft Industry*. Lexington, MA: Heath Lexington.

Rosenberg, Nathan. (1976). *Perspectives on Technology*. Cambridge, MA: Cambridge University Press.

Sahal, Devendra. (1981). *Patterns of Technological Innovation*. Reading, MA: Addison-Wesley.

Shapiro, Nina. (1981). "Pricing and the Growth of the Firm." *Journal of Post Keynesian Economics* 4, 1 (Fall): 85–100.

Simon, Herbert A. (1947). *Administrative Behavior: A Study of Decision-making Processes in Administrative Organization*. 3rd ed. New York: Free Press.

———. (1957). *Models of Man: Social and Rational Mathematical Essays on Rational Human Behavior in a Social Setting*. New York: John Wiley.

Sylos-Labini, Paolo. (1962). *Oligopoly and Technical Progress*. Cambridge, MA: Harvard University Press.

Williamson, O.E. (1975). *Markets and Hierarchies: A Study in the Economics of Internal Organization*. New York: Free Press.

Wood, Adrian. (1975). *A Theory of Profits*. Cambridge: Cambridge University Press.

Chapter 19

The Coase Theorem as a Negative Externality

E Ray Canterbery / A. Marvasti*

Abstract: The Coase Theorem (1960) states that under perfect competition, and in the absence of income effects and transactions costs, voluntarily negotiated agreements among private parties generating or being affected by externalities will lead to the same resource allocation regardless of how property rights are assigned among the parties. Coase understands that his neutrality theorem could be falsified in the presence of income effects. He also acknowledges that high transactions costs might preclude a voluntary contractual agreement. Coase nonetheless remains skeptical about such outcomes because he thinks the administrative costs of correcting externalities could be high. The theorem then borders on circularity. Externalities first are a problem because they exist, but they may persist because the transactions costs in their removal are so high. High transactions costs may lead to unsatisfactory contracts. Cooter (1982) even questons whether there is a Coase Theorem. Nevertheless, the high private and public costs of removing externalities has led to Ptolemaic epicycles extending the Coase Theorem.

Full text: In contested property rights to resources, such as those of oceans, the assignment of property rights by legal rules is allocatively neutral because all externalities are internalized. This allocative neutrality doctrine, or the Coase Theorem 1960!, can be thusly summarized: Under perfect competition, and in the absence of income effects and transactions costs, voluntarily negotiated agreements among private parties generating or being affected by externalities will lead to the same resource allocation (and output mix) regardless of how property rights are assigned among the parties.(1)

Coase understands that his neutrality theorem could be falsified in the presence of income effects. The party assigned the property rights would have to pay bribes to the other parties rather than the other way round. If the income elasticity of demand differed for one party compared with the other, the pattern of demand, and hence of equilibrium prices and of outputs, would differ under alternative assignments of rights.

Coase also acknowledges that high transactions costs might preclude a voluntary contractual agreement. In such instances, the government, imbued with legal rights and enforcement powers, could eliminate externalities. Coase nonetheless remains skeptical about such outcomes because he thinks the administrative costs of correcting externalities could be high.

The theorem then borders on circularity. Externalities first are a problem because they exist, but they may persist because the transactions costs in their removal are so high. High transactions costs may lead to unsatisfactory contracts. Cooter 1982! even questions whether there is a Coase Theorem because it is a generalization made by other economists based only on a set of concrete examples developed by Coase. Nevertheless, the high private and public costs of removing externalities has led to Ptolemaic epicycles extending the "Coase Theorem." This note searches the economics heavens for the True Theorem.

BEFORE THE THEOREM: THE PUREST COASE

In the beginning, there were no epicycles. Coase first advanced the proposition that has become the Coase Theorem in an article titled "The Federal Communications Commission" 1959!. The definition is by example. In this case, the example concerns the ownership and use of a cave. Ownership of the cave, says Coase 1959, 25!, is "no doubt dependent on the law of property." But, "whether the cave is used for storing bank records, as a natural gas reservoir, or for growing mushrooms depends, not on the law of property, but on whether the bank, the natural gas corporation, or the mushroom concern will pay the most in order to be able to use the cave."

In a second example 1960!, Coase considers the potential conflict between ranchers raising cattle and farmers cultivating crops. The cattle could roam and destroy crops, creating a negative externality for the farmers. Suppose the damage to crops with both ranching and farming is valued at less than either the rents of the ranchers or the rents of the farmers. If the ranchers are liable for the damage, they could compensate the farmers, continue their operations, and still be better off than if they abandoned ranching by an amount equal to their rents minus the value of the damage.

If the ranchers are not liable, the maximum the farmers would pay to induce the ranchers to cease would be the value of the destroyed crops. This is less than the additional sum the ranchers could earn by continuing to operate rather than moving to the best alternative employment. The farmers would therefore be unable to induce the ranchers to stop their operations. As the rents of the farmers are greater than the value of the destroyed crops, the farmers would still enjoy a net gain from continuing to farm. Whatever the legal position, both ranchers and farmers would continue to operate.

What happens if the damage to the crops is valued at less than the rents of the ranchers but more than the rents of the farmers? If the ranchers are liable, and if they compensate the farmers for their crop loss (which they could do since their rents are greater than the value of the crop damage), the farmers would earn the same as if the damage had not happened (payment by the ranchers for the crops destroyed would be substituted for marketing the crops). But, since the rents of the farmers are less than the value of the crops destroyed, the farmers would agree not to cultivate for any payment that is greater than their rents. A bargain could be struck by which, for a payment by the ranchers greater than the farmers' rents but less than the value of the crop damage, the farmers would cease cultivation.

Suppose the ranchers are not liable. Since the damage suffered by the farmers would exceed their rents, the farmers would earn less than in their best alternative activity. They would therefore not grow crops unless they could induce the ranchers to give up their operations. Since the ranchers' rents (with the attendant crop destruction) are greater than the farmers' rents, the farmers would be unable to make payments sufficient to induce the ranchers to cease ranching. The farmers would switch to their best alternative occupations, while the ranchers would continue to operate. In each case, a change in legal responsibility has no effect on the allocation of resources.

Pure and simple, these are examples in search of a theorem, and they become more and more tedius with each retelling. They could become exciting tales. The cave dweller might grow exotic mushrooms, begin to hallucinate, and turn to publishing books in the tradition of Carlos Castenada. The gentlemanly discussions of voluntary exchanges that leave resources allocated in the same way could deteriorate into range wars--cattle rustling, cowboys dying, and mothers advising their sons not to grow up to be cowboys.

In short, the examples are incredibly naive. These are not the worlds of "separate realities" or of Gunsmoke. More importantly, all of the examples are hypothetical. If it is true, as Coase claims, that "the proportion of cases in which no agreement is reached will be small" 1988, 161!, why doesn't Coase use real-world examples? Why does he resort to fiction when the economic world is populated with economic agents on contract curves?

We are left wondering. What are the true transactions costs? What numbers are involved: how many caves, how many uses, how many ranchers, how many farmers? Are all ranchers and all farmers alike? What if the best alternative opportunity for the rancher is to become a farmer and for the farmer to become a rancher? Then, all would be indifferent to their activities. What if the ranchers have guns and the farmers have only short-range pitchforks? What if the ranchers are rich and the farmers are dirt poor? These kinds of questions led to the epicycles.

THE TRANSACTIONS COSTS CONUNDRUM

Buchanan and Stubblebine (1962) create one epicycle to deal with the idea of unsatisfactory contracts. There are, they say, market solutions for Pareto-relevant externalities when potential gains are greater than transactions costs. Transactions costs consist of output sacrificed because resources are used to set up a system of voluntary exchanges and to keep it functioning. If the potential gains from a market transaction are small relative to transactions costs, however, the externality would be Pareto-irrelevant. Rather than being an indication of market failure, the lack of an observable market to eliminate externalities reflects an excess of transactions and enforcement costs over potential gains from trade.

Demsetz 1967! extends Coase's Theorem by focusing on property rights systems and their role as a guide for internalizing externalities. In Demsetz's view, the common property rights system is inherently unstable, and a private or a state-owned property right emerges in response to changes in technology and demand.(2) In the continued pursuit of the transactions costs conundrum, Demsetz and Alchian (1973) perceive transactions costs as being significantly reduced by alterations of institutional arrangements such as common property systems. For example, historical enclosure movements have reduced the cost of organizing and carrying on transactions by limiting the participants in the negotiations to those already possessing property rights.

This externalities literature abstracts from the issue of the measurability of costs and benefits. Cheung (1970) sees government regulation as an efficient alternative to the market if the costs and benefits of the market solution cannot be accurately measured and evaluated. As to the market, Cheung suggests that in addition to competitive conditions, an effective contract requires transferability of rights. Rights would have to be liquid.

Dahlman 1979! adds specificity. He identifies three groups of transactions costs that are losses of resources required to eliminate externalities and to attain a Pareto-improved position. First, search and information costs are incurred in the process of finding the parties involved and informing them of exchange opportunities. Second, bargaining and decision costs result from negotiations on the way to agreeable terms of trade. Third, policing and enforcement entail costs; otherwise, obligations might not be met according to the terms of the contract.

In short, according to this literature, when these various transactions costs are high relative to benefits from a market transaction, the exchange should not take place, for it is Pareto-irrelevant. In such a view, the market never fails; rather, transactions costs simply are excessive. Such a conclusion continues to beg the question. Do externalities persist because of high transactions costs, or do excessive transactions costs comprise an inescapable obstacle to a Paretian solution? If the latter is the case, the second-order externality cannot be internalized, obviating the need to posit the Coase Theorem. When the market is the problem in this manner, the market cannot be the solution.

"COMMON PROPERTY" OR "OPEN ACCESS"?

The fuzzy definition of "common property" in the Coase literature generates still another difficulty. Economists occasionally use the terms "common property" and "open access" to assign the legal status of a resource. Demsetz (1973), for example, refers to public roads as "common property," whereas Weitzman (1974) uses highways as an example of a "free-access resource." Ciriacy-Wantrup and Bishop (1975), p.714 define common property legalistically as "a distribution of property rights in resources in which a number of owners are co-equal in their rights to use the resource."

Under the legal definition of common property, the rights of nonusers are not lost because of nonuse. The rights of all co-owners to use the resource on a first-come, first-served basis make the property common, but the rights do not imply equality of co-owners in the use of the resource. The Grand Canyon is owned by "all the people," but a long-term obstruction of the view by the first million users would not violate the rights of the next million "late arrivals." Moreover, the term "common" refers both to the institution and to the resource subject to the institution. Ciriacy-Wantrup and Bishop contend that the concept of "common property resources," or "commons," can be used only after the institutional arrangements are made. Therefore, unowned resources such as high seas fisheries by definition are not common property resources; they are resources with free or open access.

In this strictly legal distinction between common property and free-access resources, there seem to be no implications for economic efficiency or for the allocation of resources. Even so, Runge 1986! sees such a distinction as having significant policy implications. Unrestricted entry causes inefficiency in an open-access regime, he says, while the structure of joint use causes inefficiency related to common property. Using Ciriacy-Wantrup and Bishop's legal definition of coequal access rights, Runge sees the common property rights system as providing efficient and equitable outcomes. Apparently, those who arrive at the end of the queue at the Grand Canyon had free information that would have put them first, if they had desired the preferred view.

The application of the theory of common property resources in the solution of problems related to "ubiquitous" or "fugitive" resources is inappropriate, according to Ciriacy-Wantrup and Bishop. Ubiquitous resources such as solar radiation, precipitation, and wind are not scarce and can be used by everyone until a stage of development is reached that makes these resources scarce. Thus, institutional regulations for the allocation of these resources are not needed. As to fugitive and mobile resources such as fish, their allocation to various groups cannot be decided until they are captured.

DISTRIBUTION AMONG HETEROGENEOUS PARTIES

Suppose surpluses result. Since the original Coase Theorem is allocatively neutral, it does not consider the distribution of production surpluses among affected parties. In addressing this issue, Randall 1974! finds the allocative effects of choices sometimes substantial and thus to be taken seriously. Such is especially the case when a government is involved in bargaining for the affected parties. Oakerson 1986! perceives possible collective decisions regarding the commons binding on all parties without their consent.

Such decisions become increasingly inequitable as asymmetries in bargaining powers among users increase. When the U.S. Calvary was sent west in the late nineteenth century to kill or imprison any American Indian attempting to maintain as commons what gold miners considered private property, the rifle gave the U. S. government superior bargaining power. These inequities, according to Oakerson, may cause collective actions to fail and inefficiencies to result.

In addition to asymmetries in bargaining powers, the abilities of the parties to use resources may be unequal. The greater the number of parties bargaining, the greater the probability that the parties are heterogeneous. For example, the United States has the technology to mine deep ocean seabeds, whereas Argentina does not. Completing a contract becomes more difficult with such heterogeneity Johnson and Libecap 1982; Sugden 1984!. Furthermore, Weitzman 1974! sees a private property rights system depriving some from access to an otherwise free-access resource.(3)

In most cases, the negotiations obviously become more difficult and transactions costs higher as the affected parties increase in diversity and number Randall 1974; Oates 1986!. Indeed, when the parties are many, argues Oates, the Coase Theorem is irrelevant. But if the parties are few, how can perfect competition prevail?

Cooter 1982a, 1982b! depicts the Coase Theorem as overly optimistic. That is, as long as transactions costs are zero, voluntary cooperation among bargaining parties leads to agreement. Such obviously effortless cases require no special analytics, only hypothetical examples. Cooter counters with the "Hobbes Theorem" for the difficult and interesting cases: without a third party's coercive force, individuals will react to the harshest threats. Cooter's Hobbesian pessimism or the noncooperative approach has the division of surpluses or joint benefits from transactions allocated by a government's compulsory arbitration (the American Indian solution?). Then the Coase Theorem becomes irrelevant.

AFTER THE THEOREM: THE SECOND COASE

In Coase's more recent retelling of his examples, he clearly is frustrated but undaunted. His point of view, he laments, "Has not in general commanded assent, nor has my argument, for the most part, been understood." But he continues, "As the argument in these papers is, I believe, simple, so simple indeed as almost to make their propositions fall into the category of truths which can be deemed self-evident, their rejection or apparent incomprehensibility would seem to imply that most economists have a different way of looking at economic problems and do not share my conception of the nature of the subject. This I believe to be true" 1988, 1!.

In reply to his critics, he elaborates on transactions costs: "With zero transaction costs, producers would make whatever set of contractual arrangements was necessary to maximize the value of production" 1988, 175!. But, "Once transaction costs are taken into account, many of these measures will not be undertaken because making the contractual arrangements necessary to bring them into existence would cost more than the gain they make possible" 1988, 175!.

Coase nonetheless returns to his cattle-crop example, assigns various liabilities, and shows net gains from every conceivable agreement. But, he suggests, this is not his point. For, "Economists went wrong...not to! take into account a factor which is essential if one wishes to analyze the effect of a change in the law on the allocation of resources. This missing factor is the existence of transaction costs" 1988, 175!.

Coase has shifted his argument from the assumption of zero transactions costs to the effect of various legal arrangements on the allocation of resources when transactions costs are nonzero. An optimal liability rule is impossible with positive transactions costs. But, if this is so, what can the Coase Theorem tell us in a world of suboptimal liability rules?

Coase believes that the Pigovian approach--using government to address externalities--dominates mainstream economics. Pigou becomes Coase's foil when Coase suggests, "The existence of 'externalities' does not imply that there is a prima facie case for governmental intervention" 1988, 24!. But, for proof, Coase resorts to his earlier hypothetical example of manufacturer A emiting smoke (which A has a right to do), harming C, with whom A has no contractual relations. Then, going through every conceivable configuration of benefits and costs, he finds no need for the government. He once again ignores numbers, heterogeneity, private coercion, and wealth differences.

Coase considers only those wealth effects that might ensue from the example itself. Resorting again to the cattle-crop example, if the rule of liability is known, the amount that will have been paid to acquire the land will reflect any compensation paid for the trampled crops. Thus, "There is no change in the distribution of wealth associated with the choice of a different legal rule and therefore no subsequent changes in demand, the effects of which need to be taken into account" 1988, 172!. Even granting this conclusion, the example begs the question regarding the effect of rancher-farmer wealth differences upon contracts and their enforcement.

CONCLUSIONS

Once the original Coase Theorem is surrounded by the aforementioned epicycles, the theorem itself becomes circular. The theorem's optimism derives from the allocation of legal entitlements through voluntary negotiations in a perfectly competitive market in which transactions costs are zero or nonprohibitive, Regardless of the allocation of rights, efficiency comes from the assignment of rights. But we find many objections or adjustments in the Coase Theorem that are derived from real-world conditions and practices.

Our pessimism regarding the redressing of externalities stems from transactions costs as a second-order negative externality that cannot be internalized. These high transactions costs derive from interconnections between allocative decisions and efficiencies, unequal bargaining power of the parties (in fact, a noncompetitive market), the heterogeneity of the parties in their abilities to capture the surplus, a large number of parties in the negotiations, and Hobbesian pessimism regarding human behavior.

Traditionally, political scientists rather than economists have studied the analytics of Hobbesian negotiation in which power (however defined) is not shared equally. We need not conclude that economists should not study problems of unequal power, but, rather, if they do, they cannot grant the inferences of the Coase Theorem. Coase's examples are too naive to cope with issues of power.

We arrive at the ultimate irony. The search and information costs embodied in the economics literature on the elusive Coase Theorem must have been high, even excluding the costs associated with our own literature search. Hence, the Case Theorem has generated a negative externality for economists. The search costs persist because of a theorem that wrongly presumes them to be small.

NOTES

1. Coase did not originate the phrase, the "Coase Theorem," nor its precise formulation, both of which were done by George Stigler.

2. Demsetz also supports (without direct reference) Buchanan and Stubblebine's position on Pareto-irrelevant externalities.

3. In a contrary view, under certain conditions, an individual deprived of free access to a road may be better off even in the presence of a monopoly's private property rights DeMeza and Gould 1987!.

REFERENCES

Alchian, Armen, and Harold Demsetz. "The Property Rights Paradigm." The Journal of Economic History 103, no. 1 (March 1973).

Buchanan, James, and W. C. Stubblebine. "Externality." Economica 29 (1962).

Cheung, Steven N. "The Structure of a Contract and the Theory of a Nonexclusive Resource." The Journal of Law and Economics 13 (April 1970).

Ciriacy-Wantrup, S. V., and Richard Bishop. "Common Property as a Concept in Natural Resource Policy." Natural Resources Journal 15 (October 1975).

Coase, R. H. "The Federal Communications Commission." The Journal of Law and Economics no. 2 (October 1959).

--. The Firm the Market and the Law. Chicago and London: University of Chicago Press, 1988.

--. "The Problem of Social Cost." Journal of Law and Economics no. 3 (October 1960).

Cooter, Robert, Stephen Marks, and Robert Mnookin. "The Cost of Coase." Journal of Legal Studies 11 (January 1982a).

Cooter, Robert, et al. "Bargaining in the Shadow of the Law: A Testable Model of Strategic Behavior." Journal of Legal Studies 11 (June 1982b).

Dahlman, Carl. "The Problem of Externality." The Journal of Law and Economics 22, no. 1 (April 1979).

DeMeza, David, and J. R. Gould. "Free Access Versus Private in a Resource: Income Distributions Compared." Journal of Political Economy 97, no. 6 (December 1987).

Demsetz, Harold. "Toward a Theory of Property Rights." The American Economic Review 62, no. 2 (May 1967).

Johnson, Ronald, and Gary Libecap. "Contracting Problems and Regulation: The Case of the Fishery." The American Economic Review 72, no. 2 (December 1982).

Oakerson, Ronald J. "A Model for the Analysis of Common Property Problems." In Proceedings of the Conference on Common Property Resource Management-1985, National Academy Press, 1986.

Oates, Wallace E. "Markets and Externalities-Comment 1." In Natural Resource Economics Policy Problems and Contemporary Analysis, edited by David Bromley. Dordrecht: Kluwer Nijhoff Publishing, 1986.

Randall, Alan. "Coasian Externality Theory in a Policy Contest." Natural Resources Journal 14 (January 1974).

Runge, Ford C. "Common Property and Collective Action in Economic Development." In Proceedings of the Conference on Common Property Resource Management-1985, National Academy Press, 1986.

Sugden, Robert. "Reciprocity: The Supply of Public Goods Through Voluntary Contributions." The Economic Journal 94 (December 1984).

Weitzman, Martin L. "Free Access vs. Private Ownership as Alternative Systems for Managing Common Property." Journal of Economic Theory 8 (December 1974).

*The authors are Professor of Economics, Florida State University, Tallahassee, and Assistant Professor of Economics, University of Houston, Downtown, respectively.

Chapter 20

Two Coases or two theorems? (response to article by Steven Medema in this issue, p. 208)

E. Ray Canterbery

A. Marvasti*

Professor Steven Medema (1993) has written a thoughtful, readable commentary on our recent article (1992). He suggests that our critique of the Coase Theorem "is largely on the mark"; only pathological modesty could provoke our disagreement. Medema chooses instead to deal with our treatment of Ronald Coase and his relation to the world of zero transaction costs and the Coase Theorem. In particular, Medema contends that we have "gone astray" in the view of the Coase Theorem being "at the heart of Coase's message" (1993). Rather, the "Coasian world" of zero transactions costs and perfect competition is merely a means to an end for Coase, namely, to attack the Pigouvian tradition.

"What Coase intended with his analysis of the zero transaction costs world," according to the author, "was to show that in such a world, Pigouvian remedies (e.g., taxes, subsidies, and regulations) are not necessary to resolve externality problems" (1993). Coase, according to the author, rejects the theorem bearing his name and embraces the real world of positive transaction costs. In this regard, there are not two Coases after all, apparently because Coase is not a Coasian!

Coase Theorem I: Is Coase a Coasian?

As we traverse between "The Problem of Social Cost" (1960) and Coase's later writings (1988, 1992), a shift nonetheless appears unmistakable. Perhaps the formulators of the Coase Theorem by now have convinced Coase that they misunderstood his original argument. These and "traditional" or Pigouvian economists simply missed Coase's central point regarding the critical importance of positive transactions costs. The Coasians prefer an idyllic world in which government action is not required, whereas the Pigouvians always prefer government action in the face of externalities. While we do not want to play literary critics, what the later Coase claims as his central point (the importance of positive transactions costs) is quite easy to miss in his seminal article (1960).

At the same time, Coase's disaffection with those dreaded taxes and subsidies made less arguable by Pigou and Pigouvian welfare economics is quite easy to spot. Coase (1960) opens with an attack on wrong-headed economists who use Pigou's divergence between the private and social product of a factory as the basis for a tax on pollution.(1) After devoting the heart of the article to related court decisions in which the courts end up defending the private polluters, Coase (1960, 28-44) spends the balance dancing on the grave of Pigouvian welfare economics and advocating an alternative approach. Coase favors a weighing of marginal benefits and marginal costs solely in terms of maximal production.

Coase Theorem I surely is consistent with Coase's distaste for Pigouvian welfare economics because private and social costs are equal under conditions of perfect competition. Moreover, where transactions costs are zero and there are no income effects, law and government are irrelevant because the parties involved will always bargain to the socially optimal solution once rights have been assigned. Since, if Coase Theorem I prevails, there is no need for Pigouvian welfare economics, it is hardly surprising that the "Coasians" embraced Theorem I! The hypothetical cases with zero transactions costs are the clear instances in which the Pigouvians are rebutted; the cases with clarion calls for government action are sufficiently rare as to be endangered species. If Coase's main task is to reduce the population of the Pigouvians, Theorem I is his best weapon. But, showing that there is no need for taxes, subsidies, and regulations in a hypothetical world is an empty proof.

Coase Theorem II: The Importance of Positive Transactions Costs

Let us nevertheless grant for the moment that Coase Theorem I is a misnomer and is in reality the anti-Coase. We now formulate Coase Theorem II: when externalities exist, the appropriate remedy or assignment of rights would optimize production and would take into account positive transactions costs when properly calculating marginal benefits and costs, including opportunity costs. Coase (like Pigou, incidently) favors the use of opportunity costs because these problems then can be approached "by comparing the value of the product yielded by factors in alternative uses or by alternative arrangements." In this regard, "the main advantage of the pricing system is that it leads to the employment of factors in places where the value of the product yielded is greatest and do so at less cost than alternative systems . . ." (1960, 40)

Critical to Coase's deployment of Coase Theorem II in the real world is the presence of the marginal revenues and marginal costs whereby welfare improvements can be measured. If benefits exceed costs (at the margin) by such measures, economic efficiency has been enhanced. Thus, at first blush, Theorem II seems to differ from Theorem I by the presence of positive transactions costs and the necessary use of cost-benefit analysis. Such marginal benefits and costs nonetheless are based on market prices because, by Coase's standards, social costs are not measurable. In contrast, Pigou's mantra says that market values do not necessarily reflect the social significance of goods and services.

When it comes to measuring welfare improvements, Theorem II also depends upon perfect competition (or nearly perfect, as Coase occasionally wavers on this condition (1988, 175ff). Even the transactions costs would be measured in market prices. Suppose the giant tobacco companies sue all private establishments having "no smoking" areas because cigarette production has slowed (along with the death rate from lung cancer). There will be legal fees; they become part of transactions costs. Market Failure I leads to high and positive transactions costs. In general, if voluntary agreements were reached or markets never failed, lawyers would be as extinct as dinosaurs (currently experiencing a modest revival).

Which brings us to Market Failure II. Suppose the population of lawyers were to be greatly diminished by the proliferation of "Jurassic Parks."(2) (If Coase can be fanciful, so can we.) If the surviving lawyers were to form a cartel, they themselves would be creating a negative externality, removable only by hiring more lawyers. Market Failure I leads to Market Failure II, which leads to still greater transactions costs. The cost of eliminating the second order externality depends upon the lawyers' prices. If the prices were sufficiently high (as they often are), no court action can be taken and costs exceed benefits even before society could consider the possible benefits from resolving the first order externality.

Pigouvian welfare economics has been criticized for being normative and imprecise. But, the "precision" of Coase's cost-benefit analysis really does depend upon perfectly competitive prices. After all, Paretian welfare propositions depend upon the same efficiency conditions. Coase appears to want a social valuation based upon market prices. But since prices reflect private not social costs, the evaluation of social costs with private cost data is contradictory for Coase and Pigou alike. Even when lawyers' fees are put to social purpose, those fees must remain a private cost. In the United States, legal (transactions) costs comprise the main consideration in any attempt to redress a nontrivial, negative externality. In many cases, those who can afford to pay the transactions costs decide the outcome, so that transactions costs themselves become the problem.(3)

The later Coase wants economists to enter the real world of positive transactions costs. In order to have his transactions costs and his private measure of social costs too--contradictory though it may be--Coase's "real world" nonetheless must be one of perfect competition. Otherwise, the economist must contend with the theory of second-best whereby there is nothing to choose between second, third-best, or nth best. Once this is understood, it is easy to see why precision-minded economists would formulate Coase Theorem I and why it is so difficult to believe that Coase completely rejects Theorem I while beating the Pigouvians over the head with it.(4) Theorem II has many layers, whereas Theorem I has only one; yet, between the two there is little to choose because Theorem II depends upon the marginal costs and benefits given by competitive markets. Even here, the market can turn against itself when the positive transactions costs are market determined as well.

Coase v. Pigou, or Coase v. the Pigouvians?

Pigouvian welfare economics, in contrast to Coasian economics, is openly normative and geared to practical applications in a world of great market imperfections. Pigou's original external diseconomies include occupational diseases, the employment of child labor, air pollution from untreated waste products, and unemployment from technical change. Even here, the Pigouvian vice as well is to confuse structural fractures with merely marginal divergences between the private and social product.

At first glance, Coase's antipathy for Pigou is difficult to understand. This is why we have used (above) "the Pigouvians" as Coase's true foil. Coase Theorem I can be derived from Pigou (1938, chaps. 2-9)! Like Coase, Pigou does not endorse any specific corrective tax policy or liability rule. Rather, Pigou refers to suggested taxes and subsidies as "extraordinary encouragements or restraints" heavily qualified by counterarguments. Coase's attack on these grounds reveals much more about Coase than it does about Pigou.

Perhaps Pigou is an irritant to Coase and the Coasians for three other reasons: (1) In its gestalt, Economics of Welfare confronts capitalism with one of its most glaring defects: choices as expressed in market prices do not necessarily embody the social importance of goods and services. Rock stars and professional basketball players are paid more than professors of economics; (2) since consumers' satisfactions are interdependent, Veblenesque forces--"bandwagon" and "snob" effects--can be used to justify excise taxes on J & B Scotch and Marlboros; (3) Pigou's policy ideas generally are aimed at transfering wealth from the rich to the poor under the principle of the diminishing marginal utility of income. Such transfers, of course, strongly depend upon the use of taxes and subsidies.(5)

It is easy to go too far in attributing like ideas to any two esteemed economists. In the history of economic thought, the "greatest" economists write with broad brushes. Often they are--as Coase is--contradictory. Certainly such economists cannot select their followers or define what will be important to them. Even so, it is not meaningless to say that strong differences separate the Coasians from the Pigouvians. And, as with Pigou, Coase can be expected to bear some of the responsibility for his offspring, even when they are misguided. Again, looking at the gestalt of Coase's work, it remains strongly Coasian! What's next? Can we claim Coase as an institutionalist?

Evolutionary Economics: The Importance of Being Coase

We would hope there exists a third Coase (or, a second Coase, depending upon who is counting). This Coase is concerned with the elimination (where possible) of negative externalities through the "best choice" of institutions. This is the Coase who, according to Medema, considers the importance of "economic institutions in structuring economic performance." When new legal rights and their implementation are designed, however, the margin almost never comes into play. According to the available medical data, for example, secondary smokers of tobacco die prematurely from this negative externality. Moreover, because of the direct health effects from this addictive substance, the industry loses about a half million of its best customers yearly (raising the health insurance costs of others). Even ignoring transactions costs, production is lost all the way round, not to mention the many lives. Marginal costs and marginal benefits appear in such cases to be trivial pursuits; there is nothing marginal about death.

The "institutional Coase" is best displayed in his other classics, "The Nature of the Firm" (1937) and "The Lighthouse in Economics" (1974). Since part of the firm's cost in using the price mechanism is comprised of transactions costs, the firm does organize itself in such a way as to attempt to minimize those costs.(6) However, the "firm" did not do a cost-benefit analysis in deciding how to organize itself. When the firm invented itself, the new institution was a quantum leap. And as the firm continues to evolve, the alterations are great. In the early part of this century, trusts were designed in order to eliminate the banker as the middleman (not to mention the competition). In great part, the modern transnational corporation is designed to minimize allegiance (and the associated taxes, tariffs, and other costs) to the nation state.

Coase's history of the British lighthouse system is a brilliant attack on those economists who--without research, effort, or careful thought--decided that the lighthouse was the paradigmatic public good. During the early nineteenth century, British lighthouses were undersupplied by the government, and private lighthouses were built to fill the void. As Coase suggests, charges were collected at the ports by agents for the lighthouses. Thus, enforcement in collections was no different for lighthouses than for other suppliers of goods and services to the owners of ships. This particular work also is a contribution by illustration; namely, Coase demonstrates just how detailed the study of an industry must be before economists have a complete understanding of it.

Conclusion

Suffice it to say that our original article (1992) was a critique of Coase Theorem I. If the real Coase is the one described by Medema, Ronald Coase too probably will agree that we are "largely on the mark." The confrontation of Coase Theorem I with the real world has led to Ptolemaic epicycles that now comprise the universe of the Coasians. The final epicycle, to repeat, is the negative externality the Coase Theorem has generated for economists, including (at least, according to Professor Medema) for Ronald Coase himself.

To the extent that Coase Theorem II relies upon marginal costs and marginal benefits, however, it suffers similar defects and possibly even higher-order negative externalities of its own. We stand by our view that externalities persist because the transactions costs in their removal are so high. Viewed narrowly through Coase Theorem II, nothing can be done in those cases. The "institutional Coase" or perhaps a revitalized Pigouvian welfare economics nonetheless could show us the way out of this cosmic disorder. Institutions often have to evolve or be redesigned in order to better serve human needs. As long as the Coasians search only under the lighthouse beam of Coase Theorem I, the broader institutional vision will remain hidden in the domain of darkness of the institutions of higher learning.

Notes

1. A somewhat later Coase (1974) begins in a similar fashion, inveighing against Pigou (1938) for using Sidgwick's lighthouse example as an instance of a positive externality in which marginal net product falls short of marginal social net product since services performed for third parties go uncompensated.

2. In the 1993 movie "Jurassic Park," a lawyer becomes a dinosaur's "free lunch," a scene that has left American audiences clamoring for more and attorneys demanding protection from such "hate crimes." And we think economists take themselves too seriously!

3. Although the original Coase (1960) cites many court cases, neither the original nor the later Coase of positive transactions costs consider legal fees. The absence of legal fees, of course, greatly reduces transactions costs and brings the later Coase closer to the earlier Coase.

4. In a purely analytical sense, Coase's attack on Pigouvian taxes is centered on their nonoptimal nature, and contrary to the claims to optimality of modern economists (see 1988, 179) . On this, Coase is on target. But, by what standard can he claim that his cost-benefit approach (Theorem II) is superior? He must regress into Paretian conditions.

If we were required to vote that there is only one Coase, we would vote for Coase Theorem I. In his later "Notes on the Problem of Social Cost," he upbraids Samuelson for not being able to rule out a "non-Pareto-optimal outcome" with regard to the contract curve. Counters Coase, ". . . there is good reason to suppose that the proportion of cases in which no agreement is reached will be small" (1988, 161). In rebutting Samuelson again regarding what kind of side payments would be required but not made willingly by his secretary in order to prevent Samuelson from becoming a plumber, Coase regards "such outcomes as being . . . most unlikely, particularly in a regime of zero transaction costs" (1988, 163). And, further, "most objections to the Coase Theorem seem to underestimate what costless transacting could accomplish" (1988, 163). And, in answer to a critic regarding the role of rent, "it becomes easy to show that, with zero transaction costs, the allocation of resources will remain the same whatever the legal position regarding liability for damage" (1988, 165).

When Coase (of Theorem II) does turn to positive transactions costs, he seems to be referring exclusively to those costs incurred by government in the provision of subsidies or the taking of taxes. Thus, he is continuing to attack the Pigouvians while ignoring those transactions costs that are private such as legal fees. If there are two theorems and one Coase, it is because Coase always ends up at the same destination. That is, Pigouvian taxes and subsidies are nonoptimal.

5. Elsewhere, Canterbery |1979a) has shown how the designation of "necessities" and "luxuries" in consumption necessarily infers a strong presumption of a diminishing marginal utility of income at a particular level of aggregation. Canterbery |1979b, 1980, 1981) also has explored the meaning of interdependent utility functions for individuals and for personal incomes. The implications of Rawls's principles of justice in redistribution from the rich to the poor also are explored within the context of such interdependencies |Canterbery 1981).

6. DeSerpa (1992) has formulated a mathematical proof for Coase Theorem I in its application to the "ranchers" and "farmers" dispute, but only was able to do so by introducing an "administrative function" of the Coasian firm (1937) into the production function (1960). DeSerpa does not address the objections we (1992) raised to Theorem I.

References

Canterbery, E. Ray. "Inflation, Necessities, and Distributive Efficiency." In Essays in Post-Keynesian Inflation, edited by James H. Gapinski and Charles E. Rockwood, 79-103. Cambridge, Mass.: Ballinger, 1979a.

-----. "A Vita Theory of Personal Income Distribution." Southern Economic Journal 46 (July 1979b): 12-48.

-----. "Welfare Economics and the Vita Theory." The Eastern Economic Journal 6 (January 1980): 1-20.

-----. "Income Redistribution and Rawlsian Justice." Journal of Economics and Business 33 (Spring/Summer 1981): 188-201.

Canterbery, E. Ray, and A. Marvasti. "The Coase Theorem as a Negative Externality." Journal of Economic Issues 4 (December 1992): 1179-1189.

Coase, Ronald H. "The Nature of the Firm." Economica, n.s. 4 (November 1937): 386-405.

-----. "The Problem of Social Choice." Journal of Law and Economics 3 (October 1960): 1-44.

-----. "The Lighthouse in Economics." Journal of Law and Economics 17 (October 1974): 357-376.

-----. The Firm, the Market, and the Law. Chicago: The University of Chicago Press, 1988.

-----. "The Institutional Structure of Production." American Economic Review 82 (September 1992): 713-119.

DeSerpa, Allan C. "The Pure Economics of the Coase Theorem." Eastern Economic Journal 18 (Summer 1992): 287-304.

Medema, Steven. "The Myth of Two Coases: What Coase Is Really Saying." The Journal of Economic Issues 4 (December 1993).

Pigou, Arthur C. Economics of Welfare. 4th ed. London: Macmillan, 1938.

* The authors are Professor of Economics, Florida State
University, Tallahassee, and Assistant Professor of Economics, University of Houston, Downtown, respectively.

Chapter 21

Input–output analysis

The production subsystem where virtually everything is produced is at the core of a truly viable economy. The flow of goods and services among the producing industries (inter-industry flows) is best captured by an input–output model. Since Nobel prize-winner Wassily Leontief (1941) first developed such a model, input–output analysis has been greatly expanded in many ways.

To place such a common-sense notion of what is important into 'radical' political economy seems at first strange. However, as the theory unfolds, it clearly does violate some wonderfully treasured views of what properly comprises economics. In the static or timeless input–output model, the relationship between inputs and output (the technical coefficients) is fixed. The cost of production of each unit of a product is thus set as if in concrete at all levels of output so that constant costs prevail, much as in classical economic theory. Unlike the presently fashionable neoclassical theory, marginal products (the extra output from an extra unit of input) do not decline as output rises.

A complete understanding of the *mathematics* of input-output modelling would require knowledge of matrix algebra, a daunting task for the uninitiated. My goal for the reader is less ambitious: I aim only to convey a feeling for the topic and its most important implications. For this, we need simply define a 'matrix' as a table comprised of rows and columns and a 'vector' as either one row or one column. A square matrix is one with an equal number of rows and columns. From these, all things flow.

The input–output table's *inner matrix* is comprised of the rows showing the flow of each industry's output to other industries and the columns showing the source of each industry's inputs from the same other industries. Coal flows to the steel industry and is received by the steel industry. It is a perfectly square picture of the inter-industry structure of the economy. The technical coefficients are calculated from these flows. A technical coefficient relating coal to steel, for example, would be the amount of coal needed to produce a ton of carbon steel. (In 1978, 0.95 tons of coal were required to produce a ton of US carbon steel. The technical coefficient was 0.95.)

There is a second way of viewing the inner matrix. It also comprises the ***intermediate output*** of the economy. These are outputs used strictly as inputs. It is the output–input aspect of input–output! If, for example, we consider the entire output of the lumber and woods products industry and subtract all its intermediate outputs (used by other industries in *their* production), the balance will be the lumber and woods products available to final consumers.

In a third perspective, the inner matrix (if in money value) includes all the outlays by industries for the materials used in production. The difference between total expenditures by these industries (the same as the value of total output) and the outlays for materials is equal to the industries' *value added* or income generated for the economy. This value added is the sum of wages, salaries, interest, rent and profits in the economy. In this way the value of national output will equal the value of national income. The national input-output table has been used as a periodic check on the reliability of national income accounts separately estimated.

Although the government data-crunchers construct the inner matrix in money or value terms (i.e., *PXQ*), some major theoretical breakthroughs are based upon models in which economists have sorted out the real (i.e., *Q*) values from the nominal values (the *P*s). The technical coefficients are in real or *Q* terms – tons of coal, iron ore, steel scrap or mbtus of energy. A square matrix of technical coefficients is called the *A* matrix, the list of ingredients required by the economy's technological recipes.

We can always reconstruct the inner matrix by multiplying the *A* matrix by a price or *P* vector. Once final demand is also expressed in quantities, that vector can be multiplied by the *P* vector to obtain the value of final demand, the same $C + I + G$ or aggregate expenditures of conventional Keynesian economics.

The value added (income generated) by each industry can be divided into its two major components: labour income and a residual, usually treated as 'profits'. Labour, like materials, can be expressed as technical coefficients. Continuing our earlier example, in 1978 the production of a ton of carbon steel required 8.14 manhours. This labour requirement multiplied by the wage rate for steelworkers ($11.66 per hour) and, in turn, by total carbon steel production gives us the total wage bill for the industry. If materials costs per ton and the wage bill per ton are subtracted from the price of carbon steel, we have the residual income or unit 'profits' ($29.92 per ton that year).

The reader is no doubt relieved to know that we have covered the basics. Only now does the devout technician experience enjoyment. The complete system can be solved in terms of various things, but especially quantities and prices.

The key to these and other solutions is found in the 'Leontief inverse'. The *Leontief inverse* gives not only the direct but also the indirect materials requirements for each industry. The technical coefficients included only the *direct* requirements for production such as the 0.95 tons of coal, the 1.65 tons of iron ore, the 0.10 tons of steel scrap and the 11 mbtus of energy per ton of carbon steel.

The *indirect* requirements include the tons of coal required to produce the 1.65 tons of iron ore in order to produce the ton of carbon steel, as well as the mbtus of energy to produce the 0.95 tons of coal to produce the ton of steel, and the amount of transportation to get the 0.10 tons of steel scrap to the carbon steel plant to produce the ton of steel, and so on. You can begin to understand what I mean by enjoyment.

Suppose we solve for prices. The income payments per unit of product that become price include not only the value added of those industries providing direct inputs, but also of those industries providing indirect inputs. Therefore, the prices which must prevail in the long period if each industry is to cover its costs of production will be based on directly and indirectly incurred costs of production and income payments. These prices, or the 'dual price solution' to the Leontief model of production, comprise the value added vector properly multiplied by the Leontief inverse.

What can be done for quantity and price requirements can also be done for labour requirements. The labour vector (comprised of the technical labour coefficients) can be multiplied by the omnipotent Leontief inverse to provide the hours of labour required, directly and indirectly, to produce a single unit of output for each and every industry. Moreover, we can give residual income or 'profits' the same treatment to find out the profits earned both directly and indirectly by each industry.

Can the intermediate output supplied by all industries constituting the production system be reduced to only one type of fundamental input? This central issue in value theory has divided economists from the beginning. Karl Marx, relying on a labour theory of value, believed labour to be the only source of value and thus he would multiply the Leontief inverse by the labour vector and be done with it. The neoclassicals come closer to the opposite: they would focus on the Leontief inverse times profits. The neoclassicals take the extra step of associating profits with the proper return on capital. Hence, the neoclassical theory is more a capital theory of value.

For now, let us consider the total value added required of the economy in terms of both labour value and profits. This problem was solved by Pasinetti (1981) in his vertically integrated model of production. Having derived the required hours of labour and amount of profit (both direct and indirect) per unit of production, Pasinetti multiplied these sets of values by the demand vector. Independently, Canterbery (1979, 1994) developed a similar model without sensing the vertically integrated nature of the production system.

The results are surprising. Since the direct material requirements are now reflected in larger values for the labour and profits coefficients, the inner matrix disappears. The industries producing intermediate goods also are no longer needed; this only leaves those industries that are producing for final consumption.

Of course, advanced economies actually do have vertically integrated industries. In the United States, cinema producers own both the distribution companies and the theatres in which films are shown. But the vertically integrated model of production is nonetheless hypothetical. Despite its fanciful nature, however, the model usefully shows the direct relationship between basic inputs such as labour and the net or final output of the economy. And, as we shall see, Canterbery's version serves other real world purposes as well.

Once the wage rate (unit labour cost) is known in the Pasinetti or Canterbery models, we only need to find 'profits' in order to derive the price solution. In this way the full cost of production necessary for replication or continuous expansion of the economy can be found. In this regard Sraffa (1960) has provided some wonderful insights.

Sraffa counters the neoclassical view in which the wage rate measures the marginal product of labour and the profit rate measures the marginal productivity of capital. As in Leontief, the ingredients in production in each industry are defined by technology. The total value added by the economy or national income is fixed. What is so for the nation is only so-so for any particular industry; its value added is not immutable.

The value added in the auto industry will vary as the wage rate and thus its wage bill (with those fixed technical coefficients) move relative to the profit rate. In turn, since price depends upon value added, the relative price of autos will change. (Technological improvements will also change prices.) In violation of all things held sacred by the neoclassicals, price changes alter the income distribution even as the income distribution alters prices!

Neoclassical prices allocate resources in an efficient way. Sraffian prices do not, but rather are the vehicle for redistributing income between workers and capitalists as wage rates move relative to profit rates. Since efficiency depends only on technology – not on relative prices – income is left free to be allocated by class struggle, administered wages and relative bargaining power. Also, total national output is above the fray and out of harm's way.

The printing of this book, for example, is accomplished with a computer, a printing press and a binder. The money values of capital, however, depend upon the price times quantity of all these capital goods (and others) combined. The printing press, the computer and the binder all sell at varying prices. These prices, or the 'rentals' for the services from these capital goods, in turn depend upon the distribution of income between workers and capitalists. Therefore, the value of capital (its price times its quantity) is not decided by capital's productivity after all.

Sraffa dealt value or price theory a damaging blow. By the neoclassicals' own devices, either the wage rate or the profit rate must be a 'given' that cannot be determined by the production system. If it is the wage rate that is set outside the system, then profits comprise a residual unrelated to the rate of return on capital.

Pasinetti's price solution to the vertically integrated economy highlights the dependency of prices on wages and profits. Canterbery (1979) presumes prices to be set by a percentage mark-up placed by each industry upon its wage bill, on its direct and indirect materials requirements, and on its direct and indirect profits from all industries. Canterbery makes no distinction between the mark-up and the profit margin. Later, Eichner (1987), who long before had a fully developed theory to explain mark-ups, employs Leontief, Pasinetti, Sraffa and Canterbery to build a dynamic or economic growth version of this genre. What enables the economy to grow are the introduction of investment in excess of what the economy requires simply for its reproduction, as well as the inclusion of business savings as part of industry profits. Eichner (1987, pp. 355–8) proves that we need make no distinction between the mark-up and the profit margin, even for a growing economy.

E. Ray Canterbery

References

Canterbery, E.R. (1979), 'The Mark-up, Growth and Inflation', Paper presented at the Eastern Economic Association Meetings.

Canterbery, E.R. (1994), 'A General Theory of International Trade and Domestic Employment Adjustments' in Khosrow Fatemi and Michael Landeck (eds), *International Trade: 1992 Regional and Global Management Issues*, London: Macmillan.

Eichner, A.S. (1987), *The Macrodynamics of Advanced Market Economies*, Armonk, N.Y.: M.E. Sharpe.

Leontief, W. (1941), *The Structure of the American Economy, 1919–1929*, Cambridge, MA: Harvard University Press.

Pasinetti, L.L. (1981), *Structural Change and Economic Growth*, London: Cambridge University Press.

Sraffa, P. (1960), *Production of Commodities by Means of Commodities*, Cambridge: Cambridge University Press.

Chapter 22

Cost Savings from Nuclear Regulatory Reform: An Econometric Model*

E. RAY CANTERBERY
Florida State University and Ben Johnson Associates, Inc.
Tallahassee, Florida

BEN JOHNSON
Ben Johnson Associates, Inc.
Tallahassee, Florida

DON READING
Ben Johnson Associates, Inc.
Boise, Idaho

I. Introduction

The nuclear-generated power touted in the 1950s as someday being "too cheap to meter" got dismissed in the 1980s as incapable of being both safe and cost effective. Today, less than 20 percent of American's electricity is nuclear-generated, no new plants are planned or on order, and some of the earliest units are scheduled for decommissioning within the next decade. Even so, interest in nuclear power has been revived by increasing energy demands, concerns about global warming, and the uncertainty surrounding oil resources in the Persian Gulf. As a long-term alternative to fossil fuels, atomic energy offers the important advantages of clean air and domestic availability of fuel. But these advantages will count for little unless and until the costs of nuclear power can be seen as reasonable.

Our premise is that the relevant costs are those of providing safe and environmentally clean electric energy. To the extent that increased costs have resulted from increasingly stringent regulations, they reflect the internalization of external costs. Indeed, the external costs of nuclear power (particularly safety and environmental protection) have been internalized to a greater degree than with most alternative fuel sources used by electric utilities. Nuclear construction costs are properly compared with those of alternative sources only after the latter are adjusted for environmental damage and endangerment, including, as examples, the costs of oil spills, of building double-hulled tankers, and of building off-shore offloading facilities. A shift to nuclear sources could reduce these costs whereas it would increase disposal costs for radioactive materials. We do not estimate any of these environmental costs in this article; each would be a major study in itself. We nonetheless contend that a better understanding of nuclear plant construction costs is pivotal to a balanced evaluation of the merits of uranium relative to other fuel choices.

*The authors thank an anonymous referee for several helpful suggestions that improved the final product.

Several regulatory reforms have been under consideration. At the federal level, the utilities are currently seeking to streamline and expedite the licensing process in an effort to abbreviate construction durations. Utilities are proposing pre-approved, standardized designs, pre-approved sites, one-stop licensing and legislative-style NRC hearings instead of adjudicatory proceedings. At the state level they propose the elimination of retroactive prudence reviews [11]. Our study provides insights into the effects of these proposals.

Despite the public clamor over nuclear power costs, the population of related articles in the economic literature is small. In a study by Mooz [5], nuclear construction costs are related to significant regional effects, scale economies and learning effects. Mooz also finds higher costs related to cooling towers in the plant's design. A follow-up study [6], with an expanded data base, confirmed learning effects but failed to find scale economies. Zimmerman [12] examines learning-by-doing effects both for the firm and the industry, with internal learning reducing costs at nearly twice the rate of external learning. He finds that construction costs rise in a one-to-one proportion to duration (construction start date to commercial operation date). Komanoff [3] and Cantor and Hewlett [1] respectively find reductions in overnight costs of 13 percent and 47 percent upon doubling plant size. Both studies nonetheless find scale economies are largely offset by a rise in duration associated with project size.

A U.S. Department of Energy (DOE) study [2] distinguishes resources costs and "time related" costs, attributing 75 percent of construction cost to increases in the former. Duration, however, adds to resources cost because it increases with (unmeasured) design changes as well as with safety and environmental retrofits required by regulations. DOE finds significantly higher costs for utilities using outside firms for design and engineering than for utilities performing these functions themselves. Thus, internal experience has a positive learning effect. Radlauer, Bauman, and Chapel [9] attribute a shift in construction costs from the pre-1972 era to the post 1971 era to an abrupt change in the regulatory environment.

Our model has several unique features. (1) The cost data are carefully adjusted to limit the number of remaining explanatory variables, increasing the degrees of freedom and minimizing multicollinearity. (2) Economies of scale for nuclear projects are correctly identified for the first time. (3) Learning effects are detected by an experience variable. (4) A duration variable is introduced to measure the effects of delay. Our findings comprise a bridge across the earlier findings [1; 2; 5; 6; 8; 12].

II. Theory

The real cost of nuclear power projects has greatly increased since the first plant became operational in 1957. Theory suggests three important contributors to this trend: increased regulatory requirements, changing market conditions, and lengthening construction durations.

Designed to ensure the reliability and safety of output, regulations since at least the 1960s have tended to be increasingly stringent. Their impact will differ among plants, depending on the efficiency with which each utility and architect/engineer deal with them. We nonetheless can expect that plants completed under later regulatory requirements will tend to cost more than those built earlier.[1] The consequent engineering features (e.g., a cooling tower requirement) may

1. Some analysts give the impression that NRC regulation is a new phenomenon born of the Three Mile Island accident. This is false; some regulations are as old as the industry. A realistic view of regulation should take into account the overall trend, not dwell on specific incidents.

account for a sizable part of the cost differences among nuclear power plant construction projects. However, the cost effects of NRC regulation should not be allowed to mask the effects of mismanagement or incompetence. If poor design or construction work require portions of the plant to be torn out and rebuilt, the resulting delays and increased costs may owe more to poor management than to the NRC. Therefore, project duration is an important cost variable. Unusually lengthy construction indeed may indicate a comparatively inefficient, ineffective, or incompetent project team. A short duration can imply that the team managing and building the plant is particularly effective. Presently, each U.S. plant is unique; however, intuition suggests that the experience variable would have higher values and construction duration would be significantly reduced if the industry were to repeatedly build one or two standard designs.

Demographics also play a role in nuclear plant costs. A small cost differential is attributable to climate, since very cold or wet weather can impede construction. Urban congestion can also add to plant costs, creating difficulties in the shipping of materials or forcing the imposition of additional safety requirements. Because it is often difficult to isolate the various contributors to these geographically related costs, a categorical variable is sometimes used, capturing the significance of all regional factors combined. A more sophisticated approach—the one we use—is an accounting of known wage and materials cost differentials. When adjusting the plant cost data for inflation (putting all plants into equivalent real terms), we also adjust for regional differences in cost of living and other costs of construction.

Learning based upon project design experience can lower costs. As a utility gains experience in the hiring and use of architect and engineering firms, it may gain a learning-by-doing effect in design efficiency. Construction efficiency is closely related both to design efficiency and to technological improvements shared by the entire power plant construction industry.

Economies of scale can also lower plant costs. Beyond some point, however, the scale economy diminishes as larger volumes come to require extra structural reinforcement, special materials, unusual construction techniques, or complex management or monitoring systems.

Finally, whereas there is a cost to regulatory standards, there also is a benefit. Output in terms of Mwe capacity is qualitatively improved by design enhancements (rising regulations). We assume, in the interests of simplicity, that regulations effect output in such a way that relative input shares remain constant along the expansion path (Hicksian neutrality). Paik and Shriver [8] find some evidence supporting Hicksian neutrality. The most general construction production function would be

$$q = G(R)F(L, K), \tag{1}$$

in which labor and capital are adjusted by a function of the regulatory requirements or $G(R)$. By the same token, the value of q embodies an environmentally cleaner and safer capacity. If other inputs such as materials are affected by regulation, we have

$$q = G(R)H(L, K, \mathbf{M}), \tag{2}$$

where $\mathbf{M}$ is a vector representing other inputs.

According to duality theory, we can be indifferent between estimation of the production or of the cost relationship. Either would provide full explanation of the structure of production. We select the cost function because it provides a more reliable estimate of the effects of exogenous forces and because regulation, learning-by-doing, and managerial inefficiency in the architectural engineering stages are directly related to construction inputs rather than to construction output.

The most general dual cost function (as related to equation(2)) is

$$C = J(q, N, R, \mathbf{P}, \mathbf{Z}), \tag{3}$$

where q is net reliable, safe electric generating capacity (Mwe), N is an index of learning-by-doing, R is a measure of regulation, $\mathbf{P}$ is a vector of input prices, and $\mathbf{Z}$ is a vector of special design choices.

Sometimes it is useful to "deflate" or "inflate" the dependent variable by known prices of inputs or other price differentials. Since nuclear construction projects are of long duration and are completed over different periods and with different variable price sets, an alternative version of equation (3) would be

$$L(\mathbf{X})^{-1}K(\mathbf{P})^{-1}C = J(q, N, R, \mathbf{Y}), \tag{4}$$

in which K is a function of the vector of input prices over time, L is a function of $\mathbf{X}$ which is a subset of $\mathbf{Z}$, and $\mathbf{Y}$ represents the residual subset of $\mathbf{Z}$. Then equation (4) can be simplified to

$$C^* = J(q, N, R, \mathbf{Y}), \tag{5}$$

where C^* is the adjusted cost variable.

From these equations, we estimate the parameters for two models. The initial choice for the cost equation is a multiplicative form in order to capture the interaction of variables and the expectation that cost increases due to duration and decreases due to size are nonlinear. Therefore, in Model A, ordinary least squares (OLS) is applied to

$$\ln C^* = B_0 + B_1 \ln R + B_2 \ln q + B_3 DUR + B_4 N, \tag{6}$$

where C^* is adjusted construction cost per kilowatt hour (details below), R is the number of total regulations up to the completion date of the last unit of a project, DUR is the number of months between construction start and commercial operation, and N is the number of previous nuclear projects owner-operated by the utility prior to the construction start date (the experience variable).

In Model B, OLS is applied to

$$\begin{aligned}\ln C^* = {} & C_0 + C_1 \ln R + C_2 \ln R(D_1) + C_3 \ln q + C_4 \ln q(D_2) \\ & + C_5 DUR + C_6 DUR(D_3) + C_7 N + C_8 N(D_4).\end{aligned} \tag{7}$$

This estimation allowed us to use the entire sample but distinguish values of the coefficients for two separate periods. The dummy variables (the Ds) were used to determine whether the slope coefficients differed between the two eras selected.

III. Data Issues in Nuclear Plant Comparisons

Our selection of a well-defined population avoids potentially thorny statistical problems. We include in the study all plants whose construction began after 1966 and was completed by 1987. Thus, the small number of projects built in the pre-1967 turnkey period are excluded; they were somewhat experimental in nature, and their costs were partially subsidized by manufacturers who were anxious to promote the new technology. These criteria provide a sample comprised of 53 projects.

By considering the total costs of each construction project, we avoided problems with inconsistent accounting treatments of the common costs of multiple units. By adjusting the cost data to reflect the amount of disallowances for imprudence as established by regulators, we ensured that the model would provide better estimates of the "reasonable" costs of all projects in the population.[2] We updated the Tennessee Valley Authority[3] data with more recent cost and schedule estimates obtained directly from the utilities.

Initially, the construction costs in each year are reported in current dollars of those years. Over time, of course, these are not the same dollars. The industry has developed the idea of "overnight" dollars as a method for expressing costs in terms of comparable dollars. Thus, the nominal outlays for each project, once estimated, must be inflated over time to express costs in today's like dollars ("overnight" dollars). This is done with the regional Handy-Whitman nuclear power plant construction cost index that measures cost of labor, material, and equipment.[4] The overnight costs (C^*) are

$$C^* = \sum_{\tau=s}^{f} (C_\tau / I_\tau), \tag{8}$$

where I_τ is the Handy-Whitman nuclear power plant construction index, s = start date of construction and f = finish date of construction. The index of construction (I_τ) provides a sequence of annual inflation rates where

$$I_t = \prod_{\tau=s+1}^{t} (1 + i_\tau), \tag{9}$$

for $t = s + 1, s + 2, \ldots, f$. The concept of overnight costs is a variation of present discounted value, differing in appearance only because time-f dollars comprise the numeraire rather than time-s dollars.

A meaningful comparison of project costs requires distribution of cash expenditures over the construction cycle for each period. To accomplish this task we applied an industry-standard S curve, a formula used by the Energy Information Administration [2, 89]. The pattern is established by

2. This adjustment of the data does not change the reliability of the parameter estimates. The estimated coefficients and significance levels are similar with or without adjustments for disallowances. This adjustment simply reduces the total costs of construction of projects with disallowances.

3. These data are from the TVA Office of Nuclear Power [10].

4. Individual cost components are weighted to reflect the relative share of each in the construction of a typical nuclear facility.

Marshall and Navarro [4] contend that the use of "overnight costs" contradicts accepted capital theory and such a measure biases the estimate of scale economies upward because "overnight costs" do not include inflation. This argument derives from their misdefinition of "overnight costs": such costs do include inflation. As to accepted capital theory, since rates of return for public utilities in the U.S. are regulated, such regulation encourages utilities to "overbuild" and not to minimize the cost of construction. Thus, accepted capital theory loses much of its relevance when applied to regulated public utilities. Moreover, commissions judging imprudence base the value of disallowances upon "overnight costs." The comparative estimates of what Marshall and Navarro call "true costs" are themselves seriously flawed since they separate first unit and subsequent unit costs, use a "trend" variable as the measure of regulation and fail to include "duration" as an independent variable.

Table I. Nuclear Power Plant Disallowances (000,000)

Plant	Disallowance	Plant	Disallowance
Byron 1	$101.5	River Bend	1,400.0
Callaway 1	440.0	San Onofre 2	344.6
Fermi 2	397.0	Shearon Harris	322.8
Hope Creek	489.2	Shoreham	1,395.0
Limerick 1	368.9	Vogtle 1	951.0
Nine Mile Point 2	1,803.0	Waterford 3	284.0
Palo Verde	60.0	Wolf Creek	257.3
Perry 1	628.0		

Sources: Commonwealth Edison, *Annual Report*, 1985; Illinois Power Company, Kansas City Power & Light Company, Louisiana Power & Light Company, Philadelphia Electric Service Company, Southern California Edison Company, Union Electric, *Annual Reports*, 1986; Gulf States Utilities, *Annual Report*, 1987; Michigan Public Service Commission, Final Order, Case U-7760; New York Public Service Commission, Opinion No. 86-24, Case 29124; Texas Public Utilities Commission, Final Order, Docket No. 7460; *Moody's Public Utility Manual*, 1987; *NARUC Bulletin*, January 6, 1986; *NASUCA Newsletter*, March 1988.

$$y_t = \{1 - [\cos(\pi/2)(x_t)]^{4.08198}\}^{3.24948} \tag{10}$$

where y_t = cumulative percent of total cost in year t and x_t = fraction of total elapsed construction time. The proportion or share spent during year t is $k_t = y_t - y_{t-1}$. In turn, these shares for each year are used to derive the annual costs in equation (8). With this normal pattern, total nominal project expenditures can be spread year by year over the entire construction period.[5]

Mooz [5] concluded that Northeastern region plants are the most expensive. Possible causes include a denser population, fewer suitable plant sites, and—most notably—higher construction wage rates. We adjusted the cost of all plants for differences in wage and material costs in each of the six Handy-Whitman regions.[6] By this means costs are pre-adjusted for input price differentials between regions (see equation (4)). This conversion of all plant costs to regionally equivalent overnight dollars permits use of the largest possible sample. The unique conversion ratio for each estimate is dependent primarily on the timing and duration (as well as the regional location) of each construction project.[7]

As the sample includes not only prudent projects, but also projects for which regulators have disallowed certain costs due to mismanagement and inefficiency, we adjusted the cost of imprudent plants by the value of known disallowances, thereby putting the projects on a common basis, as if all were constructed in a prudent manner. This adjustment is not perfect because regulators often lack sufficient evidence to quantify the excessive costs.[8] The plants and disallowances used appear in Table I.

5. Although widely used and accepted, the S pattern will not mirror the precise distribution of expenditures on any specific project; in some cases delays and other problems during the construction may make it a poor approximation indeed. Nevertheless, this drawback must be weighed against the advantages of consistent treatment of all plants in the sample. In any event, the actual monthly patterns of expenditure are not comprehensively available. Hence, an approximation of this sort is not only useful but also necessary.

6. This adjustment does not fully account for the cost savings one would expect in an uncongested area rather than a congested urban area. Nevertheless, it does neutralize many regional cost differences.

7. For consistency, the cost per kw figures for the comparison group excluded AFUDC, since governmental utilities typically do not accrue it (although they do incur financing costs) and there is variability in the AFUDC rates and accrual policies applicable to investor-owned utilities.

8. Regulators subjectively evaluate this phenomena based upon an evidentiary record consisting primarily of thousands of pages of qualitative evidence concerning the history of each individual project. Data limitations force us to draw

IV. Results

We reduced the set of explanatory variables to the smallest number that will adequately explain construction cost per kw of capacity. Prior to the regression analysis, costs were adjusted for substantial regional differences, disparate inflation rates at different times, and imprudent or unreasonable costs. The reduction in explanatory variables increases degrees of freedom and reduces multicollinearity. In particular, we no longer need region or inflation variables. These adjusted project costs appear in Table II.

We also tested several potential measures of the unique design characteristics of each project (e.g., the presence of cooling towers, the depth to bedrock, the type of reactor vessel). These were not consistently significant, probably because the cost of various design features varies with the method chosen by the architect/engineer. Our final equations thus include no design variables. We identified proxy variables for the remaining explanatory variables.

Descriptive statistics are reported in Table III. The final equation for the first test (Model A) is simple but powerful, containing four independent variables, all significant at the 0.0001 level. The regression results appear in Table IV for both models. We tested for heteroscedasticity, with negative results.[9] The signs and magnitude of all the coefficient estimates accord with our theoretical expectations. Regulatory requirements have a positive effect on construction cost, as the external impacts on safety and the environment have been internalized. Also, in a simulation from the model, cost per kw declines as project size increases, providing the textbook-like graph reflecting economies of scale (Figure 1). The experience variable shows large and favorable learning-curve effects. Construction duration also is significant. The greater the number of months between the construction start date and commercial operation of the final unit, the greater the cost per kw. This result fits our expectations: projects with long durations tend to have very high costs per kw.[10]

Radlauer, Bauman, and Chapel [9] have suggested that the structure of pre-1972 nuclear plant costs is different from that of post-1971 costs, attributing the differences to changes in the regulatory environment commencing with the Calvert Cliffs decision in 1972. While there are undoubtedly differences between the two regulatory environments, a properly specified regulatory variable should account for most increases in cost due to these changes. Hence, we considered it appropriate to use data from both periods.

Nevertheless, we used Model B to test for structural changes between the early (pre-1972) and late (post-1971) eras. In Model B we pooled the two sub-samples and used dummy variables to identify any changes in the slope coefficients between the two eras. In this model, D is a dummy variable having a value equal to unitary for the post-1971 era and zero for the pre-1972 era.[11] The results are reported in Table IV. Most of the nondummy coefficient estimates are significant at the 0.0001 level, a pattern consistent with that of Model A. The slope dummies are generally insignificant, suggestive of no structural differences between the two periods.

inferences about the cost of imprudent and inadequate management, rather than measure it directly for each plant in the sample.

9. The generalized least squares generated parameter estimates are not significantly different from those of OLS.

10. The additional cost per kw associated with an additional month of work is particularly important for projects with durations substantially longer than average. These also are the projects that have encountered the most problems. At the extreme, those projects that have encountered massive difficulties tend to have extremely long durations and tend to be the most costly of all, by a wide margin.

11. The complete effect of a particular explanatory variable in this specification is the sum of its regression coefficient and its post-1971 slope dummy coefficient.

Table II. Nuclear Power Plant Total Project Costs, Mixed and 1986 Overnight Dollars[a] (000,000)

Case	Project	Mixed Dollars	Overnight Dollars	Cost per KW
1	Beaver Valley 2	$2,921	$3,740	4,489
2	Browns Ferry 1,2,3	689	1,797	561
3	Braidwood 1,2	3,307	3,864	1,725
4	Brunswick 1,2	616	1,459	888
5	Byron Station 1,2	2,982	3,644	1,627
6	Calvert Cliffs 1,2	588	1,480	876
7	Callaway 1	1,613	2,093	1,820
8	Catawba 1,2	2,292	2,898	1,265
9	Clinton 1	3,350	3,978	4,187
10	Comanche Peak 1,2	6,620	7,096	3,085
11	Crystal River 3	326	796	965
12	Davis-Besse 1	507	1,161	1,281
13	Diablo Canyon 1,2	3,712	6,435	2,938
14	Farley 1,2	1,246	2,292	1,358
15	Fermi 2	2,820	4,084	3,586
16	Fort Calhoun	150	421	921
17	Grand Gulf 1	2,132	2,827	2,261
18	Harris 1	2,323	2,527	2,808
19	Hatch 1,2	798	1,768	1,126
20	Hope Creek 1	3,084	3,810	3,571
21	LaSalle 1,2	1,949	2,871	1,332
22	Limerick 1,2	4,073	4,705	2,230
23	McGuire 1,2	1,362	2,166	918
24	Millstone 3	2,649	3,607	3,137
25	Nine Mile Point 2	2,879	3,500	3,240
26	North Anna 1,2	974	1,952	1,045
27	Nuclear One 2	488	940	1,031
28	Oconee 1,2,3	374	1,041	391
29	Palo Verde 1,2,3	6,215	6,834	1,794
30	Palisades	114	337	418
31	Peach Bottom 2,3	737	2,086	979
32	Perry 1	2,926	3,593	2,982
33	Pilgrim 1	195	598	913
34	Prarie Island 1,2	349	929	876
35	Rancho Seco	282	772	841
36	River Bend 1	2,105	2,231	2,374
37	Salem 1,2	1,367	2,872	1,302
38	San Onofre 2,3	2,955	4,324	1,965
39	Seabrook 1	3,213	3,722	3,327
40	Sequoyah 1,2	1,317	2,476	1,078
41	Shoreham	2,252	2,994	3,701
42	St. Lucie 2	1,154	1,465	1,826
43	Summer	984	1,453	1,614
44	Surry 1,2	327	978	595
45	Susquehanna 1,2	2,789	4,064	1,935
46	Three Mile Island 1,2	839	2,015	1,205
47	Trojan	400	1,022	904
48	Turkey Point 3,4	174	512	396
49	Vogtle 1,2	5,269	6,081	2,665
50	WNP 2 (WPPSS 2)	2,471	3,656	3,323
51	Waterford 3	2,002	2,494	2,259
52	Wolf Creek 1	1,876	2,254	1,926
53	Zion 1,2	487	1,313	631

a. Net of imprudence—related disallowances.
Sources: [10; 2, Schedule 34].

Table III. Descriptive Statistics

Variable	Mean	Standard Deviation	Minimum	Maximum
Log of Cumulative Regulations	4.611	0.461	3.401	5.030
Log of Project Net Mwe	7.249	0.453	6.485	8.071
Project Duration	124.811	40.252	40.000	213.000
Utility Nuclear Experience	0.302	0.638	0.000	3.000

$n = 53$

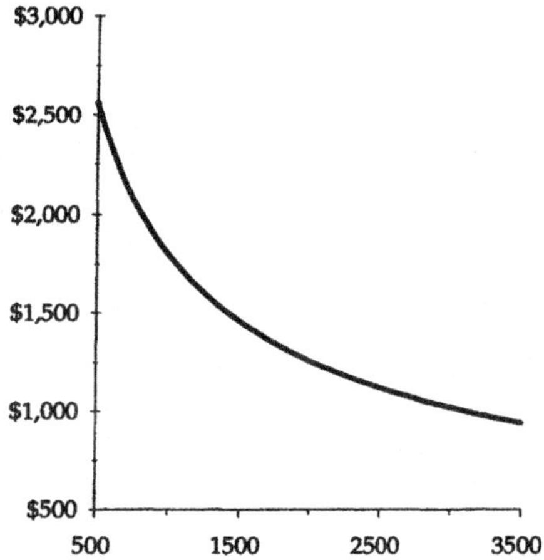

Figure 1. Economies of Scale: U.S. Nuclear Power Plants (installed cost per kW in 1986 dollars for nuclear power plants, shown in megawatts)

The predicted values from Model A are compared with actual values (in 1986 dollars) in Figure 2. As we see, only about five of the actual project costs stray far from their predicted values. Moreover, Model B should not be dismissed entirely. The insignificance of some of the variables results from multicollinearity, according to several standard statistical tests. Model B remains a good predictive model. Each time, when a single slope dummy was introduced into Model A, it was statistically significant at minimally the .1000 level.

V. Policy Simulations

We now return to nuclear policy reform proposals. If a standardized plant size and design were selected, economies of scale advantages close to a "reasonable optimum" could be gained. Then replication of standard designs would cause experience to accumulate quickly. Such homogeneity could speed the construction process greatly. Pre-approved sites, one-stop licensing, and standardized inspection procedures would also serve to reduce duration by simplifying and expediting the regulatory process. To estimate the probable effects of such policy reforms, we used Model A to simulate alternative costs per kw at different values for the independent variables. A policy

Table IV. Regression Results Dependent Variable: Log of Cost per KW

Independent Variables	Model A	Model B
Intercept	5.489150 (0.676939)[a] 0.0001[b]	6.171802 (1.049015) 0.0001
Log of Cumulative Regulations	1.111391 (0.097138) 0.0001	0.847764 (0.246081) 0.0001
Log of Project Net Mwe	−0.512734 (0.097138) 0.0001	−0.474663 (0.098971) 0.0001
Project Duration	0.003721 (0.001148) 0.0001	0.005040 (0.002248) 0.0001
Utility Nuclear Project Experience	−0.13427 (0.050057) 0.0001	−0.291892 (0.136477) 0.0150
Regulation Slope Dummy		0.085264 (0.216844) 0.6502
Size Slope Dummy		−0.029657 (0.137998) 0.5980
Duration Slope Dummy		−0.000109 (0.002424) 0.5100
Experience Slope Dummy		0.168144 (0.145461) 0.8670
n	53	53
R^2	0.893	0.903
F-Ratio	109.676275	68.652985

a. Standard error.
b. Significance level.

simulation matrix of the most plausible possibilities within and outside the sample is presented in Table V.

Across the top of the matrix the project size is varied between 800 and 2400 Mwe. The experience variable has been fixed, in turn, at 2 and 3 (within the sample) and then at 4 and 5 (outside the sample values). The value of the experience variable is assumed to increase with standardization because firms would be replicating the same prototype plant. The value of the cumulative regulations is set at its maximum of 153, which assumes no existing rule will be rescinded.

Project duration in our sample ranged from 40 to 213 months, averaging 125. Duration varies (along the vertical) from 60 to 150 in the policy simulation matrix. The larger the size of the project, the lower the costs on each line of the matrix. However, the costs per kw decline by

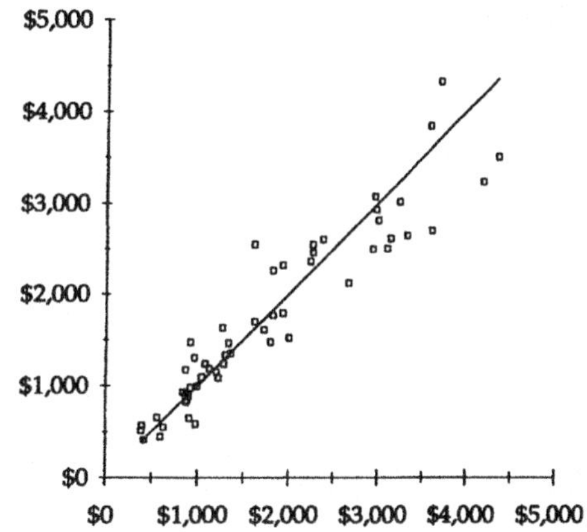

Figure 2. Nuclear Power Plants Project Costs: Actual vs. Predicted Values (installed costs per kW in 1986 dollars)

smaller and smaller percentages with each Mwe increase in scale. Moreover, these gains are achieved only if we assume a constant duration. In the real world, of course, duration is not constant. From the sample and from the findings of Komanoff [3] and Cantor and Hewlett [1] we know that duration sometimes increases with the project size. For example, returning to the policy matrix, a 2400-Mwe project completed in 60 months at sample maximal experience (3) costs $1002 per kw (1986 dollars); extended to 150 months it costs $1401 per kw. Often during the 1980s, the larger the project, the greater was the duration and the higher the costs.

Japan's experience suggests that duration need not be closely related to size, according to Navarro [7]. Exceeding the established 600–900 Mwe range raised construction time by only 10 months. Realistically, however, it seems unlikely that an extremely large plant size could be accepted as a standard by the industry, since it would exceed the needs of all but the most densely populated regions. If designs were standardized in the U.S., the optimally-sized project would probably be in the 800-Mwe to 1200-Mwe range. This would ensure usability by both small and large utilities and would allow more frequent repetition of the construction process.

The potential cost savings from more rapid construction is very significant. Duration for the 1979–86 period averaged 61.64 months in Japan versus 140.71 months in the U.S. [7,3-4). Since 1975, the Japanese utility industry has adopted a two-design program, with standardized reactors. In our policy matrix, a 1200-Mwe project would cost $1729 per kw if completed in 75 months by a utility with experience building two previous projects. Increasing the experience value to the sample-maximal value of three reduces the cost to $1512 per kw. If additional experience were gained beyond this historical maximum, the simulated cost would be reduced to $1322 and $1156 as successive projects were built, strongly suggesting the potential benefits of moving down the learning curve through replication. (The outside-of-sample extrapolations can be defended on the grounds of the near-linearity of cost and experience within the sample.)

If a policy of standardization were to achieve these changes in duration and experience, the effect on construction costs would be dramatic—allowing nuclear power to become a viable, low-cost alternative for new baseload electric generating capacity. Pre-approved sites, one-stop licensing, and standardized inspections could reduce costs even more.

Table V. Policy Simulation Matrix: Model A

	Project Size (Mwe)				
Project Duration (Months)	800	1200	1600	2000	2400
Experience = 2					
60	2013	1635	1411	1258	1146
75	2128	1729	1492	1330	1212
90	2250	1828	1577	1407	1281
105	2380	1933	1668	1488	1355
120	2516	2044	1764	1573	1433
135	2661	2161	1865	1663	1515
150	2813	2285	1972	1759	1602
Experience = 3					
60	1760	1430	1234	1100	1002
75	1861	1512	1304	1163	1059
90	1968	1598	1379	1230	1120
105	2081	1690	1458	1301	1185
120	2200	1787	1542	1375	1253
135	2326	1890	1631	1454	1325
150	2460	1998	1724	1538	1401
Experience = 4					
60	1539	1250	1079	962	876
75	1627	1322	1140	1017	926
90	1721	1398	1206	1076	980
105	1819	1478	1275	1137	1036
120	1924	1563	1348	1203	1095
135	2034	1652	1426	1272	1158
150	2151	1747	1508	1345	1225
Experience = 5					
60	1346	1093	943	841	766
75	1423	1156	997	889	810
90	1504	1222	1054	940	857
105	1591	1292	1115	994	906
120	1682	1366	1179	1052	958
135	1779	1445	1247	1112	1013
150	1881	1528	1318	1176	1071

VI. Conclusions

We use two models in order to estimate the reasonable cost per kw of capacity in the construction of nuclear projects as well as to identify the sources of these costs. The estimated models are statistically reliable and support theoretical expectations. For example, our results confirm that the cost per kw is less if the utility has already moved down the learning curve by building other nuclear plants during this era. Similarly, our results confirm the existence of economies of scale. As expected, the level of NRC regulation has contributed to the cost of nuclear projects.

Duration is critical. Higher costs per kw are associated with less efficient project management and with more complex, more costly designs. Our estimated costs depend heavily on the duration and level of experience assumed so that the policy simulation matrix adds to the case for regulatory reform—a need for pre-approved, standardized designs. Such designs would shorten construction durations and allow the industry to move more rapidly down the learning curve. Since economies of scale increase at a decreasing rate, the "reasonably optimal" size is not necessarily the largest possible; duration can be reduced and experience augmented by the selection of a standard "right-sized" project for regional requirements.

References

1. Cantor, Robin A. and James G. Hewlett. "The Economies of Nuclear Power: Further Evidence on Learning Economies of Scale and Cost Estimation." Unpublished manuscript, Oak Ridge National Laboratory, 1987.

2. Energy Information Administration. *An Analysis of Nuclear Power Plant Construction Costs.* Washington, D.C.: DOE/EIA-0485, 1985.

3. Komanoff, Charles. *Power Plant Cost Escalation.* New York: Van Nostrand Reinhold, 1981.

4. Marshall, John M. and Peter Navarro, "Costs of Nuclear Power Plant Construction: Theory and New Evidence." *RAND Journal of Economics,* Spring 1991, 148–54.

5. Mooz, William E. *Cost Analysis of Light Water Reactor Power Plants.* Washington, D.C.: R-2304-DOE (Rand Corporation), 1978.

6. ———. *A Second Cost Analysis of Light Water Reactor Power Plants.* Santa Monica, Calif.: R-2794-RC (Rand Corporation), 1979.

7. Navarro, Peter, "Comparative Energy Policy: The Economics of Nuclear Power in Japan and the United States." *The Energy Journal,* October 1988, 1–15.

8. Paik, Soon and William R. Shriver, "The Effect of Increased Regulation on Capital Costs and Manual Labor Requirements of Nuclear Power Plants." *The Engineering Economist,* Spring 1981, 223–44.

9. Radlauer, Marcy A., David S. Bauman, and Stephen W. Chapel, "Nuclear Construction Lead Times: Analysis of Past Trends and Outlook for the Future." *The Energy Journal,* January 1985, 45–62.

10. TVA Office of Nuclear Power. *U.S. Nuclear Plants Cost Per KW Report.* Washington: TVA, September 1987.

11. Yates, Marshall, "Nuclear Energy: A Failed Promise or a Promising Future?" *Public Utilities Fortnightly,* April 1, 1990, 12–13.

12. Zimmerman, Martin B., "Learning Effects and the Commercialization of New Energy Technologies." *Bell Journal of Economics,* Autumn 1982, 297–310.

Chapter 23

Cost Savings from Nuclear Regulatory Reform: Reply

I. Introduction

Since economics advances slowly, if at all, one econometric test at a time, the comment on our article [1] is especially welcome. Dismukes employs a data base that is similar to—or, at least, overlapping with—ours. Moreover, he clearly states what he has accomplished. The dramatic contrast in sample design and empirical testing enhances the comparison. Having said this, we reassert the utility of our approach and the reliability of our findings.

Dismukes levels two charges against our modeling: first, that we failed to recognize that "the construction cost data . . . has an unequal number of nuclear plants being constructed in an unequal number of years"; second, that we incorrectly used "construction costs on a 'per-project' rather than 'per-plant' basis." The claimed defects supposedly lead to two problems: irrelevance of the cumulative NRC regulations variable, since it is "perfectly correlated with time," and doubts concerning our finding of significant economies of scale.

Obviously, we know that the industry constructed an unequal number of nuclear plants in an unequal number of years. In turn, the non-linearity in the distribution of project completion dates in a cross-sectional data base minimizes the effect of any "collinearity with time" of cumulative Nuclear Regulatory Commission (NRC) regulations. Though substantial correlation exists between the log of cumulative regulations and time ($R^2 = .837$, not 1.00), the critical issues are (1) whether, in a cross-sectional data base, the log of regulations is highly correlated with commercial operation start dates, and (2) whether the model otherwise controls for time. Figure 1 is a scattergram of the log of cumulative regulations and commercial start dates from our sample. It shows that the two variables are quite distinct; they do not trace a smooth semi-log pattern. Furthermore, time enters our model as duration for each project; this controls econometrically for any residual effect of time. Finally, no significant multicollearity exists in our Model A.

II. Nuclear Projects, Cathedrals, and Time

As to economies of scale, Dismukes estimates a coefficient for *individual plants* of −.304964 compared with our estimates for *projects* of −0.512734 in Model A and −0.474663 in Model B. Using a model similar to Dismukes', but for coal-burning generation, Joskow and Rose [3], cited approvingly by Dismukes, also find quantitatively and statistically significant economies. That is, these authors find significant economies of scale despite loading the dice against them by separating projects into smaller units. Unsurprisingly, in Dismukes, the first plant is more costly by a value of 0.163435. As Dismukes suggests, ". . . multi-unit projects tend to 'front-load' a significant amount of common costs onto the first unit."

This disproportionate accounting practice, which is apparently Dismukes' rationale for using a "first plant" variable, is one reason why we prefer to study the cost of entire projects. Each utility project involves a collection of common attributes that cannot be arbitrarily severed at the

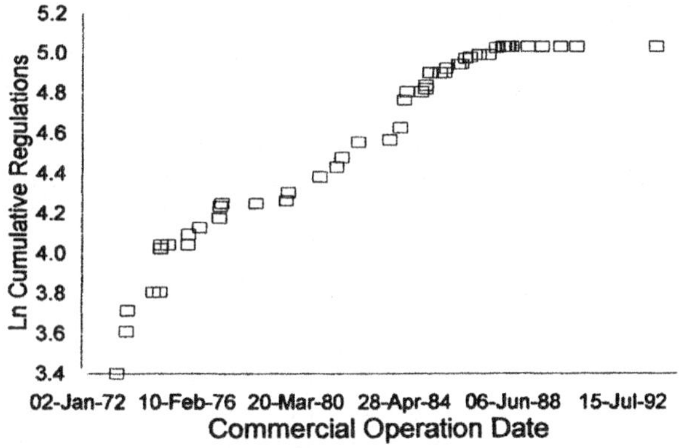

Figure 1.

first unit level. Management, site location, design, transmission lines, and substations tend to be common to the entire project. The utilities incur architectural, land acquisition, and planning costs for the entire project even before they begin the first unit. Moreover, as Dismukes suggests, ". . . current ratemaking practices do not allow utilities to recover capital expenditures until a plant has been placed into service." Management thus has incentive to "front-load" costs onto the first unit to achieve faster cost recovery. Dismukes' approach fails to distinguish between differences in the actual cost of first units and differences in accounting practices regarding first units (relative to subsequent units). More importantly, the division of a collection of overall project attributes into two or three individual "plants" arbitrarily diminishes the site's overall scale of output by 50 to 67 percent (for multi-unit projects with equal-sized units). We continue to favor the per-project approach to estimating costs and economies of scale.

Similarities, including massiveness and wall thickness, exist between modern nuclear power plant construction and the building of the great cathedrals and castles of the Middle Ages. For example, William of Sens, a brilliant French architect, was brought in to direct the extensive reconstruction of the Canterbury Cathedral in 1174. In 1179 William laid the foundation for the enlargement of the church to build a chapel (a second unit) for St. Thomas à Becket. The new foundation extended into the monks' cemetery, requiring careful exhumations and reburials (environmental reparations). In 1180 William directed the construction of the wall that encloses the choir and presbytery (third unit). He was forced to narrow the far end of the choir because of the placement of the existing towers (design error), whose massiveness precluded moving them (retrofitting).[1]

The reconstruction at Canterbury required about seven years (the average project duration in our nuclear sample was about ten years). In an accounting of the costs of construction, it would make little economic sense to use a dummy variable for the central nave costs (first unit) and then exclude the choir and the chapel in evaluating the overall scale of the project, since all areas were and are used for the production of religious services. Similarly, we would not doubt that

1. The details regarding the reconstruction of Canterbury Cathedral are taken from an observer's account, Gervase of Canterbury, in *The Medieval Reader* [2, 171–76].

duration contributed to the costs of construction (clerics meddled with the plans while William, the architect, continued to collect his handsome stipend).

Our duration variable captures the legitimate role of time (the intervals between project construction start dates and commercial operation dates). Duration adds to resources cost because it increases with inefficient project management and more complex (and changing) designs, plus safety and environmental retrofits. However, our study demonstrates that duration, as important as it is, does not explain as much as do cumulative regulations, once we have adjusted for regional differences. Our estimated cost elasticity of regulation is greater than unitary. When Zimmerman [4] earlier found construction costs rising in a one-to-one relation to duration, in part he was capturing the cumulative effect of regulation (which he did not consider separately).

All of which brings us back to Dismukes and time. In Dismukes' model, the most important independent variable is plant completion date. But unless nuclear plants have distinctive horoscopes, why should birth dates be so important—particularly since costs over time have already been normalized into overnight dollars? True, as Dismukes suggests, the final costs of plants completed in 1993 were 2.5 times those completed in 1968. Even so, knowing that units would have been cheaper if each had been completed in 1968 is less useful than knowing the causes of cost escalation. At the risk of being unfair to astrology, we submit that the greater part of those ascending costs can be laid to rising regulatory standards and increasing duration (associated with managerial inefficiency, design error, and required retrofitting). Although NRC regulations continue to accumulate, the pace has slowed considerably (as reflected in Figure 1). Assuming NRC regulations remain relatively stable over the next several decades, we would not expect a nuclear plant begun in 2010 and completed in 2018 to be 2.5 times as costly (in constant dollars) as a similar plant completed in 1993. Yet, that is the implication of Dismukes' approach, with its emphasis on the passage of time as the primary explanation of nuclear plant costs.

III. Conclusions

For a researcher or policy-maker interested only in quantifying the accounting practice of front-loading utility construction costs, Dismukes' model may be the proper tool. However, the modeling of construction costs with time as an "explanatory" variable seems to be a step backward econometrically. The passage of time does not cause anything; even rusting or aging is caused by oxidization or free radicals.

With Dismukes' model, nuclear construction costs per plant seem destined to rise through infinity regardless of how the industry, or regulators, respond. Our model suggests that perhaps costs can be controlled—if experience is enhanced, construction duration shortened, regulation stabilized, and optimal scale achieved. As our policy simulation matrix shows, regulatory reform to encourage pre-approved, standardized, and smaller designs could move the industry more rapidly down the learning curve. As we said, the "reasonably optimal" size is not necessarily the largest possible; utilities can reduce duration and augment experience by the selection of a standard "right-sized" project for regional needs. As we also said, the net benefits of future nuclear projects should be compared with alternative energy sources, including environmental costs and benefits.

E. Ray Canterbery
Florida State University
Tallahassee, Florida

Ben Johnson
Ben Johnson Associates, Inc.
Tallahassee, Florida

Don Reading
Ben Johnson Associates, Inc.
Boise, Idaho

References

1. Canterbery, E. Ray, Ben Johnson, and Don Reading. "Cost Savings from Nuclear Regulatory Reform: An Econometric Model." *Southern Economic Journal,* January 1996, 554–66.

2. Cantor, Norman F., editor. *The Medieval Reader.* New York: HarperCollins, 1994.

3. Joskow, Paul L. and Nancy L. Rose, "The Effects of Technological Change, Experience, and Environmental Regulation on the Construction Cost of Coal-Burning Generating Units." *Rand Journal of Economics,* Spring 1985, 1–27.

4. Zimmerman, Martin B., "Learning Effects and the Commercialization of New Energy Technologies: The Case of Nuclear Power." *Bell Journal of Economics,* Autumn 1982, 297–310.

Chapter 24

9

THE THEORY OF THE LEISURE CLASS AND THE THEORY OF DEMAND

E. Ray Canterbery

INTRODUCTION

Mainstream economists are of several minds regarding Veblen's *The Theory of the Leisure Class*. Few, however, would hesitate in mentioning Veblen's contribution of such evocative terms as "conspicuous consumption," "conspicuous emulation," "pecuniary culture," "vicarious consumption," and "the leisure class" to the language of economics. Though little noted, and not yet celebrated, important improvements in demand theory have emanated from *The Theory of the Leisure Class* (hereafter *TLC*). Since the enduring Veblenian contributions to our language are related to consumption, it is hardly surprising that even the mainstream has ratified Veblen with "Veblen effects."

Several of the author's phrases have resurfaced in *Bartlett's Familiar Quotations*, greatly elevating their stature. Three lengthy Veblen quotations made the 1980 edition, all from *TLC*. Notable for the task at hand, all the quotations are relevant to demand theory at both the micro and macro levels. Their worthiness bears reprinting: the first, "Conspicuous consumption of valuable goods is a means of reputability to the gentleman of leisure." The second, slightly longer, is "With the exception of the instinct of self-preservation, the propensity for emulation is probably the strongest and most alert and persistent of the economic motives proper." *Bartlett's* devotes even greater space to the third citation.

> The requirement of conspicuous wastefulness is not commonly present, consciously, in our canons of taste, but it is none the less present as a constraining norm selectively shaping and sustaining our sense of what is beautiful, and guiding our discrimination with respect to what may legitimately be approved as beautiful and what may not.[1]

In turn, I will quote much more from Veblen, phrases and ideas equally worthy of *Bartlett's*. In addition to the exquisite styling, these quotations are remarkable, too, for the phrases Veblen bequeathed to the English language. Hereafter, I will show how they have instructed mainstream economics and economics against the stream, to use Myrdal's facile expression. Now is a propitious time to restore Veblen's rightful place in the pantheon of economics. Many have forgotten his place, in his own time, at the top of his profession. In great part, Veblen endured because he illuminated modern society, a society still very much intact, with evolutionary electricity. "What is, is wrong." By applying the law of natural selection to human institutions, broadly defined to include ideas and habits of thought, he found human institutions lagging behind material change, always somehow being out of date. Habits of thought are always conservative, including those habits of thought, as Veblen often claimed, in the institutions of higher learning. Still, if we look closely, we can find Veblenian remnants in today's mainstream. We first will walk through the mainstream and, then, seek alternative vistas.

VEBLENIAN DEMAND THEORY ENTERS THE MAINSTREAM

Veblen entered the mainstream in a classic article by Harvey Leibenstein on "bandwagon, snob, and Veblen effects."[2] Leibenstein distinguishes between *functional demand* or demand for a commodity due to the qualities inherent in the commodity and *nonfunctional demand* or the portion of demand due to qualities external to it. In nonfunctional demand the utility derived from the commodity is enhanced or decreased because others are purchasing and consuming the same commodity or because the commodity bears a higher rather than a lower price tag.

The bandwagon, snob, and Veblen effects are due to *external* effects on utility. The *bandwagon effect* derives from the demand for a commodity increasing because others, too, are consuming the same commodity. *Social taboos* that effect consumption are bandwagon effects in reverse. When the wagon leaves the station, those practicing a social tabu forbidding that particular good will refuse to get on the wagon. The *snob effect* derives from the demand for a commodity decreasing because others are also consuming or increasing their consumption of the same commodity. The snob effect has an opposite but otherwise symmetrical relationship to the bandwagon effect. The snob jumps off the wagon because they do not want to associate with those jumping on. The "Veblen effect" refers to conspicuous consumption in which the demand for a consumer's good is increased because it bears a higher rather than a lower price. Since Leibenstein's operative term *is* price, he is never far from mainstream neoclassical demand theory.

Leibenstein advances the principle of diminishing marginal external consumption effect. The principle suggests that beyond a point, incremental increases in the demand for a commodity by others will have a decreasing influence on a consumer's own demand and, eventually, a zero influence. Not only do incremental increases in total demand become smaller and smaller shares of a larger and larger market demand but there are no cases in which an individual's demand for a good is infinite. Moreover, the income constraint guarantees that a consumer's demand increases eventually will cease. Taking all these influences into proper account, the most plausible demand curve is shaped like a backward S in which the schedule is upward sloping against price in some range, a range exhibiting the "Veblen effect." At some higher price for the good, the budget constraint would preclude further amounts being demanded; at some low price, the good's reason for conspicuousness disappears. From these behaviors emanate the backward S. The backward S, of course, would not apply to all commodities.

Leibenstein gives Veblen too little credit. Veblenian demand clearly includes the bandwagon and snob effects. Besides, Leibenstein defines what he identifies as *the* "Veblen effect" too narrowly. Veblen considered pecuniary emulation to be an individual's strongest motive; in this, Veblen gave everyone sufficient reason to jump on whatever bandwagon passed their doors. To Veblen the *standard of living* shared by a particular class determined the "accepted standard of expenditure." That is, contrary to Leibenstein, price is not necessarily a yardstick in demand. As Veblen put it,

> It does this directly by commending itself to his common sense as right and good, through his habitually contemplating it and assimilating the scheme of life in which it belongs; but it does so also indirectly through popular insistence on conformity to the accepted scale of expenditure as a matter of propriety, under pain of disesteem and ostracism. To accept and practise the standard of living which is in vogue is both agreeable and expedient, commonly to the point of being indispensable to personal comfort and to success in life. The standard of living of any class, so far as concerns the element of conspicuous waste, is commonly as high as the earning capacity of the class will permit – with a constant tendency to go higher. (pp. 111–112)

Not only are bandwagon effects Veblenian, the person's status within a social class commands them to consume whatever other referential persons in the class are consuming.

Moreover, Veblen rides the bandwagon much farther. Emulation dominates Veblen's Chapter VII on "Dress as an Expression of the Pecuniary Culture," where he writes that "admitted expenditure for display is more universally practised in the matter of dress than in any other line of consumption"

(p. 167). We can imagine hundreds of thousands of women jumping on the shoe-store wagon, as Veblen writes, "the woman's shoe adds the so-called French heel to the evidence of enforced leisure afforded by its polish; because this high heel obviously makes any, even the simplest and most necessary manual work extremely difficult" (p. 171). Of course, much more complex and subtle sociology is at work in *TLC*, including the woman's service as a "chief ornament" around the house and an adequately-adorned "trophy" for her husband. Women comprise an abused class in *TLC*.

Emulation, too, can explain why persons buy high-priced goods that otherwise might fail to be identified as those preferred by a higher social class. What Leibenstein calls the "Veblen effect" is only one element in the complex matrix of emulation. For a large set of reasons, persons buy more of some goods *despite, not because* their prices are higher. In Veblen, the excessive expense of such goods comes from the cost of production side. As he writes, "there are to-day no goods supplied in any trade which do not contain the honorific element in greater or less degree" (p. 157). "Honorific" refers to the amount of cost in excess of what goes to give goods serviceability for their ostensible mechanical purpose. The "proper honorific finish" is more important than price.

When it comes to emulation, the rich are more likely to take note of the higher prices of luxury goods than the middle-class emulator seeking status at any cost. In Veblen's perspective, too, "function" is in the eye of the beholder; a good that confers status serves a higher social purpose. Still, in Leibenstein's and his followers' interpretation, persons increase their demands for status goods *only* because they have higher prices. In this way Leibenstein set the standard for most of the recent mainstream contributions on prestige or status goods. It remains characteristically neoclassical to value goods solely in money prices.

The Leibenstein perspective is unduly limited in other respects. The preference for higher-priced "luxuries" rules out bargain hunters who desire to consume conspicuously as well as the upper middle class or even middle middle class who want to emulate the rich leisure class but must do so by buying cheap imitations or by borrowing, even at the risk of bankruptcy or worse, which might be called the "Gatsby effect." The Gatsby effect, of course, intimates disasters beyond bankruptcy from which recovery *is* possible.

A Gatsby effect barely pushes the Veblenian envelope. Fitzgerald's *The Great Gatsby* is the supreme Veblenian parable of conspicuous consumption, of conspicuous emulation, of pecuniary culture, and of vicarious consumption – even of waste and the leisure class itself. Jay Gatsby wanted to live with Daisy because she was a member of the *established* American aristocracy of wealth. Gatsby lacks the maturity to realize that Daisy cannot be obtained by money alone. Therefore, Gatsby flaunts, in a vulgar version of conspicuous consumption, his nouveau wealth. Despite Daisy's infinite price, Gatsby is most attracted to Daisy's voice (not the supra-price), which he describes as "full of money," because that is the most unrealistic thing about her. Then, too, Daisy is attracted to Gatsby because he reminds her of "an advertisement," the superficial illusion he represents. In the end, of course, Daisy cannot leave the trappings of the old aristocracy and Gatsby cannot escape the greatest Gatsby effect of all – paying the final price, with his life. As in Veblen's *TLC*, the cultural illusions are more important than wealth or money for Fitzgerald's central characters.

Leibenstein also apparently missed Veblen's extensive discussions of the roles of tabus in consumption. Veblen's discussions not only add cultural richness to the subject but make Leibenstein's use of a negative price range problematical. Ceremonial consumption such as "choice articles of food, and frequently also of rare articles of adornment, becomes tabu to the women and children; and if there is a base (servile) class of men, the tabu holds also for them" (p. 69). Under the tabu certain intoxicating beverages and narcotics are reserved for the use of men. Only since the 1960s has the consumption of liquor, cigarettes, cigars, and narcotics become acceptable for women in the United States, all of which remains tabu in the Arab world except for royalty.

Such tabus separate one class from another, members of the "superior class" identifying themselves not only by what they consume but by their power to prevent the consumption of the same items by others. The tabu is the fail-safe way of preventing emulation of the upper classes by the lower classes. As long as the tabu remains culturally intact, even a negative price thought to be the price necessary to pay individuals to induce them to disregard their aversion, contrary to Leibenstein's analysis, will fail to generate consumption by the "lower class." Besides, who or what institution would pay others to consume forbidden goods?

As to snobbery, Fitzgerald's Gatsby again provides instruction. Tom and Daisy Buchanan live in a Georgian Colonial mansion representing established wealth. Gatsby, not unlike the early Robber Barons, owns a pretentious, vulgar imitation of a European mansion, adorned even in brand-new ivy. Even Gatsby's ivy is not in the same league as the Buchanans'. It is clear to the establishment that Gatsby, having no sense of tradition, simply copies the style of others, much as an American university erects a library based upon a medieval Gothic chapel. Worse, Gatsby's sartorial choice is as vulgar and nouveau as his car, his mansion, and his lavish parties. Daisy could never leave Tom for Gatsby because she and Tom are partners in a "secret society" of wealth, one that Gatsby cannot enter because he does not know it. Neither this cultural richness nor the culture of the rich can be entirely captured with Leibenstein's downward shifting demand curves of individual "snobs," reducing their demands for a good because too many others are buying it.

Fitzgerald and tabus, oddly enough, bring us full circle from the *Quarterly Journal of Economics* to the *American Economic Review*. For decades, or so it seems, the *AER* has engaged in reverse emulation, even perhaps snobbery. By their rarity, references to Veblen's work appear to have long been held tabu even to the *AER*, no doubt elevating its presumed professional status. In at least one recent instance, however, the tabu has been lifted, the snobbery surrendered.

VEBLEN REENTERS THE MAINSTREAM

The mainstream has recognized some of the deficiencies in Leibenstein's theory. In particular, Bagwell and Bernheim have attempted to deal with the Veblenian cases that Leibenstein excludes. "In a theory of conspicuous consumption that is faithful to Veblen's analysis," they write, "utility should be defined over consumption and status, rather than over consumption and prices." This does not make high price irrelevant, however, "the prices that one pays for goods may affect status *in equilibrium*."[3] Since individuals like Jay Gatsby consume conspicuously to advertise their wealth, any relation between price and status should signal wealth. Otherwise, "invidious comparison" and "pecuniary emulation" cannot happen, terms insinuating a rank-order in the distribution of wealth. The upper class invites invidious comparison with the lower class whereas the lower class "emulates" the upper class. The upper class, of course, hopes that its costs are sufficiently prohibitive to the lower class that emulation is discouraged, especially by the nouveau riche class. Bagwell and Bernheim use game theory to explain the consequences of these upper-class and lower-class interdependences.

Three findings from Bagwell and Bernheim are persuasive. First, they show that some individuals might prefer to purchase a larger *quantity* of conspicuous goods at a lower price, or a higher *quality* of conspicuous goods at a higher price. For instance, social climbers do not have to be rich to buy Ralph Lauren's Polo brand clothes; yet, the label signals exclusivity. Moreover, if luxury brand "knock-offs" such as fake Rolex watches, Polo shirts, and King Cobra golf clubs cannot be distinguished from the "real things," the thrifty rich can have it both ways by buying the cheaper fakes. Veblen, who often strolled golf courses looking for golf balls, none the less would expect the King Cobra "knock-offs" to have the proper workmanship and polish.

Second, Bagwell and Bernheim rebut the "single-crossing property" of models with asymmetric information.[4] If we define the benefit ratio as the ratio of the utility gains from another unit of a conspicuous good, to the utility losses from another dollar of conspicuous expenditure, the benefit ratio is always higher for the upper-class households under the single-crossing property. (The indifference curves depicting substitutability between inconspicuous and conspicuous goods are, contrary to neoclassical theory, concave rather than convex to the origin. The "single crossing" occurs where the higher-income individual's indifference curve crosses the lower-income individual's indifference curve from below, reflecting the possibilities for cheap emulation.) Contrary to the single-crossing property, Bagwell and Bernheim show that the upper-class households can increase their utilities, without causing imitation, by purchasing more of the conspicuous good at a lower price.

Third, they show that households' conspicuous consumption need not be affected by bankruptcy *if* the conspicuous good cannot be repossessed (normally, such is the case for a house, even if it is ostentatious). There is a catch, a kind of "Catch 11": If the lower class imitates the upper-class households by matching their every luxury goods purchase, they would default on their loans, foreclosing imitation and foregoing the property protected under Chapter 11. Such an ultimate, even irrational, economic loss – the failure to retain what was pursued as well as the means of pursuit – none the less does not exclude what I have called the Gatsby effect, wherein bankruptcy is its mildest manifestation. As it turned out, Gatsby could not preserve the Daisy he pursued nor the means of pursuit, himself.

Bagwell and Bernheim are faithful to Veblen in still another way. The successful application of game theory to Veblen effects can be done only in a social setting. Neoclassical demand theory always has dismissed interdependent utility functions as either nonexistent or an unnecessary distraction.[5] Game theory cannot: in the case at hand, the upper and lower classes at the least must be aware of each other. People, not commodities, play games, games often involving subtle social nuances signaling superiority. In this sense, the Bagwell-Bernheim approach is truly Veblenian. Whereas houses, automobiles, jewelry, and clothing are often seen by many other individuals through social interaction, and are signets of resource dissipation, the Bagwell-Bernheim model is indeterminant regarding *which* durable, conspicuous goods households will choose. Veblen would have seen indeterminancy as a strength of their results.

Again, the still, cultural waters of Veblen run much deeper. Bagwell and Bernheim's use of game theory becomes an apt metaphor when we reconsider Fitzgerald's parable. Daisy's insincerity betrays her desire to play games with her husband, Gatsby, and others, rather than participate in life where she would be responsible for her actions. Empty gestures signal more to her than genuine emotions. At the center of the American dream as well as Gatsby's own is the belief that sufficient wealth can recapture and fix everything, even the ephemeral, illusory qualities of youth and beauty. Veblen, too, was writing about the great American chimeras.

In any case, though Bagwell and Bernheim do not explore price elasticities, Leibenstein suggests important implications for the price elasticity of demand as well as the nonadditivity of individual into collective demand curves. For the moment, we set aside the issue of how many of these things he describes are truly Veblen effects. If the bandwagon effect dominates, the demand curve is more elastic since reactions to price changes are followed by other reactions, in the same direction. If the snob effect dominates, the demand curve is less elastic since increases in total amounts consumed because of price reductions are countered by some snobs leaving the market. If Leibenstein's "Veblen effect" dominates, the demand curve is less elastic than otherwise, and in part may be positively sloping, making stable equilibrium improbable.

The more important implication – one that pervades Veblen, but eludes Leibenstein – is the critical role of household incomes or the ability to sustain a particular standard of living. If snob effects and conspicuous consumption are truly important, income elasticity overwhelms price effects and price becomes unimportant except as it effects relative real incomes. Moreover, the only constraints keeping persons off the wagon are income and social tabus. If price becomes sufficiently unimportant, the need for price theory (and neoclassical markets) evaporates. This conclusion was not lost on the neoclassicals during the early twentieth century in their pursuit of hegemony or, later, in their snubbing of Leibenstein, though he was closer to the mainstream than was Veblen.

AN ECONOMETRIC ESTIMATE OF "VEBLEN EFFECTS"

Going mainstream these days usually implies econometrics. Econometric tests claiming to estimate "Veblen effects," however, are sufficiently rare to be an endangered species. A small but substantial effort was made by Basmann, Molina, and Slottje.[6] They employ Veblen's distinction between primary consumption and secondary consumption. Rather than functional and nonfunctional qualities of commodities, however, Basmann *et al.* define consumption effects in utility language. ***Primary utility*** comes from the direct enhancement of life and well-being on the whole through consumption. ***Secondary utility*** comes from consumption that displays consumers' relative ability to pay, a form of consumption they ascribe to "Veblen effects."

Primary utility is measured from own-use price elasticities. Secondary utility is related to total expenditures, a proxy for real income. Since ability to pay, they say, and I concur, drives Veblen effects, such effects prevail over all social classes from the richest to the poorest. Otherwise, Veblenian emulation is not possible. Capturing both effects, according to Basmann *et al.*, requires the use of a Fechner-Thurstone direct utility function. Using this function, the authors can estimate both kinds of elasticities. A relatively large and statistically significant elasticity for durables with respect to total expenditures is found. The lowest elasticity with respect to total expenditures is for medical services. The results, they say, are consistent with Veblen effects since durables are the most visible items consumed and medical services the least visible.

Inherent in such tests is the problem with the estimated price elasticities of necessities that are necessarily low. The greatest medical expenditures usually happen during the final three to six months of life. Since the rich cannot escape mortality, no matter how much they spend on medical services, even *their* expenditures are price inelastic. As categories, we would expect, even without the benefit of econometric tests, that food and medical services would have lower price elasticities than durables (whose expected lives greatly exceed six months).

Moreover, the high level of aggregation (food, clothing, housing, durables, and medical care) makes these findings less than definitive. For the rich, surely the ownership of estate homes out of the broader category of "housing" is a form of ostentatious consumption. For the middle class, clothing with displayed brand-name labels, not "clothing" per se, is a frequently observed form of visible emulation. Many rich persons advertise their passage to grand, expensive resorts that monitor their health and try to improve it. Moreover, the middle class can advertise their ability to pay by dining, however infrequently, in fine restaurants. Still, the econometric effort was made and the results were published in another leading mainstream journal.

Veblen does write, "goods are produced and consumed as a means to the fuller unfolding of human life; and their utility consists, in the first instance, in their efficiency as means to this end." He adds, "the end is, in the first instance, the fulness of life of the individual, taken in absolute terms." What Veblen calls "secondary utility" is based on emulation which "seized upon the consumption of goods as a means to an invidious comparison, and has thereby invested consumable goods with a secondary utility as evidence of relative ability to pay." The "evidence" of ability to pay, however, is not the same as the *actual* ability to pay. Moreover, he uses the Basmann *et al.* phrase, for "this indirect or secondary use of consumable goods lends an honorific character to consumption, and presently also to the goods which best serve this emulative end of consumption" (p. 154). In what immediately follows, Veblen goes on to discuss the attendant waste or "superfluous expensiveness" in great Veblenian style.

Since so few efforts of this genre have been made, it is judged gallant. The same Bureau of Labor Statistics, however, has tapes with much more detailed consumption data. For instance, the complete data separates meals outside the home from those consumed at home. The consumption data, too, can be separated by income strata so that estimates of price elasticities may differ by income class.

JOHN KENNETH GALBRAITH: VEBLEN AGAINST THE STREAM

Most economists would agree that Veblen's logical successor is John Kenneth Galbraith. Though Galbraith is a best-selling author, he is not mainstream among professional economists. Veblen's influence on Galbraith's demand perspective is most visible in *The Affluent Society*.[7] Galbraith's "conventional wisdom," an established set of ideas used to explain the world and how it operates, providing stability, cohesion, meaning, and predictability in a highly complex environment, parallels Veblen's "vested interests." Since, by its nature, the conventional wisdom denies a change in the environment, it always and everywhere lags behind the times. This "inertia and resistance" comprise Veblen's institutional lag.

In a sense, too, the wealthy had, in Galbraith's view, and despite institutional lag, eventually learned from Veblen. The power to redistribute wealth had shifted toward unions and government. This shift made it downright dangerous for the wealthy to flaunt their wealth by consuming conspicuously, since such display increased the agitation by liberals to redistribute the wealth. Besides, the middle class now could emulate the rich in dress and even in automobiles, especially as the rich downsized to Volvos. At the time, later to be recanted, Galbraith believed economic insecurity among the masses had greatly diminished.

Galbraith concealed behind the "much reduced urgency" of consumption the idea of economic surplus, the means whereby the remaining economic insecurity could be banished. Production had now become the "solvent of the tensions once associated with inequality, and it has become the indispensable remedy for the discomforts, anxieties, and privations associated with economic insecurity." Enhanced production comes at the cost of a paradox, or, in Galbraith's words, "as production has increased in modern times concern for production seems also to have increased."[8]

Galbraith invokes the image of a hierarchy of goods whereby those required for daily living were more important to the average consumer than luxuries. Such a view, long ago advanced by the Austrian Carl Menger, is a contradiction in neoclassical economics in which no rank ordering of goods according to biological need or psychological satisfaction is possible (because cardinal utility is implied). As production surpluses mount (from rising productivity), consumers increasingly must be persuaded regarding adequate consumption. The producer must take on an ancillary role of synthesizing wants "by advertising, catalyzed by salesmanship." That wants are "shaped by the discreet manipulations of the persuaders show that they are not very urgent. A man who is hungry need never be told of his need for food."[9] Ostentatious display is impossible and advertising unnecessary without surpluses; during the Gilded Age, the rich engaged in self-advertisment.

Though it may have escaped the attention of mainstream economics, the existence of economic surplus permeates Veblen's *TLC* from beginning to end. "It has been customary in economic theory," writes Veblen, "to construe this struggle for wealth as being substantially a struggle for subsistence" (p. 24). However, he concludes, "industrial efficiency is presently carried to such a pitch as to afford something appreciably more than a bare livelihood to those engaged in the industrial process" (p. 25). Without surpluses, of course, excesses – of which Veblen finds in themselves, a surfeit – cannot exist. The motive for wealth accumulation cannot be only the satisfaction of physical comfort but must evolve from pecuniary emulation. Put differently, a Jay Gatsby in pursuit of a Daisy must distinguish himself in money terms, even if it is money disreputable for its newness, if not for its source.

In the end even "higher learning" is an expression by, of and for the pecuniary culture. Scholastic discipline conserves the habits of thought believed suitable by the leisure class. Only a leisure class can develop and pursue "esoteric" as well as "exoteric knowledge." The former comprises, as Veblen puts it, "such knowledge as is primarily of no economic or industrial effect, and the latter comprising chiefly knowledge of industrial processes and of natural phenomena which were habitually turned to account for the material purposes of life." Esoteric knowledge becomes part of the surplus, in a sense being surplus knowledge. It serves the agenda of the leisure class by demarcation "between higher learning and the lower" (p. 367). Galbraith, of course, has followed Veblen's lead in his critiques of "higher learning" in economics; Veblen and Galbraith alike have viewed the economics orthodoxy as a system of pecuniary belief suffering serious institutional lag.[10]

Veblen and Galbraith's animus is not so much for the classicals, but for the neoclassicals. After all, the classicals had workers being paid subsistence wages with subsistence often defined culturally. Wage goods provided subsistence. For those political economists, necessity was the mother of convention. The neoclassical economists, to the contrary, presume all income to be discretionary. Relieved of the burden of purchasing necessities, the imaginary consumers are "free to choose" any set of goods and services. Most important for the mathematics (and the theory), the assumption that necessities are unnecessary and luxuries are a special case, guarantees the convexity of indifference curves on which adequate budgets always yield matching marginal utility ratios.

Still, the idea that discretion is the better part of value is an incomplete account of capitalism. In a theoretical system of perpetual scarcity the capitalist can barely be a prime mover. Any self-respecting capitalist is rightly embarrassed when they fail to produce a net surplus. Since the upper 1 percent of households and individuals, *today's* leisure class, now control nearly 40 percent of the USA's total household wealth, a surplus must exist on the income side either in a reflection of production surplus or as rentier income.[11] Though many American households exist at the biological subsistence level, American capitalism is indisputably an economy of surpluses. In what I have called a "supra-surplus economy," a hierarchy of absolute physical necessities and "wants" coexist. "Higher standards of living" usually are associated with the satisfaction of a greater number of wants, not the satisfaction at the margin from one more unit of the same good.[12] The wants of least urgency can be met only by those with incomes or credit sufficient to buy more than basic necessities, a hierarchy of needs and wants implying a lexicographical utility function in which budget constraints for lower-income persons eliminate lower-order goods.[13]

Neoclassical economics has difficulty assimilating Veblen and Galbraith not only because utilities are interdependent or social, but also because surplus production pitted against the income and wealth distributions drives their economics. To the extent that prices are important to Veblen, their role is likely to be perverse; the amounts demanded of a luxury often rises with its price and the incomes of those who purchase it, though the causality need not run from higher price to greater consumption. Since emulation and display need not require a high income, the purchase of "fakes" or labels implies inexplicable waste amid a neoclassical sea of undeniable efficiency. Still, the prices of authentic luxury goods are beyond the means of the middle class. For the neoclassicals, poverty, like richness, cannot be explained except by marginal revenue products, which is not an explanation applicable to either extreme since the importance of the absolutes overwhelms that of the increments. Surpluses, of course, cannot exist in a system in which the quantities that producers are willing to supply exactly match those that consumers are willing to buy. For that matter, surpluses cannot exist where scarcity is the operative assumption defining economic theory. Neoclassical theory is about scarcity and the necessity of parsimony; Veblen and Galbraith's economics is about surpluses and the necessary implications of dreadful waste.

A PARADOX UNMASKED IN MACROECONOMIC DEMAND THEORY

Status goods and interdependent utility functions created an apparently insurmountable problem for neoclassical economics in Alfred Marshall's day. Social interdependence displacing utilitarianism foreclosed the additivity of individual demand curves into an aggregate demand curve. Keynes, like Veblen, placed greater emphasis on habits and instincts as key subjective elements in the propensity to consume[14] and even recognized the desire for ostentation and extravagance as a part of any theory of demand.[15] Keynes's remarks went largely unnoticed until an apparent macroeconomic consumption paradox related to the General Theory was discovered during the 1940s.

Keynes's "fundamental psychological law" emphasizes that as a rule and on the average, as income increases, consumption will increase, but not by as much as the increase in incomes. Thus, the average propensity to consume declines at higher incomes. He never said, however, that all historical movements in income and consumption must conform to this rule. The apparent paradox was found in the data: the average propensity to consume falls with income in cross-section data, confirming Keynes's "law," but is constant in time-series data.

The apparent paradox was seemingly resolved in the late 1940s by James Duesenberry's relative income hypothesis. His hypothesis is based on two assumptions: (1) the household's consumption depends in part upon the consumption patterns of other households (i.e., utility functions *are* interdependent); (2) consumption is in great part dependent upon habitual patterns of behavior and therefore depends in part upon past consumption behavior. These assumptions are purely Veblenian, the first being based on pecuniary emulation and the second on inertia or the unwillingness or reluctance to break with former behavioral patterns.

Duesenberry suggests that the demonstration effect has consumption expenditures by one household inducing expenditures by other households. The level of expenditures by each household is constrained by their absolute levels of income, but the ratio of consumption to income for all families is interdependent. In his second assumption, Duesenberry argues that a household's consumption pattern is irreversible. In a year when income is low relative to past income, households are inclined to sacrifice savings to protect their old standards of living. Evidently, the satisfaction from the higher standard of living influences current consumption behavior. As income rises, households consume more, but not as much more as one might expect from long-run historical data. The households are held back by their habitual patterns of lower consumption and respond only slowly to their new affluence. Therefore, Duesenberry's fundamental psychological postulate is that it is harder for a family to reduce its expenditures than for a family to refrain from making high expenditures in the first place. Such behavior seems plausible, if only because each of us has had the common experience. Moreover, spending to the point of bankruptcy and the Gatsby effect become possible.

Econometrically, Duesenberry estimates a series of short-run consumption functions that exhibit a ratchet effect. The nonlinear short-run function ratchets upward in response to a new peak level of real disposable income, but consumption backslides reluctantly along the new (nonlinear) short-run curve in response to income declines. Duesenberry's relative income hypothesis is consistent with the cross-section data results. A low-income family experiences more pressure from the demonstration effect to attempt to match the consumption patterns of a high-income household. Thus the average propensity to consume for the low-income family is higher as the family sacrifices savings for consumption. Though higher-income households spend more on goods and services, they observe fewer families exhibiting consumption expenditures in excess of their own. Therefore, the average propensity to consume falls as one moves up and through higher-income households.

Duesenberry's hypothesis *was* a mainstream view until Milton Friedman published his permanent income hypothesis in 1957. About the same time

Franco Modigliani and his collaborators (1955) were developing a slightly different explanation for the smoothing-out of consumption over the long run. In a theoretical sense, Modigliani "out-permanents" Friedman's permanent income hypothesis in his suggestion that households attempt to even out their consumption over their entire lifetimes. Friedman and Modigliani went on to win Nobel Prizes, while Duesenberry was relegated to the economics underworld. Today, no macroeconomics text with sufficient sales to remain in print even mentions the relative income hypothesis. That is a pity.

Both Friedman and Modigliani rejected Duesenberry's consumption function. The permanent income and life-cycle theories say that if the influence of the life-cycle differences and transitory earnings could be eliminated, high-income households would save the same shares of their incomes as low-income households. Study after study has failed to support Friedman and Modigliani. In his review of the evidence, Thomas Mayer concluded, "of all the many tests which have been undertaken by friends of the [equal savings shares] hypothesis, *not a single one supports it*. . . . "[16] More recently, Diamond and Hausman produced perhaps the most damaging evidence, concluding that "not only does the level of savings (wealth) rise with permanent income, but it does so in a sharply nonlinear fashion". . . .[17] For permanent incomes below $4770 per year, they found that the savings–permanent income ratio rises by 3.3 percent for each extra $1000 of permanent income; beyond $4700 it rises 5.7 percent for each extra $1000 and beyond $12,076, by 14.2 percent.

If Bill Gates' savings as a share of his permanent income is *lower* than that of another 40-year-old white male different from Gates only because he earns $18,000 per year with little hope for a significant raise, *that* would be quite surprising. Still, if the eighteen-thousand-dollar man were to become unemployed, he would likely borrow funds in an effort to maintain his family's old standard of living, possibly risking the Gatsby effect. Moreover, if Bill Gates' income were to drop a few hundred thousand dollars next year, he probably would not alter his consumption significantly. In short, habit persistence better meets the test of common sense than the permanent income hypothesis. Veblen and Galbraith no doubt would say something amusing about the habitual modes of thinking regarding permanent income in the institutions of higher learning.

VEBLEN AND AN ALTERNATIVE VISION FOR ECONOMICS

Unlike the neoclassicals, Veblen and especially Galbraith have explained why the American economy relies so heavily on advertising and salesmanship. If needs and production are exactly matched, there is no need to spread the word regarding the virtues of any particular product. The market sets the price and consumers pay it without the need for any additional information. Lonely price signals rule the neoclassical world. However, the large gap between the lowest and highest incomes inspires the corporate structure to transcend the role of a simple producer of goods. As Galbraith notes, "mass communication was not necessary when the wants of the masses were anchored primarily in physical need. The masses could not then be persuaded as to their spending – this went for basic foods and shelter."[18]

An excess of income above physiological subsistence leaves a demand wedge for producers. Imperfect competition abhors wedges. Not only does the demand gap (relative to production) lead to advertising, promotion, and salesmanship, it sets into motion forces such as the price markup on unit costs (mostly wages) to fill the space. The money wage – the wage actually negotiated – separates itself from the real wage or labor productivity. The markup depends very much on the firm's ability to further differentiate its product or service. Since products are differentiated with a particular segment of the income distribution in mind, the only relevant "price" elasticities are those prevailing within that part of the income distribution. In this vision non-price competition displaces price competition. It is difficult to imagine the existence of imperfect competition in the absence of excess production capacity.[19]

Since – to a considerable degree – we are what we consume, not surprisingly consumer tastes shape the market for labor. Thus, parallel non-wage-competing forces are found in the modern labor market, forces mirroring those prevailing in goods markets. Our ultimate sociological achievement today is not our work, much less our workmanship, but is whatever standard of living we attain (defined as what we can afford to consume). Once defined by our work and its quality, now we define ourselves by our standard of living. In a Veblenian sense we are "middle class" when we perceive ourselves as very much like everyone else. We believe that everyone is or can be on the same bandwagon. However, producers and marketing experts have much finer classifications for what we can afford and how we can be influenced in accordance with our demographic and economic characteristics. Prices and wages merely comprise background noise in this great social drama.

Duesenberry's aggregate consumption function is consistent with Veblen, Galbraith, and Keynes's visions. It signifies the importance of the income distribution in determining the level of aggregate demand. In neoclassical theory aggregate demand can only be generated by adding individual demand functions that are non-additive. Just as Veblenian demand suppresses the influence of prices at the microeconomic level, Keynes's theory of demand suppresses prices in macroeconomics. Income and output, including capitalism's natural tendency to create overcapacity, drive the system to or away from full employment equilibrium. Relative real incomes are more important than individual prices.

CONCLUSIONS

Often it is said that Veblen's ideas, and Galbraith's, for that matter, cannot be useful for economic theory because they are nebulous, diffused, and irrelevant. As we have seen, however, recent mainstream contributions to demand theory would disabuse anyone of insurmountable difficulties in the use of interdependent or lexicographical utility functions, reflecting Veblenian behaviors. Moreover, direct utility functions and extended linear expenditure systems empirically confirm the importance of standards of living in consumption behavior. Though presently inconspicuous, game theory and econometrics applied to Veblenian demand are persuasive.

That is not all: the Veblenian vision may be broad without being infinite and thereby irrelevant. To theorize about prices in competitive markets is the easy way. Thinking small, however, we are in danger of missing something big. We economists have failed to evolve with the economic system we claim to describe. Not only have technology and education greatly changed, capitalism has evolved through many stages so that it no longer bears even a family resemblance to the nascent industrialization of Alfred Marshall's time much less the merchant capitalism prevailing during the age of Adam Smith. In particular, an economy, even a global economy, with surplus industrial capacity, is not well described by a theory grounded in scarcity. As capitalism has become increasingly complex, too many economists have been content to keep everything except the mathematics simple. Our esoteric self-indulgence places us in danger of becoming the sole consumers of our own production. If that happens, economists will become part of the surplus.

NOTES

1 The three quotations are from John Bartlett, edited by Emily Morison Beck, *Bartlett's Familiar Quotations, Fifteenth Edition* (Boston: Little, Brown and Company, 1980) [1855], p. 685.

2 Harvey Leibenstein, "Bandwagon, Snob and Veblen Effects in the Theory of Consumer's Demand," *Quarterly Journal of Economics*, May 1950. The article was widely reprinted, including its appearance in Edwin Mansfield (ed.), *Microeconomics: Selected Readings*, 3rd edn (New York and London: W. W. Norton, 1971), pp. 12–30.

3 Laurie Simon Bagwell and B. Douglas Bernheim, "Veblen Effects in a Theory of Conspicuous Consumption," *The American Economic Review* 86, No. 3 (June 1996): 350.

4 See, for instance, David M. Kreps, *A Course in Microeconomic Theory* (Princeton: Princeton University Press, 1990). The single-crossing (a.k.a. the Spence-Mirrlees sorting) condition is indigenous to models using asymmetric information.

5 For a model using interdependent utility functions with implications for income redistribution, see E. Ray Canterbery, "Income Redistribution and Rawlsian Justice," *Journal of Economics and Business* 33, No. 3 (Spring/Summer 1981): 188–201. Contrary to the neoclassical conventional wisdom regarding Rawls'

principles of justice, I argue that in the real world such principles can be evaluated and implemented only if interpersonal comparisons are allowed.

6 R. L. Basmann, D. J. Molina, and D. J. Slottje, "A Note on Measuring Veblen's Theory of Conspicuous Consumption," *Review of Economics and Statistics* 70, No. 3 (August 1988): 532–535.

7 John Kenneth Galbraith, *The Affluent Society* (Boston: Houghton Mifflin, 1958).

8 *Ibid.* pp. 119–120.

9 *Ibid.* p. 158.

10 A complete survey and analysis of Galbraith's position is provided in Warren J. Samuels, "Galbraith on Economics as a System of Professional Belief," *Journal of Post Keynesian Economics* 7, No. 1 (Fall 1984): 61–76.

11 These data are from Edward N. Wolff, *Top Heavy: A Study of the Increasing Inequality of Wealth in America* (New York: The Twentieth Century Fund Press, 1995), p. 7. Wolff traces increasing wealth and income inequality to the high returns from increasingly concentrated holdings of financial wealth.

12 See E. Ray Canterbery, "A Theory of Supra-Surplus Capitalism," Presidential Address, EEA, March 6, 1987, printed in *Eastern Economic Journal* 13, No. 4 (October–December 1987): 315–332 and E. Ray Canterbery, *The Making of Economics*, 3rd edn (Belmont, CA: Wadsworth, 1987).

13 The lexicographical utility function is defined and fully explicated in E. Ray Canterbery, "Inflation, Necessities and Distributive Efficiency," in J. H. Gapinski and C. E. Rockwood (eds), *Essays in Post Keynesian Inflation* (Cambridge, MA: Ballinger, 1979), pp. 70–103. This function generates kinked Engel curves because the threshold level of income for a lower-ranked good equals the satiation level of income for the prior higher-ranked good. The value of subsistence expenditures in such a framework can be estimated through the extended linear expenditure system (also discussed).

14 As Keynes put it, the subjective factors "include those psychological characteristics of human nature and those social practices and institutions which, though not unalterable, are unlikely to undergo a material change over a short period of time except in abnormal or revolutionary circumstances" (John Maynard Keynes, *The General Theory of Employment, Interest, and Money* (New York: Harcourt, Brace & World, Inc., 1965) [1936], p. 91).

15 Keynes, *op. cit.*, p. 108.

16 Thomas Mayer, *Permanent Income, Wealth and Consumption* (Berkeley, CA: University of California Press, 1972), p. 348.

17 Peter Diamond and J. A. Hausman, "Individual Retirement and Savings Behavior," Paper presented at SSRC-NBER Conference on Public Economics, Oxford, June 1982, pp. 35–37.

18 John Kenneth Galbraith, *The New Industrial State* (Boston: Houghton Mifflin, 1967), p. 207.

19 For a more detailed discussion of the connections among a theory of demand that relates production to a hierarchy of wants and a theory of the income distribution that relates incomes to job markets as well as to other elements, see E. Ray Canterbery, "Galbraith, Sraffa, Kalecki and Supra-Surplus Capitalism," *Journal of Post Keynesian Economics* 7, No. 1 (Fall 1984): 77–90.

REFERENCES

Akerlof, George A. "A Theory of Social Custom, of Which Unemployment May Be One Consequence." *Quarterly Journal of Economics* 94, No. 4 (June 1980): 749–751.

Bagwell, Laurie Simon and B. Douglas Bernheim. "Veblen Effects in a Theory of Conspicuous Consumption." *American Economic Review*, 86, No. 3 (June 1996): 349–73.

Bartlett, John. *Bartlett's Familiar Quotations*, Fifteenth edition. Edited by Emily Morison Beck. Boston: Little, Brown and Company, 1980 [1855].

Basmann, R. L., D. J. Molina, and D. J. Slottje. "A Note on Measuring Veblen's Theory of Conspicuous Consumption." *Review of Economics and Statistics* 70, No. 3 (August 1988): 532–35.

Canterbery, E. Ray. "Income Redistribution and Rawlsian Justice." *Journal of Economics and Business* 33 (Spring/Summer 1981): 188–201.

—— *The Making of Economics*. Third edition. Belmont, CA: Wadsworth, 1987.

—— "A Theory of Supra-Surplus Capitalism." Presidential Address, EEA, March 6, 1987, printed in *Eastern Economic Journal* 13, No. 4 (October–December 1987): 315–332.

—— "Inflation, Necessities and Distributive Efficiency." In *Essays in Post Keynesian Inflation*. Edited by J. H. Gapinski and C. E. Rockwood. Cambridge, MA: Ballinger, 1979, pp. 79–103.

Diamond, Peter and J. A. Hausman. "Individual Retirement and Savings Behavior." Paper presented at SSRC-NBER Conference on Public Economics. Oxford, June 1982.

Duesenberry, James. *Income, Saving, and the Theory of Consumer Behavior*. Cambridge, MA: Harvard University Press, 1949.

Frank, Robert H. "The Demand for Unobservable and Other Nonpositional Goods." *American Economic Review* 75, No. 1 (March 1985): 101–16.

Galbraith, John Kenneth. *The Affluent Society*. Boston: Houghton Mifflin, 1958.

—— *The New Industrial State*. Boston: Houghton Mifflin, 1967.

Keynes, John Maynard. *The General Theory of Employment, Interest, and Money*. New York: Harcourt, Brace & World, Inc., 1965 [1936].

Kreps, David M. *A Course in Microeconomic Theory*. Princeton, NJ: Princeton University Press, 1990.

Leibenstein, Harvey. "Bandwagon, Snob and Veblen Effects in the Theory of Consumer's Demand." Reprinted in *Microeconomics: Selected Readings*, Third edition. Edited by Edwin Mansfield. New York, London: W. W. Norton, 1971, pp. 12–30.

Mayer, Thomas. *Permanent Income, Wealth and Consumption*. Berkeley, CA: University of California Press, 1972.

Samuels, Warren J. "Galbraith on Economics as a System of Professional Belief." *Journal of Post Keynesian Economics* 7, No. 1 (Fall 1984): 61–76.

Veblen, Thorstein. *The Theory of the Leisure Class*. New York, London: Penguin Books, 1994 [1899].

Wolff, Edward N. *Top Heavy: A Study of the Increasing Inequality of Wealth in America*. New York: The Twentieth Century Fund Press, 1995.

Chapter 25

The U.S. Motion Pictures Industry: An Empirical Approach

E. RAY CANTERBERY
Florida State University, Tallahassee, FL 32306, U.S.A.

A. MARVASTI
University of Houston-Downtown, One Main Street, Houston, TX 77002, U.S.A.

Abstract. We hypothesize that the U.S. motion pictures industry is structured so that star presence increases box office receipts and (less so) admissions, but places Ricardian limits on the output of blockbusters. The few dominant studios (majors) rely on a modified star system to generate supra-normal box office by stimulating admissions at exhibitors. Rising costs (from stars and their promotion) are required for rising revenues; that is, the majors gain revenue only at higher costs. Although the industry has unique features, the empirical results are surprisingly relevant to other industries.

I. Introduction

Empirical studies of the structure of the motion pictures industry are rare. Several simulation studies (Wildman and Siwek (1988), Frank (1992), Waterman (1993)) depict an industry greatly dependent on initial conditions, especially the initial size of the domestic market. Most non-simulation empirical studies of the industry are based strictly on samples of movies, but still reveal important stylized facts about the industry's structure. In Prag and Casavant (1994), the "quality" of a film is positively associated with costs of production related to movie stars and their publicity costs. Through advertising the studio can capitalize on the star as an input. Thus, the major studios must incur rising costs (from stars and their promotion) not only to have rising revenues, but to maintain market shares. De Vany and Walls (1997) provide further insights while supporting the Prag-Casavant findings.

Studies of the success of individual films explain the films, but not necessarily the industry. Still, from these findings we can move from individual films to a broader industry analysis. The major studio/distributors distinguish themselves through their efforts to produce "hits" or blockbusters. De Vany-Walls (1997, p. 787) find only 20 percent of a weekly Top-50 sample of films earning 80 percent of total box office receipts, with the top four movies generating a fifth of total box office revenue, and the top eight, 28.1 percent. In 1991, for example, 150 new films were released by the majors whereas 273 were "released" by other distributors, though most of the minor producers distribute and market though a major. At best, only about 30 percent of all films produced turn a profit. "In fact," as Vogel (1990, p. 29) concludes, "of any 10 major theatrical films produced, on the average 6 or 7 are unprofitable, and 1 will break even." Yet, every major studio, by definition, must produce at least one box office hit yearly.

The "star system," born with Adolph Zukor's full-length films featuring such luminaries as Mary Pickford, Douglas Fairbanks and Gloria Swanson, led to domination of the industry by a few majors. Star creation, involving national publicity campaigns, became increasingly costly. By 1916 Mary Pickford had guarantees for $20,000 weekly and 50 percent of all her films distribution profits (Murphy, 1992, p. 279). Since a star's persona cannot be duplicated, the demand for such high guarantees formed an effective barrier to entry. Although the glory days of MGM are long past, a modified star system lives on and continues to differentiate the product as it maintains a barrier to entry. In the 1960s Elizabeth Taylor and Richard Burton broke the million-dollar level and literally set the stage for the action stars such as Burt Reynolds and Clint Eastwood to begin the multimillion-dollar star spiral in the 1970s, extended by such stars as Bruce Willis in the 1980s.

Since stars are most effectively used through massive marketing outlays, in 1980 real marketing cost per new feature film (1982 = 100) reached $4.82 million, rising to $10.35 million in 1991 (Motion Pictures Association of America, 1992). Even if promotional costs could be ignored, star quasi-rents have contributed to rising production costs. In 1980 the real cost per feature film negative (master) was $10.47 million; by 1991 the cost had risen to $22.40 million (MPAA, 1992). As a result, during the 1980s and continuing through the 1990s, the circulating capital requirements of the studio/distributor have greatly increased.[1] In such a high and rising cost industry, how many major studios survive? The answer historically has depended upon box office.

In 1980, near the mid-point of our sample years, real gross box office revenue (1982–84 = 100) was about $3.3 billion (MPAA, 1992). In that year eight major studios held about 90 percent of domestic market share with miminal export receipts. If 70 percent of box office was paid to the major studios as rental fees (see Section II.3), average revenue for a major would have been $263 million. For each major, one $30 million blockbuster would have left $233 million that could be used to produce about 16 more films at "average" real costs. Eight majors could produce a total of 137 films (though they actually produced 134 films that year). As it turns out, not even the majors create equally; because "blockbusters" sometimes fail to turn a profit, four to six majors dominate the industry during any year.

[1] Although we use 1991 (the last year for our complete data sample) for these comparisons, industry data through 1999 shows real cost per film roughly doubling again.

Typically the top four studios have about 60 percent of the market. Although membership among the top four has rotated among those having blockbuster success, only six studios (Columbia, Fox, MGM/UA, Paramount, Universal, and Warner Brothers) dominated the market during our sample era. High production costs apparently require a large-scale studio or, more precisely, a very large amount of circulating capital. The oligopoly of the 1920–50 era, based upon the old star system, has evolved into its presently more complex form, but it remains an oligopoly.

II. A Model of the Industry's Structure

1. The Market Demand for Movies

The final demand for movies is found at the box offices of local theaters. Despite the growth of secondary markets for films, the economic values of films still derive from box office (Murphy, 1993, p. 290). Consumer market demand for viewing movies can be expressed as

$$Q = F(P_1, \mathbf{V}), \tag{1}$$

where Q is the number of admissions into theaters (the exhibitors), P_1 is the real price of movie tickets, and $\mathbf{V}$ is a vector of exogenous shift variables, including personal income, population of moviegoers, a measure for movie star presence, number of films available, some measure for the influence of secondary markets, and so on. We hypothesize the demand curve to be downward-sloping so $\partial Q/\partial P_1 < 0$.

The demand for films by theaters from movie producers is a *derived demand* from Equation (1). Write the generalized derived demand function for films by the theaters as

$$X^d = D[E(P_2)], \tag{2}$$

where X^d = the number of films demanded by all theaters and $E(P_2)$ = expected rental "price" of films, where E is an expectations operator (P_2, as explained below, is complexly derived since it, too, is the revenue function for the studios and contains admissions as a major component).

Theaters "produce" admissions. The main variable in the theater's production function is the number of films required (and the number of associated prints of those films) to meet its expected demand for admissions (ignoring sunk capital costs such as existing theater buildings). Although multiple showings of "a" film require multiple prints, the public and any particular theater always are demanding *a* film (book buyers behave in a similar way). Thus, neither the public nor the theater make a distinction between the master and any subsequent print.

Assume that the typical theater, the ith, uses x_i films per year to meet the *expected* demand for its admissions or $E(q_i)$, where E is an expectations operator.

The ith theater uses films as input (lower-case letters represent firm-level variables) according to a production function

$$E(q_i) = G(x_i, \mathbf{x}), \quad q_{i,M} < E(q_i) \leq E(q_{i,c}) \tag{3}$$

where $E(q_i)$ is the number of expected cumulative admissions over the film's house runs bounded by $q_{i,M}$ (the theater's cumulative minimal seating to break even) and $E(q_{i,c})$ (the theater's cumulative maximal seating capacity over the films' expected runs), x_i is the number of films per year supplied by the studios, and $\mathbf{x}$ is a given vector of other inputs. The uncertainty of the theater derives from the theater's asymmetric information regarding the preferences of its customers.

2. Production and Cost Functions of the Movies

The typical major or jth studio's production function is assumed to be

$$x_j = g_j(y_{1j}, y_{2j}, \mathbf{k}), \tag{4}$$

in which y_{1j} is the hours of non-star or "generic" labor, y_{2j} is the hours of star labor, and $\mathbf{k}$ represents other circulating capital requirements. The hours of star labor are strictly constrained by the number of stars; thus, $y_{2j} \leq y_{2\text{MAX}}$, where $y_{2\text{MAX}}$ is the maximum number of hours available from the small pool of stars. Capital requirements are continuously variable since capital is budgeted for each new movie. The major studio, having "star labor" in its production function, produces two different products, generic films and films made with stars. The main purpose for producing generic films is to supply theaters with sufficient films to remain continuously open. The main purpose of films made with stars is to generate sufficient profits to cover losses from many of the generic films plus enough to retain sufficient share of market to be a "major" studio. The probability that any particular generic film will be a "blockbuster" is small while the probability that a film with stars will be a blockbuster is large.

Write the jth major studio's implicit production function for number of films as

$$H_j(x_{1j}, x_{2j}; y_{1j}, y_{2j}; \mathbf{k}) = 0, \tag{5}$$

in which x_{1j} is the number of generic movies (of the same quality as those produced by small "independents") and x_{2j} is the number of blockbusters. We assume the production functions for the *major* studios to be identical. The observed rotation in their box office successes reflects the uncertainty regarding what moviegoers want and the occasional failure of an expensive film with stars. The aggregate industry production function for J major studios is

$$\sum_{j=1}^{J} x_j = g_j(y_{1j}, y_{2j}, \mathbf{k}) = X^s. \tag{6}$$

The studio willingly provides as many prints of a film warranted by the public and the theaters' demand for the movie. Such a demand for "reprints" from the public is even more welcome to the studio than it would be for a book publisher. In production, therefore, x refers only to the master (negative), although the supply of *any particular* x is "stretched" through reprints to meet the demands of theaters wishing to exhibit the film.

The total cost function for the jth studio is

$$c_j(x_{1j}, x_{2j}) = \mathbf{k} + (r_1 y_{1j} + r_2 y_{2j} + b r_2 y_{2j}), \tag{7}$$

where r_1 is the Theater Guild rate for cast members, and r_2 is the rental rate on "a star", including any expected share of box office receipts. "Other circulating costs", including the set or location, the screenplay, the director, and "other" required capital, continue to be represented by the vector $\mathbf{k}$. To simplify, since advertising and other promotional costs are directly associated with the stars, these costs are assumed proportional (equaling the share b) to the stars' rents. The output x_1 requires only $\mathbf{k}$ and y_1; a "blockbuster" requires the extra inputs, star presence or y_2 and a proportional amount of marketing costs.

Total production and distribution costs for a major studio requires matching circulating capital. The amount of required capital is critical because producers supply new capital for each new film. In establishing the initial conditions, Equation (7) can be simplified to

$$c_j = c(x_{1j}, x_{2j}) = K_j. \tag{8}$$

in which K_j is the annual capital required to become and to remain a major studio, including the quasi-rents paid for leasing movie stars. As we said, K_j approximated \$263 million in real dollars in 1980. The aggregate capital required by the J studios is

$$\sum_{j=1}^{J} K_j = \mathbf{K}. \tag{9}$$

In 1980 the value of K was about \$2.0 billion in real dollars.

3. The Number of Firms as Related to Market Size

To fully understand studio revenues, the meaning of P_2 or film rental fees in Equation (2), requires further explication. Since 1910, film distributors have licensed films to exhibitors for some percentage of box-office receipts. These box-office percentages have increased until they now are 90 percent of "box office" minus an allowance for the *negotiated* "theater's operating costs" or "house nut" on key first-run dates. Under these arrangements the percentage is a sliding scale, falling to about 80 percent during the next few weeks of the run, then 70 percent, and then 65 percent. Since the late 1960s, floors guarantee a maximal rental cost to the exhibitor; the percentages range from 70 percent for the first few weeks, on down to 35 percent.

Since the studio can enjoy increasing returns from longer movie runs, the declining rental rate is provided as an incentive to exhibitors to continue to exhibit the film even as its box office revenue declines. Suppose a first-run theater has a box-office take of $50,000 for the first week of a movie; take out a negotiated $10,000 "house allowance," and the studio's share is 90 percent of $40,000, or 72 percent (not 90 percent) of the consumer's dollar. If the box-office take is $70,000, the distributor's rental percentage would rise to 77 percent of the consumer's dollar. Contrary, say, to the factory price of an automobile to dealerships, p_2 or the rental fee for films *varies* with the gross revenue of the retailer. Though the larger the box-office gross, the greater the rent paid, theater owners do not complain because everybody wins.[2]

From the industry formula, the expected price of the kth film, $E(p_{2,k})$, or expected total rental fees (proceeds) from the kth movie for its studio-distributor, equals

$$E(p_{2,k}) = \sum_{i=1}^{n} \{[p_{1,ki} E(q_{ki})] - C_{ki}\} E(\pi_{ki}) \tag{10}$$

for all (n) theaters where $q_{i,M} < E(q_{ki}) \leq E(q_{i,c})$, and $E(q_{ki})$ is the expected total number of admissions to the kth movie for the ith theater (bounded by each theater's minimum and expected maximal capacity), C_{ki} is the ith theater's "house allowance" or "operating cost" of exhibiting the kth movie, and $E(\pi_{ki})$ is the expected percentage of net revenue of the ith theater on the kth film going to the studio. For the majors combined,

$$\sum_{k=1}^{m} E(p_{2,k}) = \sum_{i=1}^{n} \sum_{k=1}^{m} \{[p_{1,ki} E(q_{ki})] - C_{ki}\} E(\pi_{ki}) \tag{11}$$

for all m films produced by the majors and exhibited in n theaters. In 1980 these rental receipts by the studios was about $2.1 billion in real dollars.

Since the theater's cost (C_{ki}) is relatively fixed (by negotiation, if not in reality), the theater's rental price for a particular film depends on box office so that rental fees are insensitive to the theater's costs. Moreover, $p_{2,k}$ is highly variable, since theater receipts depend less on ticket prices and more on admissions (limited only by seating capacities over time). Ticket prices are often the same for different movies, whatever the studio's own cost of production. The studio, in turn, uses non-price means of competing (via stars, advertising, and promotion) to maximize

[2] This extended discussion of pricing practices is mostly based on discussions with industry officials.

$E(q_{ki})$. Uniquely, $E(\pi)$ percent of what is "net total revenue" to the theaters is the expected "price" paid to studios.

Although film producers' revenues depend directly on net box office proceeds, the size of the movies' market remains tightly linked to consumer demand. Assume that the admissions demand function or Equation (1) has an inverse applicable to the ith or typical theater, and

$$p_{1,i} = F^{-1}[E(q_i), \mathbf{V}]. \tag{12}$$

From the perspective of the studios the aggregate market size (S) is

$$S = \sum_{i=1}^{n} \{F^{-1}[E(q_i), \mathbf{V}]F(p_{1,i}, \mathbf{V}) - C_i\}E(\pi_i). \tag{13}$$

Now the circulating capital required by major producers to supply the requisite X films can be compared to the studios' gross revenue. Again, let K_j be the minimum circulating capital required to be a typical major studio and form the ratio

$$s = \left[\!\left[\sum_{i=1}^{n} \{F^{-1}[E(q_i), \mathbf{V}]F(p_{1,i}, \mathbf{V}) - C_i\}E(\pi_i) \right]\!\right] / K_j. \tag{14}$$

The value of s is a measure of relative market size. If $S \to \infty$ for a given value of K_j, $s \to \infty$, the market could support many studios and the industry would be perfectly competitive. If, at the other extreme, $s = 1$, a monopoly studio can supply the entire consumer market. If $s < 1$, the market is too small to allow such a monopoly studio to break even. The major studios behave alike in an important respect; they allocate great amounts of circulating capital to pay the quasi-rents of stars and to promote and advertise those stars. What certainty exists is the perception of a strong association between such capital outlays and box office. The above data on production costs and box office for the U.S. motion pictures industry suggest that $4 < s < 8$, and a sufficient interdependence of actions among the major studios to constitute an oligopoly producing films differentiated mostly by stars. Since expected net box office, $E(p_2)$, depends upon both admissions (q) *and* ticket prices, (p_1) in Equation (10), the major studios can use star power to increase the number of blockbusters (x_2) through Equation (5) even while reducing the average price elasticity of demand at the theater through the hyper-differentiation of the product.

The necessity of studios to supply "generic films" is similar to the rationale for auto manufacturers supplying an adequate number of autos to each dealer; without several models from which to chose, customers will not visit the dealerships and the dealerships will not be able to breakeven. Even during economic recessions when the three American auto producers had negative net income (totaling \$37.7 million in 1991–92), none reduced the number of models offered in those or the next few years. Theaters, too, want to deal with studios that can supply more than one or two films a year. Moreover, without exhibitors no need for movie studios exists.

III. Findings for the Industry

1. Primary Data and Hypotheses

To these stylized facts and industry data we add real-world data to test the following hypotheses. (1) Hyper-differentiation of movies (blockbusters) results in a low price elasticity of demand for admissions. (2) The main successful source of product differentiation is the movie star, who provides information regarding quality of the product to the consumer. (3) The presence of supra-specific human capital (stars) adds greatly to "quality," demand, and revenue without a strong positive effect upon *quantitative* film output (having Ricardian limits). (4) The use of generic human capital or "cast members" adds greatly to quantitative film output while affecting demand or revenue little. (5) Circulating capital affects positively quantitative *and* qualitative film output. (6) The movie experience is an inferior good for movie-goers. (7) Economies of scale exist in the production of movies.

2. A Survey of the Stars

We define "blockbusters" or "hits" as movies grossing at least $10 million in real terms (1982–84 = 100).[3] In recent film history these would include such movies as *Rambo*, *Terminator*, and *The Fugitive* – the originals and sequels. To estimate the contribution of the "star" to the blockbuster, we need an independent measure of "star".

We prepared a pretest questionnaire with the names of more than 1200 stars compiled from the lead performers in blockbuster movies during 1965–1988. We formed a small focus group of individuals of varying ages and backgrounds to discuss these names. Though we hypothesized that the stars' names provide information on the quality of those movies, we did not reveal to the focus group the basis for the selected stars. At the end of a lengthy discussion, we gave them the list and asked each: "Would any of the following names encourage you to see a movie you know nothing else about? If so, please circle the names that would have such an influence". Each star receiving at least two-thirds of the total votes, was retained on a final, greatly shortened list.

We randomly distributed the new questionnaire, containing 429 "stars", to 170 persons at a large shopping mall (a standard method used for marketing research on new products). The list includes older (and even now deceased) stars such as David Niven, Cary Grant and Olivia De Havilland as well as newer stars such as Tom Berenger, Gregory Hines and Demi Moore. A surprising result is finding the

[3] Blockbusters or "hits" data is collected from various issues of *Variety*.

great number of stars of foreign origin, suggesting that the quasi-rents of American stars attract specific human capital (stars) from other nations.[4] The raw vote count was used to measure the importance of the star's appearance in a movie. Its conversion to an integer or index number scaled this vote count down to the range 0 to 15. For example, Kim Basinger is a 10, whereas, ironically, Bo Derek, the star of *10*, is only a borderline 7. In turn, the index for each star was multiplied by the appearances of the star during a particular year. Finally, the products of the index and appearances of all stars in each year's movies were summed. These sums became the observations for the variable, "star".

The simple correlation coefficient between stars and blockbusters is 0.80. Though the original list came from the real \$10 million movies, the persons surveyed with the shorter list did not know this. Therefore, we assume that they were selecting and giving weights to information useful in their evaluation of "quality" movies. Moreover, those surveyed would have had no way of knowing how many stars had appeared in movies during any particular year. In any case, to find that 80 percent of movies with stars become blockbusters is not the same as finding that 80 percent of films with stars turn out to be blockbusters. Since star-based films sometimes have negative profits, the probability of positive profits is less than 1.00. The presence of stars nonetheless increases the probability that the film will be highly successful.

3. Output, Demand and Box Office Functions

The measure of studio production is number of films (x_1, x_2). Since the number of films is the number of masters, we cannot distinguish the production of generics from blockbusters. Besides, the number of prints (from the master) will be greater, the greater the box office generated by a particular film. Thus, in our aggregate production function estimates we make no distinction between generic and blockbuster films on the left side of the equation. We estimate the industry production function,

$$X = g(Y_1, \mathbf{K}, Y_2, \nu), \tag{4'}$$

where variables are again capitalized to represent aggregate industry values. The number of masters is X, Y_1 is "cast" or generic labor, $\mathbf{K}$ is generic circulating capital, Y_2 is supra-specialized human capital, and ν is the error term. Our index representing stars is a proxy for Y_2. The total market demand for *prints* of films by theaters is a derived demand for which data is unavailable.

We use the number of admissions to measure the *real* quantity demanded for movies or the public's direct demand for movies. Real demand is a function of the

[4] There are 75 foreign stars in our sample, including Julie Andrews, Charles Bronson, Ann Margaret, Michael Caine, Sean Connery, Dudley Moore, Arnold Schwartzenegger, and Jon Voight. The complete list of stars is available by request from the authors.

price of admissions, among other things. We estimate the real aggregate demand function from Equation (1) or, expressed in the independent variables used,

$$Q = F(P_1; Y_2, X, I, VCR, \mu), \tag{1'}$$

where Q is the number of aggregate admissions, P_1 is the real price of movie tickets, and μ is the error term. The vector **V** now consists of Y_2 or the index for stars, X or the number of masters, I or real U.S. per capita personal income, and VCR or the cumulative number of VCRs sold in the U.S. (representing secondary market forces). The number of masters is an exogenous variable because moviegoers demand a particular movie, not a particular number of films. Still, the general availability of films may influence aggregate demand. The use of an index number for stars constrains both the quantity and the quality of stars since the number of stars is limited (for any particular year) and the perceived quality of the star is embedded in the index number. Two measures of gross market size, population and GDP, could not be used because of multicollinearity (based on the simple correlation coefficients and the Variance Inflation Factors (VIF) in the initial specifications of the models).

We also estimate industry revenue as measured by box office receipts (R), the *sine qua non* of the industry. The general form is derived from the first terms on the right-hand-side of Equation (11) for n theaters and m movies, so that

$$\sum_{i=1}^{n}\sum_{k=1}^{m}[p_{1,ki}E(q_{ki})] = R = R(P_1; Y_2, X, I, VCR, \epsilon), \tag{11'}$$

where ϵ is the error term. As noted, in 1980 R was about \$3.3 billion in real dollars. Since we assume the major studios to be alike and since they dominate industry revenues, the demand and revenue functions for the industry are presumed to mimic that for the studio. The most efficient estimate of the demand function is a log-log equation, and thus a linear-log estimation is used for box office revenue. Again, we could not use the measures of gross market size.

4. Properties of the Data

Our statistical estimates are based on 1965–1991 time series data for the U.S. motion pictures industry.[5] We first examine each series for the presence of a unit root

[5] Factory sales of VCRs (in thousands of units) in the United States are derived from various issues of *Electronic Market Data Book*, published by the Electronic Industry Association. Box office receipts (in millions of real dollars), number of admissions (in millions), and number of films released are collected from the various issues of *Theatrical Data*, compiled and published by the Motion Pictures Association of America (MPAA). In addition to our own survey data on stars, data for labor (employees in thousands) and for capital (in millions of real dollars) used are from the *Survey of Current Business*. The CPI and the data used for producer price indices are from the U.S. Department of Labor, Bureau of Labor Statistics.

against the alternative hypothesis that the series is stationary around a linear trend. Since nonstationary variables do not display a "mean-reverting" property, they should be converted into stationarity processes before including them in standard regression models (otherwise, the traditional t-tests may signify false significance). The most frequently employed test for determining nonstationary (or a unit root) is the Augmented Dickey–Fuller (ADF) test. We applied two versions, one with and one without a time trend.

The ADF tests also reveal whether a data series is integrated and, if so, to what degree. A series is integrated if it requires differencing to make it stationary. A non-stationary series such as χ_t is integrated of order d, i.e., $\chi_t \sim I(d)$, if it becomes stationary after being differenced d times. After determining the degree of integration in each series, the Johansen cointegration test is used to confirm the existence of cointegrating equations (that is, have variables whose long-term movements are related to each other). If cointegrating equations are found (and to avoid autocorrelation), parameters can be estimated with a Vector Error Correction (VEC) model, a variation of the Vector Autoregression (VAR) model with an error correction term for each cointegrating equation (see notes to Table I).

5. Discussion

Based on the ADF tests, the null hypothesis of unit roots could not be rejected at the 1 percent level for the level values of variables (including their log transformations) in the production function (X_1, Y_1, **K**, and Y_2) using either specification of the test.[6] These series, however, become stationary for first differences at either the 1 or 5 percent level and therefore are $I(1)$. The ADF results for the demand and box office variables are less consistent than those for production. The null hypothesis of a unit root could not be rejected under either specification of the test for the values of real per capita income (I). However, the real price of movie tickets (P_1) and real box-office revenues (R) are stationary, at least at the 5 or 10 percent level. The ADF test results are less clear for admissions (Q), the dependent variable in the demand function. The Q series has a unit root in the ADF test with a constant term only, but seems to be stationary at the 5 percent level when a constant and a time trend are used (though not in logs). The Q series (as well as the Y_2, I, X_1, Y_1, and **K** series), however, are $I(1)$, suggestive of the possibility of being stationary in first differences.

Johansen cointegration tests were conducted for various groupings of the series.[7] The null hypothesis is that at least one cointegrating vector appears in each model. According to the likelihood ratio tests, all selected models suggest the existence of at least one cointegrating vector at the 5 percent level [even though cointegration of only two series might be sufficient to presume cointegration (Engle

[6] A table showing all ADF test results is available on request from the authors.

[7] A table showing the results of the Johansen cointegration tests for groupings of the variables is available on request from the authors.

Table I. Normalized cointegrating equations results from VEC model for production function[b]

Variables	$X_{1,t-1}$
$Y_{1,t-1}$	-10.3976^{a}
	(2.6617)
K_{t-1}	0.3894^{a}
	(0.0816)
$Y_{2,t-1}$	0.5042^{a}
	(0.2135)
Constant	1756.575
Log likelihood	430.86
Akaike information criteria	39.57
Schwarz criteria	41.73
Adj R^2	–

[a]Significant at the 1% level.
[b]Standard errors are in parentheses.
Notes: As noted in the text, we used two versions of the ADF test for unit roots and degree of integration of the time series data. Our first specification for a series such as χ is with a constant and a time trend, or

$$\Delta \chi_t = \alpha + \rho \chi_{t-1} + \phi_1 \Delta \chi_{t-1} + \cdots + \phi_m \Delta \chi_{t-m} + \delta t + \epsilon_t, \tag{I.1}$$

where t is a time trend and ϵ is the error term. The null hypothesis is that $\rho = 0$, that is, nonstantionarity exists. Our second ADF specification is similar to Equation (I.1), only without the time trend. If the absolute value of the calculated statistic is smaller than the critical value, the hypothesis of nonstationarity cannot be rejected.
The standard VAR model takes the following form for a series such as χ:

$$\chi_t = A_1 \chi_{t-1} + \cdots + A_n \chi_{t-n} + B\psi_t + \epsilon_t, \tag{I.2}$$

whereas if the series follow Equation (I.1), which has a mean and a time trend but the cointegrating equations have only intercepts, the VEC is:

$$\begin{aligned} \Delta \chi_{1,t} &= \delta_1 + \gamma_1(\chi_{2,t-1} - \mu - \beta \chi_{1,t-1}) + \epsilon_{1,t}, \quad \text{and} \\ \Delta \chi_{2,t} &= \delta_2 + \gamma_2(\chi_{2,t-1} - \mu - \beta \chi_{1,t-1}) + \epsilon_{2,t}, \end{aligned} \tag{I.3}$$

where χ_1 and χ_2 are two endogenous variables. Therefore, in this example, the cointegrating equation can be specified as:

$$\chi_{2,t-1} - \mu - \beta \chi_{1,t-1} = \epsilon, \tag{I.4}$$

where μ is the mean and ϵ is the error term. The VEC model attempts to correct for ϵ. For the purpose of presentation of the statistical results, Equation (I.4) is rearranged to: $\chi_{2,t-1} = \mu + \beta \chi_{1,t-1} + \epsilon$. Of course, normalization implies that $\chi_{2,t-1}$ ($X_{1,t-1}$ in Table I) is chosen as a dependent variable with the coefficient of unity.

and Granger, 1987)]. Since all of the variables for the production function clearly are $I(1)$, the VEC model is selected for estimating that function. The normalized cointegrating equation results for the production function, using the Maximum Likelihood method, are reported in Table I. Since the t-values for most of the lagged differenced values of X_1 in the VEC model are not statistically significant, they are not reported.

From the mixed results of the ADF and Johanson tests, the use of the VEC model for the demand and the total revenue functions became problematic. It appears, from the ADF results, that the data series for P and R in the demand and the total revenue functions are not cointegrated; that is, these series are $I(0)$. Most of the other variables appear to be $I(1)$. In any case, because of the number of lagged variables required for the VEC model that limited the degrees of freedom, we reverted to the standard VAR model for the real demand and box office revenue functions. We use OLS to estimate these VAR models.

As to multicollinearity, the VIFs are larger than 10 for $X_{1,t}$, I_t, and VCR. The values of the VIFs and of the correlation coefficients are used in the selection of the three model specifications for the demand function in Table II and for the total revenue function reported in Table III. The remaining parameter estimates remain quite stable across the three model specifications, and the tests used in model selection do not clearly favor any one of the three models.

Our preliminary unreported estimates for studio film production appeared reliable, though no increasing returns to scale were found. However, we then discovered that the population for the number-of-films data series was increased significantly, beginning in 1982. Earlier, *only* the major studios were surveyed to find number of films produced, a series highly favorable to our assumptions. The population surveyed was expanded to include films by independent producers and old, reissued films. Once we introduced a dummy variable (DUM) for the later series, our parameter estimates deteriorated, as reflected in our final results. To deal with the structural break in this series, X is regressed against a dummy variable for the break. Then, the residuals from this regression or X_1 are tested for non-stationarity.

In the reported estimates for production the coefficients of capital and star are statistically significant with the expected signs. As hypothesized, rising generic capital (K) is required to produce many films simply to feed the theater chains. The coefficient of generic labor (Y_1), on the other hand, has an unexpected negative sign, while it too is statistically significant. The perverse significance of this parameter surely is implausible; a greater number of Guild actors should increase, not decrease, total film output. Perhaps technological advances in the exhibition of films, such as multiple screens, explain the sign of labor (though using time to represent continuously improving technology does not alter the estimate). The significance and size of the dummy variable in preliminary production function estimates suggest the importance of the independents in supplying large numbers

Table II. Vector Autoregression (VAR) log-log estimates for demand function[d]

Variables	Model 1	Model 2	Model 3
Ln Q_{t-1}	0.9802[a]	0.2033	0.1300
	(0.1474)	(0.1701)	(0.1566)
Ln Q_{t-2}	−0.4279[a]	−0.2903[b]	−0.3070[b]
	(0.1467)	(0.1584)	(0.1437)
Ln $P_{1,t}$	−0.2328[c]	−0.5099[a]	−0.4155[a]
	(0.1922)	(0.1867)	(0.1820)
Ln $Y_{2,t}$	0.2740[a]	0.2521[a]	0.2889[a]
	(0.0556)	(0.0636)	(0.0594)
Ln $X_{1,t-1}$	0.0205	0.0007	0.0078
	(0.0212)	(0.0229)	(0.0218)
Ln I_t	−0.9612[a]	–	−0.2937[a]
	(0.3619)		(0.1437)
Ln VCR_t	−0.0288[b]	−0.0070	–
	(0.0145)	(0.0062)	
Constant	16.8125[a]	7.4862[a]	9.7626[a]
	(3.8040)	(1.6918)	(1.4635)
Log likelihood	50.17	45.83	47.56
Akaike AIC	−3.37	−3.12	−3.25
Schwarz SC	−2.98	−2.76	−2.90
Adjusted R^2	0.84	0.79	0.82

[a]Significant at the 1% level.
[b]Significant at the 5% level.
[c]Significant at the 10% level.
[d]Standard errors are in parentheses.
Notes: See notes to Table I.

of generic films. As a result, the efficient estimation of production coefficients is elusive.

In the demand equation the significantly estimated price elasticity of demand ranges from −0.23 to −0.51, suggesting highly inelastic demand. This inelasticity may be a measure of the success of the majors in differentiating their products though non-price competition. At these elasticities, we would expect a particular percentage real price rise to result in a lesser percentage decline in admissions and an increase in total box office. At the mean of the elasticity estimates, a 1 percent increase in real ticket prices would reduce demand by only about 4 mil-

Table III. Vector Autoregression (VAR) linear-log estimates for box office revenues[d]

Variables	Model 1	Model 2	Model 3
R_{t-1}	−0.0010	−0.0051	−0.0018
	(0.0015)	(0.0015)	(0.0015)
R_{t-2}	−0.0041[a]	−0.0043[a]	−0.0042[a]
	(0.0013)	(0.0014)	(0.0013)
Ln $P_{1,t}$	32.1130[a]	26.8211[a]	29.4007[a]
	(6.8906)	(5.8696)	(5.3827)
Ln $Y_{2,t}$	10.9612[a]	10.6693[a]	11.2097[a]
	(2.0268)	(2.0661)	(1.9579)
Ln $X^{*}_{1,t}$	−0.4002	−0.8065	−0.5483
	(0.8020)	(0.7646)	(0.7562)
Ln I_t	−17.0626[c]	–	−9.6862[b]
	(12.3547)		(4.7071)
Ln VCR_t	0.2988	−0.2887[c]	–
	(0.4614)	(0.1832)	
Constant	108.5255	−35.2123[b]	44.5527
	(105.0690)	(14.7552)	(35.2052)
Log Likelihood	−154.37	−155.70	−154.68
Akaike AIC	12.99	13.02	−12.93
Schwarz SC	13.38	13.36	13.28
Adjusted R^2	0.64	0.63	0.66

[a]Significant at the 1% level.
[b]Significant at the 5% level.
[c]Significant at the 10% level.
[d]Standard errors are in parentheses.
*To take the log of X_1, the values of X_1 are scaled up by 1,000 to deal with the negative values in some residuals.
Notes: See notes to Table I.

lion, still leaving some 1,034 million admissions. Box office revenue still would rise by between $26.82 million and $32.11 million, depending on the linear-log model selected. Thus, total revenue estimates are consistent with the estimated price-inelastic demand. Variations, at the margin, in the number of generic films produced each year (X_1) apparently do not influence the viewers decision to go to the movies.

The stars do shine. In rank order of importance, box-office receipts (R) and the number of admissions (Q) are greatly improved by an increase in the index number of stars (Y_2). A 1 percent increase in the star index raises admissions by about 2.3 million and box office by about $30 million. The "marginal revenues" from star presence, of course, benefit differentially the major studios. Since *every* film cannot have a star and since stars are limited in number or appeal, they are slightly less important for admissions as for box office receipts. Surprisingly, an increase in the star index increases the *number* of films produced (X_1), bearing in mind that our production results are weak. Perhaps a strong star showing early in a movie year enables the majors to finance a greater number of generic films.

The number of VCRs sold domestically and worldwide increased dramatically during this period, so rapidly that their standard deviation is very large. The VCR effect, while expected to be important, could be either negative (contrary to the literature) or positive. That is, the VCR provides both a substitute for "going out" to the movie theater and a secondary market for the films (including blockbusters) and perhaps positive synergistic impetus for seeing more films. The ambiguity caused by these conflicting forces may be reflected in the insignificance of the VCR variable in all but Model 1 of the demand estimates and Model 2 of the box office estimates. Where significant, the sign *is* negative but the effects small.

Per capita income (I) had significant negative effects on demand and on total revenue, suggesting that movies may be inferior goods. A 1 percent increase in per capita income results in a decline of between $9.7 million and $17.1 million in box office. These results do not dispute the importance of market size and wealth as *initial conditions* for the success of the American industry. The significant constant terms in the demand estimates may reflect a part of the effect of such initial conditions as a large population and GDP.

Would the absence of increasing returns to scale in production of number of films be a plausible finding? Unless we accept the view that the industry is dominated by "crazy artists" uninterested in revenues, either increasing returns or economies of scale are required to justify the high costs of stars and their promotion. However, since studio production creates only the master print, not the admissions leading to box office, increasing returns to scale in generic *physical* production may be elusive. However, this would not rule out economies of scale from box office within the theater system.

De Vany and Walls (1997, pp. 784–785) correctly explain how the theater system can result in economies of scale, although they estimate box office only for *individual* movies without reference to the structure of the industry. Still, Equation (3) of our model can capture increasing returns to scale through the number of admissions for the theater. If, say, a theater's capacity for the length of the run is q_c admissions (= maximum number of seats, being, for each film, the sum of the seats available during the days the film is run), economies of scale are incurred up to q_c. Uniquely, capacity itself is variable, depending on the film's length of run. In turn, the theater's economies of scale translate into economies of scale for the studio in the vertically integrated industry. Since **K** becomes sunk costs (once the master is produced, the stars promoted, and the prints made), rising admissions (q) means declining unit costs where the output unit is defined as admissions, not as number of films. That is, if the aggregate studio/theater output is defined as admissions (Q) instead of number of masters (X), the ratio $\mathbf{K}/Q$ is falling if blockbusters are successful, even though the ratio $\mathbf{K}/X$ may be constant or rising! In fact, the $\mathbf{K}/Q$ ratio exhibits a downward trend. Unfortunately, the quality of the data series for X precludes a direct estimate of Equation (3).

IV. Conclusions

We cannot falsify most of our hypotheses. The few dominant studios rely on a modified star system to differentiate their product and generate supra-normal box office by optimizing admissions of exhibitors. By filling more seats and extending movie runs, the theaters create economies of scale for the major studios. Output is properly defined as admissions rather than number of master films. We would expect star labor to be even less important in influencing the raw number of films produced, if it were not for the increase in financial capital from blockbusters that probably "subsidizes" generic films. For these reasons, rising costs (from stars-advertising) are expected to be highly correlated with rising revenues; the majors maximize revenue only with rising total costs. It is the integrated structure of the industry facilitating economies of scale in admissions that enables the majors to succeed.

The initial conditions of the industry nonetheless are critical to the success of the major studios. The requirement of a large domestic market is sufficiently clear; it is required to support expensive stars and blockbusters as well as to provide an adequate inventory of generic films for theaters. Given a sufficiently large consumer market, a few nearly identical studios can subdivide a large share of the total market. Because the star system and its promotional costs made the minimal circulating capital requirements very large, even a large domestic consumer market for movies has provided for only a few dominant majors any particular year with independent producers usually depending upon the majors for distribution. External as well as internal economies of scale, imperfect competition, and vertical integration have been critical to the success of the U.S. movies industry. Industry experts lend some support to these findings.

Despite many seemingly unique characteristics in the movies industry, the movie star model may be applicable to the recording, television, and sports industries where stars receive large rents. Doubtless, admissions (and thus gate receipts or "box office") increase in the presence of Tiger Woods, Greg Norman, Cal Ripken, Jr., and Magic Johnson. (For example, not only gate attendance but Neilson ratings for golf telecasts have roughly doubled when Tiger Woods was in contention going into the weekend.) Moreover, any industry such as beer or tobacco reliant on promotion and advertising for product differentiation plus a loyal distributorship network may come under this umbrella. Even the automotive industry, which relies on advertising and dealerships, also has "stars" of a sort. Exotic models such as the Corvette and the Dodge Viper are used to draw customers into the showroom to buy the more mundane and affordable models. More important, automobile manufacturers have to produce many models to give dealers an inventory sufficient for year-to-year profitability.

References

De Vany, Arthur S., and W. David Walls (1997) 'The Market for Motion Pictures: Rank, Revenue, and Survival', *Economic Inquiry*, **35**, 783–797.

Engle, R. F., and W. J. Granger (1987) 'Co-Integration and Error Correction: Representation, Estimation, and Testing', *Journal of Political Economy*, **55**, 251–276.

Frank, B. (1992) 'A Note on the International Dominance of the U.S. in the Trade in Movies and Television Fiction', *Journal of Media Economics*, **5**, 31–28.

Murphy, A. D. (1992) 'Distribution and Exhibition: An Overview', in Jason Squire, ed., *The Movie Business Book*. New York: Simon and Schuster.

Prag, J., and J. Casavant (1994) 'An Empirical Study of the Determinants of Revenues and Marketing Expenditures in the Motion Picture Industry', *Journal of Cultural Economics*, **18**, 217–235.

Theatrical Data (1992) New York: Motion Pictures Association of America.

Vogel, H. (1986) *Entertainment Industry Economics*. Cambridge, U.K.: Cambridge University Press.

Waterman, D. (1993) 'World Television Trade: The Economic Effects of Privatization and New Technology', in Eli Noam and Joel C. Millonzi, eds., *The International Market in Film and Television Programs*. Norwood, NJ: Ablex.

Wildman, S., and S. Siwek (1988) *International Trade in Films and Television Programs*. Cambridge, MA: Ballinger Publishing Co.

PART V

ECONOMIC THOUGHT AND METHODOLOGY

Chapter 26

WHAT DO WE MEAN BY ASKING WHETHER ECONOMICS IS A SCIENCE?

E. Ray Canterbery and Robert J. Burkhardt

The question of whether economics is a science is far more complex than one might at first believe. The answer has as much to do with our understanding of what we mean by the word "science" —how the word is applied, and perhaps what we'd like it to mean —as with comparing the "scientific results" of economics with those of "real sciences" like physics or astronomy. It is generally thought that there are two opposing camps as to whether economics is a science. On the one hand, there are those who maintain that economics is essentially a science. Economics, it is argued, meets all the defining characteristics of science, whatever those might be. In their weaker moments, adherents to this position may admit that it is perhaps more accurate to say that economics only approximates being a science. To describe it as a science merely implies a standard which economists continuously seek to realize in practice but which, at the present time, is realized in neither the whole of economics nor any part of it. Or, as the adherents to this "pro-position" might say, economics has certain basic features of a science, as physics and agronomy and biology do; yet, like these other disciplines, it is not "completely scientific" in the way it goes about generating theories and then testing them. Immaculate conceptions are, after all, historically rare.

The other identifiable party to this debate maintains that economics is not a science. Actually, if the "pro-position" stated above has been somewhat simplified and differences ignored, this simplification is even more apparent in the "con-position" described next. Those who claim that economics is *not* a science do so for a number of different reasons. One group includes those

This is part of the joint product of a grant from the National Science Foundation (Grant No. 05577-16566). Any opinions, findings, and conclusions are those of the authors and do not necessarily reflect the views of the NSF.

who were once idealists, committed to the view that economics is ideally and potentially a science. Now, however, jaded through experience, they are convinced that economics either lost the vision, didn't try, or failed miserably in the effort. Also among the economics-is-not-a-science ranks are new and different idealists. They maintain that the very nature of economics, as a *social* science, precludes it from ever being a "real science" like physics or astronomy. Typically, "cons" of the latter persuasion don't lament the plight of economics at all. Instead they praise it: damned be the day that a science of human behavior should explain, predict, or experiment. Economists should be content to "understand" human nature.

There is a seldom recognized "third" position in the debate, however—one which views the adherents of the two other camps as simply talking past each other. This third position maintains that the other two groups are both right and both wrong—though for different reasons. It depends, essentially, on whether the adherents to those two positions are talking descriptively or normatively, analytically or sociologically, historically or nonhistorically. Clearly, both camps use terms like "science," "explanation," "verification," "laws," "theories," and so forth. Yet, when we consider what philosophical commitments each group begins with, we can see that the words do not have exactly the same meanings to the two sides.

Thus, in this essay it is useful to first consider what philosophers of science mean when they say "science" and what criteria they submit for its application. Next we will consider how these views relate to the question of whether economics is a science, and, finally, we'll try to answer the question: Is it?

I

The question of whether economics is a science could not have arisen prior to the twentieth century. From ancient times through the nineteenth century, the standards according to which a body of suppositions, theories, explanations, and predictions could be judged as "adequate" might have been changing. Still, the mere organization of a body of theories in some logical fashion, aimed—accurately or not—in the direction of knowledge, sufficed to qualify it as a science. The latter term was understood to mean organized cognition. Again, a certain progress, if one calls it that, can be said to have occurred in the kinds of standards designating "good explanations," or good theories. Early criteria, such as "in accord with revealed truth" gave way to the standard "formulated according to the natural light of reason" and, later, "testable by experience." Still, the claim to be a "science" was not reserved for particular kinds of theories or subject matter. Consider the "science of witchcraft" and physiognomy, judged legitimate sciences in their times and places.

A self-conscious conception of science emerged only with the rise of the logical positivist school of philosophy in the early 1900s. This philosophical system offered not only criteria for evaluating particular theories and explanations, but also ones for evaluating whole areas of investigations as well. Depending upon the subject matter, or upon the type of explanation offered, systems of organized cognition directed toward an all-encompassing "knowledge" or "truth" were rejected, or at least told to repent their nonscientific ways. Philosophy was among the first to feel the axe; ethics later; religion, of course, had to fall; still later, sociology, anthropology, and political economy felt the pressure. The logical positivists, not to be confused with so-called "positivists" like Milton Friedman in economics, made their weight felt.

Hollis and Nell[1] neatly catalogue the major tenets of the logical positivist position. These are:

1. Claims to knowledge of the world are justified only by experience;
2. Whatever is known by experience could have been otherwise;
3. All cognitively meaningful statements are either analytic (their truthfulness determined solely by the meanings of the words) or synthetic (their truthfulness determined by facts of experience);
4. Synthetic statements, being refutable, cannot be known a priori;
5. Analytic statements have no factual content;
6. Analytic truths are true by convention;
7. A causal law is an adequately confirmed empirical hypothesis;
8. A test of a theory is the success of its predictions;
9. Judgments of value have no place in science;

[1] M. Hollis, and E. Nell, *Rational Economic Man* (Cambridge: Cambridge University Press, 1975), p. 10.

10. Sciences are distinguishable by their subject matter and not by their methodology.

A further canon must be added to these. It is that science, according to logical positivists, must necessarily *progress* if it follows the above ten commandments. Through the process of continual theory-formation and testing according to experience, "unscientific" theories will be systematically discarded while true, scientific theories and laws will be shown to be true, and accumulated.

The logical positivist had a mission, which was to unify science under these canons. It was soon realized, however, that the repeated efforts to bring diverse though legitimate areas of inquiry, such as physics and biology, and sociology and botany, under the positivist umbrella were fraught with problems. Some were internal to the project of the positivists itself; some more "external." One internal problem, which in part stemmed from the practical consequences of applying the canons, especially 1 and 7, and in part from the fact that no scientist actually does follow all of those rules, led philosopher of science Karl Popper to introduce the notion of "falsifiability" in order to save the sinking positivist ship.[2] As it turns out, this rescue mission was about as effective as throwing an anchor to a drowning sailor.

Popper argued that the insistence on empirical verification of all statements (all synthetic statements, that is) isn't realistic. It's too stringent a demand, yields certain paradoxes, and, in the final analysis, isn't the way science operates. Science is instead a moving picture of conjectures, refutations, new conjectures, and so forth, governed by the principle of falsifiability. Rather than try to prove theories true, scientists should—and do—really try to prove them false. At the very least, one should be able to imagine what it would be like for the theory in question to be false in order to retain it as a candidate for a true or workable theory. Otherwise, the theory in question is probably a piece of a priori reasoning, perhaps even a fiction. Popper retains a commitment to empirical, synthetical science, but with a major modification. We should be concerned as much with the process of scientific discovery and theory-creation as with the structure and status of the statements that we claim to be scientific.

[2] Karl Popper, *The Logic of Scientific Discovery* (London: Hutchinson, 1959), and *Conjectures and Refutations* (London: Routledge and Kegan Paul, 1963).

There is a good bit more to Popper's line of argument. He included an attempt to develop, aggressively, a logic for falsification, a normative "how-to" for systematically rejecting theories. Its major importance, however, is that it introduced a pragmatic side to the positivist project, with recognition of what we might call "sciencing"—the doing of science—and the essentially normative nature of the canons for sciencing.

The pragmatic character of much scientific research and discovery became a focal point for disputes about the nature of "real science." The positivists argued that, even with a principle of falsification supplanting that of verification, real science retains the logical structure outlined in the positivist canons. Others, especially Thomas Kuhn[3] and Imre Lakatos[4] maintained that the whole of science was process, research programs, and paradigms. Taking their clue from historical studies of science, especially the "model" science of physics, philosophers of science like Kuhn and Lakatos argue that science never actually adheres to the positivistic canons. Instead, the canons are ex post facto creations of the positivists. In fact, the historian-pragmatists contend, science is really definable not by either its content or its empirical methodology but rather by what scientists who are accepted as scientists by other scientists hold it to be. Science is whatever scientists do.

The importance of this kind of claim vis-à-vis the positivists is threefold. First, in Kuhn's view a sociological analysis is more instructive than a logical construction for understanding the nature of science. Second, both Kuhn and Lakatos, and perhaps Popper as well, maintain that the criteria for science, as opposed to fiction or philosophy or religion, are established not from "on high," but instead from within the ranks of the practicing scientists. In this sense logical positivism becomes a Trojan horse. And third, the criteria that the positivists proposed mark only one *kind* of science, not "science itself"—and a false and misleading view of that one kind of science at that. (W. V. O. Quine, a philosopher of science and logic, has persuasively argued that the analytic-synthetic distinction that stands at the foundation of empiricist science is an il-

[3] Thomas Kuhn, *The Structure of Scientific Revolutions* (Chicago: University of Chicago Press, 1970); see also M. N. Richter, *Science as a Cultural Process* (Cambridge MA: Schenkman, 1972), pp. 77-83.

[4] Imre Lakatos, and Alan Musgrave, *Criticism and the Growth of Knowledge* (Cambridge: Cambridge University Press, 1970), pp. 92-195.

legitimate distinction. Thus positivists, even committed ones in the scientific community, are operating on the basis of a fiction.)[5]

The key to Kuhn's view of science lies in his concept of the scientific paradigm. Though variously defined, a scientific paradigm is best described as an outstanding scientific achievement, one that some scientific community has acknowledged as supplying the foundation for further scientific practice. It has some of the characteristics of a world view shared by a spectrum of society, at least for the limited world of scientific research and experiment. The paradigm must be attractive enough to win in competition with other potential paradigms. At the same time, the paradigm must be sufficiently "open-ended" to leave unresolved all sorts of problems that its adherents can solve.

Paradigms thus are comprehensive and open-ended at the same time: problems generated by the paradigm remain unsolved, but the paradigm holds out the prospect of successful solutions if people simply follow the well-trodden paths of previous researchers in the community. The paradigm thus provides a certain security for those working under it, as it serves to define who, in a broader scientific context or in society at large, are like-minded and indeed "really scientists."

Sociologically, some of the marks of a paradigm are that adherents all tend to hold the same level of academic degree; all have similar kinds of education, both technical and cultural; they all read the same literature, especially journal articles, so that they can communicate with each other in a way that is relatively free of ambiguity, at least on basic terms.

In terms of the structure of science, Lakatos adds considerably to Kuhn's analysis. Lakatos sees that the paradigm, or "research program," contains two main components, the "hard core" and the "protective belt." The hard core is that portion of the paradigm that scientists have already decided is irrefutable. The protective belt is that portion that contains a degree of flexibility, as certain hypotheses are tested and rejected, others introduced, tested, and rejected. The protective belt represents the area in which Popperlian falsifiability or positivist verifiability operates. Some theories, or "explanations," never reach that point, except in periods of crisis, or what Kuhn calls a "scientific revolution." In that

[5] W. V. O. Quine, *Word and Object* (Cambridge MA: MIT Press, 1960).

unusual case, the fundamental achievement, or the fundamental world view, is challenged—and rejected. Kuhn points to the shift from Ptolemaic geocentrism to Galilean heliocentrism as a case in point.

In Kuhn's, Lakatos', and even Popper's analysis of science, a distinction must be made between a normative conception of science and a descriptive one. The positivists engaged in "persuasive definition" by using the name "science" only for those knowledge-directed organized systems that adhered to their canons, while Popper showed that the positivist criteria were both too strong and too weak—too strong as a description of science, and too weak as normative criteria. Kuhn and Lakatos augment Popper's analysis by suggesting that a "meaning of science," in either a normative or a descriptive sense, must rest upon a recognition that there are forces at work in the doing of science by scientists that make science in one respect at least an indescribable phenomenon. A particular paradigm has to be looked at, to a large extent, on its own terms to see what qualifies it to be called scientific and what does not. Normatively, we can of course maintain that all science should "look like" a particular paradigm, in terms of its structure, its assumptions, and its rules for conducting research. Even that, however, may be no more than to claim, from within a paradigm, that other paradigms are not "real science."

II

There are very few "olde-type positivists" in the philosophy of science anymore. Most philosophers of science have at least nodded in the direction of Kuhn's sociological and Lakatos' dynamic analyses. They see the canons positivists apply to "science" as values —not necessarily ethical, moral, religious, or political, but values nonetheless. They are "scientific values." The problem, when it comes to defining science, is this: are the "scientific values" of falsifiability, keeping analytic and synthetic distinctions straight, and maintaining a value-free quest for greater understanding possible?

What is interesting is that even pragmatist philosophers of science think that, to a large extent, the "values" of the positivist program are basically sound and that, within limits, it is possible to live according to them. Science, that is, can be practiced fairly well if knowledge-claims are tested against experience, say in the lab; if law-like statements are subjected to falsification-instances; and if moral values are at least kept to a minimum in the practice of theory-formation and the choice of research puzzles. Granted, a full or perfect adherence to the positive ideals would be impossible; still, they would be kept firmly in mind. The pragmatist argues that, to a large extent, adherence to these ideals has worked in the past to produce a certain movement, if not progress, in science. And, by attempting to act in accordance with these ideals, especially falsifiability, we have made even paradigm shifts, or changes in the hard core.

Economics, however, is an illuminating instance of how the values of the positivists, even as ideals and not as descriptive criteria of real science, are not always attained in disciplines that claim to be scientific. In fact, economists seem to pay only lip service to the positivist ideals, going off and doing their own thing irrespective of whatever normative criteria philosophers of science—or indeed other kinds of scientists—have found to be sound, or at least functional. In this respect, economics may be a science, but only in the bold-faced Kuhnian sense of there being a paradigm within which economists practice and according to which they self-referentially define their activity as science. Economics may thus be a pre-positivist "system of organized cognition"—much in the same way, perhaps, as Ptolemaic geocentrism.

If we look at the dominant paradigm in economics, we see, in fact, that the discipline has not progressed very far; and, despite a certain avowal of positivist values, the protective belt functions there more like a chastity belt than even Kuhn and Lakatos would consider acceptable for a practicing science.

The paradigm of orthodox economics takes its lead from Adam Smith's *Wealth of Nations*. Orthodox economists recognize that, although Smith's work is "wrong" in spots, it is nonetheless based on a great truth, the self-regulating nature of the market, which marks the book as the initial achievement in economics. Alfred Marshall's *Principles* follows in a direct evolutionary path with Paul Samuelson's *Foundations* and J. R. Hick's *Value and Capital* providing a present-day cul-de-sac. We hardly need to recapitulate the way in which the ideas reflected in Smith's invisible hand, the maximization hypothesis, the propensity of man to truck and barter, and so forth have been buttressed and tightened throughout the past two centuries. Nor do we need to note how numerous are the research puzzles and problems that have been generated at the protective belt, so that challenges to the fundamental world view have rarely if ever been taken seriously, at least by "real economists." Even the so-called "Keynesian revolution," a presumed paradigm shift, has been successfully aborted insofar as Keynes's vision has been co-opted to a large extent by the dominant neoclassical orthodoxy.[6]

Still, a look at the paradigm from a sociological perspective can show some interesting trends and can set the stage for understanding why it is that positivist values do not succeed even as ideals for the economist. One major reason is the academic prestige structure so important to economists, since academics such as Milton Friedman and Paul Samuelson are among the leading figures. The academic publish-or-perish system, the value of "pure research," and the fact that the doctoral degree is the major license to practice all justify this emphasis on academia.

The most prestigious form of publication is a quantitative theoretical article in a "number-one" journal, such as *The American Economic Review*, a journal of the American Economic Association. While workers in some academic disciplines (e.g., history, anthropology) prefer books and monographs, economists since World War II, like physicists, prefer the journal article. Journal articles are cited far more than other publications.[7] While many of those who are at the apex of the profession, including Nobel Prize winners like Milton Friedman and Paul Samuelson, have also written popular books and articles, their professional prestige derives primarily from their technical writings. Popular pieces are simply frosting on the cake. In fact, Samuelson concluded his 1961 Presidential Address before the American Economic Association by saying: "In the long run, the economic scholar works for the only coin worth having—our own applause." Later, he claimed to have meant that economists should work honestly and not for public approval.[8] Still, the need for peer recognition is something that

[6] For this story, see E. Ray Canterbery, *The Making of Economics*, 2nd ed. (Belmont CA: Wadsworth, 1980).

[7] See C. Michael Lovell, "The Production of Economic Literature: An Interpretation," *Journal of Economic Literature* 11 (March 1973): 27-55.

[8] See Leonard Silk, *The Economists* (New York: Basic Books, 1976), p. 230.

economists share with other scholars and scientists who engage in ceremonial rituals that confer status on their elite, maintain discipline, and guarantee immortality. Scientists find it difficult to bear ostracism and isolation from their colleagues, even those who live at a distance. Courage (or recklessness) is the hallmark of those who dissent from Lakatos' hard core or Kuhn's normal science.

The strict hierarchy of the economics profession is especially stark in contrast to the emphasis upon individual choice, free entry (and exit), and free competition of the price theory paradigm. Leijonhufvud has used the metaphors of the caste system and the pecking order to describe the system of relations between the subfields of economics, relations between economists and other "tribes" of academics, and ties between senior and junior economists.[9]

In the profession, there is a structure of awards. Prizes in addition to the Nobel Prize are given, including the John Bates Clark medal to the most outstanding economist under forty. The presidency of the American Economic Association (AEA) is a position that carries with it a mild measure of patronage, since the president-elect of the association heads the convention program committee in arranging the program around a central theme. This does not always bias results in favor of Ph.D.'s from his school, according to Robert Eagly, an economist who has studied these professional patterns, but it may.[10] As Eagly points out, the annual conventions of the American Economic Association are not "open conventions." In sharp contrast to the conventions of many other scientific professions, the AEA has no public call for papers and no competition among prospective authors. Who appears on the program (and who is assured publication in the highly vaunted *Papers and Proceedings* of the Association) is narrowly restricted.

The same tendency toward what Eagly calls "democratic centralism," apparently a euphemism for market concentration and control, is reflected in the journals, which are, after all, edited and refereed by established scholars following a particular mode of operation. (One usually qualifies to be a referee upon publication in the particular journal.) Moreover, the population of those publish-

[9] Axel Leijonhufvud, "Life Among the Econ," *Western Economic Journal* (1973): 327-337.

[10] Robert V. Eagly, "Contemporary Profile of Conventional Economists," *History of Political Economy* (1974): 76-91.

ing *American Economic Review* articles is more or less the same as that of the AEA convention participants.

Economics as a field has, to a great extent, been sheltered from the winds of social change. There is still a high demand for economists by government and quasi-governmental agencies, businesses, and, consequently, universities. At the same time, the hierarchical "democratic centralism" of the American Economic Association has insulated it from student revolt in relative contrast to what has happened in other academic professional societies. In the Modern Language Association, a major professional society of humanities scholars, there was a coup at the business meeting. In the American Anthropological Association, students and other members gained the right to vote and helped pass radical resolutions at business meetings although the resolutions sometimes failed to be ratified by the full membership. By contrast, at the American Economic Association meetings, those who protest are vocal but orderly.

While articles by radicals appear regularly in major anthropological journals, George Borts, the editor of the *American Economic Review* from 1969 through 1980, claims that few worthy radical articles were submitted. He noted: "I am still waiting for comments on the Radical Critique of the Council of Economic Advisors Report, an invited paper which appeared December 1975. Despite a good deal of verbal comment which I was privileged to receive, this paper has not generated any significant attention from authors."[11] In his departing Editor's Report, Borts adds a second gratuitous insult to the injury. "The radical political economists, post-Keynesians, and Marxists have their own journals. If their methodologies are fruitful, I would expect economists of all persuasions to use them."[12] All this ignores the obvious: "Radicals," including Marxists and post-Keynesians, presume that their submissions will not be acceptable to the normal science or mainstream reviewers of the "leading" journals and therefore they do not submit.

[11] "Report of the Editor, AER," *American Economic Review: Papers and Proceedings* (February 1977): 451-452. Borts repeated this claim in his final report, but added Marxist and post-Keynesian authors to those who submitted a few bad papers, all of which were rejected.

[12] "Report of the Editor, AER," *American Economic Review: Papers and Proceedings* (May 1981): p. 460.

In this sense, one needs to realize that a "radical" in economic science is any scholar unfaithful to the dominant paradigm. For those "radicals" sufficiently naive to make submissions, there is the problem of acceptance. After making clear his strong personal hand in turning down papers, Borts states his own preference for "the rational, choice theoretic aspects of whatever behavior is under investigation. This is in keeping with the type of research that is being done in the profession."[13] In general, the Establishment in economics ignores its radicals and does not take them seriously. It does not have to.

There have been a relatively small number of institutions that have granted Ph.D.'s in economics and the top universities have a marked tendency to hire their own PH.D.'s or those from other high-ranking institutions. Of the Ph.D.'s granted in economics between 1935 and 1969, the sixteen top-ranked universities accounted for more than half. The most distinguished departments (according to the widely cited 1966 Cartter study)—in rank order, Harvard, Massachusetts Institute of Technology, University of Chicago, Yale, University of California at Berkeley, Stanford, and Princeton—hire each other's graduates.[14] Furthermore, the ranking of departments is strongly dependent upon the number of articles published in the "leading" journals. Two of the leading journals are at Harvard, one is at Chicago, and *The American Economic Review* was edited by a University of Chicago Ph.D. between 1969 and 1980. The holders of doctorates from these schools also are among the majority of authors in the leading journals and among convention participants. Our updated version of this research confirms that this trend continues. Of the full-length articles in Harvard's *Quarterly Journal of Economics* in 1973 through 1978, one-third were authored by Harvard graduates. Of the full-length articles during the same period in Chicago's *Journal of Political Economy*, one-fifth were authored by the University's graduates. Although the *American Economic Review* was located at Brown University, Chicago graduates ranked first in authorship and Harvard graduates third. These data are detailed in Tables 1, 2, and 3. Almost one-half of the members of the editor-

[13] Ibid., p. 459.

[14] Allan Cartter, *An Assessment of Quality in Graduate Education* (Washington: American Council on Education, 1966).

Table 1

Ph.D. Affiliation of *QJE* Authors, 1973-1978

Ph.D. grantor	Number	Percent
Harvard	34	33.3
Stanford	11	10.8
MIT	10	9.8
Yale	8	7.8
University of Chicago	6	5.9
University of California (Berkeley)	4	3.9
Columbia	3	2.9
Princeton	3	2.9
Cambridge	2	2.0
University of Wisconsin	2	2.0
University of Rochester	2	2.0
All others (1 each)	17	16.7
Totals	102	100.0%
Affiliation unknown	(62)	

Table 2

Ph.D. Affiliation of *JPE* Authors, 1973-1978

Ph.D. grantor	Number	Percent
University of Chicago	44	20.7
MIT	22	10.3
Harvard	21	9.9
Yale	18	8.5
Columbia	10	4.7
University of California (Berkeley)	8	3.8
Johns Hopkins	7	3.3
Stanford	6	2.8
University of Wisconsin	5	2.4
Princeton	5	2.4
Oxford	4	1.9
UCLA	4	1.9
University of Pennsylvania	3	1.4
University of Michigan	3	1.4
University of London	3	1.4
All others (2 or less)	50	23.5
Totals	213	100.3%*
Affiliation unknown	(60)	

*Total greater than 100% because of rounding.

Table 3

Ph.D. Affiliation of *AER* Authors, 1973-1978

Ph.D. grantor	Number	Percent
University of Chicago	28	14.0
MIT	21	10.7
Harvard	14	7.1
Stanford	12	6.1
Yale	12	6.1
Columbia	11	6.1
University of California (Berkeley)	10	5.1
Princeton	8	4.1
University of Pennsylvania	6	3.1
North Carolina State	6	3.1
University of Wisconsin	5	2.6
Johns Hopkins	5	2.6
Brown	5	2.6
University of Rochester	4	2.0
University of London	4	2.0
New School for Social Research	4	2.0
University of Virginia	3	1.5
UCLA	3	1.5
Purdue	3	1.5
Southern Illinois	3	1.5
All others (1 article each)	29	14.8
Totals	196	100.3%*
Affiliation unknown	(52)	

*Total greater than 100% because of rounding.

ial board of the *AER* during these years were from three schools, in rank order Chicago, MIT, and Harvard. About 70 percent of the board members were from Cartter's seven distinguished departments, and some 57 percent of the members of the nominating committees (for officers of the association). Is it any wonder that the departments are "distinguished"? Thus the "best" departments are those who publish in their own journals, which are "best" since they publish the "best" departments. This academic incest would be considered genetically unsound if it involved biological reproduction.

To be fair, our school publication data should be adjusted by

Table 4

Publication Shares Relative to Ph.D. Population Shares

Ph.D. grantor	"Merit" ratio by leading journal*		
	AER (Brown)	*JPE* (Chicago)	*QJE* (Harvard)
MIT	7.0 (1)	6.8 (1)	6.4 (2)
Stanford	4.0 (2)	1.8 (4)	7.1 (1)
Yale	3.6 (3)	5.0 (2)	4.6 (3)
University of Chicago	3.3 (4)	4.7 (3)	1.4 (6)
Princeton	2.2 (5)	1.2 (6)	1.6 (5)
University of California (Berkeley)	1.0 (6)	0.7 (7)	0.2 (8)
Columbia	0.8 (7)	0.6 (8)	0.4 (7)
University of Pennsylvania	0.8 (8)	0.4 (9)	0.0 (10)
Harvard	0.7 (9)	1.4 (5)	3.2 (4)
University of Wisconsin	0.3 (10)	0.3 (10)	0.2 (9)

*The share or percentage of authors of a particular Ph.D. affiliation divided by the share or percentage of total U.S. economics Ph.D. output (1920-1961) by the same institution.

the number of economic graduates from the schools in question to provide a "merit" ratio. Once adjusted for the number of graduates, Chicago's ranking drops from 1 to 3 in its own journal and Harvard drops from 1 to 4 in its journal (see Table 4). Chicago is fourth in the *AER*; Harvard drops to ninth. If the percentage of authors equaled the percentage of Ph.D. output for a particular department, publication frequency would be based upon population only. However, Wisconsin, which has produced nearly twice the share of graduates as Chicago, has very low ratios in these leading journals. A similar pattern applies to Columbia University. Does this mean that the Chicago graduate is 16 times as brilliant as Wisconsin's and 8 times as ingenious as Columbia's? If a common standard for acceptance of papers applies, one also wonders why the representation of a department is unequal across journals.

It is difficult to know what to make of all this. One thing is clear—if we apply neoclassical price theory. Fees are required upon the submission of papers to the *AER* and the *JPE*. Moreover, the *AER* is the organization journal for the profession and is purchased by all members. Yet, in the period studied, 54, 58, and 74 percent of the authors in the *AER*, *JPE*, and *QJE* respectively were graduates of Cartter's seven "distinguished" departments. All three journals drew from the same population. It is economically inefficient to print three separate journals for the output of only seven academic departments and unfair to the masses who pay submission fees in competition for the remaining minority space and thus subsidize the handful of departments. Finally, the membership of the AEA is subsidizing a Board of Editors drawn almost exclusively from the same seven sisters.

The "truth," therefore, resides in seven academic departments whose membership constitutes a small share of the registry of all economists. This small number of individuals dominates the "leading" journals, publications financially supported by the admiring apostles of economics who genuflect when encountering a "leading" author but otherwise ignore the journals' contents. Journals are to be published in by the few and subscribed to by the many. Were it not for the need for subscribers one might conclude that most economists are superfluous.

This picture of a pro-business-competition profession which itself behaves oligopolistically is softened somewhat by the realization that, while the different universities work in similar ways, their theoretical approaches and policy conclusions are not identical. While different universities are characterized by different approaches (e.g., the University of Chicago representing the "monetarist" approach), economists *do* read and do battle in the journals. Nonetheless, in studies of journal citations, certain tendencies towards parochialism can be noted. The faculty of a particular university department is cited more by those who were students there than by outsiders, again a practice common to other disciplines. Ideological and theoretical preferences are passed on from the professors to the students. While the difference in favorable and unfavorable citations of outside authorities is not great when all universities are considered, the doctoral students of certain schools have greater antagonisms than do others. For instance, Chicago students are more unfavorable to Harvard than others, and some holders of MIT doctorates are similarly antagonistic to Chicago faculty. All in all, the studies show that, while British and American economics are marked by a common basis, there is also considerable parochialism.[15] Often economists end up talking mainly to each other and not to the world.

[15] See Eagly, op cit. Also see G. Stigler and C. Friedland, "The Citation Practices of Doctorates in Economics," *Journal of Political Economy* (June 1975):

The sociology of the profession explains in large part why, at the level of theory or hypothesis testing, the positivist program simply does not exist, even as a "value." The tendency is to continue to support theories that themselves support the paradigm, without even attempting, or at least rarely attempting, to falsify the results of a hypothesis testing a theory. In an examination of 542 full-length "empirical" articles in the major orthodox economics journals from 1973 to 1978,[16] we found that only three articles actually attempted to falsify the hypothesis proposed; since the hypotheses were (necessarily) in accordance with the fundamental presuppositions of the orthodoxy, it at least appears that there is little, if any, serious concern for challenging fundamental presuppositions.

More interesting than the fact that hypotheses in these cases were nearly always accepted is the kinds of hypotheses that were accepted. Nearly all tended to support, in relatively uncontroversial fashion, the paradigm's major tenets, the "hard core" in Lakatos' term. A complete summary of these would be beyond our scope, but a sample appears in the attached appendix.[17]

We will allow these hypotheses to speak for themselves except to focus on one illuminating subfield of the paradigm. Approximately one out of every five articles appearing in the *American Economic Review* and the *Journal of Political Economy* combined was in one specialty, human capital, which falls within the rubric of the choice-theoretic nexus of economics. The premises of the human capital school—quite distinct from those of Wisconsin's human resources school, which studies similar phenomena—are consistent with the general defense of free markets. Gary Becker's hypotheses from "The Theory of Marriage: Part 1" (see Appendix, *Journal of Political Economy*) will suffice to illustrate the point. His first hypothesis is that the gain of men and women from marrying compared to remaining single is shown to depend positively on

---

477-480. Stigler is a Professor of Economics at the University of Chicago. For comparison with anthropology, see Beverly McElliott Hurlburt, "Status and Exchange in the Profession of Anthropologist," *American Anthropologist* (February 1976): 272-285.

[16] From E. Ray Canterbery and R. J. Burkhardt, "Economics: The Embarrassed Science," National Science Foundation EVIST Research Report, 1979. Appendix 10A.

[17] Ibid., Appendix 10D.

their incomes, human capital, and relative difference in wage rates. His second hypothesis is that men differing in physical capital, education or intelligence (aside from their effect on wage rate), height, race, or many other traits will tend to marry women with like measured values of these traits. The third hypothesis is that correlation between males for wage rates or for traits of men and women that are close substitutes in household production will tend to be negative. In short, the research constitutes an exercise in economic optimization within the household.

In this and the following examples, what is purportedly being tested is not ideally being assessed. First, the behavioral assumptions are taken on faith. Second, the hypotheses—that could be formulated from quite different assumptions—are presumed rather to derive directly from those behavioral characteristics taken on faith. Third, the empirical trackings claimed to support the hypotheses (and—it is falsely presumed—the behavioral assumptions) are not inconsistent with the affirmation of the hypotheses but neither are they in conflict with any number of other quite distinct behavioral assumption sets. In other words the human capital pioneers are nominally operating in the protective belt but they accept the assumptions of the core, fail to test those assumptions, and therefore both protect and extend the core.

Another specific application is Isaac Ehrlich's "The Deterrent Effect of Capital Punishment: A Question of Life and Death" in the *American Economic Review*, in which he affirms the hypothesis that capital punishment does have a deterrent effect on crime. This finding apparently was considered so remarkable that essentially the same article was also published in the *Journal of Political Economy*. Ehrlich extended his earlier study by concluding that punishment *in general* and capital punishment in particular have a restraining effect on murders.

Still another example is Ray C. Fair's racy "A Theory of Extramarital Affairs." Professor Fair develops a model that, he claims, explains the allocation of an individual's time among work and two types of leisure activity: time spent with spouse, and time spent with a paramour. In the event the reader supposes that the human capital theorist might run out of fields to invade, one more example suffices to show that no issue is sacred, including the sacred. Corcy Azzi and Ronald Ehrenbery write about "Household Allocation of Time and Church Attendance" in the *Journal of*

Political Economy. Their hypothesis? Religiosity, the individual's religious commitment and participation in church-related activities, can be explained by a multi-period utility maximization model of household allocation of time that includes implications about the division of participation between husband and wife in the shape of the household's life-cycle religious participation profile. In all cases the hypotheses were accepted.

Situations like this suggest that the "empiricist" nature of science, which the positivists proposed, breaks down when it comes to "real testing." But further, to reflect on the positivist ideal, economists continue to maintain that they "know" the results of even "rigged" testing, or partial verification without any attempts at falsification. What is more, the maximization hypothesis that sets the tone and content for much of the work that appears in journals is simply accepted as an empirical fact, thereby violating the positivist notion that definitions, i.e., analytic truths, have no factual content. And, "supply and demand" is continually invoked as an explanation, although extensive qualifying clauses and ceteris paribus assumptions once again discredit its "empirical" nature.

One feature of orthodox economics that is positivist in its appearance is the statement that analytic truths are true by convention, that is, by agreement among practitioners in the science. If indeed positivism were accepted as a normative conception of science, such analytic truths as the maximization hypothesis, rational economic man, supply and demand, and diminishing returns would perhaps be self-consciously embraced as values, and for certain political, moral, methodological, or other reasons. Friedman, at least has suggested a pragmatic value in accepting these constructs on faith—they generate predictions.[18] However, even failing predictions—as indeed many are—do not lead to a rejection of these and of conventional truths in favor of *more* pragmatic ones. One can only believe that they are accepted for other than purely practical or "scientific" reasons. And surely our analysis of the sociology of the profession bears this out.

III

We began by asking what we have to mean by a "science" to say whether or not economics is one. We can now restate that question

[18] Friedman, *An Essay on Positive Economics* (Chicago: University of Chicago Press, 1953).

by asking, What do we have to say of economics to say whether or not economics is a science? That is, Is economics really a science under any of the descriptive or normative definitions of science from philosophers of science?

The essence of science is, according to the "pro" camp or the economists who claim that economics *is* a science, definable by the positivist vision. This vista is a normative prescription, what good science *should* be. According to the logical positivists, science is empirical, testable, synthetic, value-free; and science is defined by having a certain kind of logical relational structure, with determinate content. Definitions are regarded as either practical, operational ones or simply stipulations on how certain terms are to be understood. Above all, however, once hypotheses or theories emerge, they are subject to falsification, whether they challenge old theories or not or whether, in being tested, a "basic theory" is rejected. Economists faithful to their own prescription, therefore, will be open to the potential falsifiability of even cherished hypotheses like the maximization hypothesis, and the laws of supply and demand.

Those "cons" who maintain that economics is a science in principle but not in practice ally themselves with those wavering "pros" who maintain that we are not there *yet*, despite our following the ten commandments of logical positivism. The "cons" are more impatient and lament the fact that even after two centuries—that include higher mathematics—"yet" hasn't arrived. It all seems futile to these "cons."

The less sympathetic "cons" will maintain that, as practicing economists, all they are doing is "social philosophizing," spinning theories as ideologies or, perhaps, as "moral fictions." Others, outside the profession, might be less charitable: Economists are not doing science, but simply giving the illusion that they are knowledge-directed or organized in their cognition. Indeed, the issues of the predictability of human behavior versus free will, or of social control versus a more "naturalist" view of social life, might implicate any social science that pretends to be a science as radically misconceiving itself and human beings.

The Kuhnian view describes science as its own history without giving any explicit advice as to how the history should have proceeded. If Kuhn is right, the claims of all the pros and cons are right on their own terms, but still mistaken. If we define "science" normatively, we answer the question of whether economics is a science before we formulate it. Human activities are not identifiable before the fact as of one kind or another. We should look at what counts as science, both for scientists and for everyone else. In this regard whatever economists do is science, unless they claim to be doing something else.

Is economics a science? Economists do not in practice follow their own normative commandments for science and thus economics is not a science in terms of their own criteria. However, economics has a paradigm and devout practitioners, so that economics is a science in a Kuhnian sense of having a single overarching paradigm to which most practitioners in the field subscribe. But so what?

IV

There is a critical problem that Kuhn's analysis encounters, that of the notion of the progress of science. As we noted, the ideal science discards false theories, accumulates more information, generates new explanations and so forth. Above this, the current science or present paradigm must be in some sense "better" than the previous science. Kuhn's analysis extends the notion of progress somewhat, to focus upon the question of "progress through paradigms."

Clearly, in one respect, there is progress *within* a paradigm. Researchers develop "new frontiers" within the context of shared basic assumptions. New puzzles are generated from old, and solved; more theories and hypotheses are advanced. For economics, it is clear that the Smithian–Marshallian paradigm has generated more and more data, explanation, predictions, mathematical formulas, puzzles, and solutions. Within the orthodoxy, within the neoclassical paradigm, there has been "progress."

Kuhn's point, however, is that the idea of scientific progress, from paradigm to paradigm, makes little sense. If the orthodoxy defines scientific progress, only in-house or inside-paradigm changes constitute scientific advances. Perhaps all we can say is that there has been a certain amount of "progress away" from some assumptions or world views. However, if those who judge prior paradigms do so with the criteria of their own, the contest is rigged. This is an even greater problem when evaluating the tenets of a potential new paradigm. For example, if an orthodox neoclassical is the judge for the "scientific nature" of a post-Keynesian paradigm, it will always fall short of "scientific standards"—unless the neoclassical is able to step outside his or her own paradigm and apply criteria that are independent of the orthodoxy (see, e.g., the criteria of Eichner, this volume). Paradigms can only define truth *within them*, as they define the limits of acceptable discourse, acceptable practice. The rank-ordering of paradigms requires an Olympian vista.

In the final analysis, all we can say is that, at present, orthodox economics is the dominant paradigm. Clearly, there are challenges and questions, both from within and from without. Perhaps it is the specter of a "new paradigm" which even allows the question to be raised as to whether economics is a science, and what that must mean. Since science is paradigm and paradigm is the science, however, one can only maintain that present challenges to the dominance of orthodox economics are only attempts to show that there are problems—some within and some social—which those trained within the community find insoluable. If a scientific revolution is at hand, though, it is not because theirs is not a scientific paradigm. Rather, it is because it is not *our* paradigm. We hope ours is more reliable. We hope ours meets criteria bigger than any singular paradigm. Even so, the orthodoxy will not enter the railway carriage until the unmistakable scent of revolution is in the air or else they arrive at the station in their coffins. The shift in paradigms only once in each generation is not due to mere chance.

APPENDIX

Sample from hypotheses empirically tested in leading general journals of economics, 1973-1978*

American Economic Review

December 1973, Vol. 63, No. 5

Welch, Finis, "Black-White Difference in Returns to Schooling," pp. 893-907.

*Journals studied are *American Economic Review, Journal of Political Economy, The Economic Journal*, and *The Quarterly Journal of Economics*. The hypotheses presented constitute a non-random sample from the 340 empirical articles in these journals for the 1973-78 period.

Ho_1: Much of the gain associated with observed rise in the relative earnings of blacks in the United States is associated with tightening labor markets.

Ho_2: Part of this gain results from a coverage of completion levels.

Ho_3: The quality of schooling is an important variable.

Conclusion: Ho's [hypotheses] accepted.

March 1975, Vol. 65, No. 1

Gramm, Wendy Lee, "Household Utility Maximization and the Working Wife," pp. 90-100.

Ho_1: The marginal product of women's time in producing home goods is largest for households with young children.

Ho_2: The presence of the first child seems to be very important in explaining labor supply decisions of the wife. The second child does not seem to have a large effect on the wife's labor supply decision.

Ho_3: The age of the household is a factor affecting the labor supply decisions of the married female in this sample and this factor is distinct from the effect of the various ages of her children.

Conclusion: Ho's accepted.

June 1975, Vol. 65, No. 3

Ehrlich, Isaac, "The Deterrent Effect of Capital Punishment: A Question of Life and Death," pp. 397-417.

Ho: Capital punishment does have a deterrent effect on crime.

Conclusion: Ho accepted.

June 1976, Vol. 66, No. 3

Shishko, Robert, and Bernard Rostker, "The Economics of Multiple Job Holding," pp. 298-308.

Ho_1: The supply of moonlighting labor increases with the moonlighting wage rate and falls with primary job earnings.

Ho_2: Family size (a proxy for consumption) is significant and positively related to moonlighting hours. Furthermore, as is consistent with the life-cycle consumption hypothesis, age, which can be considered an inverse proxy for unmet family needs, shows a significant negative relationship to moonlighting hours.

Conclusion: Ho's accepted.

Frank, Robert H., "Why Women Earn Less: The Theory and Estimation of Differentials Overqualification," pp. 360-373.

Ho: The earnings differential between male and female can be attributed to a supply-side phenomenon, the overqualification differential, which measures the average fraction by which wives' earnings are reduced purely as a result of having followed their husband to a particular geographic location.

Conclusion: Ho accepted.

Journal of Political Economy

January/February 1973, Vol. 81, No. 1

Taubman, Paul J. and Terence J. Wales, "Higher Education, Mental Ability and Screening," pp. 28-55.

Ho: Education adds to income by screening people with low education out of high-paying occupations.

Conclusion: Ho accepted.

Part 1, March/April 1973, Vol. 81, No. 2

Feldstein, Martin, "The Welfare Loss of Excess Health Insurance," pp. 251-279.

Ho: American families are in general overinsured against health expenses. If insurance coverage were reduced, the utility loss from increased risk would be more than outweighed by the gain due to lower cost and the reduced purchase of excess care.

Conclusion: Ho accepted.

July/August 1973, Vol. 81, No. 4

Becker, Gary S., "The Theory of Marriage: Part 1," pp. 813-846.

Ho_1: The gain to a man and woman from marrying compared to remaining single is shown to depend positively on their incomes, human capital, and relative difference in wage rates.

Ho_2: Men differing in physical capital, education or intelligence (aside from their effect on wage rates), height, race, or many other traits will tend to marry women with like measured values of these traits.

Ho_3: The correlation between males for wage rates or for traits of men and women that are close substitutes in household production will tend to be negative.

Conclusion: Ho's accepted.

August 1975, Vol. 83, No. 4

Peltzman, Sam, "The Effect of Automobile Safety Regulation," pp. 677-725.

Ho: Safety regulation has no effect on the highway death toll and may have increased the share of this toll borne by pedestrians and increased the total number of accidents.

Conclusion: Ho accepted.

December 1977, Vol. 85, No. 6

Gronau, Reuben, "Leisure, Home Production and Work—The Theory of the Allocation of Time Revisited," pp. 1099-1123.

Ho: An increase in the market wage rate is expected to reduce work at home, while its effect on leisure and work in the market is indeterminate. An increase in income increases leisure, reduces work in the market, and leaves work at home unchanged.

Conclusion: Ho accepted.

Smith, Vernon, "The Principle of Unanimity and Voluntary Consent in Social Choice," pp. 1125-1139.

Ho: The existence of significant direct (and indirect) opportunity cost of thinking, calculating, and signaling makes strategizing in social choice uneconomical. Competitive behavior in such cases is a rational response.

Conclusion: Ho accepted.

Becker, Gary, Elizabeth M. Landes, and Robert T. Michael, "An Economic Analysis of Marital Instability," pp. 1141-1187.

Ho: Marital dissolution can be analyzed using a utility maximizing framework which incorporates uncertainty about the outcome of marital decisions.

Conclusion: Ho accepted.

The Economic Journal

September 1976, Vol. 86, No. 343

Hart, P. E., "The Dynamics of Earnings, 1963-73," pp. 551-565.

Ho: With cohort data, there is evidence that the inequality of earnings before taxes increased, but increases in inequality were usually accompanied by a clear tendency for the earnings of the poorer paid to increase proportionally more on the average than the earnings of the better paid.

Conclusion: Ho accepted.

QJE

February 1974, Vol. 78, No. 1

Straszheim, Mahlon R., "Housing Market Discrimination and Black Housing Consumption," pp. 17-43.

Ho: Racial discrimination in housing markets can be explained in terms of Blacks' responses to higher prices and to supply rationing arising from the existence of entry barriers to white submarkets.

Conclusion: Ho accepted.

May 1974, Vol. 88, No. 2

Darby, Michael P., "The Permanent Income Theory of Consumption: A Restatement," pp. 229-250.

Ho_1: The econometric techniques previously used to estimate the weight of current income in the determination of permanent income have suffered from severe upward bias.

Ho_2: The permanent income model can be formulated in terms of a simple perpetual inventory of an all-inclusive concept of wealth.

Conclusion: Ho's accepted.

February 1977, Vol. 91, No. 1

Beebe, Jack H., "Institutional Structure and Program Choice in Television Markets," pp. 15-37.

Ho: Steiner's suggestions that under limited channels monopoly will provide a more diverse program mix, greater consumer surplus, and greater total surplus than will competition depend critically on his strict viewer preferences assumption.

Conclusion: Ho accepted.

Chapter 27

Review of the Reconstruction of Economic Theory, Edited by Philip Mirowski. (Dordrecht: Kluwer Martin Nijhoff, 1986). pp.266.

The pretentious title is softened by an "apologia" in the introductory essay. Mirowski, in good humor, discusses how every scholar has faced his discontent with tradition and infers how no self-respecting mother would want her child to grow up to be a Kuhnian "normal scientist." It is far better to proclaim the "revolutionary" this or the "path-breaking" that. Mirowski defines normal-science economics as the bigemony of neoclassicism and Marxism, the center of gravity for any reconstruction era.

The editor identifies a possible "third stream" flowing from such journals as the *Journal of Post Keynesian Economics*, *Journal of Economic Issues*, *Cambridge Journal of Economics*, and *Economic Development and Cultural Change*. The contributors are drawn from those pages. Mirowski regards himself as most implacably opposed to the theoretical imperatives of present-day neoclassical theory, followed in rapidly increasing order of sympathy by contributors David Levine, Randall Bausor, David Ellerman, and Donald Katzner.

Mirowski sees the bigemony coming from attempts to appropriate the metaphors of the physics of two historical periods, bending them (like light?) to economic phenomena. Bluntly, "Marxian economic theory is a bowdlerized version of Cartesian substance theories of motion; whereas neoclassical economic theory is a bowdlerized version of nineteenth-century energy physics" (p. 5). I agree with this characterization of neoclassical theory and have so argued elsewhere. However, Mirowski's claim that Marx advanced a labor theory of value under Hegel's spell as "the pinnacle of Cartesian substance theories in economics" (p. 5) is, in my judgment, wrong. Hegel's dialectic is nonlinear and non-Cartesian. Surely Marxian alienation is not a substance, controlled or otherwise. But I quibble, for the value of this collection does not depend upon one's methodological stance. I am indifferent as to the base from which the authors ascend; it is their climb that I find exhilarating.

Mirowski identifies the third stream as: (1) not having its feet firmly embedded in tradition; (2) price not being its obsession; (3) neoinstitutional insofar as the market is an institution based upon the operation of other social institutions, its components operating in a sometimes symbiotic, sometimes contradictory way; (4) evaluating the effect of mathematical sophistication on the content of economic theory, rather than taking the mathematics as a given.

None of the contributions are bound by tradition. Levine describes a classical price theory in which persons acting in their self-interest cannot be relied upon to generate systemic coherence. The production price supposedly draws the market price toward a level consistent with reproduction of the system. As Levine suggests, the production price (based on the cost of production) often fails to do this. He writes an alternative theory of the firm in which the firm treats its profit margin and capitalization rate as variables subject to determination within an accumulation strategy designed to take advantage of ongoing market development. (His indebtedness to Kalecki is apparent.)

Bausor and Mirowski attack the "law of one price." Price cannot carry enough information to be a dependable means of economic coordination, suggests Bausor. The problem is rooted in the concept of time required by conventional general equilibrium models, where an assumed prior knowledge of equilibrium price is "a prerequisite for those acts" leading to equilibrium. Furthermore, in this model (Debreu's) events are sequentially ordered, but no formal distinction is made between motion in one time direction or the other. It is as if (reversing one of Bausor's own examples), the *Titanic* could arrive in London even though it sank on the way to New York. Each decision, being irrevocable and unrepeatable, the captain of the ship would already have decided the outcome. In any case a fallacy of composition prevents individually compiled expectations from together achieving coherent plans.

Bausor develops an alternative mathematical model in historical time using G. L. S. Shackle's idea that the present separates an unknowable future from an irrevocable past. (We know that the *Challenger* exploded, but we don't know whether the same will happen to another space vehicle.) He also employs Shackle's *kaleidics*; individuals form uncertain expectations, which lead to attempted acts. A learning curve, in turn, influences their new expectations. The model elegantly demonstrates how the rational-expectations focus upon price alone, neglecting quantity information, leads "rational" individuals into errors precluding equilibrium.

Mirowski, on the other hand, attacks the perspective that price is merely the simple ratio of physical quantities. Commodities are nonhomogeneous and cannot be properly quantified in physical units. Different characteristics of oil are used in different ways—for energy by consumers for transport, by producers to produce plastics or to lubricate ball bearings. Neoclassical economics, in which physical exchange ratios are used to express real values, requires a unit of a commodity to be equivalent to any other unit of the same commodity, further implying that the commodity will be exchanged for itself, which does not happen. An identity element must appear in every commodity set, a function that can be served only by money defining equivalence in exchange. Such "legitimate" trades, however, in a monetized economy (value being conserved in trade), preclude economic growth. Profit and growth depend upon breaking this symmetry. Credit may be the institution creating surplus value and growth possibilities.

Pride of place for neoinstitutionalism goes to Ellerman, who sees something not in neoclassical theory, namely, a theory of property appropriation. In this view the distributive-shares metaphor is misleading because in fact one legal party, such as the employer in a capitalist firm, owns all the product. As he says, "General Motors doesn't own just 'capital's share' of the GM cars produced; it owns all of them" (p. 42). Ellerman uses double-entry property accounting and activity analysis to identify appropriations (or, metaphorically, transactions with nature). Rather than income being a return to some factor of production, the whole product is a return to a contractual role, the hiring party as the last legal owner of the used-up inputs. It is a return in terms of property, a "labor theory of property" resembling the work of Veblen and Commons far more than Marx.

Levine treats the firm as a semiautonomous institution and Katzner models the firm as a case application of formalism to economic analysis. Katzner introduces a new technique that includes roles of rules and social hierarchy in production, a concern related to institutionalist labor economics. Katzner makes a distinction between arithmomorphic and dialectical notions, faithfully following N. Gęorgescu-Roegen from processes to functions to functionals. He shows that formalist metaphors are based upon dialectical perceptions of reality. In his own theorems the internalization of the values of the firm, vertical influence, and incentive motivation each helps to reduce wastefulness in production but none alone is sufficient.

In some way each essay evaluates the mathematical content of conventional theory while using sophisticated alternative mathematical techniques. Mirowski's essay, "Mathematical Formalism and Economic Explanation," is a brilliant discourse on physics, mathematics, and economics. He begins with Gödel's theorem denying the possibility of formal algebra being both fully complete and fully consistent. (The economic actors behave as if they understand the theorem better than orthodox economists, since the actors conspire to make quantities and prices things they are not supposed to be.) Mirowski closes with a wonderful reconstruction of Marx's value theory in formal group theory, a mathematics Marx was groping toward. (As Mirowski might have added, Marx ended up reinventing differential equations along the way.) Though Marx erred in the mathematics of the transformation problem, he—like Marshall and Keynes later—liked to use the mathematics as background for his verbal discourse. As Mirowski notes, Isaac Newton also originally left the mathematics out of his *Principia* (p. 191). We can only guess how economics would have turned out, had Newton followed his instincts.

The essays are extremely well written, with at least their first halves fully accessible to all economists and their second halves accessible to those trained in advanced algebra and integral calculus. The essays combine methodology, history of thought, and new concepts in an understandable but, for the impatient reader, a sometimes irritating way. *My* patience was well rewarded, but some may slide over the methodological discourses, and even the entertaining perspectives on past and recent doctrines. Such a selective reader will miss much. If time *were* reversible, I would prefer to have two short books, one on methodology and the other on unadorned expression of the authors' best ideas.

Is there a third stream? Has economics been reconstructed? Besides each author's, there are other important names attached to the essays—N. Georgescu-Roegen, M. Kalecki, P. Sraffa, J. Steindl, G. Shackle, M. Shubik, Douglas Vickers, H. Gintis, P. Garegnani, G. C. Harcourt, O. Morgenstern, J. Commons, W. C. Mitchell, and others. Many of us would agree that there is a third way, be sympathetic with most of the ideas expressed in these essays, but remain unconvinced that an acceptable synthesis has been achieved. We would not expect that from a collection such as this, one which adds to the many branches of the third stream.

I would agree with Mirowski; there are more novel ideas contained here per page than in most of the journal literature. On that basis, I recommend this book. Mirowski, who understands normal science for the protective function it serves, knows perfectly well that the third way will be barred from the "leading" journals until it too becomes the only way. That's the way normal science is.

E. RAY CANTERBERY, *Florida State University*

Chapter 28

The doctrine of inherent productivity: Keynes, Sraffa, and Kalecki

E. RAY CANTERBERY and WILLIAM McLEOD

Introduction

Capital has inherent value; this is the dominant orthodox view. The orthodox paradigm of "dual scarcity" has the price of capital determined in the capital goods market and the price of finished goods in the final goods market; the value of capital somehow straddles capital goods pricing and the maximization of consumer utility. Despite this surface unity, however, below that surface is conflict. The same orthodox sources also claim the following.

1. In the face of constant or increasing returns, there is excess capacity relative to demand. Over-capacity creates a loose connection between monetary returns and returns related to the size of the capital stock.

2. The final market value of capital is decided (long after it has been purchased) by the demand for the goods it produces. A "Value of Capital" decided *ex post* cannot be inherent in the capital itself.

3. Capital investment opens and closes entire markets over the business cycle. What is the inherent value of capital in a market that so closes and the inherent value of capital in a market that so opens? Throughout these themes runs a thread of an "economic efficiency" that cannot properly be assigned to technology or to the optimal capital/labor combination.

We trace the inherent value of capital idea back as far as David

The authors are grateful to Irvin Sobel and an anonymous referee for insightful suggestions that greatly improved the article. We reluctantly retain all property rights to any remaining errors.

Ricardo and forward through John Maynard Keynes. Keynes is found to retain from Alfred Marshall the conflation of technological and economic efficiency of capital, even though Marshall himself sensed that the value of capital could not be determined in its own market. Piero Sraffa destroys Marshall's postulate that firm supply schedules are independent so that the prices of capital goods cannot be reflections of the inherent value of capital. Sraffa nonetheless fails to link the value relation between production and sales. In reality, capitalistic production is so ordered that no values are obtained except after a lag during which its output (product) is sold. The future product market is an uncertain one (as Keynes in other contexts understood) so that no proper distinction between efficiency gained from technology (process) or economic efficiency (capital/labor mix optima) can be made. This opposition of technological and economic efficiency, like the dichotomy alleged to exist between monetary and real phenomena, is a false distinction. Kalecki properly critiques Keynes' Marshallian conception of the marginal efficiency of capital and suggests that the cumulative process of production creates and also closes market opportunities. From Kalecki's ideas emerge a fledgling Post Keynesian escape route from dilemmas perpetuated by Marshall and Keynes.

The doctrine advanced (Marshall)

In line of descent, Marshall welded a theory of value with the independent schedules of supply and demand out of a misapplication of an aspect of David Ricardo's work. In his *Essay on the Profits of Stock*, Ricardo makes the well-known claim that the marginal or poorer quality lands forced into cultivation by trade protection provide rents to the owners of the more fertile acres. This return is due to an inherent property of the soil, land's natural and indestructible capacity for production. Compare this treatment of nature's absolute and inherent productivity, however, with the vagaries which Ricardo asserts underlie the conditions of mass production.

In *The Principles of Political Economy*, Ricardo assumes uniform profit transmission across industrial sectors so that any alteration in the wage and interest rate ratio will exert unpredictable outcomes upon cost. Depending upon the machine-labor combinations involved in the direct and indirect production of a product, changes in relative costs create perturbations upon the entire network of prices. These belie any a priori cost estimate so that no measure of capital-labor intensity may be performed that is price independent (Pasinetti, 1977, pp. 82–83). Thus, produced means of production do not possess, *sui generis*, a single cost basis. Ricardo purged rent from capital valuation.

Alfred Marshall advanced the notion of a dual scarcity developing out of production with diminishing returns and out of consumption with diminishing utility. This position has dominated the analysis of the short period. To restate Marshall's position we posit an impetus ex machina from the demand side, which then places pressure upon the firm's existing short-run fixed capacity. Thus, as in Ricardian land, the firm's initial endowment of the fixed factor yields successively smaller physical productive increments, raising the difference in yields between these and the intramargins. As these returns fall, cost and supply price rises *pari passu*. This, the adaptation of Ricardian rent to the problem of industrial costs, also became the marginalist's view of why investment demand comes to a halt in the short period. Each manufacturing unit possesses a finite capacity contributing predictably smaller amounts of output when squeezed by demand.

A different interpretation of Marshall is possible, even though his confusion remains visible. Marshall does not deny the possibility of increasing returns to firms. He apparently intends to reconcile, in one way or another, increasing returns to competitive conditions. At one point Marshall has a firm increasing its size to "obtain a larger output at a lower proportionate cost" (Marshall, 1920, p. 378). However, since "this additional output will be small relative to the aggregate volume of production in the trade, it will not much lower the price; so that the firm will reap great gains" (Marshall, 1920, p. 378). Oddly, the firm still has no control over price even though it gains, through economies of scale, increased control over average costs. In his attempt at reconciliation, Marshall blurs two key distinctions: that between the short run and the long run,[1] and that between statics and dynamics.[2]

[1]The price of fish is a familiar Marshallian example. In one place he argues that the "normal price of fish would decrease with an increase in demand" because of what economists today call an enhanced "human capital" and economies of scale (no pun intended) (Marshall, 1920, p. 371). If economies of scale pre-exist, and a stationary long-run equilibrium does not, a *short-run* demand increase could reduce price. The normal short-run price relates, according to Marshall, to "a few months or a year" (p. 379).

[2]Just prior to referring the reader to Appendix H, Marshall suggests that "the Statical theory of equilibrium is only an introduction into economic studies; and it is barely even an introduction to the study of the progress and development of industries which show a tendency to increasing returns" (Marshall, 1920, p. 461). Since increasing returns characterize certain firms, however, the same argument can be extended to the theory of the firm.

Only a textual exegesis can retrace a tortured reasoning born of the frustration of dealing with increasing returns and competitive conditions at the same time.

Marshall admits to the difficulty of calculating average costs of production because fixed capital is purchased far in advance of the final sale of the finished product. The price of what he calls "appliances for production" cannot be established merely from the supply side but must be determined from a list of normal demand prices (Marshall, 1920, Appendix H, pp. 810–811). Establishing the value of fixed capital requires a circular argument; the value of capital is derived from the short-run spot prices of capital and final product.

In Book V of the text Marshall suggests that as prime or variable costs comprise only a small portion of total cost, then a substantial surplus above variable costs often forms price (p. 375). The Post Keynesian would call this "surplus" a "markup" on prime costs. Marshall goes on to say that the marginal unit of production is not the isolated individual unit of vendible output, rather the entire product line must be considered (p. 376). Thus the presence of fixed capital, with lifetimes in many cases in excess of the period of a business cycle, presents a problem for the analysis of short-period pricing. We cannot take for granted these pieces of fixed capital in the short period nor can we arbitrarily assign them values unless and until the final product (or products) is sold.

These arguments (and associated analyses in Books IV and V) show that Marshall understood the problem of inherent productivity; he knew that one cannot consider the question of value exclusively from the standpoint of source, but must also inquire as to its final use. He nonetheless did not want to throw out demand and supply analyses that depended upon competitive conditions. Even so, the inherent value problem precludes the valuation of a given stock of capital (or other productive resources) in the face of a quick and short fluctuation in demand resulting in rising marginal variable costs.

The doctrine revealed (Keynes)

The period model in Keynes' *General Theory* is powerless to explain the cumulative process of production set as it is within Alfred Marshall's short run. Keynes admits as much in Chapter 22, "Notes on the Trade Cycle." Although alterations in the schedule of the marginal efficiency of capital comprise the efficient cause of changes in the overall level of economic activity, once Keynes turns the focus to the short period, this same force becomes a passive element (Keynes, 1964 [1936], p. 313). The reversal derives from his expedient of holding constant the level of capital stock and thus severely restricting the time interval (ibid., p. 183). By placing investment in this position, Keynes is successful in showing saving for what it is—the absence of spending—rather than what the Classicals believed it to be, a kind of spending that will be deferred on schedule through the agency of investment (ibid., p. 211). As saving canceled present consumption without a compensating order placed into the future (the paradox of thrift), Keynes established income as the equilibrating force for saving and investment. The enigma of dynamic capital accumulation via dynamic income and market shares cannot be resolved with tools fashioned to solve Keynes' critical problem, namely those explaining the conditons for short-run unemployment.

Although Keynes' struggle to escape marginalism is self-documented throughout,[3] the escape is incomplete. Elsewhere Keynes asserts that as with all markets, the market for physical capital is governed by the principle of scarcity represented through production conditions prevailing under diminishing marginal productivity, and through consumption founded under the law of diminishing marginal utility (ibid., p. 213).

Keynes' theory of capital scarcity (derived primarily from supply and demand within the capital goods industry) is evident in the marginal efficiency of capital. Since the marginal costing theory is part of Keynes' explanation for capital's efficiency, he combines these conditions of productivity within the capital-producing firm with those of demand arising from the capital-using firm. To regulate capital, Keynes posits a process whereby accumulation forces excess demand to drive up capital cost because of limited capacity in the capital-producing firm, while simultaneously driving down the rate of capital efficiency in the capital-using firm. Said another way, the net present value of returns expressed as a percentage of supply price falls because the denominator—supply price—rises against the numerator—diminishing returns (ibid., pp. 136–137). Because old and new market opportunities are neglected as both cause and consequence of investment, the rate of capital accumulation implodes into a single measure, the marginal efficiency of capital. The MEC reflects both the laws of diminishing

[3]In the Appendix to Chapter 14 Keynes attacks Marshall for confusing the demand and supply of loanable funds with that of the "real" thing, physical capital (Keynes, 1964 [1936], p. 186).

returns in the capital-producing sector and the derived demand for capital based on the law of diminishing marginal utility and premised in static output markets. In this way Keynes adopts Marshall's dual scarcity.

Ricardo had purged rent from capital valuation but in the following century the Marshall–Keynes premise of rising supply price reinstated this old doctrine. Lost was the Ricardian distinction between natural, indestructible, and inherent commodity *sources* or *means* of productivity in contrast to freely reproducible commodities such as capital, for which rent and therefore rising supply price does not influence allocation. The notion that capital is like land, a factor of production possessing inherent productive capacity, does not fit well into a world where uncertain forward markets prevent the instantaneous valuation of capital.

The doctrine repudiated (Sraffa)

Whether the labor power or the actual commodities themselves are the source of productivity became a debating point once Piero Sraffa published his *Production of Commodities by Means of Commodities*. This question is mooted, however, by Sraffa's failure to take the further step of identifying those *uses* or *ends* sought for all productive activities. Thus conditions of effective demand where productivity may become validated in a final market sale closes the circle which Say and his followers left incomplete. At a particular level of effective demand, commodities are produced by means of commodities. This result precludes the fine demarcations between technological/economic efficiency and undermines the doctrine of inherent productivity.

Earlier Sraffa (1925, 1926) highlighted the very special and unrealistic assumptions required to place an individual firm within its broader industrial setting. In order to possess validity on the scale of individual production, each supply schedule must maintain independence from the others' schedules of supply and demand (Sraffa, 1926, p. 538). Should the industry within which the firm operates employ but a portion of the total amount of a fixed factor, excess demand then creates an upward and general interindustrial rescheduling of production costs and therefore supply price. In this way action undertaken by one individual firm has collective consequences. Sraffa further observes that commodities sharing a common fixed factor often stand as substitutes, so that when the previous interindustry cost nexus becomes broken, the ultimate resting place for price and quantity is unknown (Sraffa, 1926, p. 539). This lack of predictability renders a devastating blow to those efforts made in distilling a theorem of price and quantity equilibria premised in the *ceteris paribus* status of fixed capacity.

In the alternative, if the firm produces under conditions wherein the industry utilizes the entire amount of the fixed factor, Marshall's supply curve is equally damaged. Only large increases in the activity of each firm are sufficient to decrease returns and thus raise costs (ibid., p. 539). Such an outcome precludes the small incremental changes that allow for continuous differentiable supply schedules. Each scenario ends at the same place: an incremental supply schedule cannot be established from some fundamental physical law of production based in decreasing returns. As markets may expand or contract, no monocausal principle of diminishing returns can derive from increased investment activity.

Nevertheless, Sraffa's work is not merely an effort in methodological nihilism, for his 1925 paper does offer us a way out of this straitjacket, an avenue so simple one wonders why so few economists neglected its possibility (Maneschi, 1986, p. 3). Sraffa provides as an example the individual agrarian producer underutilizing a plot of available land and thereby achieving a range of output over which returns neither fall nor rise. In this way, marginal cost remains constant and equal to average cost. Earlier economists, when thinking about the short period, had interpreted too literally the fixed factor as one that could never be reduced. For a vendor who does not face the conditions established under Say's Law and thus an unlimited elastic demand, the opportunity always exists to underutilize existing fixed capacity. This would be the case for the producer who—like the farmer—faces a variable seasonal demand and so generally would underutilize his capacity.

Thus we might imagine production plans arranged in a lexicographic ordering so that inputs are utilized according to priority. If only the most urgent requirements are fulfilled and then so on down the scale, there would be no necessity for physical returns to fall in the traditional sense. In this manner, each input, although homogeneous in itself, is employed to its best use, breaking the analogy between any inherent properties of natural resources and those of the capacity utilized. The production function becomes one of processes decided by the state of industry technology. The captain of industry resides in the same economic world as the farmer, each using his resources so as to achieve constant physical returns and unit costs. Numerous studies of firms in various industries and countries disclose constant or close-to-constant costs.[4]

The doctrine replaced (Kalecki)

In reviewing Keynes' *General Theory*, Michal Kalecki's attack on the notion of the marginal efficiency of capital is in the same intellectual tradition as Sraffa's (Kalecki, 1937, p. 84). For most production scenarios capital capacity is abundant relative to demand, thereby rendering ambiguous any causal connection between the inherent ability of capital to yield a technological result and the monetary return to capital. Capital goods are not priced according to short period scarcity principles, but instead once acquired receive their value from conditions prevailing in the final market for the commodity thereby produced. Through this agency of capital both productive and market opportunities are created. As the market for finished goods always exists at a date ahead of that when capital is purchased, installed, and used, capital valuation becomes applied *ex post*.

Rule of thumb relationships nonetheless do serve to measure the profit returns to capital considered as capacity. Under these, the costs of holding excess capacity together with the opportunity costs of finance can be calculated. Each formula lends an emphasis to certain exigencies looming larger in importance, depending upon the type of industry considered and the macroeconomic-financial market climate of the period. Such institutional settings nonetheless preclude a general decision rule applicable to the cost of capital.

As Kalecki further observes, Keynes' rule for comparing the net present value of returns with supply price is also incorrect strictly within the logic of *The General Theory* (Kalecki, 1937, pp. 84–85). No guarantee exists assuring rising supply prices, and so capital accumulation may continue as the multiplier augments profits. Again the marketplace is the final arbiter, for by the time capital goods once manufactured and delivered become written down in the corporation's books, the expansion may have proved a bit overzealous. The conditions prevailing when the decision was instigated change and this is due to the decision itself. And so at first, capital goods expansion acts as a

[4]See, e.g., the works of Christensen and Greene (1976), Walters (1963), Moroney (1967), and Bell and Murphy (1968).

powerful tonic propelling advances in national income, but eventually it breaks this upswing as market opportunities diminish relative to capacity.

From this cyclical perspective Kalecki explained the self-propelling movement of dynamic capital value replacing the static doctrine of inherent productivity. Capital value is procyclical, rising when the rate of investment orders exceeds the rate of completion for ongoing projects. Several consequences flowing from this relation conspire to depress capital value through lowering rates of return. First, as new projects are launched, these augment the portfolio of existing undertakings. This rise in average accumulation creates greater profits in the aggregate through the investment multiplier. So long as total capital stock remains below its average business cycle level, the ratio of profits to capital advances. Encouraged by this outcome, entrepreneurs launch an avalanche of fresh orders. As this process continues, accumulation rises above depreciation, consequently equipment entering production exceeds equipment retiring. Now the capital stock climbs past its average level, a result contributing to the fall in rates of profit. And so a downward cumulative process of profits, capital value, and accumulation ensues until the capital stock becomes sufficiently pruned to allow increasing returns. Capital value rises again (Kalecki, 1971, pp. 8–14).

Seen in this regard, inputs possess no inherent value derived from innate productive capacity. Rather, capital enlargement underwrites value through profits expansion, only later to veto this result by driving down its own value.

The corporation's project mix in the climate of recovery will open new markets, or in the case of recession will lever to widen existing ones. The true cost of these investments, regardless of whether internally or externally financed, are not calculated in the price of capital nor do the benefits exist simply from the inherent physical productive capabilities of plant and equipment. Rather, costs and benefits derived from each fixed capital project are related to revenues captured or lost from the market, a market that itself alters in response to changes in capital composition and expansion.

Because the larger corporations are loath to dilute outstanding equity or further lever their balance sheets, finance for market expansion often is derived from retained earnings, this augmented by further marking up unit manufacturing costs (Davidson, 1981, p. 38; Canterbery, 1987, pp. 282–283). Limits to the process do exist, for while new investments create new marketing ventures, the same activity that is given birth by a price surcharge may invite consumer flight, corporate invasions, as well as government intervention (Eichner, 1985, p. 37). Thus, paradoxically, investment financing activity simultaneously opens and shuts different market doors, the question being which rooms the modern corporation wishes to walk through. In short, the cumulative process of production creates and also closes market opportunities, a process that vitiates the myopic notion that productivity is inherent within the capital good.

Keynes' redux

As we have seen, Keynes' theory of investment misstates the true costs and hence the scarcity limits facing the firm. We nonetheless may gather strength from other places in Keynes' writings. The following neatly expresses the direction to which both Sraffa and Kalecki were driving.

> In the optimum conditions . . . production should be organized as to produce in the most efficient manner compatible with delivery . . . (Keynes, 1964 [1936], p. 215).

Said differently, capital accumulation must conform to those market conditions prevailing when its product is ready for sale. Capital has characteristics similar to those Keynes considered essential to money; each standing to link the present with the incalculable future (Davidson, 1981, pp. 193–197). Like a standard of deferred payment, the accumulation process connects production as inchoate value with the later sale, giving validity to the undertaking. Keynes regarded the money contract as the vehicle for uncertainty that eliminated the distinction between real and monetary forces. Capital, which embodies this uncertainty, creates and destroys market processes, precluding the possibility of inherent productivity.

REFERENCES

Bell, F. W., and Murphy, N. B. *Costs in Commercial Banking*. Boston: Federal Reserve Bank of Boston, Research Reprint No. 41, 1968.

Canterbery, E. R. *The Making of Economics*. 3rd ed. Belmont, CA: Wadsworth, 1987.

Christensen, L. R., and Greene, W. H. "Economies of Scale in U.S. Electric Power Generation." *Journal of Political Economy*, August 1976.

Davidson, Paul. *Money and the Real World*. 2nd ed. New York: McGraw-Hill, 1981.

Eichner, A. S. *Toward a New Economics*. Armonk, N.Y.: M. E. Sharpe, 1985.

Kalecki, Michal. "A Theory of the Business Cycle." *Review of Economic Studies*, February 1937.

———. *Selected Essays on the Dynamics of the Capitalist Economy, 1963–1970*. Cambridge: Cambridge University Press, 1971.

Keynes, J. M. *The General Theory of Employment, Interest, and Money*. New York: Harcourt, Brace, and World, 1964 (first published in 1936).

Marshall, A. *Principles of Economics*. 1920. 8th ed. New York: Macmillan, 1961.

Maneschi, A. "A Comparative Evaluation of Sraffa's 'The Laws of Returns Under Competitive Conditions' and Its Italian Precursor." *Cambridge Journal of Economics*, 1986, p. 10.

Moroney, J. R. "Cobb-Douglas Production Functions and Returns to Scale in U.S. Manufacturing Industry." *Western Economic Journal* [*Economic Inquiry*], December 1967.

Pasinetti, L. *Lectures on the Theory of Production*. New York: Columbia University Press, 1977.

Ricardo, D. *The Works and Correspondence of David Ricardo*. Edited by Piero Sraffa. Cambridge: Cambridge University Press, 1951.

Sardoni, C. "Some Ties of Kalecki to the 1926 Sraffian Manifesto." *Journal of Post Keynesian Economics*, Spring 1984, *6* (3).

Sraffa, P. "Sulle Relazioni Fra Costo e Quantita Prodotta." *Annali di Economia II*, 1925.

———. "The Laws of Returns Under Competitive Conditions." *Economic Journal*, March 1926.

———. *Production of Commodities by Means of Commodities*. Cambridge: Cambridge University Press, 1960.

Walters, A. A., "Production and Cost Functions: An Econometric Survey." *Econometrica*, January–April 1963.

Chapter 29

BURKE, THE FRENCH REVOLUTION AND PUBLIC CHOICE THEORY

E. Ray Canterbery and Edgar A. Fresen

I. INTRODUCTION

By the time of the American Bicentennial a vocal minority was clamoring for a new Constitutional Convention. Among the revolt's intellectual leaders were James Buchanan and the public choice theorists. Because the U.S. Supreme Court had replaced the hallowed Constitution with anarchy, it was argued, a new Constitution with expressly economic amendments such as a mandatory balanced federal budget and a monetary rule was required. Order would replace inflation and chaos.

It was not the first time the cries for a new Contitutional Convention had been heard—nor has it been the last.

Would such a Constitutional Convention give the public choice theorists what they want, a balanced budget amendment and a fixed monetary rule? We doubt it. More likely, debates about abortion, the rights of AIDS victims, prayer in schools, mandatory drug testing, the unification of church and state and censorship of movies about the "temptations" of Jesus Christ would leave little or no time for "trivial economic issues."

Times have changed since Edmund Burke (1729-1797) delivered stirring orations in the English Parliament. But history holds some valuable lessons, and the rhetoric of modern conservatism remains the same.

The historical Burke and modern conservatism rose from the ashes of the French Revolution, a revolution that promised to enfranchise the masses at the expense of the landed aristocracy. Burke's counterrevolution against the ideals of the democratic phase of the French Revolution captures the hearts and minds of today's modern conservative.

The American Constitution was a more conservative document that originally linked the right to vote exclusively to property ownership. The greatest fear, Hobbesian by nature, remains the same: public choice theorists see private property rights being eroded by a fiat credit system and by a nasty, brutish majority using votes to redistribute income and wealth away from the pattern established by free market competition. Hands are busy and visible in the public sector but, it is believed, the "invisible hand" rules the Smithian competitive system. It is not just the hand that is truly invisible, however—it is the system, a romantic Utopia.

The French Revolution was spearheaded by an aristocratic elite that had Burke's support. But when the masses took command of the revolution, Burke used Hobbesian choice to mount a defense of the French monarchy and its attack upon the plebeian revolutionaries.

James Buchanan has based a theory of public choice upon a contract theory that begins in Hobbes' state of nature and ends in the mire of Burkean Conservatism. The public choice theorists are continuing the counterrevolution begun by Edmund Burke. The central issues raised by each run in parallel.

Burke was enraptured with the laissez-faire interpretation of Adam Smith; only during the Reign of Terror did he turn to Hobbesian fear. The public choice theorists' embracing of Smithian self-interest for the private sector stops at the edge of the public sector—the dreaded "leviathan" beyond which Hobbesian pessimism regarding man's true nature prevails.[1]

Selfishness is projected upon all economic actors, even political actors (and presumably actors who are politicians), and the outcome is pernicious. Selfishness—a motive 99.9 percent pure in the marketplace—has a pernicious denouement because votes rather than profits are maximized. What is worse, votes can overwhelm the otherwise benevolent harmony from universal self-interest played out in the marketplace.

Burke also worried about the effects of votes, except for those of the privileged. Since the public choice theorists consider Smithian free markets to be a utopian state that *should* exist, they can be understood only in the neo-Austrian tradition of *normative* economics. In this respect, Burke's most romantic notions regarding the unquestioned respect of the poor for private property that they cannot share is embodied in public choice antipathy for government redistribution of wealth or income.

II. THE FRENCH REVOLUTION AND BURKE'S COUNTERREVOLUTION

Without revolution there can be no counterrevolution. Modern conservatism, a counterrevolution against the French Revolution, continues today. The spirit of Edmund Burke lives on among those who desire to keep privileges (derived from property) the way they were. But first came the Revolutions.

The government of Louis XVI, beginning in 1774, was forever on the brink of bankruptcy because the propertied failed to bear their share of the fiscal burden and because the French economy grew slowly. The situation grew worse. By the time of the drafting of the American Constitution (1787), Louis XVI brought together an Assembly of Notables—140 leaders of the French aristocracy—requesting that they abandon some of their traditional fiscal privileges. What the king got in return was a tax revolt.

The aristocrats who benefited most from the ancient regime took advantage of the king's fiscal deficit to reverse the trend of modern French history toward a strong monarchy. Although aristocrats and their apologists, like Edmund Burke, conveniently forgot what they had wrought, the French Revolution began as a kind of Proposition 13, accelerated by the concern that the king's promiscuous selling of titles had debased the nobles' social currency. As ignoble as it indeed was, bad titles were driving out good titles.

The aristocrats hoped to use the Estates General, last convened in 1614, to draft a government of the people, by and for the aristocracy. Since the aristocrats controlled the first estate (the nobility) and the second estate (the clergy), and since they expected voting to take place by rank order, the top two estates could always outvote the third (the commoners). What happened next should serve as a caution flag for public choice theorists advocating a new Constitutional Convention.

When the Estates General met, Louis XVI contended that its sole purpose was to end the fiscal crisis (perhaps a balanced budget amendment and a monetary rule?). After weeks of egotistic chest- and brow-beating, the third estate declared itself a National Constituent Assembly and invited the other members to sit with them. The revolt of the nobles had been commanded by the commoners.

The Constituent Assembly swore (the Tennis Court oath) that they would disband only when France had a written constitution. The ball was now in the king's court. Louis XVI, whose kindness was said to greatly exceed his intelligence, legalized the extralegal actions of the commoners.[2] Voting by head count ended the aristocratic revolt and started the anti-aristocratic revolution. The National Assembly introduced reforms to meet the needs of the peasants and urban middle class while depriving the nobles of their special privileges, including the manorial obligations of the feudal system.

Then came the Declaration of the Rights of Man and the Citizen (August 1789) and the Constitution (1791) that provided for a limited monarchy operated by property owners. About two-thirds of the adult males could vote and hold office and a one-house legislature would, for all practical purposes, rule France.

Finally, to the dismay of Pope Pius VI and Louis XVI, the National Assembly took over church lands and issued bonds, certificates and paper money (assignats) with church lands as collateral. Rather than fiscal-monetary constraints, France went on a Catholic land standard complete with paper currency.

Much intrigue and one war later, the experiment with a limited monarchy failed. The democratic phase of the Revolution began. A new legislation making body, the Convention, was selected by universal suffrage (though not everyone voted—no doubt due to the "rational ignorance effect") in summer 1792. Its first act was to formally end the monarchy and to establish the French Republic.

A. Enter Burke: The First Modern Conservative

The events of the French Revolution created the historical Edmund Burke, who published his *Reflections on the Revolution in France* on November 1, 1790. This work was an instant literary success: 7,000 copies were sold within a week of its publication, and before the end of that year the book had been reprinted several times.

Such a popular publication was destined to create controversy. Burke launched an impassioned attack on a political development which embodied the aspirations of vast segments of the population of Europe and seriously threatened the established order. At this early stage, the French Revolution had been viewed favorably—particularly in England, where there was general agreement that the old French government was tyrannical and ineffective. Even members of the British parliament interpreted these events as an attempt by the French people to adopt a constitutional monarchy, following the noble example of the English Revolution in 1688. Burke, therefore, was labeled an alarmist and his denunciations and warnings considered unwarranted.

This negative perception changed in 1793 when France's Committee of Public Safety initiated "The Terror." The guillotine sharply vindicated Burke. The alarmist was now a prophet in his own time. Vested with this prophetic quality, Burke's ideas became the foundation for modern conservatism, a doctrine in defense of privilege which could serve as an antidote for future revolutions. The themes of this counterrevolution are echoed currently by public choice theorists, a coalition of academic conservatives led by James Buchanan.

Burke's political setbacks in England during the previous years caused him to shift his strategy toward "high moral issues." The National Assembly's expropriation of the lands of the French Church, and their use to guarantee the floating of a new loan, created a political opportunity. The French Revolutionaries had declared the lands of the Church to be rightfully the lands of the nation, had instituted the civil constitution of the clergy and had turned members of the clergy into salaried functionaries of the state. In eloquent orations at home, Burke defended the right of the Church of England to own property.

Burke saw no conflict between property ownership by the Church and ownership by individuals. In general agreement with the laissez-faire economics of the age, he believed that "the laws of commerce" were the same as the "laws of nature, and consequently the laws of God" (quoted by Lock, 1985, p. 18).

David Hume, in his essay "Of Public Credit," presents a vision of the dissolution of society through the proliferation of paper money. Even Adam Smith in the *Wealth of Nations* indicates that the British economy could not support the public debt; the British Revolution had created the Bank of England to issue notes to finance it. John Locke—in lockstep with Smith and Hume—expressed concern that speculators in the government debt would affect interest rates as the debt grew. Burke, however, had argued that public debt would not be a problem under a government controlled by the aristocracy. When the anti-aristocratic leaders gained control of the French government, Burke nonetheless saw the French public debt out of control.

Burke's new conservative doctrines were not simply reactions to the French Revolution. His ideas had been shaped over a period of 30 years by his observations about the emerging bourgeoisie. The Revolution represented, to him, the consolidation of power by his detested class of "sophisters, economists and calculators." (The reference apparently was to French economists not in agreement with Adam Smith.) Above all, Burke was suspicious of the role of an independent class of talented men who would exercise their intellect to experiment with a Lockean-Smithian natural social order, established through property rights to land.

Burke expressed a further fear. The economies of 18th century states were economies of public credit. The state borrowed from the economy in anticipation of future revenues. This created a class of public creditors who traded on the promises made by government to repay, *as if* these promises were commodities. Since the rate at which these promises changed hands came to determine the rates at which money could be borrowed, there was a danger that paper credit would determine the value of money, and thus the activities of the public creditors would exercise control over property itself. In an age where political power and social standing depended upon real property, this was no idle threat.

The existence of the debt created a "monied interest" which was not only inflationary but would eventually expropriate all lands. Burke's dislike for the bourgeoisie nonetheless did not extend to men who invested their capital in commerce and industry and who also subordinated their efforts to the control of the contemporary landed aristocracy. The enemies of this social order were the intellectuals—lawyers, teachers, and bureaucrats—who by inclination would comprise the group of speculators. These "men of letters" constituted the real threat.

Paper money speculators and free-spirited intellectuals would destroy the Church, property, the aristocracy, and eventually commerce. (The revolutionary conspiracy against proper manners also was a conspiracy against history.) Since the Anglican Church and the aristocracy controlled patronage, men of letters were, and should continue to be, at the service of these institutions. The social order was natural; it was an alliance between heaven and earth with property as the means by which humans assumed their place in this natural historical order. All was in its rightful place as long as intellectual energy was controlled and enlisted by the clergy or similarly by the patronage of "great men," that is, landed aristocrats who were the foundation of the social order.

Problems arise only when the "cheerful energy" of the human intellect, set free from social restraints, chooses to be destructive and asserts its own power. Once the monied interests became allied with the political right, however, Burke considered them the lesser evil. Bureaucrats and technocrats replaced the "monied interests" as the enemies of modern conservatism in their alliance with the revolutionary intelligentsia.

To Burke, the institution of private property is, in many ways, more important than the state. Since property is a natural right, the state cannot be a proprietor, only a guardian and regulator. This regulatory role, however, does not include the redistribution of property. Even if all property was equally divided, the poor would gain nothing since their shares would remain insignificant. The redistribution of wealth, therefore, is not a solution to social problems. Rather, men should be taught to "respect that property of which they cannot partake" (Burke, 1968 [1790], p. 372).

To Burke, the virtuous essence of property is inequality, the doctrine of equality having dangerous possibilities. Equality would shortcircuit the trickle-down benefits of property concentration.

According to Burke, property will always be under attack by ambitious men who use and excite the envy and rapacity of the poor to further their own ends.

Most of all, said Burke, property owners were negligent, if only in one regard: they were not sufficiently vigilant in their own interests and consequently needed to be represented as the dominant force in government. The possibility of institutionalized confiscation of property is, in Burke's view, the most injurious element arising out of the French Revolution. This activity would destroy the whole foundation and support of the state by corrupting the common people with the spoils of the superior classes.

Burke's thought may not be fully systematic, but it is highly imaginative, having sufficient elements of both order and fancy to render the great orator the founding father of modern intellectual conservatism. His brief for private property, influenced by Smith and dedicated to the virtues of inequality, is admired by public choice theorists who perpetuate Burke's synthesis of the Whig principle of freedom and the Tory principle of order. The tension between Hobbesian pessimism and Lockean-Smithian optimism is retained in the public choice phase of the conservatives' counterrevolution.

III. HOBBESIAN CHOICE

Thomas Hobbes' state of nature—or more exactly, the Hobbesian state of mind—validates Burke's view and is the point of departure for the public choice theorists. The Reign of Terror became Burke's metaphor for Hobbes' state of nature.

Hobbes' *Leviathan,* first published in 1651, begins as a treatise on psychology, then turns to ethics and finally to politics. Hobbes sees people as predominantly selfish, and, more than anything else, desperately fearful for their lives. The Hobbesian view says that the natural conditon of Man is misery. Not only are we essentially selfish, but we are all more or less equal—at least in the sense that almost everyone has the power to make life miserable and dangerous for everyone else. There is little mutual enjoyment because we interfere with one another too much. We quarrel constantly because we are competitive, insecure, and vain. With selfishness and conflict omnipresent, there is no natural justice or injustice, no right and no wrong. If you are physical, you have the power of force. If you are clever, you employ the trickery of fraud. Above all else, we are motivated by the fear of death. Hobbes' theory of ethics is perhaps the strongest case for psychological egoism—the theory that all actions, whether good or evil, noble or vicious—are motivated by our own self-interest, but especially by the fear of violent death.

Out of brutish nature comes the social contract. The ultimate law of nature is the right to life. Because of the instinct for self-preservation, each of us wants, out of self-interest, to give up any claims to everything in return for a general peace. Society, then, is based upon a social contract in which everyone gives up certain rights and privileges in return for society's protection and advantages. Hobbes' politics provides—odd as it may seem—both the case for a strong central government and the more radical (in his time) parliamentarianism that was thus gaining influence in England. (England's Glorious Revolution, which retained and revered the monarchy and was thus acclaimed by Burke, came only 37 years later.) The social contract causes us to bond together to form a society for the well-being of all, a "commonwealth" (as in "the Commonwealth of Virginia"), in which the rights and powers we once had alone are now concentrated in the hands of "the sovereign." The sovereign can use such power very effectively compared to us alone and thus make us behave "for our own good."

It is sometimes suggested that Hobbes is also an ethical egoist; he is arguing that we *ought* to act in our own selfish interests. It is natural and reasonable for each individual to aim solely at his own preservation or pleasure. Even so, people in society often act for the benefit of others. Hobbes contends that they *ought* to do so because of the unspoken rules to which they have agreed in the social contract. Such behavior is still motivated by selfish motives, by the desire to protect oneself and maximize security and power in society. The egoist need not argue that every act in itself must be for purely selfish gains. Even an egoist occasionally falls off the wagon of selfishness. What is clear and dominant is Hobbes' deeply pessimistic view of human nature—seeing sympathy, compassion, virtue, and nobleness as not only unnatural but irrational.

Hobbes, of course, was not the last theoretician to use the abstraction of the social contract.

In the following century, both John Locke and Jean-Jacques Rousseau developed other social contract theories. In fact, the intellectual impetus for both the French and American Revolutions stems from precepts developed by Locke and especially by Rousseau. Still more recently, in the last decade, social contract theory has been revived by Harvard philosophers John Rawls (1972) and Robert Nozick (1974).[3]

But where Hobbes saw a life without the controls of government and society as "nasty, brutish and short," the more modern contract theorists are more optimistic.

John Locke views government as necessary because of certain "inconveniences"—certainly a step up from Hobbesian misery—inherent in the state of perfect freedom into which men are born. These inconveniences include such things as the predilection of individuals to overestimate damages done to them and to exact greater punishment of the offending parties than is justified.

To Nozick, the main philosopher for the neo-Austrians and the public choice school, government's highest task is to protect individuals from Hobbesian harm, but individuals are free to do as they like as long as they do not harm others.

Just what constitutes "harm to others" in this age of computer technology and space age information is a question not being addressed by any modern conservatives, including the public choice theorists. Locke and Rousseau doubtless would be astounded at modern man's capability to invade privacy. Does the ability to call up a person's most intimate secrets at the flick of a computer switch constitute harm to that person? To the original Lockean philosophers, the answer most probably would be a resounding yes, but it is an issue that has so far been left alone by the public choice theorists.

IV. NATURAL LAW AND THE MARKET: THE PUBLIC CHOICE PERSPECTIVE

Once we touch the "invisible hand"—though we cannot see it—the comfort level of public choice theorists rises. When it comes to private commodity markets, Edmund Burke, the public choice theorists, and Nozick are of a single mind. This is so even though Buchanan has rolled his version of Leviathan out of Hobbes' pessimistic view of Man. Surely, Locke and Adam Smith (1723-1790) had a more optimistic view of Man's instinctive behavior than did Hobbes.

Although Locke's task was to "discover" natural laws in the political universe (as Isaac Newton had done for the physical universe), this concept of order neatly summarizes the shared view encompassed by theorists from the physiocrats to Adam Smith and Edmund Burke to the modern-day public choice theorists; i.e., that the natural advantages of free market competition should not be spoiled by government interference. (Nozick breathes new life into selfishness in order to rescue "capitalism among consenting adults.") Yet these same theorists who see no room for government in the affairs of the marketplace would obligate the state to protect private property.

People exhibit "rationality" in this metaphorical transfer of Newtonian mechanics to the social universe so long as they respect natural political laws, remain self-interested in economic exchanges and make consistent choices in terms of these guides. The consequences? Harmony and order in the social world. When the invisible hand is further invoked as theory, it is at the other end of the arm of natural law. Beginning with Burkean conservatism and continuing to this day, invisible hand theories are buoyed by the optimistic belief that nature is automatic and structured to reward persons according to circumlocutory merit.

As we turn to the public choice theorists, we encounter an apparent paradox. By their own description, public choice theorists impose the postulates of Hobbesian/Smithian selfishness and competition upon political markets. As Buchanan has put it, "Public choice is a *perspective* on politics that emerges from an extension-application of the tools and methods of the economists to collective or non-market decision-making" (Buchanan, 1988, p. 19). He goes on to say that the attainment of "such a perspective on politics" requires "a particular approach to economics" (Buchanan, 1986, p. 19).

If the same selfishness resides in the public sector as in the private sector, what is to be feared from public decisions? We would suppose that giant corporations have the funds for the best legislation that money can buy, legislation that simply would extend the arm of selfishness. Why are such transactions different from others in the private sector that are—with virtually no exceptions—exact and good? Is there some kind of slippage in the process whereby private power is poorly transformed into public choice? Otherwise we would suppose that the money of the corporate lobby is high-powered, having a multiplier effect as it raises private choice to higher powers.

Perhaps the same argument could apply to the aristocracy of the rich, since affluent Americans are the most heavily represented among those who vote. In the United States, 77 percent of property owners vote, compared to only 52 percent of laborers, or the masses (Piven and Cloward, 1988, p. 56). In addition, the United States has the poorest overall voting record of any democracy.

What then is to be feared? There are at least two possible answers, and we must speculate about which one is the more accurate.

The normative preference of the public choice school is for the Smithian solution in the private sector. As Buchanan puts it, "Public choice...is not new at all. It represents rediscovery and elaboration of a part of the conventional wisdom that informed classical political economy. Adam Smith, David Hume, and the American Founding Fathers would have considered the central principles of public choice theory to be so elementary as scarcely to warrant attention. A mistrust of governmental processes along with the implied necessity to impose severe constraints on the exercise of governmental authority was part and parcel of the philosophical heritage that they shared" (1988, p. 10).

One answer is that the private economy operates through the same pristine selfishness of yore and Smithian harmony prevails except where the government intrudes. History teaches us that Smith well understood how the economies of small farmers and shopkeepers worked and correctly observed the creation of monopolies by the Crown (Canterbery, 1986, pp. 152-153). However, Smith understandably did not have a full description of the ways capitalism can create its own monopolies and monopoly power through private market differentiation of products and various economies of scale. He nonetheless feared that the "mean rapacity, the monopolization spirit of the merchants and manufacturers" might prevail, a direct consequence of selfishness. Even Alfred Marshall, in the next century, got tongue-tied when he tried to explain how supply and demand still decide everything in the presence of increasing returns to scale. In economies in which neither selfishness nor capital accumulation are constrained, it would be remarkable if those joint forces failed to generate monopoly power. Such a failure would be enough to give selfishness a bad name in the business community.

The industrialized economies have since become far more complex in a number of ways: there are fewer corporations, competition has been largely replaced by administered prices and wages, the government has become a part of big business, industrial manufacturing is planned in advance and corporate ownership is increasingly divorced from management. In 1985, as before, the largest firms accounted for a very large share of total production in the major industries. For example, IBM produced 65 percent of all U.S. computers; GE and Westinghouse, 85 percent of heavy electrical equipment; Boeing and McDonnell-Douglas, 80 percent of aircraft; three tobacco companies, 80 percent of tobacco products; and so on. Thus far, IBM remains intact, with about $63.7 billion in assets. General Motors retains $87.2 billion in assets; Exxon, $76.1 billion; Chase Manhattan, $99.1 billion; Phillip Morris, $19.1 billion; AT&T, $27.4 billion; Mobil Oil, $41.1 billion; and so on.

Except in the smaller firms (greatly to be admired for everything save size), the owner of capital can no longer be described as a swashbuckling innovator. By the 1980s, money was to be made with money. Thus began the Age of the Raiders and the associated arbitrage—of Ivan Boesky, Carl Icahn, and T. Boone Pickens, Jr.—superimposed upon an ossified bureaucracy in the manufacturing sector.

Buchanan, like Burke, is an incurable romantic. They each were destined to cling tenaciously to the comfortable past.

Buchanan clearly prefers the conditions of the 18th century and is nostalgic for a return to the "mistrust of government" that "extended through the middle years of the 19th century, after which they seem to have been suspended for a hundred years" (1988, p. 10). Even so, normative wishing for Smithian competition in the private sector will not make it so. If the answer be that Smithian competition keeps Smith's dream alive in the private economy, it is an assumption masquerading as fact. A more consistent perspective would be that the public choice economists see nothing to fear from the private corporation, a vision comforming with that of their neo-Austrian brothers. Public choice theorists attack the monopolies and bureaucracies of government but assume away private enterprise monopolies and bureaucrats.

We return to our question: What then is to be feared? To provide a reasonable answer we must merge Smith's adopted Lockean private property view, Hobbes' state of nature and Burke's "votaphobia," or fear of majority votes.

There is *no* fear of the corporate state. "The Leviathan-state is the reality of our time" (1988, p. 9), warns Buchanan. It is a consequence of the "constitutional anarchy" of the Supreme Court. Since the constraints on government that worked well for a century seem to have failed, a new Constitutional Convention must be called. The central constitutional failure has been fiscal, a plight described by Buchanan and Wagner (1977). In that book, John Maynard Keynes and democracy (via majority voting) are blamed for the crisis. Keynes is described as an "elitist" who supposed that the government of Britain was and would continue to be in the hands of an intellectual aristocracy. He apparently presumed that the small group of enlightened men who made economic policy would act in accordance with the "public interest." According to Buchanan and Wagner, Keynes did not have the forethought to think that his policy ideas would be implemented in a democratic setting. Once out of reach of the aristocracy, Keynesian fiscal policy was bound to fail because of the unpopularity of taxation, leading to a massive growth in public debt.

Like Burke, Buchanan and Wagner fear that public debt is safe only in the hands of the aristocracy; otherwise, it grows out of control and leads to a redistribution of wealth. While Burke's nerves would have been soothed by the nobility of the "Lord of Tilton," Burke nonetheless feared the intellectual elite of *his* day because reason threatened the monarchy.

A. Conceptual Unanimity: The Antidote for Burkean Votaphobia

Buchanan's constitutional attitude requires him to merge the Hobbesian state of nature with the unanimity test of Knut Wicksell. People's preferences and resource endowments are given and so is a Rawlsian "veil of uncertainty" about what the future holds. From these conditions Buchanan asks which social contract would *conceptually* elicit unanimous consent. *This* social contract is a strict constitution to be strictly interpreted. The purpose of a constitution is, according to Buchanan, to provide constraints on political action. If we really understand why and how constitutions are written (as Burke surely did), we can understand the unanimity rule for what it is. *Any conceptual agreement* can be unanimous among whose who propose and therefore prefer it. In Rawls' original position there is unanimity. In Nozick's entitlement theory, the outcome is "just" because his utopian assumptions about human behavior hold true.

However, what thinkers believe would generate unanimous consent conceptually and what all would agree to in reality, are two quite different things.

In Buchanan's "original position," unanimity is achieved through the coercion of fear for life and property. Even at its conception the social contract is not the product of free people. When individually we fear for our lives, most of us are willing "to bargain with the devil" without equivocation. A constitution then fills the void left by people fleeing for their lives.

Collective choice is not a matter of romancing a tome, be it written by Buchanan, Rawls or Nozick; collective decisions are those impositions upon those who otherwise would not go along with the rule or the policy. Why would anyone freely agree to something specific that they do not want?

Constitutions—especially conceptual ones—are drafted and agreed to by a small elite. A real world constitution is never ratified by every member of the polity. The American Constitution was conceived by a few, drafted by fewer and ratified by a small minority. James Madison and the other Founding Fathers, so often praised by Buchanan and other public choice theorists, tied the voting privilege to property ownership, including the ownership of black slaves. The unpropertied, the women and the black people did not have even the right to vote after the Constitution was adopted. Conceptual unanimity had decreed that only a few had the right to vote on anything. If such "unanimity" is endorsed, disenfranchisement becomes acceptable. Burke would have approved—and did approve—of such an outcome. As it stands, today a large share of the electorate disenfranchises itself in democratic elections, a condition that Piven and Cloward (1988) blame on voter registration procedures. In the United States the electorate can be informed on national issues yet not know where to register to vote locally. We doubt if public choice theorists fully comprehend the implications of conceptual unanimity. After all, voting rights were gradually extended through "Constitutional Anarchy."

But the same old Burkean fear, votaphobia, underlies public choice theory. Barely half of eligible American voters cast ballots, apparently a number still too large and insufficiently propertied to be trusted. The fear of majority rule through coalitions is so strong that unanimity is required. Since unanimity is a romantic notion, public choice settles for *conceptual* unanimity. A requirement of *actual* unanimity flirts with dictatorship since an agreement among n-1 persons could be vetoed by the nth (becoming the dictator). There are few things that *everyone* would agree to in the absence of dictatorship, and Burkean conservatism relies—as odd as it may seem—upon *lack of agreement* to change. The singular advantage of constitutions is comprised of the barriers to entry, alteration and altercations.

The Hobbesian state of nature and the Reign of Terror are the appropriate metaphors. Sufficiently terrified, people will agree to almost anything—even balanced budgets. "Justice," states Buchanan, "as an attribute of the fiscal structure, must be implemented at the constitutional level," a requirement that extends to net redistribution (1977, p. 250). "Day-to-day exploitation of the fiscal process to seek income and wealth transfers must be abandoned in favor of quasi-permanent and built-in features of the structure which will implement transfers while at the same time restricting legislative authority" (1977, p. 250). In the fiscal and monetary areas, most of all, the fear of manipulation and change by shifting conditions in democratic legislative assemblies is greatest. This "constitutional attitude" is the modern conservative's answer to fiscal irresponsibility, the redistribution of income by "majority vote" and monetary expansionism. These legislative changes comprise the post-Keynesian democratic "Reign of Terror."

B. Crypto-normativism

The public choice theorist really does not dislike government any more than did Burke. They each simply like government outcomes that fit their preferences. The public choice theorist only wants limited government if that government suits his view of the way the world should be. As W. Samuels (1980, p. 57) has suggested, political theory and economics attempt "to construe 'knowledge' so as to affect government policy." Each theory has its own agenda for government. Conflicting theories comprise the intellectual war over the control of government. The government is used and is checked. Public choice theory engages a kind of what we choose to label "crypto-normativism," in which the positivistic tools of economics are used to bolster normative premises. The Constitution is the strongest conservative check upon legislative freedom. The Constitution in this way replaces the Divine Right of kings with the defining right of the invisible hand and natural law. In this respect, Buchanan has a realistic view of political democracy and an idealistic view of real capitalism.

As the history of the French Revolution demonstrates and Burke admonishes, constitutional conventions sometimes fall into the hands of those who do not have in mind the same conceptual constitution as the elite. The French peasants and the urban middle class overturned the concepts of the aristocracy and proclaimed the formal end of the monarchy and the establishment of the French Republic. In today's America—one still embodying inequalities exemplified by an underclass that has greatly expanded during the 1980s and a surprising rise in the number of homeless—could a Constitutional Convention confine its agenda to issues such as a federally balanced budget and a fixed M1 growth rule? Or would the Convention become "unruly?"

V. THE REST IS HISTORY: THE CORPORATE STATE AS LEVIATHAN

A. Romanticism vs. Reality

There is an uneasy coalition between the conceptual rationalism of the social contractarians and the nostalgia for 18th century liberalism. The conceptual rationalists believe that reality is whatever they construct in order to move forward to the past. The senses touching a world they oppose cannot be trusted; therefore, what is *real* is only what they—the conceptual rationalists and social contractarians—can imagine.

Not surprisingly, the followers of Hobbes and Locke slight history. History is unimportant compared with the passion of Burke and with imaginary utopias. By definition, utopia is "nowhere," so that only romantic ideas about yesteryear can be invoked as superior to the conditions of today. The public choice liberal prefers the Smithian utopia in the marketplace but deploys the anti-utopia of Hobbes that compels unanimity out of fear and makes law and order necessary.

The public choice liberal believes that the major threat to individual freedom stems from concentrations of political power, whether in the hands of the sovereign or of state bureaucrats. The magic wand of free market competition is moved and the malady of economic power disappears. Despite the rare admissions of "market failures," the comfortable world of Adam Smith is within reach if Leviathan is kept in check. The preferred economic policies cannot be entrusted to the *real* economic history which already has betrayed the public choice liberal (for at least a century). As examples, the public choice theorists advocate the elimination of the union shop and desire the aforementioned monetary constitution *a la* Henry Simons and Milton Friedman. James Buchanan was a pioneer supporter of a recognizable limit on "coercive taxation" and of California's Proposition 13. Constitutions provide inevitability of their own agenda, but the prior selection of that agenda reflects the preferences of the drafters.

B. The Corporate Person vs. Liberalism

The earlier Lockean-Smithian view of liberty tied freedom of the person to the individual's property, an inalienable right. No social obligations accompanied rights to ownership. This conception fit well an economy of large numbers of small entrepreneurs. Freedom implied self-contained, autonomous persons. Romantic notions aside, consider historical reality.

The corporation itself inherited the autonomy without obligation that was once—under the idealized capitalism of the 19th century—the sole privilege of the individual. This made labor weak so that it had to organize. Consumer complaints led to government regulations. Government became responsible for corporations, which otherwise had no specified civic duties. Big government was a by-product of the corporation.

For essentially economic reasons, liberalism was redefined as institutions changed in the 20th century. A law which prohibits persons from living in city parks is equally applied if rich and poor alike are viewed as its violators, but the paucity of rich offenders should not reflect adversely on the poor.

The opportunity for individual growth depended upon equal opportunities. In this way government became involved with individuals' economic chances. Business became less private, more public, so that the economic activities of individuals and corporations were also no longer completely private. It was not so much freedom that was redefined as the conditions under which liberty was otherwise handicapped—conditions leading to what Buchanan calls the "constitutional anarchy" of the Supreme Court and to what Burke would have called the failure of the lower economic classes to "respect that property of which they cannot partake."

C. State Capitalism and the 204-Billion-Dollar Man

No matter how much we might prefer it otherwise, time's arrow points down a one-way street. The 18th century association of liberty with property became an illusion once property was held in such a small number of hands so as to become a political force. By 1984, American's richest 400 people and families owned $181 billion in assets. If they had borrowed an equal amount and purchased 15 percent of the stock in as many large corporations as possible, they would have controlled 42 percent of the privately-owned factories and equipment in the United States. The protective umbrella of 19th century liberal ideology combined with the failure of 20th century liberalism has fused the corporation and the government into state capitalism.

The liberty-economics transformation problem has not been solved because it never has been recognized by liberals as a problem. Liberals have championed the sanctity of private corporations as if liberty, capital accumulation and economic efficiency are still the same things. Meanwhile, the freedom to accumulate wealth has led to a political power imbalance in which some individuals are coerced and equal opportunities denied. It is no wonder that Buchanan and his followers long for the Age of Jefferson, with its small shops and family farms (so unlike the one at Monticello).

The reliance on "rule of law" by the public choice theorists does not solve this problem, any more than that the preference for the invisible hand can transform natural monopolies into competitive firms. Ahistoric liberal principles collide with historical-industrial and wealth concentration. Public choice theorists thus far have failed to see the historical connections among law, the corporate bureaucracy, capital accumulation and political power.

Unlike the real individual, the real corporation has earthly immortality and even when nasty and brutish is invulnerable to imprisonment. Otherwise, its main difference from us—the size of corporate assets—is a source of possible coercion in the absence of effective corporate punishment. In this respect the continued trend toward industrial and financial concentration is not favorable to the liberals' claimed cause unless they are willing to turn their analytical guns against corporate bureaucracy and concentration. Citicorp is the 204-billion-dollar man.

The corporation enjoys a "privileged position." The individual citizen can fail but the government cannot allow giant businessess to fail because their size means that a single failure spells economic catastrophe. The U.S. government was compelled to save Lockheed, Chrysler, Illinois Continental, and First Republic of Dallas. In turn, corporate funds go to political campaigns, lobbying, the entertainment of government officials, political and institutional advertising, educational materials for public schools, university endowments, research foundations and litigation to influence government policies of their enforcement. Lacking such a well-financed *coalition,* the average taxpayer cannot match the potential power of the giant corporations. Coca-Cola is "the real thing;" liberal government and liberal society are the illusions.

How does state capitalism affect the liberal defense of liberty? The concentration of private property flowing from rule by law expands. With adoption of the 14th Amendment, the Bill of Rights, including freedom of speech, was extended to the corporate person. This interpretation was affirmed in the *Slaughterhouse* case [US(16 Wall) 36, 77-78(1873)] and recently confirmed in a U.S. Supreme Court Decision, *Federal Election Commission v. Massachusetts Citizens for Life, Inc.* [U.S. 238, 93 L.ed.2d 539, 55 U.S.L.W. 4067 (1986)], in which the corporation's right to spend corporate assets to proselytize its political and social preferences was affirmed. The rule by law—given the distribution of power—threatens majority rule by persons and thus endangers democracy itself.

Despite the preference by public choice theorists for unplanned market over planned economic outcomes, the prices and quantities of oil, steel, automobiles, tires, computers, soft drinks and so on are no longer freely determined in the market. These theorists presently ignore—at both their peril and ours—the symbiotic nature of corporate bureaucracy and government interests and, therefore, power. "Unplanned market outcomes" can be sustained only by selected government interventions despite the improbability of such a feat in the modern corporate state.

The corporation looks into a mirror and the Leviathan looks back. The corporate person, endowed with all the safeguards of other citizens, will not lobby or vote for an effective restructuring of industrial organization into workable competition. The massiveness of the interventionist effort required to restore Smithian competition would require the kind of "constitutional revolution" called for by Buchanan, and the revolutionaries cannot count on much financial support. Of all the people, public choice theorists should understand the power of this corporate coalition to dash the hopes of Adam Smith.

And Adam Smith, 200 years older and wiser, surely would want to do less than protect the majority from itself.

D. Liberal Choice and Conservative Power

Rawls—a more optimistic contractarian and a representative of 20th century liberalism—also impales himself on the horns of the power dilemma.[4] Freedom as equal liberty is the same for all, but the worth of liberty is not the same for everyone. Those who have greater authority and wealth have greater means to achieve their aims (positive freedom). Rawls, like Nozick, leaves us to doubt the ability of a modern industrial state to disperse its wealth, and therefore its power, more evenly. In this respect, the main hope for a Rawlsian solution rests in his "vision," which might motivate a society to gain order *and* power balance through mutual interests. Buchanan's hope for his preferred constitution also depends upon his "visions" gaining masses of conservative adherents through a political persona like Edmund Burke. Some would say that Ronald Reagan was the new Burke (but a balanced budget and steady growth in M1?)

Although it may well be that liberalism (be it 18th or 20th century) is part of the solution, it also is part of the problem. As long as the individual is assured that he lives in a liberal society (i.e., where he is free from coercion by others like himself and unenforced antitrust laws are on the books) the giant corporation (its once counterweight, the industrial union, in a now weakened and co-opted form) can survive intact. If the public choice liberal truly fears government as Leviathan, surely he must fear the Leviathan's mirror image.

Certainly, there are things in the looking glass to be feared. Why doesn't the liberal fear the concentration of information? In an increasingly complex society, information may be the greatest source of power in the future. The 50 largest U.S. broadcast chains already have three-quarters of the audience. The 50 largest cable television companies have two-thirds of all subscribers. The 50 largest newspaper chains have more than two-thirds of all daily newspaper sales. And this is only the *beginning* of a trend. With its assured civil rights, the conglomerate could blanket the country with propaganda by giving away the books of its acquired publisher and peddling its views in its newly acquired newspaper chain. Can GM, the corporation that denied Ralph Nader his civil liberties,[5] be trusted with, say, the Knight-Ridder news chain?

Why doesn't the liberal fear the multinational business corporation? The conglomerate usually is a large corporation of no nationality which does not come under the rule of law, operating in a world where "international law" is a nearly useless euphemism. Like the Church of Papal supremacy, it is above the government.

The public choice preoccupation with a Leviathan independent of the corporation bureaucracy obscures their rallying point and appears to be a highly improbable route to the balanced society. Yet a principle could be wrung from the ideal of public choice: government and other forms of coercion appear to be acceptable if they have the effect of dispersing power. However, if the public choice theorists recognize any connection between power and wealth concentration, they do not admit so. The logical end of power balance is most probably achieved by the substantial redistribution of income and wealth in a society having such inequalities. Yet the calculus of public choice consent is marshaled above all things, against the redistribution of income and wealth by the public sector.

If the government does not have sufficient power (or inclination) to reduce the power of the giant corporation or to redistribute income and wealth, then who will do it? If some new institution is established to conduct such policies, will we not have reason to fear it? An institution which can do what the government cannot is more powerful than the hated "Leviathan."

The viable answer might be political reform that breaks the tie between concentrated wealth and political power. Such reform was the impetus for the French Revolution. When reform fails, anarchy is the new void filling the old. Only then might history match conception as the Hobbesian state of nature coerces people into a social contract that most probably would be aimed at ending tyranny. The Reign of Terror ended, and the reign of Napoleon began. Modern conservatism—focused upon the clear definition of private property rights and the protection of the status quo—continues the counterrevolution. In a new Constitutional crisis, however, balanced budgets and monetarism would be trivial pursuits.

The sources of power have changed historically. The corporate managers and the corporate raiders in the land of the giants are today's landed gentry. In his time Edmund Burke could persuasively claim that the laws of commerce were the laws of nature and of God. Today, God knows, property concentration is too dense to hide behind a hand that is invisible. Tomorrow, however, may dawn with power in the hands of the information holders. What do we do then, and where do we obtain the information to do it?

ACKNOWLEDGMENTS

E. Ray Canterbery is Professor of Economics at Florida State University; Edgar A. Fresen is an Economist at the Department of Revenue, State of Florida.

NOTES

1. "Leviathan" originally was a medieval giant sea snake or whale. In Hobbes' classic, "Leviathan" had an organic meaning: the whole of society. Only its head represented the sovereign, whereas its many feet represented the governed. When used as a synonym for government, as it is by public choice theorists, it is misconstrued.
2. If further proof be needed, the king had married Marie Antoinette, the giddy and extravagant sister of the Austrian emperor, whose alleged remark about cake still is considered revolting.
3. A series of articles and commentary on Nozick and Rawls appears in Canterbery and Johnson, 1978. A more detailed, critical analysis of Rawls appears in Canterbery, 1981.
4. More detail on this is found in Canterbery, 1981.
5. General Motors Corporation hired a private detective to investigate Nader's private life in the hope of "smearing" him. Despite close surveillance, the private eye was unable to collect any derogatory information to use effectively to impugn Nader's reputation.

REFERENCES

Buchanan, J.M. "The Economic Theory of Politics Reborn." *Challenge,* (1988), *31*(2). Pp. 4-10.

———. *Freedom in Constitutional Contract.* College Station, TX: Texas A&M University Press. 1977.

———. *Liberty, Market and State.* Brighton, Sussex: Wheatsheaf LTC. 1986.

———. *The Limits of Liberty.* Chapel Hill, NC: University of North Carolina Press. 1960.

———. *Fiscal Responsibility in Constitutional Democracy.* Leiden & Boston: Kluwer Boston. 1978.

Buchanan, J.M. and G. Tullock. *Calculus of Consent.* Ann Arbor, MI: University of Michigan Press. 1962.

Buchanan, J.M and R.E. Wagner. *Democracy in Deficit.* New York: Academic Press. 1977.

Burke, E. *Reflections on the Revolution in France.* [1790]. Edited by C.C. O'Brien. Harmondsworth: Penguin. 1968.

Canterbery, E.R. "Income Redistribution and Rawlsian Justice." *Journal of Economics and Business,* ((1981), *33*(3), Pp. 188-201.

———. *The Making of Economics,* 3rd ed. Belmont, CA: Wadsworth, 1987.

Canterbery, E.R. and H.G. Johnson. "Symposium on Justice, Nozick and Rawls. *Eastern Economic Journal,* (1978), *4*(1).

Hayek, F.A. *Law, Legislation and Liberty,* Vol. 1, *Rules and Order.* Chicago: University of Chicago Press. 1978.

Lebergott, S. *The Americans.* New York: W.W. Norton & Company. 1984.

Lindblom, C. *Politics and Markets.* New York: Basic Books. 1976.

Lock, F.P. *Burke's Reflections on the Revolution in France.* London: George Allen & Unwin. 1985.

McKenzie, R.B. and G. Tullock. *The New World of Economics.* Homewood, IL: Richard D. Irwin. 1975.

Nozick, R. *Anarchy, State and Utopia.* New York: Basic Books. 1974.

Piven, F.F. and R.A. Cloward. *Why Americans Don't Vote.* New York: Pantheon. 1988.

Rawls, J. *A Theory of Justice.* Cambridge, MA: Harvard. 1971.

Samuels, W.J. "Toward Positive Public Choice Theory." *Review of Social Economy,* (1980), *38*(1). Pp. 55-64.

Chapter 30

JKG'S *ECONOMICS IN PERSPECTIVE*: REVIEW ESSAY— COUNTERVAILING PERSUASION

E. Ray Canterbery

Long before the United States began to import Toyotas, it imported high quality human capital. John Kenneth Galbraith (1908-), whose career began inauspiciously at Ontario Agricultural College, was the most important Canadian import in 1931. In that year Thorstein Veblen, Galbraith's mentor, had been two years dead. Biography is central to this essay because the Galbraithian persona makes his new book—*Economics in Perspective*—important and unique.

Galbraith became an American citizen in 1937, after earning a degree in agricultural economics at the University of California (Berkeley). He then moved on to Harvard University where he was to teach most of his career and where he is now Paul M. Warburg Professor of Economics Emeritus. Agricultural economics, like politics, was a mere extension of Galbraith's early life. Galbraith's father was a farmer and leading political liberal in the Ontario farming community where JKG was born. Perhaps his sardonic humor began to develop while still a tot when he would accompany the elder Galbraith to political meetings. Galbraith recalls an occasion where his father made a speech critical of his Tory opponents from atop a huge manure pile, apologizing for speaking from the Tory platform.

At Berkeley, JKG was introduced to the writings of Veblen, a Norwegian from rural Minnesota. Veblen's ironic skepticism regarding economic doctrines and "higher learning" made a lasting impression upon young Galbraith. An iconoclast attacks the fundamental beliefs of a society, an institution, or an academic discipline. Veblen, and then Galbraith, attacked all three. In this regard I cannot avoid believing that their common agricultural background is important. I too spent the early part of my youth on a family farm. (The latter part of my youth still is being spent.) On the farm I detected a dearth of pretense because the essence of rural life is all the more obvious for being simple. Once exposed to horse manure, one detects it easily forevermore.

Agriculture often is a fertile breeding ground for the intellectual's conscience. For centuries the otherwise "wily" peasant was kept in his place by beliefs taught by the established institutions, including the Academy. The progressive conscience directs itself at depreciating the currency of those Tories (by whatever establishment name) who want others to know only what is convenient to know for the protection of the status quo, which Galbraith has coined "the conventional wisdom." Though agriculturalists tend to be conservative on foreign policy, they founded populism. City-bred Manhattan intellectuals cannot be natural iconoclasts, much less populists. They believe that milk and ideals are both manufactured products.

So it is that Galbraith's early life was an excellent background for his later career as a social critic. He attended high school in Dutton, a village split by discord between the rural Scotch and the English townspeople. Here most of the Tories were English merchants, whereas the Liberal Party was predominantly Scotch. In the post-World War I years the village merchants prospered while the farmers suffered. The Scotch, who thought they were superior in every way to the English, believed that the merchants were better off because they were buying cheap and selling dear. This superior bargaining power to the merchants apparently made a lasting impression upon young Galbraith.

The steps from the barnyard to the American Academy of Arts and Letters, of which Galbraith is one of 50 members, are not long when one considers the origins of social criticism. Along the way, JKG got a jump start from the Franklin D. Roosevelt administration. He went on to organize the wartime system of price controls and played a central role in wartime economic policy. After the war, Galbraith continued his public service in a number of assignments, including distinguished service as John F. Kennedy's ambassador to India.

Galbraith has even been honored by the economics establishment's most powerful organization. In 1971 he was nominated by a sympathetic but small committee for the presidency of the American Economic Association. (Nomination is tantamount to election.) However, Milton Friedman (1912/2006), a perennial advisor to the Tories, organized an opposition, arguing that Galbraith should not be elected since Veblen had never been AEA president. As history tells us, Veblen indeed was nominated for the same position but refused to serve on the Marxian (Groucho, that is) grounds that he would not want to be president of any organization that would elect him. Neither Friedman nor Veblen prevailed, and today Galbraith enjoys the role of a past president of the AEA. He, whose diplomacy is impeccable, calls Friedman "perhaps the most influential economist of the past half century" (p. 271).

There are other accomplishments. Galbraith was given the Medal of Freedom for his wartime service, and accorded the high rank of *Commandeur* in the French Foreign Legion. He is also a recent president of the combined American Institute and Academy of Arts and Letters.

Now in his 82nd year, his writing remains undiminished. *Economics in Perspective* in his 25th book, even the more remarkable considering that JKG launched his literary career with *American Capitalism: The Concept of Countervailing Power* (1952) at age 44, upon deciding that going unread by economists was no longer endurable. His literary preeminence was not assured, however, until the appearance of *The Affluent Society* four years later. The tactic worked: Galbraith has leaned effectively against the winds of orthodoxy with charming countervailing persuasion.

The general theme of *Perspective* is clear. Economics as now taught and read and as it serves to guide both public policy and private decision making is very much the product of the past. It cannot be understood apart from its history. What's more, that history cannot be understood apart from the circumstances that shaped the beliefs of the time, including an understanding of those in power who bent those beliefs to best serve their financial privileges. At the risk of offending both my patrician *and* econometrician friends, I must accede agreement.

One might suppose a marketing problem exists here. Many books have been written on the history of economic ideas, including Robert Heilbroner's wonderful *Worldly Philosophers.* And, Galbraith wants to be read, wants to influence opinion. So, why read *Economics in Perspective?* Because it is a history of economic ideas from Galbraith's critical, often sardonic, perspective; the *perspective* is *his.* I recall the late Cliff Lloyd saying that the sole, unique characteristic of his textbook on microeconomics was its authorship. Galbraith's product is nonetheless further differentiated. Not only are the economic ideas placed securely in the life of their times, the focus is upon those ideas that have survived to influence our present beliefs and actions. Beliefs and actions, Galbraith would agree, are closely connected. Moreover, Galbraith has the special advantage of having known personally nearly all of the major players of the last 50 years, economists and policymakers alike. By his calculation, he has been professionally present and has known most of the economic participants for one quarter of the 200 years since Adam Smith (p. 3N2).

Perspective is typically Galbraithian because it replays his favorite themes. They are: (1) the neoclassical orthodoxy is irrelevant; (2) economics in practice is theology; (3) power, especially as it relates to industrial concentration, is important in explaining economic outcomes; (4) great inequalities characterize advanced capitalism; and (5) an incomes policy is critical to the survival of the advanced capitalistic system. These themes are the threads that make whole cloth of the ethical judgments that remain from the household and slave economies of the Greeks, from biblical thought and from the feudal world of St. Thomas Aquinas, from the prerevolutionary French philosophers in defense of agriculture, and from the merchant capitalists in the early days of modern capitalism. Also there is Adam Smith, viewing the early stages of the Industrial Revolution, and Karl Marx, reacting to the cruelties of 19th-century capitalism. Galbraith continues to Keynes, the Great Depression, and the modern welfare state. And, beginning with the administration of Franklin Roosevelt, JKG is there as an active participant. The book closes with Galbraith's own, newest perspectives.

The orthodoxy assailed by Galbraith begins with the Physiocrats' guiding rule in legislation and in government—*laissez faire, laissez passer*. This dictum, based as it was upon *le droit naturel,* remains the natural battle cry of orthodoxy. As Galbraith puts it,

> Theological *laissez faire* is a notable force in our own time, not least in the Washington of the 1980s. It is strongly operative in the way numerous modern businessmen view the state, up to the point where threatening bankruptcy, unduly severe foreign competition or some other looming misfortune requires a return to secular state action. (p. 51)

This *laissez faire* flosses the teeth of the gift horse in whose mouth the orthodoxy and the capitalists are forever looking. When John Maynard Keynes came to the rescue of capitalism, he was denounced as a Marxist, even though he never took the time to read, much less understand, Marx. Yet, as Galbraith says, "the classical system in its purest form will not be tolerated by its participants ..." (p. 209). The farmers would not accept the low incomes dictated by nearly flawless competition and the organization of manufacturing is expressly designed to avoid competition. No self-interested businessperson would do less.

As to Keynesian remedies, Galbraith contends, "religious conviction also has a role ... the classical system was—and remains—more than an arrangement for producing goods and services and defining personal reward. It was also a totem, a manifestation of religious faith. ... Businessmen, business executives, capitalists, rose above interest to defend faith. This, many still do" (p. 219). JKG sees the perfect competition retention of present-day economists in an age in which it is rejected by businesspeople (except as prescription for others), related both to theology and to the rise of mathematical economics. Mathematics gives economics a characteristic shared with the natural sciences. It is a pleasant accommodation for a nonerror apparent "science" that began with the conceptual laws of nature.

Today, no doubt, businesspeople see things in a clearer light than does orthodoxy. As Galbraith has it, "in the real world perfect competition was by now leading an increasingly esoteric [Veblen's term] existence if, indeed, any existence at all, and mathematical theory was, in no slight measure, the highly sophisticated cover under which it managed to survive" (p. 260).

Whereas Marx could not conceive of capitalism's surviving the business cycle, "Keynes lifted the incubus of depression and unemployment off capitalism, or such was his design" (p. 236). Keynes' reward was to be labeled "Marxist" and as Galbraith recounts history at Harvard, Lauchlin Currie (1902-1993), one of the kindest and brightest persons of my acquaintance, also was labeled (gasp!) a "liberal." Currie "had anticipated Keynes in some important respects, a circumstance that, at the time, could well have cost him a Harvard promotion" (p. 241). Lauchlin became the principal Keynesian voice in government and the first White House economic advisor (to Ronald Reagan's favorite president). Not so surprisingly, "once again it was events, not economists, that took charge—events silent, without voice and, since unrecognized, unresisted" (p. 250). Nonetheless, the Employment Act of 1946, establishing the President's Council of Economic Advisers, has been a lasting monument to the wartime Keynesians. Without the Act, conservative economists could not have advised "conservative" presidents officially, even though it is again fashionable among economists who defend perfect competition to malign Keynes and once again pin the "liberal" tale on the Donkey.

Galbraith's first reference to power begins with Jesus, "who showed that there was no divine right of the privileged; power could be with people who worked with their hands" (p. 20). JKG agrees with his friend Krister Stendahl, the former dean of the Harvard Divinity School, that the Roman execution proved that Jesus must have been messianic, at least sufficiently so as to constitute a threat to the Roman political order. The idea of equality promulgated by Jesus created the suspicion that wealth could be a source of unequal power. In this respect, early Christian doctrine condemned the taking of interest, since it was seen as extortion by the affluent from the impoverished. However, it recent times neither the religious right nor orthodoxy has objected to the taking of interest; this may illustrate how much both have accommodated themselves to the prerequisites of wealth and power.

With the rise of the nation-state Galbraith sees a close association between the government and the merchant class. The competitive market as religious totem deflected attention away from monopoly power. Despite the evidence of wealth—the great observable difference between the amount of property amongst those who labored and those who provided capital—orthodoxy showed "a reticence that persists to this day. The pursuit of power and its pecuniary and psychic rewards remains, as it was then, the great black hole of mainstream economics" (p. 115). During the times of Ricardo, Malthus, and Mill, the explanation of poverty was found in the moral deficiencies or sexual excesses of the poor. Their ideas "still have more than a fugitive presence in Bedford-Stuyvesant, the South Bronx and the works of the more determined critics of the welfare state" (p. 117). The "scientific" expression of the classical faith peaked with Social Darwinism in the early decades of the 20th century, traces of which can be discerned today. I would add that the 1988 Republican presidential nominee's attack upon a "card-carrying member of the ACLU" and the "liberals," a thinly disguised racism, was perhaps the meanest appeal to Social Darwinism in recent memory.

As Galbraith so eloquently relates, Karl Marx saw power as the inescapable consequence of property accumulation. Marx correctly identified the vulnerable points of capitalism—the distribution of power, the highly unequal distribution of income, monopoly, and the business cycle. Furthermore, government serves the interest of corporate or business power in Marx's paradigm. These consequences were no less important for being so obvious. The later development of the welfare state, mass education, abolition of child labor, and the Keynesian assault on the business cycle were logical reforms that addressed Marx's concerns. Paradoxically, all of these steps "in their time [would] be accorded a measure of condemnation as being themselves Marxist!" (p. 138)

Although the Marxian critique did not make the Atlantic crossing with the classical orthodoxy (at the end of the 19th century), Thorstein Veblen awaited the classical's landing with glee. In a series of short papers, Veblen held that "the central ideas of the classical system did not reflect a search for truth and reality; rather they were and are a celebration of approved belief. Any society has a system of thought founded not on what is actual but on what is agreeable and convenient to the influential interest" (p. 171). Veblen, unlike the neoclassicals, had a strong reaction to the giant American trusts. In the United States of the 1870s and 1880s, monopoly, not the competition praised by the neoclassicals, was the norm. These same trusts evoked the Darwinian "survival of the fittest" doctrine in defense of free competition. There is no contradiction here, as Veblen sensed; competition, so essential for others, is to be avoided at all costs by oneself.

Edward H. Chamberlin (1899-1967) and, more notably, Joan Robinson (1903-1983), toiled within this wide space of the competitive conditions between pure competition and monopoly. Oligopoly and differentiation of products became part of the language of economics. At the freshmen level of instruction monopoly is deplored and oligopoly accepted, but at the graduate level and in the scientific journals, the path of the mathematics of pure competition was paved with the Nobel prizes, while Joan Robinson traveled the "low road" of imperfectly competitive reality. Monopoly power is no longer a threat to the classical hegemony. Even so, the esoteric knowledge of price fixing shows once again that "the classical system in its purest form will not be tolerated by its participants, a highly significant fact of modern economic life" (p. 209). By now, about two thirds of U.S. industrial production comes from the thousand largest industrial firms.

In discussing "the present as future," Galbraith completes a thought about inequality that was begun in his *Affluent Society*. He rightly chastises Keynes for missing the point on the importance of income distribution, an error that post-Keynesians such as Michal Kalecki, Nicholas Kaldor, Joan Robinson, Abba Lerner, and Sidney Weintraub sought to correct. JKG reprises his theme of production's being sufficient to meet basic needs in the affluent society and the necessity for advertising to stimulate wants. To Galbraith, the economist by now should have shifted his focus away from individual prices and production and toward the security of employment and income. In today's advanced economies, production is more important for the jobs and incomes it generates rather than for itself. I have pursued this topic elsewhere (Canterbery, 1987) and have encountered the same resistance from orthodoxy. Price theory serves more than a ceremonial function. Though of minor interest to the rest of the better off, individual prices remain important to economists for the jobs-creation power of price theory.

The Keynesian system nonetheless served the first 25 years of the post-World II era well. Still, the *General Theory* was, as Galbraith explains, "a tract of the Great Depression" (p. 266). Once prices were generally rising from the cost side of the economy (wages, materials, and profits), the recession that Keynesianism was designed to repel became the main policy tool for fighting inflation. Keynesianism in reverse is perverse. Galbraith himself has contributed to the theory of the wage-price spiral and pushed his own remedy of price and wage controls and other forms of incomes policies as alternatives to a medicine that, in its adverse effects, rivals the disease.

Galbraith sees the distinction between microeconomics and macroeconomics—a split created by Keynes—as ultimately disappearing. It is difficult to say when this might happen; however, Galbraithian economics surely is eroding those unnatural boundaries. JKG believes that Japan will be the source of the economic thought of the future, much as it is the source of goods innovation today. Japanese business executives, high civil servants, and academic economists often begin their lives as Marxists.

This theory is plausible. American dominance in economics is closely connected with the financial support afforded by a vast, rich nation. We have carelessly squandered our academic advantage, even as our financial institutions have approached a meltdown. Japan is a rich and apparently dependable economy; the United States is precariously perched atop a mountain of household, corporate, federal, and foreign debt. Credit, the instrument of capitalism, topples us every time we become overly indebted to it.

There are American economists—Galbraith, Hyman Minsky, and Charles Kindleberger come to mind—who have identified the stresses and strains of advanced capitalism. They see a form of socialism rising from the ashes of unreformed, unrepentant capitalism, the welfare state having provided only makeshift repairs. Meanwhile, today's orthodoxy is as sanguine as it was when Irving Fisher wrote after the 1929 Crash that the American economy was expanding. The "best" of the orthodox minds will not be altered even by a catastrophe; that is the nature of normal science. Policymakers who have escaped the claws of ideology are the ones who respond to events, as Galbraith says. They do not listen to economists; Franklin Roosevelt never understood Keynes, but he did understand the needs of the average family. Once again, disaster is just around the corner, and saving posterity is far more important than saving the price theory paradigm or rational expectations. In any case, Say's law will continue to serve the employment of economists (and lawyers).

Galbraith has had the courage to deliver this kind of countervailing persuasion throughout his productive writing career. If he suffers the fatigue and loneliness of the long distance runner, it is well hidden behind a rapier wit that withers intellectual adversaries who nonetheless respect him. If the next revolution in the economic thought of capitalism comes from a Japanese economist originally trained in Marxism, we will continue to be amused and think fondly of John Kenneth Galbraith.

REFERENCES

Canterbery, E. Ray. "A Theory of Supra-Surplus Capitalism," (Presidential address) *Eastern Economic Journal,* (October-December, 1987), *XIII,* pp. 315-332.

Galbraith, John Kenneth. *The Affluent Society.* Boston: Houghton-Mifflin, 1958.

________. *American Capitalism: The Concept of Countervailing Power.* Boston: Houghton Mifflin, 1952.

________. *Economics in Perspective: A Critical History.* Boston: Houghton Mifflin, 1987.

________. *A Life in Our Times: Memoirs.* Boston: Houghton Mifflin, 1981.

________. *The Scotch.* Boston: Houghton Mifflin, 1964.

Chapter 31

E. Ray Canterbery

Reviews

The End of Economic Man: Principles of Any Future Economics. Third Edition

By George P. Brockway.

In Anglo-Saxon tradition there is a long—even glorious—tradition of celebrating amateurs. Economics itself is relatively new as a profession. As late as 1880, only three devout academic political economists resided at leading U.S. universities. More often then not, however, the amateur economist-writer today is gravely distrusted, even rebuked by professionals.

DISTINGUISHED AMATEUR ECONOMISTS

Convention aside, there are some important amateur economists who cannot be denied. Adam Smith, one of the first, was a moral philosopher who dabbled in economics only when he wrote *The Wealth of Nations*. Today, Smith would not qualify for tenure at even a mediocre state research university because he had not published enough refereed journal articles. David Ricardo was a stockbroker first, a parliamentarian second, a landowner third, and an amateur economist last. Jeremy Bentham, who laid the utilitarian foundations for modern microeconomics, would today be consigned to the belfry; he not only wrote books but best-sellers. Irving Fisher, highly regarded by today's economists, was an inventor, mathematician, statistician, businessman, reformer, and lastly a teacher.

The regrettable loss of status for the amateur as public intellectual brings me to George Brockway and his Third Edition of *The End of Economic Man*. My impression is that economists have yet to discover this remarkable writer-economist, once a distinguished business executive (Chairman of the Board of W.W. Norton, a large and successful employee-owned publisher, living and succeeding outside the orthodox theory of the firm). He writes wise, clear, and amusing essays for *The New Leader* and has contributed articles to *Challenge*, *Journal of Post Keynesian Economics*, and the *New York Times*. As an amateur historian, he wrote *Political Deals that Saved Andrew Johnson* and is an honorary fellow of the Society of American Historians. As an amateur anthropologist, Brockway coauthored a travel book on Greece. As an amateur writer, he holds an honorary Litt.D. from Williams College, from which he holds an earned undergraduate degree.

As much as there was to admire in Brockway's second edition—common sense graced with erudition, wit unspoiled by rancor, wisdom undiminished by pretense, and humanity unsullied by gratuitous moralizing—there is still more in this substantially revised edition. He has added a chapter on the "repulsive fallacy" of the natural rate of unemployment, has unmasked the "seductive fallacy" of productivity, and has further demystified money, interest, investment, saving, inflation, and speculation. And, still further in his favor, he again opens the book with a rapier attack on "the economic man."

THE LIFE AND DEATH OF ECONOMIC MAN

Brockway's ambition is no less than the burial of the hypothetical, self-interested and yet "rational," economic man. Despite the devilish difficulty of laying to rest someone who never existed, Brockway succeeds admirably. He then dances on the grave of this hypothetical for the next fifteen chap-

E. RAY CANTERBERY is Professor of Economics at Florida State University. His most recent book is *The Literate Economist*.

ters with what he calls his "Three Antinomies of Greed."

The first antinomy is summarized as follows: "Profit maximization and utility maximization cannot simultaneously rule us." The attempt to maximize both profits and pleasure is defeated by the limits of the twenty-four-hour day. You cannot do both. The profit-maximizing man, as "clever, bold, and ruthless" as he may be—is regrettably a workaholic, drinking deeply of self-inflicted pain. But the "charming wastrel," maximizing utility at the pulse rate of a strobe light, lives a life of endless pleasure, cutting a swath as wide as Elvis at 40. The profit maximizer has no time to pursue pleasure and the pleasure-seeker no time to pursue profits. Besides, the best a profit-maximizing Malboro Man can do—under conditions of competition that takes his breath away—is to generate a profit rate at cost, the profit rate he would have made if he had instead produced nicotine patches. The pleasure in that could hardly be thought substantial.

The second antinomy is "other things being equal, greed and its contrary are equally universal." Brockway finds self-interest or greed to be "on no surer footing than altruism." Energetic competition among self-interested producers would drive price down to cost; altruistic producers "would set prices at cost out of the goodness of their hearts." Prices would be at cost either way, in a society of calculating Benthamites like Dickens's Thomas Gradgrind *or* of generous souls like Jimmy Stewart in "It's a Wonderful Life."

The third antinomy is "foolish greed is unpredictable, and rational greed is absurd." In the end, therefore, greed alone is insufficient. An unpredictable greedy fool *is* the apt subject of Dickens's fiction. On the other hand, the *rational* self-interested economic man demeans himself and becomes a contradiction in terms, the Jay Gatsby of economic science.

Having defeated the idea of economic man with his own sword of "rationality," Brockway knocks down and rebuilds the pillars of the orthodox economics temple. While seldom straying from common sense basics, Brockway emerges from his duel of wits with economic man by chapter three to direct us toward a new, more humane economics. Unable to do justice to each pillar of wisdom, I shall focus on three issues of immediate policy concern.

THE SAVING–INVESTMENT CONUNDRUM AND CAPITAL GAINS TAX CUTS

Say's law once had been laid to rest by John Maynard Keynes, only to be resurrected by the supply-side economists during the Reagan years. The disaster, a.k.a. Reaganomics, sent J. B. Say back to the oxygen tent, in which a dangerous side-effect was the ensuing confusion among emerging Ph.D.s regarding saving and investment. Keynes had investment preceding saving and now, in their zeal to integrate microeconomics and macroeconomics, the economists preferred the vice versa. "Saving is a consequence of production," writes Brockway. "Nothing can be saved until it exists," he continues, "not-consuming does not mean investing. You can save or not-consume until you starve or freeze to death, but your not-consuming will not cause investment. Investment is a separate and deliberate action."

Brockway's appeal is not to Keynes's *General Theory* but to an earlier essay in which Keynes discussed economic growth. Keynes thought the Spanish propensity to convert bullion into castles during the sixteenth century to be frivolous. As Brockway relates, "the British steadily plowed 3.25 percent [yearly] of their earnings back into the shops for which Napoleon scorned them, and into mines and railways and factories and ships, all of which, in turn, produced further goods." The castles, mainly in Spain, were as much consumption as, much later, was Commodore Vanderbilt's house, the imposing Breakers.

The fallacy of composition whereby personal savings automatically create real investment is a convenient, even lethal, argument for reducing or eliminating capital gains taxes as a means of stimulating economic growth. It would be wonderful if it were true, but, aside from castles in the air, the main real-world result of lower capital gains tax rates is to increase the net worth of the fifth now owning 94 percent of the nation's financial net worth. Its main incentive is to spur speculation in debt instruments. Brockway is even less sanguine: "capital gains are an archaic form of profit . . . characteristic not of the capitalist system but of mercantilism and more primitive economic systems . . . like the various ventures of Antonio referred to in *The Merchant of Venice*. Gains (or losses) were realized as each investment ended." Indeed, too much in the way of capital gains and reductions in their taxation could end capitalism, as we know it.

SPECULATION V. ENTERPRISE

A second and related issue is the dichotomy between speculation and enterprise. Keynes made quite clear the distinction, but again not in the same literary piece. And, as Brockway notes, the difference between "investing" in debt and equity instruments such as bonds and stocks versus plant and equipment is not taken into account in the *General Theory* "or in the more austerely mathematical versions that appear in today's textbooks."

Let there be no mistake regarding the difference. When we buy and sell secondhand (not new) issues, we are speculating. We do not have the foggiest idea of what the securities are worth and neither do our brokers (with rare exceptions). Volatility in the bond market has erased even *its* safe-haven image. Brockway discards the benign view of speculation taken by Milton Friedman, among others. "Speculation is . . . like gambling in that it produces nothing but rearranges—often to the great profit of the rearrangers—wealth that already exists." By contrast, "enterprise is unlike speculation in that it uses wealth to produce new wealth." That is, as money flows into speculation or what I have called the Casino Economy, the producing economy not only loses sales but also more manageable financing.

To Brockway, that the national debt from Reaganomics and the amount lost during the 1987 stock market crash each equaled a trillion dollars was no coincidence. "These confused policies gave a trillion dollars of American money to people who couldn't use it; these people entrusted it to Wall Street; and Wall Street flushed it down the drain." He goes on to blame much of the speculative fever upon the interest-rate volatility engineered by the Federal Reserve Board. Again, real enterprise is the victim. Moreover, the triumph of speculation over real enterprise will continue as long as management and ownership are separate and unequal because ownership carries no responsibilities.

Speculation is not benign because there is a connection between it and the amount of real saving and employment. Elsewhere ("Reaganomics, Saving, and the Casino Effect" in James H. Gapinski [ed.], *The Economics of Saving*), I have suggested changes in household net worth as the correct measure of nominal personal savings. By this measure, personal savings raced ahead during 1980–88 while real business investment went lame. Where do personal money savings go when they die (in economic theory)? They go into the wild blue plunder of the casino. The denouement, to Brockway, is a moral issue: "That we Americans allot the richest rewards of our economy to speculators is a question of mores; that we allow one-sixth of our fellow citizens still to be ill housed, ill clad, and ill nourished is a question of morals." Brockway opts for lower, stable interest rates and a 95 percent tax on speculative assets held less than a year.

THE UNNATURAL RATE OF UNEMPLOYMENT

All of which brings us to the third issue. Brockway forthrightly dismisses the notion of a natural rate of unemployment or the non-accelerating-inflation rate of unemployment (NAIRU), the idea that hiring the unemployed causes inflation. Moreover, he finds the Fed's policy aimed at ending inflation before it exists as the main culprit. "As fast as Congress puts welfare recipients to work, the Federal Reserve Board," he complains, "ruled by whichever version of the natural rate of unemployment is then fashionable," will sufficiently slow the economy until an equal number of present jobholders are fired. "The cream of the jest," says Brockway, "is that a high interest rate, . . . usually with the intention of lowering prices, has actually increased costs and so has forced increases in prices."

In part, Brockway bases this apparent paradox on his own business experience. The cost of borrowing in advance of printing books rose sharply as interest rates climbed. In order to recover costs, Norton and other publishers had to raise prices. Of course, the effect is more direct in construction, real estate, and automobiles, where interest payments comprise large shares of the purchase prices. To put the point plainly, the Fed causes inflation in costs and prices, forcing households to forego durables. If this policy persists, unemployment follows.

He then comes full circle. An economy with comparatively high interest and low wages (the consequences of high planned profit) "is one marked by cynicism and greed." This suggests that when the economic man is alive the economy is not well. Such a society will make inadequate use of its labor and inappropriate use of its money as the Casino Economy swallows the producing economy.

THE VIEW FROM PROFESSIONAL HEIGHTS

Sometimes our zealous professionalism is downright silly. If economics were a truly progressive science, economists could be proud of their firm stand against the unwashed, the nonprofessionals. But, if today we professionals judge ourselves by our abilities to solve the nation's and the world's serious economic problems, some of us are the rank amateurs.

Brockway mounts sufficiently persuasive evidence—particularly on monetary policy and NAIRU—to provoke our humility.

A small but influential group, called the new classicals, discontented with the merely rational economic man, has invented the *superrational* economic man as the central actor in its theory of rational expectations. The marginal blue-collar worker on his way to the factory anticipates an increase in the money supply (apparently from something Rush Limbaugh said), then fully anticipates inflation within his monetarist model (a diagram of which lines the lid of his lunch pail) and a fall in his real wage rate. The worker does a U-turn, drives home, and voluntarily disemploys himself.

If this is insufficient cause to believe the new classicals to be reality-challenged, consider their new theory of business cycles caused by "technological shocks." All workers take into account the interest rate (say, on bonds) when deciding whether to work. If a technological shock raises the interest rate, workers are willing to work more hours today because their bonds will provide greater interest on their savings. Although the theory once again justifies NAIRU, it conveniently ignores the high unemployment caused when the Fed raises interest rates and the nearly 3 percent *decline* in financial net worth of the bottom 80 percent (surely comprised of people working for a living) during 1983–89. If unemployment exists, it is the optimal outcome of the "intertemporal substitution of labor." But, as Brockway notes in his devastating attack on the "natural rate of unemployment," the unemployment of labor and capital is wastage at its worst.

Are these theories of the new classicals really improvements over those of the amateurish Adam Smith? If the same logic dominated medical science, nothing would be done for passengers in automobile accidents (and other market-related crashes) because such events would be considered optimal for everyone. All the more the pity if economists and other citizens don't read George Brockway. We ignore his common sense, wit, wisdom, and humanity at our professional peril.

Chapter 32

Thorstein Veblen and *The Great Gatsby*

E. Ray Canterbery

F. Scott Fitzgerald's short novel *The Great Gatsby* is set in the 1920s; like its author, it is strongly identified with the Jazz Age—that temporal slice of self-indulgence sandwiched between the Great War and the Great Depression. Yet Fitzgerald's original setting for *Gatsby* was the middle of the Gilded Age (1885), and the theme of the novel is widely recognized as an indictment not so much of the Roaring Twenties as of the "American Dream," which had attained an honored place in American mythology well before the opening of the twentieth century.[1] It is my contention in this paper that much of the socioeconomic satire informing *The Great Gatsby* is not original with Fitzgerald, but reflects the influence, both directly and indirectly, of that earlier adversary of conspicuous consumption and pecuniary emulation, Thorstein Veblen.

The Dominance of Social Darwinism during the Gilded Age

During the Gilded Age (1870-1910), when cutthroat competition and unbridled capitalism led to the accumulation of wealth and capital in a few hands, a need arose to justify the excesses of the newly rich and their corrupt business practices. Thus emerged the "American Dream"—a blend of the Newtonian belief in a beneficent, finely tuned universe and the American versions of Calvinism and Puritanism, which condoned and encouraged the accumulation of wealth as a way of doing God's work.

Since the rich of the Gilded Age chose to display their great wealth in vulgar ways, their continued respectability required some blend of science with religion to

The author is Professor of Economics, Florida State University. *This paper was presented at the annual meeting of the Association for Evolutionary Economics, New York City, New York, January 3-5, 1999.*

make their wealth appear not only just, but inevitable. The American Social Darwinism of William Graham Sumner served this purpose, particularly as set forth in Horatio Alger, Jr.'s popular fiction for boys, which injects into the Protestant ethic an element from Newtonian science, the idea of a universe that rewards.

In the view of Herbert Spencer (1820-1903), the English founder of sociology, the fact that the rich get richer and the poor get poorer is just nature's way of improving the species and the economy at the same time. Spencer's books sold by the hundreds of thousands, and his reception in New York in 1882, two years before Gatsby originally was to arrive there, would have been the envy of Madonna's press agent.

Though a generation of scholars wallowed in Spencer's wake, the most eminent of the American Social Darwinists was William Graham Sumner (1840-1910), Veblen's professor at Yale. Sumner was direct, proclaiming that "the millionaires are a product of natural selection . . . the naturally selected agents of society for certain work. They get high wages and live in luxury, but the bargain is a good one for society" [Sumner 1914, 90]. Thus, while Horatio Alger's heroes could achieve in fiction the American Dream of rising to the top, the doctrines of the Social Darwinists helped to preserve a social process that made sure such successes were infrequent.

Sumner ingeniously put Newtonian natural law, the Protestant ethic, and a misunderstanding of Darwinian natural selection all on the side of classical economics. Evoking both Calvin and science, his sociology equated the hard-working, thrifty person of the Protestant ethic with the "fittest" in the struggle for survival. Monetary success in the capitalistic society was the fulfillment of an automatically benevolent, free competitive order. In the competitive struggle, people went from natural selection to social selection of fitter persons and from "organic forms with superior adaptability to citizens with a greater store of economic virtues" [Sumner 1914, 57]. Not surprisingly, Andrew Carnegie and John D. Rockefeller became disciples.[2]

Veblen's Counterpoint: The Theory of the Leisure Class *(TLC)*

Social Darwinism met its antithesis in *The Theory of the Leisure Class* [Veblen 1899]. When Veblen applied the law of natural selection to human institutions (broadly defined to include ideas and habits of thought), he found not progress, but regression. Human institutions (environment) perpetually lagged behind material change. Still, the successful individuals are those who can best adapt to changing institutions—more a Lamarkian than a Darwinian process. Because people are also creatures of habit, changes are made reluctantly and rarely. Because the leisure class is sheltered from pressures of subsistence, its members have no urgency to change and so retain their old habits of living. The social or cultural environment makes the survival of some characteristics more likely than others.[3]

A state of savagery requires people to be community-centered for survival. When technology advances sufficiently to create surpluses, predation and barbarism emerge, as do classes distinguished by wealth holdings. Barbarism promotes not only selfishness and emulation, but brutality [Veblen 1899, esp. chap. 9]. Though such characteristics assure survival in an economy of surpluses, they are neither noble nor progressive. Aggressive behavior is rewarded; the most cunning and competitive of the leisure class have the upper hand. If Veblen is correct, it is neither surprising that the "American Dream" is to become ever more affluent nor that the affluent promote exclusive institutions.

Since *pecuniary emulation* is an individual's strongest motive, the *standard of living* shared by a particular class determines the "accepted standard of expenditure." As Veblen put it,

> To accept and practise the standard of living which is in vogue is both agreeable and expedient, commonly to the point of being indispensable to personal comfort and to success in life. The standard of living of any class, so far as concerns the element of conspicuous waste, is commonly as high as the earning capacity of the class will permit—with a constant tendency to go higher [Veblen 1899, 111-112].

Emulation dominates Veblen's chapter "Dress as an Expression of the Pecuniary Culture," where he writes that "admitted expenditure for display is more universally practised in the matter of dress than in any other line of consumption" [Veblen 1899, 167]. Sharpening the edge of his sarcasm, Veblen writes, "the woman's shoe adds the so-called French heel to the evidence of enforced leisure afforded by its polish; because this high heel obviously makes any, even the simplest and most necessary manual work extremely difficult" [1899, 171]. Of course, much more complex and subtle sociology is at work in *TLC*, including the woman's service as a "chief ornament" around the house and an adequately adorned "trophy" for her husband. Women indeed comprise an abused class in *TLC*.

Taboos also play roles in consumption. Ceremonial consumption such as "choice articles of food, and . . . rare articles of adornment, becomes tabu to the women and children; and if there is a base (servile) class of men, the tabu holds also for them" [Veblen 1899, 69]. Certain intoxicating beverages and narcotics are reserved for the use of men. Such taboos separate one class from another; members of the "superior class" identify themselves not only by what they consume, but by their power to prevent the consumption of the same items by others. The taboo is a way of preventing emulation of the upper classes by the lower classes.

Parallels Between The Theory of the Leisure Class *and* The Great Gatsby

All of which brings us to Fitzgerald's *The Great Gatsby* [1925]. Fitzgerald's masterpiece is the supreme Veblenian parable of conspicuous consumption, of conspicuous emulation, of pecuniary culture, and of vicarious consumption—even of waste and the leisure class itself. Jay Gatsby wants to live with Daisy Buchanan because she is a member of the *established* American aristocracy of wealth. Gatsby lacks the maturity to realize that Daisy cannot be obtained by money alone and in a vulgar display of conspicuous consumption, he flaunts his nouveau wealth. Despite Daisy's infinite price (perhaps "priceless"), Gatsby is most attracted to Daisy's voice (not the supra-price), which he describes as "full of money," a voice fostering an illusion he considers real. Fitzgerald here has put on display Veblen's "secondary utility," based on emulation that "seized upon the consumption of goods as a means to an invidious comparison, . . . as evidence of relative ability to pay" [Veblen 1899, 154]. The "evidence" of ability to pay, however, is not the same as the *actual* ability to pay, especially in the instance of "purchasing" Daisy whose price is infinite. Gatsby attempted to display a purchasing ability that was out of his reach.

Surpluses, so essential to Veblenian economics, allow ostentatious display; they also promote advertising. During the Gilded Age, of course, the rich engaged in *self*-advertisement. By the 1920s, advertising had become an important allied industry. (Not accidentally, Fitzgerald's first post-Great War job was writing for the Barron Collier advertising agency in New York City.) Daisy, in her turn, is attracted to Gatsby because he reminds her of "an advertisement," the superficial illusion *he* represents. She sobs when she sees "such beautiful shirts" [Fitzgerald 1925, 93]. As Veblen would predict, for Fitzgerald's central characters the cultural illusions are more important than wealth.

The first dust jacket for *Gatsby* depicted the painted eyes of an oculist's billboard advertisement, the source of symbolism for a business dedicated to persuasion through fallacies and exaggerations. But the eyes look out over a wasteland. George Wilson, after his wife Myrtle's death (from the careless driving of Daisy), mistakes the "eyes" on such a sign for the all-seeing eyes of God and cannot believe that they are "just an advertisement."

As to snobbery, Fitzgerald's *Gatsby* again provides instruction. Tom and Daisy Buchanan live in a Georgian colonial mansion representing *established* wealth. Gatsby, not unlike the robber barons at the turn of the century, has purchased a pretentious, vulgar imitation of a European mansion in East Egg. Even Gatsby's ivy is nouveau and not in the same league as the Buchanans'. The establishment sees clearly that Gatsby, having no sense of tradition, simply copies the style of others, much as an American university will pattern its library on a medieval Gothic chapel. Worse, Gatsby's sartorial choice, a pink suit, is as vulgar and nouveau as his gaudy, cream-colored car, his mansion, and his lavish parties.

Daisy could never leave Tom for Gatsby because she and Tom are partners in a "secret society" of wealth, one that Gatsby cannot recognize, much less join. Daisy cannot leave the trappings of the old aristocracy. Tom, having originally "bought" Daisy with the gift of a $350,000 necklace, deploys brutality to keep her—even at the far greater cost to Gatsby of his (American) dreams and his life. Though Gatsby does not know it, no matter how great his acquisitive spirits as a bootlegger, the acquisition of Daisy is taboo.

Members of the upper-middle class or even middle-middle class who want to emulate the rich leisure class must do so by buying cheap imitations or by borrowing, even at the risk of bankruptcy or worse, which I have called the "Gatsby effect" [Canterbery 1998, 142-146]. The Gatsby effect, of course, intimates disasters beyond bankruptcy from which recovery *is* possible. After all, Jay Gatsby died for the sins of his own emulation, a conspicuous waste.

Before Fitzgerald, only Veblen seems to have captured this cultural richness and the culture of the rich with just the proper subtle balance, mixing satire, irony, and realism to expose the false values and social waste of the upper classes. At the center of the American dream, as well as Gatsby's own, is the belief that sufficient wealth can recapture and fix everything, even the ephemeral, illusory qualities of youth and beauty. It was the same kind of "beauty" satirized by Veblen.

In *Gatsby*, both new wealth (Jay Gatsby's) and old wealth (Daisy's) lead to human failings, though the failings are manifested differently. Early in the novel, Jay Gatsby is observed in the attitude of a worshipper, alone, stretching his arms toward a single, faraway green light at the end of the Buchanans' dock across the water—the visible symbol of his aspirations. Green is the color of promise, of hope and renewal, and, of course, of money. For Gatsby, ideals are wrapped up with wealth, and so the means corrupt the ends. But it turns out that Daisy Buchanan is unworthy of his vision of her, and her "vulgar, meretricious beauty," her pretentiousness, is a snare. Gatsby dies disillusioned, while Daisy lives on, oblivious. So much for Gatsby-like hope, so much for the shallow end of the American Dream.

Ultimately, Was Fitzgerald Influenced by Veblen?

The *Theory of the Leisure Class* was a scholarly yet satirical protest against the false values and social waste of the upper classes during the Gilded Age. *The Great Gatsby* was the exemplary novel of the Jazz Age in which Fitzgerald's sharp social sense enabled him to vividly depict the excesses and false values of the upper class at a time when gin was the national drink and sex the national obsession. The two works share not only a set of themes and a moral stance, they also exhibit many of the same writing qualities—humor, satire, teasing, exaggeration, poetic imagery, symbolism, allegory, and folklore. Nevertheless, the parallels might be dismissed as coincidental, were it not for two pieces of evidence directly linking the two writers.

The Direct Evidence

Fitzgerald first described an East Egg type of society in a March 30, 1924, syndicated article originally titled "Our Irresponsible Rich." Although Fitzgerald does not refer to Veblen in the article itself, his notes relating to the article make clear that he was consciously documenting Veblen's theme of conspicuous consumption and waste [Fitzgerald 1972, 104]. In May of the same year, Fitzgerald, with three chapters of *Gatsby* in manuscript, abandoned Long Island's lavish parties and escaped with Zelda to the more sedate Riviera, where he completed the draft. It is thus plausible to assume that the Veblenian sentiments explored in the article were much on Fitzgerald's mind as he wrote and rewrote the novel.

One paragraph of the syndicated article is especially revealing. In it Fitzgerald writes: "Here we come to something that sets the American 'leisure class' off from the leisure class of all other nations—and makes it probably the most shallow, most hollow, most pernicious leisure class in the world" [Fitzgerald 1924, 7].

Fitzgerald continues in high Veblenian style: "At no period in the world's history, perhaps, has a larger proportion of the family income been spent upon display . . ." And the waste goes on: "All that leisure—for nothing! All that wealth—it has begotten waste and destruction and dissipation and snobbery—nothing more. . . . He [the young man of inherited wealth] stocks his cellar with liquor and then votes righteously for prohibition 'for the good of the masses'."

Fitzgerald even appears to update Veblen's view of rich, oppressed women: "The boy watches his mother's almost insane striving toward a social position commensurate with her money. He sees her change her accent, her clothes, her friends, her very soul, as she pushes her way up in life, pulling her busy husband with her."

Overall, Fitzgerald's theme is that the American upper class had no sense of stewardship of society so that corruption, such as the Teapot Dome scandal (then afflicting the Harding administration), was to be expected, given the premises of the American Dream associating money with success. The status of the upper class is at once gracious in its advantages and privileges but not worthy of aspiration and vision in its callous treatment of those below. The inherited rich are families in decay.

An earlier direct reference to Veblen appeared in a paragraph intended for a published review of a 1921 book by H. L. Mencken. "It seems cruel," wrote Fitzgerald, "that the privilege [of reviewing Mencken] could not have gone to Thorstein Veblen" [Bruccoli and Duggan 1980, 75]. The paragraph, deleted by a party unknown, was apparently a Fitzgerald joke, given the fact that Mencken had earlier published an assault on Veblen's critique of capitalism as a "wraith of balderdash" [Mencken 1949, 273].

The Indirect Evidence

While Fitzgerald (who considered himself not only a good historian, but a practicing socialist) often refers to Karl Marx's *Das Kapital* and other socialist writers such as Upton Sinclair, none of his *published* writings cite or even mention Veblen. And when Fitzgerald designed "courses" for the education of Sheilah Graham, he did not list any of Veblen's books, though he included Marx [see Graham 1967, 213]. Nonetheless, the class distinctions made in *The Great Gatsby* are clearly Veblenian, not Marxist. We can only speculate about the motives for Fitzgerald's failure to acknowledge fully his debt to Veblen. It may be simply a matter of ego. Though he was generous in attributions, Fitzgerald prided himself in his originality. The parallels between his depiction of class, especially in *The Great Gatsby*, and Veblen's sharpest satire may have been too close for comfort, providing a motive for distancing himself from Veblen. Alternatively, Veblen's influence may have been more subliminal by the time Fitzgerald wrote *Gatsby*.

Other evidence of the Veblen-Fitzgerald connection may be lost to history. Fitzgerald had no secretary until 1932; thereafter, he retained carbon copies of his correspondence. Out of a total of 6,000 known letters, an estimated 3,000 were written prior to 1932, Fitzgerald's pre-carbon age [Bruccoli and Duggan 1980, xv]. Thus, much of the missing correspondence covers the *Gatsby* period. We may never know the extent of Fitzgerald's debt to Veblen.

Notes

1. The original time and locales—the Midwest and New York City—are characterized in a letter to Max Perkins, Fitzgerald's long-time editor [see Bryer and Kuehl 1971, 61].
2. Carnegie describes in his autobiography his troubled mental state concerning what he believed was the collapse of Christian theology, a tension miraculously relieved by his reading of Darwin and Spencer.

   > I had found the truth of evolution. "All is well since all grows better," became my motto, my true source of comfort. . . . Nor is there any conceivable end to his [the human being's] march to perfection [Carnegie 1920, 327].
3. This is a very compressed summary of my understanding of Veblen's methodology. For a full explication of anthropological influences, see Mayhew [1998]. For much more detail on Veblen, Darwin, and biology, see Tilman [1996]. For an expanded version of my views, see Canterbery [1987, 1999].

References

Bruccoli, Matthew J., and Margaret M. Duggan. *Correspondence of F. Scott Fitzgerald*. New York: Random House, 1980.

Bryer, Jackson, and John Kuehl, eds. *Dear Scott/Dear Max*. New York: Scribner's, 1971.

Canterbery, E. Ray. *The Making of Economics*. 3d ed. Belmont, Calif.: Wadsworth, 1987, chap. 14.

________. "The Theory of the Leisure Class and the Theory of Demand." In *The Founding of Institutional Economics: The Leisure Class and Sovereignty*, edited by Warren J. Samuels, 139-156. London: Routledge, 1998.

________. *The Literate Economist: A Brief History of Economics*. 2d ed. River View, N.J.: World Scientific, 1999, chap. 22.

Carnegie, Andrew. *Autobiography of Andrew Carnegie*. Boston: Houghton Mifflin, 1920.

Fitzgerald, F. Scott. *The Vegetable, or from President to Postman*. New York: Charles Scribner's Sons, 1923.

________. "What Kind of Husbands Do 'Jimmies' Make?" (also titled elsewhere, "Our Irresponsible Rich") *Baltimore American*, 30 March, 1924, p. 7; reprinted in Bruccoli, Matthew J., and Jackson R. Bryer, eds. *F. Scott Fitzgerald In His Own Time: A Miscellany*. Kent, Ohio: Kent State University Press, 1971.

________. *The Great Gatsby*. New York: Charles Scribner's Sons, 1925.

________. *F. Scott Fitzgerald's Ledger: A Facsimile*, introduced by Matthew Bruccoli. Washington, D.C.: Microcard Editions, 1972.

Graham, Sheilah. *College of One*. New York: The Viking Press, 1967.

________. *Beloved Infidel*. 1958. Reprint. New York: Quality Paperback Book Club, 1989.

Mayhew, Anne. "Veblen and the Anthropological Perspective." In *The Founding of Institutional Economics: The Leisure Class and Sovereignty*, edited by Warren J. Samuels, 234-249. London: Routledge, 1998.

Mencken, H. L. *A Mencken Chrestomathy*, edited by H. L. Mencken. New York: Knopf, 1949.

Sumner, William Graham. *The Challenge of Facts and Other Essays*, edited by Albert Galoway Keller. New Haven, Conn.: Yale University Press, 1914.

Tilman, Rick. *The Intellectual Legacy of Thorstein Veblen: Unresolved Issues*. Westport, Conn. and London: Greenwood Press, 1996, 47-71.

Tomlinson, Everett T. "The Perpetual 'Best-Sellers'." *World's Work* 20 (June 1910).

Turnbull, Andrew. *Scott Fitzgerald*. New York: Charles Scribner's Sons, 1962.

Veblen, Thorstein. *The Theory of the Leisure Class*. 1899. Reprint. New York and London: Penguin Books, 1994.

PART VI

ECONOMIC DEVELOPMENT

Chapter 33

The Green Revolution and the World Rice Market, 1967–1975*

E. Ray Canterbery and Hans Bickel

THE DRAMATIC green revolution in rice, wheat, and corn may shift economic development problems from concern with widespread starvation to concern with a potential grain glut on world markets. This unexpected technological twist foreshadows possibly some new trading difficulties for developed agricultural exporters such as the United States, Japan, and Canada plus some entirely different kinds of problems for LDC grain consumers and producers. The history of the development of the new seeds and the precise nature of the new technology has been widely discussed elsewhere (see, e.g., [1]). Barring widespread war, one realizes that what happens in terms of LDC production of rice and wheat and developed nations' responses will for the most part determine the economic destiny of the less developed world in this decade.

Methodology

Because of the sharp change in technology, many official government forecasts for grain output and trade patterns through 1975 are in error. The purpose of this paper is to attempt to remedy these difficulties by taking *explicitly* into account the yield changes from the technological advance and the impact of both production and consumption changes on the price of rice in the major producing nations and in the world.

Rice consumption and production estimates were developed both from statistical equations and, in the case of production in the miracle-grain-adopting nations, from nonstatistical techniques.[1] It was possible to estimate statistically rice demand functions for the major consuming nations and for the world because of the stability of most of the consumption functions. Two sets of equations were run for rice consumption (C_r) for each of the major nations: (1) Explanatory equations meeting relatively high statistical standards were estimated for the purpose of calculating income and price elasticities; (2) forecasting equations were developed that met only the test of "best fit." The same criteria were applied to production estimates.

The estimation for production and related elasticities was more difficult. We were in part constrained either by data availability or by the research costs of building data series for all the potential determinants of output. We were able to develop data series on total fertilizer consumption (F), total production (Q), area in hectares used in rice production (A), and various price series for 1955–1966, the period used for the regressions. We knew that irrigation expansion, labor input growth, insecticide usage, and rainfall variation would in some cases strongly influence output. As it turns out, the "package" nature of the miracle grain technology causes fertilizer usage, irrigation, and insecticide use to increase at about the same rate. In addition to their reduced sensitivity to the length of days and their early maturity, the new varieties experience diminishing returns from fertilizer application at much higher yields than the old, local varieties. Hence, the effect of the new technology can for the most part be "embodied" in fertilizer consumption in the LDC's. This of course is not true for the DC's. In the nonequation estimates of output in miracle-grain-using nations it was possible to take into account most of these factors.

The countries individually selected for both rice consumption and production analysis are those that are currently important in terms of quantities produced and/or consumed plus those having substantial potential. The statistically used consumption definitions by country depend upon the nation's rice trade balance during the observed period. For the importing nations of India, Japan, the Philippines, and Malaysia, consumption equals production plus imports. For the exporting nations of Burma, Thailand, Brazil, and the United States, consumption equals production minus

---

* The authors gratefully acknowledge financial support from the Office of Program and Policy Coordination, USAID, for the time devoted to this study. The findings were made independently and do not reflect the opinions or policies of USAID or any other agency of the U. S. Government.

[1] The statistical parameters, t-values, coefficients of multiple determination and variation, von Neumann ratios, and the nonstatistical production estimates are available on stencils from Professor Canterbery.

E. Ray Canterbery *is associate professor of economics at Florida State University. Hans Bickel is a graduate student at the University of Maryland.*

exports. South Korea and Pakistan are intermediate cases, while West German consumption equals her imports. Because of data limitations, one important nation is excluded—Mainland China—while only consumption estimates were made for Indonesia and Vietnam. Mainland China and Indonesian consumptions are discussed in terms of UNFAO projections.[2]

There is not sufficient space to detail herein all the econometric designs for the statistical estimates.[3] A formal theory of expected relations was postulated prior to conducting the final empirical tests. It was hypothesized that rice consumption is related to income, prices or relative prices, and population. Because of multicollinearity, it is necessary to combine GNP and POP into one variable in the *explanatory* equations. In addition to linear forms, log, inverse log, and semilog transformations are used to capture the actual pattern of behavior of the variables over time. A dummy variable is used for extreme observations or large function shifts. In the world equations, for example, a dummy variable is used for the 1958 dependent variable observations which apparently were affected by the Suez crisis. (Overall, the dummy variable is used sparingly.) In all consumption equations the *current period* price is used. In a few cases in which multicollinearity was biasing the "explanatory" coefficient estimates, the nominal (P_r) rather than the relative (or real) price (P_r/CLI) is substituted. In most of the LDC's there is no identification problem with price, as output depended upon price lagged. There was, however, a price-simultaneity problem in Japan and Thailand, and a simultaneous solution was required.

Preliminary statistical tests suggested a high correlation between area and fertilizer consumption in most nations. Also, in tests with these two variables and relative price (lagged one year) against Q_r, the price variable was usually statistically insignificant. A number of random variables, weather variation being one, influence agricultural output. In part this explains the often low degree of linear correlation between output and time. There is also a lag between commodity price changes and changes in output, because it usually takes a new growing season for commodity price-induced input changes to affect production. This lag is sometimes shorter in developed nations and will become shorter in the LDC's as the area that is doubled-cropped increases. As a result of these considerations both current and lagged observations of the independent variables appear in the production equations; area and yields usually are estimated in separate equations, and subsequently their estimated values are multiplied $[\hat{A}_r \cdot (\hat{Q}_r/\hat{A}_r)]$ to gain production estimates. As (Q_r/A_r) involves a function of a function, two-stage least squares (2SLS) is used in estimating yields. This specification has the further advantage of avoiding biases from multicollinearity resulting from the necessity of leaving out correlated variables.

Where no identification problem exists (price lagged in production equation), the explanatory price parameters are estimated directly by classical least squares. Then elasticities, with price as the dependent variable, can be determined by solving for price in each set of supply-demand equations. However, in those nations where both current supply and current demand determined price in an identified model, a simultaneous estimation is used. The reduced forms of these equations can be derived by solving the equations simultaneously in terms of P/CLI and in terms of C. The statistical parameters can then be estimated indirectly from the reduced form equations. Where the equations are simultaneous and not perfectly identified, we use 2SLS in estimating parameters.

The reliability of the elasticity estimates (from "explanatory" equation estimates) is not affected by multicollinearity but possibly is affected by small sample sizes. The standard errors are not biased by autocorrelation, but elasticities are biased where derived from nonlinear equations. The direction of bias from the latter source cannot be determined, but because of the "ball park" nature of the estimated elasticities the errors are believed to be relatively small.

Statistical forecasts of production at 1966 prices lead to underestimated output values in those nations adopting the miracle seeds after 1966. In such countries nonequation production estimates are initially made at assumed 1966 prices. The final projections "marry" the statistical forecasts, the elasticity estimates, price changes, and the nonequation forecasts of production.

Forecasting production and consumption at varying prices is of course most difficult; and for some nations such forecasts are not possible

[2] A summary of data sources follows: production and area, [2, 3, 4]; trade, [6]; prices, [2, 3, 5]; fertilizer, [3]; stocks, [7]; GNP, [8]; population, [7].

[3] These details also are available upon request, pending their publication.

because of unreliable price elasticity estimates. Only price-constant forecasts are provided for such nations. The process whereby estimated input-price and consumption-price elasticities are applied to the price-constant forecasts is explained in a later section.

Limitations of Purely Statistical Estimates

The listing and evaluation of certain assumptions that apply to our statistical forecasting equations perhaps describe best the limitations of the statistical part of this study.[4] In certain cases the least-squares estimates were adjusted "by hand" to account for known divergencies between the statistical path and the actual path of the dependent variable. For example, where per capita consumption has reached a "maximum" level in DC's during the estimation period, the consumption equation tends to overestimate projected consumption.

It is assumed that:

(1) The usual least-squares assumptions apply to the *initial* forecasts from the equations. Of course, the main divergence from the least-squares path for production is expected to be caused by the adoption of new technology, and this is taken care of in the nonstatistical estimates for those countries in which it is expected.

(2) Unless otherwise specified, any extremely adverse weather conditions dominating any particular year will be offset by extremely favorable weather conditions in some other year.

(3) The prices of nonlabor inputs averaged during the forecasted period values are equal to their observed averages. Because of more intensive cultivation of land in the IRRI-adopting countries, the long-run price of capital may rise relative to the price of land and labor. Such relative factor price changes, however, are not expected to have any appreciable impact prior to 1975.

Labor costs are in part accounted for in the cost-of-living index used as a commodity deflator. Hence, changing labor costs are in part taken into account in the nonconstant price forecasts. Although the new varieties are both labor- and capital-using, they are at the margin more capital-using than labor-using.[5]

(4) Labor inputs will grow at a sufficient rate to allow the expansion of the implied potential associated with land, capital, and technological availabilities.

(5) The rate of double-cropping of *local* varieties will not change through 1975. This is highly probable, as double-cropping normally can occur only on irrigated land and most of the new irrigated land will be devoted to the new higher-profit miracle grains. This potential increase in double-cropping is taken into account in the nonstatistical estimates.

(6) There will be no major war in the Far East or Southeastern Asia prior to 1976.

(7) Increases in irrigation are either proportional to the increased area cultivated or are highly correlated with a time variable.

(8) Mechanization has not had a significant impact on rice production.

(9) Current aid, government programs, and policies affecting agriculture and trade in rice in all nations will not change. ***This assumption, however, can be relaxed when we make a choice between estimates of production at the various assumed price changes.***

Estimated Price Changes and Production Behavior

Price data

The most frequently used price for both the demand and the supply equations is the milled wholesale price of rice, which in most cases is highly correlated with the retail price. It is believed, however, that in many cases the milled wholesale price may generate better statistical results with the supply equations than with the demand.[6] In all cases "free market" prices are used; that is, the price series selected for each nation is one of varying nominal prices. Beyond this the selection criterion is one of data availability.

In constructing real prices, we divided the nominal price by a cost-of-living index (*CLI*), an agricultural retail price index, or an agricultural wholesale price index. In some cases there was very little difference in the results irrespective of which index was used, but in general the cost-of-living index gave the best statistical results in both the demand and supply equations. Consequently, the cost-of-living index is used in the final estimating equations.

[4] The extra nonstatistical assumptions are also available upon request, with the nonstatistical tables.

[5] Over time, of course, this increased relative demand for capital may increase the price of capital and in the longer run may moderate expansion of IRRI 8 production.

[6] The following exceptions apply: the husked producer price is used for Japanese production *and* consumption; paddy producer for U. S. supply; paddy wholesale for Thailand and Brazilian supply; the export (to Ceylon) price for Burmese demand and supply; and the averag unit value of export for world production-consumption.

Table 1. Estimated rice consumption elasticities from structural equations[a] (at 1966 observations for nonlogs)

Nation	With respect to C_r				With respect to C_r/POP	
	GNP/POP	P_r/CLI	P_r	GNP	GNP/POP	P_r/CLI
Japan	.107	0				
United States				1.98	0.86	0
India	1.33	0				
Pakistan	7.14	3.85				
Thailand	−3.96	0				
Burma	−3.46	0	−4.40		−6.42	−3.68
South Korea	1.15	0				
Philippines	4.00	0				
Malaysia	1.27	−.89				
Brazil	2.47	0				
West Germany			0	.89		
World total	1.00		−0.50[b]			

[a] The algebraic signs of the elasticities are taken from the signs of the slope coefficients; hence a positive sign for price suggests perverse elasticity. With the exception of Pakistan, all estimates are based on equations having statistically insignificant multicollinearity. Where the price coefficient is not significant and other statistical requirements are met, perfect inelasticity is inferred.

[b] This elasticity is with respect to the world *trade* (unit value of exports) price.

Price-change estimates

Although production and consumption elasticities can be estimated from the structural explanatory equations, the current period price of rice itself is an endogenous variable, being determined simultaneously by output and consumption. Therefore the impact of the same independent variables on the price of rice is estimated by solving the supply and demand equations simultaneously for current price (except where an identification problem exists). The structural elasticity estimates appear in Tables 1 and 2; the simultaneous estimates appear in Table 3. These structural and simultaneous elasticities (where reliable) provide sufficient information to estimate price changes and subsequent production and consumption adjustments from their 1966 constant price values.

The simultaneous price elasticities are based on "final" production and consumption adjustments that have occurred as prices change. In some years in some countries the nominal price of rice is fixed at a support level for the producer or at a ceiling for the consumer. But as we move from price elasticities to estimates of price changes in those nations using government market intervention, these are the price changes that will occur as such price supports or ceilings are removed. It is of course possible and *even probable that the governments' prices will not be removed prior to 1975. In those cases the constant-price production forecasts apply.*

Forecasts of the independent variables through 1975 were made in order to estimate price changes. The "free market" estimates in Table 4 are derived by multiplying the expected annual percentage change in the independent variables—per capita income, area, fertilizer, lagged price—by their respective simultaneous elasticities with respect to current period price (from Table 3). The lagged-price variable reflects the normal "cobweb" relationship among consumption, production, and price. The price

Table 2. Rice production elasticities from structural equations[a] (at 1966 observations for nonlogs)

Nation	Elasticity definition					
	Q.A	Q.F	Q.P	(Q/A).F	F.P	A.P
Japan	0	.435	1.35*	.207	.440(−1)	
United States	1.06	.443	0(−1)	.089	−.056(−1)	0
India	3.19	.213			1.23	
Pakistan		.220(−1)		.207		
Indonesia	1.05			.007		
	0.20	.007	.061*(−1)	.016		.035(−1)
Thailand	.402		.318*	1.96		
Burma	1.04	.187	.035(−1)	.550	.150(−1)	0(−1)
South Korea	.853		.542*(−1)	1.97	.334	
Philippines			.086*(−1)			
	.169	.203	.371(−1)	.026	.113(−1)	0(−1)
Malaysia	.200	.374	0(−1)		0(−1)	
Brazil	1.06	.500	0*(−1)			
World	.93	.282			.179**(−1)	

[a] The coefficients of lagged independent variables are denoted by (−1) following the coefficient. All estimates are based on equations having statistically insignificant multicollinearity. Zero elasticity estimates are given only when the equation meets rigorous statistical tests and additional information supports this inelasticity presumption. The first letter in each case represents the dependent variable and the second the independent variable. "Q.A" is, for instance, response of output to changes in area (hectares harvested). The year 1966 was chosen as most representative for forecasting through 1975.

* Indicates that price is in real terms.

** The world price equals the unitary value of world rice exports.

Table 3. Rice price elasticities, simultaneous estimates[a] (at 1966 observations for nonlogs

Nation	P.(GNP/POP)	P.GNP	P.A	P.F	P.P (−1)
Japan	.964		.0000039	−3.92	
United States	1.45		−1.78	−.745	−.111
India	11.46		−30.19	−1.81	−.102
Thailand	.110		.110		
Burma[b]		−.787	2.96(−1)	−.421(−1)	.003
South Korea	29.30		−27.00	−18.32	−7.16
Philippines	9.34		−.433	−.520	−.953
Malaysia	1.42		−.220	−.410	−.010
Brazil	31.27		−13.42	−6.33	.139
World	2.15		−1.00[c]	−.230	−.040

[a] All elasticities are derived from solving at least two equations simultaneously (at least one demand and one supply). Where the price coefficient was insignificant but of positive sign, we assumed its actual sign was negative in order to retain the appropriate signs for various elasticities. These are shift elasticities that indicate the responsiveness of equilibrium prices to independent variable changes. Three nations are excluded: Complete estimates were not available for Pakistan; we have no consumption equation for Indonesia; West German production is so small that no output estimates were made.

[b] Nominal price is substituted for real price.

[c] No direct estimates of the aggregate responsiveness among area, output, and price was made. This estimate is based on major-producing-nations results.

changes forecasted from changes in per capita income, area utilized, and fertilizer demand will themselves have an impact on production.

In general, those nations having either price supports or price ceilings can be identified by the sign of the estimated net annual change in price. There are, for instance, price ceilings in South Korea and in Brazil where price changes are estimated as positive. All the "free market" price-change estimates (Table 4) suggest only what price changes *would be* if no nations adopted the new varieties. Not all of these estimates are viewed with the same confidence.[7]

The introduction of the new miracle grains increases output substantially. We know that, other things being equal, such output increases would reduce rice prices in the particular country. Of the current miracle-grain adopters, a complete set of elasticity estimates for post-miracle-grains free market estimates of price changes through 1975 could be generated only for India, the Philippines, Brazil, and from the world equations (Table 5). Because of the difficulty of shifting resources into alternative employment in less developed nations, we assume that in fact there would be a downward stickiness in output changes in response to price declines. The positive responses to upward price movements have been supported by government assistance and persuasion in most LDC cases. For simplicity we assumed throughout that the responsiveness on the downside would be only half as great as on the upside of price changes (the semiresponsiveness category). Except for this qualification, these estimates are derived in the same way as those in Table 4.

[7] In the Burmese equations income and area are highly correlated. The effect on prices of changes in fertilizer inputs is probably accurate. But the impact of changes in area planted is of the wrong sign. This effect is probably counterbalanced by the very small indicated impact of the lagged price. In short, while the price change attributed to area is probably incorrect, the net annual change may be very close to the true figure.

Table 4. "Free market" estimates of price changes (without miracle grain impact), 1967–1975[a]

	Japan	United States	India	Thailand	South Korea	Burma[c]	Philippines	Malaysia	Brazil	World
Average annual price change percentage attributed to changes in:										
Per capita income	5.48	3.92	22.23	.404	61.53	−3.54	13.64	1.86	56.29	4.79
	[5.48]	[2.7]	[1.9]	[4.1]	[2.1]	[4.5]	[1.5]	[1.3]	[1.8]	[2.2]
Area		−2.65	−39.85	.278	−2.97	6.93	−.344	−.678	−7.88	−1.5
	—[b]	[1.5]	[1.3]	[2.8]	[.11]	[2.3]	[.794]	[3.1]	[.587]	[1.5]
Fertilizer	−13.29	−3.32	−15.40	—	−84.09	−3.63	−18.87	−2.60	−31.65	−1.40
	[3.4]	[4.5]	[8.5]	—	[4.3]	[8.6]	[36.29]	[6.3]	[5.0]	[6.1]
Lagged price		−.23	3.37	—	183.00	.024	5.31	.014	1.68	−.08
	—[b]	[−2.1]	[−33.0]	—	[−25.53]	[7.8]	[−5.6]	[−1.4]	[16.8]	[1.9]
Net annual change (percent)	−7.81	−2.33	−29.65	.682	+157.47	+.21	−.26	−1.41	+18.48	+1.81

[a] Forecasted annual changes in the independent variables appear in brackets. Where experts disagree with these forecasts, the price changes can be easily recalculated.

[b] Negligible.

[c] GNP substituted for per capita income.

Table 5. Postmiracle-grain "free market" estimates of price changes, 1967–1975[a]

	India		Philippines		Brazil		World	
	Symmetrical	Semiresponsive	Symmetrical	Semiresponsive	Symmetrical	Semiresponsive	Symmetrical	Semiresponsive
Average annual price change percentage attributed to changes in:								
Per capita income	22.23	22.23	13.64	13.64	56.29	56.29	4.79	4.79
Area	−39.85	−78.49	−.344	−.688	−7.88	−15.76	−1.50	−3.00
Fertilizer	−18.62	−37.23	−23.71	−47.54	−39.55	−63.30	−5.31	−9.64
Lagged price	3.70	4.67	9.92	16.46	1.23	−1.59	−0.08	.107
Net annual change (percent)	−32.54	−88.82	−1.18	−18.13	+10.09	−24.36	−2.10	−7.74

[a] New marginal physical products relating fertilizer inputs to output were calculated from nonstatistical postmiracle-grain output estimates and least-squares estimates of fertilizer demand. "Symmetrical responsiveness" assumes that output response to price declines is identical to that for price rises. "Semiresponsiveness" assumes downward output stickiness and that production is only about half as responsive to price declines as to price rises.

Impact of price changes on rice output

Output changes in response to rice price changes (as percentage deviations from the constant-price forecast) can be estimated from the simultaneous price adjustments and from the input elasticities of the structural equations by multiplying estimated net annual price changes by the price elasticity of fertilizer and that by the fertilizer elasticity of output, that is, $\%\Delta\hat{Q} = \%\Delta(\hat{P}/C\hat{L}I)\cdot(F.P)\cdot(Q.F)$. Where estimated elasticities are very large, we have a special statistical problem. All of the estimated price elasticities from the original structural equations are of course increasingly inaccurate as we move from the mean values in these relations. An equilibrium shift that results in a 20 percent price decline, for example, would move the supply curve to an intersection of the demand curve that is a great distance from the estimated mean of the quantities demanded. It is virtually certain that the coefficients of elasticity at the new point on the demand curve are substantially different from these estimated values. To adjust for this, we assume that the impact of all "extreme" price changes are exhausted in a limited number of years. In terms of output changes, this turned out to be a problem only for India and South Korea.

In virtually all nations the constant-price *consumption* figures do not deviate from the consumption estimate at alternative prices. A significant price elasticity coefficient for the *nominal* world price was derived, however, and was used in estimating an adjusted world consumption total. The consequences of adjusting production and consumption estimates for price-change impact are reflected in the trade estimates at changing prices (Table 6).

World and National Production, Consumption, and Trade Estimates, 1967–1975

Total 1975 world consumption and production estimates[8] appear in Tables 7 and 8. We expect that the increased volume of rice moving in world trade (about 10 percent of total Q_r by 1975) will result in a higher average price elasticity than now prevails because rice will increasingly become a private market commodity. If world rice prices remain at their 1966 level through 1975, the total world production surplus is estimated at an annual rate of 26.56 million milled metric tons. In reality, of course,

[8] Total world and national rice production and consumption equation estimates yearly, 1967–1975, are available upon request.

Table 6. Rice trade of selected major nations at changing "free market" prices, 1975 (in millions of milled metric tons)

Nation	At premiracle-grain price changes	At postmiracle-grain price changes	
		Symmetrical	Semi-responsive
Japan	−.099[a]	—	—
United States	1.960	—	—
India	−6.560	−8.580	−3.780
Thailand	3.582	—	—
Burma	1.923	—	—
South Korea[b]	8.285	—	—
Malaysia	−.342	−.342	−.342
Philippines	.531	.331	.471
Brazil	.838	.838	.838

[a] A negative sign indicates that the nation is a net importer.
[b] There apparently are severe structural problems in South Korea unrelated to producer responsiveness that would prevent this high export figure from being attained.

the miracle grain revolution will have an impact on rice-price changes. After all producers and consumers have adjusted as expected to price changes through 1975, we expect a world surplus in rice equaling 8.74 million milled metric tons at an annual rate. The nominal world price of rice will have declined by 62 percent from its 1967 figure level by 1975.[9] The final consumption adjustment would narrow the surplus to only 2.34 million metric tons.[10] What follows is some country-by-country results.

The "most likely" national trade balance figures appear in Table 9 below, except for Indonesia, Nepal, South Vietnam, and Mainland China estimates. On the basis of FAO estimates of 1975 consumption, Indonesia is expected to import a net 2.95 million milled metric tons in 1975 at constant prices. This trade deficit would probably move close to zero if miracle grains are adopted successfully. The FAO estimate of consumption for Nepal indicates that the country will continue to run a trade surplus of an estimated 800,000 in 1975. With continued adoption of the IRRI varieties and a substantial diminution in the war by 1972, self-sufficiency by South Vietnam should be obtainable again. According to the FAO estimate of 1975 consumption, South Vietnam should be exporting an estimated 550,000 milled metric tons in 1975 at 1966 prices. Production and consumption forecasts from FAO for Mainland China include net exports of at least 650,000 milled metric tons in 1975.

The domestic farm rice price is supported by the governments of Japan, the Philippines, the United States, India, and Malaysia. The removal of such supports under the pressure of rising subsidy costs would result in the deflations estimated in Table 4. Presumably rice production in each of these nations would be lower also. In 1965 Japan's support price was more than 2.5 times the world average export price.

In all nations studied except perhaps Burma and Malaysia, most output increases are expected to come from more intensive cultivation and rising yields. In Burma and Malaysia area utilized for rice production has increased faster than in other parts of Asia. The miracle rice is expected to affect significantly production in India, Pakistan, the Philippines, and South Vietnam; for these nations we need initially

[9] To illustrate how surpluses could be influenced by the failure to take into account possible interdependencies between production and demand, we adjusted these price-influenced totals (World surplus I in Table 7) by an *arbitrary* 3 percent extra increment of consumption (World surplus II).

[10] In terms of strict statistical interpretation, these estimates are midpoints within a range of possible values.

Table 7. Total rice production at changing "free market" prices, 1975 (in millions of milled metric tons)

Nation	At 1966 prices	With non-miracle, symmetrical price changes	With miracle price changes: Symmetrical	With miracle price changes: Semi-response
Japan	14.43	12.70	—	—
United States	3.18	3.20	—	—
India	49.27	38.60	36.58	41.38
Pakistan	17.02	—	—	—
Thailand	10.97	11.16	—	—
Indonesia	9.12	—	—	—
Burma	6.41	6.42	—	—
South Korea	4.65	12.37	—	—
Nepal	2.11	—	—	—
Malaysia	1.16	—	—	—
Philippines	6.80	6.80	6.60	6.74
South Vietnam	4.78	—	—	—
Brazil	7.69	7.69	7.69	7.69
Mainland China (FAO)	72.70	—	—	—
Rest of World	13.50	—	—	—
World production totals	223.79	225.42	220.93	222.07
World consumption totals	197.23	192.07	201.60	213.23
World surplus I	26.56	33.35	19.33	8.74
World surplus II[a]	20.64	27.59	13.28	2.34

[a] This estimate is derived by increasing total consumption an arbitrary 3 percent because of supply-demand interaction.

Table 8. Total world rice demand at 1966 prices, 1975

Japan	12.80
United States	1.24
India	45.16
India (adjusted)	(47.87)
Pakistan	14.19
Thailand	7.58
Burma	4.50
South Korea	4.09
Philippines	6.27
Malaysia	1.51
Brazil	6.85
West Germany	0.24
Rest of world[a]	92.80
World total	197.23

[a] The value for "rest of world" is derived from an aggregate world equation. Of the "rest of the world," about 79 percent is attributable to Mainland China and another 14 percent to Indonesia. It was not possible to obtain accurate data for Mainland China and usable income statistics were not available for Indonesia (or Vietnam).

Table 9. Rice trade of major nations at 1966 prices, 1967–1975 (in millions of milled metric tons)

Year \ Nation	Japan	United States	India	Pakistan	Thailand	Burma	South Korea	Malaysia	Philippines	Brazil
1967	1.138	1.418	n.a. [−5.599][a]	n.a. [.337]	2.989	1.431	.270	−.239	n.a. [.598]	−.352
1968	1.192	1.483	5.187 [−5.326]	2.512 [−.738]	3.027	1.478	.251	−.252	2.252 [.207]	−.264
1969	1.246	1.549	4.555 [−3.749]	3.816 [1.032]	3.224	1.530	.353	−.266	2.361 [−.271]	−.292
1970	1.308	1.614	3.841 [−3.462]	3.774 [1.178]	3.257	1.586	.339	−.277	2.527 [−.543]	−.056
1971	1.369	1.679	4.584 [−3.180]	3.787 [1.332]	3.287	1.645	.327	−.282	2.487 [−.876]	.077
1972	1.430	1.744	4.121 [−2.903]	3.898 [1.491]	3.316	1.708	.384	−.303	2.328 [−1.285]	.231
1973	1.501	1.810	3.596 [−2.634]	4.063 [1.657]	3.344	1.774	.443	−.316	1.978 [−1.786]	.404
1974	1.571	1.875	3.564 [−2.361]	4.120 [1.830]	3.369	1.842	.503	−.329	1.320 [−2.399]	.616
1975	1.631	1.940	1.400 [−2.107]	3.826 [1.946]	3.392	1.913	.565	−.342	.531 [−3.144]	.838

[a] The trade values in brackets are based on least-squares equations estimates and hence do not include the effect of technological change. The difference in the two estimates indicate the impact of technological change (new seed varieties) on trade. A negative sign indicates that the nation is a net importer.

nonequation estimates of output.

There are only two exceptions to an estimated zero price elasticity of demand: Demand is estimated as sensitive (in the normal direction) in Malaysia; rice appears to be a Giffen-good in Burma.

Except for the above and subsequent qualifications, the reader can rely upon the tables for estimates. Contrary to the perverse response suggested by our statistically estimated output changes, a "free market" and U.S. rice price decline of 2.33 percent annually through 1975 would probably yield a somewhat lower level of production. As acreage controls and price supports have been such major factors in the American market, we have been unable to estimate accurately the responsiveness of American producers to such price declines. The responsiveness of output to both fertilizer and irrigation inputs could rise substantially in Indonesia. Because of problems including those with land tenure, production credit, effective water control, and continued expansion of cultivated land, we have discounted a similar possibility in Thailand.

Although statistically South Korean production *appears* to be highly sensitive to input changes, there seem to be substantial production-inhibiting forces in that country. The main constraint appears to be limited land availability, as we forecast a total increase in land utilized of less than 1/2 of 1 percent between 1970 and 1975. The apparent *lack* of statistical responsiveness of production to price changes in Malaysia is probably due to the fact that we were able to use only the export price in our equations for Malaysia rather than a domestic price. Elimination of the subsidy program there would result in an estimated annual decline in the real price of rice of 1.41 percent per year through 1975; *irrespective of our statistical results on responsiveness*, such price declines probably would reduce production.

Summary and Conclusions

In evaluating estimates of rice production, consumption, trade, and price changes, one should remember that the world has in the past decade produced enough rice to meet world demand. Starvation and low nutrition levels of people in less developed nations has resulted not from an inadequacy of world output capacity, but rather from unequal distribution of food output. If the green revolution is viewed with that perspective, it is clear that its first goal is the feeding of indigenous populations.

Traditionally the major Far East exporters of rice have been Burma, Cambodia, Taiwan, Thailand, and Vietnam. Other traditional exporters include the United States, Mainland China, the United Arab Republic, and Brazil. The traditional Far East importers have included Japan, Ceylon, India, Indonesia, Malaysia, Pakistan, the Philippines, and South Korea. At constant prices many of these traditional Far East importers—India, Pakistan, the Philippines, and South Korea—are expected to be net exporters themselves during the 1970's. Only India and Pakistan would be exceptions to this shift if the domestic producer price of rice in these countries is allowed to decline sharply.

Moreover, Indonesia and Malaysia are attempting to move to a surplus position or at least reduce their imports and may adopt the miracle grains. The Soviet Union, recently a modest importer, has been aiming at self-sufficiency. If *current government policies* continue, the Japanese and American rice surpluses are expected to grow substantially through the 1970's. Although Thailand's trade surplus is expected to grow slowly, we expect substantial increases in the size of Burma's surplus. South Vietnam is expected to return to her traditional role as a rice exporter in 1972. The most conservative projection of the change in trading relations indicates that the green revolution will turn traditional trading patterns virtually upside down.

Several policy implications emerge from these expected new trade patterns. The United States Government may want to plan early a severe acreage restriction program. But even if the United States and Japan were to shift to subsistence rice production, there would still be a substantial world surplus of rice at constant prices (and hence downward price pressure) in 1975.

The main problems between today and 1975 probably relate to income distribution and levels. Because the new varieties of food crops require substantial supplies of fertilizers with irrigation and modern cultivation methods, this agricultural technology has largely benefited the larger, more wealthy farmers. There is a possibility that small farmers may gradually be pushed out of the market by the large producers, and tenant farmers may be evicted in certain nations. The sharecropping peasants live at or below subsistence level, owning only a few crude farm tools; the benefits of the green revolution may never reach them.

A second income problem is one of income maintenance in a world of declining rice prices. The governments in the LDC's will have to decide whether to control production increases (by acreage, storage, or both) or to subsidize rice production at increasingly higher levels. *The problem of declining prices is related to the problem of income distribution.* When rice prices fall they will reach that point at which production of local varieties will be unprofitable much sooner than they reach a point at which production of the miracle grain rice is unprofitable. Presumably, then, it will be the smaller farmers who will be most adversely affected by falling rice prices. The precise marginal income distribution from the revolution will of course vary by nation. Income levels in the traditional exporting LDC's also will be adversely affected prior to the new miracle grain users; these nations would include Burma, Thailand, and Indonesia.

Unless substantial governmental policy changes are implemented by both the developed and the developing nations, there will be a new major source of conflict between the rich and poor countries. LDC trade gains from this production breakthrough will not be forthcoming without the cooperation of the developed nations and rational production controls by the LDC's. The foremost advantages of the agricultural revolution are the possibilities of eliminating hunger and starvation while reducing LDC import needs and perhaps generating an environment in which population growth will be slowed. To achieve these gains, however, requires a relatively even distribution of marginal income. Unless the peasant populations are induced to participate in the miracle grain revolution, widening disparities in income distribution may still leave large numbers deprived of food supplies. Then the maldistribution of grains that was once global will be national as well.

References

[1] Brown, Lester R., *Seeds of Change: The Green Revo-ution and Development in the 1970's*, Washington, Praeger Publishers, 1970.

[2] Food and Agriculture Organization of the United Nations, *Monthly Bulletin of Agricultural Economics and Statistics*, Rome, 1955–66.

[3] ———, *Production Yearbook*, Rome, 1956–67.
[4] ———, *Report of the Study Group on Rice*, Rome, 1953.
[5] ———, *The State of Food and Agriculture*, Rome, 1968.
[6] ———, *Trade Yearbook*, Rome, 1956–67.
[7] United Nations, *U. N. Demographic Yearbook*, New York, 1956–67.
[8] United Nations, Statistical Office, *Yearbook of National Accounts Statistics*, New York, 1956–67.
[9] U. S. Agency for International Development, *New Cereal Varieties: Rice and Wheat in India*, unpublished report, USAID-India, March 1969.
[10] ———, *New Cereal Varieties: Rice and Wheat in Pakistan*, unpublished report, USAID-Pakistan, March 1969.
[11] ———, *New Cereal Varieties: Rice in the Philippines*, unpublished report, USAID-Philippines, March 1969.
[12] ———, *New Cereal Varieties: Rice in South Vietnam*, unpublished report, USAID-Vietnam, March 1969.
[13] Wharton, Clifton R., "The Green Revolution: Cornucopia or Pandora's Box?" *Foreign Affairs* 47: 464–476, Apr. 1969.

Chapter 34

THE GREEN REVOLUTION: A REPLY TO PROFESSORS RUTTAN AND MELLOR*

In this reply we examine a major methodological issue implied by the criticisms of Ruttan and Mellor [7, 13] to our recent paper [2] and reassess supply and demand responses to price changes.

Methodology

Mellor [7] suggests that our assumptions are arbitrary and that policy practitioners are guided by intuitive insights which are likely to produce more accurate results than those produced with quantitative tools and data. He does not indicate which specific assumptions he is questioning or in what magnitudes such questionable assumptions might alter elasticity estimates and/or forecasts.

In retrospect our assumptions appear quite reasonable. We might be faulted for assuming that "there will be no major war in the Far East or Southern Asia prior to 1976" [2, p. 287]. We did not want to speculate about the possibility of civil war between East and West Pakistan. And the assumption of "no war" in economic models is probably as sacrosanct as assumptions ever become.

* Financial support from the Rockefeller Foundation (Professor Canterbery only) and the Office of Program and Policy Coordination, USAID, is gratefully acknowledged; both agencies are absolved of any responsibility for the results of this study. The authors also acknowledge the helpful comments of John Chang.

Among the positive results of our research is the provision of data series of area seeded, fertilizer demand, yields, prices, and trade for the major nation-producers of rice and for the world. Our methodology is unique inasmuch as the forecasting equations are not necessarily identical with equations used for estimating elasticities. Also, simultaneous estimates of rice price elasticities are made for the first time as far as we know. Non-equation estimates of output in miracle-grain-using nations take into account many of the factors that do not lend themselves to statistical formulation. The subsequent "marriage" of statistical and nonstatistical techniques also is, as far as we know, unique. Just why this methodology was considered to be so "ad hockery" as to offend Ruttan's "esthetic sensibilities" [13] is not clear. Indeed, we see several advantages of our methodology: (a) The parts of a systematic economic model are always available for reexamination. When "policy practitioners" are wrong, it would be useful to know why. Explicit statements of assumptions and procedures are useful as means of determining sources of error. (b) Contrary to Mellor's implication, policy practitioners frequently do use data and do quantify. Moreover, interactions of multiple variables defy purely mental conceptualization.

Area Response to Price Changes

In terms of specifics, Ruttan's "skepticism is greatest with respect to the production relations." In our results, commodity prices affected the amount of capital (fertilizer input) utilized for production but not the area of land. In support of our conclusions, we can only offer the statistical estimates and the corresponding tests of reliability. Details of these results were not provided in the original publication or here because of lack of space.

The authors of the supply literature listed by Ruttan [1, 4, 5, 6, 12] used acceptable econometric techniques, and their results were surprisingly consistent with ours. Only comparable elasticity estimates for the Punjab region and two regions in the Philippines (Southern Tagalog, Eastern Visayas) had significant and relatively large long-run price elasticities with respect to rice acreage. But the Punjab results are for a period, 1914–45, in which population pressures on land were not as substantial as they have been since. Therefore, Punjab results may not be applicable to a period of intense population pressures on land and none of the regional results are applicable to an entire nation. In the aggregative Philippine estimates for 1947–63, which are co-authored by Ruttan, the estimated long-run aggregate price coefficients are actually negative. Nonetheless, Ruttan's elasticity optimism may well be justified for *certain regions*.

Price Elasticities of Demand and the Zero Sum

Mellor [7] suggests that "estimation of the effects of a major new technology on trade patterns requires estimates of . . . the effect of the new technologies on income distribution and hence on the structure of demand." Our paper addresses itself to the effects of the new technology on rice trade patterns; our failure to extend the study to the patterns of trade in all other commodities and services is more a reflection of impending fatigue than a weakness in our analysis. We did indicate that new technology has a direct bearing upon income distribution. In fact, we argued that the main problems between today and 1975 probably relate to income distribution and levels. But we doubt that such income distribution changes will alter the structure of demand in such a way that the price elasticities of demand for *rice* will be greatly affected by 1975.

Our neglect of the structure of demand, according to Mellor, "probably causes substantial underestimation of the demand elasticities" [7]; he does not specify *which* demand elasticities (own-price, cross, income). We presume that the reference is to the own-price elasticities of rice demand which we estimate as zero for most nations. These elasticity estimates differ markedly from those postulated by Mellor [8, 9, 10] elsewhere. After a thorough review of these references and others [11, 15, 16, 3], we found the Slutsky-Schultz price elasticities that Mellor apparently leaned upon in his criticism of our results to be very deficient.[1] This is not to argue that we believe our research to be without flaws. Throughout the paper we identified certain problem areas and indicated which elasticities we rejected [2, p. 292].

Forecasts

Finally, we can compare our forecasts with those developed by the USDA [14]. Our total world consumption estimate is 0.82 percent below the USDA estimate for 1975. Our world production estimate is 3.3 percent above the USDA's. This latter difference is probably explained by our development of the higher-yielding-variety production tables by hand. For country estimates, only Japan's appear to differ significantly with both our production and consumption estimates under the assumption of a "free mar-

---

[1] Mellor's main reliance is upon the Slutsky-Schultz condition [15, p. 111] that the cross-price plus the own-price plus the income elasticities sum to zero. But the own-price elasticity will equal or exceed income elasticity (as Mellor presumes) only if the sum of the cross-price-elasticities for substitutes equals or exceeds the sum of the price cross-elasticities for complements. Evidence on food income shares and the composition of diets in the rice-consuming LDC in [11, p. 326] suggests the reverse.

In [9, p. 963] Mellor estimates by a different technique a price elasticity for foodgrains in India of −.55 which he compares favorably with the Slutsky-Schultz result. But Mellor's estimation process is incorrect. First, even if otherwise correct, his is an estimate of the price elasticity of *excess demand*. Second, he fails to estimate the complete distributed lag relationship. Third, if higher order differences were included, the correctly estimated price elasticity of *excess* demand would be *much less than* /.55/.

ket" being about 13 percent higher. But the price behavior the USDA has *assumed* is relatively consistent with price behavior that our model generates. We believe that our study and recent USDA studies are complementary. We hope that someone soon will build a better model. And when it comes, we do not believe it will be off the top of some economist's head or off the bottom of some policy practitioner's pants.

E. RAY CANTERBERY
Florida State University
HANS BICKEL
University of Maryland

References

[1] BEHRMAN, J. R., *Supply Response in Underdeveloped Agriculture*, Amsterdam, North-Holland Publishing Company, 1968.
[2] CANTERBERY, E. RAY, AND HANS BICKEL, "The Green Revolution and the World Rice Market, 1967–1975," *Am. J. Agr. Econ.* 53:285–294, May 1971.
[3] FRISCH, RAGNAR, "A Complete Scheme for Computing All Direct and Cross Demand Elasticities in a Model with Many Sectors," *Econometrica* 27:177–196, April 1959.
[4] HUSSAIN, SYED MUSHTAQ, "A Note on Farmer Response to Price in East Pakistan," *Pakistan Develop. Rev.* 4:93–106, Spring 1964.
[5] KRISHNA, RAJ, "Farm Supply Response in India-Pakistan: A Case Study of the Punjab Region," *Econ. J.* 73:477–487, Sept. 1963.
[6] MANGAHAS, MAHAR, AIDA E. RECTO, AND V. W. RUTTAN, "Price and Market Relationships for Rice and Corn in the Philippines," *J. Farm Econ.* 48:685–703, Aug. 1966.
[7] MELLOR, JOHN W., "Discussion," *Am. J. Agr. Econ.* 53:296, May 1971.
[8] ———, *The Economics of Agricultural Development*, Ithaca, Cornell University Press, 1966.
[9] ———, AND ASHOK K. DAR, "Determinants and Development Implications of Foodgrains Prices in India, 1949–1964," *Am. J. Agr. Econ.* 50:962–974, Nov. 1968.
[10] MELLOR, JOHN W., AND UMA J. LELE, "Alternative Estimates of the Trend in Indian Foodgrains Production During the First Two Plans," *Econ. Develop. & Cult. Change* 13:217–232, Jan. 1965.
[11] MELLOR, JOHN W., THOMAS F. WEAVER, UMA J. LELE, AND SHELDON R. SIMON, *Developing Rural India. Plan and Practice*, Ithaca, Cornell University Press, 1968.
[12] MUBYARTO, "The Elasticity of the Marketable Surplus of Rice in Indonesia: A Study in Java-Madura," unpublished Ph.D. thesis, Iowa State University, 1965.
[13] RUTTAN, VERNON W., "Discussion," *Am. J. Agr. Econ.* 53:294, May 1971.
[14] WEST, Q. M., "World Grain Production Prospects and Trade Stabilization Measures in Southern Asia," in *Agricultural Revolution in Southeast Asia*, Vol. 1, eds., V. W. Ruttan *et al.*, Report of a SEADAG Rural Development Seminar Meeting, Honolulu, June 19–21, 1969; New York, Herbert-Spencer, Inc., 1970.
[15] WOLD, HERMAN, in association with LARS JUREEN, *Demand Analysis. A Study in Econometrics*, New York, John Wiley & Sons, Inc., 1953.
[16] WU, SHIH-YEN, AND JACK A. PONTNEY, *An Introduction to Modern Demand Theory*, New York, Random House, 1967.

Chapter 35

E. Ray Canterbery,
Foreword in Bernard A. Schmitt,
Protein, Calories and Development: Nutritional Variables in the Economics of Developing Countries

---

Nuclear holocaust and mass starvation pose the greatest contemporary threats to human life. These dangers are related because the response of the affluent nations to the starving masses clamoring at their very borders may be to unleash the ultimate weapon. Thus the end of civilization may come with both a whimper *and* a bang, resolving the age-old dilemma of whether to opt for a Faustian or a Malthusian demise.

This book is about the Malthusian spectre of too many mouths to feed and too few grams of available nutrition. Bernard Schmitt cannot relieve our anxiety, but his study can provide the basis for policies that could forestall the terminal terror. He concludes that conditions in nutritionally deficient countries are unlikely to improve between the present and the mid-1980s.

The forecasts of social scientists have sometimes been criticized on the basis of the Heisenberg principle. An observer studying a problem cannot make accurate predictions because the projection itself alters the future. This does not seem to me to be a "problem" in social science; rather, it is an obligation. Nothing would please me more than to find a world food surplus in 1985, perhaps generated by policy responses to findings like the ones in this volume.

This book is the capstone to a decade of research on the world food problem in the Economics Department at Florida State University. Michael Roemer, then of the U.S. State

Department (AID), employed my services in 1969 as a consultant on the prospects of the Green Revolution. On the basis of this preliminary work, the Rockefeller Foundation and its social science director, Michael P. Todaro, funded a project on the economic aspects of the Green Revolution. Later, the U.S. State Department (AID) funded a study (with Frederick W. Bell) on aquaculture as an alternative protein source for the developing nations. The latter study was published as a book, *Aquaculture for the Developing Countries: A Feasibility Study.*

Bernie Schmitt was involved in these studies, learned from them, and went beyond them to produce a remarkable book of his own. The scope of the book is staggering. Schmitt looks at food production in 90 developing nations, including 2.5 billion persons or about 98 percent of the population of all such nations.

The book is innovative. Schmitt combines the ideas of biology and nutrition with those of economics. He introduces complex socioeconomic variables as explanatory variables, utilizing the data developed by researchers like Adelman and Morris and Harbison. He pioneers the idea of a nutritional production function.

This interdisciplinary approach generates a new concept, the cyclonutritional spiral. Levels of produced nutrition are inputs in the development of human capital. A diminished quality of human capital lowers labor productivity and the quantity of food production. Less food means less nutrition, and so on. Undernourished labor leads to undernourished labor, a vicious cycle.

The cyclonutritional spiral would seem less repugnant if it were inevitable. It is not: world food production is sufficient to feed the world's population. As Schmitt shows, therefore, production gains alone will not suffice. Inputs among nations are unequally distributed, production is maldistributed, and consumption is even more skewed. Africans run behind the grain wagons, hoping to catch the falling chaff. The affluent Americans feed most of their marketed grain to pigs and cows, which in turn are consumed as expensive proteins.

The inequality that cuts across nations also slices through them. Even when production is high in a developing nation, the gigantic income inequalities mean that nutrition also is distributed lopsidedly among its population. Even the largest share of the fruits of the Green Revolution have gone to those who already had the most, a tendency called the "Matthew Principle" by Kenneth Boulding.

The affluent nations that have met the production challenge can confront the distributional one. The Rockefeller Foundation, a private organization, has had a tremendous impact on food production in developing nations. There are reasons to be hopeful; the industrialized world is learning how it feels to depend upon others for a necessity like oil. As a result, we can perhaps have more empathy with the poor who have little nutrition. The impetus of the Green Revolution needs to be regained with more of the focus on distribution. New technologies and new products are needed. Schmitt's incisive, lucid treatise provides the information for a policy program. For better or for worse, the affluent nations literally will reap what they sow.

E. Ray Canterbery
Florida State University

PART VII

MACROECONOMICS

Chapter 36

A NOTE ON RECENT MONEY SUPPLY BEHAVIOR

E. RAY CANTERBERY
University of Maryland

By the end of April 1965, the U.S. commercial banking system had had no free reserves, in terms of daily averages, for two consecutive months. During this time net borrowed reserves exceeded a daily average of minus $100 million. This "reserve position" of the banking system was at its lowest level in five years. It is not uncommon for the Federal Reserve System to restrict credit when prices rise or when the economy experiences a boom of "unsustainable" proportions. But the industrial production index had been on a plateau since November 1964, and Fed officials were applauding the "balanced nature" of the economic expansion.

The intentional contraction of the money supply during this period of stable production and prices reflected the continuation of a System policy of placing a "floor" under short-term interest rates, attempting to slow the outflow of short-term capital in the international balance of payments. This interest rate policy was initiated by a new FOMC directive to the New York Federal Reserve Bank's trading desk on October 25, 1960. At that time the lower limit to short-term interest rate movements was pegged. The purpose of this note is to explain the effect of this policy upon seasonal-cyclical changes in the money supply and upon the domestic stabilization goal of monetary policy.

The Impact on the Money Supply, Beginning Mid-1960

Even the most casual observation suggests that setting an interest rate target will cause the money supply (demand deposits plus currency in circulation) to behave differently from what it otherwise would. Normally the rate of interest is thought of as a price determined by the demand for and supply of money. Through open-market operations the central bank can alter the quantity of outstanding bank credit and thus influence the money supply. In turn, interest rates are pushed one direction or the other. But setting an interest rate goal first results in the money supply doing essentially what the interest rate requires rather than vice versa. While the exact response in economic activity to a given change in the money supply and interest rates is uncertain, it is generally presumed that lower rates and a more rapidly expanding money supply are more expansionary in terms of GNP and employment than a slower growth in credit (and money) and higher interest rates.

But in view of balance-of-payments "considerations," the Federal Reserve placed a "floor" under the short-term Treasury bill rate from mid-1960 through most of 1961. The shift to an upward movement came late in 1961 and prompted a new FOMC policy declaration to the New York Trading Desk on December 19, 1961, calling for less expansive monetary conditions, higher short-term rates, and slower additions to banking reserves. It also was necessary for the Federal Reserve to interfere with free market forces during periods of seasonal slow-downs in business activity.

This new policy contributed to a behavior of short-term interest rates and the money supply which can best be described as "unorthodox." Prior to mid-1960, there was a definite seasonal pattern in short-term rates. When commercial and industrial loan demand is slack in midsummer, short-term interest rates normally are lower than in the winter or fall. From mid-1960 to mid-1963, however, as figures 1 and 2 illustrate, there was only a moderate seasonal movement in yields on Treasury bill rates and on bankers' acceptances.[1]

FIGURE 1

SEASONAL PATTERNS IN YIELDS ON TREASURY BILLS

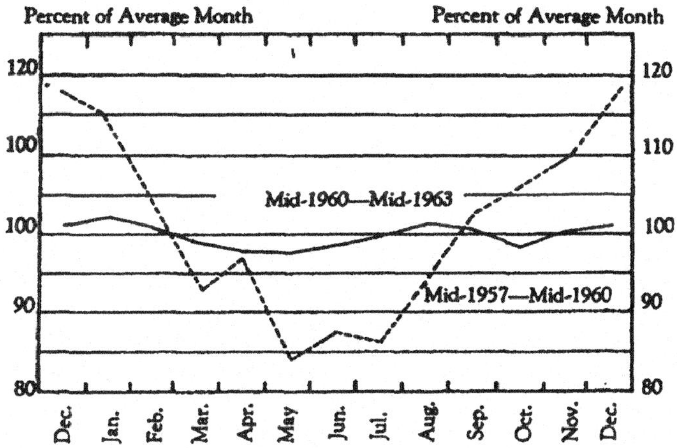

This unseasonal interest rate pattern could not be sustained without changing the behavior of the money supply. From 1951 through 1959, the average annual rate of increase in money (seasonally adjusted) from January to August was about the same as in the remainder of each year. But from 1960 through 1963 the average annual rate of advance was only 0.5 percent during the first half-year, while the rate rose to 4.7 percent in the last half (see Table 1). This new pattern began to emerge in 1960.

It is unlikely that the weather suddenly reversed itself, starting in 1960. Farm crops are still largely harvested and marketed in the fall, while retailers continue to build inventories for the Christmas season. Although there is more construction activity in winter months currently than in the distant past, building patterns did not abruptly change in mid-1960.

---

[1] This documentation of a change in seasonal patterns appears in the April 1964 *Federal Reserve Bank of St. Louis Monthly Review*. The Reserve Bank, of course, accepts no responsibility for the conclusions drawn from these data.

FIGURE 2

SEASONAL PATTERNS IN RATES ON BANKERS' ACCEPTANCES

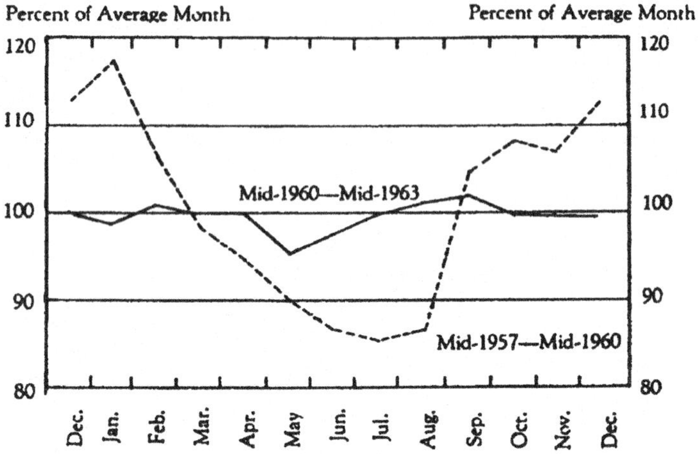

It is more reasonable to conclude that this change in the intra-yearly movement of the money stock was a consequence of the "pegging" and pushing of the short-term Treasury bill rate. In the early months of the year the monetary authorities supported higher yields by selling securities in the open market. During the fall and winter, when seasonal credit demands were strong, the System allowed the money supply to expand without endangering the support level for Treasury bill yields. The net result has been a marked alteration in seasonal movements of the money supply.

A continuation of this program means a slow addition to bank reserves and the money supply during seasonal lulls, regardless of the stage of the business

TABLE 1

CHANGES IN THE MONEY SUPPLY

Year	ANNUAL RATES OF CHANGE[a] January–August	August–January
1960	− 1.1%	+ 1.0%
1961	+ 1.7	+ 5.0
1962	− 0.9	+ 6.0
1963	+ 2.1	+ 6.9
Average 1960–63	+ 0.5	+ 4.7
Average 1951–59	+ 2.4	+ 1.9

[a] Demand deposits plus currency in circulation, seasonally adjusted by Board of Governors of the Federal Reserve System.

SOURCE: Research Department, Federal Reserve Bank of St. Louis.

cycle. Moreover, this policy has permanently changed the behavior of one of the seasonally adjusted indicators used in evaluating monetary policy, that is, the money supply itself. While the import of the latter is not altogether clear at this point, the use of the standard seasonal adjustment factors causes the money supply, between April and November of each year, to appear to have expanded faster than it actually did. The Federal Reserve Bank of St. Louis has computed alternative seasonal adjustment factors based on money supply data since mid-1960. While the number of years used in this calculation may not be sufficient for accuracy, four years is adequate for noting that a definite change has occurred in the magnitude of the seasonal factors. These alternatively adjusted data appear in Table 2.

There is also a longer-run impact from this policy. After remaining on a plateau, three-month Treasury bill rates fluctuated near 2.70 percent during the first five months of 1962, rising to a range of 2.75 to 2.90 percent in the remaining months of that year. This range was near the level prevailing in the early months of 1959 and is historically high. Meanwhile, long-term interest rates drifted slightly lower during 1962, but began to move upward in early 1963. And business borrowing costs fluctuated near their average for the previous three years.

Because the bond market is thinner, yields can be easily changed (in the short run) with a relatively moderate volume of transactions in the capital market by the Fed. This is not, however, the case with the money market which has a much larger number of buyers, sellers, and dealers. In short, interest rates are much more elastic in the Treasury bill than in the bond markets.[2]

The Economic Implications

The Monetary Contraction of 1962. In Federal Reserve efforts to accommodate its international objective of moderating short-term capital outflows and its avowed domestic goal of moderate monetary expansion, the period between the end of 1961 and the start of 1963 was most difficult. In the first quarter of 1962 the Open Market Committee had to sell, on balance, $528 million of its security holdings in order to nudge the Treasury bill rate higher (see Table 3). In the same quarter the United States lost $291 million in gold, setting the stage for a possible monetary contraction of a multiple of $819 million. Indeed, during the period January through September 1962, Open Market net purchases amounted to only $823 million, failing to offset the loss of $827 million in U.S. gold.

These open-market operations and gold losses, plus lesser factors affecting bank reserves, resulted in an extremely sharp contraction in member-bank

[2] It is extremely difficult, of course, to maintain a "floor" under interest rates during a period when the demand function for business loans shifts downward. This leads to an increased demand by banks for excess reserves and a rise in their demand for short-term marketable securities. For discussion of this process and a model describing it, see Leroy J. Grossman, "An Evaluation of the Consistency of the Defensive and Dynamic Objectives of Federal Reserve Policy." Unpublished Ph.D. Dissertation, Vanderbilt University, 1963, pp. 68–73.

TABLE 2

MONEY SUPPLY

(monthly averages of daily figures, seasonally adjusted)

	Billions of dollars				
	1960	*1961*	*1962*	*1963*	*1964*
January					
Standard[a]		141.5	145.9	148.7	154.8
Alternative[b]		140.7	145.1	147.8	153.8
February					
Standard		141.8	145.5	148.6	154.4
Alternative		141.6	145.3	148.3	154.1
March					
Standard		142.2	145.7	148.9	154.8
Alternative		142.2	145.5	148.7	154.8
April					
Standard		142.5	146.1	149.4	
Alternative		142.4	146.1	149.4	
May					
Standard		142.9	145.7	149.4	
Alternative		143.1	145.9	149.7	
June					
Standard		142.8	145.6	149.8	
Alternative		143.3	146.0	150.3	
July					
Standard	140.4	143.0	145.7	150.7	
Alternative	140.5	143.2	145.9	151.1	
August					
Standard	140.9	142.9	145.1	150.5	
Alternative	141.6	143.6	145.8	151.2	
September					
Standard	141.0	143.5	145.3	150.9	
Alternative	141.3	144.0	145.9	151.4	
October					
Standard	141.1	144.2	146.1	152.1	
Alternative	141.2	144.4	146.4	152.3	
November					
Standard	140.8	144.9	146.9	153.4	
Alternative	140.8	144.9	146.7	153.3	
December					
Standard	141.2	145.7	147.9	153.5	
Alternative	140.3	144.9	147.0	152.7	

[a] Board of Governors' seasonal adjustment based on data from 1947 through 1961.

[b] Seasonally adjusted at Federal Reserve Bank of St. Louis by link-relative method based on data since mid-1960.

TABLE 3

OPEN MARKET OPERATIONS AND THE GOLD OUTFLOW, 1962
(millions of dollars, unadjusted)

Quarter	*Net purchases or sales (–) of securities*[a]	*Gold losses (–)*
I	–528	–291
II	998	–102
III	353	–434
IV	625	– 6

[a] Includes net repurchase agreements.

SOURCE: Figures based on data released by Board of Governors of the Federal Reserve System.

reserves available for private demand deposits.[3] In turn, the nation's money supply (demand deposits plus currency) declined slightly between January and May (see Figure 3). Some analysts would say this monetary contraction contributed to the plateau in employment and industrial production from May through the end of 1962. In any case, Federal Open Market Operations clearly were not expansionary preceding a period — May 1962 to January 1963 — when the FRB Industrial Production Index and the total number of employed workers remained virtually unchanged.

FIGURE 3

MONEY SUPPLY
(monthly averages of daily figures)

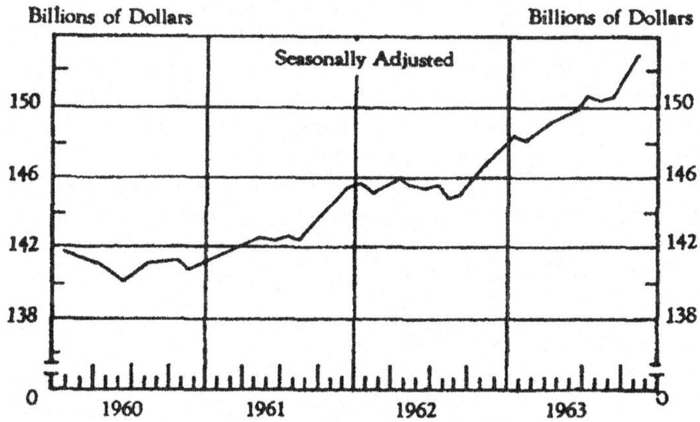

[3] During this period total member-bank reserves increased at a 3 percent annual rate, but this advance was more than absorbed by a fast growth in time deposits and, hence, required reserves behind time deposits.

The Policy in Theory. Available theory supports the view that monetary policy since late 1960 has tended to be destabilizing for domestic income and employment. It has been noted herein that Federal Reserve policy has placed a "floor" under short-term interest rates and pushed (or allowed) rates to move upward when the money market has firmed. Irrespective of whether the cause is seasonal or cyclical, if the demand for money declines, the Federal Reserve has to reduce the level of the money supply. On the other hand, it can allow the money supply to expand somewhat if the demand for money rises. This is illustrated in the simple Hicksian liquidity-preference model.[4]

Hypothetically, if real income drops seasonally, credit demands for sustaining business inventories would decline and the transactions demand for money by both consumers and producers would descend. As the monetary authorities have "pegged" the interest rate at i_0, the demand for idle money would remain unchanged; but the demand for money balances would drop. To prevent the interest rate from falling to, say, i_1 — which is below the support level — the central bank must take actions to destroy enough demand deposits to contract the money supply. This process of monetary contraction would continue so long as the transactions demand for money slumped.

Under the same policy arrangements, let us suppose that real income is rising and credit demands are stimulated by rising consumer sales. Initially, the demand schedule for money jumps upward. With no change in the money supply the new rate of interest rises sharply to, say, i_2. However, this accelerated demand for money balances enables the authorities to augment the money supply without greatly depressing the interest rate. Hence the money supply is allowed to expand, the interest rate stabilizing at, say, i_3.

This model and its more modern versions[5] describe the general seasonal and cyclical behavior of the money supply since mid-1960. Beyond this, it yields several other interesting results. First, the Hicksian *LM* curve derived herein is perfectly elastic prior to that point where the transactions demand for money ascends. This resultant curve bears a remarkable resemblance to John R. Hicks's original graph of J. M. Keynes's interest rate theory.[6] The Monetary authorities apparently have created their own "liquidity trap"! But, whereas Keynes envisaged a level below which the money market would not allow the interest rate to fall, the System has imposed its own minimum.

Second, the money supply is behaving proseasonally and procyclically. It rises when persons demand more liquidity and declines when they demand less. With central-bank policy dictated by these whims of the public, Federal Reserve actions parallel those of commercial banks rather than compensate for changes

---

[4] See John R. Hicks, "Mr. Keynes and the 'Classics,' A Suggested Interpretation," *Econometrica*, Vol. V, 1937, pp. 147–59.

[5] See especially George Horwich, *Money, Capital, and Prices* (Homewood, Illinois: Richard D. Irwin & Co., 1964), p. 369; and Franco Modigliani, "Liquidity Preference and the Theory of Interest and Money," *Econometrica*, Vol. XII, 1944, pp. 45–88, and "The Monetary Mechanism and Its Interaction with Real Phenomena," *The Review of Economics and Statistics*, Vol. XLV, 1963 supplement, pp. 79–107.

[6] Hicks, *op. cit.*, p. 153.

in commercial bank portfolios. Hence, continuing the policy into recession — when the general public and business desire to spend less — liquidity is diminished and a falling propensity to consume is reinforced. The resultant higher rate of interest and lesser availability of loanable funds also may induce businesses to curb their borrowing for inventory needs and invest in government securities, thus perhaps contributing to a slower growth in national income. Finally, it is a curious consequence of this process that, when interest rates do move up with market forces, ostensibly to slow capital outflows, this policy results in a slightly lower rate of interest than would prevail in an undisturbed money market.

Chapter 37

Galbraith symposium

Galbraith, Sraffa, Kalecki and supra-surplus capitalism

E. RAY CANTERBERY

Introduction

An interesting and forceful connection suggests itself between the economics of John Kenneth Galbraith and the economics of Piero Sraffa. In turn, there is a connection with Galbraith's work and that of Michal Kalecki, the Polish economist whose view of production conforms with Sraffa's subsistence model. These connections occur with respect to Galbraithian notions of producer sovereignty and power.

Sraffa, in his most celebrated work, nullifies demand theory and leaves open the theory of personal income distribution. In Sraffa's view, the orthodoxy's opposition of cost and demand is an untenable hybrid of objective and subjective elements. Given the notion of consumer sovereignty, the subjective elements of marginalism overwhelm the objective production elements. Galbraith, introducing something more akin to producer sovereignty, fills the demand vacuum left by Sraffa. In this way, Galbraith is the source of demand theory that derives from the extension of the objective forces of production institutions. Sraffa moves from the classical subsistence economy to a production surplus economy; Galbraith moves on to the affluent society, a *supra*-surplus economy.

Kalecki's simplification of the income distribution, dividing income only between workers and capitalists, compels us to go beyond

The author is Professor of Economics at Florida State University. He thanks Susan Williams for her superb (even dedicated) editing advice and Paul Davidson, the scissor wizard, for suggestions that shortened the article even while improving it. Paul has added new meaning to the "cutting edge" of Post Keynesianism. Both are exonerated for anything that might have gone wrong.

Kaleckian subsistence into the more complex distribution of supra-surplus capitalism, where we must recognize the role of power in economic relations—a role epitomized by Kalecki's (and Weintraub's) price mark-up. As it turns out, Kalecki's "degree of monopoly" dovetails with Galbraithian "power." The configuration of a potential paradigm is drawn with some further intimations of the most realistic theoretical constructs of demand and income distribution.

The necessary economy: from Sraffa to Kalecki

Sraffa's neo-Ricardian view of production and value

Sraffa's invocation of David Ricardo is an abstraction of the system of production only and of the way that the real value of goods is decided. After introducing a classical subsistence model in Chapter 1, Sraffa (1960) moves on to a production surplus economy, one that produces commodities in excess of labor's physiological necessities plus actual depreciation of all the means of production. In Sraffa's model of the surplus economy, basic commodities or goods that appear as inputs *and* outputs are necessities only in a technological sense.

Demand, although (abstractly) affecting the level of production, plays no role in deciding prices. Prices are production prices or physical costs, not market prices. A move in the wage (and profit) rate, one of which is given, leaves the ratio of net output or economic surplus to means of production unaltered because productivity is determined solely by the technical conditions of production rather than from the distribution of product or income between wages or profits.

In the surplus economy *non*-basic commodities or goods and services entering only into final demand include both consumer necessities *and* luxuries. Only in Sraffa's subsistence model are basic commodities necessities in consumption as well as in production. In his surplus economy, Sraffa makes no attempt to separate the allocation of the extra-subsistence wage between necessary and "luxury" consumer goods. Moreover, Sraffa's treatment of labor as neither a basic nor a nonbasic service in the surplus economy raises additional serious questions about the nature of demand. Nonetheless, his notion of a standard commodity group comprised of those basic commodities that enter into production in the same proportion that they exit production drives a wedge in the neoclassical system sufficiently wide to allow room for a new theory of demand *and* of income distribution.

What then are the central propositions from Sraffa of interest to Post

Keynesians? In an industry in which equal amounts of, say, labor are always combined with a unit of capital, the marginal product of capital evaporates. Profits can no longer be said to be a return on capital. (In an interindustry model the value of heterogeneous capital cannot be determined anyway.) Moreover, this neo-Ricardian theory tells us that relative production price movements are driven by changes in the income distribution and technology rather than by demand movements. Finally, the income distribution can be altered without changes in the economic surplus relative to the available means of production. There is little room for the usual supply-and-demand considerations so central to neoclassical price theory, because the wages-to-profits relation becomes a social-political question to be answered elsewhere (possibly by Galbraithian power).

Kaleckian income distribution within Sraffa's subsistence model

In Kalecki the national *income* is divided between profits received by capitalists and wages received by workers. The national product is divided among the investment *and* consumption spending of the capitalists and the consumption expenditures of the workers (Kalecki, 1971). If we simplify by saying that *all profits* are diligently plowed back into the business to purchase new investment goods, *saving*, as well as investment, is equal to profits. The capitalist is the lone saver in this simple economy.

A Kaleckian view of production can be made to conform with Sraffa's subsistence model, if we divide Sraffa's output sector into two distinct industries, one producing necessary consumption goods, the other producing necessary investment goods. Although Sraffa does not prefer his model of physiological subsistence, in it nonetheless the amount of business investment in capital goods and the prevailing production technology would decide the level of employment as well as the division of labor between the production of consumption necessities and production necessities (investment goods). This technology and the prevailing level of production capacity (of the vintage technology) also decide the total amount of each class of good produced.

The introduction of subsistence wages into Sraffa's subsistence model transforms it into a Kaleckian world of income distribution. Subsistence wages decide the quantity of consumer necessities manufactured. Since investment goods are combined with labor at a given technology, the demand for consumer necessities and investment goods determines the employment level. The distribution of income between workers and capitalists (between wages and profits) becomes the mirror image of the distribution of national output between consumer necessities and investment goods. We next want to consider what happens to Kalecki's theory when Sraffa's production system produces surpluses and (with a demand theory addendum) the "working class" receives a larger share of the national income than required for subsistence. When wages (perhaps bolstered by interest and rents) become substantially greater than those required for subsistence, the surplus economy is on the way to becoming Galbraith's affluent society.

Beyond Kaleckian subsistence

Ironically, then, a critical insight into the advanced economy lies hidden in the model so quickly dismissed by Sraffa, his subsistence model in which both necessary consumption and necessary capital goods coexist. Such a model reveals that labor is best treated as a basic "commodity" or, better, basic service, because labor is still necessary to produce subsistence commodities.[1] Labor is an input *and* an output in the (at least) self-reproducing economy. Nevertheless, in the long run, just as the standard commodity must change with new technology, the quantity of consumer "necessities" must change as what is necessary is redefined.

Whether necessities are a constant or a variable market basket of goods and services, their quantities and market prices will determine their value and the required value of the money wage bill. For example, in the autumn of 1976, the Bureau of Labor Statistics (BLS) estimated the annual cost of a "lower" consumption budget for a four-person family in the urban United States at $8,162. If $8,162 represented the cultural subsistence requirements for an average family in the urban United States, the wage bill paid to the household had to be at least $8,162.[2]

[1]Canterbery (1980a, pp. 306–308) took this position several years ago.

[2]The content of the BLS budgets is based upon the manner of living and actual consumer choices in the 1960s. The nutritional and health standards, as determined by scientists and nutritionists, are used for the food-at-home and housing components. Sraffa's abstraction that has real (relative) prices and output determined separately at any point in time still is relevant and so is the provision that the wage rate is not based upon the marginal product of labor. Canterbery (1979b) arrives at the same point via a different route. The "demand" for labor is the loci of money wage rates and "marginal revenue products" from given technologies and product prices. However, since the labor supply is a function of expected wage rates, a selection of technology that just clears the labor market at any moment in time is very improbable. This idea is expanded in Canterbery (1980b). Nonetheless, at full employment across all labor markets, *money* wages can be bid up by Keynesian excess demand.

Although it cannot be denied that there are many American households that exist at the biological subsistence level, Galbraith's affluent society is indisputably an economy of surpluses. The estimate for the "higher" consumption budget for a four-person family in the urban United States in 1976 was $17,048, more than twice the lower budget. In an affluent economy, we need to identify the hierarchy of absolute physical necessities and "wants." Society imposes a rank order, because the satisfaction of a greater number of wants is usually associated with "higher standards of living."

There is a certain regularity in the way that most households allocate expenditures on food, clothing, transportation, and other items. The poor, for example, spend their incomes primarily on physiological necessities. After these same needs are met by the nonpoor, the discretionary income remaining meets "needs" or wants that are difficult to pigeonhole. The uncertainty increases as we shift focus away from specific needs, such as the need to be clothed, toward the particular way these needs and wants are met, such as attempts to be fashionably dressed. Although households tend to eat more (and sometimes better) as income increases, there is a limit to the amount of extra money that people spend on food as incomes rise. That is, beyond the income level that meets basic nutritional needs, food expenditure as a share of the household budget grows slowly. This general behavior pattern was first identified as Engel's law.

Engel's law is as successful in suppressing the role of consumption prices as is Sraffa. What turns out to be important to households is the ability to meet needs and wants with their real income levels, given their budget shares. The cost of a need or want is a weighted price index for a bundle of necessary production inputs, not a single price. It is more meaningful to speak of budget shares allocated to bundles of consumer inputs than to individual consumer products (Canterbery, 1979a). Such a relation among product-service groups, money incomes, and average group prices means that, once we have identified the household's income level, we also have come close to identifying the share of the household budget that goes to meet particular needs and therefore to necessary bundles of inputs.

Discretionary income is to consumption what physical surplus (over-capacity) is to production. Both are sources of instability in the advanced economy. Budget shares in Galbraith's system are to consumption what production prices are to production in Sraffa's system. Budget shares lead to an understanding of nonprice competition that is lost when disputes are confined to market pricing. Snob appeal takes on concrete meaning in the face of the one-to-two ratio of the subsistence to the "higher" consumption budget. The large gap between the lowest and highest incomes inspires the corporate structure to transcend the role of simple producer of goods and services. Although the difference between the consumer's physiological necessities budget and the higher income budget could in theory be devoted entirely to savings, the corporation tries to divert these household dollars toward consumer goods and services. The producers create many of the wants they seek to satisfy, an economic phenomenon Galbraith (1958) calls the *dependence effect*. Not surprisingly, in such an economy, a large share of the GNP subsidizes salespeople, marketing efforts, and advertising. Only in the affluent society can wants be created in a Galbraithian manner. As Galbraith (1967, p. 207) notes, "Mass communication was not necessary when the wants of the masses were anchored primarily in physical need. The masses could not then be persuaded as to their spending—this went for basic foods and shelter."

The mark-up and supra-surplus capitalism: Kalecki to Galbraith

Kalecki is primarily responsible for the introduction of imperfect competition into macroeconomic theory in Europe, a role performed by Sidney Weintraub (1959) in America. Galbraith's conception of the New Industrial State is consistent with both notions of pricing behavior. Kalecki's and Weintraub's vision of pricing in the manufacturing sector can be dramatized in one word: *mark-up*.[3] The mark-up plays a strategic role in supra-surplus capitalism.

According to Galbraith (1967, 1973), firms in the manufacturing sector have sufficient market power to pass on to the consumer most cost increases as well as price increases required by investment needs. Somewhere between 75 and 90 percent of gross (including replacement investment) fixed capital investment in the United States is financed from retained profits, the discretionary income of corporations. The giant firm has the power to select a percentage mark-up over production costs (mostly wages) that is sufficient to complete its investment plans most of the time without going hat in hand to a banker. This configuration serves the same purpose as Kalecki's capitalist plowing

[3]Whereas Kalecki's mark-up applies only to manufacturing, Weintraub's is more general and applies to all industries, including those that are nearly competitive.

all profits back into the firm, but the capitalist is replaced by the technostructure.

Capacity utilization may move up and down with the demand for products, but the corporation will stick with the mark-up that will provide its target level of retained profits. This target depends upon its dividend payout ratio to stockholders, its amount of debt relative to its equity, and, most importantly, its perceived investment needs.[4] As long as the firm's capacity is sufficient to meet demand for its products and as long as production costs do not vary greatly from expectations, the firm will cling to the price derived from its careful planning. The margin of prices over current costs already reflects the market power of the giant corporation.

Kalecki's measure of the "degree-of- monopoly" of the firm conforms neatly with Galbraithian power. The essence of the degree-of-monopoly formula is that a firm can raise its own price in proportion to its increase in production costs, if other firms in the industry do likewise. Non-price forms of competition displace price competition so that supply-side economics cannot remain simply the theory of price.

The mark-up and investment plans are inexorably linked. Because of the degree-of-monopoly factor, actual prices charged by the industrial firms do not reflect current demand conditions; they more closely mirror the funds requirements for the planned investment expenditures the technostructure deems sufficient to increase capacity (plant size or number of machines) to meet *expected future* demand. Such a mark-up serves the technostructure's affirmative purpose of growth. When costs of production rise, the firm protects its profits-for-investment flow by raising prices according to its established mark-up over costs. A fixed mark-up serves the technostructure's protective purpose. At times the capacity accumulated with these retained profits will be in excess of that needed to meet current demand, but this situation is no problem for an oligopoly. Supra-surplus capitalism also enjoys supra-surplus capacity. The technostructure savors bureaucratic advantage and hence power.

In the updated world of Galbraith and other contemporary Post

[4]The motivation for investment "needs" has been variously attributed to market share, growth, and power goals. These explanations have been put forward, respectively, by Alfred S. Eichner (1976); Robin Marris (1964); and John Kenneth Galbraith. A further exposition on this issue appears in James Galbraith's article in this symposium.

Keynesians, money income does arise from a whole spectrum of sources. If money wages are administered by union-management agreements, the balance of income is provided by the mark-up over wages, most of which will be retained profits (profits plus depreciation) and dividend payouts. If this mark-up remains constant throughout the economy and productivity remains unchanged, any cost increase from a boost in average wages will be reflected as an increase in the price level.

If prices are set with a constant or even a variable mark-up over wage costs, money wages become central to the price level. The money wages are inflexible downward (as Keynes argued for a different reason) because to reduce money wages violates the labor contract. In the short run, therefore, market prices must adjust to money wages and the cost of production rather than vice versa. There is a revised sequence in which the price level and the rate of inflation are resolved *after* the money wage rates and increases are determined. Money wages, exogeneous in Sraffa, are endogenous in Galbraith but determined by social-political conditions, not by the technology of production.

At this juncture, if Galbraith did not exist, Post Keynesians would have to invent him. The potential paradigm requires the establishment of a connection among personal incomes, demand, and production. In Galbraith (1958, 1967, 1973), demand is, for the most part, *managed* by the corporation and the industry. Nonetheless, when demand shifts up or down, since the neoclassical response of rising and falling prices is absent, adjustments made by the firm are in output levels. If GM is not selling its inventory of cars at the current prices (based upon mark-up over unit costs), GM produces fewer Chevrolets next month and eventually may even lay off production workers. Rather than responding to lower demand by reducing prices, giant producers reduce production levels.

Where corporate and union powers exist in supra-surplus capitalism and are symbiotic (Galbraith's term), *physiological* subsistence for the labor class must expand into *cultural* subsistence. The notion of cultural subsistence brings the personal income distribution in line with a Galbraithian estate of consumption. The technology of production and the prevailing level of production capacity still decide the total potential output of two types of goods: now culturally "necessary" consumption goods and the requisite investment goods. However, realized output depends upon effective demand and the income distribution. We, of course, do not have to be content with Sraffa's "given" level of output.

The distribution of income between workers and "capitalists" re-enters the picture, but in a more complex way than Kalecki would lead us to believe. There are *two* tugs-of-war between the manufacturers and the consumers–workers; producers seem unaware of one of them and workers of the other. Displaying the instincts attributed to corporate management by Galbraith, corporations create and stimulate new demand for their goods and services. However, in the planning system, the wherewithal to fulfill both the manufacturers' and the workers' dreams is decided at the labor-management bargaining table. Only in the guise of consumers are there any losers: Goodbye Adam Smith, in which consumers wear crowns.

The planning system has succeeded all too well in convincing consumers that they should expand the number of goods and services they consider necessary. In response to these culturally determined desires, the giant labor union demands higher wages so that the workers can pay for the newly defined standard of living. The corporation capitulates, knowing that the higher cost of production from a larger wage can be passed on to consumers. The illusion that a higher wage is always a good thing—a money illusion—is enjoyed by the workers, who don't quite sense the fallacy of composition in their dual role as both laborers and consumers. These increases merely cover the "cost of living." As Galbraith suggests, it is not mere historical accident that the highest paid workers reside in the protected part of the economy, the planning system.

If the process stopped at this point, the working class would increase its share of the national income, at least in money terms, but the defensive power instrument of the manufacturers is the mark-up. The concentrated industries can use the mark-up, augmented by ready access to the largest banks and the lowest rates of interest, to generate funds for investment purposes. Throughout the history of capitalism, the idea that workers have to be employed in order to purchase the producers' goods has always eluded manufacturers. Though it is in the interest of any single producer to minimize his total wage bill, if all producers succeed in that calculus they will find there is no outlet for their products.

Given the strength of the industrial labor union, industry's ability to pay the demanded wage is enhanced by its ability to impose price mark-ups upon the consumer.[5] The industrial union's power tool is the wage rate rather than the labor supply. This means that, in the short run, employment is not related to the wage rate, and the wage rate is related to employment only if full employment extends across all labor. Therefore, a high wage can be associated with a high unemployment rate, because employment is decided by technology and effective demand rather than by the marginal product of labor. This process is so deeply imbedded in the economic system that it took a four-year global depression (1979–1982) to slow wage (and price) inflation in the United States.

In the unskilled, nonorganized labor market, there is little incentive or ability to substitute capital goods for labor. Expected wage rates are low, and unskilled workers cannot operate complex machines. The long-run supply of unskilled workers is determined by nonwage elements. Few individuals actively strive to achieve characteristics that would yield low wages. Indeed, the unskilled might be viewed as failures, so their long-term supply is a kind of residual unrelated to wage rates. An unused supply of unskilled labor is a characteristic of recent experience in the industrialized countries. The wage differentials between the union-certified skilled and the unskilled is the consequence of (at least) dual labor markets that reflect the duality between the planning system and the competitive system.

Technological change—unpredictable and not widely understood—plays a major role in these theories. Its impact is readily seen once we accept the wage settlement as largely a political solution based upon the relative power of organized labor and organized production. It is precisely the more advanced secondary or planning sector of the economy that, in the long run, shifts toward more and more complex, automated ways of delivering its product. However, there is no guarantee that productivity will grow steadily faster than the wage rate. Moreover, we cannot expect the slow productivity growth in services to offset any such tendency. Stagflation is the secular consequence.

Even though the primary sector may contain competitive industries, the planning system of the advanced economy is in charge, wielding its power in the marketplace to control production and pass on rising costs (including money wage increases) to all of us. Its symbiotic relationship with big labor and big government gives giant business an almost

[5]In the remaining paragraphs Canterbery's vita theory (1979b, 1980b) is used to amend Galbraith. Piore's (1979) dual labor market perspective is also relevant to this discussion.

inexhaustible supply of funds for investment. The usually benign countervailing power of an earlier Galbraith (1952) gives way to (as JKG admits) non-benign compensatory power (1983). The well-funded investments in new technology that replace workers have the effect of redistributing income away from the working class, particularly away from the least skilled. Although the working class receives a share of profits, most "non-earned" income from high technology is accumulated by the entrepreneurial, managerial, and professional classes.

Technological progress alters the demand for a particular labor type in two ways. First, it can change the technical coefficients and thus labor-quantity requirements. Though capital goods and labor services complement each other in the short run (two workers may be needed for each new machine), they can become substitutes for each other in the longer run. The long-run trend of wages in the planning sector is known to be upward, and it is hardly surprising that the main purpose of new equipment in industrialized economies is to reduce labor requirements. Technological change also exerts a more indirect effect on labor demand. A new, more complex technology can cause a shift to labor of a different type altogether. Workers who once combined the ingredients for frozen cakes may be unqualified to monitor the automated machines that now perform this task, and unemployment of these workers results.

We have no assurance that displaced labor will be hired elsewhere. The rehiring of such labor requires the coincidence of new products and new industries emerging quickly enough to absorb the labor reserve. Even then, it is the more skilled reserve that is needed. Meanwhile, the life plans of the more advantaged workers move inexorably toward collectively increasing their numbers and the skilled labor supply. From the viewpoint of those who wish to have the highest possible personal income, this collective response is unfavorable. Rather than "rationality" being a way out of poverty or a low-income predicament, it can be a way in.

The requisites of technology rearrange the demands for different qualities of labor. The consequent arrangement of incomes is the stage upon which demand plays. The cultural generation of wants, though not entirely separate from technology, plays out much of its destiny within this dimly lit area at the interface between the wants of labor and those of corporate management. Within that gray area, Galbraith can tell us more than Sraffa or Kalecki can.

Whether all this is good or bad depends upon the institutionalized length of the workweek and the income distribution policies of the government. After all, the motivation behind the Industrial Revolution was to reduce physical labor in the process of creating production surpluses. One important measure of the output success of industrialization is the magnitude of unemployment that industry generates in the secondary sector. What we do with the freed effort we have so diligently sought depends upon the ethics of society and collective decisions regarding alternatives to physical work effort as a source of both pleasure and income. In this regard, Galbraith finds an unevenness in development between the private and public sector.

Conclusions

In order to fill the vacuum left by Sraffa and Kalecki, a theory of demand that relates production to a hierarchy of wants and a theory of the income distribution that relates incomes to job markets as well as to other elements are required. If labor is treated as a basic service, demand can be introduced into Sraffa's model. When hierarchical demand is considered, the true nature and importance of necessities, compared with luxuries in an advanced economy producing surpluses beyond physiological subsistence, is revealed. Income earners are then viewed as allocating expenditures among goods on the basis of a budget. In this view, the personal income distribution is dominant, and we are thus able to suppress orthodox price theory.

There is a connection among income distribution, consumer budget shares, production technology, and inflation that has not been widely appreciated. In Galbraith's planning system, we find a round robin of events in which giant business firms separate the affluent from their money by stimulating new wants. There is a kind of poetic justice in this, for the organized workers in the concentrated manufacturing industries demand higher wages to indulge their whetted appetites. The Post Keynesian price mark-up enables producers to pay the wages required to purchase the products the workers have been persuaded they truly need. In this process, the basic cost of remaining in the economic system keeps going up as both what is believed necessary expands and the prices of these "necessities" rise. As such wage settlements are "political," we cannot expect them to be related to productivity.

Moving from short-run variations in economic activity to economic growth, we still find technology and the income distribution to be the deciding forces. Traditionally, investment has been a source of volatility in industrial capacity; switching to new production processes is even less predictable. Moreover, the determinants of the personal income distribution add extra uncertainty, because the quality of the labor force at any time is unlikely to match exactly the new technological requirements. Finally, where labor services and capital goods are not substituted for each other in response to short-run relative price changes, we have to look to innovations and the birth of new industries to keep supra-surplus capitalism growing. The consumers' sovereignty—lost in the decline of the market—can be regained only through political sovereignty, which is itself in jeopardy at the hand of the same groups that felled the market. Galbraith noted the former in *The Affluent Society* and appraised the alternative sources of power in *The Anatomy of Power*. This appraisal of supra-surplus capitalism returns us, ironically, to concerns of the old political economists (e.g., Ricardo, Malthus, and Marx), who saw a close connection between state policy and the economy, thus clothing economics with real-world issues. Their world, the real world, is Galbraith's.

REFERENCES

Canterbery, E. Ray. "Inflation, Necessities, and Distributive Efficiency." In *Essays in Post-Keynesian Inflation*. Ed. by J. H. Gapinski and C. E. Rockwood. Cambridge, Mass.: Balinger, 1979a.

__________. "A Vita Theory of Personal Income Distribution." *Southern Economic Journal*, July 1979b, 46.

__________. *The Making of Economics*. 2nd ed. Belmont, CA.: Wadsworth Publishing Company, 1980a.

__________. "Welfare Economics and the Vita Theory." *The Eastern Economic Journal*, January 1980b, 6.

Eichner, Alfred S. *The Megacorp and Oligopoly: Micro Foundations of Macro Dynamics*. Cambridge, England: Cambridge University Press, 1976.

Galbraith, John Kenneth. *American Capitalism: The Concept of Countervailing Power*. Boston: Houghton, Mifflin Co., 1952.

__________. *The Affluent Society*. 2d ed. rev. Boston: Houghton Mifflin Co., 1958.

__________. *The New Industrial State*. Boston: Houghton Mifflin Co., 1967.

__________. *Economics and the Public Purpose*. Boston: Houghton Mifflin Co., 1973.

__________. *The Anatomy of Power*. Boston: Houghton Mifflin Co., 1983.

Kalecki, Michal. *Selected Essays on the Dynamics of the Capitalistic Economy*. Cambridge, England: Cambridge University Press, 1971.

Marris, Robin. *The Economic Theory of "Managerial" Capitalism*. New York: Basic Books, 1964.

Piore, Michael J., ed. *Unemployment and Inflation: Institutionalist and Structuralist Views*. Armonk, N.Y.: M. E. Sharpe, Inc., 1979.

Sraffa, Piero. *Production of Commodities by Means of Commodities*. Cambridge, England: Cambridge University Press, 1960.

Weintraub, Sidney. *A General Theory of the Price Level, Output, Income Distribution and Economic Growth*. Philadelphia: Chilton, 1959.

Chapter 38

REAGANOMICS, SAVING, AND THE CASINO EFFECT

E. Ray Canterbery

Florida State University

1. Reaganomics and the Supply-Siders

During the 1980s the theory of "supply-side economics" became identified with the set of policies known as "Reaganomics," policies aimed at ending inflation without reducing output and employment and thus escaping the stagnation that afflicted the U.S. economy during the 1970s. Tight monetary policy would curb inflation, while supply-side incentives would expand employment and production. Most of all, personal saving would be expanded through the incentives of tax cuts for the highest income earners. Supply-side economics thus became the Holy Grail of savers. Reaganomics, by whatever name or design, culminated in what I call the "Casino Economy."

In retrospect, the fact that Reaganomics even gained social acceptability, much less the status of holy writ, is a revealing commentary on the state of the public psyche. Reaganomics exploited widespread disillusionment with received principles of wealth redistribution and turned them on their heads. The poor were to be disgorged from federal welfare rolls because—receiving so much on the dole—they had disincentives to work. The rich were to receive the greatest tax cuts, for their tax burden was so great they had meager incentive to save. In the name of incentives, Robin-Hood-in-reverse implied that the poor had *too much* after-tax income and the rich *too little*. This frail piece of logic had such immediate appeal that it alone was nearly sufficient to support the Reagan Revolution. But it got lots of help.

Supply-side economics was a media event begun by Wall Street journalist Jude Wanniski, writer Bruce Bartlett, and pop sociologist George Gilder. All three writers made devoted reference to the second-generation Austrian economists—von Hayek, von Mises, Schumpeter, Frank Knight—and the neo-Austrians Kirzner and Rothbard. The Laffer curve, the Rosetta Stone of Reaganomics, drawn for Wanniski on a napkin in a Washington, D.C., "insiders'" hotel bar by Arthur Laffer, was given celebrity status in Wanniski's book *The Way the World Works*.

George Gilder gave a further boost to Lafferism even while embracing neo-Austrian entrepreneurship in his *Wealth and Poverty*, required reading for the 1981 White House staff. (David Stockman distributed 30 copies immediately upon its publication.) Gilder, the chief evangelist for Reaganomics, argued that personal income tax cuts for the rich would stimulate their output; eventually, the resulting expanded production and added tax revenue would allow further tax cuts for low- and middle-income families. But Gilder went further. The welfare state that America had become, he said, motivated the poor to choose leisure over work. Because only the rich could acquire enough savings to induce capital formation, their reduced tax rates would stimulate economic growth.

Thus the neo-Austrian spirit of entrepreneurship continued to blitz the White House long after the planned tax cut had been drafted. That is, although the initial impetus for Reaganomics came from Laffer's version of neoclassical economics, Gilder's fervor kept the ball rolling. His faith in God and enterprise apparently reassured the president, even after OMB director David Stockman had become convinced otherwise, that Reaganomics would stimulate output and employment.

In short, although it stressed those elements crucial to the supply of labor and productive capacity, the full Reaganomics program went beyond tax cuts to slashes in government welfare spending and decreases in regulation. The unique proclamation of supply-side economics is its dual promise of stimulating economic growth and retarding inflation. The next section will discuss the bricks and mortar of the supply-side economics archway.

2. Say's Law Embued with Entrepreneurial Spirit

The first canon of supply-side economics was Say's law, resurrected from its presumed entombment at the hands of the Great Depression and John Maynard Keynes. Say's law connects supply-side economics to economic growth. Saving is the starter key for the growth engine because of the guaranteed transmission of saving into investment. The engine always starts, no matter how chilly the investment climate, because every dollar saved is predestined to become a dollar of investment.

Because Reaganomics viewed the upper-income class (over $50,000 a year in 1980 dollars) as the dominant personal savers, the central economic purpose of the wealthy was to save. This perspective rationalized lowering marginal tax rates for the well-to-do as an incentive to increase personal saving, which would end up as new plant and equipment. As a fail-safe, special tax benefits to corporations (larger credits, lower rates, and faster depreciation) would provide still more incentives for investment. No doubt this faith was buttressed by the neo-Austrian optimism regarding the alertness of the entrepreneur in responding to changed profit opportunities.

Thus, even though the various tax cuts would increase disposable income, their presumed effectiveness did not stem from their effects on Keynesian aggregate demand, which were thought to be nil. Rather, with neoclassical immaculateness, the effectiveness of tax reductions would come from their changing of relative prices. A reduction in tax rates would induce decision makers to substitute productive activity (investment, work, and exchange) for leisure and idleness, causing output to rise. Moreover, entrepreneurs, freed from the constraints of taxation, would play a role here. The shift from nonproduction (and consumption) toward production would enlarge total supply, causing real income to expand rapidly. The market supply of goods and services—that is, aggregate supply and hence economic growth—would be enhanced.

3. Truth in Taxes and in Lending

The 1981 Economic Recovery Tax Act cut taxes across the board for individuals: 5 percent in 1981, 10 percent in 1982, and another 10 percent in 1983. The most beloved policy slashed the top bracket from 70 percent to 50 percent. Although taxation of earned income had topped out at 50 percent in 1972, the same cap was placed on *unearned* income, providing great gains to the small set of households living off interest and rents; the top rate on capital gains was cut from 28 to 20 percent.

At the same time social security tax rates were allowed to climb from 6.05 percent in 1978 to 6.70 percent in 1982–83, 7.05 percent in 1985, and 7.51 percent in 1988–89, on a path blazed by the Carter administration in 1977. The share of federal tax receipts from this source rose from 31 percent in 1980 to 36 percent in 1988, even while the working class's share of the national income declined. The share of tax revenue contributed by the top 1 percent of taxpayers also rose, but only in step with their share of the national income; their ability to pay had been equally enhanced. According to the Congressional Budget Office, which has calibrated the effect of federal taxes by population decile for 1977–1984 and 1977–1988, the highest income households paid lower effective rates because of the tax cuts on income from interest, dividends, rents, and capital gains (table 4–1).

We pause, for practice seldom makes perfect theory. Did Reagan's advisers really believe that workers were so sensitive to small real-wage increments that meager marginal tax reductions would so energize work effort? If so, the effective federal marginal tax *increases* should cause labor productivity to nosedive!

The answer was provided by Stockman in his Christmastime 1981 "confessions" to the *Atlantic Monthly*. "The hard part of the supply-side tax cut is dropping the top rate from 70 to 50 percent—the rest of it is a secondary matter," he explained. "The original argument was that the top bracket was too high, and that's having the most devastating effect on the economy. Then, the general argument was that, in order to make this palatable as a political matter, you had to bring down all the brackets. But, I mean, Kemp-Roth (the name of the original supply-side tax bill) was always a Trojan Horse to bring down the top rate."[1]

Table 4–1. Percentage Point Changes in Effective Tax Rates by Population Income Decile, 1977–1988

Decile	*1977–1984*	*1977–1988*
1	+2.5	+1.6
2	−0.2	−0.4
3	+1.2	+1.3
4	+0.1	+0.6
5	−0.6	+0.1
6	−0.9	−0.1
7	−1.5	−0.7
8	−0.6	0.0
9	−0.7	+0.2
10	−3.1	−1.7
top 5%	−4.2	−2.6
top 1%	−7.8	−6.0

Source: Congressional Budget Office, *The Changing Distribution of Federal Taxes: 1975–1990*, October, 1987, Table 8, p. 48.

A Trojan horse? Supply-side economics was rolled into the enemy camp of labor with a horseload of entrepreneurs. For the stimulation of output the Reagan administration was counting not really on a Calvinistic response by workers but rather on Say's law. Stockman conceded as much: The supply-side theory was really new clothes for the naked doctrine of the old "trickle-down theory."[2] The main effect on the highest income quintile was to greatly increase after-tax income in the expressed belief that personal savings (and para passu private *real* investment) would rise.

Part of the plan was to give *direct* assistance to real capital formation. With reductions in corporate tax rates and liberalization of depreciation benefits, the share of federal tax receipts represented by corporate income tax revenues dropped to an all-time low of 6.2 percent in 1983, down from 12.5 percent in 1980.

The spending side of the federal fiscal ledger also became an instrument for redistribution. Reagan was elected on the platform that "government is the problem." Republicans claimed that a gigantic public sector had ended innovation and stifled creativity even as the welfare state destroyed the family. The Reagan solution was massive increases in defense spending that shifted federal funds out of human resources. Between 1980 and 1987 defense climbed from 23 percent to 28 percent of federal outlays, whereas human resources descended from 28 percent to 22 percent.

Federal deficits far beyond the lively imagination of John Maynard Keynes were the consequence. The 1981 tax bill married them to higher interest rates. The rise in federal debt interest from $96 billion in 1981 to $216 billion in 1988 virtually guaranteed that nonearned income from holding paper would rise faster than the wages of workers. The top quintile of households were receiving 80 percent of the federal interest payments made to individuals, even as the top tax rate on such receipts fell steadily (to 28 percent in 1988).

Finally, Reaganomics jumped on the deregulation bandwagon that the Carter administration had started rolling. Forces already in motion were sustained or accelerated in telecommunications, transportation, financial services, and many other industries. Removal by Congress in 1980 of deposit and loan interest ceilings had already awarded the greatest benefits to the 10 percent of families owning 86 percent of the net financial wealth.

The Wall Street raiders of the 1980s were encouraged—even cheered—as they used greenmail in the merger frenzy of the era. Between FY1980 and FY1988 merger filings soared more than 320 percent while the work-years allocated to antitrust enforcement plunged 40 percent. Raiders like

Carl Icahn, Boone Pickens, and Ivan Boesky, as well as LBO masters such as Henry Kravis, built a large, profitable infrastructure that assured huge fees from questionable ventures and an unrealistic upward spin to stock market prices.

The intent in word and deed was to redistribute income and wealth from the working class to the upper 10 percent, increasing both income and wealth concentration. Economists can defer to the Kitty Kellys to address the hypocrisy related to family values, but Reaganomics left no room for hypocrisy regarding income and wealth redistribution. President Reagan achieved what he had said he wanted. Even before the lopsided tax cuts, money income by quintile shows growing income inequality during the Reagan years (see table 4–2).

The wealth distribution is always less equal than the income distribution. The Joint Economic Committee of Congress compiled data on the total wealth held by the top 0.5 percent of U.S. households from date furnished by the Federal Reserve Board. By 1983 the share of wealth held by the super-rich had risen sharply (to 26.9 percent) after falling for 40 years. Further increases in income inequality since then, plus other evidence, suggest that this trend continues.

Average total corporate CEO compensation increased from $900,000 in 1983 to $2,025,000 in 1988 (93 times the earnings of the average factory worker). In 1988 Michael Milken of Drexel, the innovator of junk bonds, received between $180 and $199 *million*, up from a meager $60 million in 1987 and around $80 million in 1986. The net worth of the Forbes 400 (the wealthest 400 persons in the United States as estimated by *Forbes* magazine) went from $92 *billion* to some $270 *billion* between 1982 and 1989, a gain of 293 percent. In 1981 there were 600,000 millionaires. But by 1988 there were some 1,500,000 millionaires, 100,000 decamillionaires,

Table 4–2. Changes, Share of Money Income Received by Quintile

Year	*1*	*2*	*3*	*4*	*5*
1969	5.6%	12.4%	17.7%	23.7%	40.6%
1980	5.1	11.6	17.5	24.3	41.6
1983	4.7	11.1	17.1	24.3	42.8
1985	4.6	10.9	16.9	24.2	43.5
1988	4.6	10.7	16.7	24.0	44.0

Source: U.S. Census Bureau.

Notes: The 1988 income range for each quintile is 1 = Under $15,102; 2 = $15,102–$26,182; 3 = $26,182–$38,500; 4 = $38,500–$55,906; and 5 = Over $55,906.

1200 centimillionaires, and 51 billionaires. Many of these fortunes were made in finance and real estate.

To be sure, by this test supply-side economics worked. But did the income/wealth expansion and redistribution increase real saving and real investment? If so, did such increases come from supply-side tax "incentives"? Before addressing these questions, we need to ponder whether we have a correct measure of saving.

4. The Measurement of Saving

The difficulty of understanding saving at conception is exceeded only by data problems. The identity of saving and investment in the National Income and Product Accounts (NIPA) applies to *real* saving—real in the sense of a withholding of current income from consumption. It does not capture the additions in financial wealth that may result from increases in the value of existing and tangible assets. And it does not reflect creation of new credit, of which the Fed and the commercial banking system are usually capable. Having stated this caveat, we note that the NIPA show that personal savings as a percentage of disposable personal income dropped from 7.5 percent in 1981 to a low of 3.2 percent in 1987. If the truth be known, the U.S. Department of Commerce does not measure personal savings to generate its savings data. Instead, the Commerce Department measures disposable income and consumption and then subtracts consumption from disposable income to determine savings. This economists consider *real*.

Such a measure surely understates personal money savings during the 1980s, a fact that has brought tears of joy to many a supply-sider. Quite simply, the Commerce Department fails to account for changes in net worth, including that created by new credit. If an individual owns an asset that appreciates in value, such as a stock, bond, or house, are those new savings any less real to the person than savings accumulated by thrift? Not all increases in one's store of wealth are spent lavishly: That depends upon one's income class and tastes. By the same token, would not a depreciation of such assets diminish personal saving? Such personal money savings do go somewhere and influence the macroeconomy, but economists generally have been unable to determine their destination.

The Federal Reserve System also measures individual savings—indirectly, using a flow-of-funds approach. It is a much closer approximation of changes in net worth. The Federal Reserve measure adds increases in financial assets to net investment in consumer durables (such as a house purchase), and then subtracts the net increase in debts to arrive at savings. The Fed's number-crunchers attribute to households those flows not accounted for by banks, insurance companies, pension funds, and other funds handlers. Periodically, a Fed survey of consumer finance provides a direct check of some household financial behavior.

If one considers personal saving to be the increase in household net worth, the Commerce Department clearly undercounts personal savings, a discrepency that greatly widened after 1981. The similarity in the two data series during 1961–1981 suggests that they had once been measuring the same thing. Nonetheless, during 1986, 1987, and 1988 the Fed's measure of personal saving was 30.2, 45.0, and 34.6 percent higher, respectively, than that of the Commerce Department. Still another alternative measure of savings has been provided by Block,[3] who focuses on the ability of households to supply a financial surplus to the business sector for investment.

Are then the supply-siders correct? Did the supply-side tax incentives greatly swell personal savings? This chapter shall argue otherwise. It is likely that personal money savings did soar during the 1980s, but for reasons quite apart from supply-side incentives. What happened to net business savings is the rest of the story.

5. Keynes Redux

The stimulative fiscal policy of the Reagan administration came into full effect as the 1981–1982 recession was ending and an aggregate demand stimulus was needed. Because personal income rose and was being redistributed to the highest income intervals, it would be surprising if personal money saving failed to soar along with consumption, especially by the upper classes. Tables 4–3 and 4–4 reveal those consequences: These data are "real" only in the sense that they are adjusted by price indices.

Price-adjusted consumption increased at an annual rate of only .03 percent between 1972–73 and 1980–81 but soared .46 percent between 1980–81 and 1986–87 (see table 4–3). Even so, the important story is found in the distribution of these growth rates by quintile. Most of the increased rate of consumption during the 1980s can be attributed to the two highest consuming quintiles. The 1980s' increases in household money net worth as a share of slow-growing money disposable income were higher than during the 1960s but lower than during the 1970s. However, given that the inflation in *goods* prices slowed during the 1980s, the increase in price-adjusted household net worth as a share of disposable income was phenomenal, especially during 1985–1988 (see table 4–4).

Table 4–3. Real Consumption Expenditures, Average Annual Growth Rates (in percent)

	1972–73 to 1980–81	*1980–81 to 1986–87*
All consumer units	0.03	0.46
By quintile		
Lowest fifth	1.49	0.23
Second fifth	0.28	−0.45
Third fifth	−0.33	0.01
Fourth fifth	−0.17	0.32
Highest fifth	−0.08	1.59

Sources: U.S. Department of Labor, Bureau of Labor Statistics; *Survey of Consumer Expenditures*; and *Consumer Price Index*.

Notes: As the same households are not necessarily in the same income quintiles in each period, the growth rates in consumption should be used with caution. The relative growth rates of the various income groups nonetheless can be meaningly compared across the two eras. A detailed discussion of these data appear in Robert Blecker, *Are Americans on a Consumption Binge*? (Washington D.C.: Economic Policy Institute, 1990).

A Keynesian explanation for rising money and price-adjusted household saving is provided in tables 4–5 and 4–6 by estimates of the marginal and average propensities to save. Because these propensities are based on before-tax income, the MPSs for the lowest income interval are misleading. Those MPSs would be much lower when measured against after-tax income. In any case, the average propensities to save by quintile of income are the most revealing. On the average the lowest two-fifths of the consumer units during the 1980s and the lowest three-fifths during 1987 and 1989 had *negative* average saving rates. As Keynesians and the average person on the assembly line would expect, the two highest quintiles did the positive saving.

No self-respecting Keynesian would be surprised that both consumption and saving rose with incomes, nor surprised that a redistribution of income toward the highest income interval would raise the personal money savings rate. The main effect of Reaganomics was to raise the incomes of those in the higher quintiles and increase their ability to spend *and* save. Moreover, as the highest income groups increased their rates of spending, even supply-siders would not be surprised to see soaring tourism in Europe or higher sales of luxury durables, including imported luxury cars.

In conventional macroeconomics, *real* saving is measured as the value of *real* investment—private business investment in plant, equipment, and

Table 4–4. Personal Saving and Investment Rates

	1960–1969	1970–1979	1980–1988	1985–1988
Shares				
Increase, household net worth/DI	27.0	38.9	33.9	32.1
Increase, real household net worth/ *DI*[a]	14.0	8.4	11.2	28.5
Net fixed investment/ NNP	6.6	6.7	4.8	4.9
Gross fixed investment/ GNP	14.5	15.6	15.4	15.2
Growth Rates				
Growth rate, capital services, private business sector[b]	4.2	4.0	3.2	1.3
Growth rate, capital services, manufacturing sector[b]	4.7	3.7	2.2	1.5

Sources: Federal Reserve, *Balance Sheets for the U.S. Economy*; BEA, National Income and Product Accounts; and BLS, *Multifactor Productivity Measures*.

[a] Nominal household net worth is deflated by the GNP deflator.

[b] The BLS capital input series measures the services derived from the stock of physical assets. The assets included are fixed business equipment, structures, inventories, and land. Structures include nonresidential structures and residential capital that is rented out by profit-making firms or persons. Financial assets are *excluded* as are owner-occupied residential structures. The aggregate capital measures are obtained by weighting the capital stocks for each asset type within each industry using the respective rental prices. Rental prices are the sum of the real rate of return to all assets within the industry and rate of depreciation of the specific asset, adjusted for the effect of taxes. Data on physical assets and the gross product originating by industry used in measuring the rental prices are obtained from the BEA.

new inventories. If saving does not end up as such investment, it plays no further role in the economy. Table 4–4 notes that gross fixed investment as a share of GNP has remained steady for four decades. *Net* fixed investment (the really *real* part of investment) declined to less than 5 percent during the 1980s. Most importantly, the growth rates of capital services in the private business and manufacturing sectors had almost fallen through the factory floor by 1985–1988. During the 1980s the one

Table 4–5. Marginal Propensities to Save by Income Interval, Selected Years

	Income Interval						
Year	*1*	*2*	*3*	*4*	*5*	*6*	*7*
1982–1983	0.81	0.32	0.44	0.36	0.47	0.48	
1984	1.02	0.38	0.39	0.32	0.46	0.29	
1987	0.80	0.06	0.36	0.36	0.38	0.28	0.56
1989	0.83	0.13	0.36	0.28	0.26	0.52	0.24

Source: BLS, U.S. Department of Labor, *Consumer Expenditure Survey*, 1982–83, 1984, 1987, 1989.

Notes: The income intervals for 1982–83 and 1984 are: less than $5000, $5000–$9999, $10,000–$14,999, $15,000–$19,999, $20,000–$29,999, $30,000–$39,999, and $40,000 and over in income *before* taxes. The 1987 and 1989 surveys include an interval of $40,000–49,999 and a new highest interval of $50,000 and over. Moreover, the surveys beginning in 1987 integrate the results of a diary and interview portions of the Bureau's Consumer Expenditure Survey and are, therefore, more complete. The MPSs are calculated from changes in average incomes and expenditures between the income intervals. The data should be interpreted with care. The interview sample is selected on a rotating panel basis, targeted at 5000 consumer units each quarter in 109 areas of the country. The diary survey yields about 10,000 diaries a year (each for 2 one-week periods). Total expenditures or consumption are the transaction costs, including excise and sales taxes, of goods and services acquired during the interview period.

Table 4–6. Average Propensities to Save by Quintiles of Income

	Quintile of Consumer Units				
Year	*1*	*2*	*3*	*4*	*5*
1982–83	−1.03	−0.14	0.08	0.21	0.33
1984	−2.17	−0.28	0.02	0.16	0.30
1987	−1.25	−0.31	−0.04	0.11	0.29
1989	−1.12	−0.27	−0.03	0.09	0.30

Source: BLS, U.S. Department of Labor, *Consumer Expenditures Survey*, 1982–83, 1984, 1987, 1989.

Notes: See Notes to table 4–4.

thing private business did best was depreciate—lose capital to wear, tear, obsolescence, and destruction. In this view, real saving stagnated. Why—in the Gildered Age when the idolatry of capital was peaking and personal money saving was on the ascent—did so many machines commit suicide?

To solve the mystery of where personal money savings go when they die (in economic theory), we turn to a theory less conventional than Keynes's expenditures model. We need to examine the composition of savings in firms and households.

6. A Business and Household Net Worth Approach

This section follows the Fed's approach and considers the economy as a series of balance sheets. In this respect, often one household's or organization's asset is another's liability. Thus, when we speak of changes in assets, we often speak as well of co-movements in liabilities. Sometimes the co-movements occur within the same balance sheet. Banks and S&Ls that used high-interest-rate CDs and junk bonds (their liabilities) during the early 1980s to finance mortgages that began to depreciate by 1988 (their assets) have learned dearly this latter connection. There are at least three sources of change in assets. First, value appreciation or depreciation occurs as the prices of the items go up or down. Second, physical depreciation can happen as machines and buildings wear out or become obsolete. Third, exchange (which presumes a change in ownership of the asset) can increase or decrease holdings.[4]

The aggregate net worth of the private business sector (G_b) is equal to its money and money market asset holdings (M_b), plus its value of goods holdings that include inventories of finished goods, goods in process, raw materials, buildings and equipment, and land (Q_b), plus the net household indebtedness to business ($K_h - K'_h$), where K_h is total debts (such as installment credit) due to businessess from households and K'_h is the total debts due from businesses to households plus government bond holdings (B_b). The K'_h consists mostly of corporate bonds held by households. Business firms hold debt of other business firms but, in the aggregate, business-to-business debt cancels. New issues of equities increase the money and market asset holdings of the firm. Change in aggregate business net worth during any accounting period is

$$dG_b = dM_b + dQ_b + dK_h - dK'_h + dB_b = S_b \qquad (4\text{–}1)$$

Because the quantity dG_b is that part of profits not distributed in dividends, it comprises business saving or dissaving.

Net worth (saving) increases through the revaluation of assets above costs, normally at the moment of sale. Despite ritualistic chanting against inflation by business, inflation in goods prices is a reliable route to greater increases in net worth (and business saving). Money and money market assets ideally provide firms only with liquidity. Physical depreciation or value depreciation decrease net savings. Of course, an increase in debts due from households increases business saving even as it decreases household saving.

In a Keynesian-Kaleckian style model, the increased retained earnings of businesses is not only a source of investment funds but an incentive for *more* investment. A price markup is used to increase the value of the goods that businesses sell, adding to the funds flowing from household spending. Retained earnings from sales revenue becomes corporate savings, some of which will be invested. In turn, rising sales revenue nudging full capacity is an impetus to expand. These internal funds so generated by the firm can be levered by debt to finance still more capital assets. The more that is invested, the greater will be the sales of capital goods and the profits' share in the national income. In this regard it is the hope of firms that households will not be spendthrifts. Because of low transactions costs, retained earnings are a preferred source of funds to new issues of preferred or common stock or, in a tax-neutral world, to increased corporate debt (dK_h). Indeed, increases in corporate debt to households reduce business saving. In the *aggregate*, nonetheless, investment requires *external* funds.

And so, equation (4–1) illustrates how easily one can slip into the supply-side error whereby saving "causes" investment. Household saving is a source of corporate debt, an indebtedness no doubt incurred solely for *real* business investment purposes. However, these household savings only enter the firm when *new* corporate bonds are issued. Otherwise, households are merely exchanging ownership of corporate (and no doubt government) bonds with each other. In that process the value of financial assets may be bid up and the wealth and income distribution may be altered. A redistribution toward those of highest marginal and average propensities to save will diminish corporate sales revenue and the impetus for *real* investment. Moreover, there is no guarantee that any particular corporation will use retained earnings to enhance real investment.

Because real investment, when it does happen, raises the retained earnings of the capital goods industry, its employment, and the incomes of those it employs, the more believable parable is that investment "causes" saving. This view too, no doubt, is an oversimplification, but at least the *direction* of causality is clear. Moreover, for the 1980s, it is a relationship whose pattern—as we have seen—is found in the data.

A little noted component of declining saving is the slump in *business* saving. Business saving is conventionally measured in the national accounts by retained earnings of corporations. As a percentage of GNP, it fell from around 4.5 percent in the mid-1960s to 2.75 percent in the late 1970s, and to 1 percent during the late 1980s. Alternatively, the Federal Reserve balance sheet measure of corporate saving (which includes stock dividends and nondividend cash payments) suggests that corporate saving actually turned *negative* during the late 1980s. This event is related to the outbreak of leveraged buyouts and stock repurchases to fight them.

Now we turn to the ledger sheets of the household. Surely it is so that household saving equals household income less household consumption, properly measured. It is equally so that household saving is the change in household net worth. The household equation for saving comparable to that for the corporation is

$$dG_h = dM_h + dQ_h + dK_h' - dK_h + dB_h + dE_h = S_h, \quad (4\text{–}2)$$

where dB_h is the increase in the value of government bond holdings of households and dE_h is the increase in the value of equities. Any increase in goods holdings would be in durables and would include the increase (or decrease) in the value of housing.

A reminder to the unwary reader: As long as these items are expressed in nominal terms, they can rise and fall from changes in either units or prices. In fact, a positive dQ_b in a business firm's balance sheet can be seen as a price increase *only*, given that firms attempt to sell products above cost. Even though the act of exchange is merely a change in asset ownership, those holding assets rising in price enjoy increased net worth.

We now move to the national income and its distribution. Aggregate profits of business (V) is the gross increase in net worth (i.e., gross business saving), out of which interest and dividends are paid (D), or

$$V = S_b + D. \quad (4\text{–}3)$$

Substituting the components of business saving from equation (4–1),

$$V = dQ_b + (dM_b + dK_h - dK_h' + dB_b + D). \quad (4\text{–}4)$$

Since household income is comprised of wages (W) and dividends and interest paid (D), we can write

$$S_h = (W + D) - C_h, \quad (4\text{–}5)$$

where C_h is household consumption. Substitute the values from equation (4–2) for S_h and

$$W = C_h + dQ_h - (-dM_h + dK_h - dK_h' - dB_h - dE_h + D). \quad (4\text{–}6)$$

If we ignore the direct transfers to and from governments and assume the inventory of government bonds to be constant for the period, there are transfer items that flow between the business and the household sectors comprised of changes in money holdings (the M's), changes in debt (the K's), changes in government bond holdings (the B's), increases in equity holdings (the E), and dividend and interest payments (D). The transfer item (T) defined in equation (4–4) as

$$T = dM_b + dK_h - dK'_h + dB_b + D. \qquad (4\text{–}7)$$

has the lightness of being highly liquid assets and liabilities. Without denoting exact ownership shares, T can be written as

$$T = dM + dK - dK' + dB + D. \qquad (4\text{–}7a)$$

The "T" for the household differs from the "T" for the business firm by the value dE_h, or the change in equity holdings. This complication requires some elaboration. An increase in household equity holdings can come from new stock issues, existing stock in the secondary market, or a rise in stock market prices. *Only* when a positive dE_h comes from *new* issues (about 1 percent of the value of all such transactions) does the corporation experience an increase in money offsetting the decrease in household money holdings (i.e., $dM_b = -dM_h$). Otherwise, the change in equity holdings merely shifts the ownership of equity and liquidity among households. The implications of this complication can begin to be understood by defining the household "T" as XT from equation (4–6) or

$$XT = -dM_h + dK_h - dK'_h - dB_h - dE_h + D. \qquad (4\text{–}8)$$

Now, we can simplify equations (4–4) and (4–6) to read

$$V = dQ_b + T \quad \text{and} \quad W = C + dQ_h - XT.$$

Aggregate wages and profits exhaust the value of aggregate output so that national income is

$$Y = W + V = C + dQ_h + dQ_b - (XT - T). \qquad (4\text{–}9)$$

Only when $T = XT$ would nominal saving be $dQ_h + dQ_b$ and national income be

$$Y = C + dQ_h + dQ_b. \qquad (4\text{–}9a)$$

The value "T" then would simply disappear as transfers between firms and households cancel.

Anyone who has struggled to understand T and who by now associates T with "torture" no doubt must be disappointed greatly to see it disappear! The nature of equation (4–9a) and, to a slightly lesser extent, equation (4–9) as identities tends to hide everything that went on in the economy in the determination of national income and its division, including the strategic role of T. In particular, we note that a net positive value of T transfers financial resources from households to businesses.

If net savings are determined independently from dividends, then busi ness dividends are a "widow's cruse and Danaid jar": The more business distributes in interest and dividends, the more will return in profits to be distributed.[5] By the same token, the more business *pays* in interest, the lower its profits will go. Whereas the corporation can increase its cash from equities only with new issues (which were rare during the 1980s), the household can enjoy secondary-market appreciation in its equities holdings (via XT) without sharing such benefits with business.

Because XT and T differ only by dE_h in equation (4–9), the nominal national income is

$$Y = C + dQ_h + dQ_b + dE_h. \tag{4–10}$$

National saving then is bolstered by an increase in household equity holdings, even by a rising stock market. Nominal national income would rise without a matching increment of *real* investment. A supply-siders' cut in the capital gains tax rate would add to nominal national income without altering plant capacity.

Thus far, it has been assumed that the central bank and private banks are not creating any new money nor is the federal government issuing new debt. It is important to relax both assumptions. When we do, equation (4–10) becomes

$$Y = C + dQ_h + dQ_b + (dM_h + dM_b + dB_h + dB_b + dE_h). \tag{4–10a}$$

Now the *nominal* national income can increase as a direct result of credit and money creation. An increase in real national income is by no means guaranteed because real investment may not increase.

The various components of T and XT swirl about their own axes without necessarily intersecting with *real* investment and saving. Financial transactions in existing assets are not real output and not included in real national income. Still, they do exist. The values can expand and contract due simply to financial speculation—speculative real estate or corporate junk bond ventures. In turn, such appreciation or depreciation and compounding of interest can alter the wealth and income distributions. Moreover, the entire financial services industry—which greatly expanded between 1981 and 1987, only to begin a monumental collapse thereafter—revolves around T.

Banking, savings and loan, and brokerage firms are unique among businesses in holding demand deposit liabilities that are assets of other businesses and of households (M_b and M_h). During the 1980s, a period when new financial instruments such as junk bonds streamed out of Wall Street, the behavior of such accounts was the basis for what I call the "Casino Effect."

7. The Casino Effect of *T*

Financial fragility did not begin with Reaganomics; rather, the Reagan–congressional deficits and deregulation of the financial industry simply took an already fragile system and tempted its collapse. Since the late 1960s, credit or finance has become increasingly important in the United States and in the global economy. The financial disturbances of 1972–1973, 1974–1975, 1979, and 1981–1982 left the peak rate of inflation and the lowest rate of unemployment ever higher. This high-flying era was characterized by a volatile but generally upward movement in nominal interest rates, wild gyrations in exchange rates, and a general decline in the growth of consumption.

By the mid-1980s interest payments as a share of net national income had risen from only 1 percent to 10 percent. A major shift toward debt finance occurred in the aforementioned business balances sheets. Whereas in 1983 equity and debt issuance were $4.8 billion and $4.0 billion, respectively, in every year of the eighties since, net new equity issuance has been negative while corporate net bond issues have soared (to about $30 billion in 1989). The irresistible combination of a fast-rising U.S. private and public debt and soaring U.S. interest rates is responsible for skyrocketing net monetary interest. By 1991 federal government interest payments to bondholders were exhausting half of all personal income tax revenue.

During the Reagan years the entrepreneur's share of national income declined drastically even as the rentier's (unearned) income share has soared. All of the increase in disposable income during the 1980s is more than accounted for by the rise in the share of interest income, while the shares of labor and other income sources declined. Surely this is not the way the Golden Age of Entrepreneurship was supposed to unfold.

Of course, an economy can never reach a state in which 100 percent of its national income is net interest, because the sum of employee compensation, proprietor's income, and corporate profits would be zero! Even so, the interest part of *D* has been eating away at manufacturers' net worth. We can begin to picture an economy whose main industries would be printing (for credit instruments and money), financial firms, and retail outlets and in which all manufactured goods and services would be imported. The central function of businesspeople in such an environment would be speculation. The society would be a giant money market fund in which households and businesses would spend each day shifting financial assets about in their gigantic portfolios. The United States would implode into Las Vegas or Trump's Taj Mahal in Atlantic City—hence, what I have called the "Casino Economy." During economic expansion such an economy can operate almost independently of real production, but its downward spiral during a recession is dangerous.

The ownership of most interest-bearing assets is highly concentrated. Some 10 percent of families own 51 percent of liquid assets, 86 percent of tax-exempt municipal bonds, and 70 percent of other bonds. The richest 10 percent hold 57 percent of household net worth and 86 percent of net financial assets. The top 10 percent also own 72 percent of corporate stock, with the top 2 percent alone owning half.

Although the monetary system is at the core of the debt creation and repayment process, its stability depends on profit flows to borrowers sufficient to service their loans. The central problems of present-day capitalism are connected to the ownership, creation, and financing of capital assets whose distribution, in turn, has contributed to speculation in financial assets. Credit has become notoriously unstable.

What comprises net worth (or worthlessness) in the casino economy? In the financial system, we are interested in the value of net worth because such institutions are intermediaries for the savings in the economy. Consider the simplest possible balance sheet for the financial industry in which net worth (G_f) is, for the accounting period,

$$G_f = dCR_f + dK_{fh} + dK_{fb} - dDD_f - dCD_f, \qquad (4\text{–}11)$$

where dCR_f is the change in cash reserves, dK_{fh} and dK_{fb} are the changes in the values of loans to households and businesses, respectively, dDD_f is the change in demand deposit liabilities, and dCD_f is the change in value of long-term certificates of deposit. We will assume that most of the loans to the household sector are to keep it housed and most to the business sector are for commercial real estate, whereas long-term CDs are used as the primary source of funds for such mortgages. (Of course, such institutions also play a role in the creation of money to finance stock market purchases.)

The link between this financial industry and the real economy is the value of real estate. During 1983–1988 the appreciation of houses (as well as the building of more luxurious houses) was a major source of household personal savings. (The *increase* in the value of housing had nearly doubled in five years—from \$158.3 billion in 1983 to \$313.1 billion in 1988. The value of new corporate bond issues during this time pales alongside this huge figure.) Apparently expecting real estate to appreciate forever, the financial industry scurried to provide high-cost mortgage money financed from high-yielding CDs. (The S&Ls, of course, also placed heavy reliance on junk bonds.) The increased concentration of wealth or savings during this era is linked to the demand for real estate and the supply of funds for CDs.

Let RE be the value of real estate, K_f be the value of total mortgages held by the financial industry at any point in time (that change at the rate dK_f/dt), and W be the real value of wealth ("real" = deflated by goods prices) of the upper quintile of the distribution. This wealth is created by the dynamics of T and XT. These values are connected in a circular way even though the circle can expand or contract in space. In the simplest model the circles do not intersect, so that

$$[RE(t) - W(t)]^2 + [K_f(t) - W(t)]^2 = [W(t)]^2, \qquad (4-12)$$

a system of curves or circles whose position depends on the value of real wealth (W) at any point in time. The center of the circle is (W, W) and its radius is W. The following constraints define the curves: $0 \leq RE \leq W$, $0 \leq K_f \leq W$, and $RE + K_f \leq W$. As W gets larger, the center of the circle moves away from the origin along a line bisecting the angle between the axes (45° line), and the radius of the circle increases. Imagine tossing different-sized units of gold bullion (W) into a smooth-surfaced lake; the larger the volume of bullion, the greater the circle made from the ripples. (Hopefully, I will not be accused of making a circular argument.)[6]

This simple model says that an increase in real wealth in the upper reaches will increase the potential values of RE and K_f. Because the values of mortgages as financial assets are also colinear with the value of real estate, RE and K_f most likely will follow the 45° line. If the real wealth of the top quintile declines, so too will the value of real estate and mortgages. If much of the real wealth is tied to real estate and the prices of real estate drop, this event can shrink the circle. This happens if real estate prices drop faster than goods prices in the economy. The supply-siders are correct about the importance of relative prices; but it is the relative price of real estate and goods rather than the relative price of leisure that is critical in the Casino Economy.

Now we arrive at the Casino Effect. Although RE and K_f may move together with respect to real wealth, their time path need not be (and has not been) linear. Rather, with respect to time the pattern would be exponential or

$$RE(t) = a_1 e^{k_1 W(t)} \qquad K_f(t) = a_2 e^{k_2 W(t)}, \qquad (4-13)$$

where the *a*'s are positive integers and the *k*'s are positive fractions. The *k*'s, provisionally constant, are velocities at which wealth is trundled into its real estate and mortgage incarnations. The velocities, combined with the exponential nature of the function, give the Casino Effect.

Of course, as real estate values fall, the exponents will become negative. There is not a satisfactory way to model this sudden shift from asset appreciation to asset depreciation except to say that the initial state and conditions have changed. Indeed, the exponential pattern—up or down—did not characterize the era before the late 1960s. Events changed the initial state and conditions beginning at that time. First, income and wealth distributions became much more concentrated during the 1980s. Second, the Carter and Reagan administrations turned dramatically toward the deregulation of the financial industry. Third, the deposit insurance systems and the lender of last resort stance of the Fed—which had provided needed confidence to depositors after the Great Depression—now seemed to take the risk out of overexpansion by the financial industry.

Historically, speculative episodes have been preceded by rapid shifts of wealth toward smaller and smaller numbers. Why does this movement cause speculative bubbles? Why does *T* spin out of control and create larger and larger circles? One reason relates to ability to pay; the household needs wealth in excess of basic needs in order to "afford" to speculate. Moreover, such high-risk finance pays off during economic expansions, especially when there is a wealthier "greater fool" to bid assets still higher. Even generally cautious persons tend to jump onto the bandwagan. (No less a cynic than Thorstein Veblen took an uncharacteristic dive into the stock market during the 1920s but mercifully died a few months before the Great Crash.) Finally, in an environment of cutthroat competition in the financial industry, firms offer higher and higher interest rates to attract funds that in turn must be lent at still higher rates, requiring higher-risk loans. The compounding of the values of these assets and liabilities gives the exponential path.

We call such financial episodes "speculative bubbles" for their tendency to burst. Real estate values have slumped about 20 percent since their peaks in 1988. By historical standards this decline is huge. Just as sharp rises in real estate values relative to goods prices led the parade of high-yielding mortgages, CDs, and junk bonds, the decline in real estate values relative to modest inflation in goods prices has produced nonperforming loans nearly to the point of extinction of the S&L industry and to the point of grave threat to the banking industry. Even the insurance industry is threatened with a possible run, as it has about twice the share of junk-bond assets than was originally reported. Meanwhile, the prolonged recession beginning in July 1990 has led to sharp increases in bankruptcies throughout other industries as sales revenue growth has been insufficient to service heavy, existing debt. (Business failures per week have risen from 900 at the beginning of 1990 to more than 1700 by April 1991.) This contagion has spread to households, which also are filing record numbers of bankruptcies. The values of assets and liabilities in *T* indeed are connected in a nearly unbroken circle. The widening of the circle has now been reversed.

8. Conclusions

Every 40 to 50 years the policies of free enterprise's most devoted disciples bring American capitalism to its knees. The ideology renews itself as soon as the wounded generation has died or slid into a forgetful senility. Capitalism's survival—in newly directed and regulated form—speaks well of its strength. Each time it has survived the best efforts of its friends.

Properly measured, personal money *and* personal real savings soared during the 1980s. The main effect of supply-side "incentives" was to increase the disposable income of the highest-income families and in this way bolster personal savings. The other main source of personal savings is found in the speculative bubble in real estate. The explanation, however, is not Reaganometric but Keynesian.

We arrive at a dichotomy inexplicable in conventional thought: Real business saving and investment slumped. The dichotomy is explained by the Kaleckian-Keynesian tendencies within the economy. It takes rising sales from households having high average and marginal propensities to consume in order to motivate more investment, even as they provide internal funds to leverage debt that becomes *real* investment. During the 1980s retained earnings were damaged by income and wealth redistributions that shunted luxury spending toward foreign nations, by skyrocketing debt service costs, and by real investment's displacement by massive federal borrowing. Only when business is making real investments does personal saving become real saving.

With the slowdown in real net business investment, high levels of personal savings were diverted into the Casino Economy, creating speculative bubbles that have been exploding with an eerie regularity since October 1987. The American economy has shifted its focus from using money to produce goods to using money for speculative profits. Shifting tax policy to favor highest-income savers is part of the problem, not the solution. In fact, the use of public policy to encourage personal saving is based on mistaken notions regarding the true incentives for business investment.

For the first time since the Great Depression, the economy is in a downturn that has financial causes. Financial fragility has led to failing S&Ls, banks, and insurance companies. Thus far, the government has decided that it must rescue those financial institutions "too large to fail." However, the public is increasingly aware of their contingent liabilities in these bailouts. We know that the loans made by the U.S. Treasury will someday have to be paid. This awareness is coming at a time when state and local governments (having inherited the social welfare role partly abdicated by the Reagan administration) are raising taxes for mandated budget balancing. If taxpayers revolt against these continued bailouts, the failing institutions will become "too big to save."

The growing tax burden for the average household is coming at the worst of times. The 1990 recession is not an ordinary downturn. There is a danger that a rising tax burden and shrinking liquidity in an increasingly risky business environment could keep our economy in a troubled state for many years. That would be the most tragic legacy of Reaganomics. It made the rich so much richer that their speculative excesses have led to demands for their rescue. If we have so little compassion for the working poor, how can we find it in our hearts to bail out the bondholders?

Notes

1. Quoted by William Greider, "The Education of David Stockman," *Atlantic Monthly*, December 1981, p. 46. Stockman's confessions had been made to journalist-friend Greider.
2. Ibid., p. 47.
3. Fred Block, "Bad Data Drive Out Good: The Decline of Personal Savings Reexamined," *Journal of Post Keynesian Economics* 13, no. 1 (Fall 1990): 3–19. Robert Blecker also favors the use of the Federal Reserve's measure of net worth. See Robert Blecker, *Are Americans On a Consumption Binge*? (Washington, D.C.: Economic Policy Institute, 1990).
4. In this section I am following the lead—in spirit if not in detail—of Boulding (1950, pp. 243–302). Using a net worth approach, Boulding was able to integrate the income distribution into macroeconomic theory. Unfortunately, as he latter became aware, he made several errors. In this account I have attempted to correct those mistakes as well as introduce additional variables. Moreover, I express values in money rather than in real terms, whereas Boulding is using the traditional definitions of real saving and investment. In Boulding's update of his theory of distribution, he corrects his 1950 effort. See Kenneth Boulding, "Puzzles Over Distribution," *Challenge* (November/December 1985): 4–10.
5. Kenneth Boulding correctly disclosed this relationship even though he made some missteps along the way in Kenneth Boulding, *A Reconstruction of Economics* (New York: John Wiley, 1950), pp. 255–258.

6. There are other candidate equations, the most promising of which relate to the wave equation. Poisson developed a formula for the propagation of a wave with specified initial conditions that satisfied a second-order partial differential equation. A quite different method was used by Riemann in the course of his work on the propagation of sound waves of finite amplitude. Riemann considers a second-order linear differential equation that defines a curve and space. His method depends on finding a Riemann or characteristic function that satisfies an adjoint equation. The Reimann method is useful only for hyperbolic equations in two independent variables. Later the Helmholtz equation was used to represent all harmonic, acoustic, elastic, and electromagnetic waves. The work of Helmholtz was used by Kirchhoff to obtain another solution of the initial-value problem for the wave equation. These equations have since been generalized.

Chapter 39

Boulding's T, Kaleckian Power, and Minsky's Fragility Hypothesis

E. Ray Canterbery

In his classic *A Reconstruction of Economics* [1950], Kenneth Boulding goes a long way toward revising the theory of the firm, the concept of consumption, and the macroeconomic theory of distribution. It is a pity that his deepest insights encountered quantum resistance from the mainstream. In this paper, I hope to summarize the most enduring (by my judgment) of the reconstruction as well as suggest some extensions.

My focus will be upon Boulding's effort to construct a "classical" type of macroeconomic distribution theory. I will force all else through this funnel of vision. In his rejection of Walrasian equilibrium, Boulding distinguishes between the exchange process on the one hand, by which existing assets, including money, are circulated among various owners, and the processes of production, consumption, income and outgo on the other, by which assets are created, destroyed, and accumulated. As he says, marginalism treats the firm as if it has nothing but an income account. It has no balance sheet, no funding problems, and no dynamics. The firm maximizes a strange variable called "net revenue," of which no accountant has ever heard.

Boulding, therefore, uses the balance sheet as the central analytical concept of the theory of the firm and introduces asset preferences, which hitherto had been confined almost exclusively

---

The author is Professor of Economics at Florida State University. *The author thanks L. Randall Wray for helpful comments while holding him blameless for what might have gone wrong.*

to banking theory. Boulding's unique contribution is to show how the personal income distribution, effected by a potentially volatile financial transfers item (T), is a determinant of output (and, by extension, employment). Indeed, Boulding's T is a potential source of financial fragility. I proceed to integrate Boulding's income distribution theory with Kalecki's quantitative notion of economic power. Finally, I draw a connection between Minsky's financial fragility hypothesis and Boulding's T via Kalecki. As I will contend, this cluster of ideas–which brings together production and money–sheds considerable light on the leveraged nature of a "casino economy."[1]

The Macroeconomic Income Distribution Identities

Summary

The balance sheet is central. Profit-making is related to the gross growth in the value of net worth. The separate summations of business and household balance sheets provide identities for gross profits (non-labor income) and for the wage bill, the component parts of which are in some degree parameters of behavior and which can therefore be used to construct macroeconomic models.

The distribution of national income between wages and gross profits is determined by several related sets of decisions. Gross profits are greater the more business adds to its stocks of capital (investment decisions), the more it finances investment out of profits, the more it distributes interest, rent, and dividends, the more consumer credit it extends (finance decisions), and the more the money stock shifts out of household into business accounts (liquidity decisions). The more the money stock shifts out of business into household accounts, the less the increases in consumer credit and sales of securities to households, the less will be the distributions to capitalists in rent, interest, and dividends.

The conclusion is heretical. Investment, consumption, finance, and liquidity decisions decide the distribution of income rather than wage bargaining (except in so far as such bargains react on these decisions). Whereas Walrasian theory sees payments to capitalists as one side of an equal exchange, Boulding has financial transfers by the firm returning through its front door. Being one-way transfers does not mean that they are grants, as defined later in Boulding's "grants economy." In *Reconstruction*, the financial transfers by business firms to households boomerang to the advantage of the bottom line.

Business and Household Net Worth

The aggregate net worth of businesses is equal to their money holdings (M_b), plus their value of goods holdings (Q_b), plus the net household indebtedness to business (K_h - K_h'), where K_h is total debts due to businesses from households and K_h' is the total debts due from businesses to households. The latter consist mostly of the bonds of businesses held by households. From these variables, Boulding derives the business-net-worth identity, which can be expressed as the differential equation

$$dG_b = dM_b + dQ_b + dK_h - dK_h' = S_b \qquad (1)$$

in which the d's are accounting period time derivatives.

The quantity dG_b is that part of profits not distributed in dividends and can be called business saving if positive–dissavings if negative. Business saving (S_b), therefore, is generally not determined by the decisions of businesses to save, but rather result from other decisions that determine business savings such as the effort of individual firms to increase their net worth–through an increase in money holdings (dM_b), an increase in the value of durable goods (dQ_b), an increase in business credit extended to households (dK_h), or a decrease in bonds issued to households (dK_h'). As we will see, business decisions to save, reflected in dividends, determine not business savings but the level of profits.

Thus, if V is the aggregate profits of business, it must equal business savings plus business distributions in interest and dividends. Total profit is the gross increase in net worth, out of which interest and dividends are paid. Thus,

$$V = dG_b + D, \qquad (2)$$

where D represents aggregate distributions in interest and dividends. Business savings is

$$dG_b = V - D \tag{3}$$

Imagine that dG_b has already been decided by the variables of Equation 1–the increase in money and goods holdings plus net credit extended to households. The aggregate distributions are mostly governed by dividend declarations since interest payments are based mostly on past contractual obligations. If dG_b is independent of such distributions (as stated in Equation 1), business payments of interest and dividends comprise a "widow's cruse" whereby the greater the business interest and dividend distributions (Equation 2), the more will be returned to business in profits to distribute. Profits leap from one pocket into another on the same pair of pants, and business wears the pants. An increase in dividends by one firm will swell the profits of other firms.

There is a second way of explaining this apparent paradox. Once saving (dG_b) is decided by elements unrelated to the saving decision, the savings part of aggregate profits has been predetermined. If, in turn, the business sector decides to reduce its savings, it can only do so by increasing its dividends. This increase in dividends–which does not alter the original savings level at all–is added to saving and enlarges gross aggregate profits.

Substituting the RHS of Equation 1 for dG_b in Equation 2, gross aggregate business profits are

$$V = dQ_b + (dM_b + dK_h - dK_h' + D) \tag{4}$$

All items on the RHS, except for dQ_b, are "transfer items" or T. I will have more to say about T later.

Since the K's are assets in one balance sheet and liabilities in the other, and since all the net worth of businesses must ultimately be allocated to households, there is a comparable household identity for wages. In turn, household saving can be found by differentiating that sector's net worth identity, and

$$dG_h = dM_h + dM_b + dQ_h + dQ_b - (dK_h - dK_h') = S_h. \tag{5}$$

In turn, according to Boulding [1950, 248], "the values of all *titles* to property cancel out when we add up all balance sheets, and we are left with the identity that the net worth of households is equal to the 'value' of all 'real' property, including money." Thus, the change in household net worth is reduced to,

$$dG_h = dM_h + dM_b + dQ_h + dQ_b = S_h, \tag{6}$$

so that household saving is equal to the changes in the total quantity of money in the system plus the changes in the total value of the stock of real assets (goods) in the system.

When Boulding assumes a given national money supply, any increase in money holdings of business (dM_b) is a decrease in money holdings of households ($-dM_h$), and Equation 6 is simplified to

$$dG_h = dQ_b + dQ_h. \tag{7}$$

Aggregate saving, all of which ultimately resides in households, equals the increase in aggregate real capital. Later, he suggests that "relaxing this assumption does not make much difference to the argument" [Boulding 1950, 253]. This I doubt. Since there is a net accumulation of goods during the accounting period, Boulding must be assuming (though he is silent on this) that the net increase in output is financed by expanding credit (with no increase in endogenous money) or by an increase in the income velocity of money.

Obviously, household saving also equals household income less household consumption where income is the gross addition to households' net worth. It consists of wages earned (W), dividends paid (D), and business savings (dG_b) that accrue ultimately to households. Given household consumption (C_h), we can write:

$$dG_h = (W + D + dG_b) - C_h. \tag{8}$$

Taking the value of dG_b from the RHS of Equation 1 and of dG_h or $dQ_h + dQ_b$ (the total accumulation of durables and materials) from Equation 7, we have

$$W = C_h + dQ_h - (dM_b + dK_h - dK_h' + D). \tag{9}$$

The same financial transfers item $(dM_b + dK_h - dK_h' + D) = T$ appears in aggregate profits (Equation 4) and aggregate wages. Thus, we can write

$$W = C_h + dQ_h - T, \text{ and} \tag{10}$$

$$V = dQ_b + T. \quad (11)$$

We can think of the "transfer" as being from wages to profits with no necessary quid pro quo in goods.

Net Domestic Product and the Transfer Item

Aggregate wages and profits exhaust aggregate output so that net domestic product or income is

$$Y = W + V = C_h + dQ_h + dQ_b. \quad (12)$$

GDP, of course, would include depreciation, which is not distributed and is not a part of national income (Y).

Paradoxes abound and enliven *Reconstruction*. In particular, paradoxes populate Boulding's unique contribution, the "transfer item," or transfer of wages to profit (T). The first term in this transfer (dM_b) is the net transfer of money from households to businesses that reflects the relative liquidity preferences of households and businesses (measured by the velocity of money).

The second transfer term (dK_h) is the change in consumer credit. Such credit, which would include credit cards and installment credit, can shift the income distribution from labor to favor profits. Whereas an increased use of credit by a particular household can enhance its standard of living, all households doing the same thing will reduce the income/product share of labor. Could this perhaps help to explain why–at the end of the consumer-credit-fueled economic expansion of the 1980s–the income distribution had shifted in favor of the rich?

The third transfer is the increase in business indebtedness to households ($-dK_h'$), mostly comprised of corporate bonds. It is given a negative sign so that the greater the volume of securities sold to households, the more income is redistributed toward wages and away from profits. This generates still another paradox: Since the sale of bonds reduces the profits share in expectation of which the securities are offered, the purchase of bonds (usually by the upper class) benefits a particular investor to the detriment of his own class. This attraction to bonds is not fatal, because undistributed profits can be used to increase the level of business investment.

The fourth transfer is business dividends and interest payments (D). It is the source of still another paradox, the aforementioned "widow's cruse." Since business saving has been determined by other forces, each dollar increase in D swells aggregate profits a dollar. Boulding concludes that dividend policy does not affect consumption patterns, except as these are affected by the liquidity of the shareholder [Boulding 1950, 257].

Thus far, Boulding has assumed that the central bank and private banks are not creating any new money nor is the federal government issuing new debt. Later, he relaxes these assumptions. When one does [Canterbery 1993, 168], the RHS of Equation 12 becomes

$$Y = C_h + dQ_h + dQ_b + (dM_h + dM_b + dB_h + dB_b), \quad (13)$$

where dB_b comprise changes in the value of government bond holdings. As Canterbery [1993, 168] concludes, once these dynamic elements are introduced, some of the components of T reappear in the nominal national income. Now the nominal national income can increase as a direct result of credit and money creation. An increase in *real* national income is by no means guaranteed because real investment may not increase.

So far, so good. The income distribution results are similar to those of Michal Kalecki [see, e.g., Davidson 1960, chap. 5]. In particular, the "widow's cruse" is essential Kalecki. Even though these equations provide remarkable insights, an economist could easily raise the objection that they nonetheless are mathematical identities and not functions. However, Boulding does go on to develop two distributional models with functional relations.

Income Distribution Models with the Transfer Item

Distributional Model I

Boulding shows how his identities provide a foundation for a large number of macroeconomic models of comparative state equilibrium and even of dynamics. He presents two models. Model I is driven by the functions in which the more common symbols C, I, and Y are used. Household consumption (or C), however, is the sum ($C_h + dQ_h$). Consumption is a function of the wage share of output (W/Y), and business investment is a function of the profits share (V/Y). Boulding's T is viewed in two ways: One T divides profits from wages with T independent of the distributional shares and its components given; and a second T is a function of the profits share. If T is given, we have seven independent equations and seven unknowns: If T is variable, the model is overdetermined. In the latter case, we can write the consumption, investment, and transfer functions as:

$$\begin{aligned} C &= C(W/Y) \\ I &= I(V/Y) \\ T &= T(V/Y) \end{aligned} \qquad (14)$$

Then, the identities of composition are:

$$\begin{aligned} Y &= C + I \\ Y &= W + V \\ W &= C - T \\ V &= I + T \end{aligned} \qquad (15)$$

Consumption is a positive function of the wage share, and investment is a positive function of the profits share. Profits and wages also are determined by the levels of consumption and investment adjusted by transfers.

Boulding [1950, 259] provides only a geometrical "solution" for this model. A simplified version of his geometry appears as Figure 1: it reveals a remarkable intuition. Along the base O_wO_v is measured the proportionate distribution between wages and gross profits; at O_w all the product goes to wages, and at O_v all of the product goes to gross profits. Consumption, or CC, falls with the wages share, and investment, or II, rises with the profits share. Total output, or YY, initially rises as the profits share grows but peaks at Y_x, the distributional equilibrium (which may or may not be at full employment).

Vertical, parallel lines divide the distribution of total output into deciles. The loci of T's (at given values of the financial components of T) comprise what I call a factor-payments transfer curve, a curve that divides the total output into wages (the upper portion) and profit (the lower portion) at each level of distribution. At any distribution, $T = V - I = C - W$. For example, distribution O_2 represents 20 percent profits and 80 percent wages; I_2T_2 then is total profits and T_2C_2 total wages, and O_2T_2 is the equilibrium factor-payments transfer.

Now, we introduce a variable financial transfer function or $T(V/Y) = dM_b + dK_h - dK_h' + D$, wherein all components vary with V/Y. In order to identify it separately from the aforementioned factor-payments transfer curve of T's, the financial transfer item curve is RR. The changes in money holdings of business and the changes in debts due business from households is assumed not to be much affected by the wage-profits distribution. The third item, the change in debts due from businesses to households, will be closely related to the volume of investment: At the extreme, where all investment is financed by the sale of securities to households, $dK_h' = I$. The fourth item, D, is likely to be related to profits because the higher go profits, the higher will distributions be. If all profits are distributed, V = D. At the extreme, where all investment is debt-financed, not only does V = D, but $dK_h' = I$ and $dM_b + dK_h = 0$, the equation of the R-curve becomes identical to the T-curve (i.e., R = V - I = T), and the solution is indeterminate. Once gross profits exceed contractual distributions, both D and dK_h' are likely to rise. With T positive, gross profits are greater than business investment, and D is likely to rise faster than dK_h'; then, the R-curve is likely to slope upwards. (The reverse is the case, however, if there is a strong tendency to finance investment by issuing new securities, as with the corporate debt explosion during the 1980s.)

We arrive now at Boulding's incredibly prophetic intuitive insight. First, he notes, "if the slopes of the T-curve and the R-curve are similar the equilibrium, if it exists, will be highly insecure and 'shiftable'; i.e. a slight change in the underlying functions will cause a large shift in the equilibrium position or will even destroy the possibilities of equilibrium altogether" [1950, 262]. If the R-curve lies wholly above the T-curve, there will be a constant tendency to increase the profit share until the economy breaks down. Or, if the R-curve lies wholly below the T-curve, there will be a constant tendency for the wages share to increase. "The possibility," he concludes, "of a shift from a stable equilibrium to an apparently chaotic state of perpetual disequilibrium . . . has some basis in experience" [1950, 362]. He goes on to cite 1929 and the distributional shift toward wages and away from profits and the accompanying unemployment. This, he suggests, could have been caused by a shift in the investment function, say, to I'I' in Figure 1 (reducing investment) and the consequent shift in the T-curve to I'C (increasing the wage share).

Figure 1. Distribution Model I

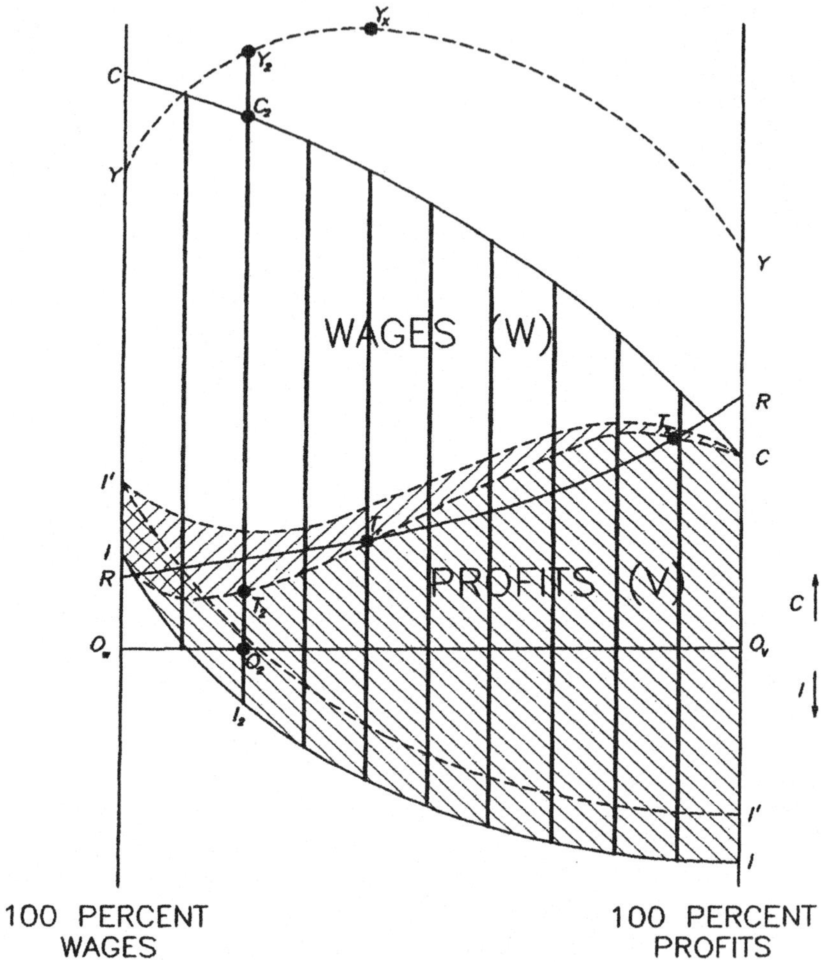

Although Boulding no doubt did not realize it, his analysis of both the relative slopes of the T- and R-curves and their separation precluding their intersection is a classic example of the use of chaos theory! The curves are S-curves that, at best, intersect more than once (multiple equilibria). In fact, in his geometry, there is only one stable equilibrium point; it rests at T_r. There exist unstable extrema at I and C, whereas T_x is an unstable equilibrium.

Distributional Model II

In Boulding's distributional model II, variables are expressed in absolute terms. These functions can be expressed as

$$C = C(Y) \text{ (consumption function)} \tag{14}$$
$$I = I(V) \text{ (investment function).}$$

The identities are

$$Y = C + I = W + V \text{ (income identity), where, again,} \tag{15}$$
$$W = C - T \text{ (wage identity)}$$
$$V = I + T \text{ (profits identity).}$$

The wage and profit levels will be different at each level of output. In turn, those differences will result in different allocations of the output between households and businesses. The level of investment (I) is a positive function of profits (V), and consumption (C) is a positive function of national income (Y). Income, output, and expenditures are simultaneously determined.

In Figure 2, output is measured along the horizontal axis, whereas the various components of output are measured vertically. The consumption function is given by CC, showing how much will be consumed at each level of output (income). If the transfer factor is independent of output, equal to CW, the wage curve, WW, lies below the CC-curve by the amount of the transfer factor. This is the absolute wage bill at each level of output, when output is at its equilibrium level. At any output $0Y_1$, Y_1C_1 is the amount consumed, and Y_1W_1 is the wage bill. If the 45° line OE_2 intersects Y_1C_1 at L_1, then actual output is Y_1L_1 (= OY_1), and profits will be W_1L_1, actual investment being C_1L_1. (In this case, there is disinvestment.) The investment function is a positive function of profits (as shown in the smaller figure). At a profits level of L_1W_1 or $0V_1$ in the smaller figure, the planned investment will be C_1E_1 (= OI_1, in the smaller figure).

This model has less intuitive appeal than model I. Suppose, Boulding suggests, transfers change so that the income distribution shifts in favor of profits relative to wages. Aggregate planned expenditures rise since consumption now is assumed independent of the wage share. In Boulding's diagrammatic example [1950, 266] and in Figure 2, the fall in wages is somewhat less than the

Figure 2. Distribution Model II

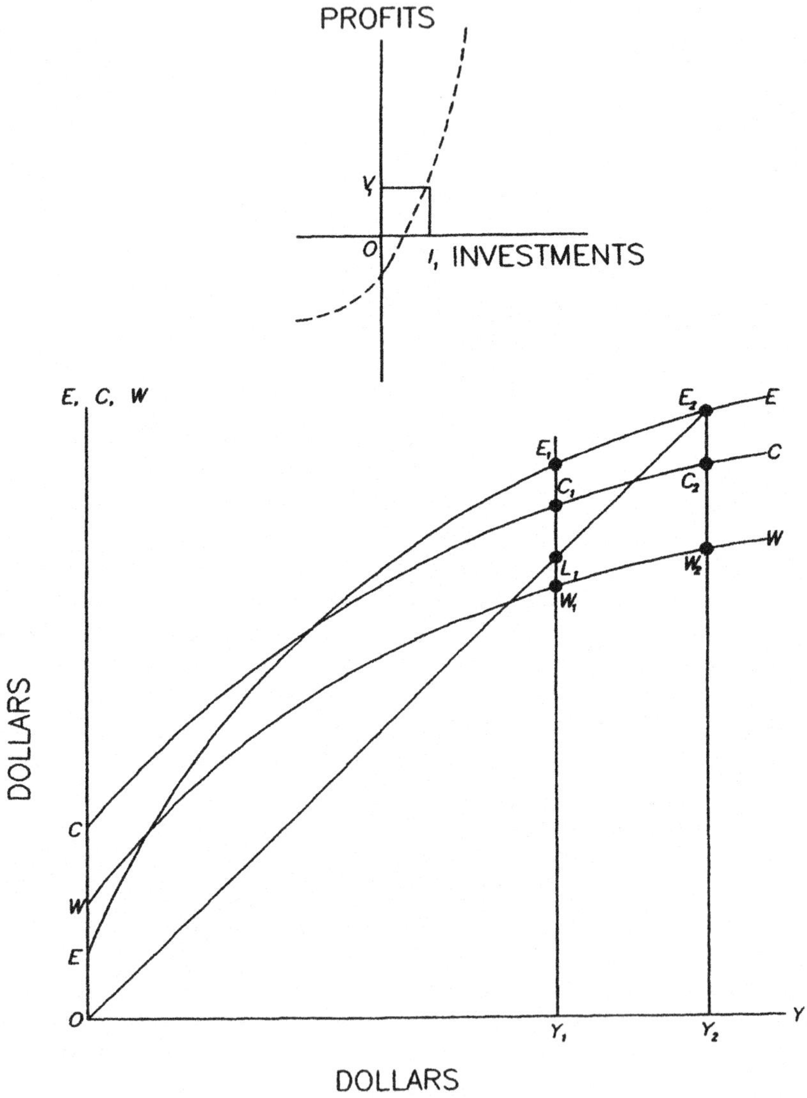

change in the transfers, while the rise in profits is somewhat greater.

Boulding separates the effect of the shift from profits to wages into a "transfer effect" plus an "income effect." The transfer effect simply is the amount of the transfer being added to total profits and subtracted from total wages. The income effect is the rise in national income due to the shift being divided between wages and profits, softening the fall in wages while hardening the rise in profits. The share of this division depends on the relative slopes of the consumption and investment functions. The steeper is the consumption function, the greater the increase in income that will accrue to wages. If consumption is reduced by the shift of wages to profits, as well it might be, this counters the output-increasing effects of a shift from wages to profits. If this effect is sufficiently large, there may be net output-decreasing effects, as in model I (to the right of Y_x).

Suppose, says Boulding, consumption rises exogenously. With no change in transfers or the relation of investment to profits, the wage curve will rise by the same amount as the consumption curve. At each output level, profits will suffer relative to wages; this is because the composition of output determines its distribution as in the identity $W = C - T$. Kalecki is clearer on this in his more complex model: A rise in the wage bill in the consumption sector has no effect on absolute profits, but it will reduce the share of a larger national income going to profits. Only if the wage bill in the investment sector rises would profits and the profit share rise. (Although he does not say it, Boulding implicitly may be assuming that the bulk of wages are paid in the consumer products sector.)

Even so, it is difficult to understand how this model generates an equilibrium output and income level. If transfers vary with business investment and with dividends that, in turn, vary with profits, where would output and income settle? Boulding says as much when he concludes that "the dynamics of all these models is likely to be complicated by the dynamic instability of the transfer factor, and even of the consumption and investment functions themselves" [1950, 269]. The modeling of this instability goes beyond the mathematics used by Boulding.[2]

Supra-surplus Capitalism and Kaleckian Power

Going Beyond Boulding

Boulding appears correct in arguing that transfers and thus the financial system can alter the income distribution and the level of national income. Increases in consumer credit, decreases in corporate bond sales to households, and an increase in dividends because of a more liquid business sector will reduce the absolute level of wages. The use of profits as the growth in net worth and the introduction of financial variables at the firm level are a fruitful means to model this interrelationship between household and business expenditures and the distribution of income between profits and wages. It has the merit of taking distribution theory out of the world of marginalism whereby factors, rather than people, receive income. At even the microeconomic level, the refinement of classical economics threw out the Ricardian baby with J. B. Say's bathwater. I would suggest nonetheless that the notion of subsistence household expenditure be resurrected as the complement of subsistence wages, leaving a discretionary wage increment that determines discretionary spending.

Classical subsistence income and neoclassical discretionary income coexist in surplus capitalism. Production surpluses are created when net output exceeds biological necessities and depreciation on replacement capital. In what I [1984, 1987a, 1987b, 1995] have dubbed "supra-surplus capitalism," production surpluses are so great that producers and governments must spend great resources in order to massage the interests and demand of the middle class (and beyond) to absorb supra-net-output. When private demands nonetheless falter, federal budget deficits financed by the Central Bank and depreciation of the international value of the currency prop up supra-surplus capitalism.

An excess of income above physiological subsistence leaves a demand wedge that provides breathing space for producers. Imperfect competition abhors wedges and sets into motion forces to fill the space. The price markup tool accomplishes the task. Within the wedge the price elasticity of demand, in part, can be manipulated by producers.[3] At this juncture we can return to Kalecki.

Kaleckian Power and the Lerner Index

Earlier I mentioned the similarity of Boulding's distributional identities and those of Kalecki. In the simplest version of Kalecki, the general income and product identities are the same as Boulding's. However, Kalecki's definition of profits, in Boulding's terms, is

$$V = dQ_b = I \tag{16}$$

Kalecki does not have a transfer item that includes the other forms in which business savings are held. However, Kalecki's idea of the degree of monopoly is something with which the later Boulding probably could agree–the Boulding of the integrative system [1978]. With only slight amendments or liberties taken, we can fit Kalecki's notion of power into the income distribution model. Moreover, this formulation provides an initial value of profits (V).

Kalecki also begins at the firm level in which price exceeds marginal cost by the unit values of capitalist income and overhead. By a standard formula of price theory, the difference between price and marginal cost can be expressed in elasticity terms so that:

$$(p - mc)/p = 1/n = u. \tag{17}$$

The small letters refer to the firm in which n is price elasticity of demand expressed as positive, and u is the degree of monopoly power or Lerner's index of monopoly power [1934]. Since a markup on average cost can be used to generate the capitalist's income and overhead profits, the equivalent markup version of Equation 17 is

$$p - ac = p/n = pu = \text{unit markup}, \tag{18}$$

where ac or average cost is substituted for marginal cost.

We can redefine pu as Boulding unit profits since the transfer item includes forms in which profits are distributed or held. Consider a perfectly competitive firm facing an infinite price elasticity: The ratio p/n becomes zero, p = ac = mc, and the firm has zero power to raise price. A firm facing a very low elasticity would have a high degree of such power. In a dynamic model, the producer would use marketing tools to differentiate a product or service–making it seem unique–in order to reduce the price elasticity of demand and increase its power over price.

At the macroeconomics level, let **U** be a unit markup vector for the entire economy [a column vector of all (p - ac)'s], and let **Q'** be a row vector of the related outputs. Then,

$$V = \mathbf{Q'U}, \tag{19}$$

and,

$$\mathbf{Q'UY^{-1}} = \mathbf{VY^{-1}}, \tag{20}$$

where, given **Q'**, the larger the elements in **U**, the greater the power of firms generally to increase the aggregate profits share or VY^{-1}. It is easy to show how **Q'** can be determined in an input-output model [Canterbery 1988; 1994] in which average cost and demand also are determined.

Profits as a share of the national product or income is a macroeconomic version of the Kalecki-Lerner measure of the degree of monopoly power, all of which reverts back to the price elasticities of demand. The $\mathbf{Q'UY^{-1}} = \mathbf{VY^{-1}}$ relationship holds because the percentage markup (from the degree of monopoly power) determines the initial profit level. Given the initial level of profits, Boulding's T would further influence the distribution between profits and wages. In this way, the role of market power can be brought under Boulding's umbrella.

Kalecki has business investment as a function of profits and profits as a function of investment (the causality running both ways). But ultimately because firms can decide how much to spend but not how much to earn, investment determines profits. In Boulding's model I, the causality also appears to run both ways. American data for the post-World War II era do show that profits and investments are closely related, but investment lags two years behind profits; that is, the real world relationship between profits and investment does not appear to be simultaneous.

The Transfer Item, Minsky, and Financial Fragility

Surprisingly, there is an unbroken lineage among Kalecki, Boulding, and Hyman Minsky. This genealogy can tell us more about Boulding's T. Minsky [1982] begins with Kalecki's accounting and accepts the Kaleckian markup. In Minsky's elaboration, however, the internal funds so generated by the firm are levered by debt to finance the acquisition of additional capital assets. In the aggregate, investment requires external financing. Thus, investment requires the issuance of bonds, which do appear in Boulding's T. Investment is financed by both internal (Kalecki) and external (Minsky-Boulding) funds.

The income distribution still plays a dominant role because Minsky sees household consumption depending upon household incomes, which includes, for the higher-income households, interest and dividend income from lending to business. The income constraint for the firm is provided by retained earnings and the amount financed by debt (loans from households). If, in the aggregate, the external funding needs of business exceed the household saving made available to finance investment, the shortfall will have to be met by some combination of an increase in the money supply and a decrease in households' money holdings (that is, by an increase in the velocity of money). Since the money supply is endogenous, private banks respond by providing finance and altering the money supply. This fits Boulding to a T!

As I suggest above, the components of T are unstable and lead to a dynamic indeterminacy in Boulding's model that may reflect the real world *and* Minsky's idea of financial fragility. Rising wage costs during an economic expansion at a constant markup elevate production costs. Since the amount of markup is not unlimited (price elasticity of demand for products at the firm level is not zero), only a generalized inflation can assure full employment. In this process, a rising share of investment is financed by debt. Bankers and businessmen go along with the rising ratio of debt to internal financing so long as they are reasonably convinced that inflation will continue.

Any slowdown in wages does not alter contractual debt commitments so that the burden of debt rises during disinflation or deflation. Debt-financed investment decreases, and purchases of investment goods financed by money supply increments decline. Business firms will begin to pay off debt instead of buying new plant and equipment. Employment falls with the decline in use of the existing capital stock.

A liquidity crisis ensues if the central bank attempts to reduce outstanding debt. Financial panics, such as stock market crashes, may occur as finance becomes more and more fragile. I would note that during the fourth quarter of 1989, the ratio of debt servicing by U.S. corporations to declining profits was about 60 percent. In Boulding's T, this heavy debt burden would have to be reflected as an increased sale of bonds, as indeed it was. An economic recession in this debt environment could lead to financial panic with devastating consequences for changes in net worth of U.S. corporations.

Recently there have been many opportunities for panic. The stock market crashed in 1987. The savings and loan industry began its monumental collapse in 1988. Many giant banks have failed since the 1970s. Giant insurance companies have been failing. Thus far, why haven't we seen a debacle like 1929-1933? Minsky [1985, 17] has provided the answer: the Federal Reserve has served as lender of last resort, as it did when it declared that liabilities of giant banks have a special, protected position in the United States (the Continental Illinois case). Of course, in the unique case of the failed S&Ls, we had a taxpayer bailout. Moreover, a chaos-like collapse of that industry and of the stock market *did* happen. A model of the private sector that provides a vision of dynamic instability is hardly beside the point. We still do not know what would happen if taxpayers refuse to bail-out banks "too large to save" or what would happen if the Federal Reserve and the Treasury end up with all the Treasury securities now outstanding.

Concluding Remarks

Why has the mainstream ignored Boulding's macroeconomic contributions? First, I offer what might be called "excuses." Boulding's theory is very complex. Moreover, his notation and his mathematics are not always clear. He does not help his cause when he uses phrases such as "the value of real capital," and he makes it difficult to make some distinctions such as that between what I have called the factor-payments transfer function and the financial transfer function. Boulding himself seemed to throw up his hands in his later *Economic Analysis*, a book that fails to mention either the effects of the distribution of income on the macroeconomy or the transfer item. Finally, Boulding's notation and awkward mathematics were faced with a new standard for the use of mathematics in economics set by Samuelson [1947], who made the mathematics of neoclassical optimization virtually unassailable.

Why are these "excuses"? Neoclassical economics has been polished by nitpickers for more than two centuries. Mainstream economists have not rejected a single intuitive neoclassical idea befitting the paradigm, going back to the earliest marginalist genes, no matter how inelegant the mathematics. No less than a John Maynard Keynes rejected only Say's law (which has experienced a revival worthy of "olde tyme" tent meetings) while committing mathematical hari-kari with his own theory of insufficient aggregate demand. Mainstream economists have not bothered to polish Boulding for the more fundamental reasons rooted in their commitment to the neoclassical paradigm.

In this perspective, the neoclassicals can find much to ignore. The mainstream does not like models that collapse, because of the dangerous inference that private market capitalism invites collapse in the absence of reforms. The mainstream does not like indeterminacy because it violates the fundamental premises of maximization (Samuelson's [1947] powerful influence again). The mainstream does not like the idea of a "microeconomic" phenomenon such as the distribution of personal income affecting the macroeconomy. If the income distribution is related to macroeconomics, the marginal revenue product explanation is lost and so too the closing of the marginalist system of markets. Moreover, a personal income distribution suggests that there may be income classes: the economist even hinting at such unmentionables can be branded a "Marxist." Finally, the implication that financial transfers can actually alter the income distribution means that, in part, the income distribution is not driven entirely by "pure" economic forces, and Michael Milken was not receiving simply his marginal revenue product.

The complete modeling of a merger of Boulding's T, Kalecki's degree of monopoly power, and Minsky's hypothesis is difficult but no doubt possible. I will stop at this point, a juncture at which I can imagine, at least, that I am ahead.[4]

Boulding's warning about the instability of T perhaps was 40 years too soon. As John Kenneth Galbraith has advised younger economists, for the sake of reputation it is best not to jump to the front of the parade until it is in front of your door. But, I suspect, if Ken Boulding had had 1950 to do again, he would still have preferred to be in the vanguard. Boulding was a genius beyond and above economics. He also was the reliable Quaker among those heading the parade for world peace; that he seemed always to be at peace with himself helped immensely in all these endeavors against the stream.

Notes

1. Canterbery [1987a, 1995] defined the "casino economy," although other writers either before or after have coined the term "casino capitalism."
2. In a later publication, Boulding [1985] seems aware of some of these problems and makes some corrections.
3. Canterbery [1984, 1987a, 1987b, 1995] has described this process.
4. Actually, I did not stop but only paused at this point. Since writing the first draft of this paper for a conference in honor of Boulding, I was inspired by his T and by Minsky's hypothesis to attempt more exact modeling [1993]. A still more mathematical version of the "casino multiplier" [1995] awaits publication. The great difficulty of modeling a dynamic T, even with today's tools, causes one to admire Boulding's pioneering effort even more.

References

Boulding, Kenneth E. "Puzzles Over Distribution." *Challenge* 28, no. 5 (November/December 1985).

________. *Economic Analysis*, 4th ed., vols. 1 and 2. New York: Harper & Row, 1966.

________. *Economics: A New Theory of Societal Evolution*. Beverly Hills, Calif.: Sage Publications, 1978.

________. *A Reconstruction of Economics*. New York: John Wiley & Sons, Inc., 1950.

Canterbery, E. Ray. "Galbraith, Sraffa, Kalecki and Supra-Surplus Capitalism." *Journal of Post Keynesian Economics* 7 (Fall 1984).

________. "The Theory of Supra-surplus Capitalism." *Eastern Economic Journal* 13 (October/November 1987a).

________. *The Making of Economics*, 3rd ed. Belmont: Wadsworth, 1987b.

_______. "Dynamics of Economic Growth." Paper given at Kaldor Conference, Hungarian Academy of Sciences, Budapest, September 3, 1988.

_______. "Reaganomics, Saving, and the Casino Effect." *The Economics of Saving*, edited by James Gapinski. Boston: Kluwer Acadamic Publishers, 1993.

_______. "A General Theory of International Trade and Domestic Employment Adjustments." *International Trade: Regional and Global Issues*, edited by M. Landeck. New York: St. Martin's Press, 1994.

_______. *The Literate Economist*. New York: HarperCollins, 1995.

_______. "Chaos Theory and the Casino Economy Multiplier." 1995.

Davidson, Paul. *Theories of Aggregate Income Distribution*. New Brunswick: Rutgers University Press, 1960.

Lerner, Abba P. "The Concept of Monopoly and Measurement of Monopoly Power." *Review of Economic Studies* (June 1934).

Minsky, Hyman P. *John Maynard Keynes*. New York: Columbia University Press, 1976.

_______. "Money and the Lender of Last Resort." *Challenge* (March/April 1985).

Chapter 40

The Theory of the Bondholding Class

E. Ray Canterbery

It is oft repeated that the world changed on September 11, 2001. Some things nonetheless remain the same. Alan Greenspan remains head of the Federal Reserve. Back in summer 1998 he had a revelation: "The current economic performance . . . is as impressive as any I have witnessed . . . It is possible we have moved beyond history."[1] The "end of history" refers to the presumably permanent dominance of US free market capitalism in the world community. Apparently Greenspan believed that the end of history would be a happy ending for the American story of the twentieth century.

By summer 1999, however, Alan Greenspan began to sense an inflationary breeze in goods prices. In June he raised the federal funds rate. Even though goods prices had been remarkably stable, Greenspan was to raise the fed funds rate six times. By the end of the century his policies had set in motion recessionary forces, and it was not the first time. In the past twenty-five years workers have seen no improvement in their overall living standards and their insecurity remains high. Meanwhile, income and wealth inequalities *have* "moved beyond history."

The Origins of the Bondholding Class

The bondholding class evolved and continues to thrive in an environment shaped for its own convenience. Its few families own not only virtually all bonds held by households but most of the value of stocks and other marketable assets. It is an elite of super- or supra-rich families, its small population strengthened by some investment bankers and security dealers on Wall Street. This new American leisure class consists of families whose yearly incomes begin at around $200,000 and go up into the tens of millions and billions of dollars (in 1992 dollars). The families number only about 1.1 million, but

---

The author is Professor of Economics at Florida State University, Tallahassee, USA. This paper was presented at the annual meeting of the Association for Evolutionary Economics, Atlanta, Georgia, USA, January 4–6, 2002.

their average wealth now is around $10.0 million. Its support group comprises a small number of professionals on Wall Street, the US Treasury, and the Federal Reserve System.[2] The bondholding class even has its own editorial page—that of the *Wall Street Journal*.

The ideology decreeing evolutionary fitness to the bondholding class emanates from Wall Street. It consists of four central ideas. First, inflation or even rapid economic growth is bad for bondholders (bad also for stockholders, but only because it initially is bad for bondholders). Second, the sole cause of inflation is an excessively fast growth rate in the money supply. Third, federal budget deficits are inflationary if fed by rapid growth in the money supply and otherwise evil because they are the by-product of the redistribution of income and wealth from the rich to the poor. Welfare payments to the poor make them lazy whereas the rich do not have *enough wealth* to keep them from sloth. Fourth, household savings, the main source of real investment and essential capital accumulation in the economy, will "trickle down" from the rich to the working class and the poor, assuring full employment. Moreover, when inflation turns from illusion to reality, the failure of enough people to volunteer for the Reserve's army of the unemployed is unacceptable.

If it is to serve the class, a *Wall Street ideology* must become a *bond market strategy* of three parts. First, since Wall Street has the most reliable understanding of inflation, monetary authorities should be selected by, from, and for Wall Street. Second, since household savings create real investment, the rich, who save more than the poor or the middle class, should have low income taxes and modest if not zero capital gains taxes. Third, since post-Reagan federal budget deficits cause inflation and crowd out private investment, it is imperative to balance, at the least, the federal budget yearly.[3] Wars, cold or hot, are exempt from this political arithmetic.

Facts need not correspond with ideology. The bondholding class was jumpstarted during the early years of the Reagan administration. While Paul Volcker's recession combined with Reagan's budgets were taking the national debt or the value of bonds outstanding to $3.2 trillion, Reagan's tax cuts had given the rich a $2 trillion windfall for purchasing securities, leaving precious few new bonds for institutional and foreign buyers.[4] Since only 3 percent of all families then directly held any bonds, the top 1 percent of wealth holders, the super rich, got half of all interest payments going to households, while the top 10 percent got virtually all of it. The yearly tax benefits for the very rich (top 5 percent) combined with *exploding* debt interest payments exceeded the full increase in the yearly pace of federal deficits beginning with Reagan's first year. Compound interest alone was creating new millionaires and billionaires.

Since "deficits cause inflation," it would be inconvenient to blame the deficits on those receiving the tax breaks used to buy the interest-earning bonds. The notion that reckless welfare recipients with no fears of inflation were the guilty parties better served the bondholding class. Moreover, coming to the aid of the rich *was* good for Wall Street. Not only had the bond issuers and bond buyers given investment bankers more profits, any future capital losses could be blamed on unemployment rates falling below the natural rate, breaking the speed limit for economic growth. It became *scientific capitalism.*

During the Clinton years the head of the Federal Reserve, two successive Treasury secretaries, and the bondholding class, itself a joint product of Washington and New York, moved Wall Street's agenda into the White House. As Greenspan outlined his new philosophy to President-elect Clinton, no single economic policy could do more good for society than a drop in long-term interest rates (*increases* in long-term bond prices). These rates matter most to businesses with large debts and to people paying mortgages. The Fed could control short-term interest rates, but long-term rates would not drop unless "*the bond market*" was convinced that the White House was going to reduce the federal deficit. With federal deficits under control, Greenspan said, market players would have more faith in their mantra, price stability, and long-term rates would drop like stones, losing their expected inflation premiums. Stock market prices would take flight like scalded geese. By the end of more than two hours of "bonding," the new president-elect had signed on to Greenspan's bond market strategy. Clinton kept his part of the bargain and even managed to create surpluses.

Gradually the 30-year bond rate did come down, from 6.8 percent to below 6.0 percent, and the *capital gains* of bondholders went up. The modest growth in the economy was only in interest-rate sensitive sectors. The Greenspan-Clinton alliance nonetheless had the life span of a butterfly. In January 1994 Greenspan told Clinton and his economic advisers that inflation expectations were mounting, driving long-term rates to 6.3 percent (bond prices *down*). By April 18, 1994, the Fed had raised short-term rates three times. The long-term benchmark rate moved up to 7.4 percent. Those interest hikes began when the unemployment rate had fallen to the "dangerously low level" of 6.5 percent and inflation had been declining. Greenspan went on to raise interest rates *in the face of declining federal deficits* four more times—guaranteeing a slow-growing economy, real wage declines, and rising bond prices.

Already on the road to a recession, a monetary policy reversal came quite by accident. Beginning in fall 1998 the real estate and stock market bubbles in southeastern Asia burst. In the United States, the Federal Reserve had just orchestrated the bailout of a giant hedge fund, Long-term Capital Management.[5] Worried about "investor anxiety" on Wall Street, Greenspan cut the federal funds rate three times over seven weeks beginning in late September. The bond and stock markets quickly rallied as foreign capital sprinted into US financial markets, helping to sustain the US speculative bubbles. Thereafter, speculation in newly minted Internet stocks created a bubble within a bubble, as Greenspan spun fables about the "new economy." Although the intent of the reversal in monetary policy was not to reduce unemployment (again, reckoned perilously low), the interest rate cuts stimulated the economy directly in the usual way and indirectly by adding to the net worth of financial wealth holders. Thereafter came the accidental acceleration in economic growth.[6]

The monetary easing proved transitory, as commodities inflation passed once again before Greenspan's eyes; upward moves in the federal funds rate returned in summer

1999, and the forced march toward recession resumed. Still, by keeping the incremental changes small, and abetted by pro-financial market policies emanating from the Treasury and the White House, the Federal Reserve managed to accelerate not only income and wealth gains for those at the top but validate the greatest bull market in stocks in American history.

The Unique Power of the Bondholders

How did the few bondholders become so powerful? First, far more wealth is made in bonds than most people are aware.[7] Second, during the past quarter century, increased volatility in the bond market made bonds good substitutes for stocks. Today, bond wealth is even more concentrated at the top than stock wealth. Worse, the unprecedented volatility in bond prices due to this heightened bond market volume has led to an explosion in speculative financial derivatives, contributing to worldwide financial fragility. Third, since shareholders time their sales with increases in bond yields, bond market conditions can cause frighteningly abrupt downdrafts in the stock market. Contrary to popular opinion, bonds are nowadays held only briefly.[8]

Fourth, since monetary policy has dominated economic policy for a quarter century, and since the bondholders decide the destiny of bond and stockholders, the Federal Reserve has been able to exercise its bond market strategy with impunity. Because of the bondholders' primal fear of inflation, monetary policy has had a strong anti-wage, anti-inflationary, anti-growth, and anti-employment bias. This bias gave rise to *the Goldilocks economy*—not too hot, not too cold, but just right. Within their fairy tale these "good news bears" want a Fed willing to raise interest rates to soften the economy so that long-term interest rates soon fall; then, the bears can sit back and enjoy the ascension of bond and stock prices. This fable not only dominated economic policy for the last decades of the twentieth century but endures.

President George W. Bush's 2001 "trickle down" supply-side income tax cuts received the blessing of Greenspan. When fully in place, at 2001 income levels, the top 1 percent of income earners will receive 31.3 percent of the tax cut while the lowest fifth will receive only 1 percent. More broadly, the top 10 percent will receive 48.3 percent of the tax cut and the bottom 60 percent, only 16.5 percent.[9] The tax cuts and the recession beginning in March 2001 combined with increased defense spending have turned budget surpluses into deficits—more T-bonds and more tax breaks to buy them. It is deja-voodoo economics all over again.

The Great Inflation Anomaly Principle

At the Federal Reserve, wages inflation is guilty by association with goods inflation. Increases in wage rates, according to recent Federal Reserve heads, require quick and brutal punishment. Since nothing causes as much anxiety as a shrinkage in the Reserve's army of unemployed, the retribution is unemployment and temporary work. Job insecurity makes the Fed's work easier. In turn, the sustained threat of unemployment and depressed wages, not to mention rising inequality, helped to breed the greatest bull market in securities in American history. This confluence of interests has created not only a class rich beyond ordinary imagination but also a great anomaly. Whereas rising prices for ordinary goods or wages signal inflation and must be restrained, rising prices of financial assets are considered good news on Wall Street! No threats are voiced; no obligatory punishment is meted out. Let the bull be; let the bull run!

On Wall Street the tripling of prices of financial assets—prices racing faster than their fundamental or underlying values—is presumed to be benign, but wages cannot be allowed to keep abreast of productivity, much less outrun it. High employment and rising wages being bad for society while spiraling financial asset prices and extravagant profits on Wall Street are good is *not* a benign anomaly. While about 5 percent of American households were becoming extraordinarily rich from financial asset inflation during the last quarter of the twentieth century, the other 95 percent of households were becoming worse off. Because of this distressing anomaly—goods inflation being bad and financial asset inflation being good—bullishness in financial markets has become the most respectable indicator of American economic well-being.

A self-serving myth on Wall Street tells us that wealth has been democratized during the past quarter century by widespread participation in booming financial markets. In truth, between 1983 and 1995 the top fifth of American households gained about 11 percent to reach an average net financial wealth value of $730,000. The second fifth *lost* 4.3 percent, the third fifth *lost* 7.8 percent, and the bottom 40 percent *lost* an astounding 68.3 percent, ending up with a *negative* net financial net worth of -$10,600. If we climb back to the top, we find the top 1 percent gained nearly 20 percent during this time, enough to elevate the average value of their financial wealth to $7.4 million—today, to at least $10.0 million.

Did the thunderous financial markets between 1995 and 1999 make up for those losses among working Americans? If the bottom 80 percent of households retained their 1995 share of net financial wealth (rather than continuing to lose wealth), the average addition to their financial health would have been about $1,500. This would be sufficient to bring the bottom 40 percent up to - $9,100. That is, the gains for each of the top million-plus households would be about $2.6 million, while the gains for each of about 89 million families would have been, at best, $1,500. In truth, rising debt has outweighed any bond or stock gains for most families. By 1997, the middle fifth of households had less net worth than they had in 1989, after adjusting for inflation.[10]

The Great NASDAQ Crash of 2000–2001

Alan Greenspan's delicate high-wire balancing act—manipulating interest rates to keep wages soft and securities prices high, while avoiding falling profits—created crosswinds that led to a devastating NASDAQ tailspin. At the mercy of the irrepressible speculative forces that he helped create, Greenspan told the Senate Budget Committee on January 28, 1999, that the rise in Internet stocks "does reflect something good about the way our securities markets work; namely, that they do endeavor to ferret out the better opportunities and put capital into various different types of endeavors, prior to earnings actually materializing. That's good for our system." Greenspan now saw "craziness" in the financial markets as not only rational but "good." Now, people placing bets on companies with no earnings was what capitalism was all about! While Greenspan continued to talk the talk, stocks and bonds did more than walk the random walk. Daily stock index swings of 100, 200, 300, or 400 points have become so commonplace that they no longer insinuate volatility. His earlier rhetoric (December 1996) of "irrational exuberance" having failed, Greenspan has since been tip-toeing through the tulips to avoid triggering the greatest and most complete financial markets crash in world history. The Dow proceeded to soar to 11,000 and the NASDAQ advanced nearly 100 percent during 1999 alone. Much of these advances was based on debt: margin buying increased 62 percent during 1999 alone and has increased 650 percent since 1990.

This stock market bubble invites comparison with that of the late 1920s that ended in the Great Crash of 1929. Really, there is no comparison. It took *two* years for the *Times* industrials, the index for the high tech stocks of the Jazz Age, to increase 1.88 times, whereas it took only a year for the NASDAQ to double (by 2000).[11] At peak volume during the 1920s, only about 7.5 percent of families were trading stocks. Yet the stock market dominated American culture during the era. Today, more than half the households in America own stocks, though only the top 5 percent of the wealth distribution own truly important amounts. Today, the market has become an important part of not only our culture but of our future. Never before has so much of consumer confidence been tied to the financial markets. Any move by the Reserve to preserve or limit growth was magnified by the reactions in the financial markets. With consumers' confidence tied to the performance of the stock market, the evolving bear market in stocks was withering.

What Is at Stake and What Can Be Done about It

If we are to know what to do regarding the reversal of fortunes for wage earners, we need first an understanding of the economy counter to the ideology of the bondholding class. Rather than providing for real investment in the real economy that will trickle down to real workers, the bondholding class diverts funds away from constructive economic roles and toward wasteful speculation. Perpetual prosperity on Wall Street requires the evaporation of personal savings, or what we may call the "angels' share" of savings. These savings are like the amount of cognac intentionally evaporated in France, an "angels' share" equal to the entire annual volume consumed in France, sufficient to assure quality for the industry and enough to keep many spirits high. Those savings do *not* become real investment.[12] That has been demonstrated by the meltdown in real investment that began late in 2000.

The impenetrable veil of money masking true knowledge of money's potentially more humane role in society, once lifted, reveals a way to have interest and principal without bondage. We need interest-free US Treasury bonds to refurbish badly frayed municipal and state infrastructures.[13] We need a transactions tax on financial instruments designed for long-term holding but actually sold in a fortnight. We need to recognize that costs are incurred when the Federal Reserve is allowed to continue as an unconstitutional fourth and unequal branch of government. Thereafter, a reform of the Federal Reserve System could free both monetary and fiscal policy to foster strong and real economic growth that benefits more than just people at the top.

Much is at stake. The energy force of traditional capitalism seeps out when Wall Street capitalism dominates the society. Capitalism thrives among puddles of inequality sprinkling down from productivity differentials, but limits to sustainable inequality exist. When a dominant new leisure class gains power through unearned income—financial capital gains and interest—speculative bubbles float where real production once ruled. When great amounts of money are made from money—not from production—real investments in factories, machines, tools, and people ultimately suffer and so do middle class incomes, employment, and wealth.

It is not so much history ending, as history repeating itself.

Notes

1. In his remarks before the Joint Economic Committee of Congress, June 10, 1998.
2. The New York area, including New Jersey, employed only about 190,000 people in the securities industry by the end of 1996, rising to 340,000 in early 1998. Employment has been receding in 2001–2002.
3. Surpluses would be even better.
4. Luckily, Michael Milken and the junk bond market were able to supply additional corporate bonds that led to leveraged buyout mania and still more bonds. For the details, see Canterbery 2000, 109–114.
5. Only ten days before the bailout, Greenspan had told a Congressional hearing why regulation of hedge funds would be a mistake. See Canterbery 2000, 183.
6. The Clinton administration's embrace of *The Bond Market* as a new American icon seems complete as we read the *Economic Report of the President* for 1995 and 1997. And, as if to validate the *bond market strategy*, Clinton signed a 1997 tax bill with a cut in capital gains taxes and other tax cuts for the rich. The richest 1 percent of households once again gained by far the most, with each paying $16,000 less in taxes. The bottom fifth of US households saw their taxes *rise* by an average of $40 a year.
7. The most recent data show that the median value of bond holdings among families with incomes of $100,000 or more is nearly twice the median value of their stock holdings. The median is such that half of these families held more and half held less than $58,000 in bonds and $30,000 in stocks.
8. The average holding period for a US Treasury bond or note is just one month, or 359 months short of the maturity of the bellwether Treasury. The average holding period for a Treasury bill is three weeks, a week short of the shortest-lived T-bill. The tight connection between the

bond and stock markets gives the bondholding class still more power—power over the fate of stock prices.

9. These estimates are based on the tax model of Citizens for Tax Justice, Februarv 2001.
10. Much more detail regarding these events can be found in Canterberv 2000. For wealth-hold ing updates through 1998, see Wolff 2002.
11. Even though radios were as popular in the 1920s as computers are today, the Radio Corporation of America, a "high tech" favorite of the era, price per share had plummeted from a "mania high" of $114 per share in 1929 to $2.50 by 1932, while the *Times* industrials closed at 58 by summer.
12. The theoretical and empirical explanation for the evaporation of savings appears in Canterbery 2000, 225–242. For a more technical treatment, see Canterbery 1993. For a clear explanation for why it takes real investment to cause real saving, see Eisner 1995, 33–41.
13. Now, during a troublesome economic recession, is the ideal time to begin to issue interest-free US Treasury loans. After the loans are repaid during the recovery, this device could be used as a "new" fiscal policy during future recessions. The fiscal policy that has been abandoned during the past two decades could be restored.

References

Canterbery, E. Ray. "Reaganomics, Saving, and the Casino Effect." In *The Economics of Saving*, edited by James H. Gapinski. Boston/Dordrect/London: Kluwer Academic Publishers, 1993, 153–175.

——. *Wall Street Capitalism*. Singapore/New Jersey/London/Hong Kong: World Scientific, 2000.

Eisner, Robert. *The Misunderstood Economy: What Counts and How to Count It*. Boston: Harvard Business School Press, 1995.

Wolff, Edward N. *Top Heavy*. New York: New Press, 2002.

Chapter 41

Necessities, the Marginal Utility of Money, and Saving

E. Ray Canterbery

This essay brings together the themes of two book chapters, publications separated by more than a decade but newly relevant. The first ties inflation in necessities to distributive efficiency; the second ties 'Reaganomics' to the Casino Effect, which generates a new kind of savings through asset inflation. The distributive effects of these two kinds of inflation - goods and asset - are linked by the marginal utility of money (or income) and the marginal propensity to save. The surprising macroeconomic implications of these relationships are explored within the context of the new welfare economics.

1. Introduction [×]

The themes of the two book chapters summarized here are separated by 14 years but are newly relevant. The first ties inflation in necessities to distributive efficiency; the second ties Reaganomics and saving to the "Casino Effect." In the 1970s goods inflation was a major problem, especially inflation in necessities. By the late 1980s goods inflation was subdued even as invisible asset inflation that I called the "Casino Effect" was

[•] *Author's note:* This paper is written as to honor the memory of Jim Gapinski and his perseverance that led me to contribute chapters to books he edited (see References). *Editor's note*: Jim Gapinski passed away in a November month about half a dozen years ago. I am grateful for having interacted with him for the short time that I did.

taking place. A new kind of savings was generated by the Casino Effect, something that I later called the "angels' share of savings." The Casino Effect was temporarily reversed by the stock market crash of 1987 only to be followed by a speculative Nasdaq bubble that burst in March 2001. We are still reeling from its effects even while observing the reemergence of a speculative asset bubble as well as inflation in necessities such as energy and food. The distributive effects of the two kinds of inflation—goods and asset—are linked by the marginal utility of money (or income) and the marginal propensity to save.

2. The Marginal Utility of Money and Distributive Efficiency

Abba P. Lerner had attempted to revitalize welfare economics with the remarkable idea of distributive efficiency. Since it presumes a diminishing marginal utility of income, distributive efficiency provides an ingenious defense of egalitarianism. Lerner saw distributive efficiency as exactly parallel to productive efficiency. In the analogy the efficient allocation of income requires the equalization of the marginal utilities of different expenditures on the various consumption goods. Lerner presumed that the marginal utility of income is derived from the marginal utility of expenditures on consumer goods and services. Then, transferring income from higher to lower income intervals is the only way utility can be maximized.

In turn, I attempted to explain why the marginal utility of income does, in reality, diminish (Canterbery, 1979). Every individual's utility cannot be determined, but that is not an issue since we are concerned only with probabilities. For that, it is sufficient to measure marginal utility between one income interval and another. Individuals have a hierarchy of needs and wants; that is, basic needs trump other needs and some wants are more compelling than others. Properly defined, a hierarchy of bundles of goods and services can be lexicographically ordered. That is, individuals would rather have some goods and services (hereafter simply goods) from bundle-type one than to have any at all from the bundle-type ranked two, and this holds for all subsequent rankings.

In this layered view personal income levels decide not only "marginal" but total utilities. Imagine these bundles stacked like the sandbags on a levee with the water level representing the level of income. All the goods and services in each bag will not be consumed until income (liquidity) rises to the top of the bag. The other bags remain dry. If income rises adequately, all the basic necessities will be consumed and the consumer moves on to satisfy wants. The threshold level of income for, say, bundle-type two, equals the satiation level of income for bundle-type one so that the satiation level of income in each case specifies a kink in the Engel curve (quantities consumed at different incomes). The sandbags at the top of the levy provide the *least extra* utility but together with those beneath, the greatest *total* utility.

As far as I can surmise, we cannot move directly from the set theory of lexicographic functions to an econometric estimate of the implied parameters. Fortunately, this appears to be both unnecessary and unwise. The extended linear expenditure system (ELES) not only is a way of measuring consumer responsiveness to changes in income, but also can identify "necessities" versus "desired goods" for a society of a particular per capita income. That income devoted to non-necessities is supernumerary or purely discretionary income, giving rise to a supernumerary function (the ratio of expenditures on non-necessities to total expenditures). This ratio is higher in higher income countries and is higher for high-income families and lower for low-income families in the *same* country.

The microeconomics of ELES provides a measure of the marginal utility of income even as it dovetails with Keynesian macroeconomics. The negative of the inverse of the supernumerary function is the expenditure elasticity of the marginal utility of expenditure or the Frisch parameter. Since the marginal propensities to consume each discretionary commodity or bundle out of income can be estimated from the ELES equation, their sum is the *aggregate* marginal propensity to consume (MPC). In turn, the MPC and the MPS can linearly transform the Frisch parameter into the income elasticity of the marginal utility of income. The integral, mathematically, of the income elasticity *is* the *marginal utility of income*. Repeated ELES estimates find the absolute value of the Frisch parameter as well as the MPC declining as income rises. The ELES provides a direct estimate of Lerner's elusive but nevertheless diminishing marginal utility of income because lower-valued commodity bundles are consumed at higher incomes.

3. Personal Savings and the Wealth Distribution – Keynesian or Classical?

Lexicographical orderings and ELES provide some special insights into savings as normally defined as well as the their macroeconomic implications. A general rise in the price of necessities such as food, public utilities and medical care (at a given money income) requires a diversion of income away from discretionary items.[1] The

[1] The slowdown in U.S. aggregate consumption during the second quarter of 2004 (and perhaps beyond) probably can be attributed to rising energy and food prices. Ironically, what is now called core inflation *excludes* these necessities from the CPI as parts of meaningful goods inflation. The one possibly commendable but unmentioned rationale for this exclusion is that energy and food prices inflation is beyond the reach of monetary and fiscal policies. In such case all necessities, including health care, should be excluded from the core. Indeed, price inflation driven by any supply-constrained goods output is immune to tightening monetary and fiscal policies (except through massive employment and output reductions). The influence of

household shifts expenditures away from those items yielding lower marginal utility and toward those providing higher marginal utility. As the subsistence share of total expenditures rises, savings will fall. The sensitivity of savings to the prices of the "most necessary" goods declines as per capita income rises. Put differently, as absolute necessities become smaller shares of incomes, savings become less responsive to price changes in the highest ranked (least desired) good. Therefore, we can expect the MPS and savings to rise at higher levels of per capita income, Keynes' long forgotten admonition.

Two contentious views of the role of personal savings in the macroeconomy exist. In the classical view, personal savings (plural) not only generate real investment but the two are always equal. Because of the direction of effects—from savings toward investment—the social purpose of the rich is elevated to uncommon heights. By the deployment of Say's law, this transmutation of savings assures a natural rate of full employment. Supply creates its own demand. The prosperity, even the survival of capitalism depends greatly on higher incomes and greater savings by the rich. It is a matter of great social convenience.

An equally compressed sketch of John Maynard Keynes' ideas has demand creating its own supply; in this view, maintaining the purchasing power of the middle class and its low MPS is critical to full employment. When incomes of the masses are too skimpy to buy industry's discretionary products, business firms have little reason to invest in plant and equipment or in research and development. When demand-driven private investment is adequate, so too is employment; when investment is inadequate, total demand in the economy is insufficient to employ everyone desiring work. Thus, to a true Keynesian, real investment in factories generates real saving (singular). These grand claims are not as remarkable as their polarity.

In today's economy, both the classicals and Keynes cannot be correct. Yet, the art of knowing which policies to deploy depends on a reliable design of the bridges between investment and savings or saving. As I will contend, Keynes comes closer to the truth inasmuch as real investment leads to real saving (singular), but he offers only an incomplete explanation of financial asset inflation and its effect on the real economy. We nonetheless correctly measure real national saving as the value of real investment. A society has not really saved unless it has a new factory, equipment, house, or highway to show for it. If personal or household saving(s) does not somehow link up with real investment as cause or effect, in the cloistered worlds of both classical and Keynesian economics they play no further economy role.

The traditional version of Say's law, buried by the Great

---

such policies on even demand-driven inflation is suspect.

Depression and Keynesian economics, was resurrected in Reaganomics and later re-energized by the George W. Bush Administration. Numerous and large tax cuts for income-earners in the top-most income brackets bolstered by cuts in the top rate on capital gains would, it was claimed, lead to a flood of personal savings (plural) and of real investment. This rehabilitation of Say's law has happened at the same time as other trends tending to lower workers' incomes while elevating those at the top. There has been a flight of manufacturing to low-wage countries that has put downward pressures on U.S. manufacturing wages and employment. At the other end of the income distribution corporate CEO compensation has soared even as corporations have been (on a net basis) buying back more common stock than they have been newly issuing. The collective consequence has been the greatest redistribution of income and wealth toward the top in peacetime American history. A bull market in bonds and the Nasdaq stock price bubble enhanced these trends during the late 1990s.

In Keynesian economics a rising national income from rising real investment leads to greater real saving. Even if "real," a portion of saving out of a rising national income should accrue to households. In classical economics a rising level of personal savings (as loanable funds) leads to rising business investment. Both views are confounded by a U.S. national income accounts measure of personal savings *as a share* of disposable personal income peaking at 7.5 percent in 1981 and since declining to near invisibility. Since the 1970s the surges in business investment came with the splurge on new information technology as a counterpart of the Nasdaq bubble that burst and the recent boomlet that has left the Nasdaq once again overpriced. There also is the quandary of a secular bull market in bonds and stocks in an era of zero or near-zero personal savings.

4. The "Casino Effect" and the Angels' Share of Savings

The saving(s) paradox cannot be resolved in the absence of a third, unrecognized form of personal savings. The national income accounts do not measure savings directly; rather, savings comprise the difference between disposable income and consumption. Properly defined, personal savings is the same as an increase in net worth. Using a flow-of-funds approach, the Federal Reserve System has a much closer approximation of changes in net worth. It adds increases in financial assets to net investment in consumer durables (such as a house purchase), and then subtracts the net increase in debts to arrive at savings. If the Federal Reserve figures are compared with the national income account figures, the Commerce Department has greatly understated savings by as much as 45 percent (in 1987).

These diverging measures suggest a defect shared by Keynesian and classical theories. Neither Keynes nor the classicals defined saving(s) as a positive change in net worth.

During periods of rapidly rising financial asset prices, personal net worth grows rapidly at the very top of the wealth distribution. If home prices also are rapidly appreciating, personal net worth of the middle, especially the upper middle class, also soars. These personal savings simply evaporate in macroeconomic theory because of the absence of financial asset prices. During speculative episodes there is an irresistible tendency to make money with money. Why take huge risks buying real assets when highly liquid financial assets are yielding exorbitant returns? I have called the exponential growth in asset prices during such speculative times the "Casino Effect" (Canterbery, 1993, pp. 171-172; and Canterbery, 2000, pp. 243-245).

Though speculative asset gains (capital gains) may not appear in macroeconomic theories, surely their reality has some real macroeconomic effects. In the vineyards of France, the angels' share of cognac is the amount necessarily evaporated to give cognac its celebrated quality. The amount evaporated seasonally roughly equals all the cognac consumed in France during the year, sufficient to keep many spirits high. In like fashion, most of the personal savings of the wealthy evaporate; it is the "angels' share" of savings (Canterbery, 2000, pp. 227, 252-255, 292-295). This "angels' share" of savings mostly benefits bankers, investment firms and brokers on Wall Street and other blue-stocking financial centres. Ironically, such savings from speculative gains divert funds from the real economy and, in that sense, do indeed evaporate. Real investment is compromised.

Even so, where the angels' share goes is the great unsolved mystery of Keynesian economics. The solution to the mystery is found in the net worth approach to personal savings. The net-worth economy is one of revolving-door finance wherein the angels' share of personal savings remains as financial assets without intersecting real investment. Since the 1970s the financial services sector of the American economy has grown much faster than the GDP. The positive growth in personal income has been rentier's (unearned) income. In fact, all of the increase in disposable income during the 1980s was more than accounted for by the rise in the share of *interest* income, while the shares of labor and other income sources declined. Such a financial services economy is quite distinct from an economy that produces goods and services for consumption and for further production (real investment). A truly efficient economy would not need more finance than production.

There is another way of looking at the macroeconomic consequences of the angels' share. GDP is measured two ways by the Department of Commerce; one estimate is from the product side (consumption, investment, government spending, and net exports), the other from the income side (wages and salaries, profits, depreciation, etc.). Capital gains, including those from the financial markets, are not counted as "income" in the national accounts. Although these two ways of estimating GDP should give the same number, measurement errors have always led to differences. The statisticians halve the difference in the two measures—adding half to the lower figure and subtracting half from the higher estimate—to arrive at one reported value for GDP. Generally, it has been said, the product side will be higher than the income side because some income will be hidden through the efforts of business firms and households to evade income taxes. In the past several years, however, the difference between the product measure and the income measure has turned *negative* with the income-based estimate of GDP exceeding the output measure by more than a full percentage point by 1997.

As noted, capital gains are not part of real output gains either. Increasingly, however, top corporate executives have been paid partly in stock options at no cost to corporations. This practice explains, in great part, why compensation of the highest paid CEOs has soared into hundreds of millions of dollars in recent times, making CEOs even wealthier. Worse, shareholders may receive inaccurate profit reports because, generally in corporate accounting, the values of stock options are not subtracted from profits. Since the Commerce Department cannot effectively check the official corporate accounts and adjust for the value of newly issued stock paid to executives, the statisticians will overstate actual profits and, more to our point, overstate the income-side measure of GDP. In fact, the discrepancy between the income and product measures of GDP is highly correlated with the growth in the S&P 500. A similar correlation exists with bond price appreciation.

The growth of net worth or wealth in the economy has apparently switched from business firms to selected families. During the 1980s and 1990s the gain in net worth of the top 1 percent was about $1 trillion (equaling about an eighth of the national GDP) or roughly an average of half a million dollars per household. If such advances in the personal savings of the wealthy were being made, Say's law says that real investment must have been soaring. It wasn't and it isn't. The savings have evaporated, sadly going the way of so much cognac. American production and employment has slowed as a few households became super-rich from unearned income. Meanwhile, the incomes of working people have declined with manufacturing prospects.

5. Conclusions

The original classical argument for the importance of rich households in the economy was based on a household-business model in which the savers and the factory owners were the same persons. Thus, the factory owner used his savings to build and equip his factory. Once, as Keynes noted, the producer and the personal savers are separate entities with disparate motives, there is no assurance that savings and investment will be even loosely connected. Keynes believed that he had destroyed the basic economic welfare rationale justifying highly unequal income and wealth distributions. Meanwhile, the social and welfare implication of a MPS rising with income was lost in econometric aggregation. Keynesians never expected classical loanable funds theory to be rehabilitated for the purpose of *redistributing* income and wealth from the lower to the higher income classes by taxing ordinary wages at a higher rate than unearned income.

The "New Welfare Economics" beginning during the early 1950s based economic welfare entirely on *productive* efficiency. Pareto optimality requires that no further economic change should occur that would leave any individual "worse off." Since *all* microeconomic optima that yield productive efficiency meet this criterion, free markets simultaneously provide productive efficiency *and* social welfare optima. A shotgun marriage between general equilibrium as economic "science" and Pareto optimality blew away Keynes' social concerns. To considerable regret, once this is understood, there is no further need for economists (or philosophers, for that matter); both would be technologically unemployed (as indeed philosophers are).

The reality of a diminishing marginal utility of income found in ELES estimates supports Lerner's idea of distributional efficiency and could revive welfare economics. In truth, it *should* revive welfare economics. Optimal income and wealth distributions can happen without impinging on optimal mechanical production optima (Canterbery, 1979, July 1979; Lerner, 1978). After all, we expect relatively free market exchange conditions to generate a "social dividend" that can be redistributed among the population. A simultaneous allocative and distributional efficiencies optimum is what I have called a "maximax" (Lerner, 1978, p. 65; Canterbery, 1981, pp. 199-201). A society with extremely unequal income and wealth distributions is *not* an optimal society since many could be made better off by a great margin while the best-off are being made slightly less well off. Moreover, highly unequal distributions and a rising MPS from a diminishing marginal utility of expenditure preclude Keynesian full employment because of insufficient aggregate demand. Worse, heavy concentrations at the very top lead to speculative financial markets destined to collapse. Thus, a redistribution of unearned income away from the top can lead to optimal microeconomic conditions move an economy toward higher employment *sans* an inordinate amount of a wasteful angels' share of savings.

References

Canterbery, E. Ray, "A Vita Theory of the Personal Income Distribution," *Southern Economic Journal*, July 1979), pp. 12-48.

Canterbery, E. Ray, "Inflation, Necessities and Distributive Efficiency," in James H. Gapinski and Charles Rockwood, Editors, *Essays in Post-Keynesian Inflation: In Honor of Abba P. Lerner* (Cambridge, MA: Ballinger, 1979), pp. 79-103

Canterbery, E. Ray, "Income Redistribution and Rawlsian Justice," *Journal of Economics and Business*, Spring 1981, pp. 181-201.

Canterbery, E. Ray, "Reaganomics, Saving, and the Casino Effect," in James H. Gapinski, Editor, *The Economics of Saving* (Boston/Dordrecht/London: Kluwer Academic Publishers, 1993), pp. 153-175.

Canterbery, E. Ray, *Wall Street Capitalism: The Theory of the Bondholding Class* (World Scientific: Singapore/New Jersey/London/Hong Kong 2000).

Lerner, A.P., "Utilitarian Marginalism (Nozick, Rawls, Justice, and Welfare)" in Justice, Nozick, and Rawls: A Symposium, edited by E. Ray Canterbery and Harry G. Johnson, *Eastern Economic Journal*, January 1978, pp. 51-65.

PART VIII

MONETARY AND FISCAL POLICY

Chapter 42

The Fine Line Between Politics and Economics

by E. RAY CANTERBERY

THERE ARE several possible roles for the President's Council of Economic Advisers (CEA), each with its attendant risks and a different shade of political meaning.

- As merely an *analytical* agency, it would gather, process and analyze data, distribute results to the President, the Congress and others, but make no recommendations.
- As strictly an *advisory* agency, it would go a step further to give suggestions to the President, possibly also to Congress, but make no attempt to seek public support for such suggestions.
- As a policy-*formulating* agency, it would go several steps further in the course of allowing itself to be heard in the early stages of drafting new legislation.
- And as a policy-*making* agency, it would move on to perform some of the tasks now performed by the President and Congress.

While the CEA cannot usurp the powers vested in the executive and legislative branches, no solid line can be easily drawn between policy making and policy formulation in the economic realm. Still, it may be said that the Council has played all of these roles to some extent. When Walter W. Heller, current Chairman of the Council, testified before Congress in support of the President's bill to grant corporations a tax credit for investment in new plant and equipment, he was, to all intents and purposes, acting as a policy formulator.

Insofar as Congress enacted the bill and the President signed it, they were the policy makers. Inasmuch as the Council helped draft the program, the Council was a policy formulator. But as a spokesman for the President before the Congress and before the public (he appeared on NBC's "Meet the Press"), Chairman Heller certainly attempts to determine the fate of legislation, though the Council has no legislative power. Even his phrases defending a sharp 1963 government deficit were often the same phrases used by the President. Thus the Council today is definitely active in the policy-making process.

This present role appears a natural evolution of the Council through a variety of problems, five chairmen and the Administrations of three Presidents. President Truman selected the highly respected Brookings Institution economist Edwin G. Nourse as first chairman when the Council was set up under the Employment Act of 1946. Under the Act the federal government is given the responsibility "to promote free competitive enterprise and the general walfare" in order to assure "maximum employment, production and purchasing power." And the three-member Council, in the Office of the President, is charged with developing and recommending policy consistent with these national goals.

The fact that its three members are assisted by a staff of other economists does not even today make this assignment any less formidable, for the Council must analyze economic trends, as well as all activities of the federal government, in the light of the objectives of the Act. The Council has, further, the duty to assist and advise in the preparation of the Economic Report of the President, and to prepare an annual report of its own for the President each December.

Dr. Nourse could not find "a single word" in the Employment Act about any responsibility of the Council to Congress. He considered the economist a scientist and therefore not the proper implement for policy making, whether for business firms or for nations. And President Truman, pressured by other duties, was indifferent to the detailed complexities of economics.

The first Council, which also included Messrs. John Clark and Leon H. Keyserling, was somewhat analogous to the research department of a large industrial firm such as General Motors. With no responsibility for drafting or promoting legislation, the advice which Truman accepted, at least up to 1948, became policy primarily through his efforts. He initiated the practice of occasionally having the Council appear at Cabinet meetings, although Nourse did not interpret this as ranking Council members on the Cabinet level. In fact, Nourse viewed Cabinet members as representatives of rival interests and beliefs, and it was not his feeling that the Council should cater to any particular interest.

Because Truman always had ample political advice, Nourse believed the Council would be superfluous in plotting policy strategy. Apparently Truman disagreed with this stewardship when the Presidential election campaign of 1948 got under way. In that battle, two of Truman's favorite targets were high prices and high profits. Nourse intentionally kept out of this debate. But Keyserling and Clark envisaged a less passive role for the government in the economy and backed the Administration.

Keyserling became increasingly

conspicuous in Democratic party affairs during the 1948 Presidential campaign. He addressed the Western States Democratic Conference, participated in the Southern Regional Conference and delivered two speeches at the "Jefferson Jubilee" in Chicago. At the latter he stated, ". . . I believe profoundly that the budgetary policies of the federal government since the first Administration of Franklin D. Roosevelt until the present moment have been basically right."

No longer strictly an analytical-advisory agency, the Council's changing demeanor drew the fire of the Republican members of the Joint Economic Committee of Congress, who expressed the fear that the Economic Report was becoming political propaganda.

The 1948 midyear Economic Report had already reflected the Truman-Keyserling-Clark policy of selective credit and price controls, the political role of the Council was confirmed by Truman's election, and disagreement was finally settled by the resignation of Nourse. His successor was Leon Keyserling.

The Council's free hand in interpreting the intent of the Act and in steering its own course explains in large part the variations in its position under subsequent Administrations and the different personalities of its chairmen. Under Leon Keyserling the Council was primarily an advisory and policy-formulating group. And Keyserling often campaigned for the Fair Deal program.

THE DANGER of economic advisers following the advice of the President rather than vice-versa is illustrated by the subsequent chaos. Keyserling followed Truman's lead and advocated a $4 billion tax increase in the 1949 Economic Report to curb the inflation of "high profit levels." As the issue reached a heated peak, the Council apparently failed to notice that the economy was in the throes of its first postwar recession. Truman and the Council had to reverse themselves as Congress rejected their program. Consequently, the 1950 Economic Report's appraisal of the preceding year is among the most ambiguous Council reviews.

Keyserling saw no distinction between the role of Council members and the position of Cabinet members and other agency heads in their responsibility of sharing in the enunciation and implementation of Presidential policy. For all practical purposes, it was by now understood that Truman's Council economists, like Cabinet members, were expendable if they were unable or unwilling to support the President's *specific* proposals before the Congress and the public.

EDWIN G. NOURSE
Truman (1946-49)

When President Eisenhower assumed office in 1953, he took to heart Keyserling's criterion that the Council head and the President share the same approach to policy and named Prof. Arthur F. Burns of Columbia University as Chairman of the Council. For a time it appeared that the Council might be dismantled, as funds were only sufficient to carry it through the end of March. But Congress provided for an "Economic Adviser to the President," and necessary staff, for the remainder of that fiscal year.

With this unique title and a small staff, Burns continued to perform the functions of the old Council. New plans went into effect early that fall providing for a clearer line of responsibility to the President. Responsibility for employing staff, specialists and consultants was transferred from the three-man Council to its chairman, as was the task of reporting the Council's views to the President. Whereas each member of the trio previously had coequal powers, the reorganization gave Chairman Burns and successive chairmen top authority.

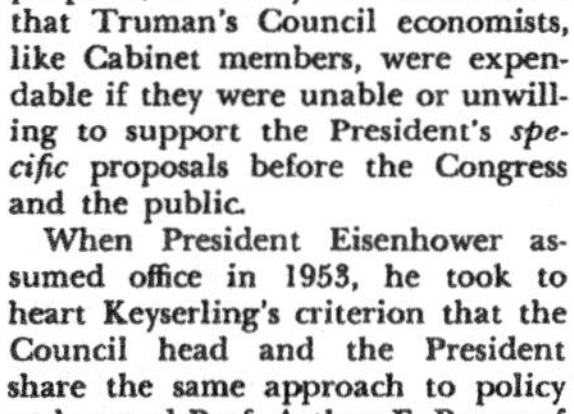

LEON H. KEYSERLING
Truman (1949-53)

The formation of an Advisory Board on Economic Growth and Stability was an important feature of the revised Council. Comprised of the heads of several departments and agencies, under the leadership of Burns, the Advisory Board evaluated the effect of government policies on the rate of economic growth. This placed the Council nearer the top policy level of the executive branch, and the Board proved effective in achieving the mutual understanding necessary for better coordinated action of these diverse groups.

Arthur Burns pictured a less political role for the Council than had Keyserling. Policy making in the executive branch was the function of the President, he argued, and his inclination was "to stay out of the limelight, make my recommendation to the President, indicate the basis for the recommendation—and then, having done that, to remain eternally quiet."

Like Nourse, he claimed that the Council could not be the President's counselor and at the same time an Administration spokesman. It was the chairman's job, Burns said, to "speak out boldly within the halls of the executive, but prudently elsewhere." And to some degree, Eisenhower's first chairman retreated to the style of Truman's first chairman. Both Burns and Nourse refused to appear before the Joint Economic Committee in public hearings. While Nourse never appeared, Burns did agree to appear at an off-the-record executive session.

THE REASONS expressed by Burns for testifying in this manner were similar to those given by Nourse for not appearing at all. If his testimony was on the record, Burns argued, the Council member would almost necessarily have to appear as a public spokesman for the Administration. And after such testimony, the Council's objectivity in handling economic facts and policies would be impaired. Like Nourse, Burns anticipated the dilemma of Council members testifying on issues in which the President had taken a position contrary to their advice. In this case the Council would have either to argue for the Chief Executive's view regardless of professional convictions or present the spectacle of disputing the President.

If the Council compromised itself by defending the Chief Executive at all costs, he might, in turn, begin to distrust their private advice. There was both the jeopardy of destroying a comfortable intellectual relationship with the President and impairing the professional standing of the Council, thus losing the public's faith in its detached analysis.

Despite their announced intention, neither Nourse nor Burns was able to remain completely divorced from politics, which suggests that, by its very nature, the Council's conduct must be in part political. Although not an Administration spokesman in the Keyserling tradition, Burns defended Eisenhower's programs in public addresses and magazine articles. In a speech before the Detroit Economic Club, two weeks before the 1954 Congressional elections, he supported Eisenhower's "comprehensive economic program."

Burns once indicated that he was "an economist who happened to be a Republican." This apology for political affiliation points up the curious dilemma for Council members. Neil Jacoby, a Council member under Burns, stated in 1956 that President Eisenhower never asked a Council member to support Administration policy "before Congress or the public." Eisenhower and his Council must always have been in political agreement or the Council chose not to be publicly critical. But with no official record, its position before the Congress remains secret.

With the exception of Nourse, no Council head has been at odds with the President's general approach to economic policy. But since each Chief Executive has used the Council in a unique way, both White House and Council personalities have contributed to the development of the Council's role. Raymond J. Saulnier [see *Interview*, page 18], who followed Burns to the helm in 1956, stayed further in the background than did his predecessor.

ARTHUR F. BURNS
Eisenhower (1953-56)

Part of the explanation was that Burns was better known nationally and in the Republican party.

Saulnier had been a Council member under Burns, and as a fiscal conservative it is no accident that he carried on Burns' cautious attitude toward economic planning. The tenor of the Economic Reports under Eisenhower placed strong trust in the private sector of the economy, reflecting both the fiscal philosophy of the President and his choice of Council chairmen.

EISENHOWER consulted frequently with his Council on an informal basis, in some instances more than once a day. He placed heavy reliance on its week-to-week judgments as to general economic conditions. To say Burns and Saulnier envisaged a limited role for the government is not to suggest that they had no influence on policy. Quite the contrary, they gave the White House arguments and data to support the fiscal views of the Administration.

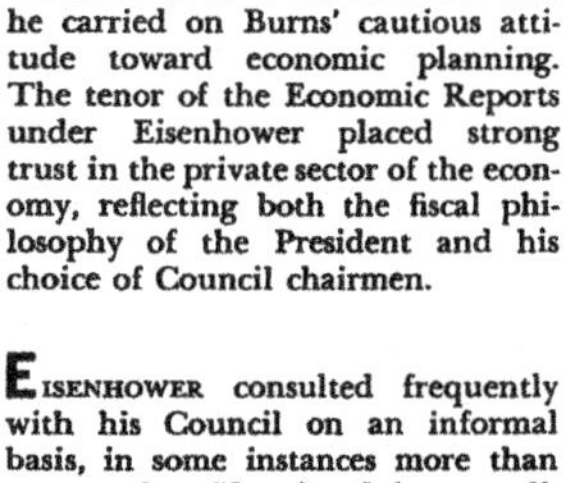

RAYMOND J. SAULNIER
Eisenhower (1956-61)

Moreover, Saulnier did not escape entirely the pitfalls of politics. Other economists scoffed when the Council denied the existence of an economic recession during the 1960 elections. The criticism usually reserved for Congress during election years was applied with equal force to the Council of Economic Advisers. But the Eisenhower economists did not share the political spotlight with the President, as did Leon Keyserling with Truman.

Eisenhower leaned most strongly on Burns for his judgment during periods of recession. The antirecession measures formulated by Burns and his economists during the 1953 downturn were agreeable to the President and acceptable to a Congress which respected Burns for his business cycle expertise. An easing of monetary policy was Burns' major recommendation, a precedent followed by Saulnier in 1957.

The Council and Eisenhower, in fact, shifted policy emphasis from the national budget to the Federal Reserve, with heavy dependence on the impersonal forces of general monetary policy.

IN 1957 Gabriel Hauge, Eisenhower's Special Assistant for Economic Affairs, and Treasury Secretary Robert Anderson arranged for informal meetings between the President and themselves, Chairman William McChesney Martin of the Federal Reserve Board, and Saulnier. Referred to informally as the "financial group" or the "anti-inflation group," they were not intended to be a policy-making combine, but their discussions of monetary and other questions undoubtedly had influence on policy decisions. Under President Kennedy, a similar committee was formed by Council Chairman Walter W. Heller, with Treasury Secretary Douglas Dillon, former Budget Director David Bell and William McChesney Martin.

Saulnier carried on Arthur Burns' practice of attending most Cabinet meetings and reporting frequently on economic developments and their policy implications. He also attended all National Security Council meetings when economic questions were discussed and participated in several international conferences.

Unlike Burns, Saulnier agreed to appear at recorded hearings before the Joint Committee, but reserved the right to edit the transcript and go "off the record" when he felt the Council would "jeopardize its position of anonymity."

As the international balance of payments problem reached crisis proportions by the end of Eisenhower's second term, relations with other countries began to occupy more and more of the Council's time. The gold outflow was to become a constraint on the domestic economic policy recommendations of the Heller Council.

Present-day concern over this problem is reflected in the Council's part in a second Cabinet-level committee, this one on the payments problem. The business of the Advisory Board on Economic Growth and Stability, formed under Chairman Burns, was transferred by President Kennedy to a Cabinet Committee on Economic Growth, chaired by the Council head and composed of the Secretary of the Treasury, the Director of the Bureau of the Budget and the Secretaries of Labor and Commerce.

President Kennedy and Chairman Heller have used history as their guide and envisaged a compromise role for the Council. Heller is attempting to make it a top-flight analysis *and* policy center within the Administration, putting equal stress on both. Hoping to combine analysis with persuasion, Heller sees his own role as "less political than it was under Leon H. Keyserling," but not as restricted as under Nourse.

In its first public testimony, the Heller Council set forth the principle that it must necessarily be "in harmony with the general aims and direction of the President," but "this general harmony is . . . consistent with divergences of views on specific issues." Thus the Council can be true to itself and differ professionally with the White House on specific policies.

At President Kennedy's urging, the Council's scope of action has been broadened even more as it has taken "its place as a key element in the Presidential office," and Heller has been actively "infighting" for his pet projects.

The Manpower Development and Training Act of 1962, accelerated Social Security payments during the slow 1962 upswing and postponement of an increase in contributions until January, 1963 were Heller victories. Also, the Heller Council has been instrumental in shifting domestic economic policy emphasis again toward the national budget.

Acting in virtually a policy-making role, the Council sent advance data and arguments to Sen. Albert Gore (D.-Tenn.) to gain public support for Kennedy's first exhortation to the steel companies to keep prices in step with the Council's productivity guidelines.

This new concept of the Council has both merits and faults. The Lilliputian Council of Nourse no longer seems realistic. The President's Council of Economic Advisers *should* appear in public testimony before the Congress. The dilemma posed by Nourse and Burns that the Council member would have to limit himself to defending Presidential policy has still to materialize. Rather, Kennedy wants the Council to explain his economic strategy on Capitol Hill, as well as formulate its own ideas and debate them in Congress and with himself. For example, after Heller suggested to Congress in early 1961 that new government spending programs were needed to stimulate the economy, the President and Treasury Secretary Dillon were in disagreement.

WALTER W. HELLER
Kennedy (1961-. .)

If the Council served a President incapable of understanding economic issues, the Council Chairman could still present alternative proposals on specific issues to the Joint Economic Committee and its contribution to economic policy would not be totally lost.

As the influence of the Council expands, the potential impact of a misstep becomes greater. Today business firms and even consumers look to the Council for policies affecting their vital interests. When the slow advance of the economy last year fell short of the optimistic projections of the Council, some businesses reversed investment plans.

The Council's obvious involvement in last year's steel price showdown did not convince businessmen of the objectivity of its economic analysis. This is true even though the Council advised the President that slack demand would not sustain higher steel prices, obviating the justification for intervention.

Finally, the tax cut policy itself might be "oversold" by a persusasive Council. Nourse, the ground breaker, foresaw the future nightmares of advisers whose forecasts had gone awry. If the public is convinced that only the new tax program will prevent a serious recession, its rejection by reluctant Congressional committees may peril consumer and producer psychology.

The Council chairman today influences virtually every aspect of the Administration's economic program plus some issues outside the realm of economics. Some of these decisions, such as the substantial Council impact on the Trade Expansion Act of 1962, affect our relations with other countries. Although this imposing role contrasts with the humble beginnings under Nourse, who was frequently ignored by Truman, each of the postwar Presidents and Council chairmen has helped shape the Council's present form.

It is virtually impossible to steer a straight course based purely on economic analysis, and it is less easy to do so in the light of political reality. But Walter Heller, heading a revitalized Council, is attempting to achieve a balanced mixture of two volatile elements—economics and politics. Many of the New Frontier's goals and the fate of the President's economic policies will be determined by the success of the polemics of his Council. ▪

Chapter 43

E. RAY CANTERBERY

The Awkward Independence of the Federal Reserve

Last spring, after long and heated debate, a liberal Congress and a conservative President finally agreed on a fiscal program to help pull the country out of what almost everyone had come to see as the Great Recession. No sooner had it been enacted, however, than there were disturbing signs that the expansionary effects of the tax cut might be negated by a restrictive monetary policy. For under the influence of its powerful chairman, Arthur F. Burns, the Federal Reserve seemed to be substituting its own judgment about economic priorities for that of the nation's elected representatives.

The United States has experienced a similar dilemma many times in the past. For the studiously "nonpolitical" Fed is in the rather anomalous position of having powers that affect, directly and indirectly, every worker and businessman in the country with no clearly defined responsibilities to the Congress, to the President, or to the American people. In the context of the most severe economic crisis since the 1930s, it is certainly appropriate to ask whether this Olympian independence has any place in a democratic society.

The immaculate conception of monetary policy

Prior to the establishment of the Federal Reserve System in 1913, the United States experienced frequent financial panics in which bank reserves were inadequate to cover withdrawals of deposits. The original purposes of the Fed, as stated by Congress,

were "to give the country an elastic currency, to provide facilities for discounting commercial paper, and to improve the supervision of banking." More recently, the Board of Governors of the Federal Reserve has recognized broader responsibilities to "counteract inflationary movements and to share in creating conditions favorable to sustained high employment, stable values, growth of the country, and a rising level of consumption."

But while the Fed has obviously governmental functions, it is a quasi-public agency, partially owned by the private commercial banks it regulates and virtually independent of the rest of the government. Members of the Board of Governors of the Federal Reserve are appointed by the President, with the consent of Congress, to a fourteen-year term of office. The theory was, of course, that since no president could expect to appoint more than two or three members, he would keep his hands off monetary policy. Unwashed politicos, it was thought, would be more responsive to the demands of debtors for a greater supply of "cheap" money and might seek monetary plentitude to cover the costs of large government programs.

During the Second World War, the highly vaunted independence of the Fed was laid aside in the interest of assuring a receptive market for Treasury issues. But the Treasury-Fed accord of 1951 withdrew this financing responsibility, and by 1956 President Eisenhower was speaking of Fed independence in terms that delighted conservative bankers: "The Federal Reserve is set up as a separate agency of Government. It is not under the authority of the President, and I . . . believe it would be a mistake to make it responsible to the political head of state."

The basic premise behind this independence is so obvious—or so embarrassing—that it is seldom mentioned: the general public is either too ignorant or too immoral to be trusted with money management. Having risen above the murky depths of politics, the "Supreme Court of Finance" is regally beyond the influence of the carping citizen. Fed officials can exert their power over the economy with no need to take account of the various special interest groups—or, if the truth be known, the general public.

Yet, it is clear that the Fed is dominated by the attitudes and interests of the private financial community. Indeed, although the Fed was created to supervise the American banking system, one might suppose that the relationship was just the reverse, given the solicitude with which Fed officials consider the views of bankers.

Intentional vagueness

Once the American public was told that tax policy should not be determined by its own representatives. The result, of course, was a revolution against "taxation without representation." But today, the public acquiesces in monetary management without representation, despite the fact that what the Fed decides touches almost everyone, almost every day.

The main reason is public ignorance of the importance of monetary policy. Federal Reserve operations are highly technical and little understood by most members of Congress—and even by many commercial bankers. In addition, the effects of money supply changes are usually so subtle that they are difficult to observe. Since the mystique of money is a useful tool in itself, the Fed attempts to cultivate this lack of understanding. Public statements on current or future policy tend to be inconsistent or vague. Statements on *past* policy normally blame economic adversity on forces beyond the Fed's control, although officials are eager to accept credit for any good news. The technical goals, as expressed for public consumption, always vacillate. At one time, Fed testimony before Congress will indicate that the target of policy is to maintain the "proper" level of free reserves in banks to meet the credit needs of the economy. At another time, Federal Reserve officials will declare that free reserves are irrelevant and point to actions taken to stabilize the money market as facilitating credit availability. Recently, Fed Chairman Burns admitted to the Senate Budget Committee that the agency had fallen well short of its own modest money growth targets in the second half of 1974. But he insisted that this was "not a serious matter" because the Fed was meeting its targets for velocity of money turnover. Some members of the Fed staff were themselves mystified, since they knew of no such "velocity targets" for policymaking.

How monetary policy works

Yet there is no basic reason why the public—and the politicians—should not understand the workings of monetary policy at least as much as they understand fiscal policy. The basic outlines of the process are not that difficult to comprehend.

To stimulate business activity, the central bank normally expands the nation's supply of money (primarily commercial bank deposits) and, therefore, the availability of loanable funds. The System can add to checking deposits by buying government securities in the open market, since this increases the bank reserves on which those deposits are based. These market transactions by the Federal Reserve have at least two potential effects on economic activity: a "liquidity" effect, which influences general spending patterns; and an interest rate effect, which impinges directly on business investment decisions and private construction activity.

Since giant firms have alternatives to bank credit that are not available to smaller businesses, the latter are the first to feel the pinch of tight money. The uneven effects of monetary stringency are best illustrated by the events of 1974, when the Federal Reserve took on much of the burden of fighting the war against inflation. Consumer credit continued to expand substantially, at least until consumer incomes began to fall during the final quarter. But the housing industry was thrown into its worst depression in several decades, and the entire construction industry plunged into a deep slump. The shocking deterioration in economic activity was reflected in widespread layoffs and a large rise in the unemployment rate. Overall, the drop in real GNP was the sharpest since World War II.

Yet, as late as June 1975, the Federal Reserve's chief policymaking body, the Open Market Committee (FOMC) saw its main priority as resisting inflationary pressures and achieving an equilibrium in the country's balance of payments. Burns insisted that an appropriate target for the increase in the money supply was 5 to 7 percent. Most economists, including many on the Fed's staff, believed 8 to 10 percent growth necessary to insure adequate recovery.

The key question now is how the Fed will respond to the recently enacted tax cut, which, added to the decline in revenues due to the fall-off in economic activity, will mean a federal deficit of perhaps \$60 billion. If the Federal Reserve purchases government securities totaling this figure—that is, if it finances the deficit through the banking system—total bank reserves will rise by a multiple of this amount and the money supply will grow rapidly. In this case, the expansionary power of the tax cut will be strongly supported by monetary policy. But what if the Federal Reserve absorbs none of the deficit? Bank reserves and the money supply will at best remain constant, interest rates will soar ever higher, and savings that otherwise would be loaned to the business community will have to be used by the government to pay debts. In effect, the monetary authorities will have confiscated much of the additional spending that Congress tried to induce through the tax cut. What the Fed *intends* to do is, as always, a secret—except for Arthur Burns's vague promise to Congress to maintain a rate of expansion of between 5 and 7.5 percent in a "key version" of the money supply over the balance of the year. Generally the Fed does not even give a hint of what it *has* done until it publishes the edited record of FOMC policy actions ninety days after the event.

A movement toward reform

Not surprisingly, Congress has become more and more disenchanted with the Fed's stiff-necked refusal to take the public into its confidence. And some influential members of Congress have suggested various measures to restrict the Fed's independence. Representative Henry Reuss of Wisconsin, the new Chairman of the House Banking Committee, has suggested a mandate to the Fed to "gently nudge" private commercial banks to lend money to homebuilders and businessmen for productive investment. William Proxmire of Wisconsin, Chairman of the Senate Banking Committee, and Senator Hubert H. Humphrey of Minnesota, Chairman of the Joint Economic Committee, support a legislative requirement that the Fed at least spell out its policy goals in some public form. But the FOMC would probably be just as evasive in writing justifications for its failures to meet congressional objectives as it presently is in rationalizing its inability to hit its own money supply or interest rate targets.

A more radical proposal comes from Milton Friedman, leader of the Chicago school of monetary theorists. Friedman would require that the Fed increase the money supply by a set amount each year (from 3 to 5 percent, depending on which money supply measure is used). His rule is based on the presumption that the Federal Reserve has caused rather than prevented economic instability—or, as Walter W. Heller has put it, "to err is human, and to live by rules is divine." But the idea that economic knowledge is so poor—or the members of the FOMC automatically so incompetent—that a rule should replace deliberate decisions is a rather anachronistic repudiation of the scientific revolution. Despite Friedman's faith in the automatic adjustments of the competitive market system, giant business exercises such strong influence on so much of the American economy that those adjustments are hardly guaranteed. The Friedman rule would probably condemn us to long periods of economic doldrums rather than produce the millennium of a stable economy.

A somewhat more modest proposal has been to put the Fed directly under the authority of the President, who is generally held responsible for mistakes in monetary policy in any case. To do this, however, would reduce one of the real accomplishments of the Fed as it is now set up: by operating outside of the vast federal bureaucracy, it has been able to develop effective machinery to carry out its policies. The Fed is a model of administration in the excellent handling of its service functions; even its mistakes are implemented efficiently. Making it merely another executive department would probably cause it to be unduly constrained by the complicated federal rules and vague regulations that often shackle other agencies.

Another proposal has been to make sure that various groups—unions, academicians, small businessmen, consumer advocates—are adequately represented on the boards of the Federal Reserve banks. These positions are mostly honorific, however, since the banks themselves are actually supervised by the Board of Governors in Washington. A part-time board has neither the time nor the expert knowledge to quarrel intelligently with the policies of the Governors.

Congressional control of the Fed

Any move to make the money managers more responsive to political pressures rests on the hypothesis that a select few do not have inherent abilities or divine rights concerning the money supply. For this reason, no institution should be given solitary jurisdiction over the tripartite functions of determining, implementing, and enforcing such an important function of government.

Prudent judgment moderated by political reality recommends that the Federal Reserve System somehow be made more responsible to the body politic without taking away the Fed's power to avoid direct dependence on the Treasury. This could be accomplished by reforms that would generally enhance congressional authority.

First, the Joint Economic Committee should be given authority to set up a watchdog committee, the Congressional Monetary Committee (CMC), comprised of academic and technical experts who would evaluate monetary policy on a continuous basis within the framework of the Employment Act of 1946. The responsibilities of the CMC would be comparable to the federal budget analysis now provided by the Congressional Budget Committees. The findings of this subcommittee, which could include dissident former Federal Reserve economists, should be published monthly, with a more lengthy year-end report issued.

In order to add force to the recommendations of the CMC, the Joint Economic Committee itself should be given authority to introduce legislation embodying reforms based on the reports of its committee of experts. The new power of Congress could be somewhat balanced by allowing the President to appoint a Board Chairman with a term that corresponds to his own.

Another reform would be to change the internal workings of the Federal Open Market Committee. The practice of placing five regional Reserve Bank presidents on the FOMC, four of whom are on a rotating basis, would be discontinued. These men are generally career Fed employees and are, in any event, subservient to the Board. This would of course remove from the FOMC the President of the New York Fed, currently a permanent member of the committee, who, next to the Chairman himself, generally has had the most to say about the course of monetary policy. This reform would also weaken the close ties of the Fed to its financial constituency, especially the New York banking community.

The effect of these reforms would be to exhume the Federal Reserve from solitary confinement and to make it a political institution, subject to appropriate pressures from the public at large, rather than permitting it to cater to the policy preferences of a small coterie. The high-handed inference that only an exclusive club of inbred alumni can understand monetary policy is at best a self-fulfilling myth that stems from the Fed's own cultivation of a cult of obscurity. The public may not at present fully understand the monetary policy alternatives. But after the impenetrable veil is removed, public knowledge will grow. And as the Fed becomes less of a mystery, its standards of economic policy—and its sense of public responsibility—will inevitably be raised.

Chapter 44

LETTERS

The Independence of Arthur F. Burns

IN THE SILLY SEASON of the nation's bicentennial celebration we perhaps can forgive Arthur Burns, the Chairman of the Board of Governors of the Federal Reserve System, for declaring his independence from the United States *(Challenge*, July/August 1976). For that is what it is: the continued independence of the Federal Reserve from effective congressional monitoring gives the Chairman almost absolute control over monetary policy. Burns attempts to focus the public's attention upon the Federal Reserve Board, but monetary policy is conducted by the Federal Open Market Committee (FOMC), which includes five regional Reserve Bank presidents who are subservient to a Board dominated by its Chairman. (Have you ever read a statement by an ordinary Board member or Reserve Bank president which was an avowed expression of Federal Reserve Policy?)

If there were doubts about the arguments against traditional Federal Reserve independence (Canterbery, *Challenge,* September/October 1975; Kane, *Challenge,* November/December 1975), they are erased by Burns' declaration. Kane and I contended that the Federal Reserve cultivates an obscurity for its own sake out of fear that the public will understand its mechanics and bring monetary policy under the congressional umbrella. I argued that the Fed views itself as the exclusive moral custodian of money, posturing as a "Supreme Court of Finance." I stated that the Fed looks after the special interests of its private financial constituency while expressing self-righteous indignation for those who would end Federal Reserve independence and make the Fed vulnerable to "special interests."

"The concept of independence of the monetary authority within the structure of government is congenial to the basic principles of our Constitution," states Burns. The "partitions between the various branches of government" are to be constructed to make one independent of the other. The truth is: a tripartite governmental structure has evolved that separates the executive, congressional, and judicial branches as well as their primary functions. Neither the Constitution nor the evolving theory of representative government recommends a *fourth* branch, a Federal Reserve whose conduct is modeled "on that of the Supreme Court." More than Burns' misunderstanding of the principles of representative government—well-intentioned though it may be—is required to establish the Fed as a fourth branch.

"[T]he members of the Board scrupulously avoid any contact with interested parties." I presume that this all-inclusive political shyness has no place for the general public and *its* interests. And yet, "every member of the Board, and every member of the Federal Open Market Committee, weighs the issues of monetary and credit policy solely from the viewpoint of the public interest and the general welfare." These members are not ordinary judicial mortals. They are angels who fly through friendly nonpolitical skies, into the marble edifice in Washington, and through the gates held open by the St. Peter of money. The monetary angels hover above the clouds (of their own creation) and yet understand fully the monetary policy needs of the man on the street. The clear implication left by Burns is that no such angels can be found anywhere in the "other three branches" of government.

A truly tripartite government assures that the functions of determining, implementing, and enforcing policy do not rest in the same hands. The Congress does not "adjudicate" (Burns' term). The Supreme Court (the other one) does not administer governmental policy, and the President does not legislate. Should we nonetheless entrust Chairman Burns with all three roles in the area of monetary policy?

While the Fed's antiseptic view of itself is used to defend its playing independently all three roles of government, it is precisely this political isolationism that requires a blind moral trust that we rightly denied to King George. In the Fed's confounding of outside observers, the public has monetary policy without representation. Moral superiority is not a legitimate claim for a branch of government, much less an *agency* of government, in a representative system. Those claims are reserved for the people. I remain unswayed from my conviction that the public needs a Congressional Monetary Committee and the other reforms that I recommend.

E. RAY CANTERBERY
Florida State University

Chapter 45

E. RAY CANTERBERY

Tax reform and incomes policy: a VATIP proposal

The United States does not have an incomes policy. It is not for want of logic, evidence, or ideas that inaction characterizes the state of incomes policy in the United States. It now has been more than a decade since Sidney Weintraub and Henry Wallich (1971) first proposed a Tax-Based Incomes Policy (TIP). At first it was opposed by orthodox economists, who saw no need for special penalties or incentives in an economy enjoying all the comforts of general equilibrium. When TIP emerged politically in October 1978, President Carter proposed a clumsy real wage insurance version because of the *perception* that it otherwise was unfair to labor. Congress rejected the proposal. Wisely so, as it turned out, for the oil price increases of 1979 provided an extra inflationary push that would have shoved the expenses (from the promised insurance payments) of the U.S. Treasury through its roof. Thus far, in the triumph of ideological purity over common sense, President Reagan has opposed *all* incomes policies. Even so, the President apparently no longer believes that Reaganomics will restore nineteenth-century capitalism.

A decade is a long time, and certain conditions have changed. For one thing the effective average corporate income tax rate, the original tax penalty base for TIP, has been approaching zero under the "Economic Recovery Tax Act of 1981." For another, net interest income has been growing nearly 18 percent per year compared with employee compensation, which has been expanding at a rate around 10.5 percent. The irresistible combination of a fast-

The author is Professor of Economics at Florida State University.

rising U.S. *private* debt and soaring U.S. interest rates (thanks to the singular reliance upon monetary policy to fight inflation, an ill-advised massive tax cut in 1981, and a federal budget deficit deepened by the resultant recession) is responsible for skyrocketing net monetary interest.[1] Indeed at the 1970s growth rates for national income and net interest income, the entire U.S. national income would equal net interest income sometime in 1996! This, of course, cannot happen. Be that as it may, it is essential to obtain a new federal revenue source to exert downward pressure on interest rates as well as a TIP that acknowledges monetary interest as a new, increasingly important source of rising production costs.

The federal deficits must be reduced in order to bring down long-term rates in order to establish conditions favorable for a sustained economic expansion. Until this happens, construction will remain in the doldrums, and businesses whose revenues and retained earnings are stagnant or falling will be unable to borrow from the bond market for productive investment purposes. In spite of what monetarists claim, there is a rate of growth in the money supply that will bring long-term rates down. However, the Federal Reserve will not shift policy gears in the absence of an effective incomes policy. Rather, with even the scent of an economic upturn in the air, the Fed will brake the rate of growth in the credit and money supply. A sustained economic expansion appears impossible in the absence of an effective incomes policy.

I would like to propose, therefore: (a) an equitable value-added tax (VAT) as a new revenue source and as the ideal tax base for the immediate implementation of TIP; and (b) a simplified personal income tax program that would satisfy those critics of VAT who view it as inequitable or as another "supply-side" trick to benefit rich savers.[2] A streamlined tax system appears to be an idea whose time has come, for Democrats and Republicans alike in the United States are busily designing various "flat tax" schemes.

[1] John Hotson is responsible for calling this to my attention. See Hotson and Hixson (1982).

[2] The latter view is expressed by Davidson (1981), who appropriately imposes a *ceteris paribus* caveat. Since we agree that gross business savings rather than personal savings comprise the strategic savings for plant and equipment investment, we presumably would agree that a VAT in the absence of other tax relief for the masses is an inappropriate tool for "stimulating" investment by constraining consumption.

In order to keep the argument straightforward, the complete theory behind my proposal will not be presented here.[3]

Equitable value-added and personal income taxes

The closing of all tax loopholes, so that all income (including unearned income) would be taxed alike, would be the first step in raising revenue. This action would be ideologically neutral because no special privileges would be granted. Indeed this reform would greatly diminish the power of special-interest groups that have given Americans Will Rogers' "best Congress money can buy."

The next step would require a second tax reform based upon the understanding that every family, rich or poor, buys necessities. A value-added tax can be introduced in slow stages (perhaps 2 percent the first year) as "revenue enhancement." Such a tax raises the price level by at least the percentage of the tax and thus must be implemented in stages. In theory, the tax base for VAT is the value added to the product at each level of production. In practice, the tax base is measured by the increase in sales price at each stage of production. Each stage in the chain collects the VAT on its sales, takes a credit for VAT paid on purchases to other firms, and remits the net amount of VAT to the IRS. At the end of the chain, the consumer pays the full amount of the tax in the sales price of the good or service and *with no other reform measure* would bear the full burden. Thus, VAT is in its effects a national sales tax. Administrative efficiency demands that all consumption should be taxed at a single, flat rate. This means that VAT should *not* be implemented without a reduction in the income taxes paid on the personal income allocated to necessities.

Exemptions for dependents under the income tax code were originally meant to cover the above contingency, namely, to provide a tax credit equal to the amount spent simply to maintain life. As a *required* counterpart of VAT, the family income tax exemption should be raised for all taxpayers to a value equal to the cost of a marketbasket of necessities. The BLS "lower" consumption budget or a share of it, say 80 percent, might be used as the measure of the necessities basket. A flat tax rate would apply to *all* income in excess of the minimal consumption budget (gross dis-

[3] A general discussion of such a theory appears in Canterbery (1980) and a technical discourse is found in Canterbery (1979*b*).

eliminate the future need for social security and ultimately the payroll tax connected with such benefits.

New incomes policy: TIP for VAT or VATIP

The combination of VAT, tax credit exemptions, and the negative income tax has two unexpected bonuses. The redistribution of income and wealth by the "Economic Recovery Tax Act of 1981" toward the *ultra*discretionary households (those with incomes $80,000 or more) reduced the size of mass markets for new products or services and therefore penalized new industry. For example, the well-to-do can now afford personal computers, but a mass market that would give economies of scale and lower prices requires that the middle class purchase not only Apple but presently higher-priced IBM personal computers. The guarantee of tax-free income for life's necessities and truly graduated income tax rates would assure that the middle class would once again enjoy discretionary income and the wherewithal to buy newly marketed products.

For the sake of keeping the inflation rate within manageable limits and of encouraging an expansionary monetary policy, we turn to a second advantage of VAT. It is the ideal instrument for immediately implementing a tax-based incomes policy (TIP). The Weintraub-Wallich TIP would penalize with an extra corporate tax bite any one of the 2,000 or so largest corporations granting an *average* pay hike in excess of the historical economywide pace of productivity improvement. As a by-product of the reliable theory behind the original TIP, we know that if value added (or net sales) grows at the same pace as *real* output, inflation would be minimized. The Federal Reserve would be free to follow an easy money policy without the fear of domestically induced inflation. VAT can fill the incomes policy void. A firm with a 1 percentage point increase in value added (its payments to the factors of production which include profits, net interest, and rent payments as well as all employee compensation) in excess of an *adjusted* real output growth norm could be penalized by adding 1 percentage point to its VAT. Why *adjusted* real output growth norm? Some 2 or 3 percentage points should be added to the historical average real output pace because some price increases simply reflect preferences for a higher-priced marketbasket of goods. Suppose we add a

4 percent historical real output growth rate (labor productivity growth rate plus labor force growth rate) to a 2 percent "conflation" rate.[5] With the adjusted output growth norm of 6 percent, a giant firm allowing its value added from wages and salaries, net interest, rents, or profits to rise 7 percent would have to pay 1 percentage point extra in value-added taxes. A firm with a value-added increase of 8 percent would pay a 2 percent penalty. In actual practice, those firms raising net prices (after purchases from other firms) by 7 or 8 percent would be penalized accordingly.

A special device is required to prevent price expectations from spoiling any incomes policy. In order to prevent the giants from passing along any penalty tax in the way of higher prices, the penalty is deliberately set equal to 100 percent of any price increase above the norm. Since TIP for VAT treats all income sources alike, it has a dual advantage. First, the employer gains no special advantage in holding down wage payments alone because all his income payments are taxed. Second, it is possible to tax away *all* value-added increases in excess of the norm so that the corporation can never race ahead of the tax collector with "catch-up" price increases.

A simple formula demonstrates the administrative simplicity of VATIP. Under VATIP, the tax rate of the *i*-th corporation (vt_i) would be:

$$(1) \qquad vt_i = vt_b + 1.00\,(v_i - q), \quad \text{if } v_i > q$$
$$vt_i = vt_b, \qquad \text{if } v_i \leqslant q,$$

where vt_b = base VAT rate, 1.00 = the VATIP "multiplier" that is always set at 1.00, v_i = the percentage increase in value added at the *i*-th firm, and q = the national norm for the growth rate in real potential output. Suppose the initial value of value-added tax (vt_b) is 2 percent, the real output growth norm (q) is the aforementioned 6 percent, and the *i*-th firm's value-added growth rate is 9 percent. The firm's value-added tax (vt_i) would be 5 percent with 3 percent-

[5] The term "conflation" comes from Warsh (1977) who has advanced a "complexity" theory of the price level. When the prices of highways, American tanks in El Salvador, and pollution control equipment are diffused into the prices of automobiles, what we are undergoing, Warsh suggests, is not inflation but "conflation" which describes "what happens to old costs when new ones are added" (Warsh, 1977, p. 205). Yet we appear to want what the new costs deliver.

age points penalty, which is to say that 100 percent of the "inflationary" value added is taxed away.

In the vintage TIP, the tax rate of the *i*-th corporation would be:

$$(2) \qquad t_i = b + m\,(w_i - n), \quad \text{if } w_i > n$$
$$t_i = b, \qquad \text{if } w_i \leq n,$$

where b = base corporate tax rate (then 46 percent for many large corporations); m = the TIP "multiplier," w_i = percentage increase in average hourly compensation at the *i*-th firm, and n = the national hourly compensation productivity norm. Even with the 46 percent corporate tax rate there was always the threat that the tax could be passed to the consumer unless the value of m were (unacceptably) large. For example, a firm that granted a 9 percent w_i at the 6 percent norm would only face a 100 percent tax rate if m were set at 18. Seidman (1979) advanced several tortured reasons why it would be "unnecessary" to set m so large, but this served only to make TIP look too complicated for implementation. Moreover, after the Reaganomics tax breaks many giant corporations paid zero or negative taxes in 1981. At a zero tax rate, the aforementioned firm would only face a 100 percent tax penalty if m were set at 33.3!

One possible objection to VATIP is that it provides the corporation with more flexibility and freedom in its distribution of value added between wages and profits than does TIP alone. Since the VATIP penalty is 100 percent for any violator, a corporation confronted with a union or nonunion labor shortage due to a sharp rise in its product demand may have to take a profits cut either voluntarily by staying within the value-added growth rate norm or involuntarily (by an equal percentage) if it exceeds the norm. Since employee compensation presently comprises the largest share of value added, however, the pursuit of moderation in all such income payments would seem a logical corporate strategy.

A second possible objection is that VATIP requires a new system of taxes whereas TIP is a more modest permutation of the extant system. VAT *would* be new for the United States, but the United Kingdom, Western Europe, and the Scandinavian countries have VATs. We should not forever lag behind the Old World, and indeed flat tax proposals are becoming epidemic in the United States.[6] The U.S. economy is at the center of the global stagflation

[6] Sidney Weintraub has gently chided me with these two objections. These statements are my response.

storm, but global stability would be further enhanced if these Old World governments also implemented a VATIP policy.

External sources of inflation

A third objection applies equally to TIP and VATIP. An incomes policy, including the VATIP proposal, is not equally effective against every source of inflation. For example, the tax penalty cannot be imposed on foreign suppliers. An increase in the price of an import necessary as an intermediary good will be deducted by the domestic corporation as a part of its purchases from other producers. However, the VATIP penalty will confine the externally induced price rise to a one-time stimulus at the front end of the price level; still there would be no "inflationary" increase in *domestically generated* national income, and inflation from an external source cannot be sustained unless the external price continues to rise.

This ability to contain but not control foreign economic shocks embodies a warning to the industrialized countries. The successful cartelization of necessary primary commodity imports still can increase production costs and raise the price levels of the industrialized countries. Therefore, supplementary policies may be required to ease external shocks.

Taxation and armament

The long-run objective for the United States would be to shift roughly four-fifths of Federal revenue sources to VAT and one-fifth to the personal income tax. Ultimately the personal income tax could be used solely for financing national defense. The main contribution of the working class to defense and war efforts has been to supply manpower. More equity could be achieved by financing defense with the progressive tax on incomes. If the rich object to their taxes going to national defense, they have the resources to lobby for disarmament or slower growth in the defense establishment. On the other hand VAT is less visible, less felt. Those presently in tax shelters apparently "feel" that too much of their taxes go to social programs. With the allocation of VAT revenues to the income grants for the poor, education, and other socially necessary programs, the currently sheltered could be painlessly altruistic. Moreover, they can see each VAT increase swell their income tax credits.

Toward industrial peace in the United States

The last weapon in this new policy arsenal is again for the longer run and would require considerable public discussion and refinement in the United States. It is widely agreed that the combination of corporate, union, and government power in the United States is unfair to the balance of society. Smithian consumer benefits have gone the way of perfect competition, so that a new social contract is needed. Federal charters could mandate the 2,000 largest corporations to include equal representation from labor, business, and consumers on their boards. Fairness requires a disinterest achievable through balanced public participation in pricing, investment, and wage setting.

Similarly, some of these public representatives could also be members of quasi-public planning panels for each concentrated industry.[7] Such panels could make indicative forecasts rather than explicitly directing investment funds. Furthermore, selected *new* growth industries could be supported by research and development foundations similar to the National Science Foundation but jointly supported by government and industry. Any revenue from the U.S. VATIP penalties could be used to start such funds. Such an arrangement bears more directly to the productivity point than the Reaganomics tax reductions for the supradiscretionary households, as such foundations could speed the shift of industry structure in its postindustrial direction. Once the new social contract is working, the VATIP can be dropped. Indeed the VATIP itself would be an incentive to move from a tax penalty system to the complete decision-making flexibility afforded by voluntary arrangements.

The Reaganomics tilt toward the supradiscretionary households is precisely the wrong direction. To restore an adequate U.S. real economic growth pace, the poor and a resurrected middle class must spend, and for that they need adequate real income. To restore health and equity to the American economy, only a policy reversal will do. And of course, this restoration is critical to the health of the entire global economy.

[7] This is an abbreviated version of an earlier proposal (Canterbery, 1979*a*). Eichner (1976) also has proposed such planning panels.

REFERENCES

Canterbery, E. R. Contribution to Symposium on "The Threatening Economy." Ed. by D. Mermelstein. *The New York Times Magazine*, December 30, 1979. (*a*)

________. "Inflation, Necessities and Distributive Efficiency." In *Essays in Post-Keynesian Inflation*. Ed. by J. H. Gapinski and C. E. Rockwood. Cambridge, Mass.: Ballinger, 1979. (*b*)

________. *The Making of Economics*. 2nd edition. Belmont, Ca.: Wadsworth Publishing Company, 1980.

Davidson, P. "Can VAT Resolve the Shortage of Savings (SOS) Distress?" *Journal of Post Keynesian Economics*, 1981, *4*(1).

Eichner, A. *The Megacorp and Oligopoly: Micro Foundations of Macro Dynamics*. Cambridge: Cambridge University Press, 1976.

Hotson, J. H., and Hixson, W. F. "Reaganomics and the Tax-Bond: An Escape Route for Capitalism?" Paper before the Eastern Economic Association Meetings, Washington, D.C., April 30, 1982.

Seidman, L. S. "TIP: Feasibility and Equity." *Journal of Post Keynesian Economics*, 1979, *1*(4).

Wallich, H., and Weintraub, S. "A Tax-Based Incomes Policy." *Journal of Economic Issues*, June 1971, 5.

Warsh, D. "The Great Hamburger Paradox." *Forbes*, September 15, 1977.

Chapter 46

THE FLAT TAX, NEGATIVE TAX, AND VAT: GAINING PROGRESSIVITY AND REVENUE

E. Ray Canterbery, Eric W. Cook, and Bernard A. Schmitt

Overview of Current Tax Reform Proposals

The ubiquitous attack on the federal income tax system has accelerated in recent years. Even economists no longer believe that modest alterations in the present system will suffice. Tax reform has come to mean a complete overhaul of a system riddled with holes. The four tax reform proposals that have received the most attention are the Fair tax (H.R. 3271, S. 1421), introduced by Senator Bill Bradley and Congressman Richard Gephardt; the Fair and Simple (FAST) tax (H.R. 6165, S. 2948), introduced by Congressman Jack Kemp and Senator Robert Kasten; Treasury I, the U.S. Treasury's tax simplification proposal; and Treasury II, the White House's modified version of Treasury I.

The present income tax is held in disrepute because it violates five basic principles of taxation:

1. The tax system should be fair, sufficiently fair to encourage compliance. Horizontal fairness, an idea that dates to Plato, requires taxpayers with the same incomes (regardless of sources) to pay roughly the same amount of tax. Vertical fairness would have taxpayers with higher incomes paying more tax than those with lower incomes. Virtually everyone agrees with these notions of fairness except apparently those special interest groups who try to control tax legislation.

Cato Journal, Vol. 5, No. 2 (Fall 1985).

E. Ray Canterbery is Professor of Economics at Florida State University. Eric W. Cook and Bernard A. Schmitt are staff economists with the Joint Committee on Taxation of the U.S. Congress. The views expressed in this paper are those of the authors and do not reflect in any way positions taken by the nonpartisan staff of the Joint Committee on Taxation.

2. The tax system should be simple and understandable to the taxpayer. The personal income tax was sufficiently complex in 1983 that $3 billion was spent on tax preparation. This may explain why H & R Block opposes tax reform.
3. The tax system should have a broad base. Tax reformers, beginning 40 years ago with Henry Simons at the University of Chicago, have argued for a broad tax base. The reason is as simple as tax simplification: the broader the tax base, the lower the tax rates required for a targeted revenue.
4. The tax system should impede as little as possible the long-run allocation of resources: this is the economic efficiency principle. Today, the well-to-do family and the corporation are at least as much concerned with what an investment will do to their taxes as they are with what it will do for production. Today, tax preferences, which generally take the form of tax expenditures, are so pervasive that they exceed the amount of revenue generated by the income tax system.
5. The federal tax system should contribute to economic stability by cushioning swings in consumer and business incomes from the business cycle. Tax revenues that decline more rapidly than incomes during recessions and rise more rapidly during expansions cushion such swings in income.

In the three decades ending in 1979 the tax system adequately funded the federal government. This is so even though the federal revenue-to-spending ratio dropped to about 91 percent during the 1970s. This latter decline is largely attributable to deep recessions during the Nixon and Ford administrations. If one uses forecasts from David Stockman, who until recently headed the Office of Management and Budget (OMB) and was notorious for his overoptimism, the federal revenue-to-spending ratio will remain at only 80 percent from fiscal 1985 onward, even with strong economic growth. Will any of the major tax reform proposals alter this future? Regretably, they will not because they are all designed to be revenue neutral, and (without tinkering) would not generate any more revenue in 1985 than the present system.

Despite its other faults the present income tax has considerable vertical equity; it is progressive in structure since the average tax burden rises with income. Those with the highest incomes receive the greatest benefits from a stable, democratic government and from the free enterprise system. It is poetic justice that those who benefit the most in terms of the government's nurture and preservation of wealth should pay the highest tax rates. There are those who contend that all taxation is a burden. Let there be no mistake about it; it is, but such antagonists (or anarchists) miss the point. Unless the federal government enforces contracts and deters crime against property, develops and maintains a national system of communications and transportation, guarantees a nationwide system of education that provides a skilled labor force for industry, stabilizes the economy, regulates trade, and protects factories from foreign enemies, individuals and businesses will not be able to utilize fully their capacities for earning incomes. Taxation is a burden that individuals agree to share in order to maintain the necessary infrastructure for corporate enterprise and a free society. No political theorist ever said that government enterprise was a free lunch or that it should be. A plane cargo without an airport, a truckload of personal computers halted by a collapsed bridge, a factory bombed by the enemy, or an information industry dependent upon illiterates are all useless.

With respect to fairness, all of the aforementioned reform proposals are generally less progressive in nominal terms than the present system. In particular, the FAST tax, the flattest of them all, would shift some of the relative tax burden to middle-class taxpayers because low- and high-income taxpayers would receive a larger relative tax reduction.

Irrespective of the relative importance of tax simplification, its limits are set by the necessity to tax net rather than gross income. All of the major tax reform proposals would simplify and broaden the tax base by eliminating many tax preferences. However, exclusions such as the personal exemption that are available to most taxpayers and serve important goals are retained. As a general principle, the tax code can only be "as simple as possible," given potential conflicts with other important goals of the tax code.

An Alternative Proposal: FLANVAT

This proposal—for a flat, negative, and VAT tax system (FLANVAT)—is a combination of a modified flat-rate system of federal income tax reform for individuals with an income-based refundable tax credit (FLAN) and a value-added tax (VAT).[1] The FLAN reform program replaces the multi-bracketed tax-rate structure for individuals with three tax rates, which range from 10 to 30 percent, and applies these rates against a substantially broadened tax base. This part of the program is structured so that it would not significantly

[1] *The overall configuration of this proposal first was presented in Canterbery (1983).* Additional detail was provided in Canterbery (1984). The present paper elaborates the specific characteristics of the proposal and provides a quantitative analysis of its impact.

change total tax liabilities, total federal expenditures, the distribution of tax liabilities, or federal expenditures among income classes (though such could be done).

The tax base under the reform program would be expanded by repealing most exemptions, deductions, and credits as well as a number of additional tax expenditures. These alterations would expand the tax base for all income classes. An income-based refundable credit would assist the same lower-income groups even as it provided about the same dollar amount of assistance as the federal income-security programs that it replaced. The refundable income tax credit would guarantee a proportion of poverty level income, which is based on a necessities budget and demographics. This credit would be phased out as an individual's income increased, although the credit phase-out would be limited by a low-level credit floor. Finally, a comprehensive value-added tax (VAT) is suggested as a means for raising net revenue and therefore as a sorely needed deficit-fighter. The regressive feature of a flat VAT would be offset by the indexation of personal exemptions and by the refundable income tax credit.

Income Taxation and Welfare: The FLAN Program

Tax Code Simplification

The first step in reform is to broaden the tax base and to simplify the income-tax system even while increasing its fairness to assure compliance. Most current deductions from adjusted gross income for individual exemptions would be repealed. Although the parental personal exemption for students age 19 or over and the exemptions for the taxpayer and spouse, dependents, aged, and blind are repealed under the proposed FLAN program, these exemptions would be converted into a credit (see below). The program also would repeal most existing credits, such as the residential energy credits, targeted jobs credits, and the investment tax credit. The foreign tax credit would be retained.

Eight present deductions would be repealed and others modified; among those eliminated would be charitable contributions, moving expenses, and contributions to Individual Retirement Accounts (IRAs) and Keogh plans. The deduction for medical expenses would be altered such that the allowable deduction would be in the amount of 10 percent of adjusted gross income rather than the 5 percent under present law. The itemized deductions that would be retained are deductions for business expenses. In addition, the statutory adjustments to income that would be retained are deductions for employee business expenses and alimony paid.

The tax base would be further broadened and the tax system further simplified by the elimination of 28 tax preferences that also would increase fairness. Gone would be such tax expenditures as the expensing of research and development expenditures and the exploration and development costs for oil, gas, and other fuels. Moreover, compensation would be taxed irrespective of source or name so that workmen's compensation benefits, unemployment insurance benefits, railroad retirement benefits, social security benefits, and contributions to employer-provided insurance and profit-sharing plans would be treated as income.

Changes in Social Security

Two significant changes would be made to social security that relate to benefits and the federal income tax treatment of those benefits: (1) The social security earnings test would be repealed. (2) Some 80 percent of social security benefits would be included in total income for federal income tax purposes.

As a result of the repeal of the exclusions for a number of employer-provided fringe benefits, the social security tax base also would be expanded such that compensation would include these items for purposes of social security taxation. Although these modifications would place social security on a more solid funding basis, the proposed negative income tax would reduce the public's reliance on social security benefits.

Necessities and the Personal Exemption (Tax Credit)

The second step makes the elements of the first palatable. Every family, rich or poor, buys necessities. Exemptions for dependents under the income tax code originally were meant to cover the above contingency, namely, to provide a tax credit equal to the amount spent simply to maintain life. Ultimately there should be only one individual exemption. The household income tax exemption for dependents would be raised to a value equal, or close to, the cost of a marketbasket of necessities for those who are poor. The value of this sole exemption, a refundable tax credit, would vary only with the cost of the marketbasket and the demographics of the household. The government annually calibrates the value of a minimal household budget by defining poverty level incomes based on the current cost-of-living and on demographic characteristics. This official poverty level would be the basis for the refundable tax credit to cover necessities.[2]

[2]In the initial proposal (Canterbery 1983), the use of the BLS "lower" consumption budget or share of it, say 80 percent, for the relevant geographic region and family size was suggested.

Four features are aimed at providing for basic necessities: (1) a defined minimum for which a zero tax-rate applies; (2) a 10 percent tax rate on all taxable income to $20,000 (single filing status) and $35,000 (joint filing status); (3) a refundable tax credit for the poor; and (4) indexation of the refundable tax credit as well as the official definition of poverty to the annual inflation rate. (The official definition of poverty income presently varies with the inflation rate.) This means that the refundable tax credit also is indexed to inflation. The zero bracket amounts would be $1,500 for taxpayers using joint filing status, $1,000 for taxpayers using either a single or a head of household filing status, and $750 for those married and filing separately.

Marginal Tax Rates: A Tri-flat Tax

The third step introduces a modified flat tax system; three statutory tax rates of 10, 25, and 30 percent would be applied to taxable income. Since most deductions and tax preferences would be eliminated, the tax rates would apply to virtually all income above the zero tax bracket. The three marginal tax rates and the complete tax schedule appear in Table 1. The maximum marginal tax rate of 30 percent would be attractive to almost everyone. In addition to modifying the rate structure, the FLAN program would abolish indexation of the tax brackets. However, the indexation of the refundable tax credit under FLAN would moderate, but not eliminate, the present-law automatic stabilization. Since this proposal attempts to insure that families can provide for absolute necessities, the indexation of the refundable tax credit is far more important than the indexation of the three tax brackets. Moreover, the automatic countercyclical effects of the federal tax system would be retained, though probably dampened during expansions.

The Negative Income Tax: An Income-based Refundable Credit

There is still a social problem with the unemployed and present unemployables who have incomes below a minimal consumption budget. Conservatives bemoan the "disincentives" of the hodgepodge of welfare services: liberals complain about the infringements upon freedom and dignity from the various "needs tests." The negative income tax, endorsed by liberals such as James Tobin and conservatives such as Milton Friedman, is an ingenious system for transferring income to the poor, and providing a minimum guaranteed income. This income should be sufficient to maintain the social minimum for necessities. A negative income tax could reduce the present burdens placed on the social security system and the payroll tax connected with future benefits.

TABLE 1

PROPOSED TAX BRACKETS AND TAX RATES, 1985

Tax Bracket	Rate Structure
	Single Filing Status
$0 to $1,000	no tax
$1,000 to $20,000	$0 plus 10% of excess over $1,000
$20,000 to $65,000	$1,900 plus 25% of excess over $20,000
Over $65,000	$13,500 plus 30% of excess over $65,000
	Joint Filing Status
$0 to $1,500	no tax
$1,500 to $35,000	$0 plus 10% of excess over $1,500
$35,000 to $100,000	$3,350 plus 25% of excess over $35,000
Over $100,000	$19,600 plus 30% of excess over $100,000
	Married Filing Separately
$0 to $750	no tax
$750 to $17,500	$0 plus 10% of excess over $750
$17,500 to $50,000	$1,675 plus 25% of excess over $17,500
Over $50,000	$9,800 plus 30% of excess over $50,000
	Head of Household
$0 to $1,000	no tax
$1,000 to $30,000	$0 plus 10% of excess over $1,000
$30,000 to $75,000	$2,900 plus 25% of excess over $30,000
Over $75,000	$14,150 plus 30% of excess over $75,000

NOTE: Indexation of the personal refundable tax credit would be introduced under the FLAN program and would begin in 1986. Present-law indexation of the tax brackets would be repealed.

Our society is committed to the provision of absolute necessities for every person in need. However, the welfare programs are comprised of a strange assortment of "incomes in kind." The government can best reduce its direct bureaucratic involvement in such programs by moving toward a cash payment system as quickly as possible. Even before the full implementation of a negative income tax, administered solely by the Internal Revenue Service, the government could convert the food stamp program into a cash program. Then the household would have the freedom to allocate such resources to best meet its immediate needs, and the government could get out of the welfare business. Most federal income-security programs—under the broad categories of unemployment compensation, housing assistance, food and nutrition assistance, supplemental security income, AFDC, and low-income energy assistance—can be eliminated under the tax reform program. The president's "Budget of the United States Government, 1985," estimates that the federal expenditures for these programs will be approximately $64 billion in fiscal 1985. Though it may be prudent to phase out gradually such programs, the need for such programs fades from the social landscape once a negative income tax is a reality. None of the other tax reform proposals provide for this social welfare reform on the expenditures side.

Under FLAN, a negative income tax, comprised of a refundable credit administered on a monthly basis by the Internal Revenue Service, would replace the present federal welfare system. The negative income tax would guarantee at least 50 percent of poverty level income to an individual electing to use the single filing status, and guarantee generally over 75 percent of poverty level income to those filing jointly. For the head of household filing status, over 60 percent of poverty level income generally would be guaranteed. To the extent income assistance is an incentive, the poor would be motivated to stay within the family unit.

The initial credit amounts that replace the current personal exemptions would be based upon both the filing status and the number of dependents. The definitions of the taxpayer, spouse, and dependents would be similar to the present tax code, although no additional credit amounts would be provided to the aged or the blind. The initial credit amount for the single person and the head of a household would be $2,800. For the joint filing status, the initial credit amount would be $5,400. To these amounts, $1,500 would be added for each dependent, up to a maximum of $6,000. The estimates provided in Table 2 and just summarized reflect averages for the population as a whole. In practice, since poverty levels vary with demographic char-

TABLE 2

ESTIMATED POVERTY LEVELS AND GUARANTEED MINIMUM INCOME LEVELS, 1985

	Family Size					
	1	2	3	4	5	6
Poverty Level (PL)	5,546	7,107	8,702	11,157	13,208	14,941
Joint Filing Status		5,400	6,900	8,400	9,900	11,400
(% PL)	NA	(76)	(79)	(75)	(75)	(76)
Single or Head						
of Household	2,800	4,300	5,800	7,300	8,800	10,300
(% PL)	(50)	(61)	(67)	(65)	(67)	(69)

acteristics, these credit amounts would be adjusted so that the same proportions of poverty-level income would be guaranteed for the different filing statuses in various geographical areas. Credit amounts would not be adjusted to reflect different ages or a variety of family structures.

The effective marginal tax rates under present welfare programs are very high. A family of four with only $8,000 in wage income, for example, would qualify for various programs under present law. This family would be qualified to receive food stamps and the earned income credit among other benefits. The effective marginal tax rate for this family would be the food stamp phase-out rate of 30 percent plus the earned income credit phase-out rate of 12.5 percent plus the federal income tax rate of 11 percent, which yields a total effective marginal tax rate of 53.5 percent.

If this family elected to receive other federal benefits such as housing assistance, supplemental security income, or low-income energy assistance, the phase-out rates for each program would be added to this 53.5 percent. Since the phase-out rates for the housing assistance programs are generally 30 percent, for supplemental security income, 50 percent, for AFDC, 100 percent, an effective marginal tax rate in excess of 100 percent is easily attainable for those receiving benefits under several programs. The eligibility requirements of the programs vary with the state and specific circumstances.

In 1981, 58.5 percent of the 11.7 million households below the poverty line received either medicaid, public housing, food stamps, or school lunch benefits, and 37.8 percent of these households received benefits from more than one of these programs. When these income-based programs are combined with the present federal tax system very high marginal federal tax rates can result—rates far in excess of the marginal tax rates of the upper middle income or even rich taxpayers. On top of this, the earnings test applied to present social security benefits reduces social security benefits by 50 cents for every dollar earned in excess of a certain threshold, which results in a 50 percent marginal tax rate. Finally, the present-law taxation of social security benefits counts income twice over certain income ranges; in such cases a $100 increase in income adds $150 to adjusted gross income, effectively increasing the marginal tax rate by 50 percent.

The marginal tax rates under the proposed negative income tax are lower. The refundable credit would be phased out at a 35 percent rate as adjusted gross income exceeded zero, but would be limited by a credit floor. Thus, if an individual's adjusted gross income increased by $1,000, the credit would be reduced by $350. The credit floor would be equal to $100 for a taxpayer and $100 for a spouse plus $100 times the number of dependents. Therefore, for a family of four filing a joint return, the credit floor would be $400.

The social security earnings test would be repealed, eliminating the implicit 50 percent marginal tax rate. Also, the present-law tax treatment of social security benefits would be repealed.[3] The proposed refundable credit, meanwhile, would be lowered by 64 percent of any social security benefits received. Consequently, for those social security recipients with incomes that place them in the phase-out range of the negative income tax, an increase in social security benefits of $1,000 would result in a combined increase in federal income tax liability and a credit reduction equal to $1,000. Thus, over certain ranges of income, social security benefit increases would be offset by equal refundable tax credit reductions.[4]

Effective Marginal Tax Rates: Low-Income Taxpayers

The combination of the highest statutory income tax rate with the income-based negative income tax alters the effective marginal tax rates. For the low-income taxpayer, the first positive income tax rate of 10 percent would be added to the negative income tax phase-out rate of 35 percent. An individual whose adjusted gross income places him in the phase-out range of the negative income tax would receive an effective 45 percent marginal tax rate, the highest attainable.[5] Of course, if an individual's income places him outside the phase-out range of the negative income tax, the effective marginal tax rate is the same as the statutory marginal tax rate. This 45 percent effective marginal tax rate may seem high, but it generally represents a significant reduction compared to the present tax system.

Revenue and Distributional Effects: A Simulation

A simulation model[6] allows a comparison of the existing distribution of federal income tax liabilities by income class with the post-reform distribution. The revenue shortfalls suggested by Table 3 and

[3]The double counting of income over certain income ranges would be repealed as well.

[4]The cost of administration of this program likely would be no more and possibly substantially less than the costs of administration of the current income-security programs because duplication of services would be lessened. The administrative costs currently are approximately 11 percent of the budgets of these programs according to Congressional Research Service estimates.

[5]The tax brackets are structured so that the credit floor is attained prior to the entrance into the next bracket and its associated higher tax rate.

[6]The estimation of the revenue and distributional effects of the FLAN program is based largely on simulations using the Individual Income Tax Model of the Joint Committee on Taxation. This model compares tax liability under present law to the reform proposal

Table 4 are not indicative of the complete proposal's impact in either 1981 or 1985. For one thing, data used in the simulation model do not contain information on the repealed provisions proposed as base-broadening measures. These "off-model" items, if repealed, are estimated to increase individual federal income tax liabilities by $5.6 billion in calendar year 1985 compared with present law. (Table 3 and Table 4 do not include these off-model items. Moreover, these tables do not address expenditure changes under the program.)

Since social security taxes also would be increased by the reform proposal, the estimated distribution of the combined tax liabilities is presented in Table 4. This distribution includes the estimated federal income tax liabilities from Table 3 plus estimated social security contributions of employees and the self-employed based upon 1985 law, excluding employers' contributions.

TABLE 3

SIMULATION OF FEDERAL INCOME TAX LIABILITIES UNDER TAX REFORM

Expanded Income ($ thousands)	Present Law	FLAN Reform Program	Change	Percentage Change
0 to 10	3,848	−66,383	−69,932	−1817.3
10 to 20	29,027	17,041	−11,987	−41.3
20 to 30	43,496	39,880	−3,616	−8.3
30 to 40	38,428	35,701	−2,727	−7.1
40 to 50	25,225	25,790	564	2.2
50 to 75	26,152	27,536	1,384	5.3
75 to 100	12,076	12,298	222	1.8
100 to 200	18,978	18,545	−433	−2.3
200 +	17,558	17,401	−157	−.9
Total	214,489	127,809	−86,680	−40.4

NOTE: Estimates are subject to rounding errors and are in millions of dollars. These figures include most of the changes made under the Deficit Reduction Act of 1984 with the most significant exceptions being changes made to income averaging and the holding period for long-term capital gains and losses.

---

using a sample of 86,052 actual returns weighted to represent the characteristics of the total population. The simulations use 1981 levels of income and expenditures to compare the reform program to 1985 law. Thus, this analysis is "static" in the sense that no change in individuals' behavior is provided for as a result of the change in law. Although this assumption may not be realistic in some instances, it does provide a consistent basis for comparing different proposals.

TABLE 4

SIMULATION OF FEDERAL INCOME TAX AND SOCIAL SECURITY TAX LIABILITIES UNDER TAX REFORM

Expanded Income ($ thousands)	Present Law	FLAN Reform Program	Change	Percentage Change
0 to 10	13,722	−54,302	−68,024	−495.7
10 to 20	50,510	40,048	−10,462	−20.7
20 to 30	69,504	67,301	−2,203	−3.2
30 to 40	58,353	56,512	−1,840	−3.2
40 to 50	35,436	36,271	834	2.4
50 to 75	33,962	35,452	1,489	4.4
75 to 100	14,297	14,536	239	1.7
100 to 200	20,842	20,421	−421	−2.0
200 +	18,022	17,868	−155	−.9
Total	314,649	234,106	−80,543	−25.6

NOTE: See note to Table 3.

The FLAN program is distributionally neutral[7] for the income classes above $20,000. For the income classes below $20,000, the net effect of the program would be such that their treatment would be essentially the same as under present law. Of course, the negative income tax requires federal expenditures in the form of refundable income credits, an outlay estimated to be $63.1 billion in calendar year 1985. The estimated change in federal expenditures from all the previously described changes would be $6 billion in calendar year 1985. The estimated impact on tax liabilities of the reform program for calendar year 1985, *excluding the outlay portion of the negative income tax*, is that it would increase federal income and social security tax liabilities by $7.7 billion as compared to present law. Thus, this income tax reform program also is revenue neutral (within 5 percent of the estimate of the tax liability under present law).

A Value-Added Tax Base for Revenue Enhancement

Still, the income tax alone is not the ideal form of taxation. An effectively progressive income tax (essential for equity) cannot be neutral in its impact on the long-run allocation of resources. A tri-flat progressive tax on discretionary income, in the absence of other revenue sources, would tax personal saving at a high marginal rate.

[7]A program generally is considered to be distributionally neutral if it does not change the distribution of tax liabilities by income class by more than 5 percent.

However, a part of this impact is mitigated by other sources of investment funds. Total federal taxes paid by corporations has steadily declined from 32.1 percent of total federal government receipts in 1952 to 6.2 percent in 1983. A large share of gross business investment is financed from retained corporate earnings. These earnings come from consumer expenditures that would be bolstered by spending from tax-exempt income and the negative income tax. Nevertheless, in the interest of neutrality and the avoidance of double taxation of corporate profits, ideally a final step ought to be taken, namely, to reduce corporate profits taxes to zero. This move, however, cannot be made in a single step because of present revenue requirements and because of the tax avoidance that incorporation would provide.

The impending death of corporate income taxation and the residual problems with even a reformed personal income tax system brings us to a needed and attractive additional tax base. For a quarter of a century public interest in a value-added tax has waxed and waned in the United States but never quite disappeared. During 1979 and 1980 Senator Russell Long and Representative Al Ullman, chairmen of the two congressional tax-writing committees, courageously supported such a tax. One cannot avoid speculating how much different economic history might have been if Ullman's H. R. 5665, the Tax Restructuring Act of 1979, had been considered and passed. Possibly, VAT failed to gain widespread support because it was not considered within the context of a larger debate on tax structure and equity; FLAN eliminates this objection.

Administrative efficiency and reasonable collection costs require that all consumption should be taxed at a single, flat rate—a flat VAT. For equity, this means that VAT should not be implemented without the recommended reductions in the income taxes paid on the personal income allocated to necessities. The VAT paid in the price of necessities simply would increase the value of the income tax credit for necessities for all taxpayers and the negative income tax for lower-income filers, much as would inflation. In this way VAT would be both administratively efficient and equitable; otherwise, a VAT on necessities such as food and medicine would be regressive.

A value-added tax would raise the price level by at least the percentage of the tax and thus should be implemented in stages. Such increases could be coordinated with the proposed changes in the income tax structure. For example, careful study might conclude that a 2 percent VAT would be appropriate in the first year of the new tax. In theory, the tax base for VAT is the value added to the product at each level of production. In practice, the tax base is measured by the increase in sales price at each stage of production. Each stage in the chain collects the VAT on its sales, takes a credit for VAT paid on purchases to other firms, and remits the net amount to the IRS. At the end of the chain, the consumer pays the full amount of the tax in the sales price of the good or service and *with no other reform measure* would bear the full burden.

The consumption-type VAT nonetheless is recommended because it is neutral with regard to prices of consumption goods as long as the base is comprehensive and there is a single rate. The consumption variant also provides the most neutral treatment of capital assets and is the easiest to administer, in part because arbitrary depreciation allowances need not be calibrated. Since value added is the value that a business firm adds in the course of its operations to the goods and services it purchases from other firms, such value is added by handling or processing these purchases with the firm's labor force, machinery, buildings and capital goods. The initial acquisition of capital goods is treated the same way as the purchase of supplies so that the consumption-type VAT is equivalent to instantaneous depreciation of new plant and equipment. Since the firm may deduct, in the year of the purchase, the full value of the capital good, the value-added by the capital equipment is not subject to taxation until later years, as the equipment is consumed in the process of production. Thus, taxation on the "value" of capital also happens only once.

Consider the following example for the tax base under the consumption variant of VAT. During the taxable year the firm's gross receipts are $125,000. During the accounting period the firm purchases $25,000 of materials and supplies from other firms and $10,000 of machines (capital goods). The tax base would be $90,000: The purchases on both current account ($25,000 for materials and supplies) and capital account ($10,000 for the machines) are subtracted from the gross receipts from final sales.

Exemption's from the VAT base should be rare. Most experts, however, would agree to the following exemptions. Exports should be exempt in order to avoid taxing our foreign neighbors (whose own VAT is refunded on our purchases). The rental value of owner-occupied homes should also be exempt because of the administrative nightmare of calculating imputed (unobserved) values. Federal government purchases also should be excluded because the government would pay the tax (as a part of prices) and derive no net revenue from it.

Under these provisions the VAT tax base would equal approximately 60 percent of Gross National Product. If 1985 GNP turns out to be $3885 billion (latest DRI forecast), the tax base would be about $2331 billion, and one percentage point of VAT would yield an additional tax revenue of $23 billion. A first-stage tax of 2 percent would yield about $46 billion.

Summary and Conclusion

The proposed income tax program (FLAN) would reform the present federal income tax system by replacing the progressive tax-rate structure with a tri-flat tax system applied to a tax base significantly expanded as a result of the repeal of a number of tax expenditures. A negative income tax, which takes the form of a refundable income tax credit, guarantees a proportion of poverty-level income. This credit would be based on demographic characteristics and would be phased out as an individual's income increased. The phase-out would be limited only by a low credit floor. Most federal income-security programs would be eliminated, but the reduction in federal expenditures would be almost equally offset by the refundable income tax credit, while assisting the same lower-income groups.

Revenue simulations suggest that the FLAN program would be revenue neutral and distributionally neutral for income classes above $20,000 for calendar year 1985. The $6 billion increase in federal expenditures, which results from both the repeal of the social security earnings test and the replacement of the income-security programs with a negative income tax, would assist mostly the income classes below $20,000, without the attendent administrative and social attitudinal problems associated with the current welfare system. The value-added tax that completes the FLANVAT program would add needed revenue for education and other programs aimed at human capital improvements. This ultimately should reduce the number of poor and thereby reduce the negative income tax credits. Eventually, VAT would replace the corporate income tax.

Economists seem to like the idea of a "use" tax. Of course, it is impossible to tie every tax to a specific use. Nonetheless, a combination of VAT and a diminished dependence on the income tax means that ultimately the personal income tax could be used solely for financing national defense. The main contribution of the working class to defense and war efforts has been to supply manpower and tax revenue. A shared social burden could be achieved by financing defense with the corporate tax (until phased-out) and the tri-flat but progressive tax rate. On the other hand VAT is less visible, less felt. Those presently in tax shelters apparently "feel" that too much of their taxes go to social programs. With the allocation of VAT revenue to the income grants for the poor, education, and other social programs, the currently sheltered could be painlessly altruistic.

PART IX

21st CENTURY DEVELOPMENT

Chapter 47

THE INTERNATIONAL MOBILITY OF LAND AND THE LAW OF THE SEA

E. RAY CANTERBERY

Florida State University

THOMAS H. CAFE

Northern Kentucky University

"As for the factor land, it is, by its very nature, immobile."

Paul T. Ellsworth, 1964

"We can distinguish between the various factors of production according to the ease with which they can move from one country to another country. Thus 'land', comprising the actual area of the country, cannot be moved from one country to another country, or at any rate, can be moved only at such prohibitive cost that the question of its movement never arises . . . . [A]nd no matter what policy may be adopted for encouraging or discouraging factor movements."

James E. Meade, 1964

"The question of mobility does not arise, of course, with regard to the third factor of production. Land is immovable."

Ragnar Nurkse, 1961

"The controlling element in local adaptation is in the long-run the fact that natural resources are immobile, while labor and capital must be distributed."

Bertil Ohlin, 1967

In the twentieth century land has been the least analyzed factor of production. Perhaps the reason is found in the above quotations, which imply that land is a pretty dull factor. Although recent empirical tests of the Hechscher-Ohlin model are quite advanced and include labor, capital, natural resource content, and even human capital, land (and thus natural resources) is assumed internationally immobile [see, e.g., 12, 11]. The purpose of this article is to show that this assumption is confronted with numerous historical exceptions, the most visible being contemporary ocean resources conflicts such as the "Cod War" in Iceland and evolving international law on the use of ocean fisheries, seabed resources, and deep-sea minerals. Indeed the exploitation of the oceans and seas may be the last major earthly "land grab" in history and thus may have a massive impact upon world trade patterns.

We (1) restate the definition of land in a precise way, and use the pioneering work of Georgescu-Roegen to identify production as a process rather than as a point function; (2) derive in a simple model the motivation for international land mobility from (1); (3) explain the political and economic manifestations of land mobility and; (4) discuss the special importance to world trade of the extension of territorial limits by coastal states.

I. LAND DEFINITIONS AND THE IMPORTANCE OF PRODUCTION AS A PROCESS

We adopt John Stuart Mill's definition of land as all those natural agents which are not

* The authors thank Frederick W. Bell, James Gapinski, Nicholas Georgescu-Roegen, William Laird, Charles Rockwood, Delbert Snider, and Philip Sorensen for helpful comments but reluctantly exonerate them from sharing with us any errors.

products of labor.[1] Thus land includes the following components: all classes of agricultural types (temperate, tropical lowlands, etc.), minerals, natural forests, wild-stock fisheries, natural water, solar energy, natural air, and air space.

We can further classify land into two general types: (1) Ricardian space; and (2) natural resources. *Ricardian space* is the three-dimensional solid geometry that for a given set of coordinates includes the globe's surface, its subsoil, and superjacent air space. Within broad limits, such space (land) is indestructable and *geologically* immobile. *Natural resources* include natural soil, natural water (including water power), natural air, solar energy, minerals, natural forests, and natural (wild-stock) fisheries.

In addition to land there are two other agents of production. Walrasian *capital proper* is the factories, warehouses, machines and tools used in production. *Labor power* is the human time of a particular human capital quality available as a productive service. Such labor power is used to manipulate resource flows with the aid of capital proper.

N. Georgescu-Roegen's [2; 3] definition of production as a process becomes very useful at this juncture. In G-R's analysis, some inputs are consumed in the process of production while others survive the process, usually with a few scars. The *fund* elements, which represent the agents of the process, provide services and can be *either* inputs or outputs. Because the use of fund services does not change a stock, funds are not depletable if proper maintenance is performed. The use of a fund requires the passage of time (duration) where the size of the duration is decided within narrow limits set by the physical structure of the fund. The *flow* elements are *used* or *acted upon* by the fund elements. But a flow element is either *only* consumed or *only* produced by the process and is only an input *or* only an output. Whether a factor is classified as a fund or a flow nonetheless depends upon the duration of the production process.

In these terms Ricardian space is the *fund component of land* that provides a service, and a natural resource is a *flow component of land* that becomes a production input. That is, this is the case when the duration of the production process is of "normal" length. Ricardian space, labor, and capital proper play similar roles in the production process: all normally are funds that provide services even though Walrasian capital requires some maintenance inputs to be kept qualitatively constant. Maintenance of labor through feeding and housing is self-applied by labor in the household at above-subsistence wages.

Natural resources that are renewable are flows that can be consumed in one kind of production process or in another process, produced. Non-renewable resources are flows that are consumed in the production process. Such input flows involve a change in the stock of minerals and wild-stock fisheries in particular. The time of depletion of the stocks of these nonrenewable resources depends upon the original stock sizes and their use rate.

From G-R's definitions the *fund elements* are: L = Ricardian space; K = capital proper; and H = Labor power. The *flow* elements are: R = natural resources; I = inputs of materials which are normally transformed into products and which come from other production processes; M = maintenance inputs for capital proper; W_i = inputs of wastes (pollutants); W_o = outputs of wastes. Further, let T = time duration of production and t = clock (mechanical) time.

The above suggests that we cannot rely

[1] By defining capital as "all external and physical requisites which are products of labour," Mill notes that natural agents are "all those which are not" products of labor. [6, 155]. He continues by saying:

"Being now about to consider the impediments to production, not the facilities for it, we need advert to no other natural agents than those which are liable to be deficient either in quantity or in productive power. These may be represented by the term land. Land, *in the narrowest acceptation*, as the source of agricultural produce, is the chief of them; and if we extend the term to mines and fisheries—to what is found in the earth itself, or in the waters which partly cover it, as well as to what is grown or fed on its surface, it embraces everything with which we need at present concern ourselves" [6, 155–156].

exclusively upon the short-run (or neoclassical) production function when T is large. The short-run production function is a point function, whereas the long-run production relation is a set of points in an abstract, rather than an Euclidean space. The latter is a functional, that is, a relation from a *set* of functions to *one* function.

For the aggregate production (q) of one commodity (Q), the G-R functional is:

$$\overset{T}{q_0(t)} = \left| \mathfrak{L} \right| [\overset{T}{R(t)}, \overset{T}{I(t)}, \overset{T}{M(t)}, \overset{T}{W_i(t)}, \overset{T}{L(t)}, \overset{T}{K(t)}, \overset{T}{H(t)}, \overset{T}{W_o(t)}]; \quad (1)$$

where $0 < t < T$ and where $L(t)$, $K(t)$, and $H(t)$ are the service co-ordinates corresponding to the designated funds and $R(t)$ is the flow co-ordinate for land resources from a resource stock.

According to G-R, the degenerate functional corresponding with (1) usually constitutes an in-line arrangement of the elementary processes represented in (1), that is, a factory system. None of the "inputs" are ever idle in, for example, an assembly line, even though they are employed in sequence. We are primarily interested in the nature of the Ricardian space fund (L) and natural resources flow (R) functions in (1).

II. THE DOMESTIC MOTIVATION FOR LAND MOBILITY

The use of G-R's concept of production as a process facilitates an understanding of the economic motivation for land acquisition by nations and the control of resources through political means.

Let us use a simple model to illustrate our arguments. Let a = size of initial stock of R; q_R = cumulative amount of R used in production of duration T through time t; and S_R = stock of R at time T. Over a sufficient total production duration, say T_n, long but finite, the stock from which the flow coordinate $R(t)$ depends can be depleted. (For example, R might be petroleum resources). The precise time at which depletion happens depends upon the size of the original stock (a) and the instantaneous flow rate in the use of R, that is, $R'(t)$.

Let us make the following assumptions about R. It is a nonrenewable resource and cannot be recycled. It is used exclusively in the production of Q in equation (1). The cost of extraction of R increases with exploitation while other Q– input costs remain constant, and therefore the quantity of R demanded increases at a decreasing rate. The decreasing rate is proportional to the instantaneous flow rate and the constant of proportionality is $1 > b > 0$.

Definition:

$$q_R = R(t)\, e^{-bR'(t)t}; \quad (2)$$

where $e^{-bR'(t)t}$ constitutes a moderating but not ultimate constraint in the use of R. The cumulative amount of R used through t in the production of Q, q_R, depends upon the rate of use of R. But there is an ultimate constraint from the finiteness given by a. At any time the quantity of R's remaining stock (S_R) is:

$$S_R = a - R(t)e^{-bR'(t)}. \quad (3)$$

At some value of t, say $t_m = T_n$, the domestic resource input coordinate $R(t)$ *disappears* from the Q-production function. Express equation (3) in logs and the stock becomes zero at $\ln R(t_m) + bR'(t)t_m = \ln a$. Domestic production of Q will cease unless production takes place under a technology that does not use R (i.e., a new production function) or R is augmented by the acquisition of more L. Otherwise, Q will become an import. To the extent that domestic production of Q is desirable, the optimum private use-rate of R (such as with petroleum products) may exceed the socially optimum use-rate.[2] The so-

---

[2] This can be demonstrated with the use of equations (1) and (2). Define the Q-production constraint curves in the use of R as $q_R = ze^{rt}$ where r = the marginal product in the use of R and z = a parameter that can take on different hypothetical values. (The marginal product of R in the production of Q can, of course, vary with technology.) Write the logs of equation (2) and the constraint equation as $\ln q_R = \ln R(t) - bR'(t)t$ and $\ln q_R = \ln z + rt$.

cial costs of continued domestic production include the cost of L-acquisition or the extra costs occurred in importation.

This exercise serves to illustrate that the exhaustion or impending exhaustion of a natural resource from the production process can be a cause for acquisition of Ricardian land or natural resources. Next we will consider the specific ways in which Ricardian space and natural resources can move.

III. THE NATURE OF LAND MOBILITY

There are three general types of international land mobility. (1) The transfer of the claims to ownership of Ricardian space and/or its associated resources from one nation to another. (2) The transfer of the claims to ownership from all nations (common property rights) to one. (3) The non-territorial transfer of natural resources through manmade or natural causes to another nation.

Inter-nation land mobility under (1) simply defines international land mobility in the same way as international capital move ments. The international transfer of common property rights under (2), however, is a characteristic of land only. Ricardian space "moves" internationally when the territory that originally encompassed it is politically redefined. In this definition land "moves" because it stays geologically where it is. In one discrete change the claims to the natural soil, natural waters, natural air, natural forests, natural fisheries, and minerals within that space (the flow components of land) have also moved internationally.

The transfer of land claims—even of Ricardian space—is sometimes only partial. For example, the use of air space for international travel, as a part of imported land claims, requires international treaty agreements. Likewise, international law may define the sea surface over which national boundaries extend and the area designated for the exploitation of fisheries and minerals (economic zone) within different geometric planes.

The international transfer of claims to Ricardian space is a common historical occurrence. Ricardian space that is under the jurisdiction of a subject of international law is referred to as "territory" in political science [11, 695]. Territorial limits are political boundaries defined by the nation-state and contemporary international law. The change in claims to territory is sometimes the result of political forces but often the dominant reasons are economic as defined above.[3]

Claims to Ricardian space and natural resources can be transferred through changes in the territorial limits of a nation-state either by peaceful or aggressive methods. Treaties usually confirm these transfers of claims. Western colonialism is an obvious illustration of *in toto* changes in territorial claims (excepting "native" land reserves). Examples of other such transfers include the U.S. purchases of Louisiana and Alaska.

Territorial limits also can be redefined by political boundary contests. The positional boundary dispute is a disagreement over the precise definition of the border. Such a dispute is usually precipitated by two or more states which simultaneously lay claim to the same border land, the quality of which makes it desirable. The state's political goal is "a change in the position of the boundary" [10, 109]. The classic non-sea boundary conflict is the historically contested area of Al-

The optimum private use of R in any particular technological state (that is, at any given value of r) occurs when $d \ln q_R/dt = 0$ and $d^2 \ln q_R/dt^2 < 0$ in the log of (2). Therefore, the optimum private use of the depletable resource R occurs at $R'(t)/R(t) = bR'(t) = r$.

To the extent that r rises as different technological mixes are used (in our example, more oil-intensive production), the optimum will be reached at lower and lower levels of q_R. This "optimum" is illusory in a social sense because even at a constant marginal product where "optimum" has been passed and $r > R'(t)/R(t)$ and $r <$ marginal social costs, the resource R continues to be used in the absence of state intervention.

[3] In international law a state exercises undisputed sovereign powers within its territory. Even if the political power remains sovereign, the precise definition of borders and the distance from shore that a coastal state exercises sovereignty, control, or other jurisdiction is sometimes in dispute. For a coastal state particularly the *definition* of its territory is often disputed.

sace-Lorraine.[4] A second example was the dispute between the United Kingdom and France about the boundary between Niger and Chad in West Central Africa.

Perhaps the most important contemporary territorial claims are under (2) and involve the use of the seas. Such territorial claims become boundary disputes that are positional if the other users of the high (or common property) seas object to the expansion of territory over or under the coastal waters.[5]

Non-territorial transfers (3) also occur through boundary disputes. Claims to Ricardian land and natural resources are changed through state policy changes at the border that do not require territorial boundary alterations. These boundary disputes are of two classes, functional and resource development. The functional dispute is concerned with state functions as they are applied to the border. Resource development disputes result from natural resources such as a water supply that parallels or interdicts a common border.

A classic example of a functional dispute is the contested use of border pasture lands between Italy and France in the Alps-Maritimes.[6] An example of a resource development dispute is the distribution of water power toward the U.S. that has occurred along the Canadian border in the use of both the Niagara Falls and the Great Lakes.[7]

A resource development dispute can result in a change in natural resources locations, such as the diversion of a water power source. If a river with its source in State A flows through State B in its travels to the sea, State A could deprive State B of the water power simply by changing the river's course. This can be done by constructing a power station near the river's source and diverting the outflow for irrigation purposes. Water also can be diverted by avulsion.[8] Even if the river forms a border between two States, and if avulsion occurs, "[T]he resulting change leaves the boundary line unaffected" [11, 625]. The international law guidepost for the settlement of the resource development dispute is the Guadalupe-Hidalgo Treaty of 1848 between the U.S. and Mexico.[9]

IV. THE SPECIAL IMPORTANCE OF THE EXTENSION OF TERRITORIAL LIMITS BY COASTAL STATES

Of all land, the most important natural resources for the immediate future may come from the world's oceans, which constitute about 70 percent of the surface of the plane that separates earthly air space from underwater and subterranean space. New technologies in underwater mining, off-shore oil and gas drilling rigs, and ocean fishing have raised new issues in international law regarding the ocean's "economic zone", the area in which a nation can mine such resources. The international law governing the ownership of such resources is still evolving.

The territorial sea and its base line are sufficiently vague in terms of their geology to invite politically-determined definitions. Even the continental shelf and the continental slope which appear in definitions of the "economic zone" and are geological definitions are not precise.[10] The width of the territorial sea was once said to be measured by the eighteenth century "Cannonshot Rule",

[4] Alsace-Lorraine is the name given to 5,607 square surface miles of territory ceded by France to Germany in 1871 at the end of the Franco-Prussian War, retroceded to France in 1919 after World War I, ceded again to Germany in 1940 during World War II and *again* retroceded to France in 1945.

[5] By tradition the sea beyond "the limits of national jurisdiction" has been open to the common use of all people of all states and could not be subjected to the sovereignty of any one state.

[6] The dispute has involved the rotation in the shared use of the border pasture land among seasons.

[7] See [9].

[8] Avulsion occurs when the process of a river, from any cause, natural or artificial, suddenly leaves its old bed and forms a new one.

[9] This dispute was with respect to the Gila and Bravo Rivers. The treaty established the international principle that no action should be taken with respect to boundary waters by one state that will diminish the waters' value and usability to the other state. See [10, 127].

[10] The *territorial sea* of a country is defined as "a belt of sea adjacent to the coast of a State and is situated between its internal water (q.v.) and the high seas (q.v.) over which the coastal State exercises a limited territorial jurisdiction" [11, 695]. A *base line* is "the inner limit

that is, the distance that a cannon ball could carry from shore (then three miles). This definition expressed a heterogeneous mixture of national defense needs, weaponery technology and the law of gravity. Not unexpectedly, the defined width of the territorial sea has changed historically as a result of the economic and political actions taken by various coastal states. Moreover, the continental shelf also has been reinterpreted as a result of the economic fund and flow considerations.

The Truman Proclamation provides the present legal doctrine regarding U.S. exploitation of the continental shelf. Concerned over World War II's demand upon domestic petroleum reserves, the President in 1945 declared that the nation owns the resources on and under its continental shelf, which for the U.S. was known to be large. But at that time the U.S. made no further claim upon either the fisheries or use of the water for transport. But the states on the West Coast of South America have little or no continental shelf, while having highly productive fishing grounds in the Humboldt Current. Therefore, such nations soon claimed up to 200 miles as their territorial waters. And in 1976 the U.S. Congress introduced legislation to extend the economic zone to 200 miles, that is, beyond the continental shelf.[11]

One of the most massive of such territorial movements in recent history in terms of direct economic impact was the extension of Iceland's fishing limit, to 12 nautical miles in 1958, to 50 miles in 1972, and to 200 miles in 1975.

The Icelandic case also illustrates the often conservational nature of such claims changes that involve fisheries. Because the extensive spawning grounds are located on the Icelandic continental shelf, other nations were depleting the adjacent fisheries stock on the "high seas". The Icelandic Government gave the following reason for increasing the size of its landholdings: "the unilateral extension of a territorial sea or fisheries zones of several states in different regions to 3, 12, 18, 25, 106, 112, 130 or 200 miles are examples of customary international law in its development. Clearly, it is unreasonable, in light of these facts, to insist that unilateral action as a method of extending a fishery or territorial limit is contrary to international law" [4, 12]. Positive improvements upon Iceland's trade position that coincided with these resource base changes are dramatized by the data in the Appendix.

Despite such attempts at unilateral extension of territorial or economic zone rights, the territorial and economic limits of coastal states still is not a settled issue. The U.S. at the U.N. Law of the Sea Conferences in Caracas (1974) and Geneva (1975) argued for a 12-mile territorial sea and a 200-mile "economic zone" for the exclusive exploitation of minerals *and* fisheries (except for highly migratory species). The 200-mile zone plea represents a claim to partial Ricardian space and particular natural resources and became a key proposal for the coastal nations at the

from which the width of the territorial sea (q.v.) is measured seaward" [11, 678].

The *continental shelf* is "the area of the ocean floor between the mean low water line and that change in the inclination of the floor, from about 1/8th of one degree to more than three degrees, that marks the beginning of the continental slope which occurs at various depths usually between 130 and 200 meters, but exceptionally as shallow as 50 meters and as deep as 500 meters. The width of the shelf ranges from less than one mile up to 800 miles. When the increase in the slope is very gradual, the point of maximum rate of change of slope is considered to be the edge of the shelf" [13, 288]. The *continental slope* is defined as "area of the ocean floor extending from the outer edge of the continental shelf to the abyssal ocean floor, usually from ten to twenty miles wide. The inclination of the slope varies widely from as little as three degrees to over forty-five degrees. Geologically, it marks the rather abrupt transition from the continental, or siliac crust, to the ocean, or a simatic crust" [13, 288].

[11] This extension could be defended by the principles of the Truman Proclamation. According to Winton, "the Truman Proclamation declared that since modern technology was capable of exploiting the resources of the continental shelf, since recognized jurisdiction of such resources was necessary and, since the exercise of such jurisdiction by the contiguous state was just and reasonable, the United States, therefore, regarded the resources of the shelf contiguous states as 'appertaining to the United States and subject to its jurisdiction and control' without this in any way affecting the character of the high seas above the shelf" [13, 41–42].

1976 Conference in New York. But while 100 or so nations have a substantial coastline, 49 have none or else only a small and crowded sea. The land-locked nations and those lacking deep sea-bed mining technology are reluctant to forever sign away any claim to the most economically productive share of what has been common property sea. In particular, conflict continues over a sharing formula for the value of mineral resources exploited in the area beyond 200 miles.

V. CONCLUSIONS

When production is viewed as a long-run process, we observe nations switching production functions, moving from domestic to foreign sources for finished or semifinished

APPENDIX

ICELAND'S FISH CATCH AND EXPORTS, 1950–1971

	(1) Total Fish Catch (000 metric tons)	(2) Exports of Fish and Whale Products (millions of U.S. dollars)	(3) Total Exports (millions of U.S. dollars)	(4) (2) ÷ (3)
1950	386.5	$ 23.29	$ 25.85	.97
1951	440.1	41.58	44.52	.93
1952	437.3	36.33	39.29	.92
1953	458.0	41.47	43.28	.96
1954	479.7	50.27	51.83	.97
1955	517.5	48.29	51.95	.93
1956	548.0	57.93	63.20	.92
1957	516.9	55.99	60.51	.93
1958	604.9	60.97	65.57	.93
1959	654.9	59.47	64.92	.92
1960	610.1	61.66	66.91	.92
1961	716.1	65.43	71.50	.92
1962	832.5	76.96	84.37	.91
1963	782.0	86.34	94.02	.92
1964	971.5	100.17	111.07	.90
1965	1198.9	122.32	129.37	.95
1966	1240.3	130.47	140.50	.93
1967	896.5	87.45	98.70	.89
1968	601.4	72.60	82.23	.88
1969	688.9	87.89	107.57	.82
1970	733.0	114.77	146.76	.78
1971	680.7	125.64	149.72	.84

NOTE: Total fish catch is by ungutted weight. Historical exchange rates follow. 1950: 1 Jan-19 March: Kr. 9.37 = $1.20 March-31 Dec: Kr. 16.32 = $1. 1951–1959: Kr. 16.32 = $1. 1960: Kr. 38. = $1. 1961–1966: Kr 43. = $1. 1967: 1 Jan–23 Nov: Kr. 43. = $1. 24 Nov–31 Dec: Kr. 57. = $1. 1968: Kr. 57. = $1. 1969–1971: Kr. 88. = $1.

Source: [4, 12].

goods, or else importing land by territorial acquisition and by non-territorial disputes. The definitions of territorial waters and air are being debated in international forums at a time when certain "national" natural resources are being depleted and new technologies are causing "common property" resources to become private to the technologically endowed nations. The settlement of the conflict between the industrialized and less-developed nations, and between the coastal and "geographically disadvantaged" nations will probably cause a massive change in the pattern of world trade. Such nations are at a historical turning point. International trade theory should treat land more or less symmetrically with international capital mobility. We suggest, therefore, that future tests of the Hechscher-Ohlin model take into account the international mobility of land.

REFERENCES

1. Ellsworth, Paul T. *The International Economy*. 3rd ed. New York: MacMillan and Company, 1964, p. 146.
2. Georgescu-Roegen, N. "The Economics of Production." *The American Economic Review*, May 1970. 1–9.
3. ———, *The Entropy Law and the Economic Process*. Cambridge: Harvard University Press, 1971.
4. The Government of Iceland. *Iceland and the Law of the Sea*. Reybjavik, 1972.
5. Meade, James E. The Theory of International Economic Policy, Vol II, *Trade and Welfare*. London: Oxford University Press, 1964, pp. 357–358. [1955]
6. Mill, John S. *Principles of Political Economy*. New York: The Colonial Press, 1899.
7. Nurkse, R. "Causes and Effects of Capital Movements," *Equilibrium and Growth in the World Economy: Economic Essays by Ragnar Nurkse*. Edited by G. Haberler and R.M. Stern. Cambridge: Harvard University Press, 1961, p. 1.
8. Ohlin, Bertil. *Interregional and International Trade*. Rev. ed. Cambridge: Harvard University Press, 1967, p. 179. [1933]
9. Piper, Don C. *The International Law of the Great Lakes: A Study of the Canadian-U.S. Cooperation*. Durham, N. Carolina: Duke University Press, 1967.
10. Prescott, John R.V. *The Geography of Frontiers and Boundaries*. London: Hutchinson University Library, 1965.
11. Schwarzenberger, Georg. *A Manual of International Law*. 5th ed. New York: Frederich A. Praeger, Publishers, 1967.
12. Stern, Robert M. "Testing Trade Theories," *International Trade and Finance*. edited by Peter B. Kenen. New York: Cambridge University Press, 1975.
13. Winton, Harry N.M. (annotator) *Sea-Bed: 1968*. New York: Worldmark Press Ltd., Arno Press, Inc., 1970.

Chapter 48

A Theory of Supra-Surplus Capitalism**

E. Ray Canterbery*

I. THE CLASSICAL VERSUS NEOCLASSICAL VIEWS

The marginal product theory supposes that employment and wages are determined at the same time in the same place by the same forces. However, there are numerous institutions—schools, training centers, family structures, governments, and so on—involved in the allocative process over long periods in many different places. It's unlikely that all these institutions would converge to equilibria simultaneously everywhere. Moreover, for labor to be paid its marginal revenue product everywhere requires that short- and long-run equilibria coincide. Finally, labor market returns must be independent of consumers' or workers' needs and wants, another way of saying that wage rates are based strictly on worker productivity rather than on physically or culturally determined needs. If money income increments are not *really* based upon marginal revenue products, neoclassical productive efficiency fades into the background and the income distribution issue dominates the landscape.

In contrast to the neoclassicals, the classicals had workers being paid subsistence wages with subsistence often defined in cultural terms. Wage goods provided subsistence. For these economists, necessity was the mother of convention. The neoclassical economists presumed that all income is discretionary. Without the burden of purchasing necessities, the imaginary consumers are "free to choose" any set of goods and services. Most important from the view of theory, the implicit assumption that necessities are unnecessary and luxuries are a special case, guarantees the convexity of indifference curves on which adequate budgets always yield matching marginal utility ratios. However, the idea that discretion is the better part of value provides a lopsided view of capitalism.

Classical subsistence income and neoclassical discretionary income coexist in surplus capitalism. Production surpluses are created when net output exceeds biological necessities and depreciation on replacement capital. Under *supra-surplus capitalism*, production surpluses are so great that producers and governments must spend great resources in order to massage the interests and demands of the middle class (and beyond) to absorb supra-net-output. When private demands nonetheless falter (for whatever reason), federal budget deficits financed by the Central Bank, combined with a depreciating international currency prop up supra-surplus capitalism.

Some pioneers have prepared the way for a modern theory of surpluses. In particular, Piero Sraffa and Michal Kalecki can help us to understand the "necessary economy" that precedes surplus capitalism and coexists with it in the global economy.

II. THE NECESSARY ECONOMY: FROM SRAFFA TO KALECKI

Sraffa's View of Production and Value

After introducing a classical subsistence model, Sraffa (1960) quickly moves on to a production surplus economy, one that produces commodities in excess of labor's physiological

*Florida State University, Tallahassee, FL 32306.

** Presidential Address, Eastern Economic Association, March 6, 1987, Washington, D.C.

necessities plus actual depreciation of all the means of production. Only in Sraffa's subsistence model are basic commodities necessities in consumption as well as in production. In Sraffa's model of the surplus economy, basic commodities or goods that appear as inputs *and* outputs are necessities only in a *technological* sense. Nonetheless Sraffa's notion of a standard commodity group made up of those basic commodities that enter into production in the same proportion that they exit production demolishes neoclassical value theory.

In an industry where equal amounts of, say, labor are always combined with a unit of capital, the marginal product of capital evaporates. Profits can no longer be said to be a return on capital. Moreover, this neo-Ricardian theory tells us that relative production price movements are driven by changes in the income distribution and technology rather than by demand movements. Finally, the income distribution can be altered without changes in the economic surplus, relative to the available means of production. There is little room for the usual supply-and-demand considerations so central to orthodox neoclassical theory, because the wages-to-profits relation becomes a social-political question to be answered elsewhere. Income distribution issues become central to economic theory and policy.

Reconciling Kaleckian Income Distribution with Sraffa's Subsistence Model and Vice Versa

Kalecki divides the national income between profits received by capitalists and wages received by workers. The national product is divided among the investment and consumption spending of the capitalists and the consumption expenditures of the workers (Kalecki, 1971). If we simplify by saying that all profits are diligently plowed back into the business to purchase new investment goods, then saving (as well as investment), is equal to profits. The capitalist is the lone saver in this simple, precorporate economy.

A Kaleckian view of production can be made to conform with Sraffa's subsistence model, if we divide Sraffa's output sector into two distinct industries, one producing necessary consumption goods, the other producing necessary investment goods. The introduction of subsistence wages into Sraffa's subsistence model transforms it into a Kaleckian world of income distribution; workers eat, drink, wear, and drive what they produce. Subsistence wages decide the quantity of consumer necessities manufactured. Since investment goods are combined with labor at a given technology, the demand for consumer necessities and necessary investment goods determines the employment level. The distribution of income between workers and capitalists (between wages and profits) becomes the mirror image of the distribution of national output between consumer necessities and investment goods.

Beyond Kaleckian Subsistence

What happens to this Kaleckian-type theory when the production system produces surpluses and the "working class" receives a larger share of the national income than required for subsistence? When wages (perhaps bolstered by interest and rents) become substantially greater than required for subsistence, the economy is on the way to becoming supra-surplus capitalism. Ironically, a critical insight into the surplus economy lies hidden in the subsistence model. This model reveals that labor is best treated as a basic "commodity" or better, basic service, because labor is still necessary to produce subsistence commodities (Canterbery, 1987, pp. 283–284). Labor is an input *and* an output (basic) in the (at least) self-reproducing economy. Nevertheless, in the long run, just as Sraffa's standard commodity must change with new technology, the quantity of consumer "necessities" must change as what is necessary is redefined.

III. DEMAND: A FUNCTON OF INCOME AND ITS DISTRIBUTION

It cannot be denied that there are many American households existing at the biological subsistence level, but American capitalism is indisputably an economy of surpluses. In a supra-surplus economy, we have a hierarchy of absolute physical necessities and "wants." The satisfaction of a greater number of wants is usually associated with "higher standards of living."

Engel's Law

There is a certain regularity in the way most households allocate expenditures on food, clothing, transportation, and other items. The poor spend their income primarily on physiological necessities in violation of the neoclassical convex indifference curve. Beyond meeting basic nutritional needs, food expenditure as a share of the household budget grows slowly. This general behavior pattern was first identified as Engel's Law. These same needs are met by the non-poor, but the discretionary income remaining meets "needs" or wants that are difficult to pigeonhole. The uncertainty increases as we shift focus away from specific needs, such as the need to be housed, toward the particular way these needs and wants are met, such as through grandiosity and elegance. Households tend to eat more (and sometimes better) as income increases, but there is a limit to the amount of extra money that people spend on food as incomes rise.

The relation between reported personal income and expenditures by category for American families in 1985 is illustrated in Figure 1. For example, the highest-quintile household spends about 9.6 percent of its income on food, whereas the lowest-quintile household's share is 62 percent. Note the pattern. First, the more "necessary" the product or service, the sooner expenditure for that product or service begins to slow. Second, this pattern suggests a hierarchy of rankings. Expenditure shares for food begin to slow down at a very low level of income; transportation at a somewhat higher income level; housing at a substantially higher income level, and clothing (a small and potentially self-indulgent budget share), as well as medical care, education, and recreation (a large, rising share) appear not to slow at all at higher income levels.

Evidently, the income distribution has a lot to do with the overall level of demand in the economy, as well as with the composition of production. Furthermore, expanded consumption by those households above the middle quintile requires that households either satisfy certain wants at a higher level, or discover new wants. This is what "being middle class" really means. The consumer once satisfied with a telephone in each room of their home must now "want" at least one in their auto.

Engel's law is as successful in suppressing the role of consumption prices as is Sraffa. What turns out to be important to households is the ability to meet needs and wants with their real income levels, given their budget shares. The cost of a need or want is a weighted price index for a bundle of necessary and complementary production inputs, not a single price. It is more meaningful to speak of lexicographically-ordered budget shares allocated to bundles of consumer inputs than to individual consumer products (Canterbery, 1979b).

Engel's law places the role of discretionary income under supra-surplus capitalism into proper prospective. Discretionary income is to consumption what physical surplus (overcapacity) is to production; budget shares are to consumption what market shares are to production. Budget shares lead to an understanding of non-price competition that is lost when disputes are confined to market pricing. The greater the surpluses, the greater the difficulty in

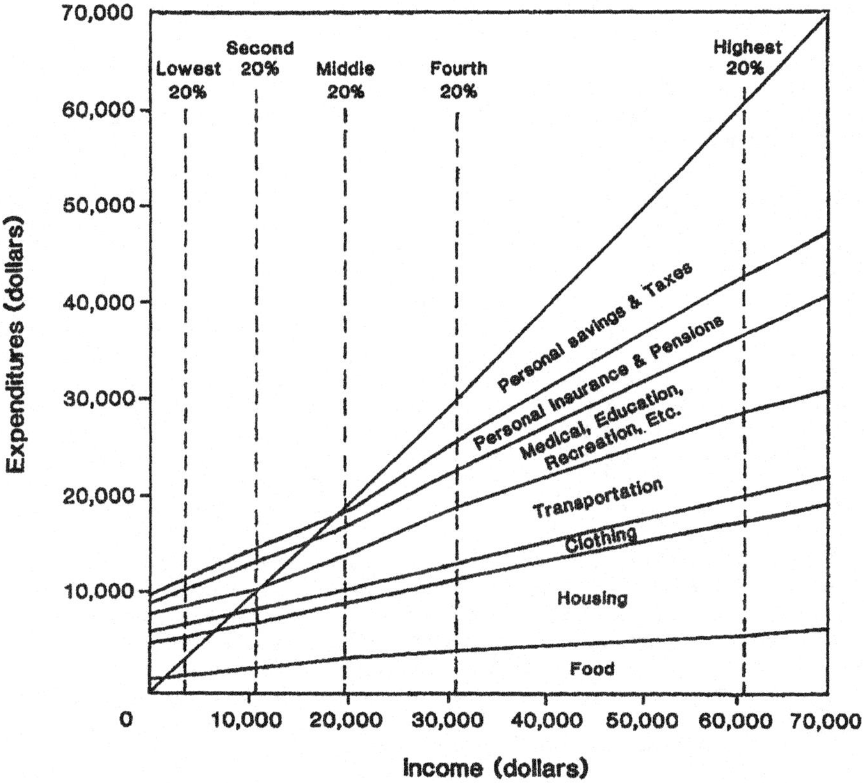

Figure 1. U.S. personal income distribution and expenditure. (Compiled from data of the U.S. Bureau of Labor Statistics, 1987, 1985 interview survey, *budget news* USDL 87-399.)

convincing households to purchase goods they otherwise feel no need for. In common sense terms, it is more difficult to show a need for a Bahamian luxury cruise than for transportation to the work place. But the large gap between the lowest and highest income inspires the corporate structure to transcend the role of simple producer of goods. As Galbraith (1967, p. 207) notes, "mass communication was not necessary when the wants of the masses were anchored primarily in physical need. The masses could not then be persuaded as to their spending—this went for basic foods and shelter."

The Mark-up and Supra-surplus Capitalism

An excess of income above physiological subsistence leaves a demand wedge that provides breathing space for producers. Imperfect competition abhors wedges and sets into motion forces to fill the space. The price markup tool accomplishes the task. In this perspective, the money wage—the actual wage negotiated—separates itself from the real wage or labor productivity. The mark-up could only be a return on capital in a "fit" of circular definition. A strategic role is played by the mark-up on unit costs (mostly wages) in the manufacturing sector. The mark-up depends upon the current number of firms in the industry and the perceived deviation of the firm's price elasticity of demand from the industry elasticity based upon the firm's ability to further differentiate its product and the firm's expectations of a market share gain from its lower relative production costs. Since ordinary price elasticities are higher at higher income quintiles because of stronger substitution effects and weaker income effects (Slutsky (1915) and Frisch (1959)), "price" elasticities at different income intervals are the relevant ones for the differentiated products aimed at the middle and upper income classes.[1] Non-price forms of competition displace price competition (rotating the demand curve) so that the economics of markets cannot remain simply the theory of price.

Given the expected "price" elasticities, the corporation sticks with the market-bearing mark-up that will provide its target level of retained profits, a target that depends upon its dividend payout ratio to stockholders, its amount of debt relative to its equity, and, most importantly, its perceived investment needs. As long as the firm meets demand for its products, and its perceived elasticities and production costs do not vary greatly from expectations, the firm's bureaucracy will cling to the price derived from corporate strategy. The margin of prices over current average costs already reflects the degree of market power of the giant corporation. This present day configuration serves roughly the same purpose as Kalecki's capitalist plowing all profits back into the firm.

The mark-up and investment plans are inexorably linked.[2] Because of the degree-of-monopoly factor, actual prices charged by the industrial firms do not reflect current demand conditions; they more closely mirror the funds requirements for the planned investment expenditures that the corporate bureaucracy deems sufficient to increase capacity (plant size or number of machines) to meet *expected future* demand. When costs of production rise, the firm protects its profits-for-investment flow by raising prices according to its established mark-up. Only upon industrial maturity—near Engel curve peaks—will the producer select new labor-replacing techniques that create still greater excess capacity.

The Money Supply and Money Wages

Rather than money entering the economic system only from the sky via Friedman's helicopter, the supply of money *comes into existence* as Keynes describes it, with private debts ("inside" money). Therefore, the money supply is related to debts created by contracts to purchase or produce goods. Production takes time, so the agreements or contracts for the goods are denoted in money units to be paid upon delivery. However, the production costs have to be paid during the time of production, so that producer debt may be incurred prior to any sales revenue.[3]

If prices are set with a constant or even a variable mark-up over wage costs, money wages become central to the price level. The money wages are inflexible downward because to reduce money wages violates the actual or implicit labor contract. In the short run, therefore, market prices must adjust to money wages and the cost of production rather than vice versa. There is a revised sequence in which the price level and the rate of inflation or disinflation are resolved *after* the money wage rates and increases are determined, though the process does not end there. Money wages, exogenous in Sraffa, are endogenous in a system in which the income distribution is determined by socio-political conditions, and not directly by the technology of production

The technology of production and the prevailing level of production capacity still decide the total potential output of two types of goods: *now* culturally "necessary" consumption goods and the requisite investment goods. However, realized output depends upon effective demand and the income distribution. Effective demand depends upon income from the industrial system that, for the most part, is decided at the labor-management bargaining table. Only in the guise of consumers are there any losers: so much the worse for the sovereignty in which consumers wear the crowns.

For the most part the industrial system has been successful in convincing consumers that they should expand the number of goods they consider necessary. In response to these culturally determined desires, labor demands higher wages so that workers can pay for the newly defined standard of living. The corporation often enough capitulates, knowing that the higher cost of production from a larger wage can be passed on to consumers. If foreign competition becomes a threat, the American corporation moves abroad to a developing, or subsistence economy and enjoys wages a fifth to a tenth of those at home, or else demands protection from foreign competition. Workers continue to believe in the illusion that higher money wages are always good; they don't quite sense the fallacy of composition in their trilateral role as wage-earners, employed persons and consumers. Wage increases merely cover the "cost of living."

There is also a fallacy of composition on the manufacturing side. Throughout the history of capitalism, the idea that workers have to be employed in order to purchase the producer's goods has eluded manufacturers. Though it is in the interest of any single producer to minimize his total wage bill, if all producers succeed in that calculus they will find there is no outlet for their products. Keynes' concept of this fallacy of composition has yet to be denied effectively. The determination of money wages brings us to the broader issue of the personal income distribution.

IV. THE VITA THEORY OF THE PERSONAL INCOME DISTRIBUTION

Despite Kalecki's remarkable insights, the reliance on a stereotyped income division between workers and capitalists is an inadequate explanation for the income distribution of supra-surplus capitalism. We need to know more about why different households occupy varied places in the income distribution. My vita theory provides a more eclectic explanation. In the vita theory, labor is not paid its marginal product and therefore labor falls into the same category as Sraffa's capital goods. The theory—fully developed elsewhere (Canterbery, 1979c, 1980b)—will be summarized briefly.

A vita is a brief summary of the main attributes and events of one's life, a kind of autobiographic sketch. The main thrust of a vita theory can be simply stated. Imagine that one labor market exists for each general class of labor, such as plumbers, medical doctors, electricians, or elementary school teachers. The individual's quality as a productive member of the economic system determines which labor market that person enters. A person "qualifies" for a particular labor market by the state of his or her vita at that time. The vita begins with birth, when race, sex, religion, national origin, inherent or initial mental and physical capacities, inheritances, and family background (endowments) are duly noted.

The autobiography is added to over the life span by education, other training, and experience. Although an individual has some control over the length and depth of his autobiography, production "recipes" change in the long run. Labor demand is related to technology as well as to product and services demand, so that only the rarest of individuals can predict with any accuracy the future demand for workers with his or her own emerging or mature biography. Beyond this, specific labor queue conditions are a collective outcome that is beyond personal control.

The Labor Market

The person's human capital type is decided simultaneously by the individual's characteristics and training, and by the labor markets and occupations currently available in the economy. If there is a one-to-one correspondence between general human capital classifications (HCs) and labor market types, there will be many homogenous and, thus, non-competing national labor types. In the short run there is no mobility among the homogenous labor markets.

Not surprisingly, the number of persons geared to a labor market decreases with increases in the skills, special aptitudes, and credentials requirements of the market. The number of persons who can qualify as unskilled labor greatly exceeds the number who can qualify as medical doctors. Formally, we can think of the members of a human capital type (say surgeons) as being in a rank order queue (for example, 1, 2, . . . , g) from most to least preferred employee characteristics, a labor force queue at either a local or national level.

In the short run the wage rate and the employment level are decided by different forces. Essentially, this separation of forces stems from the set nature of production processes combined with union and firm regulations in the short run. Union or firm rules usually specify the number of workers assigned to a machine and floor area, as well as their work speed. As employment is a fixed share of production, the amount of labor demanded is directly related to production.

The Wage Rate

Labor's instrumental variable is the wage rate rather than the labor queue over which no collective control exists. The industrial union, for example, is aware of the pricing power of concentrated industry in which higher wage costs can be passed on through a constant or rising mark-up over variable or average costs. The likelihood of full mark-up pricing increases with greater product market imperfection.

In turn, in the supra-surplus capitalistic system, discretionary spending and the production of non-essentials is not independent of the wage rate. Just as with the agricultural economy in which the classicals saw labor being paid in food supplies, the wage earners in manufacturing are paid in terms of the goods they produce. Unlike the classical system, however, there is, in part, a revised sequence in which the producer stimulates wants and often helps to define what the worker will demand in wage goods.

Given his vita and the characteristics of the applicable labor market, the individual's base wage rate depends upon the average wage for such services. Upon closer examination, however, the individual's personal income exhibits differentials from potential labor market earnings. Those differentials: occupational, geographic, interindustry, union—non-union, discriminatory, and so on—can often be traced back to the first vita stage, the birth vita. At birth one's initial or innate IQ, sex, race, and initial state of health are already determined; earning qualities nonetheless can be enhanced through education. For example, education adds substantially to the income of blacks, though not nearly as much as to that of whites. Individuals have only moderate control over their precareer vitae because voluntary schooling and training are often directly related to inherited material endowments.

In the unskilled, non-organized labor market, the longer-period queue of unskilled labor is determined by non-wage elements. Few individuals actively strive to achieve characteristics that would yield low wages. Indeed, the unskilled might be viewed as failures, so their long-term queue is a kind of residual unrelated to wage rates. The wage differentials between the union-certified skilled and the unskilled is the consequence of (at least) dual labor markets that reflect the duality between the manufacturing system and the competitive system.

V. STAGFLATION

This political-social process of wage setting means in the short run that employment is not related to the wage rate, and the wage rate is related to employment only if full employment extends across all labor queues. Therefore, a high wage can be associated with a high unemployment rate, because *employment is decided by technology and effective demand, rather than by the marginal product of labor*. This process is so deeply imbedded in the U.S. ecnomic system that it took a four-year global depression (1979–1982) to slow (not end) wage (and price) inflation in the United States.

The prerequisites of technology rearrange the demands for different qualities of labor. The consequent arrangement of incomes is the stage upon which demand plays. The cultural generation of wants, though not entirely separate from technology, plays out much of its destiny within this dimly lit area at the interface between the wants of labor and those of corporate management. Within that dimly-lit area, Veblen and Galbraith and other organization theorists can tell us more than Sraffa or Kalecki can. Neoclassical theory does not extend beyond its own lamp post.

In the Sraffa-Leontief input-output sense, the raw materials, or primary, sector feeds inputs into the secondary sector. Thus, a change in the price of raw materials at fixed price mark-ups has the same effect as a change in the wage rate—a higher or lower cost of producing manufactured goods. Moreover, the primary sector serves a dual role in production and selling because it supplies a biological necessity—food—to fuel the labor input of manufacturing as well as services.

If production techniques (technology) and the money wage rate are givens, the faster the growth rate of national income, the higher will be the rate of profit (non-wage income) relative to wages. If the relatively high level of profits result in a higher level of investment, a greater share of national income necessarily goes to "capitalists."

How can a division of income described so long ago by the classical economists be relevant to a modern industrialized economy? Because supra-surplus capitalism is dominated by large corporations, a great share of the economy's savings and leveraged debt comes out of the corporate sector. Therefore, the savings-out-of-profits behavior of large corporations is a key determinant of the distribution and level of income because profits are a prime source of disecretionary investment expenditures, just as household discretionary income is the source of discretionary consumption expenditures.

If labor is treated as a basic service, the true nature and importance of necessities compared with luxuries in supra-surplus capitalism is revealed. Income earners are then viewed as allocating expenditures among goods on the basis of a budget related to their personal income levels. In this way the consumers' budget can be incorporated into an aggregate consumption function. (As Canterbery, 1979b, has shown, the extended linear expenditure system can be used for this purpose.) As it turns out, the variety of income classes and discretionary spending power adds to a volatility of total demand traditionally assigned only to business investment.

We now will shift our attention to the very long run or the long wave for reasons that will become obvious.

VI. STAGNATION AND THE LONG WAVE (BYE BYE CAPITALISM?)

Two key assumptions of post-Keynesian growth theory must be relaxed to provide a more reliable explanation for the longer-term growth of the economy. The composition of output, as well as the methods of producing that output (technology), do change. Though the production techniques and the amount of labor relative to machines may remain constant for several years (or even decades) during a stagnation in any particular industry, at any moment *other* industries may be switching to different methods of production. It is likely that any new techniques will exhibit different mixes of inputs.

The changing composition of demand, the uncertain timing of new products and new technologies, and the uncertainty of when investment will take place, means that economic growth dependent upon investment necessarily proceeds at an uneven pace. We would not expect the private economy to perform an impossible balancing act.

Schumpeter's Entrepreneur

In Joseph A. Schumpeter's (1883–1950) theory of capitalism, the entrepreneur is the innovator, the agent of economic change. In Schumpeter's vista, the Kondratieff or long wave is spread over roughly half a century.

As Schumpeter correctly notes, there is no extraordinary opportunity for profits in the stationary state of Walrasian equilibrium; a circular flow of economic activity takes place, and the system merely reproduces itself. The entrepreneur daringly raids the circular flow and diverts labor and land to investment. Since savings are inadequate for such ventures, the entrepreneur must be provided credit created by the capitalists. Since only the more enterprising and venturesome persons act, innovations appear in "swarms." The innovations include setting up new production functions, techniques, organizational forms, and products. Even though they stand above the reluctant crowd, the heroic entrepreneurs create favorable conditions for other, less venturesome business persons to follow.

It is industrial concentration—the rise of big and stubborn business—that weakens capitalism. The maturing of an industry into a gigantic monopoly generates the political and social attitudes that ultimately destroy it. The growth of giant business deprives capitalism of its individual entrepreneurs even as it makes itself vulnerable to political and social assault. New Deal nostrums sustained capitalism by artificial means, but it was paralyzed in those functions that had guaranteed past glories. The beneficiary of capitalism's fatal disease was socialism: Schumpeter's prophecy for capitalism is Marx's denouement. Like the whale that saved Jonah, the state swallowed capitalism in order to save it.

The Product Cycle

In my view stagnation is related to the *composition* of aggregate demand and aggregate output. Although Schumpeter treated demand with non-benign neglect, he nonetheless saw some branches of industry flourishing while other branches floundered. Schumpeter's "process of creative destruction" is evolutionary: with firms and industries coming into existence, growing, declining, and disappearing. When *change* is the constant, the very long run is one of industrial evolution or even revolution.

Specialists in marketing research have known for a long time that products have a sales life cycle. Initially, a product innovation coming from one of Schumpeter's entrepreneurs will be sold (perhaps experimentally) to a handful of consumer pioneers, who are often the richest households in the society. Since a new product is usually very expensive to develop, its introductory price will be very high. However, if a middle-income class exists, Veblen's class emulation emerges, and the product is gradually diffused among a larger and larger number of families. When the product hits Main Street, the sales growth is exponential; the product "takes off." Any market thus ignited is limited only by its human population and the distribution of income.

Mass production of a product eventually turns the emulator's gold into fool's gold. When products are sufficiently diffused throughout the economy, they can be standardized in gigantic factories and produced with large-scale technology that yields low prices. When virtually every family of the society has at least one of the "new products," the market is satiated. This product cycle looks like a flattened S and is often called, appropriately enough, the product S-curve. It is illustrated in Figure 2.

Economic development brings standardized technology even as it increases the complexity of the overall production system. In the agarian society, generic goods from the land are the only goods required in consumption. Value added or the difference between the value of sales and the cost of production (and therefore economic surplus) does not exist because goods are not marketed. In contrast, the supra-surplus society relies upon a highly interdependent production system in which a longer and longer chain of suppliers supply each other—adding layer upon layer of value added—until the final product emerges.

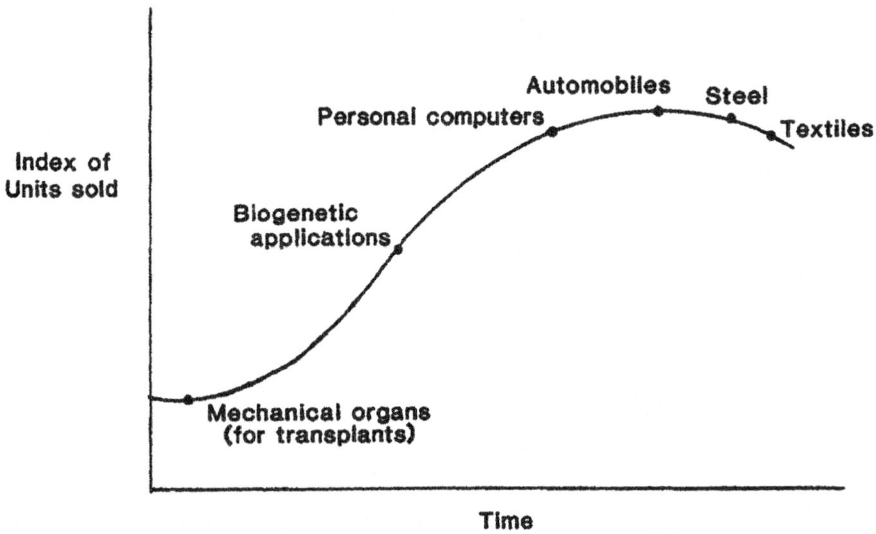

Figure 2. The product s-curve in supra-surplus countries. Note: Each product, of course, would have its own curve, each being uniquely shaped except for the generally flat-s configuration. In this illustration, however, I assume that each product follows the same life cycle in order to show where (approximately) each product is in its life cycle in the supra-surplus economies.

Budget Shares and the Size of the Firm

A reduction in income inequalities is a precondition for a middle class, and a middle class is essential at a critical historical moment in providing a product market size sufficient to warrant the standardized technology, and ultimately, the surpluses. Thus, income levels and the number of households with those incomes are related to the size of the firms and industries producing goods and services. The linkage derives from the value of total expenditures given by budget shares, which defines the overall size of the market for a particular product.

Plant size is usually decided by the lower-cost technology. Given technology, even the smallest plant may be too large for the market. If so, the plant will not be built until incomes, budget shares, and population warrant it. In some cases, the smallest plant is gigantic, and its levels of production may absorb all the revenue available for the particular product. The telephone companies, regional monopolies, fall into this category.

VII. INNOVATIONS AND STAGNATION

The long wave appears smooth over time. This is an illusion, for a set of data over a sufficiently long historical epoch is "stretched out" so much that the appearance is one of continuity. Yet, the historical reality is quite different: the world economic crises of 1825, 1929 and 1987 were a bit more like falling off cliffs than gliding through gentle valleys. Moreover,

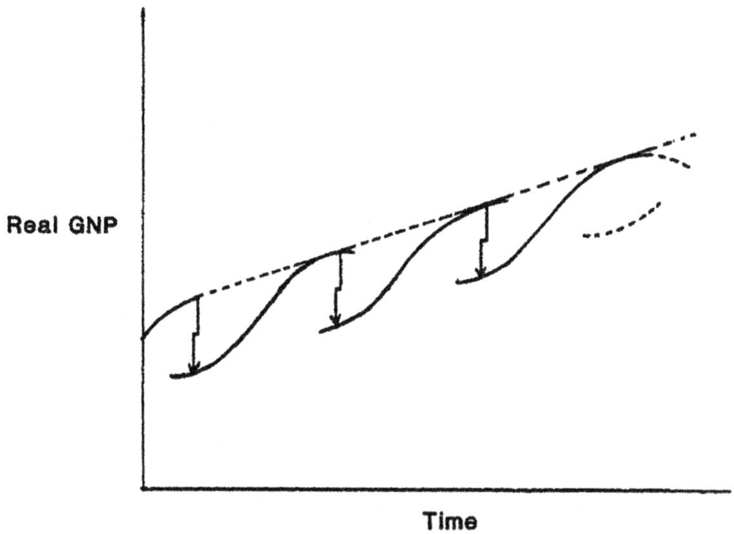

Figure 3. Mensch's (modified) metamorphosis model. Note: In the metamorphosis model, long periods of growth are interrupted by *relatively* short intervals of turbulence. Despite these breaks and upheavals over time and the variation in tempo of change, there is a regularity that conforms with the s-curves of those industrial complexes that lead the particular expansion. This is a "modification" only in the sense that general economic progress is extended over several centuries despite the sharp disruptions. See Gerhard Menach. *Stalemate in Technology* (Cambridge, Mass.: Ballinger, 1979), p. 73. for the original.

the ups and downs of the 1970s and the 1980s are enough to give continuity a bad name. A German economist, Gerhard Mensch (1979), has taken his lead from Schumpeter but favors the pattern of the discontinuous path of capitalism. Fortunately, Mensch's model, which he calls the metamorphis model, is derived from the product cycle or product S-curve. The configuration of Mensch's theory is displayed in Figure 3.

Innovations can be either of the product variety, such as laser disc recordings, or of the production-process kind, such as computer-assisted design (CAD) of an automobile or a house. We will be concerned only with technological basic innovations that produce new markets and industry branches. The lone entrepreneur is often the one who first commercializes a basic innovation, creating a temporary monopoly in the production of a new product. Eventually, an entire new industry is born. The production of electricity (1800), the first use of the coke blast furnace (1796), the first commercial use of photography (1838), the production of the jet engine (1928), and the production of nylon (1927) were basic technological innovations. An entire industry unfolds as a basic innovation generates various new industrial products. Neoclassical capital-labor substitution takes place if the long run average cost curve is viewed as a planning curve along which choices of technique are made.

The remarkable contribution of Mensch is to provide data suggesting that basic innovations do occur in swarms, as Schumpeter claimed; and, importantly for the present malaise, the frequency of the most recent swarm of basic innovations peaked in 1935 (in the middle of the Great Depression). If the average product life cycle—from basic innovation to maturity—is a half century, a large share of the 1935-centered swarm would reach maturity, or the top of their S-curves, in 1985. If so, the overall real GNP takes on an S-curve configuration that is flat by 1985. Our Engel curve analysis combined with observed satiation in automotive, airline, household appliances, and even housing markets, bolster the idea that stagnation best describes the condition of the surpra-surplus economies—Great Britain, Western Europe, Northern Europe, the United States and Japan—by 1985.

Stagnation from market saturation and inflation may be two sides of the same coin; at least, this is Mensch's claim. Stagnation describes the condition of the main branches of industry in the surpra-surplus countries since the late 1960's. Giant scale production facilities in the supra-surplus economies cannot overcome the affliction of many product cycles peaking more or less at the same time (i.e., from my demand perspective many Engel curves are flattening out simultaneously). Otherwise, the expansion in private and public credit would have fueled a sustainable expansion in real output rather than substantial inflation and the future prospect of rapid debt deflation (Postscript: Debt deflation is epitomized by the global stock market crashes of 1987).

At the end of its long expansion, the supra-surplus economy sees the number of industrial branches that are peaking exceeding those beginning with basic innovations. The sunset-to-sunrise ratio of industries means that bankruptcies and liquidation of assets are just over the horizon. Those groups whose income and wealth are threatened will circle the wagons at sunset. Coalitions demand even more subsidies and protection from foreign imports. Such coalitions in the United States, W. Germany and Japan make simultaneous expansion of such interdependent economies improbable. The compositions of their surpluses are similar.

VIII. ENTREPRENEURSHIP, THE PRICE MARK-UP AND SRAFFA-LEONTIEF

Historically, stagnation has had not only a beginning, but also an end. We must wonder why the corporate cash flow fails to lead to basic innovations. Apparently, it is because concentrated industries producing standardized products are not very innovative. The market power of these giants enable them to get by with mostly imaginary product innovations (stimulating wants) and with price increases for products whose sales no longer respond significantly to price changes. (They are producing cultural necessities.)

Fixed Coefficients

During the last half of a long-wave economic expansion, the Sraffa-Leontief fixed technical coefficients industrial model takes on an unexpected realism as neoclassical labor-capital substitution fades in importance. Once the basic process innovations that define the relations between inputs and outputs are widely diffused, the industrial branch becomes remarkably rigid in its technique. True, the size of plants and of the companies grows large, but the same technique is simply replicated on a larger scale. In the final throes of decline, ironically, the production technology finally is modified by improvement innovations; in the present wave, automation in the standardized product-manufacturing industries is being used to replace high-priced labor. Improved judgement born of necessity begins to break through the rigidities.

The Age of the Entrepreneur, however, is like Camelot; it is only here for one brief, shining moment each half century (roughly).

The Rise and Decline of Coalitions

Mancur Olson (1982) considers the "rent-seeking" coalition as "bad" because his focus is upon economic efficiency and economic growth. If, however, we shift the focus back to concerns with the income distribution, coalitions can be viewed as organized efforts to avoid the income-reducing effects of stagnation or competition. When technology is sufficient to create a surplus and inputs are complementary (as in Sraffa, Leontief, or Canterbery), it is very difficult, perhaps impossible, for even a free market to assign "marginal products" to the appropriate persons, for labor and capital goods are equally necessary. And yet, the surplus must be divided by some rule. If coalitions as "rent-seekers" design the rules, the income distribution is decided by their powers.

As long as the growth rates of wages and labor population do not exceed that of "productivity," the rent-seekers divide the surplus without creating much inflation. This could describe the first half of the long-wave expansion. Only when the swarm of innovations have been widely diffused do the rent-seekers create instability in the economy.

For the most part, we have written of economies in isolation. The integration of the global economy enables us to extend the product cycle theory to the rest of the world.

IX. THE INTERNATIONAL PRODUCT S-CURVE

The developing countries' sales normally are nowhere near the flattening-out and turning-down range of their S-curves. The global patterns of the S-curves, originally portrayed by economist Raymond Vernon, are replicated in Figure 4. The product cycle is divided among three stages: new product, maturing (growth) product, and standardized product. In the early stage an entrepreneurial near-monopoly guarantees a small number of firms and high prices. When the production plant becomes large enough and the product price low enough to satiate the domestic market of the supra-surplus economy, production levels off. Long before that happens, however, the marketeers of that product begin to look for sales possibilities abroad

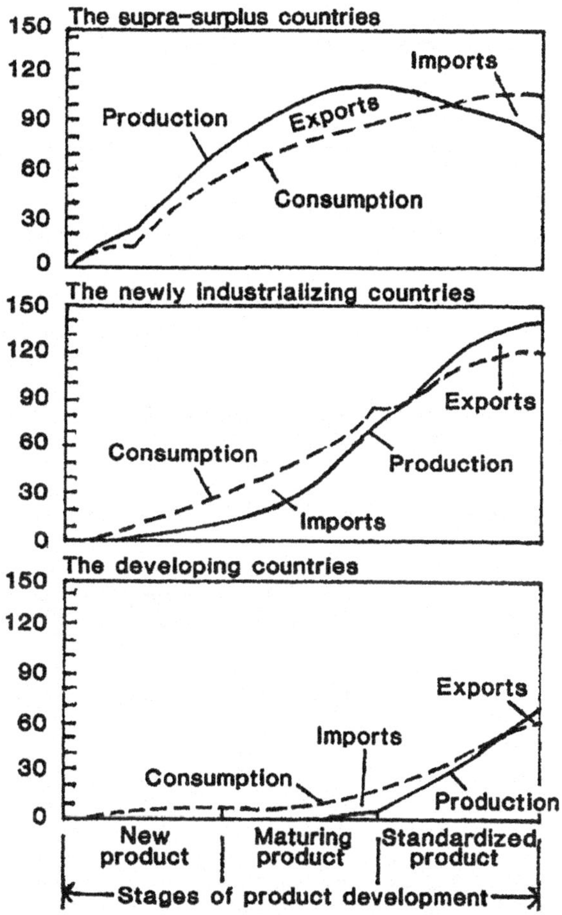

Figure 4. Vernon's international product life cycles. (*Source:* Adapted from Raymond Vernon, "International Investment and International Trade," *Quarterly Journal of Economics*, 1968, p. 199.) Note: In each region consumption generally follows the s-curve pattern. In developing nations, however, consumption is still on the exponential part of the s. In the new product stage, the supra-surplus countries are exploiting their internal markets: in the maturing stage, the supra-surplus countries' exports greatly increase (vent for surplus) and: in the standardized product stage, the technology has been widely adopted in the newly industrializing nations, whose exports rapidly grow.

(vent for surplus). In this regard, U.S. corporations established multinational empires on foreign soil; West German and Japensese firms established mostly distribution branches abroad and kept production on domestic soil.

In the standardized stage, the markets in developing countries become a vent for surpluses because the supra-surplus economy encounters competition from other surplus economies as the monopoly position is eroded. (This happened as the OECD countries became more alike in their postwar recoveries and sated each other.) The newly industrializing countries (NICS) become effective competitors because their adoption of the now-standardized technology is coupled with cheap labor. As a result, the rise in output of standardized products through standardized technology in the NICS has elicited outcries for trade protectionism.

The satiation of a particular or even a collection of product markets is a concern, nonetheless, only for those who out of necessity or ignorance take a parochial view. If one takes a global prospective, for example, there is no glut of automobiles. Around the world in 1978 only 300 million autos were available for about 4.25 billion people. The global market for autos is new and fresh, and the production technology is well defined and standardized. The developing nations are a frontier for products commonplace in the surpra-surplus countries.

Despite the setbacks of the 1980s, the drive to industrialization by the developing nations can be resumed if certain requirements are met. The standardized technologies of the traditional industries are transferable from one country to another. State-of-the-art steel and automotive plants are found in Brazil, Mexico, Taiwan, and the Republic of Korea. These NICS have gone through their "industrial revolutions" at great historical speed and are presently investing large sums in electronics research and development, an act ordinarily assigned to the supra-surplus nations. In terms of production techniques, the NICS are already surplus economies. The experience of the newly industrializing countries tells us that the diffusion of existing technology is happening much faster than in the past, mostly because information systems have improved.

We need to go a step beyond the supra-surplus economies in order to identify the next leading industries and to chart the next century. If the information network is sufficient, inventions and even innovations are available to every country that has the infrastructure to absorb them. The continued dominance of autos, household durables, steel, and other traditional manufacturers in many supra-surplus nations is based more on the power of rent-seeking Olsonian coalitions than upon domestic consumer needs; the illusion of innovation has masked the reality of stagnation.

With investment growth related to technological imperatives and interacting with the division of income, incomes earned can be explained without reference to individual or economic class productivity. As profits—flowing from a price markup—are not explained as the result of a "productive" factor called capital, the income distribution is more the result of social and political customs, including those institutions that generate special market-power privileges. This view leaves few strictly economic obstacles to a more equal income distribution. It also opens the door to policies regarding income payments as a means for controlling inflation (Canterbery, 1983, 1987; Canterbery, et. al., 1985).

The Long Run

It is far more efficient to subsidize individual human capital development, irrespective of the industry affected, than it is to subsidize indefinitely a specific sunset industry. Industries can live and die with product cycles without hurting poeple if the transition is eased through proper care and nurture of individuals. Well-designed education and training programs directing persons into skills that are in short supply could gradually reduce otherwise necessary government income credits (Canterbery, 1983, 1987).

As we shift our concerns to the very long run, we necessarily return to economic development and the problems of the Third World. The long-run view is presently blocked by the global debt and financial crises, which must be met first. But global financial fragility is more consequence than cause. Only a global realignment of industry and new policy instruments can circumvent punitive policies in the global economy. In an integrated global economy, such structural change happens because consumption patterns change with movements in per-capita income and because technological innovations alter production recipes around the world in many ways.

X. SUMMARY

The present day orthodoxy, neoclassical economics based upon marginalism, avows what it claims to prove. The core of the orthodoxy is the belief in labor markets as auction markets that always clear at full employment. From full employment all households' incomes are discretionary so that imaginary consumers are "free to choose" any qualities and amounts of goods they desire.

The reality of supra-surplus capitalism in which an hour of labor, in fact, is not paid according to its contribution to output of autos, steel, textiles and computers is quite different. Since theory should not be judged more reliable the less well it squares with facts, an alternative view requires that the usual demand and supply relations be put aside. This suspension of belief enables us to think of goods and services as either necessities or luxuries. Production surpluses are created when net output exceeds biological necessities and depreciation on replacement capital. Under supra-surplus capitalism production surpluses are so great that producers and governments must expend great resources simply to sell the supra-net-output. Since modern corporations rely upon a price mark-up for profits that can be levered by corporate debt, investment growth depends upon the ability of supra-surplus firms to persuade consumers to buy goods they initially feel no need for.

Traditional supply and demand is replaced with Engel curves and flat S-shaped product curves that depend upon the income distribution, real (price-adjusted) income changes and household budgets. As households become sated with products (a car in every garage, a computer in every household and a TV in every room), the amounts acquired no longer respond to discretionary income increases; the Engel and product curves flatten out and stagnation in those product markets and industries sets in. A simultaneous maturing of several products and industries leads to national stagnation in the supra-surplus economies. On the way to this stagnation we have *stagflation* in which "rent-seeking" coalitions (labor unions, professionals and producer alliances) help to determine wages and the income distribution; this outcome is independent of incremental products or productivity which are decided by technologies and market sizes.

The Kontratieff or long wave shows how stagnation can end. About every half century "swarms" of technological basic innovations occur which create new products, and new industries. Like in Camelot, for one brief, shining moment entrepreneurs make a difference. However, organization pushes the innovators aside and as the industry matures, only a few increasingly rigid giant firms of standardized technology remain. The short-lived Age of the Entrepreneur gives way to the Age of "rent-seeking" coalitions.

There is an international product S-curve that extends growth and decline to the global economy through international trade. The standardized technology of mature industry in the supra-surplus economies has been transferred to newly industrializing countries (NICS) such as Brazil, Mexico, Taiwan, and the Republic of Korea. Unfortunately, the supra-surpluses of the U.S. and other industrialized countries need the "vent for surpluses" provided by the developing nations.

Policies such as "bunker-state" protectionism in the U.S. are short-sighted. The global and the U.S. economies would be better served by a continued global realignment of industry aided by policies bolstering human capital that ease the transition of persons from the traditional into the new industrial branches. Moreover, an incomes policy would enable the supra-surplus economies to take the inflationary fear out of economic expansion.

FOOTNOTES

*I greatly benefited from the comments of Peter Gray and the editing suggestions of Guy Lebeda.

1. Canterbery (1985) has assumed a mark-up pricing rule of:

$$P_{jt} = VC_{jt}(1 + M_{jt}),$$

where VC is variable costs and M is the percentage mark-up. In turn, the mark-up is determined as:

$$M_{jt} = -n_t^{-1} E(N_{jt}),$$

where n_t is the current number of firms in the industry and $E(N_{jt})$ is the perceived or expected price elasticity of demand to firm j at time t. The perceived deviation of the firm's price elasticity of demand from the industry elasticity (N_t) is assumed to be based upon expectations of a market share gain from firm j's ability to further differentiate its product and its lower relative production costs. That is, if N_{jt} is greater than N_t, it is because a market share gain is expected. The perceived or expected firm price elasticity is:

$$E(N_{jt}) = N_t + INN_{jt}, \text{ where } INN_{jt} = C(VC_{mt} - VC_{jt}) + e,$$

which says that firm j's expected price elasticity equals the industry market price elasticity plus an incremental elasticity (INN) which is a positive linear function of the difference between the variable costs of the average firm in the industry (m) and firm j plus an error term (e). That is, an expected market share gain is based upon the capability of firm j in differentiating its product and the cost differential between firm j (say Boeing in aerospace) and the other firms in the industry. In this way, the mark-up potentially can be varied in order to provide funds for investment purposes.

2. The motivation for investment "needs" has been variously attributed to market share and power goals. These explanations, which lead nonetheless to similar outcomes, have been put forward, respectively, by Eichner (1976) and John Kenneth Gailbrath.
3. To the extent that borrowed funds are used to finance increments to the capital stock, new financial assets are created in the process of business investment. Hyman Minsky (1975) takes this position.

REFERENCES

Canterbery, E. Ray, "Commentary." "The Threatening Economy." *The New York Times Magazine*, December 30, 1979.(a). Ed. by David Mermelstein.

———. "Galbraith, Sraffa, Kalecki and Supra-Surplus Capitalism." *Journal of Post-Keynesian Economics*, Fall 1984, 7.

———. "Inflation, Necessities, and Distributive Efficiency." In *Essays in Post-Keynesian Inflation*. Ed. by J.H. Gapinski and C.E. Rockwood. Cambridge, Mass.: Ballinger, 1979.(b).

———. "Innovation and Its Diffusion in Industry." Working Paper, January 1985.

———. *The Making of Economics*. 3rd edition. Belmont, CA.: Wadsworth Publishing Company, 1987.

———. "Micro-economic Interdependencies Underlying Macroeconomics." Working Paper, July 1981.

———. "A Vita Theory of Personal Income Distribution." *Southern Economic Journal*, July 1979, 46.(c).

———. "Tax Reform and Incomes Policy: A VATIP Proposal." *Journal of Post-Keynesian Economics*, Spring, 1983, 5.

———. "Welfare Economics and the Vita Theory." *The Eastern Economic Journal*, January 1980, 6.

———, Eric W. Cook and Bernard H. Schmitt. "The Flat Tax, Negative Tax, and VAT: Gaining Progressivity and Revenue." *The Cato Journal,* Fall 1985.
Eichner, Alfred S. *The Megacorp and Oligopoly: Micro Foundations of Macro Dynamics.* Cambridge, England: Cambridge University Press, 1976.
Frisch, R. "A Complete Scheme for Computing All Direct and Cross Price Elasticities in a Model with Many Sectors." *Econometrica,* 1959, 27.
Gailbraith, John Kenneth. *The Affluent Society.* 2d ed. rev. Boston: Houghton Mifflin Co., 1958.
———. *The New Industrial State.* Boston: Houghton Mifflin Co., 1967.
Kalecki, Michal. *Selected Essays on the Dynamics of the Capitalistic Economy.* Cambridge, England: Cambridge University Press, 1971.
Mensch, Gerhard O. *Stalemate in Technology.* Cambridge, Mass.: Ballinger, 1979.
Minsky, Hyman P. *John Maynard Keynes.* New York: Columbia University Press, 1976.
Olson, Mancur. *The Rise and Decline of Nations.* New Haven: Yale University Press, 1982.
Slutsky, E. E. "On the Theory of the Budget of the Consumer." *Giornale degli Economisti,* July 1915.
Sraffa, Piero. *Production of Commodities by Means of Commodities.* Cambridge, England: Cambridge University Press, 1960.

Chapter 49

A General Theory of International Trade and Domestic Employment Adjustments

E. Ray Canterbery

16.1 INTRODUCTION

Peter Gray (1976, 1979, 1985) has attempted to develop a 'pragmatic theory' of international trade by including considerations related to specific human capital, or 'skill mix', the vita theory, the Linder thesis, and the product cycle.

Originally, the vita theory was developed to explain the personal income distribution (Canterbery, 1979). Even though the original version focused upon the labour market and a non-neoclassical theory of wages, the labour market was made the centrepiece of a later exposition (Canterbery, 1980).

Peter Gray saw the vita theory as the 'Rosetta Stone which enabled [him] to formulate all [his] misgivings about the interaction of rapid changes in trade patterns and the rate of employment in industrialized nations' (Gray, 1985, p. x). Gray relied not only upon the 1979 and 1980 papers but also upon extensive discussions. This version, summarized in section 16.3, has deliberate parallels with the Canterbery–Gray dialogue in Gray (1985). The vita approach is a part of my theory of supra-surplus capitalism (1984, 1987a, 1987b).

The purposes of this chapter are (i) to show how most trade theories can be summarized with a simplified production system that includes mark up pricing, (ii) to integrate my version of Vernon's (1966) product cycle theory with the vita theory, and (iii) to suggest some broader policy implications.

16.2 A SIMPLIFIED PRODUCTION SYSTEM

We begin with a production system in which the technical methods of production are given by a matrix of interindustry coefficients in physical units, denoted by A, and by a row vector of direct labour coefficients in physical units, denoted by a_n.

The meaning of the notation is familiar to input-output theorists. Each element a_{ij} (where $a_{ij} \geq 0, j = 1, 2, ..., n-1; i = 1, 2, ..., n$) of A represents the physical quantity of the i-th commodity needed in the j-th industry for the production of one physical unit of the j-th commodity. These coefficients are decided by the optimal techniques of production, processes that are given initially for the period of production.

In compact notation

$$[A, a_n] \tag{1}$$

where A is non-singular and the transpose of which can be written as

$$[A, a_n]'. \tag{2}$$

Equation 1 is only a production possibilities matrix since we have no assurance that effective demand will be sufficient to purchase the implied outputs.

In its initial stationary state the production system produces the same physical quantities of commodities each time period of production. The inputs are physical quantities of raw materials, capital type commodities and labour time. All inputs except labour are treated as intermediate goods so that investment can only be identified as 'capital-type durable goods', including Gray's traditional or reproducible capital. These commodities (as inputs) are used up in each production period so that they have to be replaced entirely. The residual replaced is the value added in the economic system. (That is, depreciation equals investment in raw materials and capital-type goods.)

The value added in the economic system equals the value of the commodities making up its net national income (or net product). This net national income is distributed as wages, net interest and profits. In general, wages are distributed in proportion to the contributed physical quantity of labour of a particular type and quality. However, a specific money wage rate is determined in the 'labour market' for the labour type and quality required. Following the vita theory, labour *is* of different qualities and therefore the wage rates will vary by industry. Shadow wages are paid to managers and professionals.[1]

The mark up over prime costs in each industry *is* the profit rate. The firm (industry) sets the mark up and thus profit rate according to the elasticity of demand for its product (an elasticity decided primarily by the degree of closeness of substitute products) and, where applicable, by rents on those inputs fixed in supply by quantity or quality. The mark up includes then the 'returns' paid to rent-earning inputs, a 'residual' in Gray (1979, p. 90). Substitution is limited from the *consumer's* perspective when groups of commodities are considered as inputs in the consumer's production function. On the other hand, the industry has some control over demand elasticity wherever products or services can be differentiated, as is presumed in the Linder thesis.[2] The rate of profit also varies by industry but can be identical over a large number of industries of a particular class.[3]

Given $[A, a_n]'$ and the assumptions regarding money wages and profit rates, money prices can be expressed as

$$P = PA(I + \pi') + a_n W'(I + \pi), \tag{3}$$

where P denotes the row vector of prices, π' the column vector of mark ups (profit rates), and W' the column vector of wage rates. The first group of terms, $PA(I + \pi')$, reflects the cost of using commodities to produce commodities and the second, $a_n W'(I + \pi')$, reflects the variable costs of labour in production.

Wage and profit rates are decided *outside* the production system and are thus 'given' in equation 3. Therefore, we have n–1 equations in which to solve for n–1 money prices. Such money prices are then decided by a combination of the 'outside' wage and profit rates and the technical conditions of production in which various commodity inputs are intermediate goods. In the special (and highly improbable) case in which perfect competition prevails and wage rates and profit rates are uniform throughout the system, relative money prices and relative real prices of commodities would be equal. However, when the prices are expressed in money terms (as they are here), we think of them ordinarily as absolute prices.

The system must be self-consistent in terms of money prices. That is, a low price elasticity of demand in one commodity market raises the profit margin and thus prices of all commodities that use the first commodity as an input beyond what their costs would be if the input were priced at zero economic profit. This consistency is reflected in the solution of the price system which is

$$P = a_n W'(I + \pi') \{I - A(I + \pi')\}^{-1} \tag{4}$$

The inverted matrix in equation 4, $\{.\}^{-1}$, is non-negative and gives the total (direct and indirect) requirements of commodities for the production of final commodities (i.e. of consumption and new investment-type goods), taking into account their shares going to real profits in each industry. The element α_{ij} $(i, j = 1, 2, ..., n-1)$ of this inverse matrix represents the physical quantity of the i-th commodity needed in the economic system as a whole (including real profits allocations) to obtain eventually one physical unit of the j-th commodity as a final good.[4] Although money wage and profit rates come from outside the production system, equation 4 shows that money price changes are also related to the interdependencies of techniques.

For example, total production of good 1 is

$$Q_1 = \{\bar{\alpha}_{11} \quad \bar{\alpha}_{12} \cdots \quad \bar{\alpha}_{ij} \cdots {}_{1,n-1}\}\{\bar{y}_1 + \bar{e}_1\} \tag{5}$$

where $\bar{y}_1 + \bar{e}_1$ is a level of real final demand, again decided outside the production system, and the $\bar{\alpha}_{ij}$s denote the *traditional* direct and indirect requirements. The $\bar{y}$s represent the demands for goods produced domestically whereas the $\bar{e}$s represent the goods exported or imported (imports being *negative* exports). For the entire system,

$$Q = [I - A]^{-1} (\bar{Y} + \bar{E}) \tag{6}$$

and aggregate output is the vector

$$Q = [Q_1 \, Q_2 \cdots Q_{n-1}] \tag{7}$$

The money price of the j-th commodity equals the sum of the costs of the quantities of the input commodities needed in the entire economic system to produce one unit of final good. Once this price is known,

$$p_j \cdot q_j = (\bar{y}_j + \bar{e}_j) \cdot (p_j) = (y_j + e_j) \tag{8}$$

gives the gross money income or gross output of the j-th industry. In general

$$PQ = (\bar{Y} + \bar{E})\, P = Y \tag{9}$$

The value added (V) in the economy is

$$V = a_n \, W'(I + \pi')\{I - A(I + \pi')\}\, Q \tag{10}$$

At any particular technology, the distribution of income depends upon wage rates and price mark ups.

We next come to the critical issues. How do labour markets and workers adjust to changes in product demand, especially when those changes are related to foreign trade? We consider the vita theory of the labour market.

16.3 THE VITA THEORY AND THE LABOUR MARKET

16.3.1 Production Labour Requirements

Let us begin with the labour requirements from the simplified production model. If labour requirements are expressed in terms of number of workers, the total employment for the stationary state is

$$a_{n1}Q_1 + a_{n2}Q_2 + \ldots a_{n,n-1}Q_{n-1} = L \qquad (11)$$

where L equals total national employment at the Q levels of physical output (some of which is exported). However, this is a gross oversimplification since different qualities of labour are used in different industries (or for that matter in the *same* industry). More accurately, therefore, the a_{nj}s represent several different types of labour. Represent each labour type by *I, II, III, ...*, *D* in which there are *D* labour types and

$$[a_{\mathrm{I}}a_{\mathrm{II}}a_{\mathrm{III}} \ldots a_D] \qquad (12)$$

are the types of unit labour requirements available to *each* industry, though not all industries will use all *D* types. The labour requirements by labour type become

$$\begin{aligned} L_{\mathrm{I}} &= a_{I1}Q_1 + a_{I2}Q_2 + \ldots a_{I,n-1}Q_{n-1} \qquad (13)\\ L_{\mathrm{II}} &= a_{II1}Q_1 + a_{II2}Q_2 + \ldots a_{II,n-1}Q_{n-1}\\ &\cdot \quad \cdot \quad \cdot \quad \cdots \quad \cdot\\ &\cdot \quad \cdot \quad \cdot \quad \cdots \quad \cdot\\ &\cdot \quad \cdot \quad \cdot \quad \cdots \quad \cdot\\ L_D &= a_{D1}Q_1 + a_{D2}Q_2 + \ldots a_{D,n-1}Q_{n-1} \end{aligned}$$

or, compactly,

$$L = [a_{jVIV}]_{n-1XD}Q \qquad (14)$$

where $[a_{JVIV}]_{n-1XD}$ is the entire matrix of labour requirements by type and Q is a column vector of output.

16.3.2 Specific Human Capital

Now, we turn more directly to the vita theory. Assume that one labour market exists for each general human capital classification. One's quantity of human capital determines *which* labour market one enters; one 'qualifies' for that market by the state of one's current vita. Determination of the vita begins at birth when one's race, sex, religion, national origin, inherent mental and physical capacity, inheritances, and family background are duly noted. The theory integrates a non-circular version of human capital and labour market theory (Canterbery, 1979, 1980).

With D labour types there are D categories of general human capital, derived from human characteristics conforming with job descriptions and meeting employer job requirements. These categories can be ranked by inherent skill requirements. For example, HCI denotes Human Capital Type 1 (the greatest quantity of human capital) and HCD the last human capital type. Each of D human capital types is potentially available in every geographically defined area. For simplicity, each industry is located in a unique geographical area so that the number of industries match the number of geographical zones.

All labour markets can be represented by a partitioned row vector,

$$HC' = [HCI_1\ HCII_1 \ldots HCD_1 | HCI_2\ HCII_2 \ldots HCD_2 | \ldots HCI_{n-1}\ HCII_{n-1} \ldots HCD_{n-1}], \quad (15)$$

in which D general human capital types are matched with n–1 labour markets in n–1 geographic areas for a total of $n\text{–}1^* D$ labour markets.

Now we place persons into the HC categories. Each cell of the matrix contains all persons qualified by vita to perform the tasks in question. Each person will place himself/herself in the highest cell desired and attainable. Within each cell, in turn, persons are ranked according to the comparative quality of their vitae.

One can imagine a long line of rank-ordered persons in each cell. There is a matrix of this description for each geographical area within the national labour market. A regional or geographical submarket precludes the spatial relocation of a worker in the short run. This is so even though the market for a professional such as medical doctor or university professor is defined as a national market.

Thus for each labour market we can write a column vector of vitae whose elements equal that vitae population. Assume that the largest number is s of the Dth HC type, representing the workforce population for the lowest skilled market. The i-th vitae vector for *all HC* types is:

$$V_i = \{VI_{1i}\, VI_{2i} \ldots VI_{gi} | VII_{1i}\, VII_{2i} \ldots VII_{ri} | \ldots VD_{1i}\, VD_{2i} \ldots VD_{si}\}. \tag{16}$$

There is a national supermatrix of vitae that includes all labour markets and associated vitae (in rank order from most to least preferred employee characteristics). This ordering can best be thought of as a labour queue, but at either a local or a national level.

Within each general human capital category are a number of 'occupations' or subspecialities. Gray (1979, p. 88) has called this 'industry specific' human capital. The separation of individual tasks into occupations depends upon the elasticity of substitution in supply. Let the category of general human capital with the most occupations – probably the category of unskilled labour – have *m* occupations. Then there exists an *n* by *m* matrix of *specific* human capital with a large number of zero elements.

Thus, for each homogeneous labour type we can write alternatively a *column* vector of occupations, also in rank order. If the lowest skilled market, the *i*-th, contains *m* occupations, this column vector is:

$$HCO_i = \{HCOI_{1i}\, HCOI_{2i} \ldots HCOI_{mi} | HCOII_{1i}\, HCOII_{2i} \ldots HCOII_{mi} | \ldots HCOD_{1i}\, HCOD_{2i} \ldots HCOD_{mi}\} \tag{17}$$

Now, a still larger supermatrix of vitae would include all occupations and associated vitae. The occupational matrix (*HCO*) could be defined as a submatrix of its labour force population.

13.3.3 Excess Supplies

There is a mirror matrix for the demand for labour. Within each of its cells is the number of workers required. With firms in each region having fixed quantities of capital goods operating under a given state of technology, aggregate demand for goods and services and the categories of that demand determine the short-run amounts of labour demanded. When more labour is demanded, the producer 'opens the door' to an *HC* cell and invites the top-ranked workers into the shop.

The demand and supply matrices coexist at a moment in time. When they are placed in opposition, the number of workers in the cells of the supply matrix can be subtracted from the number in the matching cell in the demand matrix, generating a matrix of 'excess demand'.[5] In the presence of 'excess supply' the unemployed will be those workers lowest ranked by vitae within the cell. The probability of a perfect match is very low (except in some elusive steady state), because both matrices are in a continuous state of evolution.

16.3.4 Evolution in Demand and Supply

Demand matrix evolution is related to exogenous and to induced changes. Exogenous technological change or changes in the pattern of demand for goods alters the nature of the labour demand matrix. Also, patterns of labour and capital costs can induce changes in the labour intensity and the skill intensity of the selected capital-type goods. There is even a feedback mechanism in which changes in the personal income distribution will alter the level and mix of goods demanded.[6] Long-run evolutions in the supply matrix are mostly endogenous, as persons have time to adjust to changing patterns of excess labour demand and to anticipated future changes. However, the quality of training and education can alter the supply matrix. Over a long enough period, demographic movements and changes in the skill level of the population affect the supply matrices, and the demand matrices are transmuted by alterations in the vintages of physical capital-type goods in response to new technologies, changes in relative input costs, and changes in the mix of goods demanded.

The *birth vita* is 'added to' over one's lifespan by education, other training and experience. Since the amount of labour demanded is related to product prices and a changing technology, however, only the rare person can predict with any accuracy the derived demand for workers with vitae of his or her type. Moreover, specific labour supply conditions are a collective consequence outside personal control.

The *pre-career vita* adds to the characteristics at birth both education and 'first-time' on-the-job training. The *mature vita* (the labour market vita) also carries work experience. The individual confronts a large number of homogeneous and, thus, non-competing labour markets in which each exhibit a 'wage of central tendency'.[7]

A particular individual's wage is determined by the rate paid to occupants of the highest cell to which the individual may aspire and find employment. Thus, for the highest cell in the matrix,

$$W = W(K, k, p, m, m^*, M, R, t) \tag{18}$$

where K is human capital as described by the vita, k is non-human capital available, p is the price of the end product, m and m^* are, respectively, assessments of the ease of mobility and uncertainty surrounding the costs and benefits of relocation, M is any monopoly power in the submarket due to either a labour union's or a professional association's ability to create barriers to entry, R is a factor of discrimination and t represents experience. Both k and t can be product- or skill-specific, and the variables are then identified in terms of the relevant k or t.

For our purposes, human capital can be condensed to

$$K = K(G, E, k, t, s) \qquad (19)$$

where G is biological inheritance, E is familial environment from the birth vita and s is the amount of formal education and training which the individual has received.

Gray (1985, p. 54) correctly perceives that the argument for commercial policy is based upon the quickness in which international disturbances occur relative to the slowness in which displaced workers can be dispersed into jobs in other industries, sectors and regions by the mechanism of the market. Alternatively put, exchange rates or tariffs can change faster than workers can be retrained. This is so whether the national labour market is suffering widespread excess supply or whether there are mismatches between the labour supply and demand matrices in the submarkets of the regional/industry matrices (e.g. Detroit).

16.4 INNOVATIONS, THE PRODUCT CYCLE AND UNDEREMPLOYMENT

According to the vita theory, unemployment and underemployment are related to innovations and demand changes whether purely domestic or (with Gray's extension) external.

A specific innovation is not equally likely in all countries but arises when several conditions are favourable: (i) a large domestic market (facilitating economies of scale), (ii) high per capita income fairly evenly distributed, (iii) a relatively high cost of labour. These conditions reduce the risk of introduction of a new product with high initial production costs.

Enter product cycle theory (Vernon, 1966). The early innovator will retain its lead for some time. Late-starting producers elsewhere, with a limited domestic market for the product, will be inclined to compete with established producers in their own market, where they have already achieved economies of scale. The innovator's head start derives from a magical combination of a large market and high per capita incomes. Facing little foreign competition, the innovator begins exporting, often finding the initial market for consumer goods among the high income groups in other countries. As incomes and labour costs rise abroad, foreign producers also become willing to buy new processes that replace labour. The exports or *e*'s become a more and more important source of sales revenue.

16.4.1 Wages and Price Competition

Eventually the demand in some foreign markets is sufficiently large to sustain a local production unit that can exploit scale economies, and the product becomes so standardized that price competition rears its ugly head. Cost considerations and thus wages begin to play a role in production location.

When labour is variable in type the price solution comparable to equation 4 is

$$P = [a_{jVIV}]_{n-1XD}\, Wa'(I+\pi)\{I - A(I+\pi')\}^{-1} \qquad (20)$$

where $[a_{jVIV}]$ is the labour requirements *matrix* for all industries by labour type and Wa' is a column vector of 'labour market' wage rates. (The first π is now a *row* vector.) The wage rates are now 'labour market' wage rates and therefore more than one wage rate applies to each industry.

Let E represent the complete vector of all household goods so that in the entire system the wage rate can be expressed as the vector

$$[PE] \qquad (21)$$

By substitution of PE for W' in Equation 3,

$$P = PA(I+\pi') + a_n\, PE(I+\pi) \qquad (22)$$

We now have the 'standard of living' of the workers (and managers and professionals who receive a 'shadow' standard of living). At a minimum society will expect the system to maintain a demand for consumption goods equal to E and a demand for raw materials and investment-type goods sufficient to maintain E.

Assume that the lowest wage in the system, w_1, is a subsistence wage just sufficient to buy essentials, E_1, and that the overall standard of living is measured by this wage. (The rationale is that these items or close substitutes appear in ***every household budget***.) Let PE be a price index expressed as a scaler (γ) whose initial value is $\gamma_1 = 1$. Then, by substitution of $PE = \gamma_1 = 1$ into equation 22

$$P = PA(I+\pi') + a_n\, \gamma_1(I+\pi') \qquad (23)$$

and

$$P = \gamma_1 a_n (I + \pi')\{I - A(I + \pi')\}^{-1} \tag{24}$$

so that individual prices are expressed in terms of an essentials' price index as a numeraire (γ). A necessary condition of the system to have an economically meaningful solution is that det $\{I-(1-\pi)(A-\gamma_1 a_n)\} = 0$. Now, assume an exogenous increase in the prices subsumed in w_1 so that the price index doubles to 2, and $\gamma_2 = 2$. Then,

$$P = \gamma_2 a_n (I + \pi')\{I - A(I + \pi')\}^{-1} \tag{25}$$

so that – according to a rule by which all wage rates are adjusted by changes in the cost of living – a doubling in the price index results in higher prices of *all* goods that use labour in production *including the goods subsumed in* w_1 so that wages are increased once again. The use of an iterative method gives a wage–price spiral as a consequence of standard of living adjustments in the wage rate. The change in relative prices would, of course, depend upon the *net* labour intensity of production in the various industries.[8]

16.4.2 Standardized Technology and Its Export

At this point another problem for the innovator emerges. Low wage countries can use standardized technology to produce the now standardized product. Producers in such countries can compete within their markets and even begin to displace the innovator, who may change from net exporter of the particular product to net importer (negative exports). The foreign facilities may be controlled by a foreign multinational firm (moving to low cost, low skilled labour markets) or by a local firm. Meanwhile, the stages of product development have gone from new to maturing to standardized product.

Consider, within the vita theory, how employment in an industry is altered over this product cycle. In the short run employment is a fixed proportion of production and the quantity of labour demanded of the *i*-th human capital type (HC_i) is

$$Z_i = a_i q_j$$

where q_j is the total output of product *j*, assumed homogeneous across the labour market.

If labour is paid its competitive value in production (as in Gray's 'eclectic theory'), the 'wage rate of central tendency' is

$$w_i = a_i^{-1} p \tag{27}$$

where p is the price of the product or service. Where wages are bargained, the labour market wage rate will be somewhere between the above wage and a premium wage in which all economic profits are paid to labour. That is, if product and labour markets are imperfect, the wage rate is bargained and is represented in the j-th labour market by

$$w_j = a_j^{-1} p + \Pi \tag{28}$$

where Π = the economic profits allocated to workers per hour of effort. In the short run, employment levels are independent of the wage rate and dependent upon output wherein labour competes by its position in the queue. National full employment occurs only when excess supplies of labour are zero across the partitioned occupation matrix. A high wage can be associated with a high unemployment rate.

16.5 ECONOMIC GROWTH AND EMPLOYMENT ADJUSTMENTS

Let us return to the complete production model. In order for economic growth to occur, technology must improve, net savings and net investment occur, or both. If the marginal propensity to consume is less than unitary, then

$$S = Y - D \tag{29}$$

where S = aggregate savings, Y = aggregate national income and D = aggregate demand. Investment in additional capital-type goods, raw materials accumulation, positive product inventories, and new technological innovation can happen.

With the possibility of net new investment,

$$Q(t) - AQ(t) = Y(t) \tag{30}$$

will no longer suffice as the definition of net national income because more than $AQ(t)$ will need to be set aside at the end of the production period. The net product of the system, $Y(t)$, is no longer devoted entirely to using the commodities produced, some is set aside to provide for the expansion of output capacity. The net product not devoted to consumption is assigned to new investment.

The simplest dynamic model has consumers' preferences, technology, the structure of prices, and the composition of consumption constant through time. Per capita consumption is constant so that the labour force and consumption grow at the same rate, g. Thus,

$$C(t) = cN(t) = cN(0)[1 + g]^t \tag{31}$$

where $C(t)$ represents consumption goods and $N(t)$ is population. Let $J(t)$ equal new investment-type goods. At a fixed technology, A,

$$J(t) = gAQ(t) \tag{32}$$

so that all physical quantities among the means of production $AQ(t)$ increase at the same rate. Thus,

$$Q(t) - AQ(t) - gAQ(t) = cN(t) \tag{33}$$

with solution

$$Q(t) = [I - (1+g)A]^{-1}\, cN(t), \text{ or} \tag{34}$$
$$Q(t) = [I - (1+g)A]^{-1}\, cN(0)[1+g]^t \tag{35}$$

and the total physical quantities in $Q(t)$ grow at the same rate, g, as do the physical quantities in $C(t)$. For the exponential growth of consumption, $C(t)$, this solution gives the total physical quantities, $Q(t)$, required – direct and indirect, including new investment – to keep the system in dynamic equilibrium.

The labour required (and assumed to be demanded) is

$$L(t) = [a_{JVIV}]_{n-1XD}Q(t) = [a_{JVIV}]_{m-1XD}[I - (1+g)A]^{-1}cN(o)[1+g]^t \tag{36}$$

so that full utilization of capacity and full employment (assuming initial full employment) further requires

$$L(t) = L^*(t) \tag{37}$$

where L^* is the workforce size, plus the presumption that *all* labour quality types grow at the same rate. Unfortunately, this dynamic equilibrium model generates improbable economic behaviour.

Even in the basic steady state model prices and the compositions of consumption and of labour requirements can change. That is, even a steady state equilibrium does not require such severe restrictions. Moreover, we know that in the long run technology mutates, requiring an alteration in the composition of labour and capital requirements. New technology that produces new consumer goods types (new industries) also changes the technology available to consumers for satisfying their needs and wants. The production coefficients in the A matrix of existing industries can change in the long run. Moreover, new industries give entirely new rows to the A matrix. With these new conditions the hypothesized wage rate and profit rate movements will cause different patterns of price variations. In contrast, for example, specify that

$$W'(t) = W'_a(0)[1+\rho]^t \tag{38}$$

where $W'_a(0) = I$ and ρ is a column vector of rates of growth in wage rates, as determined by labour market conditions, so that

$$W'(t) = [1+\rho]^t \tag{39}$$

By substitution of equation 39 into equation 20 the price system becomes

$$P(t) = [a_{JVIV}]_{n-1XD}[1+\rho]^t(I+\pi)\{I - A(I+\pi')\}^{-1} \tag{40}$$

This solution says that prices change at different rates (*even* if profit rates are constant).[9]

The constancy of the a_is is always provisional. In the mature stage of the product cycle, the ai's decrease even as the growth rates of the q_js decline. Rising wage rates lead to the substitution of capital for labour in increasingly automated factories. The amounts of labour demanded decrease, so that only the highest ranked vitae enter the employer's door. Employment declines. Since the product and the technology are standardized, more and more production is shifted abroad. Still greater 'excess supplies' of labour appear in the cells of the matrices.

In the standardized product/technology stage a balance-of-payments deficit accompanies rising unemployment and underemployment.

16.6 BEYOND THE STANDARDIZATION OF TECHNOLOGY

In J. Schumpeter's theory of capitalism, the entrepreneur is the innovator. Schumpeter begins his system in a stationary condition of Walrasian equilibrium (similar to that of section 16.2). There is no extraordinary opportunity for profits; only a circular flow of economic activity in which the system merely reproduces itself. The entrepreneur daringly raids the circular flow and diverts labour and land to investment goods. Since only the more enterprising and venturesome persons act, innovations appear in 'swarms'. In turn, the entrepreneurs create favourable conditions for other, less venturesome firms to follow.

Vernon's product cycle can be used to explain why the long wave comes to an end and Schumpeterian innovations can explain why the end ends. The older industrialized nations, those with great amounts of intra-industry trade, have had large numbers of product cycles peaking simultaneously. Most dramatically, standardization and mass production characterize the textile, steel, automotive and consumer electronics industries.

Not only is the income elasticity of demand for their products low, but export prospects among those countries producing the same goods are dim. Surely, clever manufacturers and advertising agencies can postpone mass realization of sameness, but eventually the cause becomes hopeless, especially when all opportunities for *real* as opposed to imaginary product 'improvements' have been made. Such is the nature of supra-surplus capitalism (Canterbery, 1984, 1987b).

Mensch (1979) provides data suggesting that basic innovations do occur in swarms, as Schumpeter claimed; and, importantly for the present malaise, the frequency of the most recent swarm of basic innovations peaked in 1935 (in the middle of the Great Depression!). If the average product life cycle – from basic innovation to maturity – is a half century, a large share of the 1935–centred swarm would reach maturity, or the top of their product *S*-curves, in 1985.

During the last half of a long-wave expansion, the unit labour requirements of the vita theory take on an unexpected realism. Once the basic process innovations are widely diffused in the economy, the industrial branch becomes remarkably rigid in its technique (fixed a_i's). True, as Vernon says, the size of plants grow large, but the same technique is simply replicated on a larger scale, at home and abroad. In the final throes of decline, ironically, the production technology finally *is* modified by *improvement* innovations (smaller a_i's); automation in the standardized product-manufacturing industries is used to replace high wage labour, at home and abroad.

A new long wave is not automatic for a particular nation. About two-thirds of the technological basic innovations that will be produced in the second half of the twentieth century will occur in the decade around 1989. The greatest surge of innovations occurred in 1985, a year comparable (on the scale of innovations) to 1825, 1886 and 1935 (ibid., p. 197). If Schumpeter and Mensch are correct, every half century or so there is a narrow window of opportunity for entrepreneurs to commercialize basic innovations, creating a temporary monopoly in the production of a new product and of new industries (new, unimagined a_i's). Thus far, however, the US, unlike Japan, has been unwilling to use positive governmental adjustment policies to speed the transition from invention to commercial application.

The integration of the product cycle and the long wave with the vita theory show the difficulties in long-term adjustments. In one view human capital augmentation policies would be added to short-term protection. Then, irrespective of the source of trade competition, multinational firms could seek US labour. In another view the US could devise policies aimed at speeding the conversion of innovations into new commercial products, processes and industries.

NOTES

1. This, of course, does not foreclose the possibility that a great number of industries may be paying identical wage rates.
2. A variation of the model would have a greater number of firms than industries so that industry structures also would influence profit rates.
3. One can abstract from monetary policy by assuming that all wage and profit distributions are made at the end of the production period. In the presence of monetary institutions, however, wages and profits can be paid in advance of production. Suffice it to assume that the money stock is sufficient to monetize the entire economic system at the given and constant money velocity.
4. The element α_{ij} should not be confused with the identical notation usually used to denote direct and indirect input requirements *unadjusted* for physical products allocated to profits.
5. Quotation marks are occasioned by the absence of neoclassical demand and supply schedules; a labour queue is *not* a schedule.
6. As we shall see, this feedback can be related to the product cycle.
7. A homogeneous non-competing labour market is defined as one bounded geographically and one in which the elasticity of substitution in production between the labour of its type and the other types within the area approaches zero. The geographic limits are set by 'reasonable' commuting distances (at current state of transportation technology) from the selected labour population centre.
8. In the more complicated version of the model, the change in relative prices also would depend upon wage changes by specific type of labour and its use by industry.

   Alternately, the model will yield a profits – price spiral that necessarily inspires a further wage inflation increment. An increase in the mark up in an industry whose output is an input in most other industries will increase the price index of essentials which gives rise to a cost of living increase for all households and a further increase in wage rates. Once again the money stock or money velocity would have to increase in order for these money wage, profit and price changes to materialize.

9. This dynamic modelling could be extended by consideration of changes (over time) in the **A** matrix coefficients as well as the introduction of new rows into **A**. Also, the theoretical structure of the system can be altered as demand requirement changes occur at different rates from growth in labour supplies by type. Moreover, it is probable that changes in the composition of consumption follows from new rows in **A** as well as from changes in prices and in the income distribution. Price dynamics are altered as consumer and producer expectations regarding future prices are included in the model.

Chapter 50

CULTURAL AND OTHER BARRIERS TO MOTION PICTURES TRADE

AKBAR MARVASTI and E. RAY CANTERBERY*

I. INTRODUCTION

The U.S. motion picture industry has long dominated world markets, but its recent expansion has been especially dramatic. Hollywood's current share of the world film market has doubled since just 1990, whereas the European film industry is about one-ninth the size it was in 1945. In the 1960s foreign films constituted 10% of the U.S. market; by 1986 they made up 7%, and today only about three-quarters of 1%. Remarkably, the global dominance of American films has evolved despite extensive protectionist efforts by other countries and virtually no barriers to trade by the United States. As to other countries, we might expect to find much more active, effective protectionism against a culturally sensitive product than against generic products and services. The characteristics of the product would suggest that the fate of U.S. motion picture exports would have at least mirrored the decline in American textiles and steel. To the contrary, the U.S. motion picture industry has been winning the global ballgame despite three strikes against it—protectionism, rising real domestic costs, and relatively stable real domestic ticket prices.

*We thank an anonymous referee for many valuable suggestions.

We address this quandary of why protectionism fails in a cultural industry where protectionism is expected to succeed. We do so first by examining the structure of the U.S. domestic motion picture industry. As it turns out, this structure provides a special impetus for exports. We next examine the nature of protectionism in a world of soaring demand for films. In this setting the American movie is a world product in a different sense than, say, the automobile. The American movie is a world product because its *presence* is dominant; the automobile is a world product mostly because its parts are interchangeable. By its nature the American movie appears to have few substitutes, even though Hollywood can use foreign locales for filming.

American movies encounter different protectionist strategies in different places. The divides fall either side of highly industrialized nations versus less developed nations, English-speaking versus non–English-speaking people, literate versus less literate people, and so on. Some countries and regions combine fees with subsidies, whereas others engage in piracy, quantitative, or service restrictions. Few countries have traditional tariffs.

Once we have defined the characteristics of the U.S. movie industry and foreign strategies

ABBREVIATIONS

MPAA: Motion Picture Association of America
LDC: Less Developed Country
GDP: Gross Domestic Product
VIF: Variance Inflation Factor

of protectionism, we can better identify the relevant variables and appropriate models to explain not only industry exports but also the failure of protectionism. We end up with a complex gravity-iceberg model as a method of estimating U.S. motion picture exports. Because of the nature of the industry, our approach shares some of the characteristics of earlier studies in which economies of scale and imperfect competition are present. Although early gravity models have focused on spatial distance, some economists have interpreted the effects of "distance" as possibly nonphysical. Thus, "cultural distance" applied to a culturally sensitive industry could be a reasonable interpretation for distance effects. After using microdata to explore protectionist strategies, we then aggregate these data for the formal model.

II. STRUCTURE OF THE U.S. MOTION PICTURES INDUSTRY: WHY EXPORT?

What determines the structure and size of market for American films? Movie studios are both producers and distributors. Though movie studio revenues depend directly on *net* revenues (gross revenues minus total costs), the *size* and extent of the movies market remain tightly linked to *gross* revenue, including domestic box office. From the perspective of the studios, aggregate market size (S) is

$$(1) \qquad S = \sum_{i=1}^{n}(R_i + X_i),$$

where R_i is gross domestic box office and X_i is the U.S. dollar value of exports (rentals, video tapes) of the ith of n movie studios. Compare the American studios' gross revenue with the circulating capital required by a major producer-distributor to supply the requisite number of films, and write the ratio

$$(2) \qquad s = \sum_{i=1}^{n}(R_i + X_i)/K_j,$$

where K_j is the optimal circulating capital (including that required to pay stars and cast) for the jth or representative studio.[1] The value of s is an important measure of *industry structure*, where generally $\infty > s > 0$. If for a given K_j, $s \to \infty$, the global market could support many studios and the industry would be perfectly competitive. If, at the other extreme, $s = 1$, a monopoly studio can supply the global consumer market.

Although our pooled trade data set will encompass 1991–95, our selected stylized facts of the U.S. motion picture industry are based on available data. Figure 1 presents gross domestic box office revenues in current dollars (Motion Pictures Association of America, MPAA) and export earnings (*Variety*) in the industry. Despite some volatility, the trend in both variables is upward. During 1980–2000 nominal domestic box office revenues have increased by a multiple of nearly 2.8. Canterbery and Marvasti (2001, p. 94) estimate a price elasticity of demand for movie attendance between −0.23 and −0.51, suggesting highly inelastic demand so that a doubling in nominal ticket prices has contributed significantly to revenues. They (p. 96) also find that a 1% increase in a "star index" raises admissions by about 2.3 million and domestic box office by about \$30 million.[2] Price inelasticity may be one measure of successful differentiation through nonprice competition (via stars, special effects, advertising, and promotion) by the major studios.[3] Canterbery and Marvasti also find significant negative effects on demand and on total revenue from per capita income increases, suggesting that movies may be inferior goods in a wealthy country.

In the past two decades the American industry has not only benefited from growth in secondary markets (because of the popularity of VCRs and cable TV) but also from Adam Smith's "extent of market." Export data in Figure 1 show a steep rise in revenues from foreign markets rapidly converging on

1. Each film project usually requires new sets, scripts, stars, other cast members, special effects, and location; thus, fixed capital is minimal compared with the circulating capital assigned to a new project. Thus the classical economists' definition of capital is applicable.

2. The Canterbery-Marvasti (2001) star index is based on star recognition from an original survey of moviegoers combined with the number of appearances of the particular star. The major studio/distributors distinguish themselves through their efforts to produce "hits" or blockbusters. In an important empirical study De Vany and Walls (1997, p. 787) find only 20% of a weekly Top 50 sample of films earning 80% of total box office receipts, with the top 4 movies generating a fifth of total box office revenue.

3. A model of the structure of the domestic industry and the complex relationship between major studios and exhibitors also is presented in Canterbery and Marvasti (2001). Domestic economies of scale are achieved through the variable capacity (number of seats) in theaters (exhibition sites).

FIGURE 1
U.S. Domestic and International Box Office Revenues

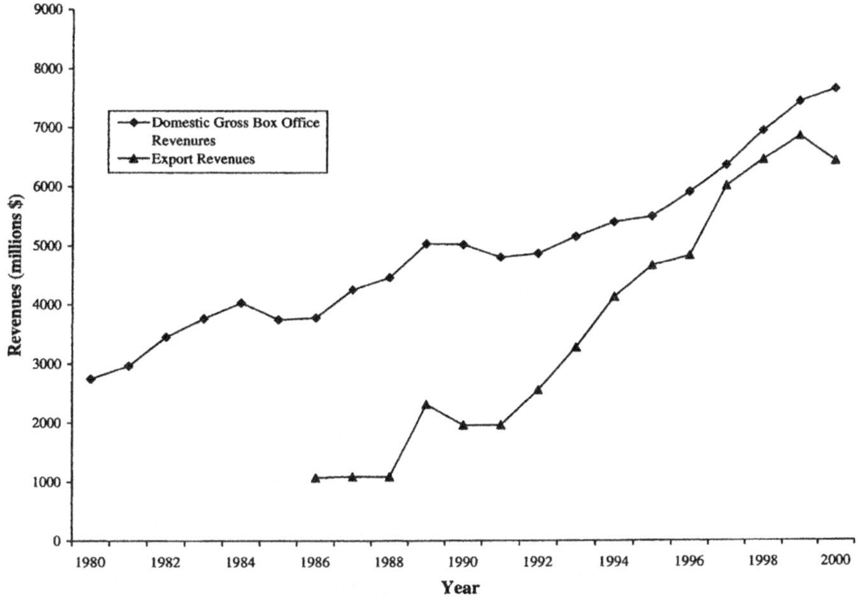

domestic gross box office revenues. Americans, however, appear to show little interest in foreign films: Imports are so insignificant that they are not even reported by the MPAA.

The American industry's motivation for seeking foreign markets is found in domestic box office, average costs, and industry structure. Cost figures (in current dollars) for members of the MPAA, comprised of the "majors" and usually including only the top seven to eight studios, are reported in Figure 2. Along with export growth, the industry has experienced remarkably rapid cost increases—a dual experience in sharp contrast to manufacturing industries, such as textiles and steel. Because most of the cost of physical production (which includes the cost of stars and cast) is incurred in producing the master copy (replicated at low cost in the United States), mostly marketing costs are incurred for exports that potentially add much more to revenues than to costs. Thus economies of scale in distribution are enhanced with increasing exports.

Because of the apparent dependency of domestic box office (R) on a high level of circulating capital (K_j), it is not surprising to find the global leader in films to be a country whose real gross domestic product (GDP) averaged 13.8 times that of its competitors during 1991–95 while the comparable per capita GDP ratio was 1.8. Although wealth levels may be important in establishing the industry, per capita income levels beyond relatively high levels have limited benefits for what appears to be an inferior good. Exports enlarge the total market ($R + X$) *relative* to optimal circulating capital costs [s in equation (2)], and therefore maintain the number of major studios that survive in a climate of soaring costs.

In 1990 the share of market for the top eight U.S. studios (the majors) was 89.2% of domestic box office and in 1997, 90.6% (*Variety*). Gross revenue for these majors, prorating exports, would have been \$6,230.4 million in 1990 and \$11,220.7 million in 1997 (current dollars). Between 1990 and 1997 nominal average costs of MPAA members more than

FIGURE 2
U.S. Production and Marketing Costs

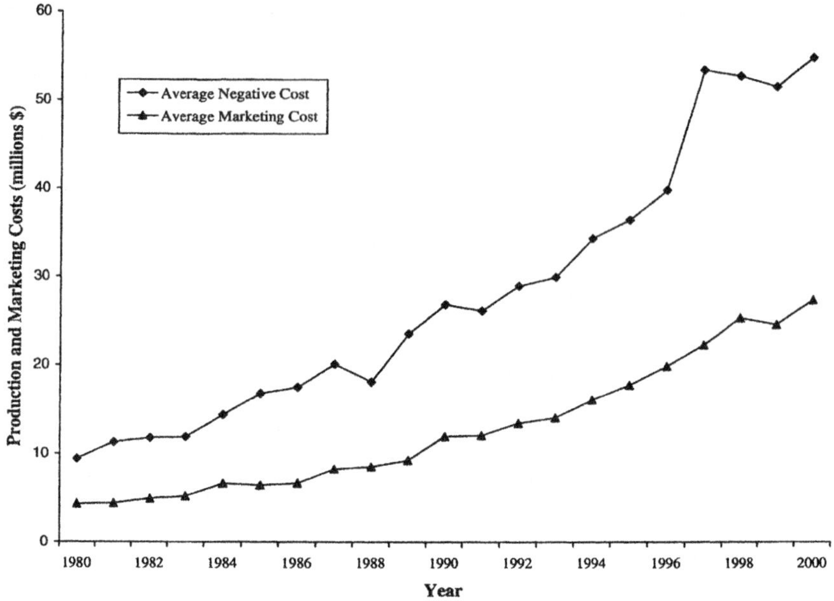

doubled. Using our formula for *s* and the average cost data from Figure 2, *s* equals 8.14 in 1990, meaning that eight major studios could have broken even but instead enjoyed substantial profits. Because of soaring costs and despite rising domestic box office revenues, the estimated *s* for 1997 equals only 5.4, making foreign revenue more critical for the profitable survival of as many as eight majors. (The majors suffered heavy losses in 1997.) As a result, by 2000 the major studios began to release films simultaneously in domestic and foreign markets.

Although the incentive for U.S. exports of films and videos emanates from the characteristics of the industry and its markets, it is beyond our scope to delve further into such details. We are content rather to suggest that major Hollywood studios can profit from product differentiation requiring rising costs accommodated by a Smithian extent of market enhanced by foreign film revenues. The foreign market further extends economies of scale in distribution.

III. PROTECTIONIST STRATEGIES IN THE MOVIE INDUSTRY

Just as movies differ from textiles or steel, trade barriers in the motion picture industry do not exactly conform to those in other industries. Although the U.S. has used tariffs to limit movie imports in the past, virtually no barriers have existed in recent years. In turn, the nature, magnitude, and strategic choices countries make to limit U.S. films vary. In Saudi Arabia, public exhibition of movies is strictly banned for religious reasons; in China, several hidden quantitative restrictions limit the importation of Western movies; in India, severe quantitative restrictions limit film imports; in Thailand, imposed duties are mostly based on number of meters of imported films; and in many European countries a complex system of subsidies and taxes exists (MPAA 1991–96). As a more general guide, various protectionist measures are defined by country in Table 1 along with the average annual number of films produced during 1991–95. Excluding India, the United States dominates in number of films.

TABLE 1
Descriptive Statistics of Trade Barriers and Number of Films by Cross-Sectional Units (1991–95)

Countries	Tariffs*	Quantitative Restrictions*	Lack of Property Rights*	Video Levy*	Subsidies*	Service Barriers*	TBN	TBI	Number of Films Produced
Western Europe									
Belgium-Luxembourg	0	0	1	1	1	0	3	6.0	8.5
France	0	1	1	1	1	1	5	9.6	155.5
Germany	0	0	1	1	1	0	3	6.0	65.8
Italy	0	1	1	0	1	1	4	9.6	106.4
Netherlands	0	0	1	1	1	0	3	4.0	14.6
Norway	0	0	0	1	1	1	3	4.6	10.8
Spain	0	1	1	1	0	1	4	8.0	55.0
Sweden	0	0	1	1	0	0	2	4.0	23.6
Switzerland	0	1	1	1	1	0	4	7.0	35.4
United Kingdom	0	1	1	0	0	0	2	6.0	58.8
Group average	0.00	0.50	0.90	0.80	0.70	0.40	3.30	6.48	53.44
North America									
Canada	0	1	1	0	1	1	4	9.0	31.0
Mexico	1	1	1	0	0	1	4	8.6	31.0
Group average	0.50	1.00	1.00	0.00	0.50	1.00	4.00	8.80	31.00
South America and Caribbean									
Argentina	0	1	1	0	1	1	4	8.6	14.7
Bermuda	0	0	0	0	0	0	0	2.0	0.1
Brazil	1	1	1	0	0	1	4	7.6	11.0
Chile	0	0	1	0	0	0	3	3.0	1.5
Venezuela	0	1	1	0	0	0	2	6.4	5.5
Group average	0.20	0.60	0.80	0.00	0.20	0.40	1.80	5.52	6.56
Middle East									
Israel	0	0	1	0	0	0	1	2.0	14.0
Saudi Arabia	0	1	1	0	0	0	2	9.0	0.1
Group average	0.00	0.50	1.00	0.00	0.00	0.00	1.50	5.50	7.05
Asia									
China	0	1	1	0	0	0	2	5.6	179.5
Hong Kong	0	0	1	0	0	0	1	2.0	197.6
India	0	1	1	0	1	0	3	8.4	827.3
Indonesia	1	1	1	0	0	1	4	9.4	37.8
Japan	0	0	1	0	0	0	1	3.0	249.6
Republic of Korea	1	1	1	0	0	0	3	8.6	68.0
Malaysia	0	1	1	0	0	0	2	5.0	14.2
Philippines	0	1	1	0	0	0	2	7.0	125.0
Singapore	0	1	0	0	0	0	1	2.0	0.1
Taiwan	0	0	1	0	0	0	1	5.0	30.4
Thailand	1	0	1	0	0	0	2	5.0	53.5
Group average	0.27	0.64	0.91	0.00	0.09	0.09	2.00	5.55	162.09
Others									
New Zealand	0	0	0	0	0	0	0	2.0	5.2
South Africa	0	0	1	0	1	0	2	4.0	0.1
Australia	0	1	1	0	0	0	2	5.0	25.4
Group average	0.00	0.33	0.67	0.00	0.33	0.00	1.33	3.67	10.23

*One denotes that a trade barrier exists, and zero if it does not.

The selected trade barriers include violations of private property rights (or existence of piracy), quantitative restrictions, tariffs, video levies, subsidies, and service barriers, such as printing and dubbing restrictions. These barriers are measured by geographical area (group averages) as well as by specific country.

The tariff, the most common barrier to most trade, is not used in Western Europe, Canada, or the Middle East. It is deployed in Brazil, Indonesia, the Republic of Korea, and Thailand. If U.S. movies demand abroad is also generally price-inelastic, tariffs probably are viewed as ineffectual in much of the world. Where tariffs are used, they may be used simply as a source of tax revenue. Otherwise, quantitative restrictions are widely used as a substitute for tariffs. Our neighbors in North America (Canada, Mexico) use quantitative restrictions more than any other region, closely followed by Asia and South America–Caribbean.

The most popular trade barrier is the denial of property rights. In 1997 the majors lost an estimated $66 million in revenues to movie piracy in India alone (MPAA). Not only does film lend itself to piracy, black markets offer a way around quantitative barriers in the presence of strong demand for movies. The denial of property rights, however, is not confined only to countries using quantitative restrictions. Piracy is virtually universal; it is the protectionist strategy of choice everywhere except for Norway, Bermuda, Singapore, and New Zealand. These countries may have especially severe penalties for this trade violation.

The closest device to a tariff is the video levy—very popular in Western Europe, where subsidies for the industry are also pervasive. Most of Western Europe, like Canada, is striving to sustain its own movie industry. Only Spain and Sweden have such levies in the absence of subsidies. Much of the motivation for video levies is the provision of funds for subsidizing the domestic industry. Only Canada, Italy, Argentina, India, and South Africa have subsidies without levies. Excepting Argentina, South Africa, Belgium-Luxembourg, the Netherlands, and Norway, countries subsidizing domestic industries also produce a substantial number of films, with India producing by far the largest number. In these countries subsidies apparently are effective in supporting local film industries. China, Hong Kong, and Japan are major Asian producers that do not subsidize their film industries; all three have very large populations, and Hong Kong and Japan have high per capita incomes. Like the United States, these countries are sufficiently large or affluent to sustain a domestic industry.

Service barriers are ubiquitous in North America and relatively important in Western Europe, South America, and the Caribbean. They are unimportant in the other geographical regions. It is difficult to generalize regarding country groupings. These complex barriers nonetheless appear along with many other barriers in individual countries, such as France, Italy, Norway, Spain, Canada, Mexico, Argentina, Brazil, and Indonesia. Spain has a complex dubbing license requirement, Argentina requires that printing and dubbing be done locally, and Brazil requires local printing even though its two printing labs operate at high costs. All these countries have expressed in various ways an interest in developing a sturdy domestic movie industry. Their motives appear to be a mixture of pride and fear of U.S. cultural dominance.

The mean values of trade barriers and average number of films that provide the most dramatic differences among population types appear in Table 2: (1) developed versus less developed countries, and (2) English-speaking versus non–English-speaking countries. The developed countries rely heavily on piracy and somewhat less on a combination of video levies and subsidies plus quantitative restrictions. A third of the developed countries use service barriers; they use *every* device *except* the tariff. Less developed countries (LDCs) rely about as much as developed countries on piracy and quite a lot more on quantitative restrictions (again, such restrictions may be much more effective than tariffs or levies, though tariffs are also deployed). About a fifth of LDCs use quite onerous service barriers. Non–English-speaking countries rely even more on property rights violations, and their quantitative restrictions are nearly twice as important as for English-speaking countries. About a third of the non-English countries also use video levies and subsidies as well as those harsh service barriers (dubbing being most relevant to these populations). Because most U.S. exports go to developed countries, the importance of piracy and subsidies infer a failing protectionist strategy.

TABLE 2
Mean Values of Trade Barriers and Number of Films by Country Group (1991–95)

Countries*	Tariffs	Quantitative Restrictions	Lack of Property Rights	Video Levy	Subsidies	Service Barriers	*TBN*	*TBI*	Number of Films Produced
Developed countries	0.00	0.47	0.87	0.53	0.53	0.33	2.73	5.72	57.31
Less developed countries	0.28	0.67	0.89	0.00	0.22	0.22	2.33	5.96	88.74
English-speaking countries	0.00	0.38	0.63	0.25	0.25	0.13	1.50	4.00	39.79
Non–English-speaking countries	0.20	0.64	0.96	0.32	0.36	0.32	2.84	6.44	85.50

*There are 15 countries in the developed countries group, 18 in the LDC group, 8 in the English-speaking group, and 25 in the non–English speaking group. If 50% or more of the population speaks English, it is categorized as an English-speaking country, otherwise it is categorized as non–English.

Although the move from these microdata to index numbers usable in gravity-iceberg models risks the loss of some information, estimations that use the individual measures of trade barriers create a multicollinearity problem. Later we will address the concern regarding possible information losses. Meanwhile, because of the descriptive and complex nature of the data on trade barriers, two broad indices of trade restrictions are developed and used in our models. One measure is based on the number of various trade barriers imposed on U.S. exports of motion pictures (*TBN*), on scale of one to six. The other measure is based on the number as well as the complexity and levels of trade barriers (*TBI*), on a scale of 1 to 10. The *TBI* measure becomes important if the aggregate effect of restrictions facing U.S. filmmakers is greater than what simply the number of trade barriers indicates.[4] We will refer to *TBN* as a numerical index and to *TBI* as a qualitative index. The values for these indices also appear in Tables 1 and 2 with summary definitions in Table 3. U.S. trading partners average about three forms of trade restrictions (*TBN*) on the imports of motion pictures, and their mean qualitative index (*TBI*) is nearly six.

The highest regional numerical index (*TBN*) is in North America (excluding, again, the United States), followed by Western Europe. Of individual countries, France has the largest value at five, followed closely by Argentina, Brazil, Canada, Indonesia, Italy, Mexico, Spain, and Switzerland with four each. The qualitative index (*TBI*) also averages highest in North America, followed by Western Europe, with the Middle East and Asia not far behind. Of countries, the highest qualitative index number is 9.6 for France and Italy, respectively; followed by 9.4 for Indonesia; 9.0 for Canada and Saudi Arabia (movies taboo); 8.6 for Argentina, Mexico, and Republic of Korea; 8.4 for India; 8.0 for Spain; and 7.6 for Brazil. Excepting Saudi Arabia, all of the countries with high *qualitative* restrictions (including levies and subsidies) tend to have strong interests in developing or preserving their domestic movie industries. Except Saudi Arabia, they also typically appear to have well-developed domestic movie industries.

As we consider developed versus LDCs, *TBN* is somewhat higher in the developed countries, and the *TBI* is somewhat higher in the less developed world. The quantitative (*TBN*) restrictions are about twice as high in the non–English-speaking countries as in the English-speaking world. The ratio for the *TBI* index for the non–English- to the English-speaking countries is similar. The LDCs generally are more protectionist by these measures and are at the same time comprised of non–English-speaking people. Thus, the LDC classification and language are candidate measures of cultural differences affecting trade barriers.

The use of levies combined with subsidies and service barriers (in the presence of piracy) as a strategy against U.S. imports in countries desiring to expand their film industries suggests

4. Because, as noted, many different methods are used to restrict imports, simply the number of trade restrictions (*TBN*) is sometimes inadequate in capturing the severity of trade restrictions.

TABLE 3
Definition, Mean, and SD of Each Variable

Variable	Definition	Mean (SD)
X	U.S. receipts from film and tape rentals in millions of dollars, each country in real terms	85.26 (133.71)
IM	U.S. payments from film and tape rentals in millions of dollars to each country in real terms	2.78 (6.83)
Y_i	U.S. GDP per capita in dollars, in real terms	22,498.41 (672.95)
Y_j	Other country's GDP per capita in dollars, in real terms	12,592.32 (9666.61)
ED	Adult literacy rate in other countries	90.78 (11.86)
LAN	Percentage of English-speaking population in other countries	14.33 (29.94)
REL	Percentage of population that is Judeo-Christian in other countries	63.46 (44.05)
TBN	Numerical index or number of trade barriers, including tariff, subsidies, quantitative restrictions, piracy, video levy, and service barriers, ranging from zero to six, six being the highest	2.83 (1.29)
TBI	Qualitative index of trade barriers allowing for number of barriers as well as their complexity, on scale of 1 to 10, 10 being the highest	5.85 (2.52)
NFP	Number of films produced in other countries	74.45 (147.37)
$INVR$	Ratio of investment in motion pictures industry in other countries to GDP in other countries	0.00015 (0.0002)
DIS	Air distance between the closest major U.S. city and the capital of each country in miles	6111.23 (11,891.34)
LDC	Dummy for LDCs, one for LDC, zero otherwise	0.5455 (0.50)
ADJ	Dummy for adjacent countries, one for adjacent, zero otherwise	0.0606 (0.24)

endogenous protectionism. The high qualitative restrictions in countries with a well-developed domestic industry suggest that the industry may have a special interest in pursuing such barriers to trade. Beyond this evidence we also consider explicit measures of the importance of film industries to countries. The ratio of investment in the motion picture industry to the level of GDP (*INVR*) as well as the number of films produced in each country (*NFP*) may represent the importance of the industry to special interest groups and thereby to policy makers.

IV. CULTURAL DISTANCE IN A GRAVITY-ICEBERG MODEL

Important characteristics of movies are consistent with the assumptions of gravity models, such as conditions of imperfect competition often associated with economies of scale in production or distribution. However, another common assumption of such models is significant transport costs sometimes used as a measure of spatial distance. As it turns out, movies have negligible transport costs, but this does not rule out other kinds of costs from distance, such as cultural distance. We normally expect audiences to prefer movies that are produced in their native languages or which reflect their cultural values. Based on our overview of the U.S. industry, the main barrier to local movie production appears to be a sufficiently large domestic market and an adequate per capita income generating the economies of scale in exhibition that warrant high production costs.

From Samuelson's original iceberg model, X_{ij} becomes the value of country i's film shipments that "arrive" at their destination, country j, having "melted down" a fraction from x_{ij} because of transportation costs and distance between the countries. Although the value of x_{ij} cannot be observed, the image of a melting iceberg affirms the inverse relation between shipments and spatial distance. Because the cost of transporting film is negligible, however, we will interpret the meltdown as most likely the effect of cultural differences between countries. Simply expressed, the total meltdown will be a weighted average from the effect of all such cultural variables for the jth importing country. Thus, in general,

$$X_{ij} = \sum_{m=1}^{M} e^{-t_{ijm}} D_{ijm} x_{ij}, \tag{3}$$

where the subscript m represents the mth of M independent cultural distance variables and t_{ijm} represents the weight of the mth cultural distance variable in the jth importing country. Furthermore, trade barriers can be included in this list of meltdown variables, barriers such as levies and subsidies in motion pictures often based on cultural considerations. Because of the nature of these meltdown variables, it can be safely assumed that $\sum_m e^{-t_{ijm}} D_{ijm} < 1$.

In Bergstrand's generalized gravity equation (1989, p. 146) and Krugman's location model (1995, p. 91) exports are positively related to the purchasing power of any country set but are inversely related to distance. By introducing Samuelson's iceberg effect from the independent variables, the complex gravity-iceberg export model becomes

$$X_{ij} = \left[k(Y_i Y_j / D_{ij}^b)\right] \left[\sum_{m=1}^{M} e^{-t_{ijm}} D_{ijm}\, x_{ij}\right], \tag{4}$$

where x_{ij} is country i's receipts from motion pictures (in real terms) from country j, the Ys are the per capita incomes in the respective countries i and j, D_{ij} is the distance between countries i and j, and b is an exponent thought to be approximately one. In our equation, k is a coefficient of the entire term in brackets; if the coefficients of per capita income and distance were estimated separately, as in much of the gravity literature, k would be a scalar. The right-hand side of equation (3) is the second term on the right-hand side of equation (4). By combining the iceberg effect with the cultural effects, we hypothesize that neither the iceberg model nor the traditional gravity model is sufficient to explain the value of movie exports. This is the rationale for conflating the two models into one.

The multiplicative market size imposes the constraint that trade between countries of equal wealth will be greater than trade between a poor and a rich country, a restriction applicable to motion picture trade. Shipments remain inversely related to distance, and will be more or less important when b is greater than or less than one. This gravity-iceberg model suggests that the volume of exports is related to domestic and foreign market sizes combined as well as *cultural* distances, *including* trade barriers. Not only is the market larger, the greater is per capita income, but the market wealth effect is multiplicative, suggesting the potential for economies of scale in distribution. The cultural effects are also multiplicative. All things considered, this model is suggestive of the imperfect competition characterizing the motion picture industries.

V. EMPIRICAL MODELS OF CULTURAL DISTANCE

A complex gravity-iceberg model and a unique pooled data set can be used to estimate U.S. motion picture exports and protectionism between other countries and the United States. As it turns out, we lose very little information in going from the particular to the general. In an apparent paradox, prior empirical gravity models suggest that both great distances and close proximity can diminish trade. McCallum (1995), Engel and Rogers (1994), and Helliwell's (1995) gravity models reveal a surprisingly large effect of the contiguity of the Canada–U.S. border in diminishing trade. Then, Anderson and Smith (1996), using a more consistent data set, find significant border effects but substantially less than those found by earlier authors. Characteristically, however, these gravity-trade studies have been conducted at high levels of aggregation—at national or regional aggregate trade amounts. Still, if border effects are important for more generic product manufacturers, they probably matter even more for cultural products. Frankel et al. (1998), as well as Frankel and Wei (1998), as examples, introduce common language as a cultural variable, we deploy still more cultural variables.

The Estimating Equations

For computational ease and for conformity with the literature, our theoretical export equation is rewritten in log transform. Thus, equation (4) becomes

$$\text{(5)} \qquad \ln X_{ij} = \ln a_{ij} + k \ln G_{ij} + \sum_{m=1}^{M} -t_{ijm} D_{ijm} + \xi_{ij},$$

where $\ln G_{ij} = [(\ln Y_i + \ln Y_j) - b \ln D_{ij}]$ and a_{ij} is a constant replacing x_{ij} in equations (3) and (4). Although x_{ij} cannot be directly estimated, it clearly becomes the constant term in the log transformation. The last term in equation (5) is an error term with a distribution to be determined statistically.

According to the theory of endogenous protectionism, higher levels of import penetration lead to greater protection because lobbying activities by domestic interest groups intensify in response to increases in import competition. In the motion pictures industry, where cultural sovereignty is a sensitive issue, the theory of endogenous protectionism seems particularly plausible. Our microdata on trade barriers as well as our indices by country (*TBN* and *TBI*) suggest the presence of endogenous protectionism. The use of subsidies (usually funded by levies) appears to be a direct way of maintaining or even growing a local industry in the face of rising imports of American films. Such culturally motivated trade restrictions become an econometric issue, especially because some empirical tests of international trade flows and trade restrictions based on cross-sectional data *have* found that such flows and barriers are endogenously determined (e.g., Ray 1981a,b; Trefler 1993; Grossman and Helpman 1994; Lee and Swagel 1997; Gawande and Banyopadhyay 2000).

To deal with the simultaneity problem of industry production growth alongside growing protectionism, the instrumental variable method is used to obtain consistent and efficient estimates of the export parameters. We sought variables that would be correlated with the trade barriers but not with the error terms in the export functions. Based on the importance of both the relative size of the import-competing industry and the cultural sovereignty dynamic in the motion pictures industry, we posit a trade barriers function for country j as it faces imports from country i,

$$\text{(6)} \qquad T_{ij} = F(\mathbf{Z}_j, \mathbf{C}_{ij}),$$

where T_{ij} represents trade barriers that indexed can take on the value of *TBN* or *TBI* and $\mathbf{Z}_j$ is a vector of measures of the importance of the industry to the economy of the importing country j. We use *NFP* and *INVR* as direct measures within Z. The second vector, $\mathbf{C}_{ij}$, contains country-specific, time-invariant variables measuring various cultural categorizing variables also present in the export functions. The more important the elements of $\mathbf{Z}_j$, the greater will be the probable lobbying activities by the interests of the import-competing domestic movie industry as imports rise. These elements determine T, but are not determined by it, and do not determine trade, other than through T. Estimates of equation (6) will be used to create the instrumental variables.

Data Base

Our estimates are from a pooled data set of annual time-series and cross-sectional observations (see Appendix for data sources). This set yields 165 observations for 33 countries for 1991–95 so that, in the estimates, $j = 1, \ldots, 33$ countries and $i =$ U.S.[5] We use common acronyms for the independent variables in Table 3. In our sample the mean number of films produced annually in other countries is only about 75 compared with 435 in the United States, spotlighting American dominance.[6] The high standard deviation of *NFP* reflects how a small number of U.S. trading partners in the industry (India, Japan, Hong Kong, China, France, and the Philippines) produce a large share of "foreign" films, whereas most others produce relatively small numbers. In our defined regions in Table 1 Asia dominates foreign production with an annual average of 162 films. The ratio of investment in the motion pictures industry to GDP (*INVR*) reflects the same reality. During

5. U.S. rental revenues from the sample countries as shares of world U.S. film exports, 1991–95, are 96%, 95%, 95%, 97%, and 96%, respectively. The share of U.S. payments for the imports of films from the sample countries as a fraction of total U.S. payments for its film imports for the same years are 97%, 94%, 96%, 90%, and 98%, respectively (*Survey of Current Business*, September 1995 and October 1997).

6. A different source suggests an even greater disparity (*Screen Digest* September 1998).

the sample period for the United States, *INVR* is 0.00091 or six times larger than the mean for the other countries in the sample (*Screen Digest* May 1997).

Traditional measures of spatial distance between countries, such as air distance between cities and adjacency, as well as various measures of cultural distance are considered. Uniquely, air distance (*DIS*) from the United States and adjacency to the United States (*ADJ*) are used both as measures of spatial distance and as naive proxies for cultural distance. Only Mexico and Canada, or 6% of the countries in the sample, however, are considered adjacent to the United States. Whereas education, religion, and language may in part define a culture, U.S. cultural influence may also be defined by geography or spatial proximity that facilitates interactions between Americans and others.

The exact number of cultural variables (*M*) depends on the model specification. We selected three direct measures of cultural distance from the United States, which are literacy rates in other countries (*ED*), the percentages of people who are of Judeo-Christianity faith (*REL*), and the percentages of populations who speak English (*LAN*). A dummy variable (*LDC*) is used to capture any remaining differences between LDCs and developed countries. Although more than half of the countries in the sample are LDCs, the bulk of U.S. motion picture trade is with highly industrialized nations. The mean literacy rate in the entire sample is 90.78%, the population that is Judeo-Christian 63.46% (the standard deviation exceeding the *REL* mean), whereas the mean percentage of English-language speaking population in the importing countries is only 14.33%.

Statistical Techniques

As noted, we generate two instrumental variables. Because the first measure of trade barriers (*TBN*) is a *count* of the number of trade restrictions imposed on imports of motion pictures, the Poisson distribution is a reasonable description for these data (Hausman et al. 1984; Greene 2000). The index of the complexity of trade barriers (*TBI*), on the other hand, is both a discrete as well as a categorical variable. If the error term is normally distributed, ordered probit is the appropriate estimation model. Otherwise, an ordered logit in which the tails of the distribution of the error term are heavier is the correct model (Greene 2000). The sample quantiles for the *TBN* and *TBI* models (not reported here) reveal small deviations for the residuals of *TBN* but a greater departure from normality of the residuals for *TBI*. Moreover, although the residuals from the *TBN* model appear to be normally distributed, the distribution of the residuals from the *TBI* model has a rather heavy tail.[7]

We conclude that Poisson is the proper choice for the *TBN* model and that the logit model is appropriate for *TBI*. However, in an initial trial we had difficulty running the logit model, and it was abandoned for ordered probit. Maddala (1983) argues that because of similarity between the cumulative normal distribution and the logistic distribution, except at the tails, the results from the logit and probit models are likely to be similar for relatively small samples. Of course, the estimated coefficients from these two alternative models are not directly comparable, and conversions are needed. Thus, Poisson and ordered probit models for the *TBN* and the *TBI* functions, respectively, are estimated, using the maximum likelihood technique.[8]

Another facet to consider in selecting a statistical technique is the nature of the sample: in this case, a balanced panel of 33 countries for five years. In pooling the data, we assume homogeneity in the parameters across all countries. Although the homogeneity assumption underlying pool models has been questioned, Baltagi and et al. (2000), in their estimates of cigarette demand among 46 American states, argue that efficiency gains from pooling is likely to outweigh the bias due to cross-sectional heterogeneity. Baltagi and colleagues contend that their assessment is particularly applicable for short time series. Finally, Maddala (1987) shows that in limited dependent variable models using panel data in which

7. Skewness and kurtosis statistics turn out to be 0.14 and 2.86, respectively, for the *TBN* function and 1.85 and 4.95 for the *TBI* function. A data series is considered to approximate the normal distribution if the value of skewness and kurtosis are close to zero and three, respectively.

8. In the estimation of limited dependent variable models, such as Poisson and ordered probit, of course, log likelihood is usually used as a measure of overall fitness of the model. Although R^2 is reported for Poisson models in LIMDEP, this statistic is not reported for probit models.

the number of cross-sectional units is large and the number of time series is short, a fixed effects model gives inconsistent parameter estimates. Because this aptly describes our pooled sample, we use a *random* effects model by assuming that individual specific constant terms are randomly distributed across countries.

The strategies revealed by the microdata suggest endogenous protectionism. Thus, as we proceed to estimate the export functions, we first need to determine *statistically* whether the trade barriers are endogenous. For this reason, a version of the Hausman specification test is deployed in a simple two-stage procedure (Pindyck and Rubinfeld 1997). First, *TBN* and *TBI* are regressed against all other dependent variables. Then the residuals from these regressions are used as explanatory variables in the estimation of U.S. exports. The null hypothesis for the lack of endogeneity is that the coefficient of the residual is statistically insignificant. The *t*-test results support our microdata findings that the trade barriers are indeed endogenous.

Following Ray's initiative (1981a), a two-stage method is used to estimate the coefficients of the structural equations. First, equation (6) is estimated with *TBN* and *TBI* as alternative dependent variables. Second, the predicted values of the trade barriers functions are used as instrumental variables in the export function estimate or equation (5).

VI. RESULTS

Expected Signs

If the theory of endogenous protectionism prevails, the expected signs for the coefficients of the explicit cultural variables (*ED*, *LAN*, and *REL*) in the trade barriers models are *negative* because an *increase* in their values would diminish the demand for protectionism. The expected sign of the coefficient for *ADJ* is positive if Canada and Mexico have a greater fear of losing their cultural sovereignty through importation of U.S. films than non-adjacent countries. If so, the gravity-iceberg model embodies a degree of apparent contradiction: Distance matters, but so does immediate proximity.

In the U.S. export equations, the expected sign of the coefficient of *G* is positive as long as transportation costs or distance as a proxy for cultural distance does not outweigh the positive influence of purchasing powers in the countries.[9] As noted, we do not expect spatial distance or transport costs to deter movies trade. The expected sign of the coefficient of *ADJ* is indeterminate because U.S. export success depends on a tension between the desires for relatively higher trade barriers in Canada or Mexico and their citizens' preferences for American movies (i.e., American popular culture). Because actual or feared import levels motivate trade barriers, the measures of trade barriers (*TBN* and *TBI*) or their predicted values would be positively correlated with U.S. exports. Finally, because *LDC* is a broad measure of cultural differences between the United States and its trading partners, and fewer cultural similarities and thereby taste similarities exist between the United States and the LDCs compared to the United States and other industrialized countries, the expected sign of the coefficient for *LDC* is negative. The expected sign of the constant term that represents x_{ij} is negative because of the meltdown effect.

Endogeneity in the Trade Barriers Equation Estimates

The maximum likelihood estimates of the trade barriers equations are reported in Table 4. Both the Poisson model (for *TBN*) and the ordered probit model (for *TBI*) are corrected for heteroscedasticity. The estimations are generally consistent with the hypothesis that both specific cultural variables *and* proximity affect the degrees of protectionism. The coefficients of the cultural variables are statistically highly significant with the expected negative signs, except for the coefficient of *REL*. The unexpectedly positive sign for religion may be the result of the large shares of Judeo-Christian population among the industrialized importers compared to those shares in the LDCs. The positive sign of the coefficient for *ADJ* suggests that adjacent nations *are* more protective of their domestic movie industry. Those nations (Canada and Mexico), as noted, are also dominant users of quantitative restrictions and have the highest average values for *TBN* and *TBI* in Table 1. These high index values are also disproportionate to the number

9. The expected sign would be negative, however, if larger domestic markets in the other nations allow their domestic producers sufficient economies of scale to effectively compete with the U.S. film industry.

TABLE 4
Random Effects Estimates of Trade Barriers Models

		Coefficients[d]					
Variables	Expected Sign	Equation (6) Poisson Model for *TBN*			Equation (6) Ordered Probit Model for *TBI*		
INVR	(+)	221.9222 (306.8140)		408.2013[c] (269.5697)	866.2376[c] (584.6599)		928.0070[b] (455.0643)
NFP	(+)	0.0006[c] (0.0004)	0.0007[b] (0.0004)		0.0002 (0.0016)	0.0007 (0.0012)	
ADJ	(+)	0.4393[c] (0.1739)	0.4210[a] (0.171)	0.4445[a] (0.1735)	1.9832[a] (0.3670)	1.8837[a] (0.3699)	1.9895[a] (0.3628)
ED	(−)	−0.0082[c] (0.0062)	−0.0063 (0.0056)	−0.0132[a] (0.0050)	−0.04182[a] (0.0160)	−0.0336[a] (0.0122)	−0.0433[a] (0.0161)
LAN	(−)	−0.0097[a] (0.0022)	−0.0094[a] (0.0021)	−0.0102[a] (0.0021)	−0.0286[a] (0.0045)	−0.0273[a] (0.0044)	−0.0288[a] (0.0045)
REL	(−)	0.0051[a] (0.0014)	0.0050[a] (0.0014)	0.0051[a] (0.0014)	0.0078[a] (0.0027)	0.0069[a] (0.0025)	0.0078[a] (0.0028)
Constant		1.4415[a] (0.5354)	1.3004[a] (0.50044)	1.9137[a] (0.4026)	4.8425[a] (1.3444)	4.2235[a] (1.0845)	4.9899[a] (1.3576)
Log likelihood		−261.93	−262.18	−262.87	−305.35	−306.72	−305.38

[a(b,c)]Significant at the 1% (5%, 10%) level.
[d]Estimated asymptotic standard errors are in parentheses.

of films produced annually in each country (31). Proximity seems to breed contempt.

To explore further the more precise individual effects of *NFR* and *INVR* on trade barriers, one of the two variables is dropped in alternative model specifications.[10] The likelihood ratio, as a measure of overall fitness of the models, remains virtually constant as one of the two variables is dropped, suggesting that the marginal contribution of each variable in the presence of the other is small. However, the size of the coefficient of either *NFP* or *INVR* increases in the absence of the other variable in the model. The coefficient of number of films (*NFP*) in the *TBN* function is statistically significant with the expected positive sign, but investment in the industry (*INVR*) appears not to be enhancing trade barriers.[11] As noted earlier, subsidies usually financed through video levies characterize protectionism in those European countries aspiring to a strong domestic movie presence. Canada, another aspirant, has subsidies sans levies. Thus, the microdata results suggesting that trade barriers are raised to protect the interests of the cultural import-competing industry (or the culture itself) gain considerable support in the functions used to estimate the instrumental variables.

We proceed to use the predicted values of the trade barriers indices from the base models in the estimation of the U.S. export function. Although we hypothesize that the cultural identity variables also belong in the export function, the inclusion of these variables in the presence of the instrumental trade barriers variables may cause a multicollinearity problem. To test for such multicollinearity, the variance inflation factor (VIF) is estimated for predicted values of *TBN* against all other explanatory variables in the original export function. The value of VIF does not exceed 0.33 in any of the estimates. Connecting the trade pattern in motion pictures to the cultural identity of countries could be informative, so we retain the cultural identity variables in the export model.

Estimates for the U.S. Export Models

The heteroscedasticity-corrected estimates of equation (5) for U.S. exports of motion

10. Because of concern about possible correlation between the measures of the importance of the motion pictures industry to the domestic economy, the zero-order correlation coefficients for *INVR* and *NFP* are considered; a coefficient of 0.31 suggests that imperfect multicollinearity is not a serious problem. Then, R^2 from the auxiliary equations for *NFP* and *INVR* are used to calculate the *VIF*; the value of 1.72 for *NFP* and 1.21 for *INVR* suggest that perfect multicollinearity does not seem to be an issue either.

11. The coefficients of *NFP* and *INVR* in the *TBN* and the *TBI* equations have varying degrees of statistically significance with the correct signs (see Table 4).

TABLE 5
Random Effects Regression Results for ln *X*[e] in Gravity-Iceberg Model

		Coefficients[d]			
Variables	**Expected Sign**	**Equation (5) Model I**	**Equation (5) Model II**	**Equation (5) Model III**	**Equation (5) Model IV**
Ln *G*	(+)	0.0925	0.1081[c]	0.1887[b]	0.1831[b]
		(0.0769)	(0.1258)	(0.1044)	(0.1065)
TBI (predicted)	(+)		0.2168[a]		0.1246[a]
			(0.0489)		(0.0430)
TBN (predicted)	(+)	0.6469[a]		0.3641[a]	
		(0.2465)		(0.1040)	
ADJ	(+ or −)	0.0751	0.1082		
		(0.3349)	(0.2714)		
ED	(+)	0.0857[a]	0.0876[a]		
		(0.0112)	(0.0099)		
LAN	(+)	0.0083[c]	0.0052		
		(0.0065)	(0.0044)		
REL	(+)	−0.0047	−0.0007		
		(0.0040)	(0.0024)		
LDC	(−)	−1.1330[a]	−1.0584[a]	−1.969[a]	−2.0916[a]
		(0.2313)	(0.2146)	(0.2987)	(0.3178)
Constant	(−)	−10.8203[a]	−10.3131[a]	−2.5305[a]	−1.8689[a]
		(1.3130)	(0.9510)	(0.6228)	(0.6958)
Adj. R^2		0.66	0.68	0.51	0.51
F		46.88	51.51	57.75	57.30

[a(b,c)]Significant at the 1% (5%, 10%) level.
[d]Standard errors are in parentheses.
[e]Heteroscedasticity corrected estimates.

pictures appear in Table 5. The Roman numerals represent successively different specifications of the initial model. In the estimate of gravity-iceberg model I, the log of *G* loses its statistical significance in the presence of *LDC* and specific cultural variables. Although the sizes of the cultural variable coefficients are only slightly altered, language (*LAN*) has diminished statistical significance. The coefficients of the predicted value of *TBN* are positive and statistically highly significant in models I and II. The numerical index TBN is replaced with *TBI* in models II and IV. The two sets of results are similar except for the insignificance of the coefficient of language (*LAN*) in model II and the significance of the coefficient of *ADJ* in model II. Protectionism abroad appears to rise with U.S. exports. As expected, the constant term representing x_{ij} is negative, and reflects the iceberg meltdown effect. Also, as expected, gravity (*G*) and *LDC* have stronger showings in the gravity-iceberg models when specific cultural variables are dropped (models III and IV). Still, by statistical standards—the adjusted R^2, the value of F, or the degrees of significance and correct signs of variables—the gravity-iceberg export models that include specific cultural variables perform best.[12]

Taken together, the estimates corroborate the strategies revealed in the microdata, namely, that particular countries desire to develop local industry and that the cultural threat of proximity of the United States to Canada and Mexico is mostly expressed through protectionism. Once the protectionist instrumental variables are introduced in the export models, *ADJ* becomes insignificant. The sizes of all of the cultural variable coefficients are surprisingly similar across the trade barriers estimates. Still, in our preferred complex gravity-iceberg export estimates wherein *endogenous* protection flows through

12. Zero-order correlation matrices and VIF estimates are used to test all of the export models for multicollinearity. The zero-order correlation coefficients are fairly low, the highest being between *LDC* and ln(Y_i+ Y_j) at 0.56. Furthermore, there is no indication of muticollinearity based on the values of the VIF.

the predicted values of *TBI* and *TBN* (export models I and II), some of the cultural variables remain significant and important alongside the state of economic development. Consumer preferences for American films are strong, but so is antitrade lobbying interests leading to levies and subsidies. There remains a tension between foreign consumers who desire American movies and foreign movie producers who have a special interest in slowing American movie imports.

VII. CONCLUDING REMARKS

The strategies of protectionism revealed by the microdata are consistent with our econometrics. The gravity-iceberg export models perform well even with aggregated indices combined with standard gravity measures of purchasing power and spatial distance. Explicit cultural variables (such as language, education, and religion) also are important indirect (via protectionism) influences on U.S. motion picture exports. Microdata as well as econometric estimates have trade barriers responding positively to growing U.S. exports as well as to aspirations for a thriving local industry buoyed by levies and subsidies, barriers that are determined endogenously. Moreover, the use of subsidies appears to be mostly a reaction to rising U.S. exports.

The United States continues to dominate the world as a popular cultural center through its export of films. Despite substantial barriers to film imports, other large economies apparently have been unable to internationally extend their domestic markets. Even India, where subsidies support the producer of the largest number of films in the world, has not successfully exported films to the U.S. market. Despite subsidies to their film industries, smaller economies have been unable to gain a competitive advantage in international markets. Europe and industrialized countries in other regions nonetheless are major consumers of American films.

Even though the English-speaking population in our sample of foreign countries is small, any increase in the use of the English language enhances U.S. exports. The absence of English speech, however, apparently deters consumption of foreign films in the American market. Presumably, even *dubbed* American films outperform the competition in the world market. This speaks volumes regarding the popularity of American films abroad even as it certifies the advantage that domestic purchasing power gives to early success and economies of scale in distribution for American film producers. The greatest U.S. barrier to foreign competition and effective foreign protectionism appears to be the gigantic production and marketing costs required to produce the kinds of films now demanded around the world. The global distributional reach of the American movie industry and the popularity of its films are formidable.

Does the recent experience of the motion picture industry provide any lessons on trade policies in the United States or other countries? Elimination of earlier American barriers to motion pictures was an efficient act because they were unnecessary in the face of weak preferences for foreign films. The U.S. music recording industry has replicated the export success of motion pictures for about the same reasons. The strategy of levies-subsidization by aspiring countries gives local producers a cultural buffer even though it does little to generate exports or to limit imports from the United States. Other industries have been able to use brand image as a way of duplicating the trademark quality of American film stars. BMW, like Mercedes Benz, has a star quality that has eluded the American big three. Chrysler's response may ultimately be effective—merger with Daimler, though it might tarnish the Mercedes as a star. Ultimately, economies of scale and highly effective product differentiation eclipse traditional protectionism, if only for distinctive products produced in economies or regions that are large or wealthy.

APPENDIX: DATA SOURCES

The data used in Figures 1 and 2 on domestic box office as well as production and advertising costs of the major studios is from the Web site of the MPAA. The data in Figure 1 on international revenues are from various January issues of *Variety*. International trade figures in motion pictures are from the *Survey of Current Business*, October 1997 and September 1995, U.S. Department of Commerce. GDP data are from the *U.N. Statistical Yearbook*, 1995. Because the United Nations does not report GDP figures for Taiwan, *Europa World Yearbook*, published by Europa Publications, 1994–98, is used as an alternative source. Figures for air distance between the closest major U.S. city and the capital of each country are from *World Almanac* 1996, published by Funk and Wagnalls, New York. Population data is extracted from *International Financial Statistics*, September 1993 through September 1997, International Monetary Fund. Literacy rates are from various sources, including *UNESCO Statistical Yearbook*, 1994–96; *Human Development Report*, 1995–96; and *World Development Report*, 1995, all published by the United Nations, as well as *Europa World Yearbook*, 1994–97. Data for religion and language are from *The Stateman's Yearbook*, 1994–97, published by St. Martin's Press. LDC identification is based on the United Nations classification in *Human Development Report*, 1998. Data for number of films produced and amount of investment in the industry for each country is from *Screen Digest* (May 1997). Number of films and investment data for some countries, for one or more years of 1991–95, are not reported in *Screen Digest*. These are typically small LDCs in which the industry is not very active; therefore, we have used the average for 1991–95 for each of these countries.

Detailed quantitative and qualitative information on trade barriers is collected from annual MPAA reports titled *Trade Barriers to Exports of U.S. Film Entertainment*, 1991–96. The countries in our sample include Argentina, Australia, Belgium-Luxembourg, Bermuda, Brazil, Canada, Chile, China, France, Germany, Hong Kong, India, Indonesia, Israel, Italy, Japan, Malaysia, Mexico, the Netherlands, New Zealand, Norway, the Philippines, Republic of Korea, Saudi Arabia, Singapore, South Africa, Spain, Sweden, Switzerland, Taiwan, Thailand, United Kingdom, and Venezuela. Although the choice of countries is based on the availability of trade data, the selected sample accounts for at least 90% and as much as 98% of U.S. motion picture rental revenue from exports and foreign country revenue from the United States during each year of our sample (see note 5).

REFERENCES

Anderson, Michael A., and Stephen L. S. Smith. "Do National Borders Really Matter: A Reconsideration of Canada–U.S. Regional Trade." Paper presented for the Southern Economics Association, Washington, D.C., 23–25 November 1996.

Baltagi, Badi H., James M. Griffin, and W. Xiong. "To Pool or Not to Pool: Homogeneous versus Heterogeneous Estimators Applied to Cigarette Demand." *Review of Economics and Statistics*, 82(1), 2000, 117–26.

Bergstrand, Jeffrey H. "The Generalized Gravity Equation, Monopolistic Competition, and Factor-Proportions Theory in International Trade." *Review of Economics and Statistics*, 71(1), 1989, 372–82.

Canterbery, E. Ray, and A. Marvasti. "The U.S. Motion Pictures Industry: An Empirical Approach." *Review of Industrial Organization*, 19(1), 2001, 81–98.

De Vany, Arthur S., and W. David Walls. "The Market for Motion Pictures: Rank, Revenue, and Survival." *Economic Inquiry*, 35(4), 1997, 783–97.

Engel, Charles, and John H. Rogers. "How Wide Is the Border?" National Bureau of Economic Research Working Paper No. 4829, 1994.

Frankel, Jeffrey A., and Shang-Jin Wei. "Regionalization of World Trade and Currencies: Economics and Politics," in *The Regionalization of the World Economy*, edited by J. A. Frankel. Chicago University of Chicago Press, 1998, 189.

Frankel, Jeffrey A., Ernesto Stein, and Shang-Jin Wei. "Continental Trading Blocs: Are They Natural or Supernatural?" in *The Regionalization of the World Economy*, edited by J. A. Frankel. Chicago University of Chicago Press, 1998, 91–113.

Gawande, Kishore, and Usrce Bandyopadhyay. "Is Protection for Sale? Evidence on the Grossman-Helpman Theory of Endogenous Protection." *Review of Economics and Statistics*, 82(1), 2000, 139–52.

Greene, William H. *Econometric Analysis*, 4th ed. New York: Macmillan, 2000.

Grossman, Gene M., and Elhanan Helpman. "Protection for Sale." *American Economic Review*, 84(4), 1994, 833–50.

Hausman, Jerry, Hall H. Bronwyn, and Zvi Griliches. "Econometric Models for Count Data with an Application to the Patent-R&D Relationship." *Econometrica*, 52(4), 1984, 909–38.

Helliwell, John F. "Do National Borders Matter for Quebec's Trade?" National Bureau of Economic Research Working Paper No. 5215, 1995.

Krugman, Paul. *Development, Geography, and Economic Theory*. Cambridge, MA: MIT Press, 1995.

Lee, Jong-Wha, and Phillip Swagel. "Trade Barriers and Trade Flows across Countries and Industries." *Review of Economics and Statistics*, 79(3), 1997, 372–82.

Maddala, G. S. *Limited-Dependent and Qualitative Variables in Econometrics*. Cambridge: Cambridge University Press, 1983.

———. "Limited Dependent Variable Models Using Panel Data." *Journal of Human Resources*, 22(1), 1987, 307–38.

McCallum, John. "National Borders Matter: Canada–U.S. Regional Trade Patterns." *American Economic Review*, 85(3), 1995, 615–23.

Pindyck, Robert S., and Daniel L. Rubinfeld. *Econometric Models and Economic Forecasts*, 4th ed. Boston: Irwin McGraw-Hill, 1997.

Ray, Edward John. "Tariff and Nontariff Barriers to Trade in the United States and Abroad." *Review of Economics and Statistics*, 68(2), 1981a, 161–68.

———. "The Determinants of Tariff and Nontariff Trade Restrictions in the United States." *Journal of Political Economy*, 89(1), 1981b, 105–21.

Screen Digest, May 1997.

———, September 1998.

Trefler, Daniel. "Trade Liberalization and the Theory of Endogenous Protection: An Econometric Study of U.S. Import Policy." *Journal of Political Economy*, 101(1), 1993, 138–60.

Chapter 51

Foreword

H. Peter Gray brilliantly depicts the dire dilemma of the United States as a waning hegemon. Prosperity in the rest of the world depends on continued growth in U.S. aggregate demand as well as an expanding gap between the value of its imports and exports. Therein sets the Catch 22: American trade deficit financing depends on the generosity of strangers willing to lend to Americans (or buy their corporate equities) so the U.S. standard of living can be maintained. If these foreigners fail – for numerous plausible reasons – to continue to recycle US dollars, the aggregate demand they depend on will collapse.

Bringing the US trade gap into balance requires roughly a third loss in the dollar's international value, which means an even greater loss by foreigners from their American financial asset holdings. If the dollar sinks to those lows, it is "exhausted" as American assets are sold in ubiquitous panic and the hegemon comes to a humiliating end, with unpleasant consequences for the global economy. This calamity can be avoided by a new global financial architecture requiring the kind of retreat into multinational cooperation inimical to a Rome or a United Kingdom in the past, much less the USA of today.

The dilemma for the global economy is sufficiently clear. As the hegemon is running a balance of payments deficit, some other nations are running surpluses. As the hegemon piles up debt, countries such as China or Japan, whose exports exceed their imports, are also exporting their "excess savings." The value of what these producers within their countries are producing exceeds the value of what their households and producers are buying, the residual being savings – savings held in the form of American financial assets.

Ben Bernanke, the Chairman designate of the Board of Governors of the Federal Reserve System, before moving to President George W. Bush's Council of Economic Advisors, finds an "unconventional" cause of this dilemma, "a global savings glut." Since economists have Keynesian amnesia these days, Bernanke can be excused for not realizing that a "savings glut" is unconventional *only* in the world of Adam Smith and J. B. Say. The current account surpluses of Japan, the eurozone, Denmark, Norway and Sweden rose some 67 percent between 1996 and 2004. The rest of the world's current account moved from a *deficit* of $99 billion to a surplus of $329 billion, an incredible swing of

$428 billion. A deterioration of confidence in the emerging market economies is responsible for this shift; they had been running deficits prior to the currency crises of 1997–98. Not surprisingly, the more recent acceleration in the US current account deficit is associated with the huge trade imbalance with China and a rising oil bill, not unrelated to China's rapidly growing thirst for oil and gas. Amazingly, the United States has absorbed about three-quarters of the "surplus savings" of the world; what is normally an unrevealed domestic Keynesian excess is unmasked as it escapes national borders.

Bernanke, being the good neoclassical economist, has "savings" driving expenditures, as if the Chinese peasant's frugality incites Americans to buy Lexus's from Japan and BMW's from Germany, as well as Donald Rumsfeld's willingness to keep his war machine humming in Iraq. Bernanke is half correct, which is a hundred percent improvement on most neoclassical economists. Economists like Peter Gray who do remember Keynes as well as understanding Mastercard might say: "If Americans were not consuming more than they were producing, Chinese, Japanese, as well as households and businesses in oil-producing countries, *would not have* surplus savings for MasterCard and Citigroup to recycle as loans." Americans are buying silk tropical shirts and skirts from China with dollars supplied by the Chinese. The United States has become the Resort Buyer of *last* resort in the global economy.

Some of the goods, such as clothing from China, Indonesia and the Philippines, are bought by low-wage American workers; other goods, such as Lexus or BMW autos, are bought by the well-to-do. A portion of US imports, of course, is comprised of commodities (Canada and the Middle East) and capital (Germany) for further production. To be fair, even the American Keynesians missed the imbalances – at home and abroad – related to income and wealth inequalities.

Peasants in China may want to consume more but have insufficient incomes; young entrepreneurs in Beijing spend as fast as they can but still have funds left over that can be used to buy not only luxury goods but IBM and GE stock. Oil-producing Saudi royals run out of time before they run out of money buying luxury goods, shares of Citigroup and high-end real estate. China and Japan's central banks buy US dollars (US Treasuries) to keep their yuan and yen cheap, making their exports even more competitive to further enhance their trade surpluses (US deficits).

At home in hegemon, the typical American wage earner cannot afford to buy most goods produced in the US so they buy "Chinese Take-Out" from Wal-Mart, produced by even cheaper Chinese labor at a low-valued yuan. After the various currency crises and the bursting of the Great American Stock Bubble, MasterCard combined with near-zero interest rates on equity loans to "clean up" credit card debt has sustained a US growth in Keynesian-style effective demand that, except for financial services and housing, has been mostly external. Although low-wage Americans needing credit the most can least afford it, the huge George W. tax cuts have supported luxury goods purchases by the rich and super-rich "to keep up with the Jones's" (the Saudi's and the new Chinese entrepreneurs) as well as subsidizing American oil and gas producers over-burdened with excess profits. Private debt has done for poor and middle-class Americans what public debt has done for rich Americans and corporations.

Not only do Americans live in a Keynesian world necessitating the odd couple of large federal budget deficits and low interest rates to avoid depression-level unemployment, so do people in Japan and the eurozone. Meantime, the emerging nations depend on America's private credit economy (indebted consumers) for their continued expansion. Despite currency and stock market crashes around the world, the instinct to buy assets remains even as purchases have shifted somewhat toward upscale or luxury primary, vacation and second homes.

Staying in a losing race as the hegemon has not been easy. US policy-makers have allowed financial bubbles to expand as a way of moving the finishing line into the future. As one bubble bursts, the world moves on to another and another. Worse, the war in Iraq has perversely helped to maintain global aggregate demand even as it has exposed the extreme weakness of the US as world geopolitical political leader. Rapid short-term policy changes are desperately required as time runs out. With this compression of time, citizens of the world have reasons to worry about the exhaustion of the hegemon on which the global economy has so long depended.

Poor countries, mostly in Asia and in oil-producing nations, are financing consumption in a very rich country. This awkward paradox can be sustained only as long as American wage earners are willing and able to borrow and buy Asian goods at low prices and Middle Eastern oil at rising prices. Abundant banking credit and low interest rates have countered the aftermath of the Great Stock Market Bubble, only to create a housing bubble.

Today the end of hegemony could come from either direction: foreigners cashing out of highly liquid American assets or Americans attempting unsuccessfully to cash out of appreciated but much less liquid properties, as US interest rates rise a couple more percentage points. Before, MasterCard debt was essential to global aggregate demand; in the aftermath Japanese and Chinese economic growth may be priceless. It is not too late to take an imposing scholar's advice – Peter Gray's urgent call for a new international payments structure.

E. RAY CANTERBERY

Chapter 52

THE MULTINATIONAL AND GLOBAL FACTOR MOBILITY

E. Ray Canterbery

I. Introduction

H. Peter Gray's purpose in his book on globalization (1999), is to develop a paradigm for the analyses of international involvement (IEI). However, he wants to avoid a formal construct, such as characterizes the Heckscher-Ohlin-Samuelson theory (H-O-S) or even the intra-industry trade models based on economies of scale and product differentiation (Krugman). He shuns the latter because their treatment of technology is too limited and they, at best, explain trade only among the industrialized nations. Gray also dismisses the "technology gap" models of North-South trade for focusing exclusively on trade between innovating countries and follower countries while failing to explain differences among technology-intensive goods and other goods.

Gray is responding to the institutional change called globalization. A movement toward freer factor movements, sharp reductions in transportation costs, the integration of financial markets, and the growth of multinational corporations (MNCs) characterize globalization. More than trade is involved, however, because technology and the factors of production have become increasingly mobile among nations. In Gray' s perspective the most important institution in this involvement is the dominance of the MNC as a production unit. Inside the MNC, proprietary technology or what Dunning (1988) calls "created assets" is a critical factor of production. Therefore, in addition to H-O-S natural resource goods and standardized goods, the technology-reliant good or S-good is added to the global market basket.

Except for the new focus on MNCs, Gray (1976, 1979, 1985) has tilled this global earth before. In his attempt to develop a "pragmatic theory" of international trade he included considerations related to specific human capital, or "skill mix," Canterbery's vita theory, the Linder thesis, and the product cycle. These concerns re-appear but with the focus on the MNC, S-goods are in the spotlight. Their production functions are more complex and they can generate quasi-rents. Imperfect competition requires mark-up pricing rather than marginal cost pricing. In the world of the MNC both comparative and competitive advantage exist.

Canterbery (1994) attempted to provide a general theory of international trade based not only on the vita theory, innovations, and the product cycle but also on standardized technology. With the expanded scope of the MNC, however, a gap exists between Gray' s (and Dunning' s) institutional analysis and Canterbery' s formal representation. My purpose herein is to begin to provide the missing links and suggest how they could be used to build a bridge to this century' s formal model. In this regard it is useful to recall that the MNC is involved in the production of *every* kind of good, including the S-good. The United Fruit Company preceded Intel and the British East India Company preceded United Fruit. In the LDCs, of course, bananas preceded the United Fruit Company, crude oil reserves preceded OPEC, and so on.

The most obvious effects of the recent growth in MNCs are three-fold: (1) With all countries much more deeply integrated into the global economy, domestic markets are much more easily supplied from abroad. In turn, with more and more services (such as telephone, travel-tourism, distribution, education, motion picture production and distribution, health care, legal, accounting, data processing, business consultancy, advertising, architecture, golf courses, engineering, transportation, and financial services) crossing borders, intra-firm trade has expanded. (2) Foreign direct investment (FDI), mostly MNC capital transfers, has been growing twice the rate of world trade, while world trade has been growing three times faster than world industrial production since the early 1980s. (3) Intra-industry trade in S-goods—reliant as they are on technology and other modes of differentiation—has greatly expanded. This expansion of MNCs could not have happened absent the blessing of the nation-states of the advanced or supra-surplus countries or even their active encouragement.

II. The Multinational Zone v. the Hot Zone

We are accustomed to think of trade as being between regions. Gray (1999, p. 31) identifies South-South, North-North, and North-South trade. However, he also denotes intra-firm and intra-industry trade. As to goods and services, he lists agricultural goods, natural-resource goods, S-goods/services, and H-O goods. Although MNCs produce and trade all types of goods and services, they specialize in the production and distribution of S-goods/services that enter into intra-firm and intra-industry trade. At only the slightest hint of oversimplification, we can say that MNCs trade *within* their firms and industries. To the extent that their powers supercede or are an integral part of the powers of nation-states, the multinationals have established their own trading region, a zone virtually unconstrained by geography or politics.

Since intra-firm services include financial services, the giant multinational banks and brokerage houses freely move portfolio and other capital around the world. Unlike the movement of goods and other services, however, this movement of funds is not under the control of the non-financial MNCs. The quick movement of such funds can dramatically alter exchange rates (witness the 1997 East Asian currency crisis and its aftermath). The rapid and unpredictable movement of international finance can either speed or slow the growth rate of the non-financial MNCs. Thus, a potential constraint on the growth of MNCs is the behavior of their financial counterparts.

Defining the MNCs as comprising a new trading zone does not obliterate the usefulness of the old trading region pairings. Since MNCs generate the greatest value-added in the world trading system, the value of their trade is mostly North-North. That part which is North-South or South-North is mostly in the emerging economies of East Asia, Eastern Europe, and Latin America. China, Taiwan, Singapore, Hong Kong, Republic of Korea, Poland, Thailand, Mexico, and Brazil come to mind. Still, it might be more analytically useful to divide the trading world into the following categories: the MNC zone (MNC), emerging nations (EN), less-developed non-oil producing nations (LDC-NO), and less-developed oil producing nations (LDC-0). In turn, the MNC zone specializes in S-goods, the EN zone specializes in standardized manufacturers and produce some S-goods based upon product differentiation rather than hi-tech specialization, the LDC-NO zone specializes in various natural-resource-intensive commodities, and the LDC-0 zone produces, of course, crude oil. In the LDC trade zone, prices and proceeds mostly are determined in competitive world commodity markets, the exception being the OPEC nations whose cartel power waxes and wanes. The price of oil is rent-based, both a mark up above unit costs *and* set in a world commodity market. Generally, however, the LDCs are price-takers.

Value added in the world trading system is the most important force driving trade growth and economic development. Except for the OPEC nations, the zone of underdevelopment relies on production whose value is decided in world commodity markets beyond its control. Wage rates and labor skills in such countries are low. Economies of scale and the use of marketing to differentiate products are the great advantages of standardized production in emerging nations. Producers then have some control over their product markets and can stabilize their own prices. Such a process adds layers of value-added in production and distribution and, by definition, grows the nations' GDPs. Though the initial impetus for "importing" standardized technology is the presence of low wages rates, wage rates in manufacturing will exceed those in commodity production.

III. A More-or-Less Formal Model

Can this simplified world trading system be connected to a formal world trade model? In this regard we shift focus to Canterbery (1994). The original model was an input-output model of an open economy that was made dynamic by introducing a product cycle. The technical methods of production are given by a matrix of interindustry coefficients in physical units denoted by A, and by a row vector of direct labor coefficients in physical units, denoted by a_n. These coefficients are decided by the optimal techniques of production, processes that are given initially for the period of production, so that

$$[A, a_n], \qquad (1)$$

where A is non-singular and the transpose of which can be written as

$$[A, a_n]'. \qquad (2)$$

Suppose we divide the world into those four major trading zones—the multinational MNC, EN, LDC_O, and LDC_{NO}. The initial production systems are different for the countries in each region. The MNC zone would be a source of dynamic change in the world system, the EN would be attempting to capture some aspects of that change, and the LDC_{NO} mostly would be at the mercy of world commodity markets. The LDC oil-producing nations would benefit from OPEC's potential to control oil production and from the growing demand for oil in the MNC and EN zones.

In each zone, a country's inputs are physical quantities of raw materials, capital type commodities and labor time. Necessary materials are treated the same as capital type goods since their functions are similar. All inputs except labor are treated as intermediate goods so that investment can only be identified as "capital-type durable goods and necessary materials," all of which is reproducible capital. The value added in each country equals the value of the commodities making up its net national income (or net product). This net national income is distributed as wages, net interest and profits. In general, wages are distributed in proportion to the contributed physical quantity of labor of a particular type and quality. However, a specific money wage rate is determined in the "labor market" for the labor type and quality required. Following the vita theory (Canterbery, 1979), labor is of different qualities and therefore the wage rates will vary by industry. Shadow wages are paid to managers and professionals. This, of course, does not foreclose the possibility that a great number of industries may be paying identical wage rates.

A. The MNC Zone

The production functions within the MNC zone are the most complex and therefore the most complete. The functions of the MNC zone are prototypical for what is *possible* though perhaps not probable elsewhere. Put differently, production relations in the other zones are derivable from those of the MNC by attrition or attenuation. Skilled and managerial labor dominate the advanced economies' labor markets even as hi-tech and otherwise differentiated goods dominate production. This analysis proceeds at the industry levels; alternatively, one could think of the production relations for each firm in an industry as decided by the best available technology and therefore either alike or comprising a monopoly.[1]

The *forms* of production relations, labor markets and price determination of each nation in any zone are identical. Only the specifics vary: the dominant industries may be somewhat different and so too the skill requirements of the labor forces. Given $[A_{MNC}, a_{n,MNC}]'$ and the conditions regarding money wages and profit rates, money prices can be expressed as

$$P_{MNC} = P_{MNC}A_{MNC}(I + \pi') + a_{n,MNC}W'_{MNC}(I + \pi), \quad (3)$$

where P denotes the row vector of prices, π' the column vector of mark-ups (profit rates), and W' the column vector of wage rates. The first group of terms reflects the cost of using commodities or goods to produce commodities and the second reflects the variable costs of labor in production. Since money prices are used, they are absolute rather than relative prices.

This system for each country (and for the world system) must be self-consistent in money prices. That is, a low price elasticity of demand in one commodity market raises the profit margin and thus prices of all commodities that use the first commodity as an input beyond what their costs would be if the input were priced at zero economic profit. This consistency is reflected in the solution of the price system for an MNC-zone nation, which is

$$P_{MNC} = a_{n,MNC}W'_{MNC}(I + \pi')\{I - A_{MNC}(I + \pi')\}^{-1}. \quad (4)$$

The inverted matrix in equation 4, $\{.\}^{-1}$, is non-negative and gives the total (direct and indirect) requirements of commodities for the production of final commodities (i.e. of consumption and new investment-type goods), taking into account their shares going to real profits in each industry. Equation 4 shows how money price changes are also related to the interdependencies of complex techniques. Consider the price of good 1 in detail.

$$P_1 = a_{n2}w_1(1 + \pi_1)\, \alpha_{11} + a_{n2}w_2(1 + \pi_{n1})\alpha_{21} + \ldots$$
$$+ a_{n,n-1}w_{n-1}(1 + \pi_{n1})\alpha_{n-1,1} \qquad (5)$$

in which the element α_{ij} (i, j = 1, 2, ..., n-1) represents the physical quantity of the *i*'th commodity needed in the economic system as a whole (including real profits allocations) to obtain eventually one physical unit of the *j*'th commodity as a final good. (The element α_{ij} should not be confused with the identical notation usually used to denote direct and indirect input requirements *unadjusted* for physical products allocated to profits.) Since the *form* of the price equations for all goods in the world system are similar, the MNC identification sub-scripts are dropped for equation 5. The wage rates reflect quality differentials in human capital as well as demand conditions in particular labor markets. For the export market, both sides of equation 5 would be multiplied by r, the trade-weighted foreign exchange rate for all other MNC-zone nations, the emerging nations (the EN zone), and the LDCs. The exchange rate, however, is not independent of the value of exports and imports.

Total production of Industry 1 in a particular nation is

$$Q_1 = m_1\rho_1 s_1\{\delta_{11}\delta_{12} \ldots \delta_{ij} \ldots \delta_{1,n-1}\}\, \{y_1 + e_1\}, \qquad (6)$$

where m_l is a cultural modifier or representation of a unique resource, ρ_l represents proprietary knowledge, s_l is a scale factor, y_l is the level of real domestic demand, and e_l represents the real value of exports or imports (imports being negative exports). Gray (1976, 1979) introduced the *m*, *ρ*, and *s* terms. In this production system the *m* and *ρ* equal either zero or one. If *m* is a cultural barrier, the industry will not exist. If *m* represents the presence of a unique natural resource such as oil or gold reserves, a product will not be produced in its absence. If the industry requires proprietary knowledge and *ρ* and is required and exists, its value is one; if *ρ* is zero, the industry does not exist If *either m* or *ρ* is zero, production of the good does not take place in a particular country. If either *m* or *ρ* is zero in every nation in a particular zone, the industry does not exist in that zone. Scale, of course, has no meaning in the absence of production; however, if production in Industry 1 takes place, $s <>= 1$.

Gray' s (1999) focus is upon S-goods in the MNC zone, goods that have positive values for *ρ* and *s*. Moreover, the more complex production functions in that zone require extensive arrays of *δs* or direct and indirect requirements. Unique resources (*m*) also can be present such as crude oil reserves and a favorable soil-climate environment for agriculture, such as in the United States.

For the production system of an entire MNC nation,

$$Q = [I - A]^{-1}(y + e), \qquad (7)$$

and aggregate output is the vector

$$Q = [Q_1\ Q_2\ \dots\ Q_{n-1}] \quad (8)$$

In turn, the value added (V) for Industry 1 is

$$V_1 = a_{n1} w_1 (1 + \pi_1)(\alpha_{11}\alpha_{12} \dots \alpha_{1,n-1}) Q_1, \quad (9)$$

or, for an entire economy,

$$V = a_n W' (I + \pi') \{I - A(I + \pi')\} Q \quad (10)$$

As noted, the type of products and industries found in the MNC zone will have high levels of value added. Such values are major contributors to high levels of net national income in such an economy.

If labor requirements are expressed as numbers of workers, total employment under static conditions is

$$a_{n1}Q_1 + a_{n2}Q_2 + \dots a_{n,n-1} = L, \quad (11)$$

where L equals total national employment at the levels of physical output. Different qualities of labor are used in different industries (or even in the same industry). More precisely, therefore, a_{nj} consists of several different types of labor. Represent each labor type by I, II, III, ..., D in which there are D labor types and

$$[a_I a_{II} a_{III} \dots a_D] \quad (12)$$

The labor requirements for Labor Type 1, the highest quality type, become

$$L_I = a_{I1}Q_1 + a_{I2}Q_2 + \dots a_{I,n-1} Q_{n-1} \quad (13)$$

and, for an entire MNC zone economy,

$$L = [a_{jVIV}]_{n-1XD} Q, \quad (14)$$

where $[a_{jVIV}]_{n-1XD}$ is the entire matrix of labor requirements by human capital type and Q is a column vector of output.[2] The net demand matrix of labor markets for the MNC economy would include a strong dependence on senior executives, professionals, upper management, middle management, and highly skilled blue-collar workers.[3] Such labor requirements mirror the production technology in hi-tech and differentiated S-goods.

A price solution comparable to equation 4 but including labor by human capital type is

$$P = [a_{jVIV}]_{n-1XD} W'a (I + \pi) \{I - A(I + \pi')\}^{-1} \quad (4A)$$

where $[a_{jVIV}]$ comprises the labor requirements *matrix* for all industries by labor type and W_a' is a column vector of "labor market" wage rates. Since the wage rates are from "labor markets," more than one wage now applies to each industry.

Wage rates for different human capital types and the size of the mark up are critical to understanding the economies of the MNC zone. Whereas Gray (1999) has "returns" to human capital and to proprietary knowledge as components of the unit costs of production, Canterbery (1994) assigns higher wage rates to higher levels of human capital and views the return to proprietary knowledge as part of the mark up. The initial costs of proprietary knowledge can be viewed as "sunk costs" that thereafter generate quasi-rents (that are included in the mark up). Not only does the existence of extensive backward and forward linkages in the MNC zone contribute to value added, but so too do high wage rates and mark ups.

The bulk of trade *within* the MNC zone is intra-industry (or intra-firm). Different countries specialize in different hi-tech products whereas most produce otherwise standardized products differentiated by advertising and marketing. All produce pharmaceuticals but perhaps only three produce large commercial aircraft. Most produce automobiles differentiated by styling, performance, and advertising, but perhaps only one or two produce space shuttles. Still, the multinational corporation largely supercedes the nation-state. Irrespective of its "home" base, it has production and distribution branches in most other MNC-zone countries. If anything, most of the governments maintain the independence of the MNCs. Moreover, because of the high returns of human capital and high profit returns from quasi-rents, most of the world' s financial capital originates in the MNC zone.

To close the model, personal incomes must be generated and consumption take place. As profits are distributed in the MNC zone, the personal income of the kth individual is

$$y_k = w_{kVIV}h + c_1\pi_1 + c_2\pi_2 + \ldots + c_{n-1}\pi_{n-1} \quad (15)$$

where w_{kVIV} is the wage of central tendency for individual *k's* HC type, *h* is the standard number of hours worked, and the *c's* are *k's* shares of the profits in the designated industries. For most workers, of course, the *c's* are all zero. The income distribution is a rank-order vector of all persons' nominal personal incomes. Total nominal person income is Σy_k $(k = 1, 2, \ldots, v)$.

An extended linear expenditure system can be used to estimate consumption. The value demanded by the kth individual for the ith commodity is

$$v_{ki} = p_i\varepsilon_{ki} + \beta_{ki}(y_k - \Sigma\, p_j\, \varepsilon_{kj}), \quad (16)$$

$$(i = 1, \ldots, n\text{-}1;\ k = 1, \ldots, v)$$

where the *p's* are given by the interdependencies of the production system with wage and profit rates. The *ε's* are parameters representing basic needs, and *β* is the marginal propensity to consume out of income. The sum of the expenditures of all individuals for the MNC country is $\Sigma\, v_i = D$ or aggregate demand while aggregate supply is given by the output vector.

The numbers of commodities that meet wants beyond basic needs as well as the amounts spent for such discretionary items are much greater in the MNC-zone nations than elsewhere in the world system. Incomes in excess of those required to meet basic needs provide the motivation for advertising and marketing efforts to sell surpluses in the MNC zone.

In their respective forms, all the above equations that represent production, value added, labor markets, and demands in an MNC-zone nation can be used to represent the entire region. That is, the MNC zone is comprised of sub-matrices of "national" economies and they are fully integrated.

B. The EN Zone, Technology Transfers and International Factor Mobility

An economy in the EN zone has the production characteristics of both an MNC country and an LDC. This amalgam is the consequence of the partial integration of the MNC zone with selected developing nations. Many of the EN countries have human capital types at least equal in quality to those in the MNC zone. Still, the EN countries are different in two important respects: wage rates, even those for comparable human capital types, are a fraction of MNC wages; and home-based financial capital is severely limited. Thus, for human capital type 1, $w_{1,MNC} > w_{1,EN}$, and the gap is substantial. As to the least skilled labor, the wage differential is even greater. Thus, the prices of MNC-type goods are less (in home currency) than they are in the MNC zone. For example, if good 1 is a differentiated product produced with standardized production functions across the regions, then $P_{1,MNC} > P_{1,EN}$, in domestic prices.

This relative status of the MNC and the EN nations leads to the mobility of factors of production, as well as standardized technology. In mature industries, two gaps—the wage and financial capital gaps—enable the MNCs to infiltrate the EN zone. Managerial labor and financial capital mobility is combined with the exportation of standardized technology or proprietary knowledge to produce cheaper production in the EN zone. Indeed, this is the impetus for economic growth that defines the emerging nation. The corporation is motivated to transfer standardized technology to the EN nations as product cycles in the MNC nations mature. Imitating the model of the MNC zone, the EN nations eventually will begin to produce home grown multinationals that will begin to export their own brands of differentiated products to the MNC zone. Examples include Korean automobiles, Taiwanese personal computers and Chinese cell phones. The critical proprietary knowledge in all three products is computer chip technology.

Free trade in finished goods becomes a moot issue in a world of multinationals. It is the freedom of movement of the multinational that defines the system. In turn, standardized technology freely moves and the changed pattern of trade depends upon its new location. Moreover, since the multinational generally produces differentiated products, the prevailing imperfect competition makes theories based on perfect competition irrelevant.

C. The LDC Zones and the International Mobility of Materials

The production functions of the LDC zones are simplest, though most distinct. Production interdependencies are not complex so that few backward and forward linkages exist. Unskilled labor dominates its labor markets and capital-type intermediate goods are scarce. Low wage rates reflect the low skills of labor. The dominant good is the natural resources good which, in some instances, can be a non-competitive good (bananas, sugar cane). For the non-competitive good, the importing nation is devoid of the required natural resource input (tropical climate and abundant agricultural land) and, therefore, has no production function for that commodity. Even though labor is abundant in the LDC, natural resources are the source of relatively higher returns, especially for non-competitive goods. Those higher returns are embedded in relatively high mark-ups and thus profit rates. The mark-up includes then the "returns" paid to rent-earning inputs such as land. Still, for exports, the domestic prices of those goods in the vector of LDC prices are multiplied by the trade-weighted exchange rate of the MNC and EN zones, an exchange rate greatly favoring the MNC zone with its high value added and its financial capital dominance, the exception being when the LDC currency is tied tc the MNC currency (read: U.S. dollar).

In what is essentially a commodity-based economy, the total production in the key industry, say Industry 5 in the LDC-NO zone is

$$Q_{5,\,LDC\text{-}NO} = m_{5,\,LDC\text{-}NO}s_{5,\,LDC\text{-}NO}\{\delta_{11}\delta_{12}\delta_{13}\delta_{14}\delta_{15}\}\{y_{5,\,LDC\text{-}NO} + e_{5,\,LDC\text{-}NO}\} \qquad (17)$$

where proprietary knowledge is not required but a unique resource ($m_{5,\,LDC\text{-}NO}$) is. If the product is mined or produced by large-scale plantations, there will be economies of scale. Very few industries are linked to the production of a primary commodity; they may be only five (5) as illustrated here. Thus, the value-added in production is minimal, domestic demand weak, and the trade balance negative. The materials exported are used like factors of production in the MNC and EN zones. The negative trade balance is a by-product of importation of high value-added goods and the exportation of low value-added goods. Such production conditions and payments deficits generally define the less-developed economy.

The price of the commodity is determined in a world commodity market, making the LDC a price-taker, so that

$$P_{5,\,MNC} = P_{5,\,EN} = P_{5,\,LDC\text{-}NO} = P_{5,\,LDC\text{-}0} = P_{5,\,WORLD}, \qquad (18)$$

where at low costs of production, the unique resource will still generate rents for the LDC. The presence of large rents often is sufficient reason to discourage the LDC from diversifying into the production of other kinds of products. Cultural conditions generally lead to the concentration of such rents in a few hands or institutions. Perfect competition surely is not an optimal condition since a major purpose of economic development is to escape the pricing and rents consequences of competitive conditions.

All of which leads us to the LDC-O zone. In the LDC-O zone where the main export product is crude petroleum, only unskilled and managerial labor may be required and the main wage rates appearing in equation 5 would be, say, w_5 and w_{10}. The main commodity inputs would be some portion of the crude oil reserves of the LDC zone plus complementary capital-type goods imported from the MNC or EN zones. The magnitude of the mark up on oil exports (and rents) would depend on the effect of OPEC on world crude oil prices. The total production in the key industry, crude petroleum (6), is

$$Q_{6,\,LDC\text{-}O} = m_{6,\,LDC\text{-}O}s_{6,\,LDC\text{-}O}\{\delta_{13}\delta_{14}\delta_{15}\}\{y_{6,\,LDC\text{-}O} + e_{6,\,LDC\text{-}O}\}, \qquad (19)$$

where, again, proprietary knowledge is not required but a unique commodity resource ($m_{6,LDC\text{-}O}$ = oil reserves) is. Economies of scale exist in the industry. Very few industries, however, are linked to the production of oil. The value-added in production is minimal, but the trade balance will be positive. The positive trade balance derives from the mostly noncompetitive characteristic of oil as an export plus the accrual of rents, especially when pricing is set by a cartel, so that

$$P_{6,LDC\text{-}O} = P_{6\text{-}EN} = P_{6\text{-}LDC\text{-}NO} = P_{6\text{-}OPEC} = P_{6\text{-}WORLD} > \text{Competitive Price} \qquad (20)$$

The LDC-zone nations are otherwise most subject to the forces of traditional demand and supply forces because such forces determine world commodity prices, whether they are for agricultural prices or for crude oil. Unlike the MNC zone nations, the LDC nations do not have sophisticated income support programs for agriculture. Thus, whatever the export, the value of both P and its fundamental r is determined in the world markets for their commodity and for their currencies. Their vector of prices are set in world markets, while their economic system has little capacity for adding value to those prices. Although rents can accrue in the LDC-O zone, the industries in the LDC zone otherwise behave like perfectly competitive producers whose prices are taken off the world markets.

The zone's materials exports are critical and mobile "factors of production" for the MNC and EN-zones. Again, free trade is an obsolete term to describe such transfers. When an import is non-competitive, competition and counter-flows of goods become irrelevant.

IV. Global Integration and Regional Trade Balances

To varying degrees every country in the world is integrated into the global economy. Even North Korea, the most isolated of nations, takes into account the possible threat of an American invasion in its nuclear production plans. The MNC and the EN zones are tightly connected to the LDC-O zone by the necessity of importing oil. In turn, the LDC-O countries receive rents in the form of hard currencies. The EN zone is connected to the MNC zone by the need for financial capital inflows and the occasional threat of outflows. In return, the MNC zone can export its excess financial capital.

In this integrated global environment it is difficult to identify fundamental values of exchange rates. Compounding the difficulty is the role the U. S. dollar serves as *the* international currency; it is the key trading and reserve currency. If its fundamental value is determined by the trade balance and net financial capital flows, then

$$r_{US} = M_{US} / (X_{US} + \text{NET FINANCIAL CAPITAL OUTFLOWS}_{US}), \qquad (21)$$

where r is the foreign exchange rate and trade values are in national currency units. Since the U.S. has been running a chronic trade deficit (mostly from consumer imports of differentiated or lower-cost goods plus oil imports priced in U.S. dollars) and is the major supplier of financial capital to the EN zone, the value of the U.S. dollar $(1/r)$ will be low relative to the value of other MNC-zone nations and even most EN-zone nations. This condition can be sustained only as long as foreigners, including their central banks and treasuries, are willing to hold dollars and as long as OPEC desires to price oil in dollars.[4]

Surplus trade balances in differentiated products characterizes the low-wage EN-zone nations as well as many of the other MNC-zone nations. As noted, the EN nations are net borrowers from MNC nations. The LDCs are running chronic trade deficits, including even the oil-producing nations. This is a consequence of their being producers of low value-added products, including exports. Their main route to economic development is the importation of standardized technology from the MNCs, something prohibited only in orthodox trade theory.

V. The World System and Global Economic Growth

The world system is a super-matrix comprised of the interdependent matrices of the MNC, EN, LDC-O, and LDC-NO zones. The final outputs, value added, employment, and demand take the same forms as equations 7 through 16. The linkages of the MNC-zone nations are though intra-firm and interindustry trade, technology transfers by the MNCs to the EN zone, and financial capital movements to (mostly) the EN zone. Obviously, the MNC zone is the most dynamic part of the world system.

To have positive economic growth, technology must improve and advance, net savings and net investment occur, or both. The net product of the MNC zone, $Y_{MNC}(t)$, is no longer devoted entirely to using the commodities produced; some is set aside to provide for the expansion of output capacity. The net product not devoted to consumption is assigned to new investment. These investments are made in human capital as well as physical capital.

The simplest dynamic world model has consumers preferences, technology, and the structure of prices constant through time. Thus, the composition of consumption does not change. Per capita consumption is constant so that the labor force and consumption grow at the same rate, g, so that

$$C(t) = cN(t) = cN(0)\,[1 + g]^t, \qquad (22)$$

where C(t) is the value of consumption and N(t) is population. Let J(t) equal new investment-type goods so that at a fixed technology, A,

$$J(t) = gAQ(t) \qquad (23)$$

and all physical quantities among the means of production AQ(t) grow at the same rate. Therefore,

$$Q(t) - AQ(t) - gAQ(t) = cN(t) \qquad (24)$$

with the solution

$$Q(t) = [I - (1 + g)A]^{-1}\, cN(0)[1 + g]^t \qquad (25)$$

and the total physical quantities in Q(t) grow at the same rate, g, as do the physical quantities in C(t). Put differently, at the exponential growth of consumption, C(t), the equation (24) gives the total physical quantities, Q(t), required, both directly and indirectly, including new investment, to keep the world system in dynamic equilibrium. Though this is what is necessary for dynamic world equilibrium, there is no assurance that all the necessary conditions will be met.

In line with the analysis of the MNC zone, the labor required (and assumed to be demanded) in the world system is

$$L(t) = [a_{jVIV}]_{n-1XD}\, Q(t) = [a_{jviv}]_{m-1XD}\, [I - (1+ g)A]^{-1}\, cN(0)\, [1 + g]^{t}, \quad (26)$$

but full utilization of capacities and full employment further requires that

$$L(t) = L^{*}(t), \quad (27)$$

where $L^{*}(t)$ is the world' s labor force and all labor quality types are growing at the same rate. Since the MNC zone countries contain the richest mix of labor qualities (including unskilled labor) the qualities in the world labor matrix is defined by that of the MNC zone. Again, there are many reasons why full employment in the world system does not happen, not the least of which is inadequate incomes of the masses of unskilled labor and thus insufficient aggregate demand, though full employment may be achieved in one or more of the MNC nations.

Even in the static model the compositions of consumption and of labor requirements can change. Moreover, we know that in the long run technology mutates, requiring an alteration in the composition of labor and capital requirements. New technology that produces new consumer goods (new industries) also changes the technology available to consumers for satisfying their needs and wants. The production coefficients in the *A* matrix of existing industries can change in the long run. Moreover, new industries give entirely new rows to the *A* matrix. With these new conditions the hypothesized wage rate and profit rate movements will cause different patterns of price variations.[5]

VI. Concluding Notes

Today' s general equilibrium theory usually proceeds from the particular to the aggregate. The input-output and initially linear approach used here shows how you can reverse this process and go from the aggregate to the particular. The central advantage from introducing realistic production, labor, and consumption relations is the ability to show how the multinational business corporation can be a dynamic force for global economic growth. At the same time, because the MNC zone is the main source for financial capital, that zone introduces exchange rate instability into the world system even as it becomes the source of financial capital for the emerging nations.

The products and services produced and distributed by the multinational in the MNC zone cannot be explained by classical or Heckscher-Olin theories that require factor/technology *im*mobility among nations and perfect competition in traded finished goods. The multinational freely moves its production, technology and management wherever it finds profit opportunities. Proprietary knowledge has no national boundaries and floats freely, making the multinational nation-free. Even LDC commodity production and export fails to conform to traditional models. There is little scope for factor-price equalization or for pricing based upon the marginal costs of production. Rather, production is demand-driven and prices are determined in world commodity markets, as producers become price-takers.

References

Canterbery, E. Ray (1979), "A Vita Theory of Personal Income Distribution," *Southern Economic Journal*, vol. 46, no. 2 (July) pp. 12-48.

_______________ (1987), "A Theory of Supra-Surplus Capitalism," *Eastern Economic Journal*, vol. 13, no. 4 (October-December) pp. 1-20.

_______________ (1991), "Growth and Inflation in a Heterogeneous Multi-sector Model," Paper presented at the Eastern Economic Association Meetings, March 18.

_______________ (1992), "An Evolutionary Model of Technical Change with Markup Pricing," in William Millberg, editor, The Megacorp & Macrodynamics: Essays in Memory of Alfred Eichner (Armonk & London: M. E. Sharpe, Inc.), pp. 87-100.

_______________ (1994), "A General Theory of International Trade and Domestic Employment Adjustments," in Michael Landeck, Editor, *International Trade: Regional and Global Issues* (London: The Macmillan Press), chapter 16.

Dunning, John H. (1988), "The Eclectic Paradigm of International Production: A Restatement and Some Possible Extensions," *Journal of International Business Studies*, vol. 19, pp. 1-31.

Gray, H. Peter (1976), *A Generalized Theory of International Trade* (London: Macmillan; New York: Holmes & Meier).

__________ (1979), *International Trade, Investment, and Payments* (Boston: Houghton Mifflin Company).

___________ (1984), "Employment Arguments for Protection and the Vita Theory," *Eastern Economic Journal*, vol. 10, no. 1 (January-March) pp. 1-13.

___________ (1985), *Free Trade or Protection: A Pragmatic Analysis* (London: Macmillan; New York: St. Martin' s Press).

___________ (1999), *Global Economic Involvement: A Synthesis of Modern International Economics* (Copenhagen: Copenhagen Business School Press).

Krugman, Paul R (1991), *Geography and Trade* (Leuven: Leuven University Press).

___________ (2004), *The Exhaustion of the Dollar: Its Implications for Global Prosperity* (Hampshire & New York: Palgrave Macmillan).

Milberg, William and Bruce Elmslie (1992), "Technical Change in the Corporate Economy: A vertically Integrated Approach," in William Milberg, editor, *The Megacorp & Macrodynamics: Essays in Memory of Alfred Eichner* (Armonk and London: M. E. Sharpe, Inc.), pp. 101-130.[6]

[1]NOTES

[1] The origins of technology and its change are beyond the scope of this paper. However, for a paper on that subject that is consistent with the modeling in this paper, see Canterbery (1992). The two models can be integrated.

[2] The labor coefficients in the advanced economies change very slowly over time. For example, Milberg and Elmslie (1992) find change in combined direct and indirect labor coefficients changing less than 1 percent across 20 industries in 8 advanced economies.

[3] For a discussion of excess demands and supplies of labor by type based on the vita theory and their implications for protectionism, see Gray (1984).

[4] This is a "quick and dirty" evaluation of the fundamental international value of the dollar. For a brilliant, complete and "exhausting" accounting, see Gray (2004).

[5] These results are demonstrated in Canterbery (1994, p. 160).

[6] In eight advanced countries, they find direct plus indirect labor requirements changing by less than 1 percent in 20 industries in a half decade.

CPSIA information can be obtained at www.ICGtesting.com
Printed in the USA
BVOW06*2018120716

455309BV00001B/1/P

9 789814 704373